RESTRICTED ENVIRONMENTAL STIMULATION

RESTRICTED ENVIRONMENTAL STIMULATION

RESEARCH AND CLINICAL APPLICATIONS

PETER SUEDFELD

The University of British Columbia

with contributions by

HENRY B. ADAMS, RODERICK A. BORRIE,
AND RICHARD C. TEES

A WILEY-INTERSCIENCE PUBLICATION

JOHN WILEY & SONS, New York • Chichester • Brisbane • Toronto

Library of Congress Cataloging in Publication Data:

Suedfeld, Peter, 1935-
    Restricted environmental stimulation.

    (Wiley series on personality processes)
    "A Wiley-Interscience publication."
    Includes bibliographical references and indexes.
    1. Sensory deprivation—Therapeutic use.
I. Title.

RC489.S44S93   616.89'14   79-26927
ISBN 0-471-83536-6

Printed in the United States of America

10 9 8 7 6 5 4 3 2 1

To
the memory of
my good friends and colleagues
Frederick F. Ikard
John P. Zubek

Series Preface

This series of books is addressed to behavioral scientists interested in the nature of human personality. Its scope should prove pertinent to personality theorists and researchers as well as to clinicians concerned with applying an understanding of personality processes to the amelioration of emotional difficulties in living. To this end, the series provides a scholarly integration of theoretical formulations, empirical data, and practical recommendations.

Six major aspects of studying and learning about human personality can be designated: personality theory, personality structure and dynamics, personality development, personality assessment, personality change, and personality adjustment. In exploring these aspects of personality, the books in the series discuss a number of distinct but related subject areas: the nature and implications of various theories of personality; personality characteristics that account for consistencies and variations in human behavior; the emergence of personality processes in children and adolescents; the use of interviewing and testing procedures to evaluate individual differences in personality; efforts to modify personality styles through psychotherapy, counseling, behavior therapy, and other methods of influence; and patterns of abnormal personality functioning that impair individual competence.

Irving B. Weiner

University of Denver
Denver, Colorado

Preface

An article in the weekly newsletter, *Behavior Today*, was headlined "Sensory Deprivation: Thoughtlessly Maligned, Needlessly Neglected" (1977). This is a valid description of how the restricted environmental stimulation technique (REST) has been treated by professionals and laymen alike, a surprising development for a research method that started out 25 years ago with great promise and fanfare. Unfortunately, the years between have been marked by a variety of criticisms, some valid, some erroneous, and some ignorant, which have overshadowed the substantial progress that was made during the same time.

In the public mind, and even in the minds of many behavioral scientists and clinicians, the term "sensory deprivation" evokes images of bizarre effects, psychological disturbance, a Svengali-like power over the subject, and torture. All of these images are far from reality, but they seem to have taken on a life of their own. Paradoxically, one line of criticism implies that REST has no real impact, with all of the results being due to subject expectancy and the awesome paraphernalia of the experimenter. Directly contrary, another and more widely publicized attack is that the technique is equivalent to brainwashing, dehumanization, and the induction of at least temporary if not permanent insanity.

Actually, stimulus reduction is a powerful way to elicit changes in a variety of psychological and behavioral processes. Even stripped of melodrama, it produces a range of reliable effects. However, the range is not as great as was once thought, and the effects are modifiable by the manipulation of a number of variables that are only now being explored systematically. Most importantly, workers are beginning to apply the technique to solving the problems of individual human beings. Such applications are to a great extent based on the person's realization that a difficulty exists and that it may be amenable to solution by his or her own actions. Whether the problem is directly due to an excess of information or stimulation, or whether its solution is made unnecessarily difficult by such an excess, at some point the decision is made to reduce the level of environmental input. At this point, the methods with which this book is concerned become relevant. While specific details vary, there is an increasing recognition that stimulus restriction can and should be tried as one form of intervention in such instances.

The purpose of this book is to evaluate the usefulness, reliability, and practicality of restricted environmental stimulation therapy. There have been many scattered reports of the beneficial uses of reduced input, ranging from periodic withdrawal to enjoy solitude and nature before returning to one's accustomed environment and its problems, to the use of dark, soundproof rooms in the systematic treatment of patients. A review of the scientific literature on the effects of stimulus reduction on both human beings and infrahuman animals, and a systematic consideration of the attempts to translate these findings into beneficial applications, should be useful guides for those who are interested in considering the feasibility of this hitherto neglected but possibly very helpful approach.

As in the case of most books, this one was nurtured by a cooperative effort. Among the individuals most closely involved in my own contribution is Jack A. Vernon, with whom I first began to do research in this field, and who during my early efforts provided an atmosphere of intellectual freedom and stimulation. My senior colleagues and friends, Thomas I. Myers and John P. Zubek, fostered my enthusiasm for the possibilities of the restricted stimulation technique. Among my own students and collaborators, Frederick F. Ikard, P. Bruce Landon, and Roderick A. Borrie have been the most closely associated with the line of research discussed in this volume. All of these people, and many other colleagues, students, and experimental subjects have contributed ideas, encouragement, and help to make our joint efforts an exciting experience over the years. None of this would have been possible without the successive institutional support of Princeton University, Rutgers—The State University, and The University of British Columbia, nor without financial aid from the universities mentioned, the National Institutes of Health Biomedical Sciences Support Program, the Canada Council, and the National Research Council.

The preparation of this book was originally suggested by Henry B. Adams, who continued to offer valuable suggestions along the way. The actual writing was mostly made possible by the supportive atmosphere provided by The University of British Columbia, The University of New South Wales, and Yale University, and by the help of a Canada Council Leave Fellowship. Carmenza Ramirez organized a great deal of scattered information into a usable format, both at the beginning and at the end of the project. Important suggestions and editorial comments were made by Gary E. Schwartz, Jean L. Kristeller, Michael J. Chandler, and Geraldine Schwartz. P. J. Johnson's careful reading of the manuscript was particularly helpful. Several colleagues generously shared unpublished data, thoughts, and questions with me. Among the most lavish were Ann Corcoran, S. P. Hersh, Paul T. Hoffman, Terry Hunt, J. D. Neill, Lee Perry, and Reto Volkart. Others are mentioned in the text. I apologize to those whose names have been inadvertently omitted, and assure them that the omission does not reflect a lack of gratitude.

It is almost routine for authors to acknowledge the services of the person who types their manuscript. In this case, both the service and the appreciation go far beyond the norm. Mirana Yu, the recipient of many hours of taped dictation that was often disjointed and sometimes incomprehensible, managed not only to transform it into clear text, but even to organize it so that it made sense. Had it not been for her ability to do this, and to cope with the vicissitudes of the postal systems of Canada, the United States, and Australia, the book would never have been finished. The preparation of the final version was coordinated, and to a great extent completed, by Rosabella Prasad.

PETER SUEDFELD

Vancouver, British Columbia
March 1980

Contents

CHAPTER 1

Introduction

Man thrives on variety. The most enjoyable dish palls when eaten for the fifth meal in succession; the most awesome scenery rates only a glance when one has lived with it for a year; the most exciting work eventually becomes onerously routine; the most enchanting companion loses some of the enchantment after long intimacy. Most of us try to design our lives so that the boredom of sameness is warded off—and, indeed, the world provides complexity and change from the moment that the infant is first immersed in its "blooming, buzzing confusion."

Sometimes, in fact, the world tends to overdo a good thing. Simultaneous variety, or complexity, is the bane of the modern urbanite. High levels of stimulation and information are difficult to cope with, and the barrage to which we are exposed sometimes becomes intolerable. Successive variety, change, can also reach painful levels. "Future shock" (Toffler, 1970) is one reaction to the accelerating rate of change in technological society where, for example, a man in whose childhood powered flight was generally considered an absurd dream and radios transmitted only dots and dashes could eventually watch a live TV program of people walking on the moon. The diversification explosion—diversification including both increased complexity and accelerated change—has preoccupied many of us. We yearn for the wilderness, for fewer consumer items, for handicrafts, for a "greening"; we desire to return to a simpler and more stable life. We are uneasy about the impossibility of "keeping up with the literature," on whatever topic; we narrow our range of interests; we are traumatized by future shock, and seek remedies for it or asylums from it.

Our lives are rich in both complexity and change—mine is, and so are those of the probable readers of this book. But we must remember that this condition is by no means universal. There are vast numbers of people whose activities and surroundings are still simple and stable, to whom diversification is mostly hearsay and not immediate experience. Even in the most technological of societies, much of the personal day-to-day life of great segments of the population is characterized by monotony. For them, diversification is vicarious or confined to impersonal societal issues.

1

Perhaps these, our compatriots in Technologia, have become more sensitized to monotony, or perhaps the threshold for boredom is becoming lower. With the attention paid to these issues by the mass media, such changes seem logical. But whatever the reason, there has been an increased emphasis on avoiding routine and sameness. From the rejection of rote memorization in the schools to the abandonment of the assembly line for work teams, from the replacement of therapeutic dyads by therapeutic groups to the growth of communes and extended families, the search for diversity seems as much a part of our ethos as the retreat from it.

Psychologists have shared the growing interest in the roles of complexity, change, novelty, stimulation, and information. It has become clear, for example, that the drive-reduction concept of motivation is inadequate to explain either human or infrahuman behavior; one set of competing theories emphasizes instead the activation level of the organism, which in turn is to a great extent a function of environmental stimulation (e.g., Berlyne, 1960; Duffy, 1957; Fiske and Maddi, 1961; Hebb, 1955), while another set focuses on the importance of successfully coping with the environment (Hunt, 1961; White, 1959). Diversity levels, under other labels, have been central considerations in research on problem-solving (see Bourne and Dominowski, 1972), child development (Hunt, 1963), social behavior (Streufert and Streufert, 1978), personality variables (Schroder and Suedfeld, 1971), environmental effects (Proshansky, Ittelson, and Rivlin, 1970), and neurological bases of behavior (Lindsley, 1961).

A MATTER OF LABELS

Among the approaches used to study the effects of changes in diversity is an experimental technique—or rather, a set of techniques—that reduces external stimulation to a minimum. The methods have included reductions of absolute levels of stimulation, of meaningful patterned perception, of changes in the perceptual field, and combinations of these, as will be discussed in the next chapter. Over the years, all of these procedures, as well as nonlaboratory situations involving stimulus reduction, have come to be subsumed under the label "sensory deprivation." This term, while convenient and now widely familiar, is inaccurate and has also become harmful to serious workers in the area.

It is inaccurate for two reasons. The first is that many studies and environments do not in fact alter the level of sensory input, as the adjective "sensory" implies. In many of the experimental procedures, this level may remain essentially unchanged, or may even be increased. As will be seen, such techniques involve limiting the variability, patterning, or meaningfulness of inputs, or restricting the range of outputs, without reduction of the gross levels of stimulation impinging upon the sensory receptors. Second, the noun "deprivation" is clearly inappropriate, if it is taken in its usual meaning of complete removal. Sensory deprivation is not analogous to, say, food deprivation. Even in those laboratories that impose restrictions of external stimulation, it is quite clear that the subjects themselves generate stimuli (sounds made by the body, physical movements, retinal firing) that would tend to compensate for the experimental manipulation. A deprivation state could be achieved only by chemical or surgical blocking of the afferent nerves, and none of the studies that we will be discussing has involved such a procedure.

Perhaps even more important than the scientific imprecision of the term is the fact that through repeated association it has come to carry a connotation of disturbance, threat, and aversiveness. The historical reasons for this development are discussed somewhat later; at this point, it suffices to indicate the almost unbelievable importance of word magic in the thinking of even highly educated and scientifically trained individuals. The appearance of the words "sensory deprivation" may be enough to reduce the chances that a research proposal will be funded, a manuscript accepted for publication, a technique included in an applied project, a comment accepted as relevant to a scholarly question, or a thesis topic approved by a committee. Many such reactions have been mentioned in conversations among people interested in this field, and in some cases have been definitively demonstrated in correspondence and at professional meetings. It is discouraging that rejection seems to occur independently of such issues as clearance from ethics committees, careful experimental designs and procedures, interesting and important results, and other normally overriding characteristics.

For these reasons, it seems time to deemphasize the term, sacrificing historical continuity and immediate recognition in order to obtain precision and objective evaluation. I would like to propose "Restricted Environmental Stimulation Technique" as an alternative to "sensory deprivation." This term was chosen after long consideration, and is a variant of one originally suggested by Roderick A. Borrie. To begin with, the proposed term is accurate: stimulation from the environment is in some way restricted by all of the techniques being considered here. For another, it is not completely novel, "restricted stimulation" being one of the 25 terms previously applied to at least some versions of the sensory deprivation procedure (Brownfield, 1965). It does not have the negative connotations of the more familiar label; and, in fact, it can be made into an acronym

(REST) with connotations that are not only pleasant but also quite valid in terms of some of the uses to which such procedures have been put. For these reasons, while in the rest of this book various terms including "sensory deprivation" will be used somewhat interchangeably for this class of methodologies, the phrase and acronym proposed above will be the labels of first choice. Where appropriate, REST may also be read as Restricted Environmental Stimulation *Therapy.*

RELEVANT WRITINGS

The voluminous literature in this area has been reviewed and summarized many times. Some of these reviews were extensive enough to cover also the older anecdotal and autobiographical material written by and about prisoners in solitary confinement, explorers in remote areas, shipwrecked sailors in rafts and lifeboats, solitary navigators on the water and in the air, and individuals who for whatever reason withdrew from the company of their fellows. The latter writings were usually by or about rather unusual people. For one thing, most of them were successful survivors: as history is written by the victors, so the individual history of successful experiences is written by those who surmount the obstacles (e.g., Bombard, 1953; Byrd, 1938; Chichester, 1967; Cooke, 1960; Graham, 1974; Lewis, 1975; Slocum, 1900). Most of the exceptions to this rule, although not all (see e.g. Tomalin and Hall, 1970), tend to appear in unpublished clinical notes, legal briefs, and diaries. It is impossible to gain from the published anecdotal literature a view of the effects of isolation and monotony uncontaminated by danger, physical privation, and uncertainty of rescue.

The response to lower stimulation appears to be culturally determined to a significant degree, in that the coping reactions to lower stimulation themselves evoke anxiety because they are perceived as symptoms of mental aberration. This definition is not universal across cultures, but it seems to contribute to the stress that most Westerners feel in such situations. Restoration of acceptable stimulation levels often takes the form of self-generation of stimuli, which may involve courses of physical exercise or mental problem-solving, but also reverie, fantasy, hallucinations, talking to oneself, and free-flowing sequences of thought and emotion. The individual's response to these phenomena is strongly affected by his cultural background and specific expectations and orientation.

In a study that does not differentiate among sources of stress that accompany, but are not a part of, isolation and sensory reduction, Gross, Kempe, and Reimer (1972) looked at several reports of experimental

REST as well as the experiences of solitary sailors, immigrants in countries whose language they do not understand, and the like. It is clear, as we already know, that there are people who experience various fears while in this kind of situation; once again, however, there is no evidence that these fears are either so overwhelming that the subject cannot cope with them in some way nor that they lead to pathological changes that persist once the individual has left the experimental environment.

The stress is a complex result of the interaction among all of the variables involved, not merely—and perhaps not even primarily—of reduced stimulation or social contact. People who because of their background interpret the unusual phenomena they are experiencing as signs of imminent or actual breakdown will experience even more stress, beginning a cycle which may lead to serious psychological problems. Conversely, those who can control, tolerate, or enjoy such experiences are more likely to survive them intact and even to benefit from them (Suedfeld, 1974; see also Al-Issa, 1977).

Suedfeld (1974) has discussed briefly the ritual isolation that many cultures have used to mark the passage from childhood to adulthood. In these cases, it is culturally expected that the candidate will experience hallucinations, vivid dreams, visits from spiritual forces, and so on; accordingly, such unusual experiences are not interpreted by either the individual or his society as being signs of abnormality, and have no adverse effects on his later functioning. The fact that low environmental stimulation may reduce reality testing and lead to a high level of fantasy is perfectly acceptable in some cultures. Problems may arise when individuals from such cultures, accustomed to this kind of psychological process, come into contact and conflict with Western society (see e.g., Devereux, 1951).

As a special variant of the rite of passage, solitude is sometimes used as a prerequisite for achieving some specific status position within the group. For example, aspiring Shamans among some Alaskan Eskimos have to wander about on the tundra, experiencing great suffering and acquiring a familiar spirit in visions (Murphy, 1964). Shamanistic healing rituals also frequently include a combination of reduced and monotonous stimulation (e.g., darkness and rhythmic drumming; Foxx, 1964) or an alternation between low and high levels of input (Jilek, 1977).

Folk healing in several cultures includes physical restraint and isolation for the mentally ill. This may range to such relatively sophisticated environments as seclusion rooms in which the patient is physically tied or shackled for some days or even weeks, as among the Yoruba of Nigeria (Prince, 1964). This incarceration is continued until the patient is calm and amenable to other forms of treatment. The Salish Indians of Western

Canada cure members of the tribe who have some kind of mental illness, or at least engage in what is considered to be antisocial behavior, through a treatment that starts with isolation for a period of four to over forty days (depending on how recalcitrant the patient is). This state of isolation follows and alternates with periods of frightening, unexpected, disorienting, and painful sensory overload. While isolated, the patient is blindfolded, covered with heavy blankets, deprived of food and water, and is not permitted to talk or move. Specific messages are also presented, including tribal legends, a spirit dance, and other rituals, which are designed to reawaken the patient's sense of responsibility towards the tribe (Jilek, 1974, 1978). The resemblance between this procedure and those described in the literature on coercive persuasion is clear, although the Salish version is less stressful in that the recipient of the treatment does not perceive its administrators as being hostile to him. Nor is the process perceived as punitive or as torture; rather, it is to kill the imperfect self of the patient and allow the emergence of a true, good traditional Indian personality.

Even a cursory check through the Human Relations Area Files finds further examples ranging from brief vigils, such as the night of wakeful silence endured upon a young boy about to enter the status of an adult Brahmin in India (reminiscent of the night of contemplation undergone by aspirants for the knighthood in medieval Europe) to over a week of seclusion among the Kikuyu, and a month among the Mossi of West Africa. Among the Jivaros of South America, a jungle vigil culminates in the taking of the head of a totemic animal, which is then brought home and shrunk in the same way that human heads used to be in that culture.

These examples of the use of restricted stimulation as part of the process of preparing oneself to take a full part in society or as a part of the treatment administered to restore someone to such participation should be kept conceptually separated from quarantine, although in some cultures the distinction may be blurred. For instance, isolating adolescent girls at menarche is a fairly common practice (the Aleuts do it for a 40-day period, in darkness). This isolation is partly an initiation and partly a quarantine. The segregation of menstruating women, also quite frequent, is a more obvious case of avoiding "contamination."

Of course, the "cultural learning experience" explanation of why solitude and stimulus reduction seem so aversive to us is not the only plausible one. Day (1920) in his imaginative extrapolation of species-specific traits, speculated on how a society of intelligent felines would differ from that constructed by primates. Among other things, he proposes that the alternative civilization would have been characterized by cleanliness, mental stability, individual rather than group endeavors, a love of adventure and exploration, originality in art, and cunning in government.

The most relevant point is the value that such a species would place upon solitude: "A race of civilized beings descended from these great cats would have been rich in hermits and solitary thinkers. The recluse would not have been stigmatized as peculiar, as he is by us simians" (Day, 1920, p. 17). It may indeed be argued that the general preference for high levels of social interaction and distracting stimulation are genetically programmed into simian species; such a hypothesis would certainly help to explain some of the unfavorable reactions voiced about restricted environmental stimulation techniques and the negative attitudes toward relatively nongregarious individuals (e.g., Parmalee and Werner, 1978). At the same time, it is obvious that a great deal of individual variation exists across ape and monkey species, and within homo sapiens in particular, and that cultural factors modify any such preprogrammed tendencies. Still, when culture and biology reinforce each other, it is particularly understandable that contrary opinions and approaches be subjected to severe criticism.

Although Day's treatment is fantasy, not science, it certainly is compatible with more scientific treatments. Prominent among these is the statement, by a distinguished writer on the subject, that it is in the evolutionary history of the human species that one must search for the basic causes of our general fear of solitude (Bowlby, 1973).

Because the relevant variables are so much better controlled than in field studies and biographical or anthropological writings, because the durations are so much shorter, and because the entire experience is designed and monitored for the very purpose of collecting data, information about the effects of experimental REST is relatively extensive, objective, and systematic. Naturally, as the research continues, reviews become in turn outdated. The most thorough examination of the relevant work appears in the book edited by John P. Zubek (1969); a shorter but more current summary was published by Zubek in 1973. The latter appeared after the high point of active research with this technique; thus, it is possible to use it as the basic framework for a current look at the literature, with only relatively few additions needing to be made. The renewed growth of interest in the area may make the chore of the next reviewer, five or so years from now, much more difficult.

METHODOLOGICAL ISSUES

Experimental Procedures

There are three major ways of achieving global sensory restriction. One category has as its goal the reduction of absolute levels of input to a minimum: the major ways of achieving this goal are confinement in a completely dark, soundproof room, and immersion in water. These techniques have been given such labels as sensory isolation and stimulus reduction (Brownfield, 1965). Many workers in the field have used the term sensory deprivation in a specific sense to mean this type of procedure (Zubek, 1969a). Water immersion in particular has been distinguished by the label hydro-hypodynamic environment (Shurley, 1963).

During room confinement, the subject usually lies on a bed for the entire period of the session, with food, water, and a chemical toilet available near the bedside. Gloves, arm cuffs, and earplugs or earmuffs may be used to reduce stimulation further; in some cases, the food is chosen to be bland in taste; and either instructions or physical restraints may be used to reduce kinesthetic stimulation (see Fig. 1-1).

Water immersion techniques may employ flotation gear so that the subject's head is above water, or a helmet or face mask transmitting air to a subject who is completely immersed. Typically, the water is close to body temperature and the tank is located in a chamber which itself is light-proof, sound-reducing, and temperature-controlled. The subject may neither eat nor defecate during the session. With both procedures, as with all other techniques in this area, the subject is monitored constantly to ensure his safety, comfort, and compliance with instructions (see Fig. 1-2).

As has been pointed out, "sensory deprivation" is not an accurate description of these techniques. With chamber confinement, the subject still has a variety of tactile, kinesthetic, olfactory, and gustatory cues; auditory stimuli are received from inside the body, from one's own movements, and (even if greatly attenuated) from the outside environment; and a variety of methods may be used to evoke pseudo-visual experiences. Auditory stimulation is also possible in the water tank, as are novel tactile and kinesthetic inputs from moving parts of the body in the water, thus setting up changes in buoyancy, water currents, and the like. Nevertheless, these are the conditions that most closely approximate what people generally think of when the phrase sensory deprivation is used. As Henry B. Adams has noted, their common distinguishing characteristic is that they both involve *reduced stimulation*, and in the rest of the book this term will be used to refer to such methods.

The second major category includes techniques that do not decrease the absolute levels of stimulation, and in fact may even increase it, but that interfere with normal pattern perception. The approach of the McGill University group is the model here: the subject lies on a bed, with constant white noise at low to moderate volume provided through earphones or over an intercom system, translucent goggles over the eyes, and gauntlets or gloves and cardboard cuffs for the hands and arms. Because of the

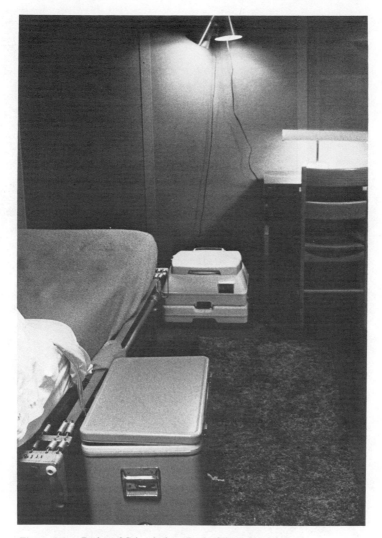

Figure 1.1. Reduced Stimulation: Dark, Silent Chamber.

constant noise and diffuse light, the general input level is quite high. However, no meaningful or patterned sounds can be heard, and no specific objects or patterns can be seen. This condition was labelled perceptual isolation by the McGill group; more recently, it has been called pattern reduction and is now commonly referred to as perceptual deprivation. Various *Ganzfeld* techniques resemble this situation, as does the method of stabilized retinal images, although of course only visual stimulation is affected in these procedures.

Figure 1.2.   Reduced Stimulation: Water Immersion Tank.

It may be argued that this technique should be treated as an overstimulation rather than as a REST treatment because of its constant high level of input. Such a change in category might lead to some clarification of REST effects, since reduced stimulation and pattern reduction have frequently led to dissimilar findings. I have felt that at this time the reclassification would be too drastic a break with the existing literature, but some of the relevant differences and their implications for the therapeutic use of REST are considered later in the book.

The last, and least commonly used, of the major approaches has been termed variation reduction (Suedfeld, 1968): it uses some device that makes the sensory input less changeable without necessarily lowering either the absolute level or the level of patterning. A prominent example is the use of an inoperative iron lung, in which the subject's body is placed with the head protruding and held in a frame so that the visual field consists only of the front of the machine and its immediate surroundings. This technique probably provides an environment closer to normal than any of the others discussed so far; however, the mechanical elimination of bodily movement introduces a new dimension of deprivation far more stringent than the equivalent in other methods (cf. Zubek, Bayer, Milstein and Shepard, 1969). In accordance with Adams's suggestion, both pattern reduction and variation reduction will be labeled by their common characteristic, *monotonous stimulation,* throughout this book. However, this may require modification in the future if pattern reduction is in fact recategorized as an overstimulation technique. For example, a two-dimensional taxonomy may be a more accurate conceptual map as well as a more differentiated and consistent basis for prediction (see Fig. 1-3).

Aside from these relatively "pure" methods, there have also been combinations using, for example, complete darkness and white noise, or silence and diffuse light, and so on. Such mixtures are used in relatively few studies, and their effects have not been systematically compared with those of the more homogeneous approaches.

Even at this early stage, the reader may have noticed the possible confusion that may arise from the multiplicity of terms used to refer to the various techniques. The convention among workers in the field has been that the term "sensory deprivation" is applied generically, as well as to the stimulus reduction methodologies specifically. This convention is helpful, but the dual use of "sensory deprivation" has led to considerable confusion, almost as much confusion as the inaccuracy of the term. This is another justification for substituting the phrase "Restricted Environmental Stimulation Technique" (REST).

Besides the techniques outlined above, all of which are directed toward global interference with normal sensation and perception, a number of

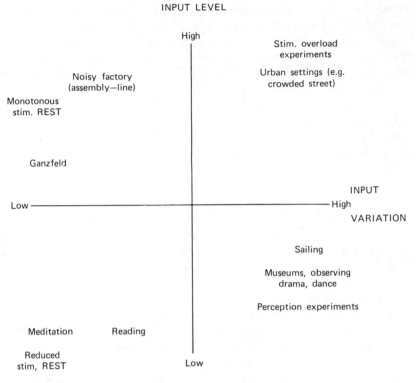

Figure 1.3.   A Two-Dimensional Taxonomy of Special Environments.

methods have been employed to obtain changes in some part of the accustomed environmental input. To begin with, global REST confounds or combines sensory/perceptual changes in the physical stimulus world with social isolation, confinement to a limited space, and monotony. All three of these variables may have effects of their own, which in some unknown way may combine with those of reduced stimulation, the result being a stew whose flavor comes from the combination and in which the contribution of any particular ingredient cannot be identified with any certainty. In order to remedy the situation, some researchers have imposed conditions of monotony, isolation, or physical restriction, each as the major independent variable and without a general reduction in stimulation. It should be noted that this appears to be the only way to approach the problem; it is difficult to imagine how one could impose a general REST condition without the other three factors.

One overlooked aspect has been the control of temperature within the experimental room. There is some incidental evidence to show that excessive heat may modify the effects of social isolation (Suedfeld, Grissom, and Vernon, 1964); and a recent paper (Gerlach, 1974) indicates that constant temperature may be a factor in sensory deprivation. If so, most experimenters have unwittingly and fortunately met this criterion, due to the ventilation equipment that is typically used. On the other hand, investigators and designers who are concerned with minimizing monotony might pay attention to providing minor variations in the thermal environment.

Within the environmental stimulus reduction paradigm itself, some researchers have addressed themselves to the problem of identifying the specific contributions of various aspects of the deprivation situation. These approaches have been mainly in the direction of imposing reductions in a particular sensory modality, while trying to maintain normal levels of input to the other receptors. The results of these unimodal deprivation experiments have shed some light on the components of the reduced stimulation effect, as well as leading to some interesting insights about the ways in which the processes of sensation and perception operate in human beings.

Obviously, one would expect results to be influenced by the nature of the experimental techniques being employed. It has been proposed that monotonous stimulation is more stressful, and should have more drastic effects, than reduced stimulation (Schultz, 1965). The evidence as to the former hypothesis appears to be negative: of sixteen categories of events that occurred significantly more among deprived than among control subjects in one experiment (Zubek, Hughes and Shephard, 1971), only two distinguished significantly between pattern and stimulus reduction. These two were loneliness and positive attitudes towards the experimenter, which do not necessarily indicate differential stress. The second hypothesis has been supported more consistently, with monotonous stimulation leading to a variety of perceptual, cognitive, and physiological changes that are either not found at all or are found only in markedly lesser degree as a result of stimulus reduction (Zubek et al., 1971).

Similarly, water immersion has been frequently cited as the most stressful of all of the techniques, a label that intuitively seems valid not because the situation necessarily imposes a greater degree of deprivation, but because being totally immersed in water is a frightening situation for most subjects. Tangential evidence for that explanation is provided by Shurley (1966), who showed that subjects floating horizontally and breathing regular room air exhibited significantly less stress and stayed in the situation longer than those who were completely immersed. Short duration times, however, do not seem to be accompanied by unusually high verbal expressions of anxiety or stress (see Zuckerman, 1969a).

One study in which water immersion and stimulus reduction in a dark room were compared indicated that duration time was shorter, and heart rate higher, in the tank; furthermore, immersed subjects overestimated the time they had spent in the experiment while room subjects (as is the usual case) underestimated it (Forgays and McClure, 1974). Subjects spending 6 hours in each situation, 1 week apart, did not produce more perceptual phenomena in one than in the other. However, physiological measures of arousal, frequently used to infer psychological stress, did differ: water immersion led to higher arousal than a stimulus-reduction chamber, as measured by heart rate, respiration, and EEG frequency. EEG amplitude and eye movements gave similar results during most, but not all, of the session (Levin, 1974).

When compared with monotonous (as opposed to reduced) stimulation in a chamber, water tank immersion results in a heightening of EEG frequencies, cardiac rate, lateral and vertical eye movements, and of the number of electrodermal phenomena (Serafetinides, Shurley, Brooks and Gideon, 1973). Unfortunately, this study—the only one in the literature comparing the two techniques directly—suffered from overlooking the methodological issue of repeated confinement just as did Forgays and McClure (1974) (see below). Each subject was used as his own control, here with a one-month period between sessions. One source of encouragement stems from the fact that the order in which subjects experienced the two techniques was counterbalanced and no order effect was found.

An interesting comparison is that in the tank the initial high rates and levels of many physiological phenomena diminish with time, while in the chamber the originally relatively low rates of arousal actually increase with time. There are no data to test any explanation of this pattern; but one might hypothesize that in both cases it accompanies the emergence of responses that are specific to REST phenomena. As time goes on, the tank subjects adapt to the originally disorienting, anxiety-arousing, and novel situation, allowing stimulus-reduction effects to emerge. For the chamber subjects, the impact of environmental reduction gradually surpasses the threshold and begins to have an effect.

Other Aspects of the Environment

Some studies have evaluated the contributions of individual components of the global stimulation reduction methodology. For example, it has been shown that severe physical confinement adds considerably to the stressfulness of the experience, and that in fact such restriction can evoke most stress effects commonly found in sensory deprivation even when no other forms of stimulus reduction are imposed (Zuckerman, 1969a). Conversely, either systematic physical exercise (Lebedinsky, Levinsky and

Nefedov, 1964; Zubek, 1963) or spontaneous bodily movements (Dittrich, 1974) can counteract and reduce the usual symptoms of stress.

The supine position which is characteristic of most room and some water tank procedures may also have an effect. For example, Beigel (1952) has indicated that lying on one's back facilitates free association. By extension, it may contribute to the reduction of stimulus-bound references and to the concomitant increase in statements relating to the self that have been found among REST subjects (Sipprelle, Long and Lucik, 1963). These in turn may be involved in the personal problem-solving and seeking for insight that is so frequently cited by patients undergoing REST. In another non-REST experiment, male subjects lying on their back were found to increase in visual field dependence as measured by the rod and frame apparatus (Lichtenstein and Saucer, 1974). While this is probably not very relevant to the majority of environmental restriction studies, it may have an effect on the outcomes of those that rely on variation reduction by such means as the iron lung. It also raises some questions, which have so far not been investigated, about the differences between the results of the most common room-confinement procedure, with the subjects lying on a bed, and the less frequently used system of having them sit in a chair (e.g., Cohen, Silverman, Bressler and Shmavonian, 1961). Another interesting point is raised by the finding that stimulus restriction per se leads to increased independence from the field (Jacobson, 1966; Kurie and Mordkoff, 1970); one might expect that if the REST situation did not involve lying supinely on a bed, the change might be even greater.

Another aspect of the methodology that may make a difference is one that has been generally neglected. This is the fact that, although the subject is in the chamber by himself, he is aware and is frequently explicitly told that a monitor is on duty, or at the very least that his responses will be examined by the researcher. Obviously, this raises all of the questions of evaluation apprehension that social psychologists have discussed at such length. According to Svab and Gross (1967), subjects who believed that only recording apparatus (rather than a live monitor) was being used showed more relaxation during the early part of a sensory deprivation session, but increasing anxiety and less euphoria toward the latter part of the session as compared to a group whose information was that they were continuously being monitored by a staff member.

The Importance of Session Duration

The results of reduced stimulation experiments are also affected by the expected and actual duration of the session. The first of these factors appears primarily to influence the degree of stress experienced by the subjects. In particular, individuals who are recruited without being told the time limit of the experiment (e.g., "for some unspecified period up to *x* hours") report a greater occurrence of anxiety symptoms. Many researchers in the field have noted informally that subjects going in for a definite period were more relaxed and more tolerant of restriction than those going in under rather vague expectations as to duration; still, in a study manipulating time expectancy and time cues (Francis, 1964), the results were not quite as expected. One of the four treatment groups received clear information as to how long to expect to be in the tank; a second was given time cues while immersed; the third got neither of these; and the last got both. As predicted, the last group found the three-hour session the most tolerable; but surprisingly, the third group was next. That is, no information was better than one or the other cue. Francis speculated that this might have been due to the contrast between the anxiety aroused in this group, which might have been very high due to the lack of information, and the actual mildness of the experience.

Experiments of set duration have lasted as little as 5 minutes to as much as 3 weeks. Unless one is really carried away by the mystical tales surrounding the procedure, one can hardly credit that real REST effects could possibly be demonstrated during the shorter periods used. It is difficult to understand how bizarre phenomena could be produced in 5 minutes to 1 or 2 hours if stimulus reduction were in fact the critical variable, given that everybody in normal life undergoes some period of darkness and silence almost daily (e.g., just before falling asleep). The fact that verbal reports of stress and anxiety are made within the first few hours seems to indicate that the deciding factor is something other than the removal of stimulation per se; similarly, reported visual sensations occurring within the first hour of deprivation are a cue that what we are dealing with are reports of spontaneous neural firing and other normal phenomena, perhaps cognitively elaborated, rather than hallucinations symptomatic of some major psychic disruption because of the nature of the environment.

True REST effects tend to develop gradually over time, reach a critical point, and then either decline or remain at asymptote. They are at first masked by other responses such as curiosity or anxiety, but as time goes on they take over an increasing proportion of the total repertoire. With respect to some psychological processes, an asymptote is reached and performance then remains relatively constant until post-release readaptation and return to baseline. In other cases, there is a peak period, after which the changes begin to disappear and the performance pattern begins to regress toward the pre-isolation levels even before the session is over. For example, physiological and behavioral stress measures do not begin to reach substantial levels until at least 3 hours have passed. Most cognitive effects either peak or have reached asymptote by the end of the first 24 hours. Perceptual and motor changes, on the other hand, seem to reach their highest levels only after 48 hours of deprivation. Bodily movements are low for approximately the first 3 hours, reach a peak at 12 hours, decrease again when the subject falls asleep, and then increase during the last stages of a 24-hour sensory deprivation session. After the first few hours of confinement, respiration rates, cardiac rate, and EEG frequencies from the occipital lobe decrease throughout at least 2 weeks of deprivation, and stay below baselines for some time after release. However, the physiological data are confused to some extent by differences in procedure among various researchers, as well as by the persistence of diurnal cycles (Zuckerman, 1969a). Most of the behaviors investigated in REST laboratories return to baseline very quickly after the session.

No parametric studies have investigated the effects of duration on the therapeutic effects with which this book is primarily concerned. Many studies have used 8 to 24 hours with good results. However, the duration times were chosen more or less on an intuitive basis. The problem calls for systematic investigation: we should establish whether we can get equally good results more efficiently by reducing REST time, or conversely increase the therapeutic impact by using longer periods. It is interesting to note that beneficial effects have been reported after as little as 2 hours of REST (Cooper, et al., 1977).

Repeated Exposure

One other question related to methodology is whether individuals habituate to reduced stimulation or whether its effects become increasingly marked with subsequent exposure. Reports are somewhat mixed. Zuckerman's review (1969a) makes it clear that subjects undergoing the experience for the second time tend to show much less drastic changes than they had during the first confinement session. This, incidentally, can be viewed as an indication that subject expectation is not the overwhelming variable in the results; if it were, one would predict that the second experience would closely resemble the first. According to Zuckerman, this erosion of the changes is most reliable in the context of verbal statements of anxiety and stress, with somewhat less consistency on other measures. At any rate, indications are that the general trend is in the direction of adaptation.

In contrast to this, we have Lilly's (1977) remarks about individuals undergoing water-tank REST for purposes of self-exploration. According to this report, the first session is typically characterized by attentional focusing upon the environment and the overt experience. It is only in later sessions, as time goes on, that the transcendental experiences begin to occur and be reported. While there were no systematic presentations of data on this issue, if one accepts the general conclusion it could be interpreted as also showing adaptation effects of a sort. That is, since the subject has become used to the rather bizarre situation, and its bizarreness has diminished, his mind is free to consider and experience a wider range of non-stimulus-bound phenomena.

Aside from the intrinsic interest of these findings, there are some implications for research. More and more individuals are participating in activities where solitude and sometimes a form of restricted (although not necessarily reduced) stimulation is involved, such as camping, spelunking, meditation, and systematic relaxation. It would be interesting to see what the effects of such prior exposure are if the individual enters a REST situation. Similarly, some of the scientific research on physiological and psychological characteristics of transcendental meditators, adepts of Zen, yoga, and similar disciplines, or members of strict monastic orders, should be extended to look at the effects of REST on such individuals. The expectation would be that there would be little if any stress response; enhancement effects, on the other hand, might be quite marked.

HISTORICAL OVERVIEW

It has now been approximately 25 years since Donald O. Hebb and his team at McGill University began reporting on the first systematic research project using experimental stimulus restriction with human subjects. The next 10 years saw a very high level of activity in the field, as the original dramatic results, which were widely if selectively publicized, attracted the attention of behavioral scientists. As Sugimoto (1976) recently pointed out, the attractiveness of the area lay in three characteristics. It was related to a wide diversity of psychological phenomena; its effects were obvious and massive; and it held forth the promise of applicability to such problems as the monotony of work situations and the loneliness of space exploration.

During the first decade, the scatter-gun approach was characteristic. Investigators used "sensory deprivation" to explore effects on almost any dependent variable they could think of. There were very few coherent programs that explored in depth some particular issue; and while some theorizing went on, it could fairly be said that sensory deprivation was a mass of data looking for a theory. Methodologically, the ancillary aspects of the procedure were frequently naive. Subject and experimenter expectation, unrepresentativeness of subject samples, failure to include adequate controls, and other such sources of artifact affected the data to some now unknowable degree.

Aside from the confusion that such flaws added to the scientific literature, they had another, and in the long run perhaps more damaging, effect. Because many of the procedural details emphasized the expectation and likelihood of adverse reactions, and because subjects as well as experimenters were sensitized to such responses, so-called sensory deprivation results were in fact strongly confounded with anxiety effects induced by peripheral aspects of the research methodology. As a result, some people concluded that REST effects were *merely* anxiety effects (see many of the misinterpretations of the results of Orne and Scheibe, 1964). Even worse, a false conception that stimulus restriction is universally and extremely stressful was broadcast both within the profession (including to some researchers in the area) and to the wider public. This misunderstanding has seriously interfered with scientific progress in the field and continues to do so even now.

The next phase of development, beginning in the late 1950s, was characterized by the departure of many early contributors but at the same time by the refinement of programs, techniques, and theories. During the subsequent 10 years, many of the ambiguities and inconsistencies of the earlier data base were removed as specific variables responsible for results were empirically identified. Important progress was made in elucidating the motivational, perceptual, and cognitive effects of reduced stimulation. At the same time, some relatively testable theories, based on concepts ranging from neurophysiology to psychoanalysis, were developed. At the end of this period, the authoritative review of research in the field was published: John P. Zubek's *Sensory Deprivation: Fifteen Years of Research* (1969a), with contributions by some of the most active workers in the area.

Strangely enough, and in contradiction to what one might expect from reinforcement theories, the volume of research began to diminish drastically toward the later stages of this period. Several reasons can be advanced for this change. One was that scientists whose interest in the field was limited to a concentration on some dramatic phenomenon had either exhausted their concern or decided to move on to other questions. Second, stimulus reduction experiments are quite expensive; systematic programs would have required substantial funds, at a time when research support was being eroded in many countries. Third, the workers in the area had failed to integrate the results of their research into the substantive fields, so that for the most part specialists in clinical psychology, perception, cognition, and so on were relatively unaware of the relevance of REST findings to these areas. Thus, the wide-flung network of communication, interest, and support that could have sustained the enterprise was for the most part missing. Last, and contributing to the effects of the previous factors, was the increasing politicization of many universities. With students knowing about "sensory deprivation" only what they read in introductory textbooks or the popular press, and identifying the area with brainwashing and stress, both administrators and researchers frequently decided that continuing work in the field was not worth the harassment they might have to suffer.

Reed (in press) adds another reason for the decline in REST research. This is that workers became increasingly aware of the complexity of the variables involved, and the even greater complexity of their interactions. As a result, they became frustrated and eventually hopeless about the possibility of eliminating artifacts, generating exact hypotheses and testing them, and identifying important and stable phenomena. This discouragement led to abandonment of the field. If this hypothesis is correct, those of us still persisting must have very high frustration tolerance, incurable optimism, or maladaptive levels of stereotyped perseverance.

Lack of funds and political problems were both exacerbated during the latest phase, which is only now showing signs of coming to an end. This period has been characterized by a severely reduced level of activity, with relatively few of the old guard still in the ranks; a constant battle against adverse propaganda; and, partly as a reaction to the latter, increasing attention to the positive implications and particularly to the applied benefits of the technique. This effort has been relatively successful, to the point where the quantity of output and the number of researchers and laboratories involved again appear to be on the increase.

At the present time, there are relatively few programs of sustained research in the experimental sensory deprivation area. In fact, of twenty prominent laboratories described in a previous review (Suedfeld, 1969a), not one is currently active within the field at the same location. This is not necessarily as drastic as it sounds: some of the same workers have merely moved to other places. Woodburn Heron, a member of the original McGill team, is still doing sensory deprivation research at McMaster University; the present author is working at The University of British Columbia with the collaboration of P. Bruce Landon, Roderick A. Borrie, and others, continuing research begun at Princeton University and then pursued further at Rutgers, The State University; John C. Lilly is using water immersion sensory deprivation as a method of self-knowledge and attainment of altered states of consciousness in California; and Thomas I. Myers, in Bethesda, Maryland, is planning to embark on a major research program in the near future. Since the untimely death of John P. Zubek, his work has been completed by his former students, in particular by Michael Bross and Dan W. Harper. Henry B. Adams, now at Area C Community Mental Health Center of the District of Columbia Department of Human Resources, is still collaborating with G. David Cooper and other researchers at George Mason University in Fairfax, Virginia. Austin Jones, after a stint in academic administration, has returned to restricted stimulation research at Arizona State University. Jan Gross, with Peter Kempe and others, has been conducting a major program at the Psychiatric Institute of the University of Hamburg; but this project was discontinued after the principal investigator was subjected to politically motivated attacks that culminated in an attempt to murder him.

In addition, new investigators in the field have appeared in the United States, Canada, Australia, and Europe, with therapists using the technique in the first three of these and in Ecuador. Nonlaboratory work on reduced stimulation in field settings is being carried on in Continental Europe, Asia, and the Americas. Thus there is reason to believe that, after a lull lasting for some years, a new and vigorous period of research and application may be near.

WHAT HAS BEEN ACCOMPLISHED?

Shallice (1972a) has charged that research on sensory deprivation has added very little if anything to our knowledge of psychology. According to him, there were some minor contributions dealing with brain functioning and motivation, and perhaps some useful implications for the psychology of perception stemming from the work of Zubek. Aside from this, he maintains that the research in the field has become functionally autonomous: that is, that it has continued only in order to explore further the implications of the methodology, without substantive pay-off. In his opinion there is very little if any justification for continuing this research, since it is not making positive contributions, while at the same time it may be used for inhumane purposes.

This analysis is persuasive only if one ignores a great deal of the relevant evidence. Restricted stimulation research has increased our understanding of a variety of psychological processes, has helped to develop theory and initiate other types of experimentation, and has contributed to the solution of important problems. To begin with, I would argue that one of the important functions of science is to explore those aspects of the world that human beings find challenging and interesting. There can be very little doubt that isolation, confinement, and reduction of stimuli are such topics. In fact, to the limited extent that Shallice is right about the functional autonomy of the technique, this development occurred because REST per se is fascinating and has fascinating effects. Wide public admiration for people like Charles Lindbergh, Joshua Slocum, and Sir Francis Chichester has much more to do with their solitude than with their technical feats. After all, there had been trans-Atlantic flights before Lindbergh's, and around-the-world sailing voyages before those of Slocum and Chichester. The frequent publication and wide readership of the accounts of prisoners, castaways, shipwreck survivors, and people in similar situations further attest to our deep interest about such experiences. This interest in itself makes the area a legitimate one for scientific inquiry.

But there is more to it than that. Results of research using restricted conditions with both infrahuman animals and human beings gave impetus to the rise of the activation/arousal theories of motivation that to a great extent replaced the classical drive theories of the 1940s. These findings helped to focus the attention of psychologists on internal processes, including cognitive and neurological functions, emphasizing the view that the organism is an active performer. This paradigm has become increasingly dominant in psychological theory, supplanting the previous focus on external stimulus characteristics and the concept of the organism as a passive responder. Furthermore, REST researchers introduced the idea that some kinds of homeostasis may be based on moderate rather than minimal levels of motivation, emotion, discrepancy, excitation, or stimulation. The work has led to increased investigation and understanding of the role of the nonspecific brain pathways. There have even been contributions to aspects of psychoanalytic theory, specifically in the strengthening of ego psychology and of the standpoint that the ego can put to its own uses events in the external world and the primary process generated by the id (for brief reviews and references, see Suedfeld 1969c; Zuckerman, 1969c).

The influence of reduced stimulation research on the development of psychological theory further includes those formulations that were specifically designed in response to sensory deprivation results. The two most prominent of these are the theory of sensoristasis (Schultz, 1965) and the optimal level of stimulation theory (Zuckerman, 1964, 1969c), both of which have much more general applications than merely to explain the results that give them their original starting point. In particular, the explanations proposed by Schultz have important implications for the way in which the perceptual and sensory systems function; some of these implications have been supported by empirical research. Zuckerman's theory, while it in many ways incorporates aspects of sensoristasis, goes further and deals with the factors of unexpectedness, habituation, individual differences, and biological cycles. Unfortunately, this theory was proposed and published in full form for the first time in 1969, and there has been very little subsequent research designed to test its postulates. Zuckerman's widely cited work on sensation-seeking (e.g., 1974) also originated in his REST research.

The role of external cues in cognitive and perceptual information processing has been explored by sensory deprivation researchers. Among the results have been strong support for the interference theory of forgetting —with REST on the human level functioning as the equivalent of various chemical and electrical procedures with infrahuman animals—and an indication of the importance of measuring and specifying task complexity as a critical variable in problem solving. Zubek and his associates, using both multimodal and unimodal sensory restriction techniques, have demonstrated interesting relationships between deprivation and sensory acuity. Not only have they shown an intriguing connection between the blocking of input in a particular receptor organ and improved acuity in its contralateral equivalent, but they have also confirmed the existence of a temporal pattern of depression and enhancement of acuity, which when further explored may shed new light on the functioning of the sensory systems (Harper and Bross, 1978).

Research on attitude change as a function of sensory restriction has demonstrated important moderating functions of intelligence and cognitive style, showed the importance of anchor points in determining the amount of yielding to propaganda or group consensus, and demonstrated the possibility that individuals experiencing high levels of stimulus hunger may exhibit behavioral compliance without internalization of a new attitude. Research in the area of personality has also benefited, with contributions to the study of ego functioning (as mentioned above) and cognitive personality styles including field dependence, conceptual complexity, and intelligence, among others. There have also been useful additions to the literature on experimental design and procedure in psychology, particularly with regard to the effects of subject and experimenter expectation, unintended effects of recruiting material, orientation, and pre-experimental procedure, and the confounding of these variables with the effects of the independent variable.

Restricted stimulation techniques have also contributed to research in applied settings. Reduced or monotonous stimulation characterizes the living and working conditions of many people. The first systematic demonstrations of some of the adverse effects of such situations led to further investigation under field conditions, with resultant suggestions for amelioration. Among the areas thus affected have been the arts and sciences concerned with the design of built environments, the structuring of physical and procedural conditions for monotonous work (e.g., Frankenhaeuser and Johansson, 1974), and the design of total environments for individuals who are confined, either alone or in small groups, for long periods of time in polar stations, space vehicles, submarines, and the like (Flaherty, 1961; Fraser, 1966). Another major applied field in which restricted stimulation is important is that of recreational environments; the importance of stimulus reduction among people who are chronically overstimulated is implied by the growth of interest among psychologists in the functions of the natural wilderness (Olsen, 1975–1977, Wohlwill, 1973). Similarly, suggestions for child rearing both at home and in institutions have come from studies of infrahuman and human infants reared under restricted conditions or subjected to reduced stimulation because of perceptual handicaps (Hunt, Mohandessi, Ghodssi, and Akiyama, 1976; Warren, 1977). Last but not least, of course, is the use of restricted stimulation in psychotherapy, the discussion of which forms the main portion of this book.

Clearly, it should not be necessary to defend the existence and continuation of research on restricted environments, including laboratory "sensory deprivation" as well as isolation or reduced stimulation in non-experimental situations. Unfortunately, the necessity does exist, and during the past few years an increasing effort is being made by workers in the field to combat the misleading negative aura that has surrounded their efforts. Articles and letters have appeared in a variety of popular publications, the common distortions presented in many psychology textbooks have been documented, and prejudiced condemnations of the technique have been openly challenged. It is to be hoped that these initiatives will help to dispel false impressions, and will make it possible for unbiased evaluation of the benefits and shortcomings of REST research to be made and understood.

THE PLAN OF THIS BOOK

The contents of this book reflect the wide range of topics to which stimulus reduction is relevant. Some of these are closely and obviously tied to the clinical use of REST. They include the effects of experimental stimulus reduction on persuasibility, theories of psychopathology in which the maintenance of optimal input levels is a crucial mediating variable, and the use of monotonous conditions as part of established psychotherapeutic methods. Others are more remotely related—for example, the characteristics of feral children, the reactions of campers going into the wilderness, or the way in which infant rats mature under different levels of environmental complexity. Still, the underlying commonality is there: the question of what we know, and what we need to find out, about the effects of restricted levels of environmental stimulation. Some of these effects are—or may be—useful in treatment; some may pose problems to be solved; some may appear irrelevant at our present state of understanding. But they are, at the least, interesting and potentially significant.

Chapters 2 through 5 present a review of research findings relevant to stimulus reduction. Chapter 2 considers the results compiled by researchers working in restricted stimulation laboratories with adult subjects. Aside from the very complete coverage presented in Zubek (1969a), the most recent review of the sensory deprivation literature appeared in a chapter by Zubek (1973) with a Spanish version published in the *Revista Interamericana de Psicología* (1972). This was a painstaking and thorough examination, compiled by the individual who, by virtue of his editorship of the definitive book and his own involvement in the field, probably had access to more of the current literature than anyone else. Chapter 2 summarizes the main points of Zubek's review and brings the discussion up to date. In general, it follows Zubek's outline and gives relatively brief resumés except where substantial new developments have occurred in the recent past.

Chapter 3 deals with two major instances of restricted stimulation that are not usually induced for experimental or therapeutic reasons. One such experience is that undergone by patients who are isolated, immobilized, or otherwise sensorially restricted as a by-product of treatment for physical illness, usually in hospitals. This occurs in order to allow better healing of traumatic injury or surgical incisions, to maintain the patient in an infection-free environment, to reduce physical stress on the cardiovascular system, and so on. Although these periods of restricted stimulation are associated with hospitalization, they are not considered a component of the actual treatment. Solitary confinement in penal institutions is a somewhat related situation and is also covered in the chapter.

Chapter 4 discusses some of the links between restricted stimulation and human development, including possible causal relationships between failures to encounter or adapt to normal levels of stimulation on the one hand and problems of psychological adjustment on the other. Such theories have been advanced to account for major psychiatric illnesses, sometimes with very different suggestions as to appropriate therapeutic tactics.

Chapter 5 covers research on infrahuman animals. It was written by Richard C. Tees, an active contributor to investigations in this field. Much of the literature deals with stimulus deprivation during the organism's infancy or early life, sometimes over periods that are quite long compared to the lifespan of the animal. Accordingly, the effects are frequently severe and may involve gross neurological and physiological changes. Deleterious effects may also be due to the failure of some developmental advance to occur during a critical period. A recent book (Riesen, 1975) has addressed itself in some detail to these effects. However, it does not cover another topic that is even more closely related to the central theme of this volume: the behavioral and psychological deficits occurring as a result of interference with normal stimulation, which can be reversed by appropriate intervention techniques later in life. Such interventions are the equivalent of therapy with individuals who as children suffered from sensory handicaps or other forms of environmental impoverishment.

The second half of the book focuses on deliberate attempts to obtain beneficial results through the use of systematic stimulus restriction. Chapter 6 is concerned with self-improvement, enlightenment, and other quasi-therapeutic goals. Among such uses we find the use of solitude in the course of religious rituals, in the search for a deeper understanding of oneself or of the universe, and during periods of contemplation and meditation. The experience may be sought in a variety of locations, ranging from the individual's own home to monasteries or wilderness campsites. A growing subset within such approaches has been the use of actual REST chambers or immersion tanks to pursue self-fulfillment and personal growth. The material discussed in this chapter is open to criticism by workers dedicated to a more orthodox scientific paradigm; however, the volume and consistency of the reports appear to warrant at least an open-minded consideration.

Chapter 7 addresses itself to REST components in commonly used psychotherapeutic techniques. Many such approaches, ranging from psychoanalysis to meditation and biofeedback, involve conditions that have much in common with restricted stimulation therapy. The role of the environment in the effectiveness of these methods has seldom been tested or considered independently.

Chapter 8 is devoted to the use of the restricted environmental stimulation technique with noninstitutionalized adult patients. This kind of treatment has been carried on in relation to a range of neurotic symptoms. There has also been extensive work in the use of stimulus reduction to enable individuals to initiate and maintain modifications of health-dysfunctional behaviors such as smoking.

Chapter 9 covers the use of REST as a therapeutic method with children. Such applications have been recommended as desirable in the perinatal environment, as well as in the medical treatment of various physical and psychological dysfunctions. The most common institutional use, involving timeout from positive reinforcement, is also examined in this chapter.

Chapter 10, written by Henry B. Adams, reviews studies using REST with institutionalized adult psychiatric patients. It has been found that many such patients are helped by restricted stimulation, and that they may derive even more benefits when stimulus reduction is combined with verbal inputs. Patients who are the most susceptible to this approach are those whose initial diagnoses are the least favorable, whose symptoms are the most severe, and who are the least likely to benefit from standard psychotherapies. One section of the chapter covers the treatment of patients who are hospitalized as emergency cases because of drug-induced psychosis.

Chapter 11, written by Roderick A. Borrie, presents detailed technical information for researchers and practitioners who are interested in setting up a REST facility. Mechanical, financial, and procedural points are discussed. Dr. Borrie has been associated with many projects in this field, including both basic research and clinical work. He also participated in the provision of REST as a therapeutic technique available to clients from the general community. This practical guide should enable interested researchers and clinicians to avoid many of the problems that previous workers have had to learn about by trial and error or through informal exchanges of information.

The final chapter considers and evaluates theories related to the status of REST as a therapeutic method. It notes areas of demonstrated strength, of demonstrated weakness, and of ambiguity or ignorance. It also examines the issue of whether the technique is safe and ethical, aside from its effectiveness or potency in particular contexts. Some suggestions for applied research needed to put this approach on a firm footing are indicated.

CHAPTER 2

Experimental REST Research
With Human Subjects

The fact that reduced stimulation has wide-ranging consequences on human behavior is one of the reasons for the rapid growth of the experimental REST literature during the 1960s. The review in this chapter is a condensed representative sampling of the relevant findings, with emphasis on research published since the Zubek (1973) review.

The reader should be aware that the topic headings are somewhat arbitrary. For example, there is one section on perceptual processes and another on cognitive processes. Workers in these fields will recognize that this is at best an uncertain distinction. There is doubt as to whether these two kinds of functions can be separated at all, and in any case there are certainly important psychological phenomena in which it is impossible to discriminate between them (see e.g., Erdelyi, 1974). Memory, reasoning, and comparison processes always intervene in determining how one experiences external stimuli, while the cognitive functions themselves are in turn affected by sensory inputs. Similarly, there are cases in which a motor response is a complex outcome of perceptual and cognitive functioning. Clearly, if one is going to follow a taxonomic scheme, all of the data must be assigned to one category or another. This Procrustean set of categories is a necessity for clearly organizing the body of material, but for a real understanding of the effects of REST a holistic approach would be more valid.

PERCEPTUAL EFFECTS

One of the problems with the research on the perceptual and motor effects of REST has been methodological. As has been pointed out, early sensory deprivation researchers tended to view the field as a substantive one rather than as a technique by which various substantive problems could be investigated. Thus, they become relatively isolated from developments in the more basic areas of psychological experimentation. For this reason, much of the research has employed procedures that have been excessively simple and in some cases even obsolete by the standards of the general field to which they belong. For example, the work on perception done in Zubek's laboratory has been criticized for failing to use the current tools of signal detection theory, ROC curves and information theoretical analyses. All of these are now standard in the perception literature, and could have added significantly to the meaningfulness of the findings (e.g., Richardson, 1972; Swets, 1973). We must also remember the other side of the coin: scientists doing research in particular substantive areas frequently have little if any knowledge of the contributions that restricted stimulation research has made or could make to their field.

Subjective Reports

One of the most widely publicized outcomes of the first perceptual deprivation studies was that many of the subjects had experienced visual, auditory, tactile, or kinesthetic hallucinations. Most striking were the visual phenomena. Many of these were very simple (flashes of light or geometric forms), but some were quite complex, highly integrated, and meaningful. The latter included, for instance, a miniature spaceship shooting pellets at the subject who could actually feel the impact of the missiles, and a line of animals with sacks on their backs marching across the visual field. In one study, 25 of 29 subjects reported some kind of hallucination (Heron, 1961).

The Controversy About "Hallucinations." Reports of hallucinations remained quite common throughout the early years of REST research. Even more recently, both REST and Δ^9-THC (an hallucinogen) led to more visual sensations than did a placebo condition (Dittrich, 1975). In such reports, with no qualitative or criterion-referenced data, it is difficult to establish what the differences between treatment groups really mean. Increasingly, workers in the field began to question the appropriateness of using the term "hallucination" for the experiences described by their subjects. Denotatively, in the sense of a perceptual event that seems to have no external counterpart, the word may have been reasonably accurate; but its connotations, and its common use in psychology and medicine as associated with the effects of psychoses and of some psychoactive drugs, were thought to be possibly misleading. The importance of this issue was highlighted by the fact that writers who wanted to emphasize the disruptive nature of sensory deprivation frequently cited hallucinations as evidence that the environment generated a "model psychosis."

While the duration of confinement is associated with the occurrence of such phenomena, with longer periods resulting in a higher frequency of reports than shorter sessions (Zuckerman, 1969b), the crucial factor appears to be how one defines hallucinations. There is certainly no doubt that subjects in restrictive stimulation conditions experience perceptual phenomena. Among these are extremely vivid dreams, daydreams, fantasies, hypnagogic and hypnopompic imagery (that is, experiences that occur in the borderline state from wakefulness to sleep and vice versa), spontaneous firing in the retina, and the perception of endogenous, residual, or low-intensity stimuli of which the experimenter is not aware. Such experiences are not the same as hallucinations. Nor are they precursors or correlates of hallucinatory psychoses (Starker, 1979). Several investigators have used a more exact definition of hallucination, usually demanding that the percept have an "out-there" quality, be uncontrollable by the subject himself, and be perceived as real by the subject. Very few REST participants turn out to have experiences that meet such criteria. In one example (Schulman, Richlin, and Weinstein, 1967), 74% of the subjects experienced some visual percepts while in darkness, but only 2% reported phenomena that met the requirements for apparent reality and lack of control.

As a result of the controversy over definitions, recent examinations of this question have adopted the neutral terms "reported visual sensations (RVSs)" and "reported auditory sensations (RASs)." The most recent thorough review of this area (Zuckerman, 1969b) has indicated that reported sensations during REST progress from simple, meaningless percepts to more complex ones. They are primarily visual, thus differing from psychotic hallucinations, while at the same time being less vivid and persistent than drug-induced hallucinations. Most RVSs "seem to be transient impersonal phenomena of no dynamic or pathological significance" (p. 125). The occurrence of RVSs is increased if the subject is lying down and is in a state of medium or high arousal. It does not seem to be affected by the particular stimulus restriction technique employed, nor by such details as intermittent visual stimulation and amount of activity. Anxiety and expectancy on the part of subjects make relatively little difference, except that a positive set fosters more reports of simple RVSs. Subject personality, at least within the aspects measured so far, has not been reliably tied to the phenomena, although some people report unusually high numbers of sensations. Whether the subject is instructed to report RVSs as soon as they occur or only after the end of the experiment is irrelevant.

Sugimoto and Kida (1968) attempted to distinguish between illusions, defined as false perceptions of an objective stimulus, and hallucinations, defined as subjective perceptions of what does not exist in the environment. The environment in this study included buzzing from an air-conditioner. Thus, all comments related to a buzzing noise (e.g., "I heard buzzing, like an airplane") were classified as illusions; "hearing a cricket chirp" as an hallucination; and phenomena of whose reality the subject was unsure (e.g., "I thought I heard motorcycle noises . . . although it's doubtful whether I did or not") as "hallucination-like experiences." All eight subjects reported a wide variety of perceptual experiences, although none of them reported any visual sensations. This may be explained by the fact that there was only a moderate reduction of visual input in the experimental chamber. The frequency of illusions and hallucinations was a curvilinear function of REST duration, increasing from none during the first day and decreasing again on the third.

Heinemann (1970), apparently using himself or a colleague as the subject in two separate experiments, attempted to evaluate the causes of various types of RVS. The first deprivation session lasted 108 hours and consisted of diffuse light, social isolation, and extreme immobilization. The second, a year later, lasted for 128 hours and consisted of complete visual and periodic auditory perceptual deprivation as well as social isolation. RVSs were related to the degree of illumination and the duration of reduced perceptual input. To some extent, the usual progression from simple to complex percepts was found, the latter appearing in full variety only after 3 days of deprivation. The data indicated that geometric figures were seen relatively frequently, in regular arrays which had qualities of depth and perspective. The author interpreted this finding as support for Gestalt explanations of the perceptual process.

One important point that has frequently been overlooked is that several studies have demonstrated a high frequency of RVSs reported by nondeprived control subjects. In fact, REST-related "imagery" seems neither reliably more frequent nor qualitatively different from nonveridical sensory experiences found under nonexperimental conditions (see Goldstein, 1976, Horowitz, 1976; Myers et al., 1966; Zuckerman, 1969a). Siegel (1977) found the occurrence of hallucinations to be associated with high arousal and "a functional disorganization of the part of the brain that regulates incoming stimuli." In view of the fact that REST may be associated with both these components, one might expect that it is one of the list of situations in which reported sensations would be found.

Another approach that would predict a high occurrence of such phenomena under sensory reduction conditions is the dual-input model (Arlow, 1969; West, 1962). While the original versions of this model focused on psychological control of perception, an environmental counterpart would lead us to the internal/external balance theory discussed elsewhere in this book (see also Schultz, 1965; Zuckerman, 1969c). That is, internal experiences become more vivid as the organism attempts to maintain a moderate level of overall stimulation in the absence of external input. Had this fact been taken into proper account in the literature, it would have been clear that REST is not unique in leading to such changes, and that their occurrence carries no implication of dysfunction, breakdown or other melodramatic trauma.

It has been argued that hallucinations, as well as other REST phenomena, are symptoms of regression in the service of the ego. In this view, the reduction of sensory inputs brings about the emergence of primary process, reestablishes feelings of dependency and lack of control, and thus returns the subject to more childlike patterns of functioning. This point of view has been used to explain not only the occurrence of reported sensations, but the other cognitive and therapeutic consequences of REST as well (Azima, Vispo, and Cramer-Azima, 1961; Rapaport, 1958). The explanation is intriguing, but has not been well supported by data.

Like visual hallucinations, regression (whether "in the service of the ego" or not) can frequently be found in normal environments. Furthermore, regression may be a function of anxiety, including the anxiety of subjects who went through the early versions of orientation to sensory deprivation experiments. Shapiro (1972) demonstrated that these facts cast some doubt on the idea that sensory deprivation per se induces regression. Obviously, the issue deserves further exploration.

The Role of Set.   Gross, Kempe, and Reimer (1972) emphasize that one must try to separate the experience of "hallucinatory" phenomena from the willingness to report such experiences. These authors feel that, given similar conditions, the phenomena are experienced about equally by most subjects. It is the reporting of the event that tends to differ. There is a personality difference, for example. Those who did report "hallucinations" under REST conditions scored on the MMPI as more extroverted, less self-justificatory, and lower on the lie scales than subjects who did not report this kind of phenomenon. All three of these differences seem logically related to one's readiness to admit having had an unusual and even "weird" experience.

Several studies have established the importance of experimentally-induced set in the reporting of RVSs (see Zuckerman, 1969a). In one recent social isolation study (Hunt, 1971), some of the induced sets—e.g., suggestions for experiencing altered states of consciousness, similar to the instructions used in a number of sensory deprivation experiments—elicited reports of perceptual anomalies and other unusual phenomena in as little as 5 minutes. Hunt and Tagefurka (1976) found that 10 minutes in an isolation room resulted in reports of "altered states of consciousness" (including nonveridical sensations) when the student participants had been instructed to concentrate on immediate subjective experiences. The rate was significantly higher than similar reports emanating from a group in the same situation but with a nonsensitizing orientation.

In an even more revealing experiment (Coon, 1973), the highest rate of RVSs was found when subjects were led to believe that such phenomena, while relatively rare, were primarily experienced by individuals of high intelligence. This goes a step further than previous attempts to induce specific sets, which manipulated primarily the expectancy that nonstimulus bound perception would or would not occur. As Coon suggests, it appears that the dual set induced in his subjects made them particularly alert and careful to note and report every event that could be classified as an RVS. Subjects who were led to believe that such experiences were rarely reported by intelligent individuals gave the fewest reports. Set made no significant difference in the accurate reporting of actual stimulus lights. Incidentally, every subject reported "a spontaneous rate of continuous ideoretinal 'noise' (i.e., tiny specks and flashes of 'light')." Apparently, what was manipulated by the different instructions was the criterion whereby subjects either did or did not classify such experiences as reportable RVSs.

Although percepts of questionable reality have been reported in all sensory modalities during REST, only visual and auditory sensations have been investigated at all systematically. Because of the relative difficulty of eliminating or even identifying real sources of noise, smell, taste, or touch in the experimental room, there are problems in doing precise studies on phenomena in these modalities. As a result, aside from a summary table of simple and complex reported auditory sensations (Zuckerman, 1969b, pp. 87–92), the literature has generally ignored them.

Objective Measures

Many of the findings of pioneer investigators have proved not to be replicable in subsequent studies, an idiosyncrasy for which no adequate explanation has yet been found. At the present time we must accept and perhaps extend to other early papers Zubek's conclusion that the results "were produced by some unique interaction of several variables of a procedural, personality, or motivational nature" (1973, p. 14). One of the great values of original programs was the extensive recording of anecdotal information that became the groundwork for later, more systematic, investigation. Many of the phenomena were unexpected, and thus appear only in spontaneous reports by the subjects. Such reports gave clues for the inclusion of objective measures in later work, measures that did not necessarily confirm the original statements. The McGill data originally showed dramatic changes in the appearance of the visual world after 2 to 6 days of monotonous stimulation. These included changes in the saturation and luminosity of colors, movements and angular distortions of objects in the environment, and unusually strong afterimages. However, subsequent researchers, using as much as 14 days of confinement in both reduced and monotonous stimulation experiments, have failed to confirm these reports. Impairment of depth perception, visual acuity, and size constancy featured among other early reports that were not substantiated by subsequent research. Stimulus reduction has also failed to produce reliable changes in stereoscopic estimates of size and distance (Lawson and Frey, 1971). Other phenomena not reliably affected by reduced stimulation include shape and brightness constancy, brightness discrimination and contrast, various visual illusions, auditory thresholds, and kinesthetic acuity.

Color discrimination does deteriorate consistently, as does the ability to copy accurately figures ranging from the very simple (Vernon, 1963) to the quite complex (see Zubek, 1973). There is also an impairment of the ability to recognize figures when they are embedded in more complex designs.

Among the visual illusions, a number of studies have found the autokinetic effect to be increased, decreased, or unchanged. The inconsistency is probably due to methodological differences as well as to the complexity of the phenomenon and of the variables that can influence it. The aftereffect of the Archimedes spiral consistently increases in duration, the magnitude of the Müller-Lyer illusion decreases, and phi-perception is impaired. The perception of reversible figures generally becomes less flexible, although it appears that different results are obtained depending on whether one uses the Necker cubes or the faces-vase figure (Zubek, 1969b). The apparent speed of a moving line has consistently been found to decrease, regardless of whether the experiment involves reduced or monotonous stimulation. The autoscopic illusion, the perception of one's own features in another person, has been ascribed to sensory reduction (Sperber, 1969), although no attempts have been made to measure its occurrence in that situation.

Considerable research has been done on the phenomenon of fusion, or the speed at which stimuli must alternate or repeat in order to be perceived as one continuous stimulus. Critical flicker frequency (CFF) decreases after 2 days of pattern reduction, although no such effect is found at longer or shorter durations. Visual deprivation alone produces significant increases in acuity in critical flicker frequency, critical frequency of percussion (the tactile equivalent), and in auditory flutter fusion (Harper and

Bross, 1978). Similarly, unimodal deprivation in other modalities leads to improved discrimination. This is true of the effects of auditory deprivation on visual and tactile discrimination, and of nonexperimental cutaneous deprivation (using amputees as subjects) on the visual CFF measure. Discrimination also improves when a particular sensory receptor is occluded (e.g., one eye or an area of skin on the forearm). The change occurs both for the occluded organ after the termination of the condition and for the contralateral organ or area.

The most exhaustive aspect of this research, directed by John P. Zubek and summarized after his death by two of his former students (Harper and Bross, 1978), was concerned with the effects of monocular deprivation on the acuity of the other eye. There is a rapid decrease in CFF, followed by negatively accelerated increase up to about 11 days and then leveling off, a pattern that Zubek called the depression-enhancement phenomenon. The changed CFF persists for approximately as long a time after the end of the session as the occlusion itself lasted. It is found only when the experimental procedure involves sensory reduction, and does not appear with monotonous stimulation. The CFF of the occluded eye itself, by the way, does not change consistently.

These findings, which are quite reliable across experiments and subjects, provide an interesting test of current theories of the perceptual apparatus. In particular, while demonstrating the central mediation of perception, they cast some doubt upon theories based on general arousal phenomena and a sensory equivalent of homeostasis. If this were the actual mediating process, the occluded as well as the contralateral areas should exhibit increased sensitivity. Zubek and Bross (1972) have indicated that reduced stimulation may be equivalent to functional denervation which, like physical denervation, leads to a brief lack of sensitivity followed by supersensitivity. This analogy may be either a more accurate analysis of the situation or one that should be combined with the centralist theories.

Although general visual acuity and auditory thresholds do not change, tactile acuity and pain sensitivity do increase. The latter phenomenon seems to be restricted to stimulus reduction techniques, since the white noise usually present in pattern reduction experiments is in fact an analgesic, and appears to result in decreased sensitivity to pain stimuli (Zubek, 1969b; Zubek, Aftanas, Hasek, Sansom, Schludermann, Wilgosh and Winocur, 1962). With monotonous stimulation, gustatory sensitivity improves at least in the sweet and bitter ranges; visual deprivation alone produces similar effects for salty and sweet tastes but not for sour and bitter. Olfactory acuity consistently increases, while there seem to be no changes in kinesthetic acuity. Spatial orientation while blindfolded appears to be impaired after pattern reduction, particularly as regards the judgment of angles and directions.

The failure of REST researchers to use the most current techniques and theories in the area of perception has evoked criticism. It is expected that this situation will soon be corrected (Harper and Bross, 1978). Meanwhile, the one attempt to use signal detection theory to separate motivational from truly sensory changes resulting from reduced stimulation (Gendreau and Carlson, 1974) applied stimuli to occluded areas on the skin of the arm. An actual threshold change, rather than merely a shift in criterion, was found.

EFFECTS ON MOTOR FUNCTIONING

In his review of the literature, Zubek (1973) concludes that the deleterious effects of restricted stimulation on various kinds of motor performance have been established beyond reasonable doubt. The instruments used to measure the effects have included pencil mazes, numeral cancellation, speed and quality of handwriting, placing dots or checkmarks inside printed geometric figures, the MacQuarrie Test of Mechanical Skills, mirror tracing, rotary pursuit, and walking along a wooden rail. Some of these effects, particularly the more complex ones, appear only after 2 days of confinement, and may diminish thereafter; some of them can be produced by long durations of social isolation without any other environmental interference.

One recent study used a factorial manipulation of light and noise to look at reaction time to a tactile stimulus (Kallman and Isaac, 1977). The two environmental conditions interacted to produce the curvilinear function reported by previous researchers, with performance decrements when light and sound were both present or both absent. This was interpreted as an indication of a change in arousal level. As is usually the case, a replication indicated that performance improved during the second session (cf. Zubek, 1973). In this particular study there was also a sex difference, with males performing better and improving more on the second testing.

Since most of the research on motor effects was done early in the history of REST, it was reviewed fully by Zubek (1969b, 1973).

VIGILANCE

Performance on vigilance tasks spans cognitive, perceptual, and motor functions. Visual measures after REST have shown decrements related to the impairment of reaction time, with 2 days identified as a critical period.

Auditory measures have shown that deprived subjects perform as well as controls tested in normal conditions, and better than controls taking the test in darkness. This finding seems quite reliable and is not greatly affected by duration time from 1 to 7 days using reduced stimulation. Monotonous stimulation, however, seems to lead to impaired auditory as well as visual vigilance. The crucial mediating variable may be subjective feelings of boredom (see Thackray, Bailey, and Touchstone, 1977).

Kemp (1973) used monotonous stimulation in an attempt to increase the performance speed of aged subjects. The theoretical argument was that age-related differences in speed of behavior are related to decreased activation levels and activation capacity among older subjects. A group of subjects with a mean age of 26.5 years was compared with a group with a mean of 68.1 years, and test-retest changes under experimental and control conditions were noted. Contrary to the hypothesis, pattern deprivation had no significant main effect on auditory reaction time. The two independent variables, age and stimulation, interacted. Some adverse emotional reactions to deprivation were reported.

The findings could have important implications for our knowledge of how age affects one's responses to the environment, except for one problem. The duration of the REST session was only 2½ hours. Previous experiments had shown that such short periods were sufficient to elicit anxiety-related verbal reports, but not to cause reliable changes in auditory reaction time. Thus, the procedure did not adequately test the hypothesis on which it was based. It is to be hoped that the idea, which bears upon an important theoretical and practical problem, will be further explored. This is only one example of a creative hypothesis that may not have been supported by the data because of such problems as the wrong confinement duration, an excessively long test battery, or some other overlooked procedural factor.

Perhaps the most stressful monotonous environment is that in which stimulation is low in information value (highly predictable, invariant) but in which a vigilance task must be continuously performed. The effects of such a condition should be compared to those of a control treatment consisting of a no-task, monotonous environment. This comparison would help to explain at least some of the differences between natural and laboratory REST situations, since the former do usually involve the necessity of task performance.

COGNITIVE EFFECTS

Research concerning the effects of REST on cognitive processes has been marred by procedural problems. Investigators use different tests and call them by the same name, or conversely use the same test and call it by different names. Although differences between pre- and post-session scores have been cited as showing treatment effects, they may actually have been due to repeated testing or to the nonequivalence of supposedly equivalent test forms. Another source of confusion is that REST effects probably diminish during the administration of long test batteries. In some cases, testing is not begun until some time after the termination of the session. Even when there is no delay, the test administration may completely disrupt the REST conditions. For example, the lights may be turned on, and writing materials may be used, sometimes in the acutal presence of an experimenter. All of these procedures drastically increase the level of stimulation. In addition to these problems, the interpretation of data is made more difficult by a deplorable tendency to discuss nonsignificant trends in the predicted direction as though they actually supported the hypothesis.

Summary of Findings

The original McGill studies set the tone for much of the next decade of research on the intellectual effects of restricted stimulation. Subjects in the first studies reported that they found it difficult to think in a clear, organized and persistent way, a finding that has been replicated numerous times. However, recent research in the clinical context has implied that this is not a universal phenomenon. Although no explicit test has been performed, the anecdotal literature seems to warrant the hypothesis that the inability to concentrate on and cognitively explore particular topics is at least to some extent a function of the motivation of the subject and the purported reason for his participation in REST.

When people enter the reduced stimulation environment because they feel that it might be helpful with regard to some personal problem that they are highly motivated to solve, their ability to concentrate on it and on possible ways of dealing with it seems to suffer no impairment. On the contrary, subjects have reported that they are much more capable of sustained pursuits of insight and problem-solving techniques in the REST environment than under normal conditions. This might be expected because of the elimination of distracting stimuli from the outside. However, research is needed to explore the interaction between this effect and the general reduction of complex cognitive processing that emerges in purely experimental studies. The crucial difference may be that clinical subjects do not experience the feeling that "concentrating was too much trouble" (Suedfeld, 1969b), and thus may have either overcome or not experienced whatever disruptive effects stimulus restriction may have on cognition per se. In fact, the findings may support previous suggestions that experimental subjects are actually showing motivational, rather than strictly cognitive, impairment.

The detailed review of this literature (Suedfeld, 1969b) indicates that monotonous stimulation leads to more disturbances of cognitive processing than does stimulus reduction, and that a 24-hour confinement duration appears to be the critical period. The verbal behavior of confined subjects varies tremendously, both on a spontaneous basis and in response to questions permitting long answers. Although there appears to be a desire to continue talking and thereby maintain contact with another person, several studies have indicated that subjects actually manage to speak no more, or even significantly less, than do controls (Suedfeld, 1969b; but cf. Leff and Hirsch, 1972). Since socially isolated but not sensorially deprived subjects, who presumably experience the same motivational changes, do significantly increase their level of verbal output, one might hypothesize that the REST data do actually indicate a decrease in the ability to maintain connected verbal discourse. This phenomenon, like so many others, tends to diminish with repeated confinement.

One of the most interesting effects of REST on cognitive processes is that related to memory. There are relatively few experiments in which memory decrements were reported. On the contrary, most workers have found either no significant effect or significant improvements. The specific stimulus restriction technique does not affect the outcome. Although the type of material being remembered also does not seem to be crucial, there is some indication that decrements occur primarily with nonmeaningful stimuli. The fact that a period of REST after learning improves later recall of the learned material is not surprising: time to consolidate memories without the interference of other stimuli should lead to greater accuracy. Stimulus reduction not only prevents the forgetting that occurs among control subjects over a 24-hour intertrial interval, but in fact leads to a reminiscence phenomenon. REST participants remember more of the material at the end of a 24-hour session than on a test immediately after the original presentation (Grissom, 1966).

This research has important implications in areas related to educational psychology as well as to clinical practice. In situations where retention of material is important, the use of a stimulus-reduced environment as soon as possible after learning may be beneficial. Furthermore, such a condition may be used to reduce forgetting that may be a result of other treatments or experiences—for example, electroconvulsive shock (ECS) (Robertson and Inglis, 1977). It has already been shown with animals that sensory deprivation after electroconvulsive shock reduces or eliminates the retrograde amnesia that ECS normally produces (Calhoun, Prewett, Peters, and Adams, 1975; Peters, Calhoun, and Adams, 1973). This beneficial effect can occur even if the animal is isolated for only one hour following ECS (Hinderliter, Smith, and Misanin, 1976). So far, no equivalent work has been published with human patients, but in view of the serious criticisms of ECS as a memory-disrupting experience, such research is clearly warranted.

Investigations of more complicated intellectual processes, such as problem solving, reasoning, and arithmetical calculation have come up with less clear-cut results. In fact, the most that can be said about performance on such tasks is that in the overwhelming majority of instances REST seems to have no statistically reliable effect. Some data indicate that monotonous stimulation is a bit more consistent in bringing about deficits than is stimulus reduction, particularly when the duration of confinement is at least a week. The effects can be counteracted by exercise. This research, reported from Zubek's laboratory, is at best indicative because of the failure of other laboratories to arrive at consistent findings.

Evaluations of even more complex cognitive processes, on the other hand, have found quite reliably that REST impairs performance. The data are based on measures of divergent thinking, various projective tests, and situations where relatively long and detailed verbalization about a particular problem is required. This category of tasks comes closest to justifying the popular impression that sensory deprivation results in cognitive decrements.

The Importance of Task Complexity

These results have been interpreted in terms of an arousal U-curve (e.g., Landon and Suedfeld, 1972). Stimulus restriction is conceived of as an arousal-inducing manipulation, with cognitive effects similar to those of other such manipulations, including competition for a financial incentive (e.g., Suedfeld, 1968; Suedfeld, Glucksberg and Vernon, 1967). As such, it results in the increased dominance of responses already high in the subject's repertoire, as was posited by Yerkes and Dodson (1908) and by Hull-Spence behavior theory. In consequence, tasks whose correct solution is already near the top of the response hierarchy—that is, simple problems—are solved even more efficiently. Complex tasks, whose correct solution is either low in the repertoire or completely unavailable (so that the subject must generate a novel response) become even more difficult to solve.

Suedfeld (1969b) arranged the tasks used in REST studies on a dimension of complexity. Simple tasks are those that depend "on the use of overlearned, structured, logical steps to reach a definite, clear answer . . . to the degree that new combinations must be made, uncertain approaches tried, new material generated, on the way to an unknown, self-defined, unstructured goal, the problem lies on the complex or open-system half of the complexity continuum" (p. 147). Each task used by REST researchers was assigned to one of three categories: *simple,* consisting of learning and memory tests; *moderate,* including tests of rapid problem-solving, numerical problems, logical deductions, anagrams, and the like; and *complex,* subsuming projective measures, word association, and tests of verbal fluency and creativity.

In the "simple" category, one-third of the reports indicated significant improvement in performance, as opposed to only one such report in the other two categories. In the "moderate" category, 76% of the studies showed no significant effect due to REST, half again as high a rate as in the other two categories. The "moderate" category being a rather diverse catch-all, its lack of consistency may reflect weak or contradictory effects. Over half of the "complex" task reports showed decrements, about twice as many as in the other two categories.

A later review (Landon and Suedfeld, 1972) showed that in the interim, data had accrued that even more strongly supported the hypothesized relationship between task complexity and REST effects (see Fig. 2-1). The modal outcomes were now almost 40% for improvement of simple performance, almost 80% for no effect on moderate performance, and close to 60% impairment on complex tasks. These data were compiled from more than 80 published studies, many of which used more than one task.

Landon and Suedfeld (1977) have indicated that the interaction between complexity and restricted stimulation affects not only performance level but response bias. Deprived subjects evidenced less bias than controls on a simple concept identification task and more when the task was complex. Although this finding may have been partly artifactual, since the simple and complex tasks were both so easy that virtually all subjects learned to solve them, it points to a possible refinement in our understanding of the cognitive effects of reduced stimulation.

Complexity is not, of course, the only relevant variable. As has been mentioned, type of deprivation may affect the results, as may the timing, duration, and modality of the test battery. Deprivation duration is also important, with 24 hours appearing fairly regularly as the range around which both positive and negative effects have become markedly evident. Other parameters—set, personality characteristics related to cognition, and so on—probably also have some impact; but no systematic research of these influences has yet been published.

There have been a few studies looking at the impact of REST on tasks of somewhat indeterminate complexity but high affective relevance.

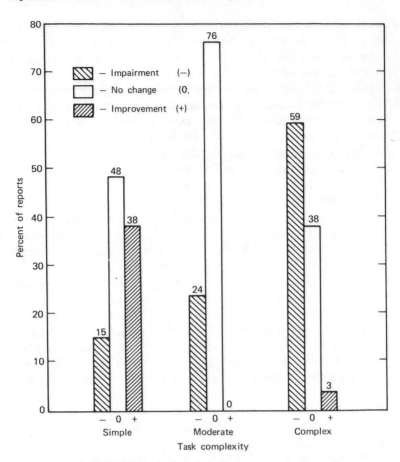

Figure 2.1. The effects of REST on cognitive performance as a function of task complexity. Based on data published by Suedfeld & Landon, 1972.

Myers, Murphy, Smith, and Goffard (1966) did several studies testing the meaning of words before and after stimulus reduction or a control condition. They found that for the most part there was no change attributable to the environment. Measures included indices of anxiety and commonality of responses to a variety of stimuli, as well as the MMPI validity scales to see if cubicle subjects were somehow less confiding in their answers. To relatively neutral stimuli, such as those used in word association tests, the responses of deprived subjects tended to be less creative than those of controls. To some extent, this appeared to be the result of lower motivation rather than of cognitive disruption. However, there were changes in associations to words which were related to REST and thus had some emotional impact. In another study, Adler (1973) found that the way subjects scaled a variety of affectively loaded pictures was related to the amount of stress being experienced as well as to how relevant the particular picture was to the current experience. Once again there was no general disruption, even though this study involved four weeks in social isolation in an underground bunker.

One kind of cognitive performance that has remained untested is that involving high-level creativity. There is no scarcity of self-reported creative thinking while under conditions of isolation and reduced stimulation. Examples range from Descartes (1637/1912) laying the groundwork of his philosophy while staying in one isolated room "undisturbed by any cares or passions" (p. 10) and building upon it afterwards "as solitary and as retired as in the midst of the most remote deserts" (p. 25) to Raymond B. Cattell (1972) citing the solitude needed for intellectual incubation, which he found among the lonely moors of his childhood and later in "an eyrie" in the Rocky Mountains. The list includes a great number of artists, scientists, philosophers, and religious and political leaders. Actual REST facilities can have the same effect: we have seen reports of profound sensory reduction being used by a mathematician and a tournament-level chess player to work out problems, and by a dancer to conceptualize choreographic ideas (Bernstein, 1976).

There is certainly no doubt that a great increase in fantasy can be experienced under REST conditions. To the extent that creativity is a function or consequence of a relaxed and free flow of images and ideas, one would expect it to be facilitated accordingly. Using 2 hours of monotonous stimulation, Shore (undated) studied the reports of three graduate students in physical chemistry. Among other topics of thought, the problems encountered by the individual in his own research, and his feelings about his work and about science in general featured prominently. Some of the comments quoted in the paper communicate a feeling of great excitement and ecstatic pleasure about scientific work. Shore concludes that "the sensory deprivation procedure can participate in the formation and modification of scientific concepts" (p. 11). Clearly, the usefulness of REST in facilitating the productivity of artists, scientists, and other creative individuals deserves careful exploration.

Cognitive Change and Brain Functioning

The findings of REST research are quite compatible with recent theoretical and methodological shifts in experimental psychology. In particular, the current view of perception and cognition as active constructive processes has been significantly advanced by this set of data (Reed, in press). Contradicting Shallice's (1972a) criticism about the lack of contributions that reduced stimulation research has made to theory, Reed recognizes that this line of work has played a part in the radical transformation of cognitive psychology during the past twenty years.

As Reed shows, some of Shallice's (1972b) ideas on consciousness and information processing have clear implications that can be tested by reduced stimulation research. Specifically, Shallice's theory argues that there are selectors in brain functioning that determine whether a particular action system becomes dominant and, if so, toward what goal. While this idea and its predecessors have been tested to some extent on the stimulus input side, there has been relatively little investigation into the characteristics of decision-making and behavioral output in the absence of determining external stimuli. It is ironic that Shallice, aspects of whose theory could be so well tested by this technique, should have originated a general political assault on "sensory deprivation" research (1972a).

Reed interprets the REST literature as indicating that logical, analytical thought, based on verbal symbols, deteriorates at the same time that there is more involuntary imagery in various sensory modalities, particularly the visual. In the theoretical part of his chapter, he further elaborates the idea that the change in information processing as a function of REST is essentially an impairment in sequential ordering rather than in parallel processing (cf. Paivio, 1971). Reviewing data on cerebral hemispheric functioning, he argues that stimulus deprivation appears to increase the kind of information processing that characterizes the right hemisphere: a prevalence of intuitive, configurational procedures at the expense of analysis, language, and logic. The hypothesis that REST is an environmental way to achieve the temporary dominance of right hemisphere functioning is certainly an intriguing one, and is compatible with the view that the situation is an externally structured analogue of meditation and similar states.

Reed himself points out some of the problems with this formulation. One of these is the exclusive concentration on the cerebral hemispheres, while ignoring the brainstem for whose involvement in REST effects there is both evidence and theoretical argument (cf. Lindsley, 1961). Second, the hypothesis accepts the reductionist argument of the equivalence between certain mental processes and cortical hemispheres, an assumption that is rejected by many people as unproven at best and fallacious at worst (as one extreme example, see the rejection of the "contained mind" hypothesis presented by Lilly, 1977). Specialization of the hemispheres itself is somewhat dubious, since it has not been demonstrated in a wide range of functions with intact, normal human beings. The cerebrum typically works as a unit, and it is risky to assume that when the system is disrupted, specific operations can be ascribed to one part of it or another. In spite of these difficulties, the approach is certainly an intriguing one. Reed echoes my own regret that the decrease in REST research came before major advances in other areas of psychology. In his opinion, the work on altered states of consciousness, imagery, and the split-brain technique are obvious developments that are related to REST but have not been applied to it.

TIME ESTIMATION

Like vigilance, time estimation is a compound task. It cannot easily be assigned to cognition or to perception. Marum (1968), using water immersion, found that there was a general tendency under both REST and control conditions to overestimate stimuli of brief duration and underestimate those of longer duration (the range being from 2 to 32 seconds). However, while there were significant effects for the actual duration of the stimulus and for the methods used to estimate that duration, there was no significant difference between the REST and control conditions.

The data on estimation of long duration times are striking. Logically, one would expect that, REST time being "empty," durations would be greatly overestimated. In fact, the opposite has usually been the case. Subjects in reduced stimulation conditions underestimate the time that they have spent in the tank or chamber. This finding remains consistent even though changes in time estimation vary across individuals. Extraverts underestimate elapsed time more grossly than introverts, and subjects who are particularly stressed by the reduced stimulation environment overestimate time spent in the chamber. Underestimates can be as much as 40 or 50% of the actual time (Zubek, 1969a). They occur primarily during the early part of a session, and tend to disappear later or during repeated exposures to REST.

In view of the importance of cultural background in a wide variety of other psychological functions, one might expect Japanese subjects to react differently to REST than Westerners. But the differences do not seem to be overwhelming. For example, Japanese subjects spending 72 hours in reduced stimulation showed relatively small errors in time estimation during the first day (Sugimoto, Kida, Teranishi, and Yamamoto, 1968). Errors increased markedly during the second day and then fell off again. Greater involvement in activities was associated with greater time estimation error in either direction. As in Western studies, 6 of the 8 subjects underestimated time in confinement. This failure to find cultural differences has been quite common in Japanese REST experiments.

Fraisse (1973), finding similar results in cave studies of extremely long duration compared to laboratory REST, follows the theory of Sturt (1925;

Ornstein, 1969) in hypothesizing that the estimation of elapsed time is a function of the number of changes occurring during a given period. When the subject is confined, with both the incoming stimuli and his own responses being relatively unchanging and/or low in intensity, it takes longer for a particular level of change to occur. This period is estimated to be longer than an objectively equivalent duration in a more diversified normal environment. This psychological explanation seems preferable to a purely physical one because there is no physiological evidence for changes in the biological clock. For example, body temperature, including the circadian changes, does not seem to be affected.

The Sturt explanation is contradicted by the findings of Sugimoto et al. (1968), as well as by a study in which isolated but not otherwise deprived subjects were asked to estimate the hour and day several times per day during a 2-week session (Lavie and Webb, 1975). It was found that a group undergoing intense scheduled exercise underestimated the elapsed time significantly, while this was not found among a free-activity group. According to Sturt's hypothesis, required exercise subjects should have shown less underestimation since they would have experienced more changes than the free-activity group. Lavie and Webb postulate that there is a change in the diurnal cycle, so that the period experienced as one day actually becomes more than 24 hours long, but people continue to give their estimates by anchoring them around normal experience. Thus, a subject waking up from a long sleep would be likely to say that it is approximately 8 o'clock in the morning, if that is his normal time for awakening; but if his day has been lengthened, the actual time may be several hours later. Since the exercise group in the Lavie and Webb study had more periods of sleep per day, this might have exacerbated their problem in making accurate estimates.

As Reed (in press) has pointed out, the consistent and systematic underestimations do not give the full picture of what the effects of REST on the time sense really are. While estimates of time duration can remain fairly accurate, this does not necessarily depict the actual experience of the flow of time. In Reed's own earlier study (1962), this experience became so changed that even in a session lasting less than an hour approximately a third of the subjects said they had a feeling of timelessness. His 1978 review supports this finding, in that many subjects in several laboratories felt disoriented in time. Reed, who accepts Sturt's hypothesis, feels that it is possible for a subject to underestimate elapsed time while simultaneously feeling that time is going by very slowly (see also Wessman and Gorman, 1977).

A cognitive dissonance explanation is also plausible. Subjects may protect themselves against the discovery that they have an unexpectedly long period of deprivation still to go by underestimating the time that they have spent in the chamber. Thus, they will not encounter the unpleasant surprise of thinking that the session is almost over when in fact that is not yet the case. Tangential evidence compatible with this hypothesis can be found among subjects who quit REST ahead of schedule. When tested early in the experiment, such subjects overestimated the time they had spent in reduced stimulation significantly more than did REST-tolerant individuals (Murphy, Hampton, and Myers, 1962)—a failure to use the self-protective cognitive manipulation described above. This failure may have increased their feelings of stress to the point where they had to leave the chamber.

INDIVIDUAL DIFFERENCES

One frequently asked question is whether personality differences affect the response to restricted stimulation. The interactionist point of view would logically imply such differences, since the response to any environment should be mediated by the customary behavior patterns of the individual. Yet, surprisingly little agreement has been found on this question. Even characteristics that on theoretical grounds should be extremely relevant have failed to correlate highly and reliably with responses to REST.

Demographic Data

Demographic characteristics such as age, educational and occupational level, and ethnic background have generally been ignored as independent variables. It is difficult to understand this lack of data, since REST experiments have included subjects representing wide ranges on many such variables. The only major demographic factor that has received attention is gender.

Zuckerman's review of sex differences in the response to REST (1969a) indicates that there are either no differences, or that differences have been found in some studies but not others, on such dependent measures as reported stress, perceptual phenomena, time estimation, body movement and changes in body image, verbal reporting, and endurance. Among physiological measures, heart rate has shown no difference in either tank or chamber settings.

Using the water immersion technique, McClure and Forgays (1975) reported that subjects of both sexes stayed in the tank for about the same period of time, underestimated the time spent almost equally, and had approximately the same mean heart rate. Walters, Shurley, and Parsons

(1962) found that male subjects were less introspective, more stimulus oriented, and more field dependent than females. Women were more willing to report having had pleasant experiences in the tank (men reported such experiences only to a male interviewer). It was hypothesized that these differences may have been due to different cultural expectations and sets. Interestingly, responses were affected by whether the post-session interview was conducted by a male or a female experimenter. Psychological content scores on sexual feelings and the total experience encountered in restricted stimulation were higher when subject and interviewer were of the same sex. The investigators also concluded that the responses of the male group were more homogeneous. It should be noted that all of these subjects were medical students, obviously not a representative sample, particularly of females.

Although REST research has been conducted in many countries, data on the effects of different cultural backgrounds are even more scarce. There are some indications that Japanese subjects tolerate reduced stimulation more easily than Westerners, although this is a very tentative finding and may be to some extent a function of different experimental procedures. In one study (Schwitzgebel, 1962), a group of black African students, by definition somewhat acculturated to European norms, showed fewer changes on measures of simple perceptual and cognitive processes than a group of white Africans after 8 hours of either monotonous stimulation or social isolation.

One might also expect that differences in occupation (or field of study, in the case of students) would be relevant. This assumption has not been well tested. Zuckerman (1969a) refers to two relevant studies. One compared the sensory deprivation tolerance of US Air Force officers and seminary students. While there were reliable personality differences among groups, there was no significant difference in requesting early release from the chamber (Peters, Benjamin, Helvey, and Albright, 1963). The other (Holt and Goldberger, 1961) compared a group of education students with a group of unemployed actors living in New York. All of the actors (but not the students) completed the scheduled session successfully without coming close to quitting. Very few of them complained that they were unable to concentrate. In fact, this group "found the whole situation . . . much less threatening and unpleasant than the students did" (p. 259). In the student sample, there was a correlation between the ability to adapt comfortably to monotonous stimulation and a pattern of personality test scores that indicated passivity, high esthetic values, nurturance, dependence, and intellectual flexibility, among other characteristics. The authors summarized the more adaptable pattern as acceptance of the feminine side of one's nature (all of the subjects were male).

The attempt to replicate this finding with the group of actors was a failure. On some scales, in fact, the relationship was statistically significant in the opposite direction. This was explained in terms of the different meaning of masculinity to the two samples. Among the education students used as a comparison group, high masculinity scores indicated orientation toward high activity. Individuals who fit this pattern were threatened and stressed by the monotonous stimulation condition. Students with "feminine interests," disposed toward introspection, found the situation quite tolerable. By contrast, the authors felt, actors scoring high on masculinity were similar to the low-masculinity student group, in that they had a reasonable balance of interests. The actor sample included a high proportion of overt homosexuals (at least five of the 16 subjects). A study using newly-developed measures of androgyny would be able to shed further light on these hypotheses.

In one other study on demographic differences, Haggard (1973) found that individuals from remote, socially isolated farms in Norway were less disturbed by monotonous stimulation in an experimental chamber than subjects from an urban background. Rural subjects had significantly fewer visual, auditory, and bodily sensations and post-experimental perceptual distortions. They showed a trend toward less movement during the first hour of confinement, and significantly less during the third and fifth hours. They reported less fear and anxiety, and tended to have a lower incidence of thought disturbance and reported stress.

Very little work has been done with such special subject groups. It would be interesting to study the effects of REST on spelunkers, prospectors, SCUBA divers, and other individuals who are used to similar kinds of environments. The perceptually handicapped would also be an interesting population. In one experiment, Mendelson (1964) put 20 deaf college students into a monotonous stimulus condition for one hour and compared their responses with those that they emitted in a control condition administered exactly one week earlier or later. The primary dependent variable was imagery, communicated by sign language which was then transcribed. There were more visual images during the REST session than during the control session, and during the first than during the second session, regardless of treatment condition. These differences were significant only with subjects whose deafness was congenital. The quality of visual imagery apparently did not change, regardless of timing or condition. Congenitally deaf subjects also had more auditory images in the first than in the second session, a pattern that was reversed among subjects who had become deaf relatively late in life. While these findings are interesting, they fall far short of any comprehensive analysis of the effects of experimentally reduced stimulation on the deaf. There is no evidence as to the reactions of individuals with other forms of perceptual impairment.

Personality Data

Several tests have been made of the effects of REST on those processes that make up what is traditionally called cognitive style. Most contributors to this area are essentially personality theorists, and tend to emphasize the trans-situational, unchanging aspects of information processing that supposedly characterize each individual. An alternative viewpoint is that cognitive styles either change as a function of situational demands or are determined by interaction between such demands and individual disposition. One of the few examples of a cognitive theory of personality that has also led to considerable research on situational effects has been conceptual complexity theory (e.g., Schroder, Driver, and Streufert, 1967); but other such constructs (see Schroder and Suedfeld, 1971) can also be viewed in the same way. This is an unusual approach. The standard procedure is to investigate how personality affects one's responses to the environment, not the other way around. REST researchers have been among the few to take the concept of person-environment interaction seriously enough to reverse the traditional definition of which is the independent and which the dependent variable.

Jacobson (1966) showed that field independence, as measured by the Rod and Frame Test, increased after a one-hour session in REST. An alternative measure of field independence, the Embedded Figures Test (which relies exclusively on visual cues rather than on a combination of visual and bodily feedback), did not show changes after two hours of reduced stimulation (Culver, Cohen, Silverman, and Shmavonian, 1964). However, monotonous stimulation for over two days led to increased field dependence on this measure in the McGill studies. A direct test of these phenomena (Kurie and Mordkoff, 1970) showed that reduced stimulation for 45 minutes improved performance on the Rod and Frame but not on Embedded Figures. Another condition, in which subjects were told to concentrate as much as possible upon their somatic experiences, led to more accurate performance than REST, but again only on the Rod and Frame Test. We may therefore conclude that brief stimulus restriction may lead to better integration of information from visual and somatic feedback. The evidence is limited, since field independence is unusual among cognitive style approaches in providing other than verbal measures.

The effects of REST on other personality variables has not yet been ascertained. Any such research would have to control for the more basic changes that stimulus restriction brings about in verbal fluency and in the ability to concentrate. In the one study that attempted to measure changes in a variety of cognitive styles, McKenna (1971) found inconsistent effects. McKenna used three environmental conditions, each for 3 hours.

These were a control condition, with the subject socially isolated and lying on a bed; a perceptual monotony condition with translucent goggles and white noise; and a perceptual variation condition, in which the environment was programmed to be highly stimulating. Amazingly, the difference in environments did not produce changes in either field dependence or scanning-focusing. The author speculates that the lack of significant results may be due to insufficient differentiation among the three conditions. The so-called control condition may have been quite similar to the monotonous one, and the perceptual variation condition may not have been stimulating enough compared to the normal experiences of college-student subjects. It is difficult to accept the second explanation. If the subjects were used to a high level of stimulation, both the control and the perceptual reduction treatments should have had magnified effects. Since previous researchers had found significant Rod and Frame changes after even shorter periods of deprivation, the brief duration used here does not explain the lack of effects. Thus, the inconsistency must remain unexplained for the time being.

The more orthodox question focuses on the effect of personality differences on the response to REST. As indicated in the major reviews (Zubek, 1969a, 1973), the data have been unexciting and inconsistent. Even some variables that intuitively appear likely to affect the subject's response to stimulus reduction have failed to do so consistently. For example, what prediction would seem safer than to hypothesize that introverts would adapt better to such a situation than extraverts? Yet, in spite of a valiant effort to interpret the data as conforming to this hypothesis (Eysenck, 1976), neither the likelihood of volunteering for REST experiments (Francis and Diespecker, 1973) nor one's performance and emotions in the chamber (Myers, 1969) are predicted accurately by measures of introversion. There does seem to be an advantage to the introvert in some studies, but data on tolerance of stimulus restriction tend to go in the opposite direction. The findings are contaminated by the possibility that extraverts violate the experimental restrictions, thus reducing the severity of stimulus reduction. Outside the laboratory, the same confusion exists. As one illustration, introversion does not seem to be related to the attitudes of children toward social isolation and corporal punishment (Parker, 1972).

A variety of other personality traits have also been explored. Studies using field independence as the personality variable of concern have failed to obtain reliable results. Field dependent individuals may react adversely to the uncertainty involved in stimulus restriction procedures, without a differential response to the lack of stimuli per se (Zuckerman, 1969c).

Stimulus augmenters and reducers (Petrie, 1979) have not been found to differ significantly in reacting to restricted stimulation. Even the theoretical relationship of this variable to behavior in REST conditions is open to debate. The obvious hypothesis is that augmenters would be less adversely affected, since they can make the most of whatever stimulation is available by enhancing its intensity. But Buchsbaum (1976) suggests that reducers would tolerate stimulus reduction better than augmenters. This hypothesis is based on the finding that reducers have lower sensory thresholds and larger amplitude average evoked responses. The apparent contradiction is resolved by viewing reducers as individuals who are quite responsive to low stimulus intensities, but who attenuate inputs of high intensity. This formulation contrasts with Petrie's original theory, in which both reduction and augmentation are uniform across the stimulus intensity continuum.

Conceptual structure (Harvey, Hunt, and Schroder, 1961; Schroder, Driver, and Streufert, 1967) has been used in only a few studies. Apparently, individuals who are simple in structure find reduced stimulation less unpleasant than do the relatively information-oriented complex subjects. When given the opportunity to hear messages in the chamber, people at lower levels of conceptual functioning prefer simple messages while individuals at higher levels prefer complex ones (MacNeil and Rule, 1970). Last, there is some evidence that conceptually simple REST subjects show greater increases in persuasibility than do more complex subjects (Suedfeld, 1969b). Other major cognitive style variables—authoritarianism, dogmatism, personal constructs (Goldstein and Blackman, 1978)—have been unexplored in this context.

A few studies have explored other measures, mostly with the hope of predicting REST tolerance, and mostly without success (see Zubek, 1969a, 1973). Among these traits have been ego strength, neuroticism, and anxiety. A variety of multitrait batteries has also been used (see Myers, 1969). One would certainly expect that a need for high levels of stimulation, activity, and/or arousal (Mehrabian, 1977; Myers et al., 1966; Zuckerman, Kolin, Price, and Zoob, 1964) would be strongly related to reactions in REST. There are some positive findings; but again, the picture is by no means clear.

Cox (1977) compared a group of subjects who scored high in sensation seeking and low on a measure of socialization—as would be expected from psychopaths—with groups whose test scores fell into different patterns. Although all of the subjects were university students, the reasonableness of the analogy with psychopaths was supported by the fact that the focal group reported having poorer occupational and academic records, less satisfactory family lives, a greater incidence of alcohol and nonmedical drug use, and more frequent problems with the law than did the more highly socialized participants. During and after 1¹/₂. hours of monotonous stimulation, the psychopath-like subjects showed less reduction in state anxiety than the others, which was interpreted as a relatively low ability to adapt to the experimental situation. Unlike the highly socialized group, they seemed to concentrate on their own experiences rather than on the characteristics of the environment, and used this focusing of attention as a relief from boredom and drowsiness. They also showed less autonomic arousal than the other groups.

Stimulus-hunger is related to the variable of general activation and arousal. There seems to be general agreement that REST is a situation in which arousal is nonnormal (e.g., Fiske and Maddi, 1961; Solomon et al., 1961; Zubek, 1973), but there is controversy as to whether the level is displaced toward the low or toward the high end of the well-known U-curve (Berlyne, 1966; Hebb, 1955; Suedfeld, 1969c; Zuckerman, 1969c). Physiological measures have yielded inconsistent results (Zubek, 1973), and the behavioral measures are inferential at best (Suedfeld, 1969b). There is some question as to the usefulness of the arousal construct as anything more than a conceptual convenience; but to the extent that the need to restore optimal levels of arousal can lead to perceptual, cognitive, emotional, and behavioral change it may be relevant to REST research and therapy (see Chapter 12).

Among other findings with measures that have been used in only one or two studies each, we have reports that high scorers on a creativity test (like conceptually complex subjects) have greater needs for stimulation under stimulus restriction conditions (Levin and Brody, 1974). Their cognitive performance shows fewer decrements, again like that of complex people (Busch, 1966). REST subjects whose Rorschach score showed high oral dependency performed poorly on a simple cognitive task, showed relatively high stress which was reduced when they were confined together with another subject, and were more likely to have considered leaving the chamber before the end of the 40-minute session (Price, undated). Last but not least, Blazer (1962) reported that more mature individuals found a 48-hour REST session more enjoyable than did those who on a battery of tests scored as less mature and well adjusted.

MOTIVATIONAL EFFECTS

"Sensory deprivation" research was originally conceived partly to test the then-current dominance of the theory that the initiation of behavior was generally traceable to disruptions of physiological homeostasis. A radical version of drive-reduction theory would certainly posit that individuals in a restricted environment, but with sufficient food, water, and oxygen, would not be motivated toward mental or physical activity. The findings, of course, thoroughly contradicted this hypothesis. As a result, they gave rise to a number of theories that contributed significantly to ending the dominance of drive reduction as the foremost system of explanation in behavioral psychology.

However, one must admit that the new explanations had much in common with the old. The major differences were that tissue needs were not involved in these motivational constructs, or at least could not be identified; and that the homeostatic level that was sought as optimal was a moderate rather than a minimal one. The exponents of such new motives as the need for stimulation, change, novelty, and exploration were either content to keep their hypotheses on a behavioral level, or referred to neurophysiological and neurochemical conjectures about the functioning of the brain. They one and all agreed that organisms needed and sought situations in which there was no great discrepancy from a moderate amount of stimulation, information, or novelty. Thus, we went from the gut to the brain and from the urge to remain quiescent to the need for some amount of excitement.

These developments had, of course, been foreshadowed within the behavioral framework. Drive-reduction theories had considerable trouble explaining complex human behavior and even with behavior clearly related to some of the primary drives, such as sex. Not only were the biochemical balances involved sometimes obscure or unidentifiable, but it was clear that some levels of drive arousal could be quite pleasant. Furthermore, it had been demonstrated in some cases that organisms preferred nondrive-reducing reinforcers. The patchwork quilt of hypothesized secondary drives and their conjectured derivations from the more basic systems could hold together only so long, and Hebb's data on monotonous stimulation came along at the right time to contribute to its disintegration.

Need for Stimulation and Information

Clearly, "stimulus-action hunger" (Lilly, 1956) is a construct that has observable consequences. For example, Sugimoto (1967) indicated that the 3 subjects in his experiment showed attempts to maintain normal ego functioning by moving and vocalizing, but that deterioration appeared to be unavoidable. During the middle of the 72-hour session of reduced stimulation, primary process thought became dominant and led to high rates of both speech and impulsive behavior. Toward the end of the experiment, however, there was a general replacement of activity by quiescence and sleep. This was interpreted as a "loss of motivation" presumably similar to that frequently reported by subjects in studies performed in Western laboratories.

One of the questions with which REST researchers have concerned themselves at some length is the exact nature of the motivational state aroused in the situation. Obviously, restricted stimulation techniques are complex and multimodal. The subject encounters changed levels of stimulation and/or perception. These alterations affect not only total input levels but also variety, novelty, change, information, and challenge. Furthermore, they are usually combined with social isolation, reduced motility, and confinement in a small space. Another major aspect, frequently ignored, is that stimulus deprivation also involves response deprivation and deprivation of feedback from the response. In normal environments, we are not only used to encountering certain levels of input, but also to emitting certain levels of output. Each behavior in which we engage produces feedback that is monitored and used to test the appropriateness of the behavior. This aspect of human information processing has been conceived of by some theorists as being crucial to adaptive functioning (see e.g., Miller, Galanter, and Pribram, 1960). In REST, there is at the very least a disruption of visual feedback, which for most people is constant and important in the normal environment.

Among the researchers who have addressed themselves to the difficult question of motivational consequences, perhaps the most prominent has been Austin Jones. In a series of studies that has tended to dominate the field (summarized in Jones, 1969), he parametrically manipulated the characteristics of light sequences varying in color. The results indicated that the least predictable sequence was maximally valued by subjects. The complexity and alternation of the sequences was not important. Furthermore, incentive value was an increasing function of how long the subject had been in REST prior to the availability of the stimuli. In a study using tones rather than lights, previous satiation with highly unpredictable sequences resulted in increased preference for more predictable stimuli. Rogers (1975) essentially replicated these findings in the tactile modality, one of the few studies not using visual or auditory stimuli. The research shows that the need for information generalizes across modalities. Satiation with visual information reduces the desire for auditory information, and vice versa. On the basis of these findings, Jones (1969) concluded that "the information drive in humans mediates a homeostasis of information transmission, and that the homeostasis, once disturbed by extreme values of stimulus information in a particular modality, may be reinstated, at least in part, by compensatory adjustments of the information value of the stimuli in another modality" (p. 201).

In another series of studies on the motivational effects of reduced stimulation, Leckart and his colleagues have collected data that support some of Jones' propositions. For example, the complexity of slides depicting a variety of objects was positively related to how long people looked at each slide. A period of darkness prior to stimulus presentation increased looking time, but did not interact with complexity (Leckart, Glanville, Hootstein, Keleman, and Yaremko, 1972). In other words, while complex visual inputs were more interesting, REST did not increase the previously existing preference for complexity (a finding replicated by Bearwald, 1976). Rather, it led to prolonged looking times for all categories of stimuli. One of the things that makes this particular study intriguing is that the duration of darkness was varied from only 2 seconds to 30 seconds prior to each stimulus presentation. This study extended the concerns of an earlier one (Leckart, Levine, Goscinski, and Brayman, 1970), and replicated its findings with regard to deprivation duration. Later investigations indicated similar effects of duration in the tactile (Yaremko, Glanville, Rofer, and Leckart, 1972) and auditory (Levine, Pettit, and Leckart, 1973) modalities.

Drake and Herzog (1974) measured the incentive value of randomly generated complicated polygons. Looking time was significantly higher when the figure was presented following a period of darkness than when it followed either homogeneous white light or the presentation of similar figures. However, there was also a strong correlation between looking time and the duration of the foreperiod. The authors attributed the former datum to the transition from darkness to light, rather than to the level of illumination itself. They therefore concluded that there was no evidence of a "perceptual deprivation effect," in contradiction to the work of Leckart and his colleagues.

Most of the work cited above used nonmeaningful stimuli. Let us now look at the results of research with meaningful inputs. Here again, there seems to be no doubt that a state of stimulus hunger appears after some period of restriction. Subjects in many experiments have shown a wish to listen to stimuli even though these are monotonous, repetitive, and familiar. Among the best known findings of this nature were those of the original McGill researchers, whose deprived subjects requested to hear repeated presentations of excerpts from old stock market reports, children's primers, and popular songs. Control subjects preferred to avoid this material after the first presentation. These findings have been replicated by other researchers. Stimulus-restricted subjects are also more willing to listen to counterattitudinal propaganda messages, an activity that attitude theorists normally consider to be aversive. It appears that a REST participant may consider any input to be better than none, as a hungry person may eat food he normally detests; but this does not clarify the nature of the crucial motivational factors.

With relatively complex stimuli, one may posit a more sophisticated alternative to the information-drive hypothesis. The subject may be responding on the basis of some sort of competence motivation. An unpredictable, novel, or dissonant series is preferable because it poses more of a challenge for puzzle-solving and integration. A study by Landon and Suedfeld (1969), in which originally meaningful phrases were scrambled to various degrees of randomness, indicated that this is a tenable explanation. The greatest incentive value was attached to those stimuli that were intermediate in randomness, unusual enough to be nonobvious but systematic enough to be decipherable. This hypothesis may also explain the preference for an unstructured complex visual stimulus, such as a Rorschach card, over an unstructured complex auditory stimulus such as a tone mixture (Goldstein, 1965). In this case, the modality difference itself is likely to be relevant. Other findings that can be explained from either the information or the competence motivation standpoint are the greater stress reported by conceptually complex REST subjects (Suedfeld, 1964), and the rapid appearance of stimulus hunger among highly creative subjects compared to its more gradual increase in less creative individuals (Levin and Brody, 1974).

The data are not entirely consistent, however. In one study using a series of slides differing in meaningfulness (Rossi, Nathan, Harrison, and Solomon, 1969), subjects who had experienced two hours of REST increased their desire to see the least meaningful and least predictable series. They did not demonstrate any greater wish than control subjects to see meaningful and moderately meaningful sequences. And in the study by Landon and Suedfeld (1969), meaningfulness and predictability were unrelated to change in operant rate although moderately meaningful and moderately unpredictable stimuli were rated as the least boring.

At this stage, the data are insufficient for a real understanding of what we vaguely call stimulus hunger. It may be that this is a pseudo-question. The alternative definitions may be merely matters of different emphases, in that material that is high in information value is also challenging, or vice versa. Ignoring the theoretical issues, each investigator can follow his or her own interest in choosing to concentrate on the measurable information properties of the presentation or on the response preferences of the recipient.

On the basis of the exhaustive review by Jones (1969), it does seem fairly clear that the need has demonstrable drive properties. There is a preferred homeostatic level, deviations from which in either direction elicit increases in the operant rate of responses that change the existing level towards optimum. This response rate increases with the duration of deprivation and perhaps of satiation. Under REST conditions, responses are emitted at a high rate both for informational stimuli presented in the chamber and for early release from the situation. Subjects who are less tolerant of the condition, as indicated by eventually quitting the experiment, are more responsive for even minimal stimulation. Performance on substantively irrelevant tasks is affected in the same way as it is by other drives, and the effects of REST on irrelevant performances summate with those of other drives (Jones, 1969; Suedfeld, 1969b). Central mediation is demonstrated by the fact that satiation in one modality can compensate for deprivation in another.

This set of findings is fairly persuasive. At least one motivational consequence of restricted stimulation is analogous to the classical drives. Furthermore, the data indicate that this motivational effect is not equivalent to arousal or activation, in spite of the great reliance placed on this latter construct by many theorists (see Suedfeld, 1969c; Zuckerman, 1969c). For one thing, different measures of arousal show opposite changes as a result of restricted environmental stimulation. For another, some of the energizing effects of the drive occur and increase even while physiological measures of arousal show successive lowering.

Reinforcer and Incentive Characteristics

As to the specific stimuli that can act as reinforcers, the research is less conclusive. It appears that visual presentations have the most impact, with auditory inputs somewhat lower. No systematic research has been done using other modalities, although there is some evidence that even working a lever has some incentive value (Goldstein, 1965). As noted above, the predictability of nonmeaningful stimuli appears to be associated with a drive variable. Both predictability and fluctuation serve as incentive dimensions, whereas complexity does not.

The incentive value of meaningful materials also changes as a result of REST, but there has been relatively little research on the relevant stimulus aspects of such materials. We know that some value attaches even to counterattitudinal, boring, and repetitive messages, as has been shown at McGill and in the work of Myers and his colleagues (e.g., Myers, Murphy, Smith, and Goffard, 1966). There is also evidence indicating that the crucial incentive characteristic is in the realm of general, rather than of specifically social, stimulation. This is true even when the treatment consists of confinement and social isolation without stimulus reduction (Suedfeld, Rank, and Rank, 1977). As has been mentioned, the confounded variables of novelty, information value, and cognitive challenge also seem to be associated with the incentive value of meaningful stimuli.

While the measure of stimulus need or attractiveness has usually been an operant behavior such as button-pressing, and somewhat less frequently a rating, one experiment used an increase in GSR as the operant. Rossi (1971) presented slides showing scenes from different countries whenever the subject, who had been confined for 2.5 hours, produced a drop in skin resistance averaging at least 1500 ohms. During REST, the occurrence of criterion-level GSR changes increased significantly. The increase remained stable over time when the visual stimulus was not contingent upon the operant during a control period, but continued to increase throughout the duration of contingent reinforcement. Incidentally, given the reliance upon visual stimuli in this and many other motivational studies of reduced stimulation, someone should follow up the report that individuals whose uncorrected visual acuity is good prefer higher levels of stimulation and produce more novel stories on a projective test than do those whose eyesight is less acute (Palmer, 1970).

One would expect the degree of stimulus hunger to vary across individuals, and this indeed seems to be the case. For example, Gale (1969) reported that extraverts maintained a higher response rate for sound reinforcers than introverts, and also changed more frequently from one kind of reinforcer to another. However, the total duration of earned auditory stimulation did not differ between the groups.

Individuals who scored high on a measure of sensation seeking (Zuckerman, Kolin, Price, and Zoob, 1964) emitted significantly more button-presses than low scorers when the button-press was reinforced with a 15-second slide exposure depicting a wide variety of objects (Lambert and Levy, 1972). In a study by Suedfeld and Vernon (1966), subjects who were rated as conceptually complex were more likely than conceptually simple individuals to report agreement with one side of a bivalent attitudinal message when such agreement was reinforced by stimulation (the presentation of the next message). However, this compliant behavior was not accompanied by actual attitude change. This finding is compatible with data showing that conceptually complex individuals find REST less pleasant (Suedfeld, 1964), and bears out the relationship between subjective stress in REST and the seeking of whatever stimulation may be available (see e.g., Vernon and McGill, 1960).

PHYSIOLOGICAL EFFECTS

Relatively little has been added to this portion of the literature since Zubek's (1973) review. However, some of the newer results are quite relevant not only to experimental but also to clinical REST.

Changes in CNS Functioning

The effects of restricted stimulation on EEG seem to be both reliable and relatively long-lasting, although there are individual differences. Progressive slowing of mean alpha frequency persists for up to 4 days after the subject is removed from the chamber. Such changes have been found with schizophrenic patients after as little as an hour and as much as 2 days of restriction (Smith, 1962; Marjerrison and Keogh, 1967). The relationship of this effect to the positive reactions of schizophrenics to REST has not been investigated. The EEG change is progressive during confinement. It is interesting to note that the progressive change is not found when a cross-sectional approach is used (that is, when different subjects are tested after different periods of REST, rather than when the same subject is tested repeatedly over a period of time). The phenomenon is also affected by the specific experimental technique being used. Monotonous stimulation leads to larger changes than reduced stimulation. Neither a control condition nor restricted movement produces the same effect. Reduced and monotonous stimulation lead to similar degrees of increased theta wave activity, especially in the temporal region. This finding has been replicated, although not as many times as the change in alpha waves.

Sugimoto, Kida, and Teranishi (1969) showed that changes in EEG were a joint function of the subject's behavior and increasing time in isolation. Lower frequencies of alpha waves were associated with increasing time spent in the monotonous stimulation condition, and with behaviors characteristic of low cortical activity such as sleeping and resting (Serafetinides, Shurley, Brooks, and Gideon, 1972). The mean frequency of occipital alpha waves went up when the subject was thinking or playing.

Heron, Tait, and Smith (1972) reported that most of the change in alpha occurs during the first 4 days of REST, and reaches asymptote or in some cases reverses direction slightly thereafter. One subject, who experienced vivid RVSs during the fourth day of confinement, also showed marked increases in alpha frequency during that day. During the last 4 days of the 7-day study, there was a great deal of variation from day to day. Frequencies increased toward normal as each day passed. The authors conclude that their results "are not directly related to level of arousal and are not easy to interpret in terms of our present understanding of neurophysiology. It is possible that the effects are due to the establishment of some new organization" (p. 284).

Several theoretical viewpoints lead one to expect that both sleep patterns and dreaming would be altered as a function of the REST environment (see e.g., Suedfeld and Borrie, 1978b). Many subjects actually have mentioned such effects. It is particularly unfortunate in view of recent advances in sleep research that these changes have not been investigated more systematically. In one of the few studies that considered dreams as a major variable, Dallett (1973) divided subjects on the basis of introversion-extraversion. A test of the importance of intuition in the subject's usual functioning, and other personality measures from the Myers-Briggs Type Indicator were also administered. Subjects served as their own controls in a baseline and in three experimental conditions. The latter were sensory monotony, social isolation and forced social stimulation. These conditions did not significantly affect dream content across the total group, although the length of dream reports increased significantly after both of the restricted environmental conditions. Jungian type was related to this phenomenon: the difference was found among those who scored high in thinking and feeling. The sensory richness of the dreams of high intuition subjects decreased in the monotonous stimulation condition and increased after social stimulation, contrary to the compensation hypotheses advanced by Dallett. However, the compensation hypothesis was supported among those subjects who were particularly involved with or emotionally affected by the restricted environment. These findings are an interesting complement to the theory that REM sleep functions to discharge drive (Baekeland, 1970), and that this function explains increases in the amount of REM sleep among environmentally restricted and socially isolated subjects (Van der Kolk and Hartmann, 1968; Wood, 1962).

Restricted stimulation also seems to affect physiological phenomena during sleep. There are bursts of alpha during REM sleep in some subjects (Heron et al., 1972). The number of fast sleep phases and the amount of REMs are increased in both night and daytime sleep, although more markedly in the former (Salzarulo, 1971, 1972). There is a marked increase of slow eye movements during the onset of sleep, a finding that Salzarulo (1972) thinks may be related to hypnagogic imagery. The findings also indicate the existence of EEG, muscular tension, and eye movement patterns that do not fit the definition of descending Stage 1 sleep, but do occur at a time when that would normally be expected. These anomalies cannot be explained on the basis of currently available data. Last, it appears that there is no evidence for an internal cycle regulating fast sleep phases. In REST, the rhythm of these phases is highly variable and unreliable. Subjects undergoing REST fall asleep faster during the night but more slowly during the afternoon than subjects in the normal environment (Salzarulo, 1971, 1972). The total amount of sleep is usually estimated to be normal, or at most slightly increased. No quantitative data have been collected, however.

It seems a pity that most of the research on the psychophysiological aspects of REST was done so early in the history of the field. As a result, the more sophisticated techniques of recording and analysis now common in investigations of this sort have seldom been applied to the effects of stimulus restriction. For example, telemetry would reduce the stress and other artifacts associated with being wired to the apparatus for long periods, and could provide much more convincing evidence about the changes caused by REST. Among the few experiments that have used current methods is a detailed study of the effects of monotonous stimulation on the EEG, using computer power spectral analysis (Tait, 1977). The findings disconfirmed Zubek's original prediction of a more gradual alpha decrease when subjects were in deprivation for longer periods, and implied that the generally accepted common substratum between alpha waves and sleep spindles may not exist.

In another study, which may have great significance for the therapeutic use of REST, Lloyd and Shurley (1976) demonstrated a significant increase in the speed of acquiring a single motor unit conditioned response after one hour on an "activated, air-fluidized, ceramic-bead bed" in a dark, sound-attenuated chamber with a masking hum. This finding supports the suggestion made in Chapter 7 that such procedures as biofeedback could be enhanced by the concomitant use of stimulus reduction.

Relatively few investigators have taken an integrated systems view of the biopsychological effects of REST. Physiological and behavioral aspects are frequently isolated from each other in the literature—as one must admit them to be throughout psychology. Still another gap is the failure of scientists working with human subjects to take a lead from fascinating data generated with infrahuman animals. There seem to be implications for REST applied to gastrointestinal disturbances in reports that long-term interference with normal sensory inputs reduces gastric secretions in dogs (Schapiro, Gross, Nakamura, Wruble, and Britt, 1970; Schapiro, Wruble, Britt, and Bell, 1970). It might be useful to replicate with human beings the finding that even very brief visual deprivation reduces cerebral blood flow in chickens (Bondy and Morelos, 1971). Some of the data related to changes in the CNS as a function of stimulus deprivation have been followed up with human subjects (e.g., Glass, 1977). But once again, there are exciting findings whose trans-species generalizability remains unexplored. One is the possibility that some neurons are environment-dependent, and develop only in the presence of adequate amounts of stimulation (Cummins, Livesey, Evans, and Walsh, 1977).

One other change, with important therapeutic implications, is related to drug effects. It appears that REST inhibits the effect of at least some psychoactive substances—for example, LSD and phencyclidine (Sernyl).

The experimental data are not completely consistent (see Panton and Fischer, 1973; Kristeller, 1978; Zubek, 1969c); but coupled with the clinical evidence (Chapter 10), they are quite persuasive. It would seem that this effect could be the basis of REST therapy for drug overdose or abuse.

Changes in Autonomic Functioning

In this area, practically no recent research has been reported. Thus, Zubek's (1973) review gives a fairly complete presentation of what is known, and this section is primarily a summary of the early findings. Data on changes in skin resistance are fairly consistent, indicating increases in the GSR. This change is progressive over the time of confinement. Skin conductance is also related to some aspects of behavior in the chamber. For example, high GSR reactors seem to exhibit more stimulus hunger. The change in GSR accompanying deprivation in either the visual or the auditory modality is much less than the change caused by deprivation in both modalities. Visual deprivation leads to slightly more change than auditory.

Other physiological measures, including temperature, blood pressure, heart rate, respiration, and muscle potential, do not seem to be reliably affected by the restricted stimulation experience. Some preliminary data do show that heart rate, respiration, and blood pressure change during very long periods of social isolation (i.e., after 20 days). London, Schubert, and Washburn (1972) reported that GSR and heart rate are positively related to feelings of boredom. This finding implicitly supports the hypothesis that experimental REST is an arousal-inducing environment. More importantly, it leads to some interesting research questions. Are there, for example, differences in subjective boredom, and therefore in the arousal effects of REST, as a function of personality characteristics? Or as a function of whether the participant is merely an experimental volunteer or a client trying to solve an important problem? And how may such differences mediate the effects of REST on behavior? No researcher has yet attempted to answer such questions.

Attempts to measure biochemical activity show no consistent changes in the production of catecholamine nor of 11-oxycorticoids, indicating a lack of adrenal activation by monotonous stimulation in these studies. This research suffers from considerable contact between the subject and the experimenter. Had this contact been reduced, thus increasing the degree of stimulus reduction, the results might have been different. Individual differences also appeared. Eventual quitters showed lower levels of adrenal secretion prior to confinement than did those who successfully completed the scheduled session. Subjects who quit after 2 days but prior to the scheduled end of the experiment demonstrated increases in adrenal production after the second day. The output of 17-ketogenic steroids and 17-ketosteroids was higher in reduced stimulation and in a social isolation treatment than on tests made in a normal environment several months later, with each subject serving as his own control. Urine excretion and gross body weight also decrease reliably during time in REST, apparently regardless either of calorie or liquid intake differences within the normal range.

SUSCEPTIBILITY TO INFLUENCE

There is no doubt by now that REST increases the susceptibility of most subjects to influence from external sources. This may be one of the major reasons for its effectiveness as a therapeutic technique. The literature in this area will not be discussed in detail in spite of its importance, as it has grown relatively little since it was reviewed ten years ago (Suedfeld, 1969b).

Empirical Findings

In summary, primary suggestibility (e.g., body sway, autokinetic effect, figure-copying) generally increases, as does hypnotizability (Ritchie, 1976; Sanders and Reyher, 1969; Wickramasekera, 1969, 1970). In the study by Ritchie, the basic hypnotic susceptibility of REST subjects remained higher as much as 21 days after the session, although their advanced susceptibility had returned to normal. A stress-treatment group showed decreases on both kinds of hypnotic susceptibility, another differentiation between stress and stimulus reduction.

A number of experimenters have investigated the effects of REST on attitude change. Among the more systematic experimental programs have been the original McGill studies, work at the Army's Human Resources Research Office—HumRRO—(Myers et al., 1966), and research in my own laboratories. Clinical analogues were provided by Henry Adams and his colleagues. Persuasibility in response to actual messages is affected by many variables, but almost all researchers find a general heightening of susceptibility. In fact, such increases are among the most consistently found effects of stimulus reduction. One of the complicating factors is that increased attitude change as a function of REST has been found to be highest among less intelligent and conceptually less complex subjects. This finding may be related to Adams' hypothesis that REST is a more powerful therapeutic technique with individuals who are not as verbal as those usually considered to be the best candidates for psychotherapy.

One important methodological point, discussed further in Chapter 8, is that the experimental research deals exclusively with attitudes of little importance or relevance to the subject. While this kind of research provides interesting experimental data, one should be extremely cautious in generalizing from it to the possibility of inducing changes in opinions and beliefs that involve a firm commitment on the part of the subject. These latter, of course, are typical in clinical situations.

Theoretical Formulations

Explanations of the phenomenon have varied, but for the most part do not seem to be mutually exclusive. One that is clearly inappropriate is that based on the supposed parallels between reduced stimulation and "brainwashing." This argument ignores the well-documented fact that coercive persuasion techniques in fact rely on excessive stimulation. Another hypothesis whose status is somewhat dubious is that involving stimulus-hunger as the crucial mediating variable. While the early McGill studies showed that normally disliked and boring materials were frequently requested by confined subjects, this merely indicates an increased desire for stimulation. It does not imply that the messages were actually liked, nor was there any direct evidence of such a change. Thus, the findings may not have involved actual attitude change. On a more complex level, one might propose that stimulus-hunger would lead subjects to listen more closely to messages that might normally be warded off because they are cognitively dissonant, and also to remember such messages better. At the present time, there is relatively little evidence to support this hypothesis. Still, it has not been investigated thoroughly enough to be discarded.

Another explanation is that restricted stimulation induces cognitive disorganization, particularly when complex information processing is involved, and that dealing with a persuasive message is such an activity. The argument here is that in order not to give in to a counterattitudinal message, the recipient must evaluate the contents of that message with a fairly high level of intellectual efficacy, perceive its weaknesses and strengths, generate or recall counterarguments as appropriate, perhaps assimilate some aspects of the presentation without grossly changing his original attitude, and accurately judge the implications of particular points in the presentation. If, as our review of cognitive changes has shown, such complex processes are impaired by REST, one would expect that the stimulus-restricted subject would be more likely to fail in his attempts to maintain the original attitude structure in the face of attack. The result would be the "unfreezing" of the previously established belief-opinion structure (Lewin, 1952; see also Zajonc and Morrissette, 1960).

The disorganization hypothesis is, along with the stimulus-hunger proposition, part of the two-component theory of REST effects on susceptibility to influence proposed by Suedfeld (e.g., 1972). Recently collected data tending to support the importance of this component include a demonstration that 24 hours of stimulus reduction, even without the introduction of any persuasive messages, induces disorganization in the stability of opinion-belief structures related to both peripheral and central attitudes (Tetlock and Suedfeld, 1976), and that restricted stimulation can inhibit the generation of arguments against a counterattitudinal message (Suedfeld, Tetlock, and Borrie, in preparation). It has also been shown that while REST may strengthen the impact of an attitude change attempt, it does not magnify the power of a message designed to inoculate subjects against future persuasive attacks (Suedfeld and Borrie, 1978a). In other words, it can cause unfreezing but cannot "superfreeze" existing attitudes.

SOME METHODOLOGICAL PROBLEMS

Although the reduced stimulation technique can cause great changes in a number of psychological and physiological functions, the literature is not completely clear. We have seen that there is controversy as to exactly what changes may be expected, and some unreliability in the data collected by different experimenters or by the same experimenter in different studies. One reason for these inconsistencies is the complexity of the technique itself. Among the relevant variables that have already been discussed are the exact type of environmental restriction used; the expected and actual duration of the session; demographic, cultural, and personality differences among participants; and differences in measures, definitions, baselines, and controls used in different investigations (see also Rossi, 1969; Zuckerman, 1969a).

Two other issues that are ubiquitous in psychological experimentation may be particularly salient in this area. The first of these is the relevance of Heisenberg's Uncertainty Principle. The very act of measuring a phenomenon alters that phenomenon. This is a critical issue when one is dealing with reduced stimulation, since any testing procedure introduces new stimuli to the environment. A brief look at some aspects of the research will serve to illustrate just how important this problem may be in considering the data from REST experiments.

Data Collection as a Disruptor of REST

As we have seen, workers in the field have looked at a wide variety of dependent variables. These have included EEG patterns, hallucinations, cognitive functioning, persuasibility, emotional changes, perception, spatial orientation, and motor activity. In many cases, all or most of them were measured in a given experiment. This shotgun pattern was adopted for several reasons. One was intellectual: with such a bag of exciting possibilities, everyone wanted to grab as big a handful as possible. Another was organizational: most teams consisted of researchers with a relatively wide range of backgrounds and interests, each of whom had to include some pet variable. Perhaps the most important reason, however, was economic. When reasonably large samples are needed, and each subject represents from 1 to 15 full, 24-hour days of monitoring, feeding, stimulus presentation, and data collection, it is wasteful not to collect as many types of data as possible.

Unfortunately, many nonphysiological effects of restricted stimulation tend to dissipate quite rapidly after return to the normal environment. Long test batteries therefore reduce the probability that the actual REST effects will be accurately observed or understood. This is particularly a problem when a possible change is tested relatively late in a battery where test order is not counterbalanced; and lack of counterbalancing has been more the rule then the exception.

This disrupting of the effect by observing it may outweigh the influence of other variables. For example, Oleson and Zubek (1970) used a 24-hour sensory reduction session to measure changes in complex cognitive functioning. In the past, that kind of intellectual process had been found fairly consistently to deteriorate under similar conditions (Suedfeld, 1969b; Suedfeld and Landon, 1970). Nevertheless, Oleson and Zubek did not find reliable changes. The reason for this failure may lie in their use of a battery lasting about an hour, as opposed to previous research in which the dependent variable was measured in 15 minutes or less. In addition, their measurement procedure was particularly disruptive (see below), which probably exacerbated the problem (Suedfeld, 1971).

The extent to which testing affects the results is theoretically a function of environmental disruption. With the continuous presentation of problems and tasks, the low level of external stimulation is replaced by increasingly more normal levels. It is this substitution of varied stimulation for the experimental conditions that presumably leads to the dissipation of REST effects. In the same way, the more stimulating the measurement procedure is, the more it disrupts the condition. Oleson and Zubek, and many other researchers, used written tests. Such tests require that the chamber be illuminated, that the experimenter enter and communicate with the subject, that the subject sit up and manipulate paper and pencil. There are instructions to read, the subject may speak to the experimenter, and so on. Aside from the stimulus increase itself, the change from low to higher stimulation levels may also have its own "abrupt-change" effects that lead to the erosion of REST phenomena (Miller, 1948; Rossi, 1969).

Less disruptive procedures used in other research may present the questions over an intercom. The subject can answer either by merely pushing a button or switch, or by a brief spoken response. Quite obviously, this method leads to much less change in stimulation level. It maintains the elimination of visual inputs, which (as implied by Zubek's extensive work on visual deprivation) may be critical. Social isolation is also maintained.

One last issue involved with testing at the end of the experiment is the delay between the end of the REST session and the beginning of the measurement procedure. There have been some studies in which the collection of data occurs only after the subject has been removed from the chamber, debriefed, washed, and dressed. One would not expect the effects observed at this point to be as great as those seen if the dependent measures were administered immediately at, or just prior to, the end of the session. Once again, the disruption of the environmental conditions is probably crucial. This error may lead to failures to replicate previous findings (e.g., Robertson, 1965).

Set as an Artifact

Another problem that is particularly difficult to deal with in the REST literature is that of expectation, whether on the part of experimenters or of subjects. In a number of studies, Orne and his coworkers (e.g., Orne, 1962) and Rosenthal (e.g., 1964) have demonstrated the wide-reaching effects of this artifact. Subjects may be affected in a number of ways, ranging from the desire to make themselves look good to the experimenter to wanting their data cither to support or to oppose what they think the experimenter wants to find. The investigator in turn is presumably motivated to collect data that support some a priori hypothesis, or that at least will be novel and interesting (and publishable). Deliberately or not, both parties may as a consequence alter some aspect of the experimental situation to maximize the probability that the prophecies will become self-fulfilling.

In research with human subjects, unlike in some of the rat experiments used by Rosenthal to demonstrate his experimenter-bias hypothesis, it is difficult to separate the two kinds of expectation. In particular, if the individual designing and conducting the experiment has strong anticipations as to the results, he may structure his procedure so that the expectation is communicated to the subject and becomes the latter's own.

Recent studies have indicated that in REST subject expectation is a more important factor than experimenter bias and that some phenomena are more vulnerable to this influence than others (see Zuckerman, Persky, and Link, 1969). For example, one experiment (Suedfeld, Landon, Epstein, and Pargament, 1971) provided essentially similar orientation materials to student experimenters and student subjects. The material emphasized either the stress and aversive symptoms or the reports of relaxation and positive affect reported by previous subjects going through restricted stimulation. A third group in each category received no initial bias. The set induced in the experimenter proved to have no effects. Subject expectancy did reliably alter the degree of stress that participants reported having experienced during the session, but did not influence performance on a cognitive task.

A less elaborate study by Raffetto (1968) found experimenter set effects on reports of complex RVSs. The nature of the dependent variable, coupled with the fact that only an hour of reduced stimulation was used, implies that Raffetto's results were also primarily a function of the subject's willingness to report certain experiences. More recently, Landon (1976) introduced a variation on this design. In his experiment, the individuals running the study were misled as to whether any particular participant spent the 24 hours between two testing sessions in restricted stimulation or in a control condition. Once again, the set of the experimenter did not influence the outcome of the study.

Subject set may strongly influence the results of restricted stimulation experiments before the study even begins. The vast majority of individuals likely to participate in REST experiments will have been exposed to some writings on the topic. Many subjects are students who have read introductory psychology texts, and both they and the general public have encountered popular novels and journalistic accounts of "sensory deprivation." Both of these sources tend to emphasize the bizarre and negative effects ascribed to isolation and confinement. It would be expected that such a background would set up anticipations that might lead subjects to magnify certain kinds of experiences and phenomena out of proportion. Jackson and Pollard (1966) found that 75% of their student sample knew something about sensory deprivation studies prior to reporting for an experiment, and that their knowledge emphasized the more dramatic early findings. These authors (see also Jackson and Pollard, 1962) have emphasized subject expectation as a major explanatory variable in accounting for REST results. Although the evidence on this issue is mixed (see Suedfeld, 1969c), the argument is plausible and is likely to apply in at least some cases.

The researcher has more control over another factor: the recruiting materials for subjects appear to influence potential volunteers. Specifically, the proportion of first- and later-born subjects appearing for an experiment may be a function of these materials. First-born subjects volunteer in different proportions depending on whether the experiment is made to seem stressful or not (Dohrenwend, Feldstein, Plosky, and Schmeidler, 1967; Suedfeld, 1964). With anxiety-arousing orientation material, they actually expect to be more stressed than do later borns (Suedfeld, 1968), and are less likely to participate in isolation studies. In one study, such conditions also led them to report having experienced greater anxiety (Dohrenwend and Dohrenwend, 1966), although this was not confirmed in a later report (Suedfeld, 1968). In contrast, reassuring instructions reduce the amount of anticipated stress for first-born subjects (Suedfeld, 1969d).

Still other sources of subject expectancy can be minimized by appropriate procedures. The beginning of the REST session may serve as an example. In early studies, it was routine for participants to be asked to sign an impressive legal form, which purported to relieve the laboratory staff and the institution from responsibility in case of psychological or other damage suffered by the subjects during the study. Most chambers were equipped with a prominent and easily located "panic button," which the subject was instructed to push if he wanted instant release from the REST situation. The laboratory itself tended and still tends to be on the awesome side. It is usually located in the basement or some other relatively unpopulated location. The chambers have massive walls and doors (sometimes double walls and doors). There is a lot of impressive wiring, instrumentation, and elaborate soundproofing. In addition, some laboratories made it the rule that the subject never actually saw the chamber illuminated until after the experiment. All orientations and instruments were given under REST conditions. As a result, the subject did not know the dimension of the chamber, and could not establish a cognitive map based on visual memory as to where different equipment and facilities were located.

As one might expect, these features of the laboratory and the procedure tended to induce high anxiety in most subjects. Not to know the dimensions of a room nor the placement of objects within it is generally disorienting. When the outside of that room is unusual and technically complex, when it is located in an unfamiliar area, and when one's entry into it is preceded by indications that the experience to be undergone inside may be quite unpleasant or even harmful, one's thoughts, emotions, and activities will unavoidably reflect states of disorientation and fear. These reactions are above and beyond any effect produced by the environment itself—that is, by stimulus restriction. For these reasons, it is quite likely that much of the early REST literature actually dealt with the joint operation of the three variables. It should be no surprise that later studies, in which disorientation and anxiety were greatly reduced if not avoided, should be unable to replicate some of the original findings.

While it is difficult to demonstrate conclusively that non-replicability is due to these factors, there is at least some inferential evidence from a study by Orne and Scheibe (1964). The procedure closely resembled those just described. There were release forms, a panic button, experimenters in laboratory coats, impressive equipment. But this awesome introduction was followed by an innocuous stay in an illuminated and comfortable room. Nevertheless, subjects showed some of the same striking effects that sensory deprivation investigators had reported. Orne and Scheibe called this phenomenon "the psychology of the panic-button." However, it took a while before workers in the area realized that the panic button was ancillary and that REST experiments could be conducted without it, thus eliminating its effects and finding out with as little contamination as possible the changes wrought by REST per se.

The issue of demand characteristics and subject expectations is particularly important because of the demonstrated ability of restricted stimulation to increase susceptibility to persuasive messages and other forms of influence. This effect, as has been shown, is quite consistent across a wide variety of specific techniques and contents. It may play an equal role in making the subject vulnerable to information that leads him to expect a certain kind of experience while in the chamber. As has been shown in the studies on birth order cited above, people who are either generally or temporarily more persuasible than the average are particularly at risk in this context. It therefore seems important for researchers in the area to be particularly careful to minimize these sources of artifact.

CONCLUSION

This brief review of the literature serves to demonstrate some of its major characteristics. REST research has looked at a wide spectrum of phenomena, which is good, but has tended to substitute diversity for system, which reduced the impact of the results. As the historical summary indicated, the volume of research has diminished in recent years. This is regrettable not only because it hinders the information-expansion process, but perhaps even more importantly because as a result this field is benefiting only slowly from current progress in theory and technology. Much of our knowledge about REST effects is based on now-obsolescent methods. Furthermore, some very important theoretical and empirical questions have not even been asked, much less answered. However, the published work has certainly contributed intriguing new thoughts and facts to the psychological repertoire, and continuing research will further clarify and expand these contributions.

CHAPTER 3

Stimulus Reduction in Hospitals and Prisons

Chapter 1 mentioned some of the natural (that is, neither experimental nor therapeutic) environments in which stimulus reduction or monotony may be important characteristics. Among these are situations experienced by groups that are isolated in remote locations, such as polar weather stations, nuclear submarines, spacecraft, small mining or lumber camps, and isolated ranches or villages. In others, we find individuals in social isolation: explorers, hermits, prospectors, and solitary sailors or flyers (both those who set out on single-handed voyages and those who end up alone as a result of some accident). A third group involves short but frequently recurring periods of monotony, such as routine and repetitive work—for example, on an assembly line.

The literature dealing with such environments is not thoroughly reviewed in this book, for several reasons. To begin with, the degree to which stimulus restriction is involved varies widely, and in most cases is so thoroughly confounded with other factors as to be practically impossible to estimate. It may in fact be that many of these situations involve unusually high levels of stimulus experience, or rapid and frequent fluctuations in stimulation, rather than a steady state of lowered input. In the case of factory workers, for example, fair amounts of distraction and recreation are at least periodically available both on and off the job. Perhaps an overwhelming majority of people who find themselves in the more drastic versions of such situations have chosen to do so, and may be extremely uncharacteristic of the general population, making their subjective reports questionable as a basis for generalization. For example, the remarks of solitary sailors reflect a great variety of unusual motives and reactions (see e.g., Heaton, 1976). These range from a chronic asocial life style to the desire to test oneself against an extreme challenge, to a truly transcendental perception of being one with the sea and the boat, and a completely dedicated scientific investigation of survival factors under such conditions. Several of them suffered from periods of great fear, others (most likely because of physical illness complicating their already difficult tasks) from strange dreams and hallucinations. Many single-handed sailors claim never to be bothered by solitude. This is likely to be a result of self-selection into the activity, as well as of denial. Of course, in recent years the use of radio transceivers, tape recorders, and so on has reduced the feeling of isolation significantly. At any rate, psychological problems resulting from monotony or aloneness seldom seem to be major aspects of single-handed sailing (Henderson, 1976).

There is another set of reasons for not covering this material thoroughly here, related to the existing literature. Much of it has already been painstakingly analyzed elsewhere (see e.g., Caplan, Cobb, French, Van Harrison, and Pinneau, 1975; Parsons, 1976; Rasmussen, 1973). This applies to almost all of the scientific data collected about people working at boring jobs, groups wintering over in the Antarctic, submarine crews, and the like. Many of the remaining situations in these categories have not been objectively studied at all, and are represented in public knowledge primarily by autobiographical writings. These have two drawbacks. First, they are very scattered and unsystematic, making it difficult to draw general conclusions. Second, they are by definition the products of relatively intellectual, educated, and verbal individuals, who are very likely a small and biased subsample of those who have participated in this kind of experience. For example, very few solitary prospectors or self-exiled itinerants have left records of their reactions to solitude and environmental restriction.

However, there is a "natural" kind of environmental monotony that is experienced by large numbers of people who do not volunteer for the experience, and about whom a considerable amount has been written. It involves at least a temporary stay in a total institution, a stay that can be imposed suddenly and unpredictably on a wide sample of the population. Monotonous or reduced stimulation may be a byproduct of the institution's major function. The types of institutions that share these characteristics have been listed by Ellenberger (1971, pp. 192–199): general hospitals, tuberculosis sanatoria, leprosaria, mental hospitals, hospitals and homes for infants, homes for aged persons, camps for prisoners of war, prisons and penitentiaries, and extermination camps.

Several of these settings have disappeared under current conditions, while others have not yet been the foci of systematic study. This chapter considers the two that may loom most common in our society, and that perhaps best represent the images and experiences that many of us associate with closed, total institutions. These two are confinement in a hospital or in a prison. Some of the similarities between these two types of institutions are noted above. Others that should be borne in mind are that in both cases the environment is unusual in many other ways besides stimulus restriction. For example, it is largely unpredictable and uncontrollable by the individual, a condition that has been found to cause emotional arousal, distress, and maladaptive behavior in both infrahuman animals and human beings (e.g., Joffe, Rawson, and Mulick, 1973; Mineka and Kihlstrom, 1978). Another similarity is that a high level of negative affect is frequently aroused by the very fact of being placed in the institution, regardless of how pleasant or unpleasant, stimulating or unstimulating, interesting or boring, the environment itself may be. The contribution of such factors to the total experience has not been specifically measured, but would intuitively appear to be substantial.

STIMULUS RESTRICTION AS A BYPRODUCT OF MEDICAL TREATMENT

In his analysis of "clinical sensory deprivation," Jackson (1969) identifies four major classes of this phenomenon. The first covers hospitalized patients who undergo more than the average degree of reduced stimulation, social isolation, and/or physical confinement. These are people suffering from eye disorders, orthopedic patients, quarantined patients, individuals in reverse isolation (protective environments), people on voice rest with laryngeal problems, neurological disorder patients, and those undergoing long-term care. Individuals in intensive care units and those recuperating from serious surgery can be added to the list. The second form of clinical stimulus reduction is that suffered by individuals whose sensory-perceptual apparatus is impaired. These would be people who are deaf, blind, paralyzed, anosmic, and so on, either completely or to some appreciable degree. The third group in Jackson's taxonomy covers patients who underwent REST as part of a psychiatric treatment. The last and fourth category is made up of patients who participated in REST experiments similar to those usually run with normal subjects: that is, experimental procedures which have no particular explicit relevance to the patient's medical or psychiatric condition. Since there are obviously major differences among these categories, the term "clinical sensory deprivation" or "clinical REST" seems to be overly general.

I think it would be more useful to differentiate among these categories. For the first group, I propose the term "iatrogenic restricted stimulation." This implies that stimulus reduction, monotony, confinement, or a combination of these, come about as a consequence of medical treatment. The treatment is presumably necessary for the amelioration of some illness, for recovery from surgery, for the prevention of infection, or the like; but these goals cannot be reached without restricting the patient's physical and social environment in some way. For the second category, I would use the term sensory or motor handicaps. The third category, of course, is what we are now calling Restricted Environmental Stimulation Therapy. The fourth refers essentially to restricted stimulation research; the nature of the subject sample can be specified when discussing the experimentation, without necessarily categorizing some such investigations separately from the general literature. The section that follows deals with the first of these classifications, iatrogenic restriction.

Iatrogenic Stimulus Restriction

The current section examines the literature on the effects of iatrogenic interference with normal stimulation. By iatrogenic stimulus restriction, I mean a disruption of the normal level and kind of stimulation that occurs as a consequence—usually an unintended by-product—of certain therapeutic methods. Some of these have been considered before in the "sensory deprivation" literature. For example, the elimination of visual stimulation that results from eye-patching patients after certain kinds of ocular surgery has been examined in some detail (e.g., Jackson, 1969). Similarly, iatrogenic stimulus reduction occurs in many cases of severe illness. For example, Sargent (1971) notes that many tubercular patients, treated by minimal stimulation and activity for long periods, reported that they used this time to examine their past lives and to gain new insight on what aspects of experience were really important to them. Among other individuals—for whom this source of stimulus restriction may pose some problems—are patients recovering from cardiac surgery or major cardiac trauma, confined in laminar flow rooms to prevent infection, or immobilized for orthopedic damage or procedures.

Friedman and his colleagues (Friedman, Handford, and Settlage, 1964; Friedman, Sibinga, Steisel, and Sinnamon, 1968), drawing on the then popular view of "sensory deprivation" research, were among the first to emphasize the similarity between the laboratory deprivation situation and those imposed by such medical procedures as oxygen tents, immobilization for intravenous feeding, quarantine isolation, and the use of casts on limbs. One of the crucial things to remember is that, once again, the analogy with experimental REST must be used with great care. The patient hospitalized for surgery or major illness is experiencing a whole host of events, of which stimulus reduction or distortion is a relatively small part. The phenomena may include fear, anxiety, pain, the effects of medication, feelings of helplessness (with their resultant reactions possibly including frustration and anger), and uncertainty about the future. The severity and duration of confinement and reduced stimulation may be widely different. Unlike patients, experimental subjects are volunteers.

There may be significant differences between the laboratory and hospital groups on such variables as age, educational level, distribution across gender, and personality characteristics (Jackson and Ellis, 1971).

One should also be aware that there are environmental characteristics that can add to the stress and consequent problems of the patient. Some of these may be related to the level of sensory input (e.g., putting the patient in a windowless room; see Wilson, 1971). Others, however, may be related to other factors that environmental psychologists have determined to be important. For example, both in isolated groups and in prisons, intrusions upon what a particular individual perceives as his own territory and personal space can be extremely arousing, leading to both anxiety and anger. The same effect can be observed in hospitals, where encroachment on personal territory is routine, frequent, and uncontrollable (Allekian, 1973). This is a factor which has been largely ignored in the medical and nursing literature.

As with prisoners, shipwrecked sailors, and sufferers in other uncontrolled sensory reduction situations, we cannot at this stage specify the relative contributions of these factors nor the outcomes of their interactions. The situation is exacerbated by authors who on the basis of preconceived ideas define certain symptoms as "sensory deprivation phenomena," and proceed to treat and discuss them on that basis, without ever bothering to assess whether stimulus reduction actually plays any causal or contributory role in the problem. Perhaps one flagrant, but by no means unusual, example will illustrate this error. When a patient suffering from extremely serious spinal injuries following an automobile accident reported that he kept dreaming about the accident, these dreams were categorized as "sensory deprivation signs" (Johnson, 1976, p. 31). This approach may be consistent with prevailing prejudices, but is neither empirically nor logically justifiable. The extent to which any particular response pattern is caused or even affected by environmental stimulus reduction is seldom if ever known, and cannot be established without further data.

The Effects of Iatrogenic Immobilization

Major medical techniques that involve immobilization include orthopedic surgery, bed rest for a variety of illnesses, and postoperative recovery of various sorts, prominently including that from heart surgery. There seems to be no doubt that many immobilized patients, like many immobilized subjects in laboratory research (Leiderman, Mendelson, Wexler, and Solomon, 1958; Zubek, Aftanas, Kovach, Wilgosh, and Winocur, 1963; Zubek, Bayer, Milstein, and Shephard, 1969; Zubek and MacNeil, 1967), do exhibit some aversive and adverse reactions. For example, subjects in bed rest situations have reported sensations in various modalities without observable concomitant external stimuli (Downs, 1974; Leiderman et al., 1958). It has also been claimed that immobilization has a variety of negative somatic outcomes, varying in severity. One of these is an increasingly negative nitrogen balance as immobilization goes on for six days or more, resulting in anorexia (Olson, 1967).

Bolin (1974), in interviews with a number of immobilized orthopedic patients, found that nightmares of various sorts were fairly frequent, particularly during the first week in hospital. In two instances, the patients behaved in noncompliant ways, that is, by performing movements that were prohibited by the treatment plan. Since the patients may have been dreaming at the time, the degree of deliberate disobedience is open to question.

Stewart (1977), in a study of a total of 39 orthopedic patients, found a decrease in negative affects including depression and anxiety, but not hostility, regardless of degree of immobilization or social isolation. Interestingly, objective tests of locus of control and memory, and an Affect Adjective Check List, showed no differences as a function of whether the patient was or was not immobilized or isolated. However, there were substantial differences in phenomenological reports, with the isolated and immobile patients indicating decreased concentration, impaired memory, disorientation, suspiciousness, feelings of helplessness, and increased frequency of vivid and unusual dreams. They also evidenced noncompliant behavior during hypnagogic states. These individuals underestimated elapsed time, just as do REST subjects, and gave more frequent reports of sensations not tied to observable external stimuli. Stewart concluded that among orthopedic patients, those who are both immobilized and socially isolated are more likely to show adverse reactions, and that such responses may be found in subjective reports even where they are not clearly revealed through the use of standardized tests. One contributor to the differences among patients may be that those people who are both immobilized and isolated may have, or may think they have, more serious and dangerous physical problems. This factor could lead to greater negative affect, anxiety, and resultant behavioral difficulties.

It appears that personality and family characteristics, and staff behavior, can exacerbate the problems leading to "traction intolerance syndrome" (Putnam and Yager, 1978). Among the former are denial or minimization of the disability, which is seen as a threat to the patient's self-image. This may be aggravated by visitors who focus on the disability or blame the patient for it. The resultant hostility and sullenness may bring the patient into a cyclically deteriorating relationship with staff members.

However, the problem can be avoided or at least reduced by appropriate medication, brief individual and family psychotherapy, appropriate staff training, and the providing of accurate information and environmental enrichment (Johnson, 1976; Putnam and Yager, 1978).

Temporary Occlusion of Sensory Receptors. One major overview of some of this literature is the summary by Jackson (1969). In looking at a large number of studies concerning patients hospitalized for eye surgery, Jackson found a high level of behavioral disturbance. Symptoms include unusual emotional, physiological, cognitive, and sensory-perceptual events, some of which are quite bizarre and adverse to the recovery of the patient. These frequently begin by the second day after the operation, and last from a few minutes to several weeks. Demographic and personality differences are relevant to some degree. While symptoms appear among patients of both sexes, there seems to be a positive relationship between such occurrences and age, inability to speak English (in studies conducted in the United States), and a history of alcoholism—in other words, with variables frequently associated with psychological isolation (Ziskind, Jones, Filante, and Goldberg, 1960). Aspects of the illness are also relevant. For example, patients with detached retinae are much more likely to experience adverse symptoms than those being treated for cataracts. The completeness of eye patching is positively related to symptomatology. Psychological symptoms of fear, dependency, and aggressiveness, coupled with bodily unrest, demands for attention, verbosity, and noncompliance with medical directions, seem to be related to preoperative personality adjustment (Klein and Moses, 1974). Among patients with adjustment problems, the symptoms may not disappear even after the bandages are removed.

It is clear that individual differences affect the way in which people respond to sensory impairment. In one study, for example, 12 of 21 patients who had undergone stapedectomy reported that the development of their hearing loss had caused significant changes in their social life. The effects included reductions in the amount of entertaining in which they engaged, reluctance to meet new people, and frequent feelings of anger or of being the target of anger. The other 9 patients reported no social change. These differences, which obviously were major ones in the lifestyle of the individual, were not related to average hearing ability, vision, or age. Patients who reported that their lives had changed also scored as being more unhappy, stressed, subject to sleepiness and dizziness, and less accepting of their hearing problem than the other groups; and they scored as more neurotic on the Eysenck Neuroticism scale (Eysenck and Eysenck, 1963). Thus, the hypothesis that the effects of stimulus reduction are mediated by individual variables, which are not necessarily known, appears to hold for adult individuals with sensory handicaps as well as for experimental subjects and children (Jackson, Ellis, Hughey, and Schlotfeldt, 1971).

Authors have recommended a variety of remedies, including attempts to sensitize the patient to input from nonaffected modalities combined with open discussions of the problem with family and a psychiatric consultant (Klein and Moses, 1974), preparing patients to expect unusual experiences and encouraging them to interact openly with the nursing staff about such phenomena (Ellis, Jackson, Rich, Hughey, and Schlotfeldt, 1968), and a variety of medical, sociopsychological, and psychiatric techniques (Jackson, 1969).

As is usual in iatrogenic situations, it is not possible to establish whether or to what extent reduced stimulation is in fact responsible for the symptoms. There may be postoperative pain, and there is certainly discomfort and a high level of fear, particularly among patients who are not sure whether the operation was a success or whether they will be permanently blind or deaf. Some problems are caused by the hospital experience: the novelty of the environment, the exigencies of the routine, feelings of helplessness, and dependence on the staff. Others are related to future social adjustment: the possibility of major changes in family, work and other relationships which might be dictated by the new health situation of the patient after release. It may well be that with eye surgery patients, and perhaps with others as well, reduced stimulation per se is not highly significant (Ziskind, 1965). While this may be overstating the case, one can at least say that the importance of the condition remains to be elucidated.

Gerdes (1968) has generalized from her reading of the "sensory deprivation" literature to the treatment of patients who are delirious or cognitively confused because of physiological illness, hypoxia, brain injury, changes in the contents of blood and other cells, and/or chemical poisoning. She recommends that any appropriate medical treatment be supplemented by psychosocial approaches. These include the provision of familiar objects to help the patient orient himself, as well as planned increases in social and sensory stimulation. Physical restraints should be used only as a last resort, since in some patients they evoke either resentment or dependency.

Although the recommendations are probably quite useful, their theoretical base is questionable. The equating of delirium caused by infection or other illness with the effects of reduced stimulation is extremely far-fetched, and it is quite doubtful that the average hospital patient in fact suffers from stimulus restriction. On the contrary, it is probable that the actual levels of stimulation are high. Medical personnel and visitors are constantly coming and going, and considerable stimulation is involved in the hospital routine and the medical treatment. Actually, Gerdes recognizes this, but chooses to blur the issue: "Mr. G endured deprivations from loss of sleep, from sensory losses, and from the social isolation that existed in spite of, and perhaps because of, the number of persons who came and went at his bedside. For, no matter how pleasant and kind they may have been, they did unpleasant things to him like inserting needles to draw blood. . . . " (p. 1231). Obviously, loss of sleep is not a form of stimulus reduction; sensory losses were not demonstrated to have occurred as an outcome of the illness; and both the "number of persons who came and went at his bedside" and the "unpleasant things" that they did to him were in fact highly stimulating. It is unfortunate that such confusions are perpetuated in the literature. False analogies may be relatively harmless in some instances, but they can become quite misleading and counterproductive in others.

Iatrogenic Stimulus Reduction Following Surgery or Trauma.   One of the more common findings in postoperative wards has been the relatively high incidence of emotional and other psychological disruptions. Many studies have been conducted on patients recovering from heart surgery, obviously a particularly traumatic experience. Patients in intensive care coronary units clearly suffer from pain, fear, and discomfort induced by their condition and from dependency on the medical personnel and equipment as well as from social isolation and reduced input and motility. All of these factors are probably stressful, but almost certainly not equally so.

Negative symptoms are typically found in around 40% of adult patients, but relatively rarely among children. Ellis (1972) concluded from her study that no particular factor, either demographic, medical, or iatrogenic, could explain the differences between the experiences of different patients. Kornfeld (1971) suggested that the psychiatric problems are to some extent due to a combination of sensory monotony and sleep deprivation, while Goldstein (1976) blamed sleep deprivation, drugs, and anxiety. Downs (1974) argues that some of the symptomatology found among cardiac patients has to do with the restricted environment imposed by bed rest, but that the hallucinatory and other disturbing experiences under such conditions are heightened by the patient's realistic fears and increased introspection. The monotony of the environment may be less at fault than those components of hospital routine that increase the efficiency of the institution but may in fact be counterproductive from a medical point of view: depersonalization, dependence, lack of control over one's own daily routine, and violations of privacy (Lewis and Coser, 1960).

A number of authors have mentioned reported sensations, frequently characterized as hallucinations or illusions, among intensive care patients (Ellis, 1972; Kjarton and Kay, 1964; Kornfeld, Zimberg, and Malm, 1965; Lazarus and Hagens, 1968). But, as in REST, it has been found that even while the experiences were occurring, the patients could describe them and discuss them rationally, so that the commonly used terms "delirium" or "psychotic reactions" do not seem to be applicable (Ellis, 1972).

Different individuals have different ways of adapting to this situation. In a revealing article, Lee and Ball (1975) characterize the most frequent coping styles as follows. The first is "obsessive compulsive: the patient deals with stress by attempting to structure the situation, place it in order, systematize it, and study its conditions minutely in order to subjugate it to intellectual mastery" (p. 1499). Another is "repressive," with the individual attempting to put his problem out of his mind and wanting the physician to be firm and definite with him. "Dependent" patients similarly want to invest their full faith in a particular medical practitioner, sometimes to the point of observably regressive behavior. Other patients are "hyperindependent," denying their fear and helplessness, and wanting to be actively involved in their own treatment. Still another group becomes "paranoid," which the authors consider to include a generally angry and resentful attitude. The last common style is depression—feelings of hopelessness and despair—sometimes accompanied by guilt

Besides adopting the rather dubious use of psychopathological diagnostic terms for coping styles that seem to range from extremely reasonable to at least helpful in adjusting to such a stressful situation, the authors also seem to have based some of their conclusions on an inadequate reading of the literature. Surely, in a paper published in 1975, there is no longer any reason to say that "a 'panic button' is always part of the equipment in sensory deprivation studies" (p. 1500). Still, the paper is valuable in alerting treatment staff to potential problems and sources of problems, including those that may involve social and sensory restriction.

Lazarus and Hagens (1968) modified the intensive care unit environment and treatment so as to reduce anxiety, sleep deprivation and stimulus reduction, and found a significant decrease in illusions, hallucinations, disorientation, and paranoid reactions. Even the remaining phenomena usually disappeared within 2 days after the patient was transferred to a standard hospital environment. Fickess (1975) provided systematic sensory stimulation for one half of a group of patients who had received abdominal surgery under general anesthesia. The treatment, which consisted of breathing and movement exercises, oral hygiene, and back care, resulted in more rapid postoperative recovery than was exhibited by the control group. Age, sex, and severity of illness were not related to differential effectiveness of the treatment program.

Unfortunately the literature is by no means definitive. Only a few systematic studies have been done, control groups are usually omitted, and there is a lack of clear criteria for deciding which symptoms are relevant or meaningful. For example, one recent author (Oster 1977) drew attention to something that too few of his predecessors have considered: the possibility that postoperative symptoms ascribed to "sensory deprivation" may in fact be due to physical causes. In his research, Oster found that it is quite possible for some symptoms to be the results of head injury that the physician had not been aware of. A careful analysis revealed seven such cases in a group of 57 skull and other fracture patients who had been admitted to the hospital with no suspicion of damage to the brain. It is in fact not unlikely that some of the behaviors that were the sequelae of this kind of trauma might be diagnosed as those of restricted stimulation.

Severe Iatrogenic Isolation.   The use of severe isolation as a preventive against infection has increased during the past several years, with applications in such situations as leukemia, various tumors, and postsurgical recovery. Among the techniques are laminar air flow rooms, frequently used in operative and postoperative situations and also with patients who are at significant risk from infection for other reasons. In laminar flow rooms, the air is forced through highly efficient filters, and there is a uniform velocity of air flow with a minimum of turbulence. These rooms are clearly effective in reducing the survival of bacteria and consequently the occurrence of infections (Schimpff, Greene, Young, Fortner, Jepsen, Cusack, Block, and Wiernik, 1975; Turner, 1974). Schimpff et al. indicate that this effectiveness is increased even further when the patient is also given antibiotic medication. Their literature review concludes that this result was obtained in every controlled study using these techniques. In the Schimpff et al. study, furthermore, leukemic patients undergoing the combined treatment showed a higher number of complete remissions. This has not been the case in all reports, although it is not unique (Freireich, Bodey, Rodriguez, Gehan, Smith, Hester, and McCredie, 1975).

In other situations, laminar flow may not be necessary. Patients can be kept in a room under conditions of isolation and air filtration, a procedure that also seems to have significant beneficial effects on the prevention of infections (Levine, Siegel, Schreiber, Hauser, Preisler, Goldstein, Seidler, Simon, Perry, Bennett, and Henderson, 1973). There has been some question as to the relative effectiveness and the appropriate use of the more elaborate laminar air flow technique and a relatively simple isolation room. Schadelin (1975) reports that there is no difference between the two procedures when the dependent measure is time to onset of infection among leukemic patients.

Parenthetically, it is clear that the medical profession has a much better approach to terminology than do experimental psychologists. The environment used for the prevention of infection in these cases is usually called a "Life Island," or a "protective environment," or "reverse isolation" (because the patient is being protected against infection from the environment rather than the opposite, as is the usual case in quarantine situations). Thus, the negative connotations of phrases such as "sensory deprivation" are avoided from the onset. We might regret in passing that early investigators of experimental stimulus reduction techniques did not use equally positive terms!

Most of the literature in this area appears to concentrate upon the biological effects of the environment. Only recently have the psychological effects been of major concern, partly because of actual observations of psychological distress and partly because as physicians and nurses became familiar with the restricted stimulation literature they came to feel that this was a relevant variable that should be considered. Furthermore, since there is already some awareness of the sometimes deleterious psychological effects of bed rest and reduced stimulation in intensive care units (Kornfeld, 1971; Lazarus and Hagens, 1968; Thomson, 1973), it would seem logical that the apparently even more stringent conditions of reverse isolation rooms be evaluated.

Gordon (1975a, b) reported on a study of ten patients suffering from acute leukemia who were treated in a plastic tent isolator. To prevent serious psychological disturbance, each patient received a careful orientation about the environment and was gradually adapted to the procedures during a 72-hour preliminary phase. Unlike in some protective environments, the routine of the treatment was not severely stimulus-reducing. The patient was encouraged to move about within the tent, was given formal physiotherapy twice a day, various leisure pursuits were available, two visitors were permitted each day, and each isolation unit had a private telephone. Nevertheless, all of the patients were anxious and apprehensive about going into isolation. This anxiety disappeared quickly in eight of the 10 patients, and eventually in the other two as well. It recurred only when a patient was experiencing physical problems.

Interestingly, the patients' feeling of being socially isolated did not increase as time went on. Four participants, in fact, admitted that they were using the environment as an excuse to avoid social contacts and to escape from responsibility in interaction with others. The major complaints centered around restricted mobility, the unchanging nature of the stimulus world, the monotony of the cuisine (exacerbated by the fact that all food was irradiated in order to sterilize it, thus changing the taste), and lack of physical contact with other people. The last two of these factors appeared to be the most unpleasant. The importance of touching other people is an aspect that looms especially large in the reports of Gordon's patients. After their release from isolation they exhibited a considerable increase in the tendency to touch others. Yet, this particular variable of sensory reduction has been very little studied in the experimental tradition. Other problems of a psychological nature included an excessively euphoric reaction, some examples of regression and denial, and ambivalence about the dependency imposed by the environment. However, there were no severe affective disturbances, no hallucinatory activity, and none of the adverse symptoms that have been found in some isolation situations.

In view of the facts that these individuals were quite ill, that two of them had histories of psychiatric problems, and that they stayed in the isolation environment from 21 to 99 days, this lack of symptomatology is quite encouraging. Gordon (1975b) indicates that even though the isolator treatment had its problems, none of the patients felt either socially isolated or deprived of privacy, none requested termination of the treatment, and all of them were willing to reenter the isolator if it were to be medically advised on future occasions. Of course, there was some distress and unhappiness, but certainly not enough to outweigh the medical advantages of the technique.

Haenel and Nagel (1975) reported on 31 severely ill cancer patients who spent a total of 767 days in a germ-free isolator. The patients ranged from 8 to 76 years in age, and were screened for both physical and psychological characteristics before being admitted to the unit. The psychological requirements were agreement to the proposed therapy, willingness to cooperate, and freedom from any psychological problem that might be exacerbated by isolation (this may be compared with the remark of Gordon, 1975b, that previous psychiatric illness was not a contraindicator for isolation treatment).

The major finding was that psychological reactions depended primarily on the physical condition of the patient, there being a direct and positive relationship between severity of the illness and severity of the psychological reaction. Women were more likely to react badly than men, contrary to the finding of Gordon (1975b). While nine patients had fairly serious psychological problems, none had to be removed from the isolator for this reason. None of the patients reported feeling isolated (in fact, some of them asked for a reduction in the number of visitors permitted), and only one reported feeling bored. Two of the patients reported that they were bothered by deprivation of human tactual contact, in both cases with particular individuals. One was a mother who missed touching her small child, and the other was an engaged man who missed the contact with his fiancée. A need for physical activity was noted by almost half of the individuals. Aggressiveness, rebelliousness, regression, and dependence were observed fairly frequently.

After being released from the Life Island, several of the patients expressed insecurity in the normal environment. Some were interested in extending their isolator treatment either because of fear of infection or for psychological reasons. One, in fact, upon her return home, set up with the cooperation of her family a kind of equivalent of the isolator. Almost all patients who were asked indicated that they would be willing to go back into the environment if this were considered medically advisable.

Another study, reporting on nine leukemic patients treated in a Life Island, reports that isolation, physical inactivity, and dependency were, in combination with medical problems, contributors to a psychological problem in the patients' dealing with their severe illness (Köhle, Simons, Weidlich, Dietrich, and Durner, 1971). Apparently, at least some of these patients were not aware that they had leukemia until they entered the hospital, so that the tremendous change in environmental circumstances was combined with the traumatic impact of the diagnosis. The patients in this case tended to be quite assertive, and to try to control those with whom they came into contact. Spontaneous emotional responses were denied, isolated, displaced, or inhibited. A great deal of emphasis was placed on activity and fitness. These were apparently considered to be normal for leukemic patients, rather than being the results of the isolation treatment.

Among twenty acute leukemia patients with an average isolation time of almost 38 days, there was a "surprisingly low incidence of more serious psychological complications" (Köhle, Simons, Dietrich, and Durner, 1973). The major symptom observed was dependency upon the medical staff, perceived by the patient as temporary and necessary for successful treatment. If the patient eventually finds such dependency to be intolerable, social withdrawal results. During prolonged confinement, there were signs of withdrawal, depression, and apathy, probably as a result of the long duration of the severe illness combined with social, sensory, and motor restrictions. Nevertheless, the authors posit only a few criteria for excluding patients from reverse isolation. These are refusal to participate, insufficient intelligence or severe physical impairment which make it impossible for the patient to cooperate adequately, or a history of psychiatric illness.

Holland (1971), in an analysis of a number of reports on the reaction of patients to different kinds of protective environments, found that general adjustment was relatively good. In fact, contrary to the expectations of some workers, there seem to be no symptoms that could be directly attributable to stimulus reduction per se, although of course the stress of illness and fear of death combined with various aspects of the complex treatment do result in some psychological problems.

In a more recent review of the literature, a group of authors sent questionnaires to the directors of 17 medical institutions that were known to use laminar air flow units quite commonly (Kellerman, Rigler, and Siegel, 1977). Of these, 13 questionnaires were returned, covering institutions that treated patients from childhood on up, with a range of 6 to 260 patients having been treated by isolation and with time in the treatment environment lasting from 2 to 240 days.

None of the institutions had performed systematic studies on the psychological effects of the isolated protective room. However, some psychiatric symptoms were reported. In 6 of the 13 institutions, some patients had to be removed because of such symptoms. Some of the specific reasons were destructive behavior, anxiety, severe regression, and depression (frequently related to the failure of treatment).

It is impossible to separate the psychological effects of the isolation from those of the illness itself and from other aspects of treatment. For instance, the only symptoms mentioned by more than half of the directors were depression, anxiety, irregular sleep, and psychological withdrawal. It would seem logical to expect that all of these problems would be found as a result of cancer and other life-threatening illnesses, regardless of environmental stimulation. Less common reactions included "hallucinations" (no criteria for this category were mentioned), spatial and temporal disorientation, regression, and nightmares. Other symptoms were reported by 2 or fewer of the 13 respondents.

Severe Iatrogenic Isolation of Children

Kellerman et al. (1977) reported on the basis of a survey of 13 medical institutions that children adapt quite well to protective environments, and in some cases like the situation so much that when they are rehospitalized they ask to be returned to isolation (a situation that the authors for some reason choose to label as a display of "psychological dependency"). Most of these requests come from children who are hospitalized for the treatment of cancer. No child in any of the institutions had to be removed from the environment because of adjustment problems.On the other hand, adolescents frequently showed regression, dependency, and—conversely—aggressive noncooperation. They apparently found isolation particularly stressful because of the lack of privacy involved, a point that institutions using these techniques should bear in mind.

There have been several reported cases in which infants have had to be brought up for long periods of time in germ-free conditions that necessitated a high degree of isolation. Of course, the situation arouses fears as to the developmental progress of such children, since the literature on restricted rearing with infrahuman organisms has repeatedly shown deleterious effects, some of which were permanent (see Chapter 5). Similarly, the supposed adverse consequences of institutionalization and other types of environmental restriction in childhood (Chapter 4) have been thought to be applicable in the case of iatrogenic isolation with children. In some cases, this fear has affected the course of treatment. For example, one child who spent four years in isolation waiting for a bone marrow transplant was finally taken out of the isolator by his mother, who felt that continued isolation could have done irreparable mental damage to him (English, 1977).

One extended systematic study dealt with a pair of fraternal twins who were kept in a protective environment for $2^{1}/_{2}$ years (Teller, 1973). During this period they were treated with antibiotics and with attempted transplants. Because their immune responses improved over the course of isolation, they were eventually gradually inoculated with bacteria and finally released into the normal environment, apparently with good results.

An evaluation of the isolation room indicated that there was no great lack of external stimulation, although the physical environment was somewhat monotonous. The major situational problems originally appeared to be a lack of complexity and stimulation, confinement to a relatively small space, and a lack of tactile contact with human beings. The twins' experience, unlike that of most other children brought up under restricted conditions, was part of a systematic and scientifically controlled treatment. This made it possible for factors in the environment to be varied when necessary, and for the results of these variations to be observed.

Isolation characteristics were identical for the two children, but their reactions were quite different.Development during the first year was fairly normal, although with some problems. At the beginning of the second year, one of the children was relatively delicate and passive, and had a developmental quotient of 80. The other was more active and healthy-looking, and scored 100. These children engaged in very vivid and intense eye contact with others. They had less than average ability to handle play materials and to learn and remember information. Since toys were almost completely unavailable, the lack of skill in handling objects was understandable. The problems in learning and memory may have been partly due to the novelty of the items used in the test, and partly to the concentration of the children on watching the psychologist rather than looking at the test materials. As a result, toys and play therapy were introduced into the treatment program, with subsequent improvement in the handling of play material. However, learning ability and intellectual capacity remained low throughout the second year of life. This began to be remedied about midway during the third year, after the play-therapeutic approach had begun to focus on encouraging spontaneous activity and the development of autonomy.

The children had some problems in establishing close relationships with adults, although the stronger one did show a definite preference for one particular nurse. He behaved aggressively when frustrated, and exhibited both separation anxiety and fear of novelty.

The other child seemed to be more creative, or at least more variable, in his play activities. His behavior showed sudden changes in mood and he liked to perform rhythmic movements. He also very much enjoyed being touched and caressed when nurses put their hands into a pair of rubber gloves attached to the inside wall of the isolator. In general, he remained small, physically weak, and developmentally retarded as compared to his twin. It should be pointed out that at the age of 4 months he had suffered a convulsive seizure, and a hypothesis of brain damage was advanced to explain the difference between the two children.

The authors conclude that long-term isolation led to the impairment of intellectual capacity, due to a lack of experience and the monotony of the environment. Rhythmic rocking, indulged in by both children for some time, disappeared when physical restraint became less severe. Play therapy helped the boys to reduce the adverse effects of isolation and prepared them for their eventual emergence into a normal environment, with the consequence that at the time of release the therapist felt that the twins "were approaching a favorable stage of their psychological development" (p. 41).

Freedman (1975; Montgomery, Wilson, Bealmear, and Salve, 1976) studied a child born with a congenital defect of the immunological system and therefore brought up in a protective environment. The last report was made when the boy reached the age of 52 months. This child demonstrated very rapid development of motor skills, hand-eye coordination, motility, and large-muscle activity. His social and emotional development was close to average, but his verbal behavior was somewhat retarded. The institution of a program to increase speech behavior and establish emotional ties with a specific other person resulted in a rapid improvement in verbal ability. Although he did some rhythmic rocking, he was in general considered to be at the age of two "a happy, outgoing, mischievous little boy" (Freedman, 1975, p. 77). At the age of 52 months, he was essentially normal for his age both physically and psychologically.

Freedman and his colleagues decided that psychological development does not necessarily suffer as a result of isolation in a protective environment of the sort used for germ-free rearing. Furthermore, the inability to experience close bodily contact with other human beings, to speak face to face without any intervening barrier, and to feel the breath and warmth of others also did not seem to result in observable handicaps. It is true that this child had a more stimulating environment than did the twins studied by Teller's team. There may also have been constitutional and/or genetic differences of major significance (see Freedman, 1975). At any rate isolation of this sort, even when it goes on for a fairly long time early in life, does not appear to be necessarily damaging or even uncomfortable for the child.

Reducing Adverse Consequences

Many of the writers whose research is described above also made suggestions about the proper structuring of stimulus-restricting medical settings. Gordon (1975b) suggests that psychiatric assessment should be used to identify patients who may react poorly to isolation and that attempts should be made to reduce some of the stressful aspects (for example, by trying to maintain the normal taste of food). The advance identification of patients whose intolerance of isolation might interfere with their therapy, and the preparation of staff members for dealing with the psychological problems that might result, would be two useful contributions of a psychologist or psychiatrist in a treatment unit using iatrogenic isolation. Gordon pointed out that it is not only the patient who suffers in these conditions. Because of the complex technical problems, the seriousness of the illness, and the relatively low emphatic contact with patients, staff members also work under an unusual level of stress. This, too, should be anticipated and dealt with.

Köhle et al. (1971) suggest that therapists should encourage the patients to enjoy the feeling of dependency on medical staff, and to engage in "regression in the service of the ego." As the reader will recall, this process was also hypothesized to be relevant to adaptation to reduced environmental stimulation (e.g., Goldberger and Holt, 1961). Köhle et al. (1971) further propose that the patient should be oriented in great detail about the procedures, techniques, and task assignments involved in his therapy, and should also be invited to make suggestions and ask questions. It was suggested that each patient be encouraged to establish a particularly strong relationship with some team member, preferably one who is not providing direct care or supervision for him. Unfortunately, the article did not go into detail about the results, even though an unusually elaborate battery of personality measures was administered to each patient.

The suggestions made by institutional directors (Kellerman et al., 1977) to foster better adaptation included detailed pre-entry orientation, which we have already pointed out to be an important factor in the adaptation to novel environments, including REST. Further, the family and the patient should be encouraged to participate in the therapeutic process, and a great deal of stimulating experience should be provided (for example, occupational and play therapy; windows with views). Time cues and structured daily schedules are important. Because of the problems that are encountered by these patients, which in turn can cause difficulty for the staff, it is also suggested that staff members be given extensive training and support before and during their assignment to such units.

REDUCED STIMULATION IN THE PRISON SETTING: THE QUESTION OF SOLITARY CONFINEMENT

This section takes up what is currently perhaps the most controversial aspect of the use of stimulus reduction in nonlaboratory and nonclinical settings. The use of social isolation—and some degree of stimulus deprivation—in prisons is an important issue, because the correctional system is so significant a part of any society. Further, it is controversial because isolation in this setting is clearly not voluntary, and is only questionably for the benefit of the inmate. Unlike in some cases of psychosis or other behavioral problems, the involuntary seclusion of prisoners is not used merely as a short-term crisis management technique. Another reason for the high visibility of this particular debate is that in some jurisdictions the correctional system is closely tied in with governmental repression, and the distinction between the incarceration of criminals and the silencing of opponents or dissidents is frequently blurred by polemicists on one side or another of the political spectrum.

The Prison Environment

Being in prison necessarily imposes some reduction of the range of available environmental stimulation. At the very least, geographic mobility is circumscribed and the number of different individuals with whom one can interact is limited. The ability to engage in diversified activities, flexible scheduling, and wide choice-making is certainly lowered. Most large prisons, particularly those that maximize security, are designed without any consideration for ameliorating these factors. As a rule, the scale of architecture in such institutions is inhumanly large, the colors of walls, furniture, clothes, bedding, and other objects are drab and monotonous, the surfaces of any open area are either concrete or sparse grass, windows are small and are made functionally even smaller by bars or shutters. Thus, the visual environment is usually uninteresting. So, too, is the array of auditory inputs, which for the greater part of the day is restricted to the voices of other men, with the occasional radio or television program to break the monotony. Movement is within this same environment day after day, from cell to mess hall to work to recreation, with very little change. Indoor and outdoor surfaces are mostly hard, and do not vary highly. Even in well-funded institutions in wealthy countries, where the food is nutritious and palatable, it is hardly exciting. Thus, the total sensory impact is one of low stimulation at any given time and low level of change over time. The resultant boredom may reach substantial levels of stressfulness, which may be alleviated by bursts of sometimes violent activity.

This brings up a point that in some ways contradicts the above. The contradiction is resolved when one realizes that any global environment is a complex one, various components of which may be inconsistent with each other. The factor that I am referring to is that prison life, while so pervasively monotonous, can also be high in certain kinds of stimulation. For example, there are stringent demands for compliance with the rules of life, both the official ones promulgated by the institution and the unofficial ones that govern the convict culture. These sets of rules, often in conflict with each other, pervade and govern most of one's daily activities. Sanctions for violation can be severe, and monitoring is ubiquitous. Trying to satisfy the institution and the convict codes, as well as one's own preferences, can be traumatic. There is very little privacy, emotions run high, and many of the individuals in the social group are dangerous. As a result, both the chronic and the fairly frequent acute levels of anxiety and tension tend to be above those usually experienced in free society.

Monotony and tension are not the only problems related to the surroundings. Another major source of stress is the lack of control that the prisoner has over the environment he inhabits. As Glass and Singer (1972) have shown, the variable of control and the related one of predictability are crucial in making a reasonably good adaptation to unpleasant situations. Both are minimized in the prison setting. In most prisons, furthermore, there is little recognition of and even less allowance for the need for personal territory (Altman and Haythorn, 1967; Ardrey, 1966). As Ardrey has argued in his popular book, and as Altman and other researchers have demonstrated, people in any environment seem to need and rapidly claim a particular area that is undeniably theirs. In home and work places in the normal world, the implicit assignments of territory are quickly learned, and markers such as personal possessions, photographs, and the like are utilized to indicate the boundaries of one's space. In the prison, the use of personal markers is frequently restricted or even forbidden, and one's territory can be intruded upon or changed for no stated reason and with very little notice.

The correctional institution also violates the inmate's interpersonal space, the need for which has been documented in a great number of studies (e.g., Barash, 1973; Hall, 1966). Here again, the protective bubble that each of us carries wherever we go is frequently breached in prison by close, often aggressive or at least assertive, physical contact with others. Another central issue is the human need for a reasonably low density of population per unit of space, and the desire for privacy associated with communal living (Stokols, 1972; Freedman, 1975; Milgram, 1970; Bossley, 1976). These requirements, too, are more frequently violated than observed in prisons, particularly in institutions where the population is much greater than the original designers had envisioned. The adverse effects of crowding on the health of prisoners have been empirically demonstrated (McCain, Cox, and Paulus, 1976; D'Atri, 1975). More research needs to be done on its psychological and behavioral consequences, as well as on those of the other factors noted above.

Serious infringement of these needs would be a stressor in any situation, not only in penal institutions (Rasmussen, 1973). But the violations are not only more pervasive and severe in prisons; to make things worse, incarcerated individuals and groups may be even more sensitive to damage from such environmental factors than the average person. Monotony is one example. Psychopaths and violent individuals in general, who are obviously overrepresented in the prison population, apparently have a higher need for stimulation than the average (Cox, 1977; Emmons and Webb, 1974; Quay, 1965). In addition, violent prisoners have been shown to have a body-buffer zone or personal space bubble almost four times as large as non-violent convicts (Kinzel, 1970). Minority groups that tend to be overrepresented in prison populations have both larger buffer zones (Baxter, 1970) and more strictly defined and observed group territories (Hall, 1971) than the majority of white North Americans. Thus, it appears that the very people who are most likely to end up in prison are also those who are most stressed by the environmental conditions that prisons impose. No wonder then that these environmental conditions are contributors to the generally high level of violence and frustration in correctional institutions (Suedfeld, 1977b).

It should be pointed out that there have been recent attempts to modify the situation, and to provide milieux that increase variety, diversity, control, predictability, and the availability of privacy and territorial security. Among North American institutions where these principles have been taken into consideration are the Regional Psychiatric Centre (Pacific) of the Canadian Penitentiary Service, Abbotsford, British Columbia, and the projected Minnesota institution that will house the most hard-core violent prisoners in that state's correctional system (Schoen, 1977). Of course, the maximum security facilities with which this discussion has been concerned tend to frustrate environmental needs much more than medium and minimum security institutions do. In such places as prison farms, camps, and the like, the level of tension is much less exacerbated by environmental problems and is typically quite tolerable for most inmates.

Solitary Confinement

Let us turn from problems that are inherent in the average penitentiary setting to look at what is perhaps the most prominent and publicized situation of low environmental stimulation in prisons: solitary confinement. The history of prisons indicates clearly that solitude has been considered to be a powerful rehabilitative technique. For example, isolation was not used in systems that considered imprisonment to be primarily a custodial function; but where incarceration was intended and expected to have beneficial effects on the prisoner, seclusion was usually advocated to encourage repentance (Walker, 1968). This practice is probably related to the use of "excommunication" in monastic orders, where offenders against the rules may be isolated from the community while they live in "penitential sorrow" and ponder their behavior. It should be noted, incidentally, that corporal punishment is recommended for those who do not mend their ways after isolation, or those who are perverse and do not understand the seriousness of being cast out (e.g. Doyle, 1948).

It seemed only logical that, when the Philadelphia Society for Alleviating the Miseries of Public Prisoners was formed by Quakers who were repulsed by the use of the whip, the stock, and the gallows, the reformed prison system adopted the religious tradition of using social isolation to foster reflection and repentance. This tradition, incidentally, was and still is particularly important to Quakers, silent contemplation forming a major part of their religious observances. It has been emphasized that in the Philadelphia system and its variants, solitary confinement was neither viewed nor imposed as vengeance. Rather, its use was meant to prevent prisoners from further corrupting each other, to foster religious contemplation, and to teach the habits of productive labor (Smith, 1833; Sommer, 1976). The efficacy of this approach is difficult to evaluate. Some observers (e.g., Dickens, 1843/1907) were horrified by the deterioration that they felt was evidenced by the prisoners. Others, however, supported the system, which in their opinion was a successful, humane, and productive one (deBeaumont and deTocqueville, 1833/1964; Smith, 1833). In fact, several very progressive social reformers expressed this positive view (see Clifford, 1978; Tobias, 1972).

The Civil Commandant of the Port Arthur prisons in Tasmania, in one section of which the separate system was very strictly enforced, said: "[eight to twelve months of the system] produces a powerful effect in changing the evil tendencies of the convicts' minds and inducing an amelioration of character as must ultimately lead to a thoroughly practical reformation—there are, of course, exceptions to these desirable results, but my considered conviction is, that the generality of convicts, do derive the greatest advantage from the discipline of the Separate Prison" (from the report of James Boyd, January 1854; cited in Brand, 1975, p. 72). This evaluation was corroborated by advocates of the Philadelphia prisons (Smith, 1833). At any rate, the system was found to be uneconomical and inefficient from the point of view of prison work, since it made it impossible to engage the prisoners in cooperative, team, assembly line, or other modern kinds of endeavor. Because of this problem, combined with the work of reformers, the separate system was gradually abandoned.

A recent analysis (Suedfeld, 1974b) categorized the most common current uses of segregation under four major headings. These are: indoctrination and interrogation, quarantine, punishment, and rehabilitation. The categories are obviously based on the purpose for which solitude is imposed. The application of solitary confinement might also be analyzed, for example, on the basis of duration, physical conditions, type of prisoner, and so on. But since in most cases the treatment is applied because of some specific goal that the authorities wish to reach, the nature of that goal seems to be a reasonable basis for a taxonomy of solitary confinement.

Indoctrination and Interrogation

There is evidence that solitary confinement has been used in attempts to reduce the resistance of political and other prisoners in the Soviet Union (Hinkle and Wolff, 1956; Krivitsky, 1939; Weissberg, 1951), Nazi Germany (Burney, 1961; Gross and Svab, 1967), and various countries of

Eastern Europe (Leites and Bernaut, 1954; Paloczi-Horvath, 1959; Sedman, 1961). It seems clear that this use of seclusion was derived from well-established practices in the police and prison systems of these countries. For example, it is well known that the treatment of political prisoners in the Soviet Union is directly traceable to techniques used by the Czarist secret police. Seclusion has been used for centuries in various kinds of prisons, particularly for important political captives. One of the functions that it has served has been to prevent the individual from communicating with his supporters, so that he cannot participate in a revolutionary group, plan his escape, or get support (moral or material) either from the outside or from other prisoners. There is no doubt that isolating a prisoner makes him easier to manage and thus has real value from the point of view of the authorities. There is a less tangible benefit as well: the isolated prisoner cannot get psychological support from his peers any more than he can get material support. As a result, he does not know whether they are still loyal to him or to their common cause, a factor that presumably would lead to weaker resistance in the face of his captors than if he were completely secure about the solidarity of the group.

There seems to be little reason to believe, however, that isolation per se breaks down the resistance of prisoners. Overstimulation is much more common, more stressful, and has more impact (see Sargant, 1961). For example, in the cases mentioned above, there was probably a general state of disorientation and anxiety. The surprise arrest in the middle of the night, the lack of knowledge as to the fate of one's family, confusion about the reason for being incarcerated and as to one's own future, frequent and prolonged intense interrogations (which impose a state of stimulus overload contrasting harshly with the monotony of the interim periods), were all part of the environmental stress. This was then used as the groundwork for the success of a very skillful and systematic interrogation technique, including a wide range of psychological techniques for inducing feelings of guilt, a desire to cooperate, identification with the interrogator, and so on (see e.g. Koestler, 1940).

Even with this highly sophisticated technique, the actual rate of submission may not have been impressive. Krivitsky (1939), a former officer of the Soviet secret police, estimated that for every prisoner from whom a public confession could be elicited during the Moscow purge trials of the 1930s a hundred others failed to reach that level of reliability. There is no way to estimate success rates for "thought reform" procedures in China, although it is quite clear that both with foreign and with native prisoners there are quite a few individuals who manage to go through the procedure without being converted (Lifton, 1961; London, 1977; Schein, 1961). Anyway, it is significant that all descriptions of the Chinese Communist techniques indicate a heavy reliance on constant overstimulation, and only extremely rare use of periods of solitude. For those who feel that the descriptions based on interviews of refugees and defectors may be distorted by hostile authors (e.g., Federal Prisoners' Coalition, 1972/73), it might be interesting to read a book which was written by someone sympathetic to the Chinese regime (Hinton, 1972). In this discussion of the course of the Cultural Revolution of the late 1960s, the process whereby people were brought to confess their wickedness, to recant, and to accept the "correct" line are depicted uncritically; the gross overstimulation involved in the procedure is quite obvious.

There is not much point in reviewing the literature on "brainwashing" here. Briefly, the techniques typically involve weakening the victim's power to resist by inducing a state of physical weakness, fear, and dependency upon the captors (Farber, Harlow, and West, 1957). Weakness can be brought about by such techniques as starvation, lack of medical treatment for illnesses and wounds, hard labor or long marches, interruption of sleep, and actual torture (see e.g., Biderman, 1963; Conquest, 1968; Lifton, 1961; Sargent, 1971). Of course, in many cases prisoners are already suffering from one or more of these conditions, so that these need not necessarily be imposed explicitly as an aid to interrogation or indoctrination (Berg and Richlin, 1977). Fear is aroused by the circumstances surrounding the event of capture or arrest, and the event itself, by threats, beatings and deprivations, uncertainty about the eventual outcome, and the removal of supportive social ties and information (Lifton, 1961; Schein, 1961; Amnesty International, 1977). Dependency is a natural outgrowth of the fact that the prisoner is completely in the power of the detaining authority, a fact which is brought home by harsh treatment, or alternating harsh and lenient treatment, sometimes apparently at random and sometimes in response to the prisoner's own behavior (Biderman, 1963; Krivitsky, 1939).

Added to this are techniques that make the prisoner completely dependent upon less recalcitrant peers for such basic necessities as food and elimination of waste matter (Lifton, 1961). Keeping the individual incommunicado also emphasizes to him the fact that he has only the good will of the authorities to protect him, one reason why the work of such groups as Amnesty International is so important. Last, a state of disorientation is brought about by the combination of all of the previous treatments, plus the factor of informational bias. This consists of presenting, repeatedly and forcefully, the point of view that the captive is supposed to accept (whether this be the point of view that continued denial is useless and he might as well cooperate, or an actual political ideology), while at the same time denying to him information favorable to opposing conclusions (Schein, 1961).

A large and, by now, empirically supported literature exists on this topic. Two general points should be made. One is that probably without exception the techniques have been known and used for centuries. Those that are dependent on modern technology are merely offshoots of older methods that accomplish the same ends. I have seen no convincing evidence that physiological or psychological research has significantly increased either the range of methods used or their effectiveness. The second point is that solitary confinement, and in some cases general stimulus reduction, have in fact been used as components of this process (again, following tactics that have been used for hundreds of years). Their usefulness appears to reside mostly in that they contribute to disorientation, since they remove from the prisoner the support of family, friends, and comrades both inside and outside the prison or prison camp. There seems to be no reason to think that this is a crucial component. In fact, seclusion has been applied very sparingly indeed in some of the most systematic Chinese attempts at conversion (see Lifton, 1961; Schein, 1961) but used quite routinely in Vietnam, a superficially similar historical situation where, however, very little attempt was made to subvert the prisoners (Deaton, Berg, Richlin, and Litrownik, 1977).

The content of the propaganda itself varies of course with the particular situation. But a combination of overt and subtle techniques is used in most cases to induce feelings of guilt, a recognition that resistance is futile, a desire to search one's own thoughts and past behavior for evidence of misdeeds, rote learning of attitude-related materials, and an identification with the authorities as opposed to fellow-prisoners who still resist (see e.g., Dolliver, 1971). In this brief account, I have not drawn the distinctions that a more detailed look would require among techniques designed to elicit useful information, to obtain confessions of guilt, to induce cooperation with the authorities (acting as a double agent), or to bring about actual conversion.

There have been reports that solitary confinement in one or another form has been used in eliciting confessions in the Union of South Africa (Mathews and Albino, 1966), and newspaper and other reports have confirmed its use in Portugal, Chile, Cuba, North and South Vietnam, and Syria, among other countries. These reports agree in listing a great variety of brutal treatment procedures that were applied to prisoners; isolation was imposed in conjunction with forms of torture. Perhaps the most publicized situation of this sort has been in Northern Ireland. One reason for this publicity is that the mistreatment there occurred in an open society, whose journalists, scientists, and ordinary people (including released prisoners) feel free to bring their case to public attention.

Some reviewers commit a basic error. That error is the complete misunderstanding of the nature of the intensive interrogation procedure (or conversely, of the REST environment). Shallice (1972a), whose paper may stand as a characteristic example of this kind of attack, describes the Ulster procedure as follows: the head of the suspect is covered with a black cloth bag and he is dressed in loose overalls; a constant extremely loud white noise of approximately 85 to 87 db is imposed within the room; the suspect is not permitted to sleep and is not given food except for dry bread and water for the first several days; and he is forced to stand against the wall in an uncomfortable and unnatural position and up to 16 hours at a time. Secondarily, it was reported that some suspects were physically assaulted, insulted, and threatened. Another publication concerned with the treatment of Ulster detainees (McGuffin, 1974) also attacks what it calls the "sensory deprivation treatment," but obviously uses the term as shorthand for a whole conglomeration of techniques. This is revealed when the author lists a total of 33 types of mistreatment (pp. 133–134), of which only two at the most (blindfolding and staring at a white wall in a small cubicle) could be identified as stimulus reduction by any stretch of imagination, and 23 of which have to do with physical pain inflicted on the prisoner by various techniques. Furthermore, neither of the two sensation-reducing techniques can in any way be ascribed to experimental research in the area, both of them having been features of the mistreatment of prisoners for many decades if not centuries.

It appears fairly clear, and is admitted in the official British investigations into the Ulster situation (Compton Committee, 1971; Parker Committee, 1972), that detainees suspected of being IRA adherents were subjected to harsh treatment while under interrogation. It is equally clear from any objective reading of the treatments (see also Association for Legal Justice, 1972–1974) that, just as in China, the major aspect of the treatment could much more accurately be characterized as excessive stimulation than as "sensory deprivation."

One really interesting demonstration of just exactly where the stress is appears in a paper by Levinson, Ingram, and Azcarata (1968). These writers specifically used mandatory participation in group therapy as an aversive reinforcer for juvenile inmates who had committed some act for which they were sent to solitary confinement. In other words, the psychologists—interpreting comments that they had heard from inmates—perceived that it was not segregation, but enforced group therapy, that was the powerful aversive situation. The requirement was for any boy who had been in segregation at least once a month for three successive months to attend a weekly $1^1/_2$-hour group meeting until he had gone for 3 successive months without being sent into segregation. The analysis was in fact correct. Being forced to attend group therapy was sufficient punishment to extinguish behavior that had previously led to solitary confinement. Eleven of the 16 members of the group earned their way out of therapy. Others were sent out of the institutional setting for other reasons. Only one participant chose voluntarily to remain in the group even after he was eligible to leave it. It would be interesting to see the critics of REST, and the advocates of group therapy (frequently the same people) work this finding into their discussions.

While group treatments differ widely, it is among them that the analogues of the Chinese coercive persuasion techniques can be found. The closest parallel that I have seen in the literature was reported by Church and Carnes (1973). The book describes the experiences of a group working for a large national company. The employees were put through a 4-day session in the Leadership Dynamics Institute. The procedures included degrading criticism and self-criticism, beatings, food and sleep deprivation, alternate expressions of strong approval and strong rejection, and a general persistently high level of stimulation. To read this account gives one perhaps the most realistic flavor of the thought reform technique transferred from China to the United States. Incidentally, even the goals sound very similar: "The idea of LDI was to rid us of our hang-ups, to force us into complete self-honesty, to make better members of society out of us" (p. 5). One person left during the session, several others sued the people who conducted it, and one wrote a severely critical book; but according to the authors quite a few went home maintaining that it had been the best experience of their life.

We have to conclude that governments bent upon indoctrinating, interrogating, or forcing confessions from political prisoners typically use techniques whose aim is to debilitate the prisoner physically, inducing in him a state of thoroughgoing fear and anxiety and convincing him that his only possible salvation or any amelioration of his condition will come only if he pleases the powers that be (see Farber, Harlow, and West, 1957). The techniques for producing these effects include starvation, beating, humiliation, unexpected acts of kindness, threats, the example of other prisoners, and so on through a long list. For the most part, the methods rely on excessive and stressful stimulation, which is high in intensity and low in predictability and controllability. These conditions are known to maximize environmental stress (Glass and Singer, 1972; Suedfeld, 1979).

It is quite possible that methods heightening the sense of stress, aloneness, and disorientation in this context may include varying periods of solitary confinement and/or general sensory reduction. However, there is no reason to believe that these conditions in themselves will induce some kind of breakdown, nor that they represent a form of torture (cf. Lucas, 1976; McGuffin, 1974; Suedfeld, 1978), nor that sensory isolation drives people insane (Dicks, Williams, Storr, and Wall, 1972). This is not to deny that severe monotony can be stressful, and that for some people it may be extremely so, nor to condone its use in conjunction with torture. Rather, it is a reminder that it is torture itself that needs to be eliminated, and that the appropriate campaign would be directed toward that goal.

Quarantine

Isolation as a form of quarantine, to protect the prisoner from being harmed by his fellow inmates, to protect other individuals from the prisoner who is being isolated, or to facilitate observation in order to prevent the prisoner from harming himself, does not seem to be very controversial. The potential harm resulting from contact may be physical or psychological. The former situation, which usually involves violence, is self-explanatory; in the latter category, we can put those instances where it is felt that interaction among prisoners would in some way damage the adjustment of one or the other party.

It is of course possible that in the second kind of case protection may become a euphemism for preventing concerted effort by the prisoners where such cooperation might cause discomfort to the authorities (see e.g., Hirt, 1973; Wilkins, 1973). Provisions for administrative dissociation, used in many jurisdictions including the Canadian Penitentiary Service, establish a category of solitary confinement for the "maintenance of good order and discipline in the institution." This is not necessarily considered punishment, since it is used rather as a preventive measure when the administration of the institution feels that an inmate may cause trouble if he is not segregated. If one accepts that the institution does have the basic right to try to prevent outbreaks, and that isolation of potential disruptors may be such a preventive step, then one must agree with a recent report of a committee struck by the Solicitor General's Department of Canada that both protective and administrative segregation should be retained as necessary tools in managing institutions (Vantour Committee, 1975).

Punishment

The third major category of use is in the context of punishment. While there are very few reliable data on the frequency of use of solitary confinement for this purpose, the almost ubiquitous nature of relevant regulations and facilities seems to indicate that it is quite common. In fact, it has been claimed that solitary confinement "is the single most used punishment in prison today" (Singer, 1971, p. 1251). This statement, of course, refers to the situation in the United States, but it probably can be generalized to many other countries. The difference between administrative and punitive segregation is sometimes merely semantic, sometimes a matter of procedure in that no one can be sentenced to punitive isolation without being convicted at some kind of hearing, and relatively rarely a matter of significant difference in the conditions of confinement. In some cases, inmates being isolated for punishment have fewer amenities in their cells (furniture, bedding, private property, and the like), have less access to bathing and entertainment facilities, are allowed out of their cells for exercise for a shorter period of time every day, or may be given less varied and balanced diets. Some of the conditions imposed in segregation cells are clearly degrading and inhumane, and in many cases have been held unconstitutional as amounting to cruel and unusual punishment (McAninch, 1973). There are also many claims by prisoners of brutal treatment, including beatings, the unnecessary use of Mace, and so on, but the extent to which these are reflections of administrative policy is highly arguable. In North America, at any rate, explicit prison policies forbid such practices, although there may be institutions where they are condoned implicitly.

Once again, as in the case of indoctrination, interrogation, and the elicitation of confession, we see the confusion of social isolation and/or stimulus reduction per se with the adverse conditions that it may accompany. There should be no argument that such things as harassment by guards, uncomfortable temperatures, inadequate diets, lack of exercise, and deprivation of clothes and possessions, are indeed highly stressful, and should be eliminated from the repertoire of prisons. At the same time, there is no evidence that being segregated has a universally, or even commonly, negative effect. Yet, once again solitary confinement is attacked as though it necessarily involves all of the injurious conditions mentioned (e.g., Thoenig, 1972; Singer, 1971).

Rehabilitation

The last use of isolation, which in prisons has frequently been confused with punishment, is rehabilitation. There have not been many attempts to use solitary confinement in this way. Of course, we may refer back to the original designers of the nineteenth century prisons in which every inmate was isolated from all others, to the argument that solitude made it possible for the prisoner to hear the inner voice of his conscience, leading to repentance and the ability to resume a blameless way of life after release (Ignatieff, 1976). Even John Howard, the great prison reformer of the eighteenth century, recommended solitary confinement for his own son, who had gone insane after a prolonged bout of drinking and debauchery.

In recent years, there have been a few systematic approaches to this problem. Perhaps the best known, which was aborted before its effects could be evaluated, was the United States program known as START (Special Treatment and Rehabilitative Training). This program, began at the U.S. Federal Prison in Springfield, Missouri, was designed for particularly intractable prisoners. The assumptions of the program were that offenders involved were not mentally ill but had been guiding their behavior by a maladaptive (criminal) set of responses, that this criminal behavior had been learned and could be unlearned, and that unlearning and retraining could take place within the institution.

The procedure was to begin with solitary confinement in a small room and with very few privileges. If the prisoner spent 20 days in these conditions without violation of the prison regulations, he was to be rewarded by being moved to the next level, which included meals outside the cell, a short period of work daily, and some time for recreation. As good behavior continued, the inmate would move upward to increasing levels of privileges and release from solitude, with the entire program lasting $7^1/2$ months if no infractions occurred. Progress to the next higher level required acceptable behavior in twelve areas. Demotions to a lower level occurred in cases of serious infractions of the rules, including attacks against staff or other prisoners, use of a weapon, and deliberate destruction of government property. There were provisions for daily feedback, for appropriate behavioral models, and for the use of positive tangible and social reinforcement.

Selection criteria for prisoners were that the participant had repeatedly violated institutional regulations, exhibited aggressive and rebellious behavior but was not psychotic, and was referred by the solitary confinement unit of an institution. Of 19 individuals who were admitted to the program, 10 successfully completed the requirements and were returned to their original institutions. In the follow-up, three of these were found to have been released from prison and to be functioning adequately in their communities. Two others were "functioning at an above average level in regular institutions" (Scheckenbach, 1976). The other five were back in segregation. Three of these had been maintained in the general inmate population for at least 6 months before being sent into isolation. Of the nine individuals who did not complete the program, two had been indicted for attacking other prisoners with weapons, six were back in segregation, and only one had managed to remain in a general prison population for as long as 3 months after release from the START program. Eighteen months later, six of the 10 successful completers had been released to the outside community, and only two were in segregation; of the nine noncompleters, five were still serious management problems in their institutions.

Scheckenbach's (1976) paper shows that at a $2^1/2$ year followup 63% of the participants had shown some improvement. This is quite impressive in view of the nature of the sample. All of the men had been convicted of serious crimes, mostly involving actual or potential violence. They had had an average of 21 disciplinary reports, with an average of 12 per man involving major incidents such as arson or assault. An average of 49% of their total time in prison had been spent in segregation, and 11 of the 19 had been convicted of further serious offenses committed in prison.

However, the program attracted a great deal of unfavorable publicity, partly because of complaints by some prisoners. The program was accused of using such techniques as psychosurgery, drugs, brainwashing, and so on. A court ruling held that monitoring the individual's behavior, an obvious necessity for feedback and reinforcement, was not permissible. After a generally negative evaluation by a panel of experts, the program was terminated, ostensibly because there were so few inmates who met the criteria for inclusion as to make the procedure uneconomical (Carlson, 1974).

A second, somewhat similar but less systematic attempt, was made in the Washington State Penitentiary at Walla Walla. Here again, the participants were the most recalcitrant prisoners to be found in the institution, primarily those with a repeated record of procedural violations and punitive segregation. The conceptual basis of the program was that the prisoners' lifestyles had been maladaptive. The goals were to bring them to realize this fact, and to teach them new and more acceptable behavior patterns. Here, again, the program began with segregation. This lasted 3 to 7 days, during which the prisoner was visited periodically by Dr. Hunter, the psychologist in charge of the ward, and by other inmates who had been there for some period of time. These visits had the dual purpose of preventing self-injurious behavior and reiterating the basic message of the program's philosophy.

After this initial period, which in a way was somewhat like the first phase of Morita therapy (see Chapter 7), the prisoner was taken out of solitary confinement and permitted to participate in group projects and sessions with the other members of the ward. All of the techniques were aimed at inculcating the idea that antisocial behavior is childish and a sign of failure to behave as a responsible adult, and at rewarding and fostering a sensible observance of rules for living in a group. When an individual violated these rules, the group could send him back into segregation for a day or two, while he again confronted his failure to live up to the norms. A distinguished psychologist, a member of the committee that visited the Walla Walla penitentiary to evaluate the program, called it "probably the most effective rehab program that may well exist in the prison system" (Brady, 1976).

Particularly interesting features of the program included the initial chance for the new arrival to think about his problems and whether he desired to reform, the explicitness of the regulations under which the ward was run, and the autonomous nature of the prisoner group. The last of these aspects included the facts that most of the rules of the living unit were decided upon by the group itself, that courses were offered as they were chosen and taught by the prisoners (each one being required to teach something), and that the group was actively involved in monitoring the progress of each member. The rules were very similar to those of the outside world, rather than to the usual convict code, and among other things led to significant cooperation with the institutional staff as well as to the elimination of the foul language usually found in such settings. Unlike the START program, the procedure at Walla Walla attempted to prepare its participants for life on the outside rather than in the prison population. Actually, this became a necessity, since inmates who adjusted to Dr. Hunter's unit were no longer "good cons," and would probably have needed protective segregation had they been returned to the prison population.

This program, too, attracted unfavorable attention, at first because of one prisoner who did not desire to participate in the program and who brought a court case against the institution based on his treatment while in the ward. He, like some other destructive and self-destructive prisoners, had been kept restrained to his bed during the initial phase of his stay there, and this was a major aspect of his complaint. Unlike some of the other prisoners who had gone through that treatment, he did not at any time agree with its rehabilitative and violence-preventive purposes. With the support of an inmate committee and of legal counsel, he managed to be returned to the regular segregation unit and then to the population. While the institution was exonerated in court, this litigation laid the publicity groundwork for a subsequent spate of criticism. The incident that triggered the final attack on the program was brought about by the insistence that the inmates themselves should control the system: they had decided that one persistent transgressor should receive corporal punishment, and accordingly beat him. When this became known, adverse publicity in the newspapers led to the termination of the program.

It is clear that self-determination by the prisoners was carried too far in this instance, and several other aspects of the treatment were questionable. However, it appeared that the program was quite successful in several cases, and my own discussion with its participants at one stage certainly supported the impression that they believed in it strongly and felt that their experience in it would help them to adjust to outside society on their release. What is unfortunate is that there was no review of the techniques used, and no systematic evaluation of their effects.

Another, much smaller scale, use of social isolation in a rehabilitative setting in prison was reported by Suedfeld and Roy (1975). In this instance, four inmates of a Canadian psychiatric center for maximum-security prisoners had been sentenced by means of the usual procedures to periods of punitive segregation. Instead of allowing this time to pass in an unstructured way, as was usual, a program of social reinforcement was devised. According to this system, any change in the behavior of the prisoner while he was in segregation was reinforced by short periods of conversation with nurses, an extra cup of coffee, or something of that sort. All four prisoners exhibited some symptom remission by the end of the confinement period and during the rest of their sentences, one of them occasionally requesting further periods of solitude. In a followup over a year later, significant improvements in adjustment to the outside community were demonstrated by those members of the group who had been released. Obviously, this sample is too small and nonrandom for any conclusions to be drawn from the outcome.

In one Canadian institution for adolescent and young adult offenders, isolation has been used as the response to a variety of rule violations (most prominently drug use and assaultive or other antisocial behavior). An analysis of 12 individuals who were segregated during a 1-year period showed that the use of the technique with drug offenders, perceived by both staff and inmates as essentially a removal from contraband rather than as punishment or rehabilitation, had no particular effects on the behavior or attitudes of the individuals. However, of six others who were isolated because of non-drug-related violations, four evidenced "remarkable and positive and immediate changes in behavior that lasted for the duration of their stay" (J. D. Mill, personal communication, April 25, 1974). These 4 were individuals who reacted badly against any sort of authority demands, which led them into difficulties in the institution. A brief "cooling out period" in isolation (for 2 days each), followed by group therapy, was judged to be very helpful in enabling them to adjust both to their peers and to the staff. The two other members of this category were individuals who had long histories of assaultive behavior, not associated with the use of alcohol. The aggressiveness and hostility implied by this behavior continued, although the inmates came to behave so as to avoid further isolation. Thus, while once again no systematic quantitative data were collected, the indications for the use of isolation with at least some types of inmates are positive. As usual, there are not enough data to demonstrate convincingly that isolation was the causal, or even a major, factor in the outcome; and as usual, the data that could test that hypothesis remain to be collected.

A paper by Glynn (1957), which is discussed in detail in Chapter 9, presents an example of how one can convert isolation as punishment into solitude as a therapeutic measure. Glynn used seclusion in a treatment unit for adolescent girls as a method to protect the staff and patients. Isolating the focal person not only helped to calm her down, but in addition prevented contagion and escalation of potential violence within the entire group. Glynn claims that "with growing experience, the staff found that seclusion could be much more than a practical management device. It could be a genuine therapeutic tool, a crucial factor in a girl's growth" (p. 157). As staff members became convinced of the therapeutic value of seclusion, they discussed the various aspects of this application both among themselves and with the girls. Apparently, both groups became convinced of the validity of this point of view, which was stated and restated whenever the topic was discussed.

Some major characteristics of the procedure are worth noting (and imitating). The girl being isolated was always told in detail exactly why this was being done, and there was no set period of time for how long she would be kept in the seclusion room. There was some social contact, mostly in the form of continued and sometimes even increased psychotherapy sessions and attention from the nursing staff. Depending on the nature of the behavioral problem, such stimulating material as books and a radio could also be provided. It became quite common for inmates to ask to be put into seclusion for a while, and also to urge each other to do so when it appeared that a violent episode was about to occur. Although no outcome data are presented in the article, it is clear that the author is quite satisfied with the effects of this use of isolation.

One interesting sidelight, reflecting rather accurately on current attitudes toward prisoners and their keepers, was a comment made to me by a spectator at the Walla Walla trial mentioned above. Basically, the case at one point seemed to boil down to a dispute between the prisoner who had brought the suit and the director of the program, Dr. Hunter. The former had been convicted of crimes including bank robbery, burglary, car theft, armed robbery, and assault with a deadly weapon, had spent a large proportion of his adult life in correctional institutions, and even in those institutions was considered to be a particularly violent and troublesome inmate. The psychologist had spent approximately 25 years of his career helping hospitalized veterans (including paraplegics and quadruplegics) suffering from tuberculosis and polio or from the aftereffects of major combat wounds, followed by about five years in rehabilitative attempts with convicts. But at one point, a fellow spectator at the trial leaned over to me and said, "It is so easy to make Hunter look like the bad guy."

In a recent article, Tittle (1974) argued that rehabilitative efforts in prisons can never be expected to gain public approval. Anyone who has followed the popular press on this issue recently must certainly agree. Unfortunately, there seems to be relatively little point to incarcerating people and then releasing them after some period of time, unless some significant and socially desirable change has occurred in the interim. Thus, while rational criticisms of particular rehabilitative efforts are useful (e.g., Comptroller General of the United States, 1975), the increasingly popular view that rehabilitation is doomed to failure—or even that it is unethical—appears to be self-defeating.

There has not been sufficient research to demonstrate how useful restricted stimulation may be as a rehabilitative technique. But there appears to be enough in the way of preliminary data to indicate that it is worth a thorough test. Obviously, this would have to be done very carefully. It would be necessary to divorce the program from any implication of punitive, administrative, or protective segregation, and to avoid the degradation ceremonies, deprivation of amenities, and harassment that are sometimes associated with solitary confinement. Furthermore, the participants would have to be carefully screened to keep out individuals who may react badly to reduced stimulation, and those who are included would need to be monitored carefully while in isolation. Just as a responsible physician would terminate the use of a normally beneficial drug if he found that a particular patient exhibited an allergic reaction to it, so must the administrators of any such procedure terminate it in the case of a participant who exhibits adverse reactions.

This would have to be done particularly carefully in view of the evidence that many psychopathic criminals are particularly high in need for stimulation (Farley and Sewell, 1976; Quay, 1965). Research may show whether this quest for constant stimulation is one way to escape thinking about one's problems, implying that reduced stimulation may be used as a period of concentration, and whether stimuli presented during REST could be effective positive reinforcers in a rehabilitation program. Based on experiences with nonprisoner clinical populations, it also seems important to investigate whether there would be a benefit in combining stimulus reduction with other techniques, including group therapy (Bruner, 1977).

The Effects of Solitary Confinement

One thing that must always be borne in mind is the wide range of conditions lumped together under the term "solitary confinement" or its variants (segregation, dissociation, and the like). These range from quite comfortable cells, essentially identical to the normal living quarters of the prisoner except with somewhat reduced privileges and exercise time, to small, extremely cold or hot, poorly ventilated holes, sometimes located beneath ground level, kept completely dark or continuously illuminated, in which the prisoner sleeps on the floor or on a hard platform, without bedclothes and sometimes without clothing, in which he is not permitted to have his own possessions, and in which not only exercise but sanitary facilities and all activities are greatly restricted. Changes of social contact in so-called isolation range from no reduction at all, with the inmate able to see and converse with other prisoners in the same unit and with members of the staff, to severe restriction, when the prisoner is behind a solid door through which he can neither see nor hear another human being except during his brief periods of exercise or meals. Similarly, total sensory stimulation may vary from essentially normal to greatly reduced.

It should be obvious that solitary confinement areas should be designed and governed with humane considerations in mind. Adequate space, ventilation, light, and heating should be provided. Facilities for exercise, sanitation, work, study, and recreation should be available. Treatment by guards should be in accordance with basic codes of human rights. These issues have nothing to do with isolation per se, but are sometimes ignored in such units.

Solitary confinement as currently practiced in most Western prisons involves very little real social isolation, and even less "sensory deprivation." Those who are familiar with routines in most segregation units are well aware that there is a considerable amount of variety and stimulation in the environment. Prisoners can usually communicate reasonably freely with others in the "isolation" unit as well as with guards, trusties, food handlers, and so on. Furthermore, they have routine procedures for exercise and sanitation, leaving their cell and sometimes even the building for these purposes. Last, but very important, they have a wide variety of privileges that have the same effect: sick call, visits from relatives, conferences with their lawyers, checkups by institutional administrators. It is very rare indeed for prisoners in segregation in the normal penitentiary really to have extremely low levels of stimulation.

I would like to mention one example, which has been widely publicized as much worse than anything that is standard in Western prisons: the purportedly extreme isolation of the Red Army Faction prisoners in West Germany. This group was for some time held under truly drastic levels of social and stimulus deprivation (Komitee gegen Folter, 1974; Kramer, 1978). However, more recently these prisoners were regularly permitted to share their cells with others, during which time they could have exercise; were given access to a variety of newspapers, magazines, television and radio programs, records, and the library; were allowed to supplement the prison diet and buy other objects that they wanted; and had liberal visiting privileges with a variety of people including their lawyers (Amnesty International, 1977; Kramer, 1978). It was this last privilege that allegedly enabled them to coordinate activities both outside the institution (as in various terrorist attacks carried out by those members of their organization still at large) and inside (culminating in their apparently coordinated suicides when a break-out plan failed). Thus, the picture that some critics have attempted to disseminate—of the segregated prisoner sitting alone, out of communication with any other human being, and staring for 24 hours a day at the four bare walls of his cell—is rarely found in the ordinary Western prison.

In addition to research evidence, there are many anecdotal reports, both negative and positive. Many of the former come from political prisoners who had been incarcerated by the German, Russian, or some other secret police (e.g., Burney, 1961; Grey, 1970; "Jailed Cubans Tell," 1978). The others have been generated by convicts engaged in attempts to get out of segregation and by critics who would like to see the procedure abolished (e.g., Enzenberger and Michel, 1973; Lucas, 1976; Pell, 1972). Favorable comments have usually (although not always—see, e.g., Sheehan, 1977) been the reports of former prisoners (including some very prominent political and religious leaders) who, looking back upon their careers, have decided that solitary confinement was a major factor in their personal development (e.g., "Ex Viet POW," 1978; "Friar Jim Reborn," 1975; Sadat, 1978; Wurmbrand, 1969). Incidentally, some of those who have suffered greatly under torture and isolation have also reached important decisions and insights during their imprisonment. Both views are highly personal and biased; neither can be accepted as objective.

In discussing solitary confinement, many writers implicitly equate the experience of the individual who spends 1 to 2 days in such an environment with the prisoner who is segregated for years or even decades. Thus, it is easy to overgeneralize one's conclusions from reading material that does not clearly indicate the nature of the conditions that are being discussed. As a matter of fact, there are no systematic investigations into the relative roles of these different variables. This is one of the concerns of the research project, discussed later in this chapter (Suedfeld, Ramirez, Clyne, and Deaton, 1976), that is currently under way.

We know that prisoners who voluntarily enter solitary confinement for brief periods of time do not respond adversely, and in fact may find the situation beneficial. For example, Walters, Callaghan, and Newman (1963) found that at the end of a 4-day session in isolation such subjects were more favorable about solitary confinement, although less so about society in general, than they had been prior to the experiment. No severe degree of deterioration was found on any measure, although there was a decrease in verbal output and a small increase in anxiety. Attitudes about a variety of topics related to prison life did not change greatly. There were no observable adverse effects on mental ability, motor performance, or suggestibility.

In another study (Gendreau, Ecclestone, and Knox, 1972), convicts volunteering to spend 7 days in social isolation showed an increased proportion of slow waves on the EEG. This change, which is usually associated with sleep and relaxation, approached asymptote after the first 4 days. In a later experiment, the same authors (Ecclestone, Gendreau, and Knox, 1974) used 10 days of isolation. There was relatively high early termination (seven of the first 16 subjects quit within the first 2 days and were replaced). Biochemical and other physiological measures showed low levels of stress among the group completing the scheduled session, and there was an increase in the consistency of cognitive differentiation as measured in the Repertory Grid Test (Kelly, 1955).

Weinberg (1967) studied 20 prisoners who were sentenced to 5 days of severe restriction (isolation, darkness, silence) and 12 others in partial restriction. No significant effects were found on any of a number of tests. These included IQ subtests, cognitive flexibility, language usage, time estimations, and the Rorschach.

There has been one published study of dangerous inmates who, during the 5 years covered by the investigation, experienced long periods of segregation (Cormier and Williams, 1966). In fact, only four of these subjects had spent less than 40% of these 5 years in solitary confinement. The main reactions to "excessive deprivation of liberty" are mentioned as aggression (physical and/or verbal), self-punishment, and withdrawal. The majority of these men had exhibited psychotic symptoms both before and during segregation. Neither solitary confinement, corporal punishment, nor other disciplinary methods reduced the aggressive behavior of these individuals. Unfortunately, no systematic examination of these prisoners has been published. Thus, we do not know whether there have been any signs of either deterioration or improvement anywhere along the course of the study; much less do we know what specific effects segregation really had.

During the past 2 years, a research team under my direction has been engaged in collecting data from prisoners themselves concerning their reaction to solitary confinement. So far, inmates have been interviewed in one American and three Canadian institutions. Many of them have had experience in more than one solitary confinement unit. At the moment, two phases of the study have been completed. One of these used primarily semi-structured interviews (Suedfeld, Ramirez, Clyne and Deaton, 1976), and the second added to the interviews a number of psychological tests. The interviewers, most of whom were originally convinced that solitary confinement is universally debilitating and aversive, were surprised to find that this was not the case. Some respondents did support the original expectations by reporting the conditions to be anxiety-arousing, frustrating, and disorienting. Others mentioned that segregation was a chance to meditate, concentrate, and work out personal problems. A relatively high proportion felt that a week or two in solitary confinement can be beneficial, but that months or years of segregation are harmful. People who spent a long time in the setting reported increased fantasy life and growing withdrawal and apathy. This may be an adaptive response to isolation (see Suedfeld, 1974a), but it is obviously counterproductive upon return either to the prison or to free society. We do not know, of course, to what extent the symptoms persist, but it would be advisable to measure this factor and to attempt to reduce this kind of behavior when the individual is released from segregation.

Many subjects reported feeling hostility toward the institution. This arose primarily from the feeling that they were isolated unjustly and without a fair hearing, and/or from harassment by the guards in the solitary confinement unit, rather than from the experience of the isolation per se. Several subjects said that they appreciated the relief from communal living and daily pressures that was afforded by segregation, and that in fact they deliberately violated institutional rules upon occasion just so that they would be separated from the population. This, incidentally, was also found by Suedfeld and Roy (1975), and even among the student "prisoners" in the well-known Stanford prison simulation (see Zimbardo, 1969). The American Civil Liberties Union, certainly a group sympathetic to the problems of prisoners, has recently stated that isolation wards are more comfortable than the "normal," overcrowded prison environment ("News Roundup," 1979).

In the second phase of our work, several personality tests were administered to three groups of inmates. Group I had experienced a severe type of solitary confinement, Group II a milder version, and Group III had never been segregated from the prison population. There were no significant differences among the groups in intelligence or creativity, contradicting the claim that major intellectual deterioration occurs as a consequence of solitary confinement. Of course, one might argue that segregated prisoners are more intelligent than the average inmate to begin with, and that their equivalence after segregation in itself indicates deterioration. This is an argument that we are unable to evaluate, since we have no pre-post measures at this time. Psychiatric and psychological testimony presented in cases challenging the use of solitary confinement, as well as the testimony of the prisoners themselves, frequently indicates adequate verbal intelligence on the part of these convicts even after months or years of segregation. The anecdotal evidence, concerned with such outstanding individuals as Edith Bone (1957) and Robert Stroud (Gaddis, 1957), also attests that at least some prisoners maintain high levels of intellectual activity in isolation.

The California Psychological Inventory indicated that Group I was the most aggressive, assertive, persistent, industrious, resourceful, masculine, ambitious, manipulative and opportunistic toward others, and rebellious towards rules. The two isolated groups were equally high on verbal fluency, outspokenness, and persuasiveness. The never-segregated group was the most apathetic, conventional, mild, conscientious, and alert to ethical and moral issues. All prison groups were significantly different from the standardization group in being undercontrolled, defensive, demanding, resentful, insecure, and rebellious. On the Multiple Affect Adjective Checklist, there were no significant differences among the groups on the anxiety, depression, and hostility scales. The isolated groups indicated significantly more displeasure with their environment on the Subjective Stress Scale, although interestingly Group II was higher than Group I. Also, in line with stimulus restriction research, it was noted that second and subsequent confinements in segregation were less stressful than the first.

On the Solitary Confinement Questionnaire, adapted from a research instrument originally developed for use with returned prisoners of war from Vietnam (Deaton, Berg, Richlin, and Litrownik, 1977), convict respondents felt that sleeping and thinking about the future were by far the most useful activities engaged in during segregation. Thinking about the future had also been high in rated usefulness among the original POW sample. Differences between the answers of the two groups indicated the higher mental activity and social orientation of the POWs.

The conclusions from the first two phases of the study are that prisoners who have experienced solitary confinement are not significantly different from other convicts in most ways, except on variables that are probably antecedents (and perhaps causes) of being removed from the prison population. However, the effects of segregation on personality cannot really be evaluated until a future phase, when pre- and post-segregation measures will be administered. In general, the tests showed no serious deterioration among solitary confinement prisoners, even those who had been isolated for fairly long periods of time. However, this latter experience did tend to make the individual more bitter and resentful toward the institution. Most of the complaints were directed toward the treatment received from certain guards, and the missing of work or academic activities which, once interrupted, were difficult to resume.

The initial days of the first solitary experience seemed to be the most difficult, a reasonable adjustment being reached after about 72 hours by most inmates. A few days of segregation were seen by many as a good opportunity to reflect on past and future behavior. As noted, thinking about the future was high on the list of activities; reliving the past and self-analysis/improvement were both within the first 10 on the list of 30 items. Later phases of this project will enable us to gather evidence from a wider sample of institutions and prisoners, to improve and widen the measurement techniques, and to track changes over time as a function of segregation. Our hope is to develop some guidelines as to the optimal use of solitary confinement for rehabilitative purposes, including some bases for predicting which prisoners would benefit from the experience and which would merely find it stressful.

CONCLUSION

Iatrogenic stimulus restriction is obviously a problem for some individual patients in some treatment categories. Although the data are inadequate for a definitive analysis of the exact role of this phenomenon vis-á-vis the psychosocial and physical consequences of the illness and the medical procedures, even the possibility of negative effects is enough to warrant preventive and remedial steps. These include appropriate training for the staff, the patient, and the family as well as attempts to make the environment simultaneously as interesting and as nonintrusive as possible. When restriction is likely to go on for a long time, such precautions are particularly important; and when children are involved, it is crucial to make proper plans to prevent interference with normal developmental sequences.

The prison and solitary confinement settings are more problematic. Any objective review of the existing published evidence on the effects of solitary confinement can come to only one conclusion: that our ignorance is overwhelming. This whole area is one in which specific research, using the conditions, populations, confinement durations, and other variables extant in the actual solitary confinement procedure, must be conducted much more intensively than has been done so far.

One of the recommendations that I would be ready to make right now is that there should be relatively isolated facilities within every prison where inmates who feel the need can volunteer to spend a few days or even weeks, without having to disrupt the good order of the institution by violating rules. This recommendation, incidentally, agrees with one recently made by a well-known prison reform group, the John Howard Society (John Howard Society, Ontario, 1975).

Whatever the reasons for imposing segregation may be, they should be explained to the prisoner in some detail. If the reason is punitive or preventive, the prisoner should be given to understand how he may earn release from isolation. The institutional staff needs careful training and procedural guidelines to ensure that no unnecessary harassment, deprivation, or brutality takes place in solitary confinement units. I would also advocate that inmates coming out of segregation, particularly after long periods, be reinserted into the population gradually, in the same way that convicts coming to the end of their prison terms should be gradually readjusted to the outside world. This procedure would provide both a period of decompression (H. Popp, personal communication, 21 June 1977) and a chance for monitoring the adjustment of the prisoner.

As to the use of solitary confinement in general, I have argued (Suedfeld and Roy, 1975; Suedfeld, 1974b) that its transformation from a punitive to a rehabilitative technique is worth testing. This argument is generally supported by the tentative evidence cited in this section. With some willingness to innovate, solitary confinement—or even profound REST—might become a tested and effective rehabilitative technique. REST, appropriately presented and structured, may have for at least some prisoners the impact that has been proposed for meditation: "With a change of consciousness people can begin to see prison as a monastery and their sentence as a time for spiritual growth" ("Spiritual paths basis," 1978).

CHAPTER 4

Environmental Stimulus Factors In Human Development

This chapter considers some possible long-term effects of inadequate stimulation on human infants and children, and the relatively sparse data available on old people. We shall discuss the data on the effects of separation from the family, frequently in the course of institutionalization, of severe social and stimulus reduction, and of major sensory handicaps. Therapeutic interventions, including environmental enrichment for certain problems and reduced environmental stimulation for others (and sometimes for the same ones as well), will also be examined. A related type of environmental restriction, imposed on children in the course of medical treatment, was discussed in Chapter 3.

SOCIAL SEPARATION AND ENVIRONMENTAL RESTRICTION

It is generally accepted that children who are separated from their family and who are placed in an environment that provides insufficient stimulation are likely to evidence disturbances in both physical and psychological development. Exactly what aspects of the environment are responsible for such outcomes has not been established. One of the best illustrations of the vagueness of explanation is a famous although presumably apocryphal anecdote frequently used to illustrate the phenomenon. This is the attempt, ascribed by different authors to a number of monarchs, to discover the original language of human beings by having a group of newborn infants isolated and cared for by nurses who were under strict instructions not to speak. The ideas was that, in the absence of learning through imitation, the children would eventually begin to communicate in some innately transmitted language; the outcome was that all of the children died. Were this a true story, and were we in the position of the king (or perhaps his consulting psychologist), to what would we ascribe the result? If we were anachronistically familiar with the literature, we could pick among the following hypotheses: separation from the mother; inadequate opportunity to establish cathectic bonds to some particular adult; failure to learn the survival skills that are served by the ability to commu-

116

nicate one's needs and responses verbally; and inadequate stimulation in the sensory environment. All of these hypotheses, and combinations of them, have in fact been advanced for the observed negative outcomes of maternal deprivation, institutionalization, isolation, and similar circumstances.

Maternal Separation and Institutionalization

The idea that separation from parents and siblings causes severe damage was noted in reports as early as the eighteenth century (see Vives and Reyes, 1978); but it was most emphatically brought to the attention of psychologists during World War II (Freud and Burlingham, 1944). Spitz (1945; 1946a, b), observing hospitalized children, noted a set of symptoms identified as "hospitalism." These included the frequent occurrence of negative emotions, fearful reactions to adults, and social withdrawal. In the last of these papers, Spitz referred to the syndrome as "anaclitic": that is, as being centered around the relationship between the mother and the child. Fifteen years later, Azima, Vispo, and Axima (1961) used the same term to describe their version of REST therapy, since in their opinion the situation created a bond between the patient and therapist that was modeled on the original mother-infant relationship.

Leiderman and Seashore (1975) support the view that early separation from the mother has deleterious effects. The article reports consequences that lasted for between 11 and 15 months after the separation had occurred. Although there were differences as a function of family constellation, sex of the child, and socioeconomic status of the family, most of the early effects of separation had disappeared. And it is reassuring to find that feelings of incompetence as a mother and lowered attachment to the infant are only temporary. However, one difference persisted: mothers who had been separated from their infant tended to touch the child less than mothers in whose families no such separation had occurred.

Banks and Cappon (1963) found that psychiatric patients reliably reported having been "deprived" in childhood to a greater extent than did nonpatients. However, the definition of deprivation (to say nothing of the question of accuracy of these reports) leaves the significance of this finding rather vague. The same differences were found, but subject to the same methodological problems, among a group of depressed women by Jacobson, Fasman, and DiMascio (1975).

There is abundant evidence available as to the deleterious effects of institutionalization. Information about the mental and physical problems of children in orphanages and similar establishments has shown beyond much doubt that the phenomenon is a real one (e.g., Dennis, 1960; 1973;

Dennis and Dennis, 1951; Goldfarb, 1945; Lowrey, 1940). Its most striking aspects are a high death rate and severe mental retardation. Other
characteristics include marked slowness in developing perceptual and
motor abilities, linguistic skills, and the ability to bring about desired
effects in the environment; inability to adapt to novel stimuli; concrete-
ness of thinking; disruptions of attention, including the inability to separate irrelevant from relevant aspects of the environment; and inadequate
or excessive responsivity to social reinforcement (Dennis, 1960; Taylor,
1968; Gibson, 1969; Zigler and Butterfield, 1968; Yarrow, 1961). It should
be pointed out, however, that not all of these phenomena have been
found by all investigators (see e.g., Yarrow, 1961).

Goldfarb (1955) compared children who were brought up in an institution under conditions of almost complete isolation for the first year and
very little stimulation for the next two years, at the end of which they
were put into foster homes, with children who were given to foster parents from the beginning. In spite of the fact that the family background of
the institutionalized children seemed if anything to be better, the foster
children were superior in IQ, conceptual ability, intellectual and emotional richness, and activity. The institutional children were found to be
hyperactive, restless, unable to concentrate, less able to inhibit responses, and lacking in affection for others.

In the most recent publication emanating from a longitudinal study of
65 children whose first years have been spent in institutions, Tizard and
Hodges (1978) reported on follow-ups at the age of eight. Several differences in social behavior that had been apparent at age four had disappeared by this time, and some of the remaining intergroup differences
could be ascribed to the extreme scores of a very few children. Still
others were apparently related to social class differences among the families with whom children were living at the time of the follow-up. There
were still some differences, some of which differentiated among parents
rather than among children. For example, parents who had retrieved their
children from the institution felt less affectionate toward them than parents who had adopted children from the institution. The same pattern was
reported by the mothers when they were asked to rate how attached the
children were to them. Children who had returned to their own families
were also more likely to have problems in behavior. In general, teachers
reported children who were still in the institution to be having more
difficulties than were cited for either those children who had been adopted
or those who had been restored to their family.

The authors' major conclusion is that a crucial variable in whether
institutionalization has irreversible effects is the environment to which
the child goes after leaving the institution. However, both in social and in

intellectual development there was some evidence for critical periods or stages, the question of whether there are rigid minimum and maximum ages being unresolved so far. The social behavior differences included more desire for physical contact among the adopted and the still-institutionalized children, and school problems that may have been related to the same need for social contact (e.g., attention-seeking behavior). A high level of need for approval and attention from adults was coupled with problems in peer relations, the children finding it less problematic to get along well with people either younger or older than themselves. These effects persisted for as long as 6 years after the child had left the institution.

The question of whether the absence of a maternal bond is truly the crucial issue is difficult to resolve. Once source of confusion is the untested conceptual leap from "separation distress" (the unhappiness of young children, associated with the mother's temporary departure) to the permanent consequences of long-term separation (see, e.g., Weinraub & Lewis, 1977). This question is the equivalent of whether one can extrapolate from laboratory stimulus reduction to its long-duration "natural" counterparts. At the very least, there is evidence that some of the long-term effects may be counteracted by a variety of stimuli. Thus, even if maternal absence (either physical or psychological) is the cause of dysfunction, the treatment does not necessarily involve a mother or a mother substitute.

Pinneau (1955) has criticized the argument put forward by Spitz that drops in developmental quotient among children suffering from "hospitalism" were a function of separation. Rather, these changes apparently began before the separation occurred, while the mother and the child were still together in the institution. Another, and major, criticism of this type of explanation is that most studies in the field have ignored such issues as the preinstitutional characteristics of the child, constitutional/genetic factors that may differentiate at least some samples of institutionalized children from their family-reared counterparts, age at separation, the nature of the post-separation environment, the reason why the child is placed in the institution, and the reason why he stays there instead of, for example, being adopted rapidly (see e.g., Casler, 1968; Zigler et al., 1968).

In his classic work, Bowlby (1973) argued that a "warm, intimate and continuous relationship" with a mother or surrogate is crucial for the psychological health of young human beings. The frequently observed sequence of separation protest followed by despair has been hypothesized to have long-term effects on both social and nonsocial behavior. A recent review (Clancy and McBride, 1975) goes so far as to propose the "isolation syndrome" as a diagnostic category. This approach is also based upon the idea that infant-caretaker bonding is crucial. The sequelae of its disruption supposedly include disorders of social interaction, communication, and perceptual-motor functioning, excessive self-stimulation, and general developmental retardation. These characteristics are explained as the result of the focusing of the attention of the child upon himself, resulting from his inability to focus it upon the mother or substitute person.

Conditions under which such problems are likely to arise include separation from the mother because of illness or other reason, distorted family relationships, an abnormality of the child which in turn leads to disruption of the relationship, and autism. Clancy and McBride (1975) argue that the isolation syndrome must be given primary attention for treatment, since its amelioration must precede accurate diagnoses, prescriptions, and prognoses related to the other problems of the family and the child. Pseudo-retardation and pseudo-autism can be part of the isolation syndrome, for example, and may disappear or at least be substantially reduced if the syndrome is treated.

Leiderman and Seashore (1975) warn that the effects of separation on the mother may be lasting and may influence her behavior toward the child in many ways (see also Jenkins and Norman, 1972), leading to results that may be incorrectly ascribed to the impact of separation on the child. There is some supporting evidence for this point of view. Klaus and Kennell (1970) have ascribed child abuse to separation shortly after birth. They found that a relatively high percentage of children who are later physically abused by their parents had been separated from them for relatively long periods in infancy, either because of prematurity or because of illness requiring hospitalization. The authors argue that such separation may disrupt the development of positive emotional ties between the parent and the child, and may make the parent less likely to be tolerant and affectionate. This hypothesis is indirectly supported by the finding that children whose birth weight is low, and who are therefore more likely to be kept in the hospital longer and/or to be kept in incubators, are also more likely to be battered (Klein and Stern, 1971).

One question that must be dealt with is that of critical periods or developmental stages. It may be that—as Piagetian theory maintains—the role of stimulation and related factors is only to modify when and for how long a given stage of functioning is paramount. Equilibrium—the match between cognitive capacity and environmental demands that makes the attainment of a stage possible—may occur at different ages, for example. Conversely, there may be a period, fixed at both ends, during which particular experiences must occur for normal development to continue. At this time, there is insufficient evidence to select either of these alternatives, although if the second hypothesis is valid the data imply that the limiting ages are not rigidly or clearly defined. Physical parameters of the environment become important at different ages (Wachs, 1978). More generally, Spitz (1950) has indicated that the cathectic bond emerges at approximately eight months, so that a disruption at even so early an age may have deleterious effects. Other workers have cited different periods, the differences for the most part being the function of empirical observation. There is evidence that different environmental conditions may result in slower or faster progress through developmental stages, but that the usual order of progress is not changed (e.g., Piaget, 1976). While environmental deprivation may be involved in slower attainment of particular levels of cognitive operations, this inhibition can be lifted, at least in some cases, by appropriate intervention at a later time (Inhelder, 1968).

Freedman (1972), attempting to remedy the vagueness of psychoanalytic theory in this regard with the relative precision of Piagetian concepts, has argued that the critical period in this context must be related to the age at which object permanence is achieved (normally 8 to 12 months). Since Freedman's paper is primarily concerned with perceptually handicapped children, and since Piaget's writings on object permanence are based on children who are not afflicted in this way, this theoretical linkage is not established; but Freedman has observed that blind infants as young as 2 weeks can distinguish the mother's voice from that of someone else. Freedman is quite pessimistic about the possibility of successful therapy for problems arising out of early perceptual deprivation, regardless of the particular therapeutic technique employed. But this is not an unchallenged position: other writers argue that the effects of maternal separation and of sensory reduction in early life, like those of institutionalization, may be quite temporary (e.g., Leiderman and Seashore, 1975).

Severe Isolation and Restriction

It does appear that some isolated children manage to catch up to their age peers. Dennis and Dennis (1951), reporting on infants who were brought up in complete silence until the 27th week and with minimal social stimulation until the age of 13 months, reported some retardation in motor behavior, but essentially normal emotional development. Two children who were kept in almost total isolation by a psychotic mother seemed to act quite normally very soon after their situation had been improved, at the ages of four and six (Freedman and Brown, 1968). However, their behavior indicated a lack of monitoring of their own bodily processes (e.g., insensitivity to pain, lack of control over eating) and an affectless, indiscriminate form of interaction with other poeple. Some of these characteristics remained even 2 years later. The parallel between such findings and those of researchers such as Harlow and Scott with infrahuman animals is obvious. Another child, who spent the first 6 years of her life in a semi-darkened attic room and was reared by a deaf-mute mother with no other social contacts, was doing average work in school 2 years after her transfer to a normal home (Davis, 1947; see also Curtiss, 1977). Presumably, 6 years is past any critical period before or within which cognitive and social developments must begin; yet the degree of deprivation experienced by this girl was not sufficient to prevent her from reaching at least some degree of normality.

The recently published case study (Curtiss, 1977) of a child who was brought up in a small room, alone and with a minimum of perceptual and motor stimulation, is forcing a revision of traditional thought about critical periods in language development. The girl, who was in this deprived situation from the age of 20 months to that of $13^1/_2$ years, had practically no language ability when discovered. During the next 5 years, when intensive efforts were made to remedy the situation, she made significant progress. She learned many words, as well as the linguistic rules for putting them together into comprehensible sentences, and also learned to understand the speech of others quite well. While at the time of publication of her history she had not yet acquired completely normal language usage, it is still quite possible that she will do so with further work. At any rate, it has become clear that the generally accepted critical period is not a stringent one for language learning per se, although it may hold for the learning of certain aspects of language. This may imply that those children who did not catch up, particularly if they were discovered early in life, may in fact have been congenitally deficient.

Kagan and Klein (1973), reviewing a series of studies performed by themselves and their coworkers in an Indian village in Guatemala, described child-rearing patterns that are not only widely divergent from the North American norm but may also represent extremes of routinely applied sensory reduction. Infants in this village spend most of their first year of life in a small, dark, windowless hut, not allowed to crawl on the floor nor to go outside, and are rarely spoken to or played with. There are no toys or manipulable objects provided for the child's particular use, and he spends most of his time either sleeping in a hammock or on his mother's lap or back. The children are extremely passive, quiet, fearful, and in fact some exhibited the symptoms that Spitz called "marasmus" in the institutionalized infants whom he observed. As compared to children in the United States, Kagan's group paid less attention to colorful and moving stimuli, and were significantly slower in attaining object permanence, fear of strangers, and vocalization. Meaningful speech was reported by many Guatemalan parents to appear approximately 1 year later than it first appears in North American children.

One would feel confident in saying that the extreme sensory restriction suffered by these children from birth had resulted in severe retardation of development. But when the child becomes mobile, the environment changes drastically. He now leaves the hut at will, and begins to explore his surroundings. The researchers found that at ages ranging from 5 to 12, the performance of these children approximated those of middle-class North American groups on such tasks as object recall, recognition memory, embedded figures, and perceptual and conceptual inference. The drastic permanent differences that one might have expected from an examination of the first year of life did not occur.

Followup studies, summarized in Kagan (1976), indicated that even after the most isolated rearing conditions, by the time of adolescence the level of performance was quite comparable to those of individuals brought up in North American or in intermediately stimulating environments. Kagan uses these data to criticize what he calls the "tape-recorder" theory of development, the idea that the environment produces clear-cut and irreversible changes in the developmental process. Rather, behavioral systems emerge, dominate development, and then give way to other systems at a rate determined by constitutional individual differences interacting with experience and temperament. If the environment changes for the better, so does development, exhibiting a great deal of flexibility and susceptibility to remediation. Of course, this does not negate the possibility that a child who is brought up and remains in an extremely stimulus-poor or otherwise adverse environment will fail to overcome the handicaps resulting from the experience. No good data are available on this question, since no examples have been reported where at least the observation and testing procedure did not modify the level of stimulation in the world of the person being studied. Also, very little cross-cultural data are available about the later effects of such childrearing practices as swaddling. These procedures (see Fig. 4.1) have been found in many areas; the work of Kagan should serve as a model for a thorough, objective study of their impact upon children and adults in societies where infantile stimulus restriction is the norm.

Medical Problems Related to Stimulus Reduction

The discovery that children subjected to physical restraint and to other forms of stimulus-response restriction may thereafter suffer from a variety of symptoms—including extremely high or extremely low reactions to

Figure 4.1.   Stimulus reduction of infants as a cultural norm: Interference in visual, auditory, tactile, and kinesthetic modalities. Portrait of Caw-Wacham (Flathead Indian woman and child) by Paul Kane. Reproduced by permission of the Musée des beaux-arts de Montreal.

environmental stimuli, lower cognitive, perceptual and motor skills, and disruptions of social relationships and communication (see e.g., Davis, 1940, 1947; Freedman, 1968; Friedman, Handford, and Settlage, 1964)—has led a number of investigators to look at the possible involvement of stimulus restriction in situations where this had not been considered as an etiological factor. Developmental problems to which these factors have been linked include the sequelae of premature birth; mental retardation, *spasmus nutans*, a perceptual-motor disturbance; and major components of PKU. The linkages in most of these cases are primarily hypothetical, with only limited empirical support.

Premature Birth.   There is little doubt that premature children suffer disproportionately from behavioral problems. Sameroff (1975) describes prematurity as "another of the classic perinatal hazards that has been related to later deviancy in behavior" (p. 271), but points out that the data are not completely conclusive. Still, there appears to be a fair bit of evidence to support the diagnosis, starting with the 1939 finding that premature children are relatively irritable, negativistic, and shy (Shirley, 1939). In contrast to many previous writers, Rothschild (1967) points to a restricted environment as at least one possible cause of behavioral mal-adaptation among premature children. This restriction comes about be-cause premature (i.e., very low birth-weight) infants have typically been isolated in incubators from birth. Such an environment not only greatly reduces the range, intensity, and variety of sensory stimuli impinging on the child; it also severely interferes with social interaction, reduces the learning of mastery because the environment is relatively unresponsive, and limits the number of manipulable objects available. This is quite different from competing explanations based on difficult births, over-protective parents, and so on.

Mental Retardation.   It has been proposed that mental retardation not induced by organic causes may be at least in some cases ascribed to social deprivation (Rosenheim and Ables, 1974). Deprivation is described as a function of either lack of adequate social stimulation, sudden disruption of and reduction from a normal level of stimulation, or a sudden drop in the level of stimulation from very high to lower, even if the final level is relatively normal. While the authors realize that the animal literature on this topic is not necessarily generalizable, and that the human research relies greatly on case studies and uncontrolled observations, they con-sider the evidence to be at least suggestive. Their own case study is that of a little girl who was used to an extremely high level of social stimula-tion and caretaking, and developed somewhat more rapidly than the norm. This situation changed when she reached the age of two with alterations in the family constellation. There was a further reduction in attention when the child reached age three and was afflicted by a new-born sibling. The lowest point was reached when she was scheduled to begin a classroom program at the age of $5\frac{1}{2}$.

According to the authors, the difference between the original adaptation level of social stimulation and that reached at the last of these points was so great that maladaptive behavior emerged aimed at gaining more stimulation, and appeared to have that effect. As a result, both cognitive retardation and psychotic behavior were adopted by the child. The therapist and the mother met the problem by giving a great deal of attention, but not as a reinforcement for bizarre behavior. In fact, social interaction was given as a reinforcer for normal behavior. Both psychological adjustment and academic performance improved temporarily after this intervention, but the improvement (and possibly the changes in stimulation contingencies and levels) failed to become permanent.

Spasmus Nutans.   Among the negative effects ascribed to an interruption of the normal stimulus environment has been *spasmus nutans*, a syndrome consisting of rhythmic head rolling, a nodding movement of the head, and nystagmus. The phenomenon, which has become relatively rare in recent years, occurs at the age of 3 or 4 months, and usually remits spontaneously by the age of $2^1/_2$ years. No neurological causes have been identified. Etiology has been variously ascribed to rickets, a virus, and a lack of visual stimulation coupled with a disturbance of the feeding relationship (Gruneberg, 1964). Gruneberg, examining five children suffering from the syndrome, indicated that the infants were routinely awakened to be fed, which he interprets as leading to a state of low arousal during meals. In agreement with the well-known U-curve hypothesis, he indicates that either excessive or insufficient stimulation, brought about by the lack of light in the environment and the peculiar procedures for feeding, leads to very high tension which the infant attempts to reduce by self-stimulation.

A more recent study (Fineman, Kuniholm, and Sheridan, 1971) ascribes the etiology to a disturbance of the mother-child relationship. This disturbance takes the form of inadequate tactile contact, and a refusal on the part of the mother to engage in intimate and continued visual interaction with the child. To this is added a lack of stimulation in the environment: dim light, restricted availability of toys and other manipulable objects, and discouragement of exploration on the part of the child. Strange motor behavior is accompanied by developmental lags in physical, motor, and possibly social development. Incidentally, it is interesting that *spasmus nutans* does not seem to appear in institutions, although one might have expected it to do so given the pervasiveness of understimulation in the environments of the affected children.

Phenylketonuria.   It has long been known that phenylketonuria (PKU), a metabolic disturbance, leads to a wide variety of psychological and behavioral symptoms. Severe mental retardation is a prominent one; others include emotional disturbances, distractibility, and impaired interpersonal relations and communication skills. For a long time, these characteristics have been ascribed to either the primary physiological abnormality or its direct derivatives. However, Friedman, Sibinga, Steisel, and Sinnamon (1968) proceeded from the observation that the behavioral symptoms varied widely, and that their severity did not seem to be correlated with aspects of the basic PKU metabolism error. In their study, they separated a group of PKU children whose parents had reported hospitalization or other forms of sensory restriction occurring before age 3 and lasting a mean of almost 15 days, and compared them with another group whose parents reported no such restriction. The groups were roughly matched on initial physical differences and on severity of mental retardation caused by PKU. Using both psychometric instruments and clinical observation, the investigators concluded that the group of restricted children displayed significantly greater impairment in interpersonal relations, object relations, and communication skills. They also exhibited lower performance on intelligence test items.

While the conclusion that the adverse effects of PKU are mediated by early stimulus restriction is quite tentative, given the wide range of restriction durations represented in the stress group and the difficulties of equating children on other relevant variables, this study certainly is an intriguing one and leads one to wonder about the way in which restriction —or, for that matter, other variables—may be important as intervening events. The possibility that such problems as PKU make the child more vulnerable to adverse effects of stimulus restriction, or that stimulus restriction is an exacerbating or catalytic factor in the development of some psychological sequelae of physical syndromes, is certainly worth investigating.

THEORETICAL APPROACHES AND THERAPEUTIC EFFORTS

Some of the variables involved in restricted rearing are beyond the scope of our interest here; but the nature of the institutional environment certainly is within our focus. It appears to be unwarranted from our point of view to treat institutionalization as an undifferentiated variable, as though all institutional environments were alike. Obviously, if one assumes that the crucial issue is the affectional bond with the mother, then any institution where no mother-figure is available is the same as all other such institutions, including those with diffuse mothering (communes, kibbutzim). However, to take this point of view is to assume that which should be empirically tested. Nevertheless, quite a few investigators have been guilty of this practice in the past. It is certainly the case that the effects of restricted and institutional living are not uniform, and furthermore that its specific nature is not well understood.

Conceptual Analysis of the Effects

The inadequacy of the gross categories used in much of the early research is now clear. Yarrow (1961) was among the first to argue for a better differentiation of environmental variables in the institution. In a later study (Yarrow, Rubenstein, Pedersen, and Jankowski, 1972), he and his coworkers analyzed children's home environments on the basis of three dimensions of inanimate stimuli (variety, responsiveness, and complexity) and four basic dimensions of social interaction (level, variety, contingency, and expression of positive affect). The characteristics of the inanimate environment showed no relationship with language and social behavior, but were significantly correlated with cognitive-motivational and motor performance. Particularly affected were the child's efforts to evoke feedback from the environment, behavior to produce changes in stimulation, reaching and grasping, fine motor development, and preference for novel stimuli. Variety in the environment, the most significant factor, was related to most of these, and was the only dimension of inanimate objects related to object permanence and problem solving. It was also very highly correlated to exploratory behavior.

Stimulation level and variety, and contingent response to stress in the social environment, were significantly related to mental development and to measures of goal-directed behavior. One measure of contingency was also related to vocalization. Goal orientation and behavior to produce changes in the environment were also related to social stimulation factors. The complexity of the pattern of these findings helps us to understand the inconsistencies found when the environment is either defined or manipulated globally (e.g., institutionalized vs. noninstitutionalized, control vs. enriched), and when only gross changes or differences in changes of the dependent variable are recorded.

Rutter (1972), like Skinner (1972), thinks that the occurrence of developmental retardation is caused not merely by institutionalization or separation from the mother, but by the fact that this separation frequently leads to inadequate levels of social, perceptual, and linguistic stimulation. How the child reacts to this is a function of the duration and severity of deprivation, and also of the relationship that existed between him and his mother before the separation occurred. The age at which separation occurred is also important. The same variables are crucial in whether and to what extent the effects are reversible.

Putting the evidence together, it may be concluded that the absolute restriction of sensory stimulation undoubtedly can impair development, including intellectual development. All forms of perceptual restriction affect different intellectual skills. However, human beings differ from animals in the additional, and crucial, importance of language with regard to intellectual development. Perhaps the single most crucial factor for the development of verbal intelligence is the quality of the child's language environment; how much he is talked to, but more than that the richness of the conversational interchange he experiences. . . . In all ordinary circumstances it is necessary for the verbal stimulation to be provided by people (Rutter, 1972, pp. 91–92).

J. McV. Hunt (1976), in his review of some of this literature, identifies information processing and action as the crucial variables. When the environment hinders the child in becoming accustomed to adequate levels of these fundamental behaviors, deterioration or failure to develop normally can be expected. The idea that institutional or other mother-deprived rearing achieves its deleterious effects by means of infantile trauma or overwhelming anxiety is dismissed, primarily on the basis of the well-known animal studies showing that animals that are stressed in infancy become better adapted to dealing with stressful situations later in life.

Casler (1968) was one of the early proponents of the argument that disabilities occur as a function of the perceptual restriction characterizing many institutions. The high rate of self-stimulation found among children in such places could certainly imply that inadequate stimulation is provided by the environment, and that the level of inadequacy is above some response threshold. We do not know whether the underlying problem is that the restrictive environment prevents the infant from receiving necessary information so that behaviors based upon that information are never learned, that it destroys cognitive and other organizations already attained, or that it fosters competing emotional responses that hinder adaptive ones from emerging. Supporting the first possibility, animal studies have shown that severe deprivation during early rearing prevents the emergence of some adaptive behaviors, and in fact prevents the establishment of appropriate neural substrata on which such behaviors could be based (see Hebb, 1949, 1955; Riesen, 1975). As to the second hypothesis, it is also true that learned behaviors are disrupted by perceptual restriction (Lessac, 1965). And last, the competing response model is harmonious with some of the work on adult environmental restriction—for example, with the data that experimental stimulus reduction interferes with complex cognitive processes, theoretically because it increases competition among responses of which none is dominant in the subject's hierarchy (see e.g., Fuller, 1967; Suedfeld, Glucksberg, and Vernon, 1967).

Among the theories as to the mediating mechanisms leading to developmental malfunctioning as a consequence of reduced stimulation, we have the hypothesis that such stimulus-restricted conditions lead to disturbances in the development of the nervous system. This position has been taken primarily by workers with infrahuman species. The authors contributing to a recent overview of this field (Riesen, 1975) exemplify the approach. "Stimulation contributes to shaping the rapidly growing nervous system anatomically and physiologically under the overall guidance of a genetic code" (page 277). Early stimulus deprivation can be brought about in lower animals not merely by manipulating the environment, but by surgical or chemical deafferentiation, thus producing real deprivation that cannot be obtained in experiments with human subjects. With such procedures, gross changes in the brain cells, sensory receptors, and limbs can be found, as can alterations of the biochemical environment of the nervous system. Changes in electrophysiological processes such as visual evoked potentials and EEGs are also quite common. Behaviorally, deprived animals show disturbances of emotionality, orientation, learning ability, perceptual and motor accuracy, social and sexual behavior, and so on (see Chapter 5).

Theoretical explanations include Casler's (1968) point that stimulus variety is needed to alert the reticular formation (see also Lindsley, 1961, and Rimland's 1964 hypothesis that autism is the result of a reticular system dysfunction), which must be aroused in order for learning to occur normally. White's famous paper (1959), which is quite compatible with the point of view espoused by J. McV. Hunt (1976), suggests that stimulation and interaction with the environment are required for a person to become competent in solving cognitive, perceptual-motor, social, and conceptual problems.

Still another theoretical point of view is that of Zern (1974), who has argued that stimulation is in fact experienced as unpleasant, a point of view that is compatible with an intuitive evaluation of some of the kinds of stimulation found to have had beneficial effects on infant rats. If this is the case, the primary function of stimulation may be to induce disequilibrium in the interaction between the infant and the environment. The baby is motivated to reduce this state. His attempts to reduce it lead to greater involvement with the environment and to increasing competence. Incidentally, the potential danger of providing experiences that are not modifiable by the individual has been nicely demonstrated by the work of Seligman on learned helplessness (e.g., 1975).

The behavioral and developmental changes are not merely simple decrements. It has been argued that one important way of interpreting the results, particularly when restricted rearing and social isolation are used as opposed to complete sensory deprivation, is so-called "novelty enhancement," a tendency of the animal to overreact to novelty (Konrad and Melzack, 1975). Because such organisms had been exposed to restricted and relatively unvarying environments in early life, they are unprepared to deal with novelty and higher levels of stimulation. The hypothesis implies that differences in behavior between normally reared and restricted animals should hold across a wide variety of environments, even relatively normal environments; and that the differences should follow a curvilinear function, diminishing at one end when the environment either is or becomes familiar to the experimental animals, and at the other where it is also extremely novel to the controls.

Findings supporting these hypotheses have been generated with a number of species, and in both feral and laboratory settings. It is important to note that recent work from the Wisconsin Primate Laboratory, where much of this research was pioneered, takes an increasingly complex view. Current analyses emphasize individual differences in optimal stimulation level, the mediating role of maturational level, the fact that no particular stimulus environment is always good or always bad, the importance of comparing pre- and post-intervention behavior in the same setting, and the crucial role of the way in which other individuals react to the subject. The feasibility of overcoming deprivation effects through appropriate "therapeutic" interactions with others has also been demonstrated (see Suomi, 1978). The long-term effects, in monkeys as in human beings, are not simple outcomes of separation. Rather, pre-separation experiences and specific characteristics of the separation environment mediate the response (Mineka and Suomi, 1978).

Riesen makes an intriguing comment in the conclusion of his book, where he compares the effects of sensory stimulation and nutrition in early life. Nutrition may be taken as one specific example from a range of other characteristics. It appears that the two types of event may have very similar effects, with neurological changes that can be irreversible when the deprivation is severe. Conversely, adequate stimulation and appropriate nutrition have additive favorable effects, and it may be that an adequate supply of one could at least to some extent alleviate a shortage of the other. In view of the recent attention paid to malnutrition as a cause of mental retardation in human beings, this is a particularly interesting possibility. It it clear that the effects of malnutrition, either of the pregnant mother or of the child, are moderated by other environmental factors (Richardson, 1976). While dietary remedies may be helpful (see Levine and Wiener, 1976), appropriate modifications of sensory and social stimulation parameters may also be relevant. Here again, we have a stimulating hypothesis that has not been systematically explored.

It is clear from the work of Hunt and others that the situation is more complex than could be explained merely by stimulus deprivation or by any other single factor. Sameroff and Chandler (1975) have elaborated the argument that the child and the environment are in a complex pattern of transactions. Development is partly a function of genetic programming and partly—in fact, to a great extent—an outcome of the way the child orients and reorients himself in response to the environment, changes the environment, and then responds to those changes (see also Sameroff, 1975). Experimental studies with infrahuman species fail to demonstrate this process, not only because it is less complex in those species but also because the laboratory environment is structured so as to be unresponsive to the infant animal's attempts at manipulating it. It appears to be an error to generalize too freely from such experiments to low-stimulation environments in which human children may find themselves.

This point of view is not necessarily incompatible with an optimal level of stimulation theory, but it implies that the effects of "nonoptimal" levels are quite complex and variable. One relatively recent contribution that bridges the gap is a short paper by Ashton (1976), in which he pleads for arousal theorists to recognize that they are dealing with an interaction between environmental stimulation and the internal state of the child, and that neither chronic nor momentary arousal levels can be inferred from knowledge of only one of those factors.

A Proposed Treatment: Environmental Enrichment

There is a long history of animal studies demonstrating that stimulation, whether gentle or painful, can enhance development, particularly in the ability to handle stress. The reviews of Beach and Jaynes (1954), Levine (1960), and Thompson and Melzack (1956) demonstrate this effect quite convincingly. Behavioral measures such as open field performance, biochemical ones such as hormonal secretion, and physiological ones such as the occurrence of ulcers and mortality rate indicate that mature rats that have been manipulated, mildly shocked, thermally stressed, or otherwise stimulated in infancy adapt to stressful situations more effectively. This phenomenon appears to be mediated by improved maturation of the central nervous system. When young, the stimulated animals develop faster, grow larger, and so on.

One of the points that makes this line of research relevant to human child-rearing is that the control animals in most of these studies are in fact brought up under what we would call restricted conditions. That is, the normal animal colony is not equivalent in stimulation to the surroundings of an infant rat in the wild: it is both socially isolating and severely limited as to stimulus and response potentials. Thus, the added stimulation received by the experimental groups remedies the effects of restricted rearing, as opposed to being an increment over development that might be

expected from normal infancy. An indirect test of this position was provided by Bernstein (1972), who attempted to overcome the effects of early
isolated rearing by a long period in a highly stimulating environment later.
As expected, he found that a stimulating environment early in life led to
the most beneficial effects on the discrimination learning of rats, but that a
group isolated for the first 45 days of life and then stimulated during the
next 90 showed no differences from the early-stimulated group by the end
of the experiment. The duration of the remedial period is apparently
crucial. When both the restricted and the later stimulation periods lasted
45 days, the deleterious effect of early deprivation was not overcome
(Bernstein, 1972; Hymovitch, 1952). More recent research (e.g., Suomi,
1973) has established that with animals higher in the phylogenetic scale
the consequences of even long-lasting infantile deprivation can be remedied. Furthermore, the previously deprived animal can learn adaptive
behavior by observing and imitating a normally-reared companion. It is a
charming thought that these findings came from Harry Harlow's laboratory, one of the earliest to explore the effects of isolated rearing in the
first place (and the source of some of the best-written articles in modern
psychology).

Theorists have argued that with human beings, too, extra stimulation
may overcome early deprivation. As so often happens when a theory is
tested empirically, some crucial parameters are not adequately defined.
These include such central concerns as the nature of the deprivation. This
variable has been defined in terms of everything from early hospitalization to low socioeconomic status. Still, there is good reason to think that
damage resulting from early stimulus restriction of children can be reduced or averted.

In a classic study, Skeels and Dye (1939) reported that two mentally
retarded children transferred from an orphanage to a ward for mentally
deficient women showed significant increases in intellectual growth. This
finding was confirmed and extended by a later study using 13 children
transferred to similar wards and comparing their development with 12
others who remained in the orphanage. Nine of the 13 experimental subjects showed substantial gains in developmental quotient, whereas 11 of
the 12 controls showed sizeable decreases. In later years (Skeels, 1966),
the experimental group children maintained and even enlarged these differences. Eleven of the 13 had been adopted, all were self-supporting,
they had completed an average of 12 years of school (one had a Ph.D.), 11
had married, and the children of the 9 who had become parents had
average IQs and satisfactory school performance. Of the controls, half
were in institutions. Five of the six exceptions were unskilled laborers;
the median educational level reached was under Grade 1; only two had

married, one of whom was divorced. The differences are clear-cut and striking, although some criticisms can be made on the basis of sampling.

There may be many reasons for these differences. Children who were transferred to the ward got more attention from adults, and according to the authors particularly from the less retarded adults, so that both the establishment of affective bonds and some adaptive modeling could occur. They were involved in many more verbal and nonverbal communications. And, of course, they received considerably more sensory stimulation. Most likely, all of these factors played a role in the development of the children. It is intriguing to speculate as to the relative impact of each factor, but speculation is all there can be at the moment.

The hypothesis that perceptual deprivation is at the root of the trouble has led to a variety of attempts to prevent or remedy the problem by providing supplementary stimulation. Sayegh and Dennis (1965) provided objects to be manipulated, and also engaged infants in extra motor activity, finding considerable and rapid gain in developmental age. Casler (1965a, b), White and Castle (1964), Irwin (1960), Solkoff, Yaffe, Waintraub, and Blase (1969), Korner (1973), and Scarr-Salapatek and Williams (1973) were among other investigators who provided various kinds of stimulation, including tactile, vestibular, linguistic, and so on, finding that such inputs helped to bring premature or otherwise deprived children closer to normal developmental patterns.

Brossard and Decarie (1971) compared the effect of increased perceptual stimulation (mobiles and taped sounds) with that of extra social stimulation (somebody talking and playing with the child) in physically normal infants 2–3 months of age. Both groups had higher developmental quotients than a matched control group of unstimulated children; up to the age of 5 months, at which time the study ended, both types of extra stimulation had the same effect on cognitive development.

It appears that intelligence is affected by early environment, and that environmental manipulations could be used to ameliorate some environmental and perhaps other problems. Wachs (1978) related information about the milieux of infants collected in the course of a longitudinal study to the IQ scores of the same children during their third year of life. Visual decoration of the child's room, lack of overcrowding, and particularly the availability of "audio-visually responsive toys" (all of which are quite likely to be related to socioeconomic status in any broad sample) were positively correlated with IQ. These three factors showed a consistent relationship, while some others had only temporary effects. Another interesting finding was that little girls were affected by environmental conditions at earlier ages than were boys, and were also more sensitive to environmental change and variety.

It has been shown that enriched tactile stimulation of premature infants leads to greater improvement on a variety of developmental scales (Solkoff and Matuszak, 1975), while a program that combined tactile stimulation with kinesthetic and visual inputs also reported greater alertness, better grasping reflexes, more weight gain, and relatively rapid developmental progress (Powell, 1974; Scarr-Salapatek and Williams, 1972). Auditory stimulation in itself, using the mother's voice, led to better development and improved perceptual functioning (Katz, 1971). The findings are not completely consistent, since weight gain is found in some studies but not others, and in some cases developmental scales show only limited differences—for example on motor but not on other kinds of development (Kramer, Chamorro, Green, and Knudtson, 1975). It may also be that specific stimulation-presentation schemes should be used. Ramey, Starr, Pallas, Whitten, and Reed (1975) found that stimuli presented contingent upon noncrying vocal behavior, coupled with improved nutrition, significantly remedied developmental retardation in children from families where there was evidence of inadequate mothering. However, the degree of original deprivation may be relevant: Vives and Reyes (1978) found that even pleasant stimulation—a visit to Disneyland—was beneficial for only those institutionalized children who had an early history of a good maternal relationship.

It appears that ill infants benefit from extra tactile, visual, and verbal stimulation as well as from specifically social contact (Brown and Hepler, 1976). These authors, working with 15 critically ill infants, found significant benefits from a special stimulation program in which the parents were closely involved so that both the emotional attachments and the knowledge of the child's abilities and response tendencies were established early and could be maintained when the infant went home. Children who are slow to develop can also benefit in important ways from programs of early stimulation in which the mother is involved, and which are rationally developed to encourage desired interactions with others and with the environment (e.g., Godfrey, 1975). Similar programs of stimulation and activity can be therapeutic for mentally ill children (Wilson, 1977). Whether such approaches can overcome broader social handicaps appears to be a very different question. Basically, stimulation per se is probably irrelevant to this problem, given the high levels of stimulation encountered by children in homes of low socioeconomic characteristics (see Hunt, 1976); this is not to say, however, that specific programs of enrichment, particularly those that encourage the utilization of feedback and the manipulation of the environment, cannot be useful (see Bromwich, 1977).

It has been noted that continuous stimulation, even at high levels of intensity (e.g., 80 db white noise) has deactivating effects on infants. Among the changes found have been decreases in heart rate, reduced latency to sleep, shorter awake states, and less active sleep, accompanied by increases in quiet sleep (e.g., Brackbill, 1975). The extent to which these data represent monotonous stimulation phenomena cannot be ascertained at this time. One really interesting aspect of this research is that it relates to lines of investigation demonstrating that (a) noise is stress-inducing, (b) monotonous stimulation is stress-inducing, and (c) in some situations, monotonous noise at high intensity has been shown to be very stressful for adult human beings. Yet the same kind of noise is soothing for newborn infants. It is clear that there are many variables, including age of subjects, receptor sensitivity, situational context, and so on, that need to be investigated in some detail before we really understand the nature of the response to this kind of stimulation.

The effect appears to transcend modality. It has been found with auditory, visual, proprioceptive, and tactile stimulation. Furthermore, the combination of several modalities being stimulated simultaneously results in greater reduction of arousal than stimulation in a single modality. There do seem to be differences across species, although the effect is not specific to human beings (see e.g., Brackbill and Douthitt, 1976). There are also differences as a function of age, with adult human beings apparently not demonstrating the same patterns of change as infants. It would be interesting to explore the relationship between such findings and work on the motivational effects of stimulus deprivation and satiation (e.g., Jones, 1969; Schultz, 1965; Zuckerman, 1969c).

Prescott (1971) has argued that ameliorative tactics may work only for the young, and that in adults the deleterious effects of restricted rearing may not be amenable to treatment. He also takes the position that changes in the nervous system may occur even with only moderate degrees of environmental differences, so that child-rearing techniques well within the range spanned by human cultures may in fact lead to differential neural development among members of those cultures. Prescott also points to the cerebellum as a major locus for such changes, and argues for the importance of that structure and of response restriction (rather than merely stimulus restriction) as being involved in consequent psychological and developmental disturbance.

One set of therapeutic prescriptions (Clancy and McBride, 1975) includes careful counseling of the parent when there appears to be a significant risk of isolation syndrome (e.g., with premature or perceptually handicapped children). The actual treatment emphasizes maximal interaction between the mother and the child (see also Robertson, 1958), who join a residential program, although other family members are also encouraged to make daily visits and to participate in the treatment. The mother is always maintained as the person in control of activities, the channel of reinforcement, the teacher of skills, and the source of games and of pleasure. According to Clancy and McBride, this treatment brings about substantial changes in social and intellectual development, even when isolation has been of relatively long duration. This optimistic assessment is noteworthy, not only because it is at variance with the prognoses for truly autistic or retarded children, but also because it is in agreement with the views of observers who have studied children brought up in stimulus-restricted environments in various cultures.

The idea that remediation of infantile sensory reduction lies in subsequent enrichment has been to some extent supported by data that functions damaged by early sensory deprivation can be improved by "reafferentiation," a process that involves exercising the relevant parts of the body to a greater extent (see e.g., Ganz, 1975; Lacey, 1967). In this context, Schultz's (1965) sensoristasis theory has been used to develop suggestions as to the role of play in human behavior (Ellis, 1973), and to make recommendations aimed at preventing or overcoming handicaps suffered by children living in high-rise apartments or suffering from sensory or motor problems (Lewis, 1978).

Among the reports showing the complex nature of the child-environment relationship was a study in which a group of preschool children, some of whom were in classrooms with an enriched environment, was measured on a variety of scales (Busse, Ree, Gutride, Alexander and Powell, 1972). The enrichment materials were specifically chosen because they were expected to produce gains in various perceptual and cognitive abilities. As it turned out, the control group gained more in performance ability and in visual perception; the experimentals gained more in visual memory; and there were no differences in verbal ability and auditory perception. The authors concluded: "A 'properly' equipped preschool classroom is apparently not a panacea for the problems of disadvantaged children" (p. 21); we may generalize the statement to say that a stimulus-rich environment is not a panacea for the problems of children who are disadvantaged in a broad sense.

Hunt's (1976) approach to improving the competence of children concentrates on providing a variety of toys that foster both information processing and motor behavior, training caretakers to encourage and reward such behavior, and in general making the environment richer in variety and change while retaining a comfortable degree of familiarity. He comments that empirical "findings are highly dissonant with the view that retardation of development in children of the poor derives from stimulus deprivation" (Hunt, 1976, p. 232); rather, an excessive lack of structure and *superoptimal* levels of stimulation and change may be involved. This point of view is compatible with the kind of enriched-experience environments provided by a number of intervention approaches, several of them described in Walsh and Greenough (1976).

In perhaps the most systematic program (Hunt, 1976), successive interventions with groups of institutionalized children consisted of: (a) repeated administrations of developmental scales, (b) an aborted attempt to provide auditory and visual stimuli controlled by the infant himself, (c) social enrichment, with major improvement in the infant-caretaker ratio and increased attention from student nurses, (d) a combination of self-controlled auditory and visual stimuli, plus responsive materials and playthings, (e) social enrichment as in (c), but with the caretakers trained in Badger's (1971) techniques for facilitating behavior to explore the child's interests and developing abilities.

One of the interesting aspects of the Hunt project (Hunt, 1976; Hunt, Mohandessi, Ghodssi, and Akiyama, 1976) is that it took place in the same city, Tehran, where Wayne Dennis (1960) performed a now classic study showing that institutionalization was associated with major developmental problems, including extreme retardation in development of locomotor skills. While there had been improvements made in the childcare techniques of orphanages in the almost 20 years since Dennis's study, there nevertheless appears to be poetic justice that the children of the same area should have been the focus as well as the beneficiaries of Hunt's intervention.

In the Hunt project, intervention (a) had something of a facilitative effect as compared to a test-retest control administration of the developmental measures; (b) having been incorrectly administered, seemed to have few if any beneficial effects; (c) led to significant improvement in posture and locomotion, with some less marked changes in other behaviors; (d) led to more rapid achievement of the later stages of object permanence, facilitated the development of the ability to achieve desired environmental events, and led to earlier development of some language skills. Posture and locomotor abilities, however, were slower than in group (c). The last group, (e), with human enrichment, the Badger program, plus special procedures designed to encourage vocal imitation, "achieved every step on every scale at a younger average age than did the infants in any of the other four [groups]. Moreover, they achieved top-level object construction and vocal imitation at slightly younger mean ages than did the infants from predominantly professional families" in an American study (p. 238). Their vocabulary also developed rapidly and more richly than those of the other children in the study, and in other studies. According to the investigators, these children were "lively, socially responsive, and very attractive" (p. 239) to the degree that 5 of the 11 children in the group were adopted during a two-month period compared to 2 children out of 55 in the other groups.

Some theoretical propositions from the REST literature could be helpful for workers in this area. One, already mentioned, is the concept of sensoristasis. Another, which might clarify the effects of enrichment, is Austin Jones's (1969) analysis of the motivating aspects of stimulation. For example, the distinction between information value and other stimulus characteristics is routinely ignored, and the variables confounded, in the work on remedial enrichment of children's environments.

The data do not clearly demonstrate that either stimulus deprivation or maternal deprivation per se is at the heart of the adverse effects of institutional rearing. What we appear to be dealing with is a failure of acceptable interactions between the infant and the environment. The specific components of this failure can differ from situation to situation and from child to child. They may include such things as excessive change, so that the child is unable to orient himself to familiar aspects and use these as an anchor from which to explore new ones; a breakdown in the predictability of sequential events; an environment which is not responsive, so that the child does not learn that his own behavior may have causal impact upon his surroundings; insufficient opportunity to manipulate objects and/or to communicate with people in the environment; a lack of models from whom appropriate reactions can be learned; and so on. When more than one of these conditions exists, the amelioration of any one will bring about only partial improvement. It appears to be futile to prescribe social enrichment only, or sensory enrichment only, when a much more complex and multimodal deficit exists in the environment and requires a complex and multimodal approach to treatment. Once again, we are reminded of the dictum that valid explanations of a pretzel-shaped universe require pretzel-shaped theories.

"FERAL" CHILDREN

One aspect of stimulation during the early life of human beings, a source of considerable interest and controversy, is the development of so-called feral children. Feral or wild human beings, as opposed to *Homo sapiens*, were supposed by Linnaeus to be hairy, unable to speak, and restricted to moving on four feet. The idea that feral man represents a separate species was, of course, abandoned long ago. Most modern writers who accept the concept at all use the term to refer to children, apparently lost or abandoned at an early age, who spent their early life in the wild alone or with infra-human animals. Approximately 60 such youngsters appear to have been identified, in literature ranging back to the third century but, except for a few cases, referring to children found since 1600 (Favazza, 1975, 1977).

Malson (1972), in his review of the literature, listed a total of 53 feral individuals whose cases have been described between 1344 and 1961. Two of these lived in the fourteenth century, four in the seventeenth, nine in the eighteenth, 19 in the nineteenth, and the rest in the twentieth; two in the United States and a few in Africa and in the Near East, the rest in Europe or India. The first half of the book, written by Malson, is a simplistic political diatribe purporting to "prove" that nurture rather than nature is the overwhelmingly important aspect of human development. Furthermore, the author never bothers to examine—although mention is made of—the shakiness of the evidence in at least some of the examples of questionably feral children. Nevertheless, the case descriptions are interesting.

Typical characteristics of feral individuals include walking on all fours and inability to speak. Many of the children eventually walked erect, but only seven learned to communicate adequately. Some never learned to eat anything but their original raw food (plants and grass, or conversely raw meat) nor to wear clothes. None of them apparently developed much interest in sex, although some learned such sex-related norms as that against nudity in public. Their visual acuity was low, particularly in bright light; some of them had very good night vision and acute senses of hearing and smell. They were relatively insensitive to changes in temperature. Overt signs of anger and impatience were displayed, but humor (laughing and smiling) was totally absent. Many of them became highly attached to various kinds of animals.

In explaining the phenomena, two major points of view emerge. One is that the children may have suffered from some sort of deficit to begin with; the second, in opposition, holds that their repertoire was limited by their environment. Dennis (1941) and Lévi-Strauss (1968) argued that feral children were abandoned because they had exhibited some congenital or developmental defect that led their parents to want to get rid of them. Gesell (1941) and Malson reject this explanation, since according to them none of the more prominent cases with which they were familiar showed schizophrenic dissociation, compulsive or manic symptoms, or fantasies (although it is difficult to see how the children could display these if they were in fact nonverbal). Malson adds that Lévi-Strauss did not acquaint himself fully with the literature.

Two more sophisticated versions of the environmental hypothesis have been advanced. Smith (1953) argues that mental degeneration of the children was caused by the emotional trauma of abandonment or isolation itself. Pribram (1971, 1973) is unusually explicit about the mechanism involved:

> The feral child has no language because his isolation has interfered with the growth of his brain, which depends on his being exposed to a verbal community—much as the child fails to read when, during the first two years of life, he suffers, due to a congenital cataract or severe squint, from a lack of patterned visual input, which has been shown to be necessary to the development of the human visual system. (Pribram, 1973, p. 111; see also Pribram, 1971; Skinner, 1972.)

The argument seems to be unresolvable. There are no data that would enable one to choose between the two theories. But it seems reasonable—at least as a working hypothesis—that complete isolation from human society during a prolonged period in early childhood may have long-lasting, and possibly permanent, effects. Perhaps the best report is that of Itard (1894/1962) of the so-called wild boy of Aveyron. This boy, Victor, was discovered in 1799 and was turned over to Itard, who kept working with him until 1806. Using various kinds of sensory training with an emphasis on manipulating objects and discriminating between stimuli, Itard (1807) reported a significant improvement in Victor's sensitivity to tactual, visual, and gustatory inputs. The boy also demonstrated increased ability for abstract thought and for verbal communication. On the emotional level, he showed greater ability to develop affection and to respond to social reinforcers. There are also some anecdotal comments that one might interpret as signs that Victor felt sexual interests, despite Itard's explicit failure to perceive such a development. In general, Victor developed into a much more "human" organism than he had been at first.

Victor seems to have been the most radically isolated of the feral children whose existence was reasonably well documented. Actually, he was originally seen in 1797, but escaped. He was recaptured in 1798 and escaped, and then was finally and permanently caught in 1800. He was estimated to be about 11 years old at that time. Pinel diagnosed him as being a congenital idiot, but Itard disagreed because he felt that "idiocy" was due to the environment. When Victor reached the age of 18, he was taken in charge by a woman who had worked with Itard. He died at the age of 40 in 1828.

Favazza (1977), in his review of the literature, is quite skeptical about the concept of feral children. Several of the specific examples referred to in other works have been demonstrated to be hoaxes; in other cases, there was a high likelihood that the individual was mentally abnormal to begin with (for a recent example see Lane and Pillard, 1978). Favazza notes in passing the proclivity of the French press (which, as can be seen in these pages, finds an echo among French social scientists) to publish enthusiastic and uncritical reports on feral children. The review leans to the interpretation of Bettelheim (1959) that autism could lead to many of the behavior patterns common to feral children, and adds the observation that even among children living in the midst of technological society the symptoms of running on all fours, not speaking, and so on, are not unheard-of (see, e.g., Hrdlicka, 1931). Favazza's conclusions are that the importance of this area lies in its relevance to children isolated early in life, rather than in the possibility that they were brought up by animals; and that the evidence seems to give cause for optimism about rehabilitating such children even after prolonged and severe social deprivation.

Maybe it is human contact that makes the difference. In fact, one may take a different attitude toward the whole issue. Instead of looking at the socialization of captured feral children as a process of education or adjustment, let us consider it as an attempt at conversion. The obvious analogy is the degree to which an urbanized, sedentary, TV-reared child could manage to adjust to living in the wilderness. Had the great apes adopted Lord Greystoke after his first year at Eton, would he still have been able to grow into Tarzan, or would he have been doomed to eternal inferiority? Skinner may be implying this relativistic point of view when he comments, "The feral child has no language, not because his isolation has interfered with some growth process, but because he has not been exposed to a verbal community" (Skinner, 1972, p. 141).

The analysis offered by Armen (1974) is even more explicit in its refusal to assume that nonadaptation to human customs is per se a deficit. Rather than emphasizing the shortcomings exhibited by such children as compared to the human norm. Armen focuses on the adaptation that one such child made to the herd of gazelles with which he was living in North Africa. Apparently, the boy had a well-established and recognized place in the herd. When Armen slowly made social overtures to him, he proved to be shy but friendly, trusting, and apparently physically healthy. The author cites with relief the fact that several later attempts to "rescue" (or, by Armen's lights, capture) the child failed. He also refers to a similarly well-adjusted individual who lived among a group of ostriches, was then returned to human society, and was eventually integrated sufficiently to write his own autobiographical account of his experiences (Monod, 1945). While Armen's account, like that of Malson (1972), is marred by dogmatic environmentalism (e.g., he appears to think that the reason why the Kelloggs' chimpanzee was eventually outstripped by their human child was purely cultural), the book is a salutary reminder that lack of adaptation to one set of environmental circumstances does not necessarily imply a lack of adaptability in general.

CHILDREN WITH SENSORY HANDICAPS

One extreme form of reduced stimulation encountered by children, in some ways closest to many of the animal studies, is the experience of being blind, deaf, or both, from birth or shortly thereafter. It is closely related to the animal studies in that stimulus reduction is complete or nearly so in the particular modality, begins very early, and continues for a long period. In the study of institutionalized or otherwise environmentally deprived children, the first of these characteristics does not obtain. The other two may or may not, to different degrees and for different periods of time.

Sensory and motor handicaps that are either congenital or begin in early life are more complete and permanent than environmental manipulations. Blindness and deafness, which affect what we usually consider the major senses and have very dramatic effects, have been the most thoroughly studied; but of course, reduced sensitivity in other modalities and limited response capacity because of motor handicaps are also relevant.

In the discussion that follows, the two primary forms of sensory diminution will be taken as prototypes. Both "blindness" and "deafness" will be used to include the range from severely reduced sensitivity to complete absence of perception in the appropriate modality. As insensitivities in the minor channels may be a milder version of blindness and deafness, so multiple handicaps are a more severe one. The prevalence of such multiple handicaps is relatively high, particularly among children whose deficits are caused by problems occurring before or shortly after birth (Freeman, 1977). Furthermore, in such cases brain damage may also have occurred, and may not be diagnosed until fairly late.

These types of deprivation have peculiar characteristics of their own, which make it dangerous to extrapolate from their effects to those of environmental restriction. Perhaps most obvious is the fact that handicaps change the way in which caretakers and others treat the child, and the ways in which the child is permitted or encouraged to explore the social and physical environment in which he or she lives. For example, handicapped children whose parents suffer from the same handicap exhibit considerably fewer adjustment problems. Labeling, or stigmatizing, leads to differences in the development of the self-image and in a whole range of personality characteristics associated with such feelings as security, self-esteem, and competence.

From a scientific point of view, one of the consequences of such modified development is that it becomes impossible to distinguish between the direct effects of the sensory handicap (i.e., the effects of stimulus deprivation) and those that are mediated by the reactions of other people and of the child to the fact that the handicap exists. This is a much more intense and extreme version of the situation that characterizes solitary survivors of catastrophe, where the effects of isolation and sensory monotony are confounded with fear, hunger, pain, uncertainty of rescue, and so on, again presenting a combination in which it is impossible to identify the contribution of any particular variable. But here the experience is usually a temporary problem for reasonably well-functioning adults whose personality characteristics are already somewhat stabilized, which would reduce the catastrophic effects of the environment. This, of course, is not the case with the handicapped child.

Blindness

It appears reasonably clear that, aside from multiple handicaps, blindness is one of the most significant types of sensory reduction affecting children in the major areas of cognitive, perceptual-motor, and personality-social development. Much of the literature has concentrated on the handicaps evidenced by blind children; with increasing evidence it appears that these outcomes are highly variable and for the most part are mediated by various social factors rather than being the direct outcome of the diminution of sensory input.

One of the problems with research on the effects of blindness on children is that the complexity of the variables is frequently overlooked. For example, on many tests congenitally blind children behave differently from those who had normal vision for some early period and then became blind. As one would expect, in the latter case the child was able to develop various kinds of learning sets and organizational principles. When blindness occurred, much of the central information previously used became unavailable. This may have bidirectional effects. On the one hand, the child has to learn a whole new information processing approach. On the other, he remembers the tactics and principles learned previously, and positive transfer may occur at least after he has become adapted to the new situation (Warren, 1977). Furthermore, age at the onset of blindness is obviously related to the duration of the time that an individual has been blind. This in turn may affect the degree to which alternate sensory modalities have come to be used, and to which the individual is sensitive to stimuli in these other modalities.

Another point is that the cause of blindness may itself be related to behavioral variables. Such illnesses as rubella affect other parts of the sensory system and of the central nervous system, so that children in this category are not only blind but have other problems as well. Other factors —hospitalization, repeated surgery, the rate and trauma of blindness onset—are also relevant. Degree of blindness is important: visual impairment is a continuum, a fact that is sometimes ignored in the research. Related to the previous point is the difficulty of defining appropriate control groups. In many of the sensory/perceptual studies, the controls are normal children who are blindfolded; whether this is in fact an appropriate comparison treatment is arguable (Warren, 1977). Another problem, which is shared with the sensory deprivation literature, is the use of different tests under the same heading (e.g., "spatial relations," "learning ability").

Personal Adjustment and Social Relationships. It has been argued (Norris, Spaulding, and Brodie, 1958; Fraiberg and Freedman, 1964) that a relatively high percentage (approximately 25%) of congenitally blind children develop a syndrome resembling autism. Among the symptoms are difficulties in learning, verbalization, and establishing social relationships. Freedman (1968) developed the thesis that this syndrome, like that presented by some of the thalidomide infants and institutionalized children, is a function of stimulus deprivation parallel to the behavioral problems of animals reared under deprived conditions. In each of these situations, and even in those where the child suffers from malnutrition, the emotional and social relations problems are considered to be paramount. It is obvious, of course, that the deprivation per se is not a sufficient cause. Even aside from such famous cases as Helen Keller (Dahl, 1965), who in spite of extreme sensory handicaps beginning very early in life grew up to be a successful and well-adjusted adult, it is still the case that only a minority of all handicapped children seem to develop severe symptoms.

Personality development clearly suffers, and there is a massive literature on the problems exhibited by the blind. Blank (1975) has stated that blindness in itself does not necessarily impair major ego functions. The high incidence of such disturbances among the blind is due to other physical handicaps—including deafness and brain damage, frequently associated with blindness—and the disruption of the relationship between the mother and the infant. These conclusions are compatible with the seminal work of Fraiberg and her associates (e.g., 1968). Warren (1977), in his review, cites a number of studies that conclude that blind children tend to have higher neuroticism scores and lower emotional adjustment scores on standard instruments, but also points out the shortcomings of these data: over-generalization from high scores on particular components such as anxiety, possible inappropriateness of the test format, and the assumption that adjustment means the same thing for blind and for sighted children. The assumption, given the differences in life circumstances, may be quite erroneous.

It does seem to be the case that serious emotional illnesses are considerably more frequent among blind children than among the sighted. Several authors refer to such symptoms as disturbances in verbal communication, abnormal sensitivity and bizarre responses to perceptual stimuli, and difficulty in maintaining social relationships. There appear to be many similarities between the syndrome exhibited by blind children and autism, but responsiveness to treatment and therefore prognosis are more favorable for blind children (Elonen and Cain, 1964).

Rogow (1973) has argued that disturbances of normal speech development in blind children suffering from multiple handicaps may be affected by sensory reduction. Her point is that sensory stimulation is crucial in the development of vocal behavior, feedback, and play because it rewards the child for learning to make sounds and to voice his thoughts. Nonspeaking blind children do not learn this sequence, perhaps because the mouth area is somewhat insensitive or the child has a reduced capacity to discern sensations from the mouth. Blind nonspeaking children have not learned to associate different kinds of sensory information, so that while they may understand many words, and may like to listen to music and singing, they do not engage in active vocal communication.

Cognitive Abilities.   Until recently, there has been relatively little research on the cognitive development of visually handicapped children, although it is known that blind children who also have other handicaps are unusually likely to be mentally retarded (Moor, 1970; Rogow, 1974). Rogow feels that this phenomenon is caused by a variety of factors, including difficulty in exploring the environment, the relative monotony of inputs, lack of clarity in differentiating between self and nonself, the low expectations of those with whom the child interacts (resulting in withdrawal, low aspirational level, and fear of rejection), and difficulty in integrating information from other modalities, a function that vision usually serves. However, Rogow suggests that these effects are preventable with appropriate parent counseling and good educational programs. Whether they are remediable is left an open question.

Some investigators have reported a deficit in abstract reasoning ability, and blind children seem to lag in the development of conservation principles, although this evidence is not conclusive. A detailed study (Hatwell, 1966) shows lags among the blind on a whole range of Piagetian developmental stages. The author ascribes this to psychomotor problems, difficulties in the development of spatial concepts, and the breakdown in the feedback loop between the child's own behavior and environmental events. A recent report (Lebron-Rodriguez and Pasnak, 1977) demonstrated that this problem can be remedied by appropriate learning exercises, which also lead to increases in IQ score. It should be noted, by the way, that many standard IQ test items are not appropriate for blind children, depending as they do to a great extent upon visual experience. Tactile discrimination and similar problems require a blindfolded comparison group, which again is of dubious validity. Thus, IQ scores probably should not be compared directly. In studies where this is done, the blind tend to score significantly worse than do the sighted, although not on all items. Halpin, Halpin, and Torrance (1973) found that blind children were more fluent, flexible, and original in verbal behavior. While the evidence for this difference is not completely consistent, the results of the Halpin et al. study are compatible with the hypothesis that the blind may have better than average verbal abilities (Dauterman, Shapiro, and Suinn, 1967). Of course, much of their verbal behavior deals with phenomena for which the blind individual may not have sufficient experiential background. This kind of communication, which tends to be glib and superficial, has been labeled verbalism; most writers derogate it, although its development seems to be a logical outcome of blindness and it may reduce the social isolation of the individual.

On the other hand, Singer and Streiner (1966) reported that the dreams of blind children had less imaginative content than did those of sighted subjects. In general, one might expect that imagery, particularly visual imagery, would be relatively depressed among subjects blind from early childhood or birth. However, while there are some data supporting this hypothesis, other studies have found no such difference, and methodological problems make it difficult to draw any firm conclusion (Warren, 1977). There seems to be relatively little literature on nonverbal or artistic creativity among the blind (Warren, 1977), although both anecdotal and case history evidence demonstrate that some individuals are able to develop high levels of creative performance (Bornstein, 1977).

Perceptual/Motor Problems. Adelson and Fraiberg (1974), studying ten blind infants who seemed otherwise intact, found that they were slower than sighted children in developing behaviors that required self-initiated movements or changes in posture as a reaction to distant external stimuli. The one exception to this pattern, which the authors could not explain, is that both groups learned to roll from the supine to the prone position at approximately the same time. In behaviors that had merely to do with posture and control of the body, the blind and seeing children were approximately equal. There was no overall retardation in motor development as a result of blindness. These data are quite compatible with others found among larger groups of blind infants. The authors conclude that while blind children, who miss important distance cues, in fact are unable to learn certain kinds of behavior as early as do other children, the effects are restricted to only some aspects of development.

It has been shown (Freedman and Cannady, 1971) that severe environmental deprivation greatly exacerbates delayed mobility in blind infants. Changes in the emotional and social ties with the parent could also be involved. Gillman (1973) argues that retardation in growth and development is not really a function of the blindness, but rather of the disturbances of parent-child interaction and other environmentally caused problems. Since among these may be a lack of coenesthetic stimulation (Freedman, 1971), it is suggested that multimodal sensory stimulation be systematically included in the treatment of such children. This point of view is supported by Goebel (1975), who has shown that blind children do not suffer only from the lack of visual information. The vestibular information system is also affected, resulting in nystagmus, dizziness, and similar symptoms. This latter factor is held responsible for the retardation of some aspects of motor behavior.

In his review of the literature, Warren (1977), investigating the performance of sighted and blind children on perceptual and motor tasks, noted the heterogeneity of the data. The blind do better on some types of [1] tasks, worse on others, and about equally well on still others (see Table 4.1).

Theories and Treatments.   The theory that reduced stimulation is a critical factor is so obvious as to be inescapable, and few authors on this topic have neglected it. However, it is very rarely presented as the sole explanation, and theorists have increasingly emphasized other (mostly social) variables. Certainly the evidence for identifying the relatively low global level of stimulation as the major cause of disturbances of learning, cognition, social relationships, and adjustment has not been convincing.

Carolan (1973a) emphasized the importance of reduced stimulation in the developmental problems of the blind, arguing that without special help from the mother it is difficult for sightless infants to feel the mastery and competence that exploration can bring about. He also recommended a treatment in which special attempts are made to vary the available stimulation.

It is, of course, difficult to separate the effects of reduced sensory stimulation from those of the social problems that it may cause. Schaffer and Emerson (1964) have argued that the important thing about social interaction between parent and child in early life is that it provides stimulation for the infant. Conversely, Berkson (1973) showed that even when the physical environment is stimulating, social isolation can evoke some of the motor behaviors usually judged to be caused by sensory depriva-

TABLE 4.1.   Perceptual and Motor Development of Blind Children (After Warren, 1977)

BEHAVIOR	PERFORMANCE DIFFERENCES BETWEEN BLIND AND SIGHTED SUBJECTS
Cutaneous sensitivity	No differences in 2-point threshold and light-touch threshold; blind children worse than sighted in cutaneous localization in one study, with opposite results in another; blind children better in perception of rhythmic tactile stimulation.
Form discrimination	In a number of experiments and using various tests, mixed results: blind better than sighted in some studies, with no difference in others. Ability to read Braille well apparently positively correlated with tactile form discrimination.
Size and length discrimination	Mixed results, depending on age of subjects and particular tasks utilized. Sighted children apparently developed some of these abilities more slowly than blind.
Weight discrimination	Mixed data, with blind children more accurate but not consistently across studies; size-weight illusion (perception of smaller of two equal-weight objects as being heavier) apparently less prevalent among blind children.
Form identification (tactile)	Mixed results; blindfolded but sighted subjects do better than the blind on tasks that involve complex spatial relations.
Auditory perception	No consistent differences between blind and sighted children in auditory discrimination, generalization, vocalization (except for children who became blind at a later age, and were superior on this task), musical ability; blind children better on recognizing auditory patterns from a background.
Other modalities	No data.
Spatial relations	Mixed results, due partly to the use of many instruments which may be measuring different things. In maze learning, no general differences, although late-blind individuals tend to do better than early or congenitally blind; mixed results on block tests, no difference in using geographical directions, the blind superior to sighted children in measures of perceived tilt.
Cross-modal functions	In relationships between sensory modalities, sighted individuals tend to organize information with a spatial-visual schema, whereas the blind use kinesthetic, motor, temporal, or some other organizational mode.

tion. According to Stone (1964), stereotyped behaviors exhibited by blind children are in fact a form of providing one's own inputs. He identified two uses for this type of behavior: as a way of withdrawing from the environment, and as a method for alerting oneself to novel objects in the environment. EEG characteristics differentiated between these two kinds of stereotyped behavior. Wakeful and drowsy patterns were associated with alerting and withdrawing, respectively.

Some investigators have concentrated on the large group of children whose blindness was the result of retrolental fibroplasia (RLF). These subjects had been put into incubators because of premature birth, and went blind as a result of the high oxygen level in that environment. (This syndrome is no longer a major problem, since the discovery of the etiological factors led to preventive procedures.) Social isolation and environmental stimulus reduction were coupled in the early days of these patients. Thus, whether the crucial factor is social stimulation (Berkson, 1973), sensory stimulation arising from social interaction (Schaffer and Emerson, 1964), or sensory stimulation regardless of specific source (Prescott, 1976; Freedman, 1971), any group of blind children that includes RLF individuals will demonstrate the necessary antecedent condition, making it difficult to partial out relevant components.

In addition, blind children are sometimes ignored by their parents, either because of parental rejection or because the parents are afraid of damaging the child further (Warren, 1977). The extent to which rejection is a problem is not known, although it is mentioned in many case studies. Parental fear may be one reason why RLF children seem to have a significantly higher incidence of emotional disturbance than even blind children with different etiologies: their prematurity makes them seem more fragile. It should be noted, however, that Chase (1972) found a negative correlation between time spent in incubation and the likelihood of emotional disturbance, as well as between initial time of hospitalization and likelihood of emotional disturbance. These findings tend to undermine the sensory deprivation/social isolation hypothesis.

Proposed treatments have been as diverse as those suggested for any other group of performance decrements and emotional disturbances. One of the major proposals is for training the parents to maximize their interaction with the child, as well as to encourage him to explore, manipulate objects, achieve mastery over the environment, and develop stable and reliable coping patterns. Sensory awareness exercises, directed at making the individual more aware and therefore more confident of his own sensations, have been successfully used with blind adults (Behar and Zucker, 1976), and can obviously be adapted to children. Similarly, environments have been designed so as to make it easier for the blind child to use his remaining senses as much as possible in orienting himself in the environment and coping successfully with it (Morris, 1974). These and similar procedures for increasing the level of social and physical stimulation in the milieu of the blind child seem to follow logically from the hypotheses as to the causes of behavioral dysfunction. However, their effectiveness has not been systematically evaluated; and to the extent that the hypothesis may be wrong in focusing on global input levels, remedies based on equally global increases may be inefficient. In fact, one might argue that specific treatments for specific problems would be a more effective approach. As an example, Lopata and Pasnak (1976) set out explicitly to increase IQ scores and to accelerate the acquisition of the concept of conservation, and succeeded in achieving both of these goals. A control treatment, which could be characterized as moderate environmental and social enrichment, produced significantly less improvement. It would seem reasonable to adopt such relatively restricted goal-directed tactics, at least in the absence of conclusive evidence that general stimulus enrichment is effective.

Many authors have recommended that specific sensory training procedures be provided for blind children, and that parents be taught to facilitate the child's locomotor behavior. There seems to be agreement that vigorous physical activity and exploration, and a variety of enriched perceptual experiences in the nonvisual modalities, would ameliorate the retarded motor behaviors that have been found among the blind.

The 10 infants in the study by Adelson and Fraiberg (1974) were involved in a developmental guidance program. Their parents were trained to provide various kinds of stimulation, to speak as much as possible to the child, and to encourage the child to explore and manipulate objects as well as his or her own body. These interventions, which lasted from the first through the second year of life, may well have helped to ameliorate some of the effects of the handicap.

In general, one might expect that appropriate interventions could prevent or remedy the situation, and this is in fact the case (see Freedman, 1972). With animals, at least, certain kinds of unpredictable stimulation may be helpful in remediation (Mason, 1968), and this type of adjunct to other forms of psychotherapy should be tried with handicapped children.

Deaf Children

As in the case of studies of the blind, a number of problems are obvious in the literature on deaf individuals. To a great extent, the problems are the same as those found in the previous category. One is that many standard tests are of questionable appropriateness for deaf subjects, and that some of the definitions of appropriate response may also be doubtful. Another is that studies and reviews do not sufficiently differentiate among their subjects on the variables of severity of deafness, age of onset, and so on, thus combining very different types of individuals, experiences, and handicaps under the generic label of "the deaf." And again, the cause of the handicap may be an illness that has other results as well, thus confounding any data collected from such individuals. In the case of the deaf, rubella is an obvious example that may lead to retardation, stereotyped movements, and other symptoms that may be incorrectly interpreted as being due to the hearing loss per se (see Williams, 1972).

Freedman (1972) argues that congenitally deaf infants reared in a favorable environment do not differ significantly from those with normal hearing, except of course in the area of language development. Although some evidence is cited for this conclusion (Freedman, Cannady, and Robinson, 1971; Furth, 1966; Vernon, 1967), it is not universally accepted. Plantade and Girardin (1976), for example, present several cases in which infantile deafness is associated with psychopathological symptoms. The latter consists of atypical behaviors, high levels of anxiety, communication problems, and difficulties in establishing social relationships. Plantade and Girardin argue that the relationship of the child to the mother is disrupted by deafness, which may be a causal factor in the development of personality problems. As in the case with emotionally disturbed blind children, here too the prognosis seems to be more favorable than it is for autistic or other psychotic children.

In their review, Goldberg, Lobb, and Kroll (1975) list similar symptoms, and also note problems in the development of gender identity (see Myklebust, 1964). Kennedy (1977) has used Erikson's model to explain some of these problems. It is more difficult for the deaf child to develop basic trust, autonomy, initiative, industry, identity, intimacy, generativity, and ego integrity than it is for those with normal hearing. These difficulties arise primarily from disruptions of interpersonal communication and from rejection or perceived rejection on the part of significant others. Societal factors also play a role, in that the tendency until recently was to isolate the deaf, either among themselves or with other handicapped groups, thus resulting in stigmatization and feelings of inferiority.

Difficulties in adjustment later in life, even though not necessarily reaching the severity of psychosis, also seem relatively frequent among the deaf. Rainer and Altshuler (1967) report that deaf individuals seem to lack empathy and insight in interpersonal relationships. Some of the characteristics ascribed to deaf people who have such problems are impulsiveness, egocentricity, and rigidity (Meadow, 1975). Narcissism, agitated depression, obsessive-compulsive neurosis, and schizophrenic symptoms have also been reported (Wright, 1969; Kohut, 1968; Lesser and Easser, 1972). Rainer and Altshuler (1971), who pioneered the first psychiatric program specifically for deaf patients, found that while the risks are not different for hearing and deaf individuals as regards a number of mental problems (including schizophrenia), deaf patients tend to stay longer in hospitals and nonpsychotic deaf individuals are more likely than their hearing counterparts to experience auditory hallucinations (Altshuler, 1971). Some behavioral disturbances persist even when the auditory handicap is remedied (Eisen, 1962).

In a study that was unusual for separating its deaf subjects into groups on the basis of their linguistic ability, Levine and Wagner (1974) found that psychotic and illiterate deaf subjects differed significantly from those whose communication skills were more close to normal. The illiterate group showed stereotyped and repetitive behavior, but maintained a reasonably acceptable social facade at the expense of individuality, flexibility, and creativity. They felt psychologically inferior, adopted compulsive modes of behavior, and frequently found the environment too complex to deal with. They in fact are identified as the only group in this study that was so aberrant as to have no normative counterparts on the personality measure used (the Hand Test). The psychotics, all of whom were in-patients, resembled long-term psychiatric patients who had no hearing difficulty. The two groups that had normal and exceptional communication skills respectively were quite similar to normal-hearing samples. One particularly important point about this study was that all of the subjects suffered from congenital profound hearing loss, so that the effects were not mediated by pre-deafness experience with auditory input.

When one turns to the question of other aspects of development, problems in language development are, of course, the major focus and the major problem, since most language learning by children is done through oral speech (Suppes, 1974). Children with hearing losses have been shown to suffer deficits in visual information processing and even in auditory information processing with stimuli above their own threshold, implying that the cognitive impairment caused by deafness generalizes beyond the fact that some stimuli are not heard (Sterritt, Camp, and Limpman, 1966). Buss and Roberts (1976), on the other hand, did not find major lags in development except in vocal imitation. This makes sense if one takes the current point of view that thought appears first in development and that language, while it becomes the main channel of thought, can appear somewhat more slowly and more flexibly than was previously thought (but cf. Vygotsky, 1960). Substituting some other symbol system for oral speech enables deaf children to avoid the developmental lags previously found in several studies. In the recent literature, there is typically no significant retardation when nonverbal symbols are used (Tomlinson-Keasey and Kelly, 1974).

The role of deafness in communication disturbances is obvious. What is not so clear-cut is the reason why adjustment difficulties should go beyond the lower ability to communicate with others. It has been argued that this is a result of disturbed relationships between the child and the parents, and in fact it does not appear reasonable to hypothesize that the difficulties are due directly to reduced sensory input. This point of view is supported by Furth (1966), who found that the maladaptive personality characteristics ascribed to many deaf people are most likely to be the results of the fear and guilt that deafness induces in the child's mother, and a subsequent lack of closeness between the two. Furth and others (see Schmale, 1974) reject the position that reduction in sensory input per se produces these adverse effects.

Michal-Smith (1962) pointed out that it is the absence of contact with the environment that seems to be the major problem. The interference with language functioning results in isolation from others, because both the deaf person and other people suffer frustration and disability in communicating with each other. The sensory deprivation itself is ameliorated by a shift of attention to other senses, a factor that can be taken advantage of in teaching the handicapped (Halliday and Evans, 1974; Yarmolenko, 1976).

These hypotheses are supported by findings that deaf children whose parents are also deaf, and who are therefore taught sign language from infancy onward, show much less disturbance of social and personality development than those whose parents have normal hearing (Meadow, 1975). Children who are integrated at school age with those who have normal hearing learn rapidly to the point where their cognitive development and components of interpersonal behavior are essentially similar, while deaf children who are segregated with each other show deficits in these areas (Mallenby, 1974; Raviv, Sharan and Strauss, 1973).

Proposed Treatments.   Fortunately, the issue tends to be primarily of theoretical importance. As a general rule, the remedies proposed are of such a nature that both communication and sensory stimulation per se are facilitated. Rubin (1972) presents a therapy program for infants that starts out with auditory training and then adds visual and tactile inputs, with the intense involvement of the parents or other caretakers. Reviews of educational programs used with deaf children tend to conclude that most of the approaches are multimodal and high in social and physical stimulation. Best and Roberts (1976) have found that rate of sensory/motor development in the deaf correlated positively with a number of measures related to stimulation in the home environment and the relationship of the mother to the child. Enrichment (Halliday and Evans, 1974; Yarmolenko, 1976) seems to be helpful.

Gaines (1969) took one unusual point of view in emphasizing the need to offer help to the parents of perceptually handicapped children. Presumably, this kind of help would also reduce the feeling of isolation and some of the actual rejection experienced by such children, thus reducing both the deviation from normal levels of social and physical stimulation and the developmental problems that may arise from the deficit.

REDUCTION OF SENSORY INPUT IN OLD AGE

The vast majority of the research and applied work described in this book has used young to middle-aged adults as the participants. The same has been true of the massive literature of stimulus reduction as it affects environmental stress in the workplace, the psychological aspects of architectural design, performance and well-being in unusual situations, and so on. As we have already seen, and as any thorough review will indicate, environmental effects are complex and are mediated by many factors. This is true of the consequences for adults as well as for children. One important example is the consistent finding that subjective states of loneliness are by no means directly related to actual solitude (Peplau and Perlman, 1979). In fact, various creative uses of time alone have been identified as being among the most frequently used techniques to stop feeling lonely (Paloutzian and Ellison, 1979; Rubenstein and Shaver, 1979).

Let us now look briefly at what has been written about the impact of environmental restriction on the aged. Little if any systematic work has been performed with this population until lately. The recent growth of interest in the psychological aspects of gerontology has led to more consideration of these problems. In addition, there has been increasing concern because of revelations about substandard nursing homes and similar living arrangements.

For old people, reduced sensory stimulation is usually the result of deterioration of the sensory-perceptual apparatus, increasingly restricted mobility, a reduced circle of social contacts, and in at least some cases chronic confinement to relatively unstimulating environments. Levels of social and physical activity decline in old age as engagement in passive and solitary pursuits increases (Gordon and Gaitz, 1977); however, those old people who report higher than average involvement in social and active behaviors also express more satisfaction with life. This finding indicates that it may be beneficial to increase such involvement by using motivational interventions and by providing good facilities and the opportunity to use them.

The specific role of reduced sensory acuity in the adjustment and health of the aged has not been established, but that it has a role seems probable. O'Neil and Calhoun (1975) studied a sample of nursing home residents all of whom were at least 70 years old. Symptoms of senility were significantly correlated with losses in sensory acuity among the subjects. It is possible that both the sensory deficits and the senile behavior are symptoms of some underlying deterioration process. On the other hand, senility may at least partly be caused by interference with external stimuli as the sensory receptors become less acute. The "emphatic model" developed by Pastalan (1971; Pastalan, Mautz, and Merrill, 1973), which involves the simulation of reduced receptor sensitivity by mechanical and chemical means, provides an impressive demonstration of these losses.

As has been mentioned, confinement in a monotonous environment may also lead to adverse psychological symptoms with stimulus reduction as a possible intervening variable. This problem may exist in a wide variety of institutional and noninstitutional settings. For example, Mills (1978) has reported that elderly patients in an extended care hospital spent 86% to 90% of randomly selected observation periods by themselves. Stephens (1974) described similar levels of isolation among elderly tenants in a single-room occupancy hotel in a large Midwestern city.

Social isolation has been related to behavioral deterioration in old people. For example, Norris (1978) notes that verbal inconsistency is associated with aloneness. Once again, it is impossible to give a definite explanation of this phenomenon. Abrupt and unexplained changes during conversation may lead others to shun the individual, so that inconsistency may cause isolation; prolonged isolation may lead to a lessening of the self-monitoring process when one does engage in discussion, so that the causal explanation may be reversed; or there may be some central process which leads the person to withdraw from others and at the same time results in rambling or inconsistent speech patterns.

There seems to be general agreement that sensory reduction, regardless of cause or type, is undesirable for the elderly. Carolan (1973b) ascribes severe psychological symptoms to long-term bed confinement and monotonous environments, saying "if this bastion [sensory input] is lost, then all is lost" (p. 128). Ernst and Badash (1977) have also proposed that emotional, social, perceptual, and sensory isolation contribute very significantly to the psychological disturbances of old age. This point of view, which fits so well with the general bias of our society, has logically led to suggestions for intervention tactics. Most writers on the "applied psychology of aging" describe ways in which to get old people more involved, engaged, and active (see e.g., Fozard and Popkin, 1978). Among such remedies have been encouragement to participate in exercise programs, sensory training, and social activities, and environmental enrichment through an appropriate variety and intensity of colors, textures, illumination, music, and food (Oster, 1976). McClannahan and Risley (1975) have proposed making available a range of hobby materials and similar manipulable objects, and encouraging elderly individuals to participate in activities involving these objects. Carolan (1973b) also recommends a program of orientation and mobility that would introduce a sensorially enriched environment into nursing homes. Such programs should be directed by a specialist who can work closely with the elderly and who could give particular attention to those whose vision is severely impaired. In some situations, more than mere encouragement and help is needed: for example, for old residents in single-room occupancy hotels, which in many cases are located in areas where the aged feel that it is dangerous to come out of their own rooms. Some elaborate remedial procedures were described by Varela (1977), who succeeded in substantially increasing the proportion of individuals willing to leave their rooms and participate in group activities in a run-down and crime-ridden hotel in New York City.

A bit of caution is in order. To begin with, the hypothesis that isolation and stimulus reduction are causal factors in the psychological disturbances of old age has not been validated. Isolation and stimulus reduction are not the only psychologically relevant environmental variables. Schulz (1976) showed that the predictability and controllability of positive events have a powerful effect on the aged. In this study, the event was a visit from college undergraduates recruited for that purpose. The visit reduced isolation and increased stimulation in all conditions; but its positive effect on the emotions and activity of the subjects was greatest if they had previously been informed when they would be visited or if they themselves could control the timing and duration of the visits. Predictability and control are, of course, among the factors that are generally considered important in the psychological response to negative as well as positive aspects of the environment (see also Chapter 3). Incidentally, the study by Schulz is unusual in that a long-term followup was conducted. It turned out that within the $3^{1}/_{2}$ years following the original study the members of those groups who had been given predictable and controllable visits declined markedly in health and mood, while subjects in a random visit and a no-visit group did not show such a change (Schulz and Hanusa, 1978).

Of course, the fact that low input levels per se may not directly cause (nor higher levels directly prevent) deterioration does not necessarily negate the desirability of increasing environmental enrichment. Intervention may have positive effects even if it is based on incorrect assumptions. For instance, when patients showing signs of senility and deterioration are treated from the point of view that environmental factors are causally involved, both the therapist and the patient may become more hopeful about the possibility of improvement than they would be if the symptoms were ascribed to irreversible physiological deterioration. Cognitive functioning may then improve, and even symptoms ascribed to organic brain deterioration may be alleviated (Ernst, Beran, Safford, and Kleinhauz, 1978). Further, the patient may feel encouraged to take an active part in the treatment (Ernst and Badash, 1977). It is also true, of course, that such an approach might result in considerable improvement of the environment in which the elderly patients live.

Even so, enrichment should be undertaken with care: bed rest, quiet, and solitude are beneficial in many conditions, so that what may be needed is the identification of appropriate durations and conditions of stimulus reduction (see e.g., Goldman, 1977). And, as with individuals at other age levels, many of the elderly actually prefer solitude. A number of studies have shown that aged subjects whose isolation is marked led essentially solitary lives long before they reached old age, and further that many of them fiercely defend their privacy and accept loneliness as the price they pay for independence (Lowenthal, Thurner, and Chiriboga, 1975; Stephens, 1974). In fact, many studies have found that old people seldom rate themselves as feeling lonely (Peplau and Perlman, 1979). Whether this very consistent and unexpected finding (cf. Weiss, 1973) reflects lower needs for social interaction, better ability to cope with isolation, stoicism, or some other factor, the well-meaning social engineer must consider it carefully before applying intrusive and perhaps unwanted techniques for eliciting higher rates of socializing among the elderly.

CONCLUSION

This chapter reviewed the literature related to maternal deprivation, institutionalization in childhood, feral children, and the effects of sensory handicaps. There is no doubt that severe stimulus restriction, social isolation, and the absence of important adults in early life can have deleterious effects. These include a wide variety of psychological and physical problems, some of which may be permanent. At the other end of the life-span, negative consequences of social isolation and sensory impairment have also been documented with old people. The literature in this area is much less extensive, and much more recent, than that with children. Therefore, theoretical analyses and remedial suggestions are quite tentative. However, empirical data collected from both age groups indicate that the obvious simple explanations, and prescriptions based on them, are inadequate.

It appears reasonable to draw some conclusions at this stage. Perhaps the most important one is that the purely sensory effects of environmental impoverishment or sensory handicaps do not seem to be crucial causal factors in developmental problems, nor in problems with later adjustment, except in the most direct sense (that is, problems such as those of isolated children establishing good social relationships, deaf children learning how to speak, or blind children developing spatial orientation). The problems that most people would consider to be truly important ones tend to come about as a function of disruptions in the social interaction of the child with significant others, particularly the parents. It would seem, therefore, that the analogy between the effects of experimentally-induced elimination of sensory input with infrahuman animals (see e.g., Riesen, 1975) and those of naturally-occurring environmental or physical handicaps in human children is strained to say the least. While we cannot rule out the hypothesis that sensory deprivation is a contributing factor in some of the problems—for example, the deaf seem to experience a rather high incidence of auditory hallucinations (Altshuler, 1971), and visual phenomena often occur among recently blinded individuals (Fitzgerald, 1971)—it is clear that this is not where the main effect is to be found.

As to ameliorative techniques, general increases in the level of stimulation would not seem to be the treatment of choice. Rather, two major approaches appear to be indicated. One of these is an educational and training program that attempts to overcome the specific adverse consequences of whatever kind of abnormal stimulus experience the child has encountered, as well as the more indirect social problems that may result from these. The other approach, particularly salient in the case of physically handicapped children, is to prepare and train parents, siblings, and other relevant individuals in how to treat the handicapped child without distortion of the normal social relationships.

Perhaps the last word should be left with Lenneberg (1967): "The only safe conclusion to be drawn . . . is that life in dark closets, wolves' dens, forests, or sadistic parents' backyards is not conducive to good health and normal development."

CHAPTER 5

The Effects of Sensory Deprivation on the Behavior of Infrahuman Organisms[1]

RICHARD C. TEES[1]
The University of British Columbia

INTRODUCTION

The sensory deprivation paradigm has been put to quite different uses depending on whether infrahumans or humans have been employed as experimental subjects. There has also been relatively little interaction between the two "kinds" of investigators and their research literatures, in spite of many similar assumptions about basic motivational and other processes affected by sensory deprivation, at least one major theoretical-historical figure in common (i.e., D.O. Hebb), and in spite of repeated attempts to point out the importance of comparison and "integration" of findings and interpretations (e.g., Jones, 1969; Suedfeld, 1974a).

A prime cause of this separate development has been the fact that researchers working with humans and infrahumans have focused on different aspects of Hebb's (1949; 1955) neurophysiological hypotheses concerning the role of sensory stimulation in the behavior of normal organisms. Hebb proposed that, early in the life of an organism, variation in sensory stimulation resulted in the initial establishment or development of complex neural processes (e.g., phase sequences) that underlay normal, integrated perceptual and cognitive behavior. In discussing the role of variability in sensory stimulation later in the life of an organism, he emphasized its homeostatic function in terms of arousal or activation in maintaining integrated behavior involving the already well-established complex neural substrate.

The major theme of those employing the sensory deprivation paradigm with infrahumans has been in terms of the role early sensory stimulation plays in the perceptual, cognitive, and affective development of the or-

[1]The preparation of this chapter was aided by a National Research Council grant as well as Canada Council Leave and Killam Senior Fellowships. The help and suggestions of Peter Suedfeld, Glenda Midgley, and John Nesbitt are gratefully acknowledged.

ganism—a thrust which presented animal researchers with a promising methodology to dissolve the constraints of the continuing controversy between nativist Gestalt and empiricist S-R theorists and to develop a true examination of the interaction between hereditary and environmental influences in behavioral development. On the other hand, the experimental use of the paradigm with humans, obviously limited in regard to manipulations of early experience, concentrated on the homeostatic role of sensory stimulation, a theme more resonant with the high interest in problems of adult humans working in isolation or in low "variability" situations such as radar operators or spacecraft personnel, and in the supposed effects of sensory deprivation experiences studied during the Korean War (e.g., Suedfeld, 1969a).

Methodological Considerations

In spite of these differences, the importance of certain methodological considerations and essential design features has been consistent across both human and infrahuman research. In each case, there have been attempts to reduce or restrict overall sensory stimulation, to simply reduce stimulus variability, and to look at the effects of variables such as social isolation and immobilization or confinement separately.

Attempts to reduce overall levels for experimental infrahuman subjects have most often been unimodal manipulations. Because of the uniqueness of the degree to which afferent processes can be controlled experimentally, and because of the stress Hebb (1949) placed on visual experience, the reduced stimulation paradigm has been utilized most systematically in exclusion and manipulation of visual stimuli (e.g., Riesen, 1975; Tees, 1976).

These manipulations have involved several procedures, each with its own goals, advantages, and disadvantages. The most frequently used method of restriction has been dark-rearing; that is, raising the organism from birth or shortly thereafter to adulthood in total darkness. Its goal is the elimination of light-produced activity in the visual system until, and usually through, testing. The animal's visual experience is restricted to that activity occurring in the test situation itself. Its advantages lie in its relative convenience and its potential comparability in many other respects (e.g., handling) to "normal" rearing conditions. A potential disadvantage is basic deterioration or atrophy of the visual system that would interfere with normal functioning, such as retinal disc pallor (Chow, Riesen and Newall, 1957). To prevent this from happening, diffuse light-rearing conditions, consisting of either white translucent contact lenses (Ganz & Riesen, 1962) or translucent globes (Fig. 5–la) in which the

Figure 5.1(a).   Rats wearing two diffuse light producing occluders. (From Cooper, *Brain Res.*, 1974, 79, 47).

animal's head is secured, have been used (Riesen, 1965). In addition to eliminating patterned light stimulation, the light intensity itself is also reduced by 1–2 log units. Such a diffuse light "supplement" usually has been given for a limited period of time daily, with the organisms remaining in the dark the rest of the time. These conditions result in less severe changes than complete dark-rearing in the more obvious measures of the neural substrate (Riesen, 1965) but are time consuming, entail potential damage due to the occluders, and involve the introduction of differences in other experiential variables into the situation. Diffuse light-rearing conditions also have been produced by suturing the eyelids together (which reduces light intensity to the eyes by 4–5 log units) as a more expeditious strategy (Wiesel and Hubel, 1965).

The technique of limited and/or biased exposure to patterned light stimulation has also been employed. "Dark-reared" animals, presented with a normal visual environment for a short (e.g., 1 hour) daily period during which they might move freely, have been compared with other animals exposed to the same visual environment, but prevented from moving during the exposure period by head-holders or similar devices (Held and Hein, 1963; Riesen and Aarons, 1959).

More currently, the stimulus array presented during the limited exposure to patterned light (Blakemore and Cooper, 1970; Bruinsma and Tees, 1977; Hirsch and Spinelli, 1971) has been restricted to a particular shape or pattern (Fig. 5–1b and 5–1c) or even a particular direction of stimulus movement (Daw and Wyatt, 1974). The importance of such manipulations is readily evident if an investigator can show substantial changes in perceptual functioning and/or the brain which relate in a predicted or specific way to the controlled exposure history of the organism. However, there have been attempts to reduce overall sensory stimulation or its variability in other modalities, including the auditory (Tees, 1967), somesthetic

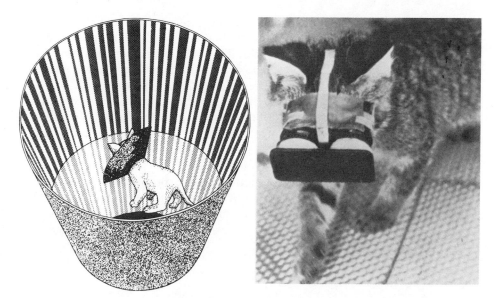

Figure 5.1(b).   Selective visual stimulation is presented by a visual display consisting of an upright plastic tube about 2 m high with an internal diameter of 46 cm. The kitten, wearing a black cuff to mask its body from its eyes, stands on a glass plate supported in the middle of the cylinder. The stripes on the wall are illuminated from above by a spotlight (from Blakemore & Cooper, *Nature*, 1970, *228*, 478).

Figure 5.1(c).   A kitten wearing one of the masks used to provide selective visual stimulation. The stimulus patterns are mounted on the inside surface of the black rectangular sheet of plastic at the end of the two white cylinders (from Hirsch & Spinelli, *Exp. Brain Res.*, 1971, *12*, 511).

(Nissen, Chow and Semmes, 1951), and olfactory modalities by various means including surgical deafferentation (Batini, Palestini, Rossi, and Zanchetti, 1959). Multimodal reduction of levels of sensory stimulation or its variability comparable to that achieved in human stimulus restriction studies (Carpenter, 1960) has also been employed. Attempts to examine the effect of physical confinement or motor restriction per se have been made with infrahumans as with humans (Lore, 1968)—perhaps with more success in the sense of isolating this particular variable from other variables associated with a deprivation experience.

Some of the same methodological problems and considerations have been encountered in animal work as in studies employing humans, albeit viewed in a somewhat different manner (Rossi, 1969). Researchers working on the effect of early stimulation history on perceptual capacity in infrahumans have become concerned with either "missing" transient effects that involve impeded or accelerated development (Fig. 5-2b) but yield no appreciable differences in adult levels of ability (Tees, 1976), or with being unable to distinguish retarded or nondevelopment (Fig. 5–2c) from deterioration in those experiments that do reveal differences in adult abilities (Solomon and Lessac, 1968). This concern is similar to one expressed by human REST researchers about missing fluctuations in effects over the time course of the experience because of the exclusive use of post-session experience tests (Rossi, 1969). The concern over ascription of post-treatment performance differences to a hypothetical REST effect, or to effects of the abrupt change per se (i.e., emergence trauma) expressed in the human literature, also has a long history in the infrahuman literature (Melzack, 1962; Miller, 1948).

On the other hand, a number of methodological problems and considerations are not common to both research areas. Unlike most human REST studies, attempts to restrict sensory stimulation in infrahumans have been

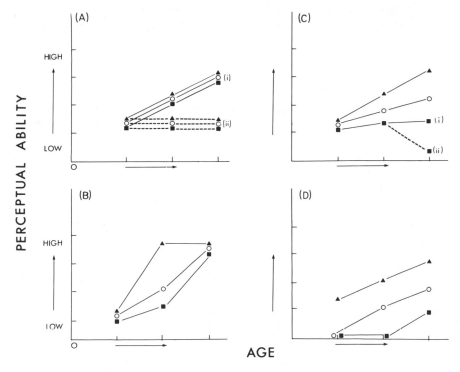

Figure 5.2. The effect of stimulation history on a perceptual capacity: some hypothetical outcomes. Environments: ▲——▲, enriched; o——o, normal; ■——■, deprived. (A) Controlled rearing results in little alteration on either (i) a capacity showing age-related changes or (ii) a relatively stable capacity. (B) A transient effect involving impeded or accelerated development but no appreciable differences in adult levels of ability. (C) Augmented or reduced levels of ability either through (i) lack of development or (ii) deterioration. (D) Delayed or advanced appearance of capacity (as well as adult levels). (From Tees, 1976, p. 299).

viewed by researchers as a rather systematic endeavor. Control groups have been consistently run to assess the role of each particular manipulation on the behavior in question, which in a sense resulted in the establishment of "baselines" for the appearance of a particular behavior. Hence, an absence of concern about "baselines" and the "automatic" systematizing of sensory stimulation manipulations by animal researchers has contrasted with that expressed by researchers working with humans. However a different kind of "baseline" problem has existed with respect to infrahuman research. In trying to measure effects of a sensorily reduced or enriched environment on behavioral development, the problem of an appropriate baseline or "normal" sensory environment can be of concern. If the control group is actually "impoverished," then the normal (N) condition may produce all or most of the important effects of deprivation, leaving no appreciable effect for the condition labeled deprived (D). Conceivably, the condition that is enriched (E), or supposedly above baseline, may also be impoverished on an absolute scale of sensory environments (Rosenzweig, 1971). If the terms D, N, and E have some validity but the rearing conditions representing them do not, then potentially sharp, qualitative differences in perceptual development due to rearing might be missed (though presumably graded effects would not be). In addition, there has been little concern expressed by infrahuman researchers about the appropriateness of test measures used to measure effects. Perhaps this is primarily because of the rather limited goals set by the animal researchers and the background of relatively crude tests of animal behavior in general. In any event this lack of concern has contributed considerably to the sometimes inconsistent and even contradictory interpretations of particular experimental findings.

The kinds of behavior examined by animal researchers looking at the effects of sensory reduction have, at least superficially, been comparable to those looked at by people working with humans. Changes in problem solving, learning, memory, affect and arousal, sensory and perceptual effects, and stimulus-seeking behavior have been examined. Some important areas of research such as susceptibility to propaganda and attitude change have obviously been neglected. However the relative impact on a sensorily restricted organism of a short period of biased or restricted stimulus exposure could be viewed as a comparable experimental situation (e.g., Hirsch, 1972).

In addition to the important "species" differences in the use of the paradigm outlined previously (e.g., age at exposure), sensory deprivation experiments with infrahumans have consistently used much longer periods of time in restricted environments than have human studies. Zubek (1969a, b) is considered to have employed a long period in his research with humans—usually one week (occasionally as much as several weeks).

This period of time would be considered very short in terms of most of the animal research programs (e.g., Riesen, 1965), many of which look at the effects of months of sensory restriction.

The plan of this particular review of the effects of stimulus reduction on infrahumans is to concentrate on the research findings of studies that are somewhat comparable or parallel to those resulting from research on humans. Some of the most important animal work—particularly that involving the effects of long-term restriction from birth on later adult behavior, neurophysiology, neuroanatomy, and neurochemistry—will necessarily be treated briefly (see Gottlieb, 1976; Riesen, 1975 for more complete reviews). The effects of several kinds of sensorily restrictive environments will be looked at in terms of changes in stimulus-seeking behavior, social and emotional behavior, exploratory activity, perceptual and intellectual behavior, and other related kinds of processes to see what conclusions can be drawn and what illustrative parallels can be made to those consequences of stimulus reduction reported in the case of humans.

REDUCTION IN SENSORY STIMULATION

The distinction between reduced levels of stimulation (sensory deprivation) and reduced stimulus variability (perceptual deprivation) made by early human REST researchers is somewhat arbitrary and misleading in terms of effective stimulation (i.e., activity) of the central nervous system (CNS). With the exception of the visual modality, control of environmental stimulation for a particular modality is very difficult. Moreover, spontaneous activity in afferent neural processes results in continuous activity in primary projection areas. Finally, since stimulus related activity in the CNS is not tightly related to the presence or absence of a particular form of energy (e.g., light) but to change or variation, absence of stimulus change as well as absence of the stimulus itself both lead to reductions in afferent activity. However, experiments can be roughly classified into those attempting to eliminate or reduce extroceptive stimulation in one or more modalities and those attempting to eliminate or reduce only variability. It should be clear that the two kinds of attempts to manipulate stimulation represent clusters of points relatively close together on a hypothetical continuum of sensory-perceptual or afferent neural activity. In terms of behavioral consequences, one could also make the distinction between *privation*, the denial of the opportunity for normal sensory experience, and *deprivation*, the interruption of sensory stimulation; however, again, such a distinction tends to become blurred under close examination and has not been emphasized in this review.

The Effect of Neonatal Sensory Restriction

As indicated earlier the consequences of early sensory experience has been a matter of intensive interest (e.g., see Riesen, 1975). Most infrahuman research has involved attempts to restrict sensory input unimodally. The ability of rodents, rabbits, cats, dogs, and monkeys reared from birth in total darkness for several months (but with "normal" auditory, tactual, etc. stimulation histories) to discriminate between complex visual patterns (e.g., N vs X) as adults is impaired compared to that of normally reared animals (Riesen, 1965; 1975; Tees, 1968, 1976). Similar findings have been reported in the case of the deleterious effect of early auditory restriction on later complex (temporal) auditory pattern discrimination (Patchett, 1977; Tees, 1967).

Although apparent irreversible loss of basic visual abilities is reported in the case of chimpanzees dark-reared for 18 months or longer, dark-rearing of the cat or monkey for shorter periods is found to produce a slight (but significant) deficit in visual acuity and visual-motor coordination when first tested, but a rapid development to normal levels with brief periods of patterned light (Hein, Gower, and Diamond, 1970; Riesen, 1961; Riesen and Zilbert, 1975). The time course of this development is no more—and sometimes less—than that observed for their controls kept under normal light conditions from birth. Slower recovery after long periods of binocular deprivation has been reported in the case of a variety of other abilities (Chow and Stewart, 1972; Van Hof-Van Duin, 1976). The evidence suggests that the extent and rate of recovery is dependent in part on the nature of the task, with complex pattern discriminative abilities being the most resistant to improvement (e.g., Tees and Midgley, 1978). In any event, these findings as well as others have been used to illustrate the differential collaboration of innate and experiential factors in the development of various perceptual abilities and their neural substrates (e.g., Tees, 1976).

Other evidence has indicated that early light deprivation also results in subtle changes in the ability to selectively attend to various aspects of a visual stimulus situation and to form associations between stimuli (Creighton and Tees, 1975; Tees and Cartwright, 1972). It has been proposed that the development of cognitive and higher-order perceptual abilities is impaired by unimodal visual deprivation (Tees and Cartwright, 1972).

Intermodal Consequences of Early Sensory Restriction

A number of observations, including the fact that sensory systems do not become functional at the same time in development (Gottlieb, 1971), have renewed interest in the more general question of how sensory systems and their stimulation histories relate to one another. Although the systems may develop relatively independently so that interference with one would not result in significant consequences for the operation of others, adult organization in one modality may depend in some way on the functioning of another developing modality (Schneirla, 1965). For example, early blindness in humans has occasionally been shown to produce impairments in a variety of nonvisual perceptual and learning tasks (Axelrod, 1959). These findings have been used as evidence of a reduced general intellectual functioning in early-blind subjects. More recently Walsh and Cummins (1975) have argued that the mechanism mediating changes due to experience is a general arousal mechanism (see discussion on pp. 189). Sensory reduction within one modality could hence result in cross-modal interference with respect to the ontogenesis of sensory systems. Visually restricted organisms have also been thought to show greater "sensitivity" in other senses than visually experienced subjects (Drever, 1955). Some fragmentary evidence exists which supports this "sensory compensation" hypothesis (e.g., Spigelman, 1969). There are also several studies of the effects of visual or somatic deprivation on the developing anatomy of the auditory cortex which seem to suggest intermodal hypertrophy and utilization (e.g., Ryugo, Ryugo, Globus, and Killackey, 1975).

However, surprisingly, there is not a great deal of systematic evidence available on potential developmental interdependence. What is clear is that neither of the above general propositions is fully supported by available research. One is faced with evidence that sensory deprivation within a late developing (visual) system can result in either acceleration (Spigelman, 1969), deceleration (Riesen and Zilbert, 1975; Spigelman, 1969) or no change (Tees and Cartwright, 1972) in the development of behaviors mediated by earlier developing (tactual and auditory) systems (see Tees, 1976 for details). With respect to the effect of manipulation of early developing systems, MacDougall and Rabinovitch (1971) have found that performance of rats deafened at birth does not differ from that of normals on either of two basic tests of visual ability (unfortunately the rats were not tested on a complex pattern discrimination). Turkewitz, Gilbert, and Birch (1974) have attempted to manipulate the experiential history of the first sensory system to develop. Tactile experience was reduced by clipping the vibrissae of newborn kittens and measuring the effect of this manipulation on the development of visual depth perception. Unfortunately, although the performance of the tactually deprived animals was superior to that of nonclipped animals at 28 days of age, the appropriate control group (clipped at time of testing) was not run. Clearly, more carefully planned studies on the intermodal consequences of controlled rearing need to be done.

Long term dark-rearing from birth (along with partial auditory, tactual, and social isolation) can also result in (1) hyperexcitability and (2) increased susceptibility to convulsive disorders (e.g., Riesen, 1961, 1975). This "cross-modal" effect has been most consistently interpreted as a consequence of abrupt change or emergence trauma—that is, the result of increases in sensory input in the absence of an established integrative organization available to supervene the necessarily incongruent sensory input (e.g., Konrad and Melzack, 1975). This effect will be discussed more fully in later sections.

In addition to these behavioral changes, a considerable amount of research has been done on the electrical, anatomical, and neurochemical changes caused by deafferentation in various modalities (e.g., reviewed by Riesen, 1975). The relationship between the pattern of changes in behavioral development caused by deprivation and those revealed, for example, electrophysiologically has been somewhat elusive (Riesen, 1971; 1975). Behavior is clearly overdetermined. Many antecedent conditions are necessary but not sufficient in regard to a particular behavior. Physiological and anatomical substrates are interchangeable to some extent and may shift during development. Ignorance of the ideas of multiple determination and interaction has led to naive and overoptimistic statements about cause and effect in regard to a particular perceptual capacity and its neural substrate. Several further points need to be made. The use of a longitudinal (rather than a two-group cross-sectional) design involving several groups of subjects would provide better information than most of what is available currently. Using such a design, Fantz (1965) measured preference in monkeys for visual targets using the amount of visual fixation as his indicator of the motivational properties of stimuli. He found that more than 2 months of dark-rearing resulted in a "deterioration" in the development of preference for increasing stimulus complexity (see Fig. 5-3). Moreover, the longer-deprived infant monkeys did not cease to have preferences but seem to have developed abnormally, revealing a shift toward a preference for color and larger size targets.

A final qualifying point about the role early experience plays in the development of the motivational properties of visual stimuli has been made by Sackett (1966). The dependence on specific sensory experience in the ontogeny of stimulus-seeking may hinge on the nature of the visual stimuli themselves. Sackett reared monkeys in social isolation and found that they began to show differential behaviors, including bar-pressing, toward specific types of visual stimulation (pictures of infant and "threatening" monkeys) at $2^{1}/_{2}$ to 4 months of age in spite of their lack of experience with such complex visual stimuli. The motivational mechanisms underlying the evocation of these differential behaviors (approach and avoidance) seem to represent the maturation of a species-specific

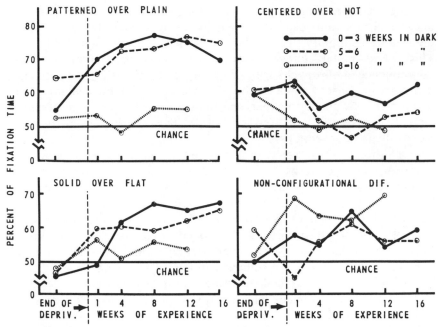

Figure 5.3. Postdeprivation development of visual preferences in each of four categories of stimulus variables by groups of infant rhesus monkeys with different lengths (●——●, 0-3 weeks; o----o, 5-6 weeks; o·····o, 8-16 weeks) of dark rearing (the most significant category is patterned over plain). From Fantz, 1965, In Schrier, Parlow & Stollnitz, *Behavior in nonhuman primates*, vol. II, New York: Academic, 1965, p. 383.

structure (and behavior) similar to releasing mechanisms, such as those identified by ethologists for avian species. In general, the influence of sensory restriction (if any), on the establishment of any of the neural processes underlying the organization of higher-order perceptual and cognitive abilities (Tees, 1976) may be characterized in terms of *atrophy*, *retarded development* or the *induction* of different patterns, capacities, and behaviors.

The Effect of Sensory Restriction in Adult Infrahumans

Surprisingly few studies have measured the behavioral impact of a period of adult stimulus reduction. However, long-term (several months) dark-rearing of adult cats and monkeys does not result in impairment in the capacity to perceive depth perception (at least as measured by performance on the visual cliff) and in the ability to learn even complex visual form discriminations (Ganz, 1975; Jones and Pasnak, 1970; Slomin and Pasnak, 1972). The ability of rodents to learn nonspatial auditory discriminations also appears to be unaffected following a period of several weeks of visual deprivation (Spigelman and Bryden, 1967; Tees and Cartwright, 1972).

Perhaps these findings are not unexpected. The tests do not approach the limits of the animals' abilities, and, more importantly, the comparable tests of learning and memory have been the most resistant to the effects of REST in humans (Zuckerman, 1969a, b). Interestingly, there are a number of reports of short-term restriction in adult rats which has resulted in an "improvement" in later performance. Spigelman and Bryden (1967) found that visual deprivation of several weeks results in better performance than that of controls on an auditory localization task—a task which was in part a measure of vigilance. The finding of improved auditory vigilance is certainly similar to that of Zubek's (1969b) with human visually deprived subjects. Facilitation of tactual and pain sensitivity also found by Zubek has not been tested in infrahumans; hence Schultz's (1965) proposition about an intermodal change in central regulation of threshold has not been put to an unequivocal test.

While most reviews (e.g., Greenough, Fuss and DeVoogd, 1976) on the influence of pre- and postoperative experience on recovery following brain damage in infrahumans cite studies emphasizing the therapeutic value of arousal-inducing, enriched environments, there are a few studies in which a short (5 day) period of sensory restriction (e.g., dark-rearing) preoperatively resulted in less impairment than normally might be expected. For example, Harrell and Balagura (1974) have examined the effect of lighting conditions on motor deficits associated with the lateral hypothalamus syndrome. Rats who spent the last preoperative period in darkness were less impaired than controls on measures of stability, waxy flexibility, and ability to step down from a platform. Short periods of postoperative visual or tactual deprivation or restriction have also been found to enhance recovery from the effects of limbic lesions under certain circumstances. This enhancement has been related to the notion of attenuating the emergence trauma normally associated with the syndromes during a period of abnormal reactivity to normal environmental stimulation (Greenough, et al., 1976). Enhanced social docility has even been reported in the case of unoperated mature rodents following 5 days of tactile sensory deprivation (Thor, 1975).

The most extensive work done in regard to the consequence of short-term sensory (i.e., light) deprivation has been in regard to the changes in the motivational properties of the sensory input with increasing amounts of deprivation. For example, Fox (1962) reported that the rate of bar-pressing for light increased with the duration of previous light deprivation asymptoting at 4 hours. Similar results have been reported in the case of the light deprived rat (Lockard and Haerer, 1968) and chick (Meyer and Collins, 1971). Wax (1977) reports that the bar-pressing behavior after short-term light deprivation of mature mice fit more closely that predicted by a stimulus change theory than did the behavior of young and juvenile mice whose behavior fit more closely to the prediction of an illumination preference theory (stimulus change theories would predict that illumination changes of large magnitude would be more reinforcing to the animal than small changes, regardless of direction. Following illumination preference would mean animals would spend more time in a particular preferred illumination intensity situation). These short-term effects of such stimulus reduction may not be as persistent or as strong (Lockard, 1963; Wendt, Lindsley, Adey and Fox, 1962) as the effects of early visual restriction on self-maintained visual stimulation. Rearing from birth in darkness can result in persistent long-term motivational changes in later responses to stimulation within the previously deprived modality (see next section).

The marked structural, biochemical, and electrical changes reported in the case of early sensory restriction or deprivation have not often been reported in the case of restricted adult animals (Globus, 1975). Changes in electrical responses such as slowing of the EEG and evoked potentials after one week or longer of dark-rearing are found to be slight and short-lived in comparison to those produced by early deprivation (e.g., Fox, Inman and Glisson, 1968) lasting less than a week, but are very comparable to those reported in the case of human REST research (e.g., Zubek, 1969c). However, recently several reports (e.g., Salinger, Schwartz and Wilkerson, 1977) have suggested a hitherto unrecognized degree of plasticity in the CNS of adult mammals.

A related investigation of short-term effects on multimodal sensory deprivation is that of Sprague, Chamber, and Stellar (1961), who attempted by discrete lesion to sensorily deprive the forebrain of adult cats, thus "eliminating" tactile, proprioceptive, auditory, and probably gustatory afferent processes. These cats showed hyperactivity and impairment, particularly in regard to attentional processes (i.e., failure to utilize visual and olfactory information in making adaptive responses). The authors interpreted their results in terms of nonspecific effects of variations in sensory stimulation in maintaining the already established neural processes related to perception, attention, and cognition. On the other hand, surgical interruption of sensory input from a single modality (i.e., auditory, somatosensory) in adults has not been reported (Buchwald and Brown, 1977; Taub, 1977) to have the same deleterious impact as multimodal deprivation.

REDUCED STIMULUS VARIABILITY: STUDIES OF
MULTIMODAL SENSORY RESTRICTION

While almost all of the attempts to reduce or eliminate stimulation in infrahumans have been unimodal, many of the experiments examining the effects of reducing stimulus variability have been multimodal, similar to those undertaken in the case of humans.

The Effect of Early Restrictive (Monotonous) Environments

The effects of early perceptual and social restriction are most readily seen in experiments involving comparison of sensorily enriched and restricted (or normal) environments. (It is reasonable to assume normal colony environments represent a considerable degree of multimodal reduction in stimulus variability.) "Enrichment" represents a second experimental strategy to test propositions related to perceptual development and a second source of information about the effects of reduced stimulation. If early deprivation is hypothesized to impede perceptual development, then enrichment involving exposure to augmented stimulus input complexity and/or variability can also be examined as to the possibility of accelerated development. Enrichment has been less frequently used than deprivation; however, cut-out "complex" stimulus patterns or three-dimensional shapes have been pre-exposed on cage walls or floors, both early and late in the life history of the organism (Forgus, 1956), both with or without the opportunity for tactual and self-regulated motor experiences with the stimuli (Forgus, 1955). Exposure to regularly changed stimulus objects and shapes has also been incorporated into experimental designs. Many of the experiments employing enrichment have tended to confound manipulations of visual experience with manipulation of opportunities for social interactions and general motor experience (Rosenzweig, 1966, 1971).

The consequences of these early, long-term manipulations of stimulus variability are reflected in some impairment of problem solving ability (Thompson and Heron, 1954), changes in exploratory behavior (Fox, 1962), emotionality (Melzack and Burns, 1965), stimulus-seeking behavior (particularly with regard to stimulus complexity preference—e.g., Dodwell, Timney, and Emerson, 1976; Sackett, 1965, 1967), social and sexual behavior (Harlow and Harlow, 1962), and in terms of electrical, chemical, and anatomical measures of brain activity (e.g., Rosenzweig, 1971) but not necessarily reflected in differences in basic sensory abilities (Angermeier, Phelps, and Reynolds, 1967). These effects are often dramatic and persistent (e.g., Melzack and Burns, 1965) and have been used to illustrate the importance of a varied environment in the development and establishment of the neural substrates underlying these kinds of behavior (e.g., Riesen, 1965; Tees, 1976).

A recent (and preliminary) attempt to examine the effects of various degrees of early reduction in stimulus variability in monkeys has focussed on somatosensory stimulation (Riesen, Dickerson, and Struble, 1977). Riesen et al. (1977) report a lack of neural development in motor control areas as well as increases in self-clutching, bizarre bodily orientations, and idiosyncratic stereotypic behavior which became evident over the first few months after birth. The effects were most pronounced in animals with restricted opportunities for manipulative-somatosensory experiences as well as restricted opportunities for social interactions and visual experience. Visual restriction and/or social isolation per se had less of an impact on these measures of brain and behavior than did the more completely restrictive regime.

Ontogenesis of Memorial Processes

In terms of alterations in the course of behavioral development produced by experimental manipulations, available information (e.g., Tees, 1976) is consistent with the idea of early experience being relatively more important than later. However, there is an apparent paradox. Early experiences appear to have important consequences for adult behavior and yet there is considerable evidence that many early acquired behaviors appear to be quickly forgotten. Investigators working on "infantile amnesia" have speculated on the mechanisms that underlie the phenomenon (reviewed by Campbell and Coulter, 1976). Suggestions have focused on changes in information processing during development. Specifically, memories for tasks learned at any early stage of development would be less accessible because stimulus information of that particular type would now be processed in a different fashion. Citing the close parallels existing between neural development and the emergence of long-term memory, the case has also been made that some kind of postnatal neural development could either cause obliteration of memories acquired during the early postnatal period or be the substrate itself for long-term memory.

If some version of the above interference hypothesis is correct, sensorily restricted animals should retain memories better than enriched animals because their information processing mechanisms are more like that of an infant than a visually experienced adult, due to retarded neural development (e.g., see Globus, 1975; Riesen, 1975). In indirect support of this crude idea is Parson and Spear's report (1972) that, at least with respect to long-term retention of avoidance learning, rearing in an enriched environment prior to a retention test of neonatal learned information accelerated forgetting. On the other hand, if general or specific neural development is necessary as the substrate of long-term memory, and is retarded by lack of stimulus variability, deprived animals may retain neonatal learning less ably than their enriched controls. There is little in the way of useful data (Kulig, 1977) to suggest that this may be the case. One important observation regarding the effects of environmental (i.e., stimulus) pre-exposure (or of controlled rearing) on subsequent behavior needs to be made. Whether this pre-exposure involves neonates or mature animals, the limited stimulus experience has been shown to enhance subsequent learning or change behavior *only* when a new stimulus is presented in an old environment or an old stimulus is presented in a new environment (Lubow, Rifkin and Alek, 1976). The consequences of such exposure may be to increase the *relative* rather than the absolute arousal inducing properties and distinctiveness of the stimulus environment situation (i.e., to increase the salience of the stimulus), which would lead to an increased likelihood of the stimulus in question to enter associations with other events. This obviously has important implications in terms of designing therapeutic situations and in making sense of apparently conflicting data.

The Effect of Reduction on Adult Infrahumans

As indicated earlier, the proposition that environmental influences on the brain and behavior of mature infrahumans are slight has come under some attack. In adult cats, 2 weeks of deprivation with restricted exposure (for 1 hour a day) to a visual environment consisting of only vertical lines resulted in a significant long-lasting change in the electrophysiological properties of the cells in the cortex of the brain (Creutzfeldt & Aeggeland, 1975). Similar reports on the effect of such special environments have suggested that the loss of normal plasticity need not accompany maturation (Salinger, et al., 1977). A recent series of experiments (e.g., Riege, 1971) have shown that the brains of mature and even geriatric rats are susceptible to the effects of a period of 30 to 60 days of multimodal reductions in stimulus variability and isolation (reviewed by Walsh & Cummins, 1976). Not only do the brains of these differentially exposed adult rats show the effects of unvarying, restrictive environments, but so does the performance of these rodents in learning mazes and on active avoidance reversals (e.g., Doty, 1972). Not only does a long period of sensory restriction in adult rats produce significant neural and behavioral effects, but it also makes these animals more susceptible to stimulation upon subsequent exposure. Periods of behavioral testing after restriction and isolation have been found to be "more arousing" and themselves produced changes in the brain larger than would be produced by such behavioral testing in the neonate or previously "enriched" animal (Cummins, Walsh, Budtz-Olsen, Konstantinos, and Horsfall, 1973).

The behavioral consequences of short-term restriction to a monotonous, stimulus impoverished situation have been more fully investigated in older studies. The infrahuman experiments which received a considerable degree of notice in this regard are those of Butler. In studying curiosity in monkeys and motivational processes related to responsiveness to environmental stimulus variability, Butler (1957) utilized a monotonous, visually and auditorily restrictive, and socially isolated chamber and found that, over a period of 4 hours, responsiveness to visual incentives (12-second "look" into the lab) increased as a function of length of perceptual restriction. These findings were highly similar to those reported for the sensorily deprived (dark-reared) adult monkey bar-pressing for light (Fox, 1962). In that case, the rate of response increased with the degree of previous light deprivation and also levelled out at 4 hours of deprivation.

More recently Levison, Levison and Norton (1968) found operant responding for complex visual stimuli by adult monkeys increased over several weeks of monotonous visual stimulation. Dodwell et al. (1976) report that stimulus seeking for visual features (e.g., lines, angles) also increased after a few days of such a regime in the adult cat. However, Levison et al. (1968) did not observe stimulus seeking behavior for the same complex visual material in the case of neonatally restricted monkeys also being tested. The early-restricted monkeys only exhibited high response rates for unpatterned light. Moreover, a brief daily period (10 minutes) of patterned and variable stimulus material resulted in "supernormal" stimulus-seeking behavior for complex visual material (Levison & Levison, 1971) in the one monkey reared under such a regime. This short, daily period of stimulus variability or "enrichment" was sufficient to result in the establishment of the neural substrate underlying complex visual pattern appreciation or perception but not to affect the motivational changes induced by the restriction. Melzack (e.g., see Konrad and Melzack, 1975) has developed the concept of novelty-enhancement-arousal to explain some of the effects of multimodal reductions in stimulus variability and isolation. A basic assumption of his hypothesis is that the different behavior patterns of deprived and normal subjects in fact lie on the same novelty-behavior continuum. Konrad and Melzack (1975) have outlined the evidence that after habituation to novelty, deprived rodents, dogs, cats, and primates come to behave like normal animals and that, in extreme cases of object or situation novelty, normally reared animals can display the behavior (e.g., freezing) of the deprived animals.

In addition to reports of changes in visual stimulus-seeking behavior resulting from decreased stimulus variability (primarily visual), changes in responsiveness to other kinds of stimuli have been found. Changes in the incentive value of auditory stimulation with short-term multimodal stimulus reduction have also been reported (Butler, 1958; Isaac, 1962). Harrington and Kohler (1966) observed that rats raised under conditions of reduced sensory variability and social isolation showed greater preference for mild electric shock when tested as adults than did normally reared animals. Lichstein and Sackett (1970) also made the same observation in the case of the similarly reared primate. This change in preference for mildly "aversive" stimuli did not depend on neonatal or long-term perceptual restriction, nor was it restricted to shock stimuli. Increases in preference were obtained for short-term (1 day) restricted adult rats using normally aversive bright flashing lights and loud pulsing tonal stimuli as well as electric shocks (Harris, 1969). Moreover, reduced sensory variability and social isolation of adult rats for as little as 3 hours has been reported to increase bar-pressing for pleasurable intracranial self-stimulation (Peretti, Suss, and Aderman, 1971) under a variety of conditions. These findings seem to show that the change in the positive reinforcing value of a wide variety of stimuli of quite different original "values" is a general consequence of reduced sensory stimulation. Such changes have also been reported with humans (e.g., Goldstein, 1965; Jones, 1969).

Not only is there evidence that the preference for a variety of kinds of stimuli changes as a function of short-term multimodal restriction, but other changes in behavior are produced by such manipulations as well. Carpenter (1960) found $22^1/_2$ hours of reduced sensory variability and isolation increased the mean times and variability of rats attempting to emit the bar-pressing responses necessary for reinforcement on a fixed ratio schedule in simple operant conditioning situations. Pishkin and Shurley (1966) confirmed this finding. For example, 10 hours of such multimodal restriction diminished the ability of the water-deprived rat to initiate and maintain satisfactory behavior to obtain the vital water during a 2-hour test-period following the restrictive experience.

More complex kinds of behavior have also been changed. Several weeks of preparturitional deprivation involving social isolation and auditory and partial visual restriction disrupt the subsequent maternal behavior of female rats and lead to poorer survival of offspring and reduced weight of surviving pups. Postnatal stimulus monotony also had a significant effect (Levine and King, 1965) on maternal behavior. Attention, as measured by the detection of changes in intensity of a light in an operant situation, was affected by a unimodal manipulation in 100 day-old albino rats. Venator (1967) found that a few hours of restriction to constant white noise resulted in poor detection compared with the performance obtained after exposure to a variable complex auditory stimulus environment. Somewhat indirect evidence as to the possibility that rhesus monkeys kept in a monotonous sensory environment undergo visual imagery or hallucination has also been reported (Vaughan, 1966). An environment which provided restriction of movement, monotonous (white noise) auditory stimulation, constant temperature, and diffuse nonpatterned white light (via cornea contact lenses) was utilized to provide 74–96 hours of reduced stimulation. Rhesus monkeys, previously trained to press only in the presence of visual patterned stimuli, bar-pressed during and after termination of the monotonous stimulation period in absence of the visual training stimuli as well as exhibiting other inappropriate behaviors during the subsequent presentation of visual stimuli. Whether or not the inference of the author as to hallucinatory behavior was justified, it was clear that the experience disrupted and changed the behavior of the adult rhesus monkey considerably. Even more clear were the long-term results of as little as 30 days of deprivation resulting from placement of adult rhesus monkeys in a narrow vertical chamber (Figure 5-4) with limited visual stimulation, social isolation, and partial confinement. Basically the apparatus was a simple stainless steel chamber, open at the top, with sides that slope towards a rounded bottom.

Harlow and Suomi (1971, 1974) found dramatic deficits in social, locomotive, and exploratory activities, excessive contact clinging, and self-directed behavior paralleling those of anaclitically depressed humans

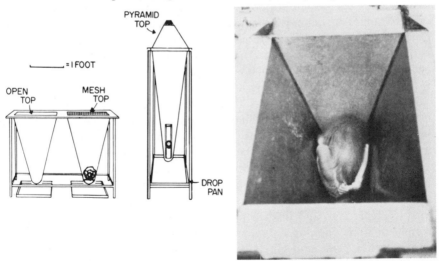

Figure 5.4(a).   The vertical chamber apparatus. From Harlow & Suomi, *Behav. Biol.*, 1974, *79*, 284.

Figure 5.4(b).   Typical subject posture within vertical chamber. From Suomi & Harlow, *Behav. Res. Meth. & Instrum.*, 1969, *1*, 247.

Figure 5.5(a).   Contact clinging in adolescent monkeys subjected to vertical chamber confinement. From Harlow & Suomi, *Behav. Biol.*, 1974, *12*, 287.
Figure 5.5(b) & (c).   Monkeys raised in social isolation develop abnormal behavior patterns including self-clutching (b) and self-biting (c). From Sackett, 1968, In Fox, M.W., *Abnormal behavior in animals*, Philadelphia, Saunders, 1968, p. 317.

which lasted for months after the experience (Figure 5-5). The deficits were not as dramatic as those produced by such vertical chamber confinement in younger monkeys restricted from birth, particularly with respect to the self-directed behavior (Figure 5-5b and c). Harlow and Suomi (1974) initially assumed that 6 to 12 months of this vertical chamber confinement/restriction, or even a period of less severe sensory reduction and social isolation from birth (see section on Isolation), produced severe and permanent deficits in behavior. Recently the syndrome has been found to be reversible (Novak and Harlow, 1975) even after 12 months of restriction. The rehabilitation program of these animals is interesting. The use of equal-age peers as therapists and an enriched environment were found to be highly ineffective, if not counterproductive. Too many stimuli for the withdrawn, isolated animals resulted in even greater huddling, self-clasping, and so on. The use of younger, socially less complex monkeys, a gradual adaptation to post-deprivation environmental stimulation, and a crude attempt to introduce self-pacing of stimulation, present less of a stimulus overload, less emergence trauma, and greater rehabilitation. Such findings would be very consistent with Melzack's ideas concerning the concept of novelty-enhancement discussed earlier, and consistent with at least one report of successful treatment of autistic children through exposure to REST experiences (Schechter, Shurley & Toussieng, 1970—see Chap. 9). The idea is that Melzack's and Harlow's restricted infrahumans as well as autistic children are unable to adequately filter incoming stimuli except by autistic behavior.

On the other hand, as in the case of more complete stimulus reduction, later monotony seems to have little or no effect on some kinds of behavior. Although it is possible that the lack of effects is due to the potential insensitivity of the measures used by researchers, the tests appear to be no more insensitive than those used in other kinds of animal research, and are sensitive enough to reveal differences due to *early* sensory and perceptual restriction of a comparable period of time (Riesen, 1965). Cats reared in diffuse light from 5 months of age through to 10 months of age learn complex pattern discrimination as rapidly as normally reared cats (Riesen, 1965). Forty-day-old rats, restricted to a monotonous environment for 3 weeks, compared favorably with rats "enriched" with visually complex material during that period in learning to discriminate between visual shapes (Forgus, 1956). Comparison of animals receiving enrichment, social as well as sensory, with those receiving multimodal restriction for several weeks during adulthood, has revealed some impairment in maze learning (Walsh and Cummins, 1976) but little effect in performance on pattern discriminations (e.g., MacDougall and Rabinovitch, 1971), although these same manipulations early in the life of the organism do have a considerable deleterious effect (Hymovitch, 1952).

SOCIAL ISOLATION

Neonatal Isolates

In addition to differences such as those due to unimodal versus multimodal stimulation reduction, attempts to examine the importance of some other experimental variables being manipulated in these conditions have been made in the case of human REST research. Primarily social isolation and confinement/immobilization have been looked at and in this regard, a considerable amount of evidence has been collected as to the effect of early social isolation on later behavior of infrahumans. As in the case of naturalistic and somewhat anecdotal reports with children (O'Connor, 1968), relatively long-term and early isolation of a variety of species such as birds, rodents, dogs, and monkeys has severe effects on later sociosexual and emotional behavior and related physiological indicators (e.g., Beach and Jaynes, 1954; Harlow and Suomi, 1974; Thompson and Heron, 1954; Sackett, 1967) as well as on adaptive behavior in stressful situations

(Fox, 1968). The dramatically inadequate and inappropriate social and sexual responses to peers as well as exploratory and approach-avoidance responses have been so widely and consistently reported (e.g., Thompson and Heron, 1954) that they have been termed the "Isolation Syndrome" and the consequences interpreted (as have those for human isolates) even in terms of disturbances resembling depressive and autistic behavior (Fox, 1968). Social isolation conditions have inevitably involved less multimodal stimulus variability (see Figure 5-6) and the consequences of such sensory restriction and isolation have been discussed to some extent in the previous section.

Successful rehabilitation has not only involved the procedures (i.e., a social therapy) outlined earlier (Novak and Harlow, 1975), but also phar-

Figure 5.6. Total social perceptual isolation chambers which deny visual and tactual contact with the environment with the front panel open. From Morrison & McKinney, 1976, In Walsh & Greenough, *Environments as a therapy for brain dysfunction,* New York: Plenum, 1976, p. 145.

macological treatment of socially isolated monkeys involving administration of chlorpromazine (CPZ) and the anti-anxiety drug diazepam (reviewed by Morrison and McKinney, 1976). In comparison to CPZ, diazepam more consistently led to improvements in social, aggressive, and exploratory behavior. The effectiveness of both agents perhaps argues against a premature acceptance of the social isolation syndrome as a model of human affective disorders. However, the antidepressant imipramine and ECS (useful in the case of human depression) also were found to be valuable therapeutic treatments when the behavior of appropriate control groups was compared.

In spite of many of the similarities between the effects of early social isolation across species (e.g., Suedfeld, 1969a) dramatic deficits reported in intellectual capacity (O'Connor, 1968) for socially isolated children have not been found in the case of socially isolated monkeys (Sackett, 1968), in spite (or perhaps because) of rather sophisticated testing. The performance of rhesus isolates is not deficient on tasks involving discrimination learning of complex shapes or delayed responses. They show normal improvement over a series of discrimination problems each of which involves only 6 trials with new pairs of objects (learning set), and only a slight impairment in the case of an "oddity" version learning set task involving 3 new objects (Harlow and Suomi, 1974). It is more than likely that this apparent species difference reflects the degree to which social isolation and sensory restriction are more confounded in the case of the "socially isolated" children than in monkeys (e.g. Riesen et al., 1977)

Adult Isolates

However, all of the above studies demonstrate little about what changes in behavior result from short-term social isolation of adult animals and hence provide little in the way of information comparable to findings of the short-term human isolation experiments. Early observations of behavioral distress (i.e., high activity, vocalization), then despair (i.e., inactivity, withdrawal) arising from temporary separation from peers and mothers (Köhler, 1927) have been made of juveniles, but systematic study of the effects has been a more recent development (Harlow and Suomi, 1974). Fox (1967) has reported that one week of social isolation in juvenile dogs produces increased levels of general activity and exploratory behavior. The change in the state of animals is also reflected in EEG activity. All of these changes gradually disappear by 7 days after emergence from isolation.

Adolescent (6-to-8 month-old) male rhesus monkey pairs, separated and isolated for two weeks, also reveal short-term changes in activity and exploration in the 4 days following emergence similar to those observed in the case of the isolated dog (Bowden and McKinney, 1962).

A series of studies (Latané, Nesbitt, Eckman and Rodin, 1972; Walton and Latané, 1972) has revealed the role of some of the important variables related to the effect of short-term social isolation in the rat. Rats housed in pairs were compared with animals both physically and visually isolated and animals only physically isolated from peers for one week. Completely isolated animals were significantly more gregarious over an 18-day test period following emergence from isolation than either of the other groups. Differences in social interaction between visually and physically isolated animals did emerge during an additional week of isolation. This effect of social deprivation was observed when either relatively young (30-day-old), middle-aged (240-day-old), or aged (450-day-old) animals were isolated and tested. A period of social isolation as short as 24 hours resulted in motivational changes that reflected themselves in increased exploration and gregariousness in the open field (a sensorily enriched environment), as well as a home cage situation (e.g., Hewitt and Hill, 1967). These effects probably represented short-term changes in rats' predisposition or motivation to approach other animals. Experiments in which animals are switched from one housing situation to another have indicated that the immediate level of social deprivation is more important overall than the prior social experience (Latané et al., 1972). Short-term social isolation has also been used in connection with the testing of psychotropic drugs as a tool or treatment to increase intra- and interspecies aggressiveness as well as gregariousness (Barnes, 1959; Valzelli and Bernasconi, 1971) and other behaviors (e.g., Davis, Beighley, Libretto, Mollenhour and Prytula, 1975). Social isolation of an adult rodent for a period of 1 to 2 weeks is perceived as being stressful, increasing activity, changing social interactions and adrenocortical activity, and having a relatively predictable effect on the action of drugs (e.g., Valzelli, 1967). This "isolation stress" is thought to facilitate subsequent performance of simple tasks while retarding it on more complex tasks (Wood and Greenough, 1974). One could argue that high arousal causes attention to be focused on the dominant aspects of the stimulus situation at the expense of less salient aspects, facilitating or retarding performance as the case may be.

Some of the same kind of interpretations (Suedfeld, 1969c; Zuckerman 1969a) have also been made in the case of the short-term human isolate research (e.g., stress inducing heightened social drive). The kind of indirect data generated to support this interpretation in humans has been increased verbal productivity in an open-ended projective test—a situation in which stimulus reduction itself leads to impairment; that is, to reduced verbal productivity (Suedfeld, Grissom, and Vernon, 1964). This kind of evidence seems no better or worse than that cited above to support similar conclusions for infrahumans.

CONFINEMENT OR IMMOBILIZATION

Human subjects in most REST experiments are confined in some way and the effects of restricted motor activity have been investigated as a potentially significant factor in producing stress and other responses observed in experiments. For example Zubek and MacNeill (1966) observed post-immobilization EEG changes as well as some behavioral deficits in tests of recognition and recall. They related these effects to the reduction in level of kinesthetic and proprioceptive stimulation that resulted from immobilization, and suggested that differences between the consequences of stimulus restriction itself and immobilization lay largely in terms of magnitude. Examination of such immobilization studies also reveals the difficulty in separating confinement from the partial reduction in variability that had to result in regard to stimulation of other modalities (e.g., Stewart, 1977).

Animal work in this area has not focused on the same kind of wide-ranging test employed by Zubek and his coworkers. A series of experiments involving sensory deprivation has revealed the importance of visual feedback from self-produced movement in perceptual development of cats and monkeys (Held and Bossom, 1961; Riesen, 1965). Most of these experiments have involved restraint of animals in body holders, but although these studies may at first appear to be relevant to the present discussion of the effects of confinement, they really are not. All involve animals who are restrained from birth during a short period (e.g., 1 hour) of daily light exposure. The remaining time is spent without restraint in "normal" visual deprivation circumstances. Nissen, Chow, and Semmes (1951) do report striking abnormalities in adult motor behavior and perceptual motor coordination of the chimpanzee following early extended rearing involving restriction of the activity of limbs in conjunction with tactual-kinesthetic and social restriction (Fig. 5-7). The considerable degree of confinement reported in the case of the early restricted McGill dogs (Melzack and Scott, 1957) has also been utilized (Suedfeld, 1969a) to illustrate the possible role of confinement in the overall effects of sensory deprivation. It is clear that maladaptive responses to novel stimulus situations were found in the case of these dogs, but the role of lack of tactual-kinesthetic stimulation or physical confinement itself is not clear. Indeed, Prescott (1971) has argued that a major factor in studies of social isolation which yield inept social behavior and motor stereotypes is the somatosensory deprivation due to this early confinement. The preliminary report by

Figure 5.7. Rob at 30 months of age, as reared in conditions of somesthetic restriction. The cylinders permitted fairly free joint movement but radically limited his tactual experience. Note the abnormal sitting posture. From Nissen, Chow and Semmes, *Amer. J. Psychol.*, 1951, *64*, 488.

Riesen et al. (1977) cited earlier would support this proposition. Several early studies (e.g., Hymovitch, 1952) have reported that small cage-reared rats perform less well than do normal rats on maze problems, but later studies seem to indicate the results were more a function of (1) total amount of sensory experience, or (2) the particular test circumstances, than a direct effect of early confinement on intellectual functioning (Forgus, 1955; Henderson, 1976; Meier and McGee, 1959; Walk, 1958).

Several experiments have involved short-term continuous confinement or immobilization of adult animals, and the results are inconclusive. Although Riopelle (1963, in Draper and Bernstein, 1963) found that rhesus monkeys released from total body casts after 48 hours show temporary perceptual as well as motor impairments, Draper and Bernstein (1963) themselves failed to find differences in social and nonsocial activities or perceptual impairment following release (although they did observe the temporary motor impairment). There is one clear-cut result that is somewhat inconsistent with the finding with humans that confinement is less stressful than sensory reduction (Ader, 1965). A short period (6 to 18 hours) of immobilization in the rat resulted in an increasing incidence of gastric ulcers in proportion to the duration of exposure. Ewbank's (1968) review of the behavior of animals in restraint also suggests confinement is stressful in most species examined. However, the intriguing though some-what anecdotal reports of trance-like state exhibited by some confined and restrained infrahumans (e.g., sheep, chickens, and cows) seem worth further, more systematic, investigation.

The other source of information about the consequences of activity restriction on animal behavior arises out of early work done on the activity drive hypothesis (reviewed by Lore, 1968). Activity deprivation (e.g., Hill, 1961) was believed to result in motivational changes in the organism's autonomous need for activity which would then be observed in increased activity following motor restriction. Unfortunately, in most of these studies, confinement consisted of restriction to small cages which does not prevent movement. However, evidence has been generated that activity reduction for 1 to 8 days did result in increases in activity following release from confinement. Lore (1968), reviewing the question of activity deprivation for the short term (5 hrs to 8 days), reported this change in activity is only found in the case of novel situations and related the effects to a change in emotionality rather than in an activity drive. It is clear from the animal research that short-term confinement can be stressful to the adult animal and results in increased activity and emotionality following release, but little else in terms of behavior has been systematically examined.

SUBJECT VARIABLES

In addition to differences due to variations in experimental variables such as type, duration, age of deprivation, and so on, and the kinds of behavior examined, subject variables have been studied in human REST studies and found to play an important role in terms of the consequences of the experience (e.g., Zuckerman, 1969a). Some important subject variables such as subject expectation, selection (volunteering), and cultural background have necessarily not been investigated by animal researchers. Other variables, such as the effect of prior exposure to REST, which are potentially interesting and testable with infrahumans have also not been looked at very systematically. However, McKinney (1974) does observe that the effect of a prior (and early) vertical chamber exposure significantly influences the response of the rhesus monkey to a subsequent period of deprivation 18 months later.

There are other data which bear on the question of subject variables. There is a reasonable amount of evidence (e.g., Fuller, 1964; Krushinski, 1962) that genetic factors are important in determining the potential effect of sensory deprivation and isolation. One should expect the susceptibility of an organism to change as a result of environmental manipulation, and to vary with genetic constitution of species. Some organisms should be expected to be strongly buffered and others weakly buffered against the lack of sensory stimulation (Thompson and Grusec, 1970). With respect to multimodal sensory restriction and isolation versus enrichment, Konrad and Melzack's (1968) work reveals real within-species differences in the consequences of such rearing for Scottish terriers versus beagles. Several studies indicate monkeys and dogs may also be more susceptible to arousal disorders due to light deprivation than are cats and rats (Riesen, 1961, 1975). Genetic differences with respect to "buffering" also appear to be the case in rat strains. Strains of rat which were selected for maze ability (or lack of it) are differentially responsive to early environmental manipulation (Cooper and Zubek, 1958). The "dull" rat strain gains much more than the "bright" strain in maze ability as a result of exposure to an enriched early environment. In a restricted environment "brights" lose much more than "dulls."

Fox (1967) has suggested a genotype-treatment interaction in which potentially overfearful animals (having an inherited "timidity" trait) will develop abnormally in the "experimentally-imposed" state of isolation. Indeed, fragmentary reports of considerable differences between certain strains of mice and rats, in the changes due to isolation in brain biogenic amine metabolism, would suggest social isolation might be expected to produce very different behavioral consequences (Stolk, Conner, and Barchus, 1974). The infant bonnet monkey's response to separation from its mother is considerably less than it is in the case of the pigtail and rhesus monkey. (Pigtail and rhesus mothers are "possessive," maintaining an exclusive relationship with their infants, while bonnet mothers are "permissive," allowing their infants to form affective relationships with other adult females soon after birth.) While this interstrain difference in the responses of bonnet versus rhesus infants to social isolation from the mother is likely an illustration of the marked differences in natural relationships between infants and mothers in the two species of monkeys (as suggested by Hinde and Spencer-Booth, 1971), the intergenera difference found between infant rhesus and patas monkey reactions to separation are harder to explain in terms of prior infant-mother attachment since both patas and rhesus mothers are "possessive." This may better be attributed to genetic contributions.

Differences between the stimulus-seeking behavior of early deprived monkeys and normal monkeys, both undergoing stimulus reduction as adults, are also interesting (Levison and Levison, 1971). The monkeys deprived from birth exhibit stimulus-seeking behavior towards unpatterned light and not necessarily towards vital complex pattern stimuli (involving less change from background illumination), while the "normal" monkey undergoing stimulus restriction showed a preference for both. Thus the importance of this subject variable (previous stimulation history) in determining the outcome of experiments is clearly revealed.

CONCLUSIONS AND SUMMARY

Evidence, albeit briefly presented in this paper, indicates clearly that unimodal or multimodal sensory restriction early in the life of an organism retards the establishment and consolidation of the substrates directly underlying particular kinds of perceptual-cognitive processing (Tees, 1976) and those subserving arousal filtering mechanisms (Melzack and Burns, 1965). I have argued elsewhere (Tees, 1976) that one can distinguish between kinds or levels of perceptual and attentional processes which are qualitatively different in terms of the demands that they place on the nervous system, and that such distinctions are related closely to differences in the responsiveness to environmental stimulation. Some of these processes involve higher-order multimodal concepts of space and time. Their neural substrates are likely to be late developing (Mayers, Robertson, Rubel, and Thompson, 1971) and thus have the maximum chance to be modified by various kinds of sensory experience. Whether or not these same higher-order processes are also the ones most affected by sensory restriction in mature organisms is still open to question.

Neonatal sensory reduction and social isolation also have dramatic and persistent effects in terms of later "personality" and social (including sexual and maternal) behavior. Presumably this is a result of the failure of the environment to provide the experiential stimulation to build up the somewhat overlapping and different structural-functional components (e.g. limbic circuits) underlying these behaviors (Fox, 1968). It is also clear that environments such as "vertical chamber" and social isolation are environments which do not provide the social-tactual stimulation nor opportunities to learn from social-role models. Nondevelopment of normal patterns of behavior as well as induction of different patterns involving stereotypic responses such as self-clasping, rocking, and huddling are the consequence. Obviously these stereotypic behaviors provide, in response to these impoverished environments, reinforcing, tactual, manipulative stimulation. The reversibility of the deleterious effects of even 12 months of perceptual and social isolation undercuts any simple ideas about the critical importance of this early period of life and atrophy-without-maintenance-stimulation (Suomi and Harlow, 1972) with respect to the development of these processes. It underlines the importance of examining more closely the effects of periods of stimulus reduction on mature infrahumans.

The major research efforts and hence findings of experiments that have utilized relatively short-term sensory restriction of adult animals have been in terms of motivational changes related to stimulation-seeking behavior. Restriction has been reported to cause increases in exploratory-social behavior, activity in general, and self-stimulation for a wide variety of stimuli including intracranial brain stimulation and stimuli normally aversive or "neutral." The effects seem to be consistent with a more general role played by the level of sensory stimulation and variation—that is, restriction of stimulation within a modality results in changes not confined to processing of information within the same modality. These studies are also beginning to point up the "super normal" impact of certain brief stimulus experiences embedded in or following a period of reduced or monotonous stimulation (e.g., Cummins et al., 1973).

In addition, there are some reports of effects of short-term stimulus reduction on other more complex behaviors—such as attention and vigilance, maternal behavior, social interaction—and even on presumed hallucinatory imagery. Most of the findings are directly related to the understanding of, or at least to the demonstration of, the homeostatic role played by sensory stimulation later in the life of an organism whose previous stimulation history has provided it with the fundamental processes underlying the organization of perceptual, cognitive, affective, and attentional behaviors. Moreover, the weight of infrahuman evidence regarding the effect of sensory deprivation is clearly consistent with that reported for comparable human research and supports the kind of optimum level of stimulation-activation theorizing proposed by Hebb, Fiske and Maddi, Schultz, Lindsley, and Zuckerman (reviewed by Zuckerman, 1969c), each of which differs in terms of specificity of detail, neurophysiological emphasis, and level of analysis. These concepts of arousal response and arousal homeostasis have also been utilized as a fundamental (but not exclusive) mechanism mediating the neural changes induced by exposing infrahumans to perceptual and social isolation throughout their early life (e.g., Walsh and Cummins, 1975). Moreover, recent evidence (e.g., Riege, 1971) of the neural changes induced in mature infrahumans after periods of sensory deprivation makes more plausible the attempts to look for common mechanisms underlying REST effects produced at any stage of life.

What evidence exists as to the separate roles of such factors as subject variables, social isolation, and confinement also appears consistent with related human REST studies. For example, subject variables such as species and strain, previous stimulation histories, and age have all been found to play a part in consequences of sensory isolation.

To some extent the infrahuman data do not provide a special illumination on sensory deprivation as a phenomenon. There are, however, a few areas of research in which important work could be done with infrahumans, particularly in regard to physiological recording during and after short-term sensory restriction and the combination of behavioral and physiological testing of the effects of arousal manipulating drugs on the deprivation experience. The effect of prior stimulation histories (including prior short-term REST experiences) and systematic study of strain and species differences perhaps based on their endogenous capability also need to be examined. In outlining a proposal for the application of behavioral principles and techniques to the modification of abnormal behavior in infrahumans (i.e., for an animal "clinical" psychology), a course of therapy involving short-term environmental manipulation such as REST was not cited (Tuber, Hothersall, and Voith, 1974); however there are clear indications that such a therapy is worth exploring (Novak and Harlow, 1975).

Most importantly, researchers studying the effects of short-term stimulus reduction in adult animals will have to begin to ask more subtle questions of their experimental subjects to uncover the effects on high-order complex processes in the same way that, for example, researchers working on frontal and temporal cortex functioning have had to increase the demand characteristics of their behavioral testing to examine slight, quantitative, intersensory changes in cognitive, perceptual, and motivational processes (e.g., Wilson, Wilson, and Sunenshine, 1968).

CHAPTER 6

Quasi-Therapeutic Applications of REST

This chapter is concerned with uses of reduced stimulation that are not therapeutic in the strict sense, but nevertheless have the goal of improving the individual's life. The improvement may be in any of several realms. It may include the abandonment of material desires and ambitions; achieving unity with the divine, with the universe, or with nature; or, more prosaically, raising one's self-image, finding novel and interesting experiences, or exploring more deeply facets of one's own personality. These goals have been pursued in caves, deserts, and forests as well as in water tanks and anechoic chambers. As we shall see, there is a mass of evidence testifying to the effectiveness of environmental reduction in these quests.

First, we shall look at the use of standard REST equipment (sensory reduction chambers and water immersion tanks) by people seeking to improve their adjustment to the world or to themselves. This activity may be related to therapy, but it is not undertaken as part of a formal treatment for any kind of diagnosed illness or behavioral dysfunction. Rather, the participants are trying to reach deeper insights into their own personality, or into their relationships with the social, physical, and spiritual environment in which they live. The closest approach to the classical ideas of treatment that this involves is that some individuals may hope to reduce or eliminate sources of psychological stress or discomfort; but for the most part, the goal is the more positive one of personal growth.

REST AND SELF-IMPROVEMENT

I should start this section with a warning. "Self-improvement" is not used here in a technical denotative sense. It subsumes self-exploration, self-actualization, and changes in self-image. For the most part, the section discusses the use of REST techniques by individuals who are neither patients nor subjects. They are, in the truest sense, participants who use the environment for personal growth or problem-solving. In those few studies where this was not the case, the researchers rather than the participants selected the goal; but the goal was the same.

Increasing Self-Esteem: Experimental Studies

Chapter 10 discusses studies of restricted stimulation with hospitalized psychiatric patients in which the desired outcomes of the treatment included an increase in self-esteem. While low self-esteem cannot generally be characterized as an illness, nor raising it as a treatment, such a change can be beneficial for many people. I shall leave aside at this stage the tempting philosophical discussion as to whether an improvement in one's feelings about oneself is necessarily good, although I would like to note at least in passing that a cogent argument can be made for advocating appropriate, rather than maximal, levels of self-approval. In other words, it may be proposed that individuals should be encouraged to view themselves relatively objectively. In some cases this may imply no change, or even an actual decrease—rather than an increase—in self-esteem.

The ability of REST to bring about self-concept changes in a nonpatient population has not been completely established, but there are indications that it is effective in at least some instances. Hewitt and Rule (1968) conducted an experiment in which normal subjects underwent $3^1/2$ hours of monotonous stimulation. At the end of this period a communication designed to improve the person's self-concept was played over the intercom, and a half hour later a test measuring self-concept (among other things) was administered. There was a main effect for REST, with greater changes in the positive direction on self-concept and acceptance of the self among confined subjects. There was also a significant decrease in the discrepancy between scores on how the person viewed himself and how he would like to be, showing an interaction between the treatment condition and conceptual structure (Harvey, Hunt, and Schroder, 1961). Similar interactions, in the predicted direction but not reaching statistical significance, indicated that the REST condition had a greater impact on individuals who were at the low end of the complexity continuum, and who therefore are generally hypothesized to be more dependent on external anchors to guide their behavior in unusual or unstructured circumstances (see also Chapter 2). Thus, personality differences may significantly affect the response of at least nonpatient samples to treatments designed to change the self-concept under restricted stimulation conditions.

Antista and Jones (1975) put 54 female university students into reduced stimulation. They found that over a 45-minute period, subjects became less anxious—contrary to the prediction and to early reports from sensory deprivation laboratories, but in harmony with more recent research—and there was a significant reduction in the discrepancy between the participants' perception of their actual self and their ideal self. In other words, the treatment led to better self-acceptance.

Kammerman (1977b) used the water immersion technique in a project relevant to self-concept change. This version of REST, even without any specific inputs, led to increases in enthusiasm and optimism, in the ability to cope with threatening and novel experiences, and probably in ego strength (although for this last phenomenon, an alternative interpretation of an increase in defensiveness is also feasible). When combined with self-enhancing messages, the treatment resulted in decreases on several clinical scales of the MMPI, increased self-insight, and an increase in the scope of the ego, all of which persisted during the 4-week followup period.

Negative evidence comes from three studies. In the first (Henrichs, 1963), the MMPI and a self-rating scale were administered three times: before, immediately at the end of, and 1 to 2 days after a 5-hour session. A taped message (identical to that previously used by the Adams group with hospitalized patients) and the REST treatment were varied independently, so that four different conditions were included in the study. Of the two major self-ratings, one (rate yourself as others see you) showed an improvement as a result of the messages, but not as a result of reduced stimulation nor of the combination of the two treatments. The other (rate yourself as you really are) showed a lower score for the two groups that had gone through REST than for the other two.

A number of explanations could be advanced for these findings. To begin with, the period of confinement may have been too brief for normal subjects to unfreeze so central a concept as self-evaluation, even though a similar period was sufficient for mentally disturbed patients and worked in some of the other studies described above. It is also possible that the message, which was strong enough to modify the subject's belief about what others thought of him, was not sufficient to change the more stable self-perception, even though again it had been effective with patients.

In a more recent study, Bentz (1978) reported essentially negative findings in a factorial investigation of the effects of a brief message and 40 minutes of stimulus reduction. Enhancement of self-concept was found for a group that heard the tape under normal environmental conditions, while there were no significant changes for the other three groups. The same pattern was found in a followup session 4 weeks afterwards. The author explained these findings on the basis of the difference between "normal" and clinical groups, suggesting that the college students used in his study were not highly motivated to change. This would be in contrast with patients or clients, who recognize that they have a problem and wish to solve it. The brief duration of the session contributed to the lack of effect.

The third paper to report a failure to find increased self-actualization (Wathney, 1978) used three tank sessions of $1^1/_2$ hours each. In one condition, REST was preceded by a taped message focusing on inner awareness and openness to new experiences. Neither the tank plus message group nor the tank only group showed higher increases on a measure of self-actualization than a control group. The author reports that many of the tank participants enjoyed the experience and claimed to have used the time to learn about themselves, solve problems, and make productive changes. Relaxation and calmness were frequently mentioned as the major effects of the REST session. The negative results on the written measure may have been due to an abnormally high mean pretest score, so that a ceiling effect on any increases was operating.

REST and Self-Exploration

In several programs using immersion, chamber confinement, or both, data were not collected in a structured fashion. However, the reports of the participants indicated changes that appeared to be relevant to the self-concept. These included increases in insight; more acceptance and/or understanding of one's own behavior, thoughts, relations with others, and place in the universe; greater confidence in one's ability to cope with problems; openness to a wide variety of novel experiences, some of them related to altered states of consciousness; and a general decrease in tension and anxiety. Some of the findings of such programs are summarized below.

As has been discussed before, the water immersion (tank isolation) technique invented by John C. Lilly has been billed as the most profound and the most stressful of REST methods. Reports had indicated that subjects could tolerate this situation for only a few hours, compared to several days or even weeks in the chamber. However, Lilly has apparently never held the view that the situation in itself is psychologically traumatic. In 1960, he wrote that in the tank "one gains an increased awareness of, and a willingness to move with, power, speed, and integrity along the lines of one's life situation along which one really and truly wishes to move."

Lilly has repeatedly argued that negative consequences are essentially a function of expectations. In this, he has consistently dissented from prevailing opinion, particularly during the early years. His recent book, *The Deep Self* (Lilly, 1977), is perhaps the most detailed exposition to date of the work that he has done with the tank, and supports by argument and anecdotal evidence the view that water immersion is not necessarily stressful and that it can in fact be beneficial and extremely enjoyable. Apparently he has not used the technique as a form of psychotherapy; rather, the people who have experienced it under his aegis use it for self-exploration and psychic growth.

Lilly's original starting point, before he opted for a paradigm shift from the standard concepts and methods of science, was a logical one. One principle of experimental science is that any phenomenon is best studied in isolation from as many potential contaminating factors as possible. Accordingly, Lilly concluded that the appropriate way to study the "body-brain-mind" system was to isolate it from the influences of the external world, thus permitting the examination of only the system itself. As he says, and as many researchers in the field can confirm (even though they may disagree with his particular approach), "This method gave a new source of data of great richness" (1977, p. 71).

His later theoretical approach is founded on the concept that the current view of the mind as essentially contained within the brain is an inadequate paradigm, and that the tank situation has the potential for allowing the mind to operate at a much higher level of degrees of freedom than does any other commonly encountered setting. Lilly draws a parallel between the states of detachment and enlightenment emphasized in Eastern religions (e.g., nirvana, satori) and the effects of the tank. As discussed in Chapter 7, REST may indeed serve as a rapid, environmentally produced analogue of meditation states, not requiring the long training and developed competence upon which the latter depend.

In Lilly's recent work, the individuals involved were volunteers who requested a chance to experience the tank, and paid for the use of the facilities, often as part of a 5-day workshop in self-exploration. The isolation tank was located in a dark and soundproofed environment, with body temperature water mixed with Epsom salts so as to increase flotation. The tank was considerably smaller than the rather large facilities used in the original immersion research. Apparently, no monitors were provided, so that each individual in the tank was completely isolated until somebody came to inform him or her that time was up. After emergence from the tank, each person was asked to write out a report concerning the phenomena encountered during the isolation period.

Lilly sees the tank as having two major uses. One is for individuals who are satisfied with and thoroughly tied into modal Western concepts about the relationship between the individual and the external world: that is, for whom the external world is the only reality, and for whom the internal world of imagery and fantasy is perceived as something unreal. If the individual is satisfied and content in this mode, the isolation tank can be used as a place to rest and relax and also as a place to consider one's problems and work out solutions with a minimum of distraction. This is, of course, the approach most similar to those for which chamber isolation has been utilized, as in the cases of individuals with personal problems such as smoking and overweight. Some of Lilly's subjects have also used the tank in this way, as quotations in the book point out.

For another group of people, the distinction between external circumstances and internal processes is not so clear-cut. They perceive both sets of phenomena as partaking of the quality of realness. These people may be interested in self-analysis, meditation, transcendental experiences, and altered states of consciousness. For them, the isolation environment is useful because it minimizes interactions with the external reality and allows the internal domain to be more fully explored. This, too, has been reported in chamber confinement, and noted in the tank logs of Lilly's group.

There is, of course, no reason why any particular individual cannot have the REST environment function in both ways, although perhaps not simultaneously. Still, it is likely that differences in personality and cognitive set will lead to an asymmetrical division of these two uses for any particular individual. The different, but not incompatible, approaches to the use of REST with essentially normal individuals are well encapsulated in Lilly's summary: "The tank experience is a very refreshing one, a resting one. If one wants to push further than this, one can do so to the limits of one's mental discipline and to the limits of one's imagination" (1977, p. 31).

Lilly's theoretical argument is that the tank enables one to separate the mind from the body and to become aware of "hundreds if not thousands of other states of being in which one's consciousness is unimpaired and apparently disconnected from the brain and the body" (p. 104). These states include dream travel to other worlds, the appearance of extraterrestrial organisms, and the individual himself changing into such an organism. While all of the experiences are dreamlike, awareness, consciousness, and participation are much more vivid than usual. The many unknown aspects of the human mind, which we have been "metaprogrammed" to ignore and which water immersion permits to emerge, are what Lilly means by the phrase "deep self."

Whether or not the theory is valid, and whether or not the data support it or are even relevant to it, the excerpts from post-immersion essays are fascinating. The book contains 78 such excerpts taken from people ranging in age up to 70 years who have spent as much as 10 hours in the tank (the pressure of time in Lilly's workshops has been such that only 1 or 2 hours per session could be permitted as the outside limit). In the beginning, subjects concentrate on the environment and on their own physical and psychological reactions; but as tank time increases, the participants more and more note such things as relaxation, feelings of love and warmth, and vivid, novel and pleasant imagery. The aftereffects are apparently also quite positive, mostly consisting of vivid memories, deep relaxation, restfulness, and pleasant sleep. Many, although not all, of the participants wanted to repeat the experience, and quite a few have had the chance to do so. Five of the respondents eventually went on to obtain their own private immersion tanks. The excerpts, of course, are selective, which may explain why there are so few negative comments.

One very helpful and informative aspect of Lilly's book is a list of considerations that would help individuals to run their own tank installation, including building directions and information about maintenance. There is also a discussion of factors such as various aspects of physical health, drug use, and other characteristics that might affect one's experience in the situation. Addresses are given for several sources of prefabricated or custom-built facilities. Lilly's book also reprints, as have several previous ones, some of the technical publications concerning his first experiments in the area.

Lilly's work leaves a number of questions unanswered. It appears to indicate that set was indeed a crucial factor in the "stress" results of early water immersion studies. It does not tell us to what extent the relaxation and vivid imagery found in his current project are also the effects of expectancy, although it does seem likely that the individuals participating in his workshops are those who find altered states of consciousness and similar unusual experiences to be both pleasant and nonthreatening. The results are compatible with the hypothesis that the disorganizing effects of isolation on such people as castaways are a cultural artifact (see Suedfeld, 1974a); but the exact role of isolation and stimulus reduction, as opposed to the orientation that the subject brings into the situation with him, still remains to be elucidated. One thing, at any rate, seems clear. Even the supposedly most stringent experimental REST situation can be personally beneficial (at least by the evaluation of the subjects themselves), enjoyable, and relaxing.

In a similar program, using both a water tank and chamber REST, Hoffman (personal communication, 1976) quotes several of his subjects as having had self-fulfilling and transcendental experiences. These include a feeling of harmony with the universe, mellowness, complete relaxation, a realization of chronic sensory overload in normal life, total enjoyment, and so on. In fact, one subject said:

Let me tell you why I think the authorities or the wider society or the 'higher class' groups, you know, whatever, *wouldn't* want this out on the street, available to the everyday consumer, like you can buy a washing machine. This would not only bring people to a political awareness and consciousness of the things around them, but it would also bring them to an awareness of themselves and their direction in society today, civilization today. It would bring them to an awareness of producing positive things and going into positive directions and looking for positive answers. And I think it would serve—to have people walking around like people are supposed to be. You would have people walking around in the society undoubtedly giving a critical analysis of what's going on, of what's going on you know in day to day life around here, what we represent as a country and what we are doing around the world. People would have the critical analysis and it would serve the purpose of the working class people of America and the working class peoples of the world. . . . It's not just an escape, although some people could use it as an escape, but they already have so many, drugs . . . I think this machine is like a drug, in that it brings people to this 'high,' brings unto this conscious high. I think that this is definitely a road to consciousness. There are many roads to consciousness, but I think this one is positive, inexpensive, profitable to the individual, at his own pace and time, at his own level of awareness. . . .

Following the path laid down by Lilly, Taylor (1973; 1977) emphasized the effects of the "scientific approach" and "behavioral frame of reference" that have characterized most research on the effects of stimulus reduction. Taylor argues that the negative expectations of the experimenters overwhelmed any other variables involved, resulting in the frequent findings of performance deterioration and aversiveness in the early literature. This, he feels, has led to the decline and fall of "sensory deprivation" research.

Taylor took the attitude "that inner exploration and inner experience could be a situation of exciting self-discovery rather than a fear-provoking event" (1973, p. 70), and that REST could be an environment in which this kind of exploration and experience could be facilitated. His thesis research, in which a total of approximately 120 subjects spent varying periods of time in an anechoic chamber, was designed to test these hypotheses. There was little attempt to standardize subject characteristics. The participants included high school and college students, yoga instructors, a prisoner, and a one-year old child going through the experience together with her parents. Some of these individuals went into the chamber alone, others in groups of up to seven. The last 49 participants made up the "core sample of the study."

Approximately 90% of the sample indicated that they had enjoyed the experience. Significant decreases in heart rate and blood pressure were found from before to after REST. There was the usual tendency toward underestimating time spent in the chamber, with less accurate estimates being positively correlated with enjoyment of the experience. There were no differences between the experimental and the control group on a multiplication task, both groups improving significantly from the pre- to the post-test. Taylor (1973) also reports that followup interviews as much as a year after the experience indicated that many participants judged the session to have had a lasting positive influence. Two cases reported in detail indicate that the long-term effects included increases in the ability to make autonomous decisions independently of social and other external pressures (see also Chapter 8).

These findings are not terribly novel, being quite compatible with the major thrust of the experimental literature. The subjective reports of the participants were more striking, reminding one very strongly of those made by people going through the water tank immersion project described by Lilly. There was a great deal of pleasant fantasy and imagery. Most subjects began the chamber session with a keen awareness of the environment. The focus of attention eventually switched to physical sensations from the sensory receptors, and then became increasingly inner-centered. Some subjects eventually reached a point of separation from the self that Taylor has called "psychological suspended animation." Some of the descriptions of this state sound very much like those found in deep stages of meditation and contemplation.

The use of self-imposed REST, aside from such mildly stimulus-reducing activities as camping, has found more formal means in the marketing of isolation chambers (e.g., by Neiman-Marcus) and water immersion tanks (Bernstein, 1976; Lilly, 1977). In at least six states of the United States ("Tanking it up," 1978) it is now possible—and quite cheap—to rent tank time. The requirements and expenses for a stimulus reducing room are, of course, even lower.

A letter from Lee Perry (personal communication, August 1, 1978), one of the owners of the Samadhi Tank Co., indicates that approximately 300 people have used tank facilities owned by the company. About 40 people have used the tank between 10 and 30 times, for 1 hour per session, and 60 others have used it between 3 and 5 times. Some of these individuals later went on to buy their own tanks. Apparently, over 200 people now possess their own facilities, and the average use is reported to be several hundred hours of tank time. Some people who own tanks use them for an hour or more every day. Many of the users are engaged in creative work, and feel that the tank experience is useful in facilitating their productivity. Students and mothers of small children are also reported to be among the satisfied customers. One newspaper article on this growing practice notes the possibility that water immersion can help alleviate physical ailments. According to an unnamed company in Arizona, people who suffer from chronic illnesses find that the weightless feeling of floating in the tank is accompanied by relief from pain, a relief that sometimes persists even after their return to normal environments. On the other hand, a California couple who had used the tank regularly was quoted as claiming that it did something bizarre to their relationship. A psychiatrist stated that unstable participants might be precipitated into a psychotic state, and that "medically, the treatment does nothing more than an ordinary warm bath." The data—if any—on which he based these two assertions are, unfortunately, not presented in the quotation nor in the article.

Perry points out that almost everyone first enters the tank with some anxiety about darkness and confinement, apprehensions about drowning, and a fear of "finding out something about themselves that they don't want to know." Apparently, however, most people find the actual experience relaxing, satisfying, pleasant, and even exciting. One typical participant reported, "Being at one with yourself and so aware of your body and mind in total darkness. It's total bliss!" (Perry, personal communication, August 1, 1978).

REST AND SELF-TRANSCENDENCE

Traditionally, seekers of transcendental experience have used solitude and stimulus restriction as a road to that goal. The use of this procedure by the ancient Greeks is mentioned in Chapter 7. Obviously, while communion with the Oracle was in many instances a therapeutic effort, it was equally a communication with the gods. Nor were the Greeks the only ancient people to perceive that the deity could be approached best under circumstances where there were no distractions.

Mystical Experiences

From the beginning, both Eastern and Western religious traditions have maintained that transcendental experiences are best sought in solitude. In her classic treatment of mysticism, Underhill (1911/1961) says: "Hence something equivalent to the solitude of the wilderness is an essential part of mystical education" (p. 173). The thousands of mystics who have pursued this course in the Himalayas, the Indian jungles, the Arabian desert, and the Alps, give full support to this point of view. In isolation and sensory reduction one becomes able to empty the inner self so that it can be filled with God. The efficacy of this precept can be seen in the uniformity that underlies many of the practices of yoga, Zen, Tao, Sufism and Christian monasticism (Arberry, 1950; Goleman, 1977; David-Neel, 1965; De Ropp, 1968; Hilliard, 1946; Merton, 1957; Naranjo and Ornstein, 1971; Pelletier and Garfield, 1976; Suzuki, 1956; Watts, 1957).

The varieties of meditation will not be reviewed here, since a large number of such analyses are already available and some discussion of this literature is presented in connection with the use of meditation as a psychotherapeutic technique (Chapter 7). One interesting point should, however, be made. That is the fact that altered states of consciousness may be reached through meditation either by the use of stimulus reduction or, on the contrary, by very high levels of input. In the latter case, the stimuli are typically rhythmical and repetitive, resulting in an environment best described as high-intensity monotony. Such procedures include, for example, rhythmic drumming, chanting, and dancing (Carrington, 1978); and in a more mundane setting, long-distance running (Solomon and Bumpus, 1978). Long-distance swimming can have the same effect ("Woman fails," 1975).

Solitude, with or without the additional trimmings, has widely been thought to put the individual in touch with the Infinite. Whether this metaphysical contact is with something inside the person or out in the universe appears to be defined largely in terms of cultural norms. Frequently, the major outcome is an enhancement of magical-religious power or communion with beings that hold such power. Among many North American Indian tribes, the expectation was that the young man on a lonely spirit quest would discover his totemic animal, his magic symbols, songs, and visions (Cooper, 1956; Fortune, 1932; Honigmann, 1949; Murie, 1914; Sapir and Swadesh, 1955; Tabbel, 1967). In the Near East, the isolated wanderer could encounter God, as did Moses and the Old Testament prophets (Berdyaev, 1938; Exodus 3:24–33); the devil, as did Christ (Matthew 4); or demons, succubi, and incubi, as did St. Anthony and the other early Christian hermits (Anson, 1964; Kingsley, undated; Waddell, 1942).

Not only did Moses and Jesus first achieve the insights that led to their ministry while isolated in the wilderness—so did Mohammed and the Buddha, thus marking a noteworthy similarity among the founders of the four great religions of the world. Toynbee has said that in his opinion neither heredity nor environment, nor the combination of the two, can "fully account for the behavior of Hosea, Zarathustra, Jeremiah, the Buddha, Socrates, Jesus, Muhammad, and St. Francis of Assisi" (1973, p. 119). Little is known of the personal lives of Hosea and Jeremiah. But contemplation and meditation in solitude are known to have played an important role in the spiritual development of each of the others named, with the exception of Socrates (see the Bible; Bishop, 1974; Potter, 1958).

Toynbee's proposition is difficult to refute, especially with the word "fully" included; but it is interesting that seminal experiences in conditions of aloneness in the wild have been recorded in the lives of five of these spiritual giants, as well as of many less well-known religious figures.

Modern mystics similarly use periods of isolation in the desert or in other remote locations to achieve altered states of consciousness and transcendence (e.g., Lilly, 1972). Many orders of monks, whether Oriental or Western, have found that, in the words of Thomas Merton, "It is in silence, and not in commotion, in solitude and not in crowds, that God best likes to reveal himself most intimately to men" (1957, p. 38). Merton, who is probably the most lyrical of the proponents of solitude in this context, draws many parallels between the early desert fathers and the European monks, as well as between these latter and their Oriental counterparts. Extolling the role of aloneness as a contributor to the religious life, Merton remarks on the growth of cenobitic and eremitic orders in modern America despite the essential philosophical hostility between the monastic life and our societal norms. Religious retreats, for laymen and clergy, frequently incorporate periods of solitude for the same purpose (e.g., Havens, 1969).

Initiation Rites

Analyzing literature that is popular among adolescents, Tyre (1978) argues that 90% of the novels are constructed along the same six points. These six are the characteristics that define "the archetypal initiation rite," and solitude is one of them. A period of isolation has been a central feature of the initiation rituals of a large number of societies (see Chapter 1). The fact that this phenomenon has been found in North America, the Middle East, Africa, Asia, and Australia seems to indicate that there is a universal appreciation of the possible values of being alone in a natural environment, even one that is demanding or dangerous. The specific features of the natural surroundings do not seem to be a crucial issue. Whether the young man went into the desert, the prairie, the forest, or the mountains, his experiences closely resembled those of adolescent members of other cultures who undertook the same quest in their own, possibly very different, habitat. This similarity is frequently obscured by the individual characteristics of the ritual, and by the different interpretations that were placed upon the subjective experience of the initiate.

To begin with, we must not ignore the challenge to survival posed by the wilderness rite of passage, and its contribution to tribal cohesiveness and pride. In a way, it may have served as the equivalent of a final examination: the culminating test of the youngster's ability to apply the hunting, food-gathering, shelter-building, and other skills that he had been learning from his elders. While in the normal course of events he would relatively seldom have to exercise these skills in isolation, it was as well to be prepared for the eventuality of being separated from the group and thrown upon his own resources. The experience may also have served to heighten feelings of identification among the group of young people who underwent it at approximately the same time, increasing the cohesiveness of hunting bands, war parties, and similar cooperative groups. In much the same way, other age-related male bonds based on common hardships simultaneously undergone were to be found in the *impi* of the Zulu kingdom and the conscript classes of nineteenth and twentieth century European countries. The coupling of such in-group comradeship with feelings of self-reliance, communion with nature and with oneself, freedom from societal restrictions and intrusions, and escape from everyday life, has characterized many movements throughout history. The most well known to modern Westerners are the scouting movement begun by Baden-Powell in Britain in the early part of the century, the German *Wandervögel* who took to the roads in great numbers in the period between the two World Wars, and the current interest in camping and hiking as well as in more permanent returns to isolated rural settings now being observed in North America.

In some tribes, it was the custom for the solitary individual to fast, and sometimes to torture himself or be tortured by such means as driving thorns into the flesh. In some cases, hallucinogenic plants were ingested. Some cultures confined the individual to a very small area, while in others he wandered about. The timing and duration of the initiation also varied widely. In some cultures it lasted only a few days, in others as much as a month. In most societies it was an ordeal that adolescents, mostly males, had to go through once in their lifetime; in others it was performed repeatedly, either at more or less set times or at periods of particular importance or crisis; in still others it became an accepted way of life for at least a recognizable subgroup within the culture. It then lost the role of a puberty rite and instead became an alternative lifestyle. In some Australian aboriginal groups, almost complete isolation was imposed for periods of several months at a time, again and again, during a long initiatory phase.

REST may also be seen as a rite of passage, just as it is in the case of the adolescent tribesman. Many of our participants have repeatedly invoked their experience as a marker than delineated their earlier selves from the new, healthier, self-efficacious individuals who were successfully coping with problems that previously left them helpless. In this sense, there is some kind of rebirth that occurs in REST, just as it does among people undergoing the procedure in ritual ways in other cultures.

Reduced Stimulation and Altered States of Consciousness (ASCs)

What are we to make of the mystical experiences reported in this litera-ture? We can, of course, take them at face value, but several alternative interpretations also present themselves. One of these is that solitude—in combination with hunger, chemical agents, physical pain, and perhaps a strong expectancy set—induces an altered state of consciousness that includes visual and auditory hallucinations, delusions, and vivid fanta-sies. A tribesman may interpret such occurrences as demonstrating divine or magical intervention, while the modern Westerner would view them as signs of mental breakdown (cf. Suedfeld, 1974a). Alternatively, we may make due allowances for the stress factors involved, and particularly for the differences in interpretation which the cognitive styles of different cultures impose on any class of experiences. We might then agree with an American youth commenting on "solo," the solitary component of the Outward Bound wilderness experience: "I did not meet God during Solo, I met myself" (O'Conner, 1974). The creative and ethical insights ob-tained by solitary initiates and mystics may, in fact, reflect their ability to reach deeper levels of thought and emotion than is customary under normal conditions. The way in which the results of this ability are inter-preted differ, of course, as a function of the person's learning and socio-cultural background.

Altered states of consciousness have been defined as situations in which the individual "clearly feels a *qualitative* shift in his pattern of mental functioning" (Tart, 1969, p. 2). This is going substantially beyond the changes on measures of self-esteem and even the general feelings of relaxation and serenity described by many REST participants. But it does fit the mental changes that characterize meditation states and the tran-scendental experiences reported by Lilly and similar investigators. Such events have been noted even in the course of traditional REST research. In our program of experiments, for example, a number of out-of-body experiences have been reported (including one by a member of the re-search team during a stint in the chamber; see Suedfeld and Borrie, 1978b). One problem with the scientific paradigm followed by most work-ers in this area is that it tends to concentrate on group results and quanti-tative data, so that such occurrences usually do not appear in the pub-lished research even when they have been mentioned by subjects. However, unpublished comments of several researchers and subjects have convinced me that this is not by any means a very rare phenomenon.

REST researchers have concerned themselves but little with the ques-tion of altered states of consciousness. The major exception, of course, is Lilly (e.g., 1972). His early work in this area includes the description of his own transcendental experiences while undergoing water immersion (frequently under the influence of LSD) while his later reports, as described above, present similar experiences on the part of other REST participants. These results are not peculiar to the water immersion environment. Hoffman (personal communication, 1976) and Taylor (1973), whose subjects went through chamber confinement, also tabulated significant alterations in the state of consciousness.

One thing that should be noted is that these projects, which proceeded from a "humanistic psychology" paradigm rather than from the more standard experimental or clinical approaches, had several things in common. All three of the project directors are people who themselves have used the REST environment as an aid to self-exploration and personal growth, and have had pleasant and important experiences, including ASCs, while in the chamber or tank. As a consequence, their expectations were probably quite different from those of most experimenters in the field. Second, and again contributing to possible expectation effects, the participants in these projects were also attuned to humanistic psychology. Many of them had experimented with various psychedelic drugs, meditation techniques, group procedures, and other aspects of the human potential movement. Many of these people had had previous ASC experiences, sometimes under conditions similar to REST, and were obviously open to further experiences of the same sort. Does this make a difference? One example may illustrate how it can affect the literature. Reported visual sensations, when experienced by subjects in traditional laboratory experiments, have frequently been categorized as hallucinations symptomatic of a temporary mental disturbance induced by REST. The same sensations reported by REST participants who are familiar with altered states of consciousness are interpreted as signs of an ASC and are responded to as exciting and pleasurable phenomena.

Altered states of consciousness develop only gradually in REST (see Taylor, 1973). As I have already mentioned, the initial reaction is heightened alertness to features of the environment and to bodily sensations. At least for some people, the focus of attention then switches to internal cognitive and emotional experiences. This state is probably the most frequent and most conducive to therapeutic progress in the REST situation. But some subjects go further, to vivid imagery (which Taylor calls "visual translation and projection of cognitive and emotional states" 1973, p. 125). Some such transcendental experiences, by the way, have also been reported by patients near death in hospital. The extremely vivid relieving of past experiences reported by such patients, by isolated explorers, and by subjects in isolation research, has been compared with "retrocognition" as one of the forms of higher knowledge in Buddhist philosophy (Sharma, 1978). Beyond this phase comes a state of flowing imagery, interspersed with mental blankness and eventually a state of detachment, serenity, tranquility, and unity with the infinite. This state has been reported by subjects in several REST projects, by mystics and meditators, and by pilots flying alone at extremely high altitudes for long periods of time (Clark and Graybiel, 1957).

One major problem, of course, is to find an acceptable definition of when a shift in the pattern of mental functioning is "qualitative." To a great extent, this can be a function of individual differences in expectancy or in definition. For the most part, drastic ASCs are not found except among subjects who have experienced them in other situations before they went into REST, and who were expecting them to occur during the session. A dream, reported sensation, or fantasy may or may not be considered as fitting the criterion by a particular researcher or participant. But the REST setting does appear to elicit fairly high proportions of what one might call low-level ASCs—changes in cognition and perception that do not represent a drastic break with normal experience but are different enough to be worthy of notice (Suedfeld and Borrie, 1978b). In this, the effects of REST are quite similar to those of hypnosis (Weitzenhoffer, 1978).

REST IN NATURAL SETTINGS

One aspect of the modern uses of reduced stimulation is the recent growth of interest in leaving the urban environment, for either long or short periods, in order to return to a less stimulating and less crowded natural milieu. Visits to wilderness areas in North America have grown at least 15-fold since World War II (Lucas, 1978). We should think of this movement as being once again on the upward portion of a cycle. It has been with us probably since the first cities began, and has waxed and waned throughout recorded history. As we have seen, it has always been an integral part of some religions and cultures; but in those with which we are most familiar, its strength appears to be related to the stresses involved in coping with the modal way of life which is highly social and rich in stimuli.

Camping Alone

Perhaps the closest to the original initiation rite aspect of wilderness solitude is the solitary vigil as practiced in some summer camps for adolescents, and the "solo" experience incorporated in many of the programs of Outward Bound. An expert in the field has estimated that there are over 300 organizations in North America alone that have wilderness programs, most of which include some period of solitude (Alistair McArthur, personal communication, 1977). In established summer camps, this may involve a few days on an island or similar geographical feature within the boundaries of the camp. In some cases, this practice originally involved a variety of somewhat artificial features. These tend to drop out as the intrinsic value of the experience, without embellishments, is realized. For example, one Canadian summer camp began with a "lonely vigil" lasting only overnight. Upon his return, the camper was expected to recite an Indian legend and was then awarded an Indian name which was inscribed on a permanent plaque. While the results of this experience for most campers appeared to be positive, it was felt that the artificial Indian trimmings "detracted from what was meant to be a very personal experience" and they were therefore dropped (David Campbell, personal communication, June, 1974).

In contrast to the relatively sedate vigil conditions of most commercial camps, the Outward Bound schools tend to put the individual into a highly demanding and challenging natural environment. Unlike summer campers, Outward Bound members do not have the easy option of terminating their solo experience on account of bad weather. They stay out for several days living off the land, and are usually not continuously monitored by counselors. Some of the literature emphasizes the solo's function as a survival experience and as an initiation rite (e.g., Katz, 1973). But physical survival is not the major issue, any more than it was for the prairie Indian adolescent. The focus is on character development, self-appraisal, and reflection (Colorado Outward Bound School, 1977; Katz, 1973).

The preparation of participants for the solo experience has undergone some criticism. In an interesting pamphlet, excerpted from a book by Katz (1973), the solo is compared to the Indian vision quests mentioned previously, to Jesuit spiritual retreats, and to Zen meditation sessions. One criticism is that while the staff carefully trains students for physical survival and competence, there is relatively little emphasis on readiness for psychological coping and growth. The author recommends that the training should be expanded to prepare participants for experiencing altered states of consciousness and for deriving insight and personal growth from such occurrences.

This is an exact counterpart to the suggestion that Westerners who are cast into solitude abruptly and without preparation, such as shipwrecked sailors or stranded explorers, may suffer significant psychological stress even though they may be perfectly competent to cope with physical problems. It has been noted that such reactions may lead to early death among a high proportion of physically uninjured survivors of shipwrecks and plane crashes (Bombard, 1953; Terence O. Moore, personal communication, November 30, 1978). Much of this high level of stress is presumably the outcome of shock, uncertainty of rescue, and sudden and dramatic change in circumstances. However, in some unknown percentage of cases, there may be a contributory factor arising from those unusual experiences that we have characterized as hallmarks of altered states of consciousness: extremely vivid dreams, illusions, hallucinations, reverie, inexplicable storms of emotion, and the like.

It has been hypothesized that these experiences occur as the organism tries to generate internal stimulation. Such actions are needed to bring the general level of information and stimulation up to the accustomed norm, compensating for the paucity of external inputs (Suedfeld, 1974a). Recommendations for training to cope with or even to enjoy such experiences should relate both to the avoidance of psychological breakdown in cases of traumatic episodes involving solitude and to the maximization of personal growth and benefit from planned and voluntary periods of aloneness. This suggestion is quite compatible with experimental findings that "sensory deprivation" is most poorly tolerated by those who find primary process phenomena (including strong fantasy and emotions) anxiety-arousing and uncontrollable (Goldberger, 1961; Goldberger and Holt, 1961a, b; Myers, 1969; Myers and Kushner, 1970).

Wilderness Therapy

So far, this section has been concerned with beneficial, but perhaps not therapeutic, uses of the wilderness experience. Although the literature is relatively scanty, there is an increasing use of what has been termed "therapeutic camping." In this situation, children with emotional or physical problems are removed from their normal home and school environments and given a chance to practice social and physical skills in the camp situation. The practice is still in its infancy and has not been systematically evaluated, although some positive results have been documented (Bchar and Stephens, 1978). Fortunately, the Devereux Foundation appears to be interested in this technique, and further research may result from its involvement (Quackenbush, 1977).

Heck (1976a; personal communication, June 20, 1978) has been conducting wilderness workshops in which small groups go into a desert or mountainous area for either 3 or 7 days. During this time, the emphasis is on unstructured time for contemplation, coupled with some instruction in neuropsychology, existential psychology, and the mythology of the American Indian. Basic instruction in survival and camping techniques is also included. The benefits to participants derive from the opportunity to reflect, to enjoy the beauty of the natural environment, and to explore and learn to appreciate solitude.

In his dissertation, Heck (1976b) studied the way in which people responded to three events: a wilderness trip in which a therapist drew their attention to natural features and interspersed self-exploration and solitary contemplation with group discussion of their experiences; a structured group interaction in which the subjects listened to encounter tapes designed for personal growth; and a control condition covering normal sleeping hours. Data were generated by before- and after-treatment administrations of the Fundamental Interpersonal Relations Orientation-Behavior scale, from which Heck derived three measures. The first, an index of loneliness, was the sum of expressed inclusion and expressed affection from the FIRO-B; the second, solitude, was the sum of wanted inclusion and wanted affection; and the third, aloneness, was the difference between the solitude score and the loneliness score.

There were intergroup differences before the treatment. For example, the group of volunteers for the wilderness experience was younger, included more women, and had less graduate education (which is probably related to the age difference). There were also initial differences among the groups on the FIRO-B scales.

The interpretation of the results depends on whether one accepts the author's setting of the alpha level at .30, or insists on a more conventional level such as .05. On the basis of the less stringent criterion, Heck concludes that "therapeutically induced isolation" (i.e., wilderness) led to the highest degree of positive affect about being alone, with the control condition being higher on this measure than the structured group treatment (encounter tape). The encounter tape condition, which fostered self-disclosure, also led to a higher desire for solitude than either of the other two situations.

Unfortunately for those who may want to be more traditional in the use of the F test, none of the differences reached a significance level of .05 or better, although several were between .07 and .10. The use of one-way analyses of variance rather than more complex techniques (given the initial intergroup differences, preferably including analyses of covariance) adds to the reader's problems. The fact that participants could select which experience they were willing to undergo not only confused the numerical data but also makes the interpretation of the results conceptually difficult. Perhaps the most useful view of this study is that it is an intriguing pilot attempt, which should be followed up with a less problematic design, procedure, and analysis.

Actually, very few of the empirical studies provided more useful data than Heck's. In fact, even the attempt to provide a control treatment is unusual. A recent review (Kahoe, 1979) showed generally positive results from over 30 studies using "wilderness therapy" with adolescents and young adults. Only three reports included control groups, and the majority failed to control the relevant personality, treatment, and environmental factors.

Theoretical Bases of the Wilderness Phenomenon

Lance Olsen, founder and editor of the *Wilderness Psychology Newsletter,* has argued that the wilderness is therapeutic in general. To begin with, the natural environment does not reinforce behaviors that are maladaptive, interpersonally exploitative or deceptive, or that substitute emotional reactions for solutions. This aspect of wilderness therapy apparently combines the virtues of behavior modification and Rational-Emotive Therapy. Second, the evaluative neutrality of the natural environment frees the individual from artificial normative restraints and invidious comparisons, allowing each person to cope with his surroundings in harmony with his own preferences, personality, and abilities. Third, Olsen mentions the difficulty of successfully projecting one's own feelings and philosophy upon the environment. Unlike in social situations, our projections upon nature are so obvious that they eventually bring us face to face with ourselves. Incidentally, Olsen has spent long periods living in solitude in undeveloped areas, an experience that not many professional psychologists have had. As a result, his insights are the more impressive for being based on both personal reactions and behavioral science training. He is one of several workers in this area who emphasize that isolation is a crucial component of the beneficial aspects of the wilderness experience (see Kahoe, 1979).

One writer in the *Wilderness Psychology Newsletter,* Silvestri (1978), identified two of the aspects that wilderness shares with REST. One is stimulus reduction, which Silvestri sees as necessary to overcome the defense mechanisms developed to protect the self from the sensory bombardment of normal life. In his view, these defense mechanisms have become too efficient, so that even desirable and "human" messages fail to get through. The wilderness experience, sometimes coupled with other techniques such as meditation, overcomes this block. The second factor, to which I shall refer later in regard to REST, is the remediation of what Schwartz (in preparation) calls "disregulation." In the wilderness one recognizes again the inescapable relationship between one's behavior and the results of that behavior. As Silvestri says, "I think one of the most valuable aspects is that [the wilderness experience] provides one with a sense of security in that Mother Nature is always just. Whatever one does, or fails to do, one pays the price; sometimes dearly. When my life dangles at the end of a rope over a two hundred foot cliff, I had better not made a mistake. If I do, I pay—unquestionably. If I make a mistake at home, there's a good chance I can wrangle out of it whether it be a ticket, my taxes, or whatever."

Hummel (1977), in considering the response to what he calls "solitude-in-wilderness," emphasizes personal autonomy and the ability to survive as sources of reward associated with that environment. By analyzing some of the reports of famous individuals who have discussed such experiences in their own lives, Hummel identifies another benefit: people gain the ability to address themselves to questions of self-identity and self-actualization. These, of course, are issues that also engage the interest of many clients undergoing REST. Hummel's ideas concerning appropriate research directions on problems raised by the wilderness experience include the need for representative subject samples, the study of individual differences, the desirability of establishing whether literal solitude is necessary for the effects to occur, and a variety of other questions relevant to the work of environmental psychologists.

Kahoe (1979) has argued that the responses evoked by the wilderness are more "natural" in an evolutionary sense, and Rolston (1975) sees the wilderness as a place where human beings can be reunited with their ancient roots. This explanation is quite similar to the sense of the "walkabout" to the sacred places of creation that Australian aborigines periodically undertake. But the pattern formed by man in nature is not wholly complete, because the human being is conscious of himself, of his surroundings, and of the consciousness of other beings. He is a shaper and may be a protector of the environment through which he moves. He further uses solitude to gain both distance from and psychological togetherness with his fellows: "Alone we cannot be human. Yet we cannot be human until we are alone" (p. 125).

Other explanations for the beneficial effects of solitude in natural environments have been based on a variety of theoretical approaches. One that has close links to experimental psychology is based upon optimal levels of stimulation. The argument here is that the normal environment of technological societies is chronically overstimulating, and that the retreat to nature serves to balance out the load of stimulation and information impact until it reaches a more tolerable level. Such explanations may or may not use arousal as an intervening variable that reflects the state of the organism as it responds to environmental conditions. The crucial variables may be absolute levels and kinds of stimulation, information, social density, complexity, problem-solving and decision-making requirements, stimulus diversity or change, or any combination of these and other factors; the basic theoretical standpoint remains the same. As the reader will have seen throughout the book, I find theories based on optimal levels of stimulation fairly persuasive, although not yet sufficiently specific. In consequence, I think it is quite likely that as the levels of arousal or stress stemming from conditions of modern urban life increase, more and more people will seek periods of time-out. In view of the intrinsic attractions of nature, one would predict that many such people would look for relief in that direction.

Wohlwill's (1973) version of this approach argues that the major attraction of the wilderness is that it is a "non-responsive environment." He proposes that a major, but largely overlooked, difference between natural and man-made milieux is that in our normal daily life we are constantly involved in person-environment feedback loops. Everything the individual does causes some responsive modification in his environment, to which he must in turn respond. As a consequence of this reaction, the environment changes again. These interactions may be impersonal and physical, as in driving a car, or interpersonal and symbolic, as in a debate.

If these interactions are prolonged to the point that they overload the capacity for continued adjustment, they may lead to fatigue and depression. Equanimity may be restored by going into the wilderness, where both the inanimate and the animate environment tend to be nonreactive to individual human beings. The mountains, streams, and trees are stable and unchanging; the animals are elusive and distant. The individual may act upon the environment as he wishes, by passively enjoying it, by seeking to test himself against it, or by trying to blend into it. All strategies are possible, and all fail to make a dent in nature. It is this characteristic that makes the wilderness so therapeutic for some people, and at the same time so stressful for those who depend upon consensual validation and reinforcement from others to maintain their psychological balance.

Of course, the wilderness is one milieu where the techniques adopted by city dwellers to deal with excessive information input are not necessary. Thus, the individual is able to attend to fine distinctions in the environment, to regard ground as well as figure, and to involve himself in the problems of others. All of these behaviors would be time- and attention-consuming luxuries in more highly information-loaded environments (Milgram, 1970). The wilderness ethic of appreciation without exploitation, and cooperative altruism, is made possible by these conditions, as are the contemplative attitude and willingness to help strangers that characterize many dwellers in solitude (see e.g., Hill, 1940).

The wilderness also provides privacy, a condition which otherwise can frequently be found only by making oneself anonymous in a crowd or by erecting psychological barriers against others (Westin, 1970). If one accepts Altman's (1975) definition of privacy as the selective control of access to the self, it become obvious that the individual's ability to exercise this kind of control is maximized under conditions of relatively low social density. To begin with, there may be a temporal balancing system similar to those hypothesized to exist for arousal and information load. Periods of relatively low privacy (or privacy achieved only with difficulty) experienced in the normal urban setting may be redressed, and any stress resulting from them dissipated, by periods of solitude with no intrusions. Second, a period of withdrawal may increase the feeling of autonomy and freedom from territorial intrusions that are such important aspects of privacy (Proshansky, Ittelson and Rivlin, 1970; Westin, 1970). Last, there is a possibility that after a solitary period the individual may be much more open to intimate interaction with others than he was before. If we accept the idea of a homeostatic moderate level of privacy, it would seem logical that after a period of interaction motivation would shift in the direction away from aloneness (Altman, 1975; Wohlwill, 1974).

Finally, the wilderness induces a feeling of independence from others. It is one of the conditions under which the individual can do essentially what he wants without being restricted and without violating the usual norms that define and dictate courtesy, conformity, and face maintenance (Goffman, 1959; Kelvin, 1973). This quality of wilderness, leading to freedom from prescribed roles and behaviors, is also mentioned in Kahoe's (1979) review.

In considering the effects of natural REST environments, two major sets of findings must be considered. Although they are qualitatively quite different, both have been reported by many writers and both appear to be important. One of these is the transcendental, mystical state of mind that some isolated individuals, as well as some tank and chamber subjects, seem to enter. These altered states of consciousness are difficult to evaluate from the point of view of traditional experimental psychology, and even from that of traditional Western rationalism. Nevertheless, they have a major impact on those who experience them. Furthermore, developing norms both among behavioral scientists and among the population at large have increased the degree of open-mindedness with which such phenomena are being regarded, so that attention is increasingly being paid to this particular set of reports.

The second group of findings is that of more mundane, but equally meaningful, changes in self-esteem and in one's perceived relationship to the rest of the world. Such changes, just like the dramatic ones mentioned above, have been experienced by participants in formal REST studies as well as by people spending time in the wilderness either on their own or in structured programs. Here again, the systematic investigation of the effects is relatively new. Not much information is available, and most of that is primarily indicative rather than definitive; but the indications are that something beneficial is happening and should be fostered.

Sane Asylums

Treffert (1976), in an insightful and interesting paper, has proposed the establishment of what he calls "sane asylums." He points out that the word asylum means "a place of security and retreat." In modern society, troubled and harried people use such techniques as rest cures, encounter groups, and retreats to find such a place. These, however, are expensive, and may not be readily available to all. Frequently, they also impose extraneous requirements (see e.g., Goodacre, 1970). Treffert's proposed solution is a place, "remote, pastoral, modest, inexpensive, and away," where people called participants (as opposed to patients) could check in and out and take part if they want to in group activities, therapy, recreation, and so on. Alternatively, they could just sit alone and explore their own needs and selves. Schedules, routines, and pressures would be minimal.

It is a beautiful idea, offering an opportunity of which many people would want to avail themselves. Let us hope that any such asylum will include, for those who want to experience solitude at a very profound level, the possibility of chamber and/or water immersion REST.

CONCLUSION

It is clear that REST, in its many varieties, has been successfully used in self-improvement projects by normal individuals. The transcendental experiences and altered states of consciousness described by religious visionaries, mystics, and meditators in natural environments with reductions of social and physical stimuli have much in common with those reported by participants in projects using systematic water tank immersion or chamber confinement. The involvement of the natural environment and solitude in adolescent rites of passage in tribal cultures around the world has much in common with its impact on Western adolescents participating in wilderness trips or in recreational and therapeutic camping.

The benefits include improvements in self-esteem, whether as the result of explicit messages presented during REST or as a consequence of having singlehandedly overcome the challenges of nature. A feeling of serenity, calmness, and insight into the workings of the universe or the deity, of union with the transcendental, can occur among people attuned to such possibilities, whether they are engaged in contemplation on a mountain top or floating in a tank. The sheer excitement of vivid fantasies and deep self-exploration provides another positive experience for many participants.

One effect that has been largely ignored in the literature is the possibility that reduced stimulation leads to increases in creativity. There have been many autobiographical reports to this effect, with great artists, scientists, and scholars commenting on the necessity for solitude and a lack of distraction as being prerequisite to creative endeavor. It would seem logical that the incubation phase of creativity, during which ideas are explored and freely manipulated, could best occur under such conditions. However, no test of this hypothesis has been made in the research literature. Studies on the cognitive effects of REST (Chapter 2) have never incorporated measures of high-level originality and creativity. The closest they have come to this is to administer tests measuring the commonality of word associations, the ability to suggest multiple uses for common objects, and originality in making up short paragraphs, all far removed from what goes on in the production of a great work of art or a brilliant scientific theory. The effects of REST on high-level creativity clearly represent an area where systematic investigation is warranted.

One last point, by now obvious to most of us, is that reduced stimulation provides a refuge. People whose lives are characterized by chronically high levels of social and physical stimuli need an occasional change to a lower level of input. This can be accomplished without the formalities of going into a water tank or a REST chamber. Alternatives range from as drastic a solution as isolating oneself in a wilderness cabin for the rest of one's life to one as mild as shutting the door to the bedroom for an hour or so. But an increasing number of people do use the clear-cut tactic of using, or even acquiring, standard REST environments for this purpose. One intriguing thought: as more people use isolation and stimulus reduction for recreation and self-fulfillment, and as they become more aware that they and others are doing so, will the public image of REST as a scientific and therapeutic tool improve? Students of attitude change processes know the relative futility of disseminating information, no matter how valid, and of presenting logical arguments, no matter how rational. In contrast, personal experience may persuade people that their current beliefs about the aversiveness of REST are incorrect and that the attitudes based on those beliefs need to be modified.

CHAPTER 7

Components of REST in Psychotherapeutic Practice

In considering REST as a therapeutic technique and a useful component in multimodal treatment programs, clinical researchers and practitioners should be reminded that its use is not a complete departure from traditional methods. In some cases REST occurs as the by-product of a treatment whose primary goal was something else: one prominent example is the use of seclusion to prevent patients from doing others an injury. An examination of several modes of treatment currently in use, some of them for many years, reveals that components of reduced stimulation have been incorporated in other approaches. Almost any therapist will find his work facilitated if the patient is receptive, concentrates on the interaction, introspects about his problems, remembers relevant material from his own previous experience, and seriously considers the comments of the therapist. All of these reactions are facilitated by REST. I shall also point out parallel applications, problems, criticisms, and theoretical concepts where these link REST with one or more standard therapeutic procedures. These do not necessarily establish underlying connections, but they help to emphasize the place of restricted stimulation therapy within, rather than outside, the broad historical tradition of clinical research and practice.

HISTORICAL ROOTS

The recognition that a period of solitude and quiet can be beneficial in the treatment of mental illness is not new. In fact, it is as old as almost any treatment for mental illness. Kouretas (1967) reported that at the Oracle of Trophonius there was a sequence of steps that led to either divination or the curing of psychological problems. The procedure began with a strict diet, imposed while the supplicant was lodged in a special building near the shrine. He then performed a sacrifice, and drank from the Fountains of Forgetfulness and Memory. This sequence first assured the good will of the Oracle, then caused the patient to forget his past, and finally

216

enabled him to remember what followed. Next, he descended through a small opening into a subterranean chamber. There, isolated and cut off from external stimulation, he underwent some striking experience, now unknown, that led to regression, personality change, and "rebirth." Coming out of the chamber into the normal world filled him with confusion which dissipated gradually. In his discussion of the psychotherapeutic approaches used in Greek antiquity, Papageorgiou (1975) proposes that the function of the diets, special environments, and other treatments was to induce supernatural dreams, which had the power to foretell the future and/or to cure illness. Apparently, vestiges of the tradition still exist in some monasteries and churches in Greece, although they are now disappearing.

"Dream psychotherapy" or "incubation" very closely resembles the divinatory and other magical apparitions so common in puberty rites among North American Indian and other cultures. But the use of stimulus reduction in a less mystical context has also been reported in folk medicine. Margetts (1968), for example, has listed covering the patient completely with a blanket and similar methods of environmental restriction among the healing practices of sub-Saharan African tribes. Recently, Klein (1978) mentioned the induction of complete relaxation, including bedrest, in the treatment of *susto,* a stress syndrome common in Latin America and among Latin American immigrants to the United States. In his extensive work dealing with the native Indians of the American Northwest and the Canadian West Coast, Jilek (e.g., 1977) discusses in detail the curing of "spirit illness," a diagnosis which is based on chronic depression, antisocial behavior, and substance abuse. To Jilek, a Western-trained psychiatrist, the term "anomic depression" seems the closest to spirit illness as defined by the Indian ritualists. The treatment consists of alternating stimulus reduction and overload, the former including darkness, immobility, and isolation and the latter achieved by rhythmic drumming, singing and clapping, pain, and vigorous dancing. Approximately two-thirds of a group of 24 spirit dancers initiated between 1967 and 1972 showed significant improvement of the original symptoms.

A more comprehensive review (Jilek, 1978) indicates that darkness and forced immobility are also used in the healing ceremonies of Southwestern tribes, as they are among the Eskimos (Margetts, 1975). In many of these cases, the line between healing and religious ritual is difficult to define and in fact may not be very meaningful. For the most part, the use of stimulus reduction appears to be related to increasing the susceptibility of the patient to persuasion and major personality change, rather than the achievement of a state of relaxation which is usually a major goal of the use of REST in formal clinical practice.

The treatment of the mentally ill by the use of "darkness [which] quiets the spirit" was already ascribed to the ancients in a medical treatise written by a first century Roman, Aulus Cornelius Celsus (cited in Garrison, 1921, p. 96). It was still the practice in the Middle Ages, along with reduced social and sensory stimulation (Bromberg, 1975). As Bromberg's review of the history of psychiatry makes clear, solitude, darkness, silence, immobilization, and other forms of REST were frequently recommended and used during the Renaissance, the Enlightenment, the Industrial Revolution, and so without interruption to today. Sometimes they were used excessively, and under physical conditions that made it clear that the purpose was management rather than treatment; sometimes, as in the "tranquilizer" invented by Benjamin Rush (1806), the founder of American psychiatry and a signer of the Declaration of Independence, the procedure could be uncomfortable and used in conjunction with then-standard medical techniques that would no longer be acceptable. In Rush's technique, the patient was strapped to a chair with his head enclosed in a box so that light and sound inputs would be severely reduced (Reidman and Green, 1964).

In other cases, the treatment was more gentle. In Mitchell's Rest Cure (1877/1905), patients showing hysterical and neurasthenic symptoms were put into isolation except for one attendant, in a dimly lit and quiet place, with a great deal of rest. Mitchell's approach was novel and far-sighted; it recognized the need for multimodal treatment, and prescribed careful procedural guidelines to make sure that isolation and REST were carried out humanely and that negative effects would be prevented (Dercum, 1917). Dercum, a follower of Mitchell, discussed in great detail various forms of rest treatment and their applicability to different categories of mental illness. His table of contents makes clear the wide utility that he envisaged for the technique, ranging from the then-common neuroses including neurasthenia, hysteria, and hypochondria, through more severe behavioral problems such as depression ("melancholia") and delirium, to such problems as epilepsy and the abuse of alcohol and other drugs. In fact, he argues that "in the management of mental disease, the first and cardinal principle is *rest*" (p. 180, emphasis in original). That this was not a unique view is shown by the fact that Janet (1919) also refers to rest and isolation as one of the major psychiatric treatments. In addition, he prescribes the economizing of effort, which in its emphasis on routine, stability, and monotony presents a less dramatic but still recognizable version of REST. Guthrie (1938), in his chapter on psychotherapy, gives some flavor of the great role that stimulus reduction and related techniques played in the psychotherapeutic dramas of the early twentieth century.

This school of thought specifically perceived the REST situation as therapeutic. As a consequence, for the most part the mistreatment, lack of care, degradation, and callousness that were combined with seclusion and restraint in the large mental hospitals such as Bedlam and the Salpê-triére did not obtain among its adherents. It is important to modify the idea that early practitioners dealing with the mentally ill generally wanted their patients to suffer as a way to bring them to their senses. As Bromberg says, "There is evidence to show that the management of mental cases rested on a spirit of humanitarianism" (1975, p. 29) during the medieval period, and the judgment is equally true of later years.

The idea that excessive stimulation can result in maladjustment is not a new one, and in fact underlies some of the pioneering uses of stimulus reduction by early psychiatrists. Mitchell, writing toward the end of the nineteenth century, warned against restless living. Dercum, during World War I, said: "In the civilization of our day, no cause is more potent than *overwork* and *nervous overstrain*. In many cases, if merely so much of the strain be taken off as is in excess of the patient's strength, nature will gradually reestablish a normal equilibrium, provided, of course, that the overstrain has not been too long continued" (p. 26; emphasis in original). The logical progression from here to ideas such as information overload, "attractive stimulus overload" (Lipowski, 1970), and "future shock" (Toffler, 1970) is clear. So is the progression from the partial and complete conditions of rest prescribed by Dercum to the various uses of REST discussed in this volume.

Seclusion as a Means of Clinical Control

As has been stated, one reason for isolation being used so widely has been that it is a convenient way to manage disruptive or dangerous patients. Of course, this is still the case; fortunately, recent workers have made progress in identifying the behavioral problems, environmental conditions, appropriate durations, and other circumstances that should govern these applications (e.g., Plutchik, Karasu, Conte, Siegel, and Jerrett, 1978; Rosen and DiGiacomo, 1978). Patients who go into seclusion tend to be those who are relatively difficult to handle and relatively severely disturbed, such as schizophrenics and manic depressives in the manic stage (Mattson and Sacks, 1978). Apparently, seclusion does not necessarily work smoothly in the control of patient behavior. Mattson and Sacks report that a high number of assaults on staff and self-destructive acts occur during isolation. So does deterioration in mental and physical condition (apparently as a consequence of failure to receive adequate medication). Just what the effects are seems difficult to establish: there seems to be a lack of attention to maintaining medical records while the patient is in solitude. Apparently, what happens is that the staff perceive seclusion as a technique for maintaining a good environment in the rest of the ward, and to some extent as beneficial in itself for the isolated patient. As a result, the continued therapeutic efforts that in other studies have shown REST to be a potent helping environment may be missing when it is used as a routine technique for controlling difficult individuals.

The use of seclusion with psychiatric inpatients is a controversial issue. There is no doubt that, even with the availability of many drugs, there are appropriate instances for the use of an isolation room. These include situations where drugs are contraindicated for some reason, where the therapist prefers to leave the cognitive and affective processes of the patient unimpaired by chemicals, and where it is judged that the participation of the patient in his own treatment would be hampered by medication (Fitzgerald and Long, 1973). It should also be pointed out that, as in the case of solitary confinement and in the use of REST as a therapeutic technique, the duration and intensity of seclusion and its effects are much more easily controlled and adjusted than those of medication. The treatment can be easily interrupted for various purposes. Furthermore, the patient in seclusion is more capable of taking care of his own personal needs. Most important, the patient can introspect and converse with therapists and other staff, actively participating in his own therapy. All of these are significant advantages over chemical sedation. Seclusion—and, in more drastic cases, physical restraint (Rosen and DiGiacomo, 1978)— also works immediately to protect others from assaultive or agitated patients, with whom drugs may work too slowly or in some cases not at all. Furthermore, the decreased sensory stimulation imposed by seclusion rooms may itself be therapeutic (Reusch, 1964). Staff members and both secluded and nonsecluded patients agree that isolation is successful in calming down aggressive individuals, even though the isolated patients themselves rate the experience as boring and frustrating (Plutchik et al., 1978).

Accordingly, even in very advanced institutions, isolation in a quiet and generally stimulus-reducing environment is used to enable the patient to regain his internal controls. Wells (1972), in a study of the use of seclusion in one particular university psychiatric ward, found that 15 (approximately 4%) of the patients were isolated at some time. Fourteen of these patients were discharged from the hospital in 8 weeks or less. Whether or not this period could be reduced by a different treatment, seclusion would certainly not seem to be an extremely traumatic experience. It is important that staff members be trained to accept not only the fact that solitude is not necessarily aversive, but also that it is not meant to be punitive (Cahn, 1975). Such an attitude certainly makes the procedure more palatable to all, probably more therapeutically effective, and less liable to gross distortions by critics.

Of course, seclusion can be an experience with great impact, which is remembered for a long time. In one study, carried out by Wadeson and Carpenter (1976), psychiatric patients were asked to draw pictures showing themselves and various aspects of their illness. Of 41 patients who had spent time in isolation, 20 drew scenes depicting that situation. Affective responses were mixed. The patients drew pictures of "visions of light, peace, God." Although it is difficult to tell, it appears that psychotic hallucinations occurred during seclusion, although there is no indication that these were any different from what the patients experienced on the wards. Negative reactions were apparently based on a feeling that seclusion was punishment, a feeling that persisted in some patients for as much as a year after admission. Once again, this fact emphasizes the importance of structuring the experience appropriately, both for the patients and for therapeutic personnel.

In the absence of adequate preparation, both medical staff and patients sometimes find the idea of seclusion rooms unpleasant. This problem may be largely a function of the conditions that frequently surround isolation, which in some cases resemble those that apply to solitary confinement in correctional institutions. As a rule, patients are placed in seclusion because their condition is severe, and the individual may confuse the direction of the cause-effect relationship. Furthermore, it may be that during removal to the seclusion area some patients are handled somewhat roughly, and once they are secluded they may not be attended to as well as they should be (see Mattson and Sacks, 1978). In all of these cases, blame may mistakenly be placed on seclusion itself rather than on the other factors, leading to some amount of misinterpretation. Another relevant point is that in general, the seclusion area in both hospitals and prisons has a negative aura, with frightening labels (e.g., "the hole"), rumors about how bad the experience is, a tendency on the part of staff members to threaten individuals who are difficult to control with being put in isolation, and the like. Thus, there is a strong negative set. It is no wonder that the experience is unpleasant for some individuals (Wadeson and Carpenter, 1976). Still, in both settings the favorable aspects of REST are recognized: there have been calls for isolation to be made easily accessible to residents who voluntarily request it (John Howard Society of Ontario, 1976; Plutchik et al., 1978).

PSYCHOANALYTIC THERAPY

The physical setting in which psychoanalytic therapy has been traditionally performed is one that imposes some degree of REST. The environment is low in variability, and low in general stimulation level; the patient's behavioral task is an open-ended one, without clear-cut learned norms, just as is the subject's behavior in a REST situation; there is encouragement to concentrate on one's inner experience; and the other person, on whom one is dependent for authority and guidance, while present in the room, is unseen and speaks relatively seldom (Kubzansky and Leiderman, 1961). This situation, which was retained when psychoanalysts moved from hypnosis to free association (Freud, 1913/1924), increases the level of relaxation of the patient. It also facilitates fantasy and regression, and makes it easier for transference to occur as the patient projects and displaces upon the analyst the feelings and attitudes that he has toward figures from his own past (Blanck, 1976). The fact that the patient lies on his back, and is prevented from moving, encourages a high flow of verbal output (Beigel, 1952). Kubie (1950) has also pointed out that the procedure increases the anonymity, or as he calls it the incognito, of the therapist. This again is supposed to make transference easier; we may also hypothesize that it reduces self-censorship of the patient's comments. The use of white noise to reduce the perception of sound from the outside, dim lighting to reduce distraction in the visual field, and the use of muted colors, unadorned walls, and sound baffles have recently been reported as explicit devices to help the patient to concentrate on the therapeutic process (Bendheim, 1979).

Let us look at what happens in REST, and note the parallels. The participant lying in the chamber is relaxed. His motor activity is restricted, and he communicates only with an unseen and somewhat unknown other person. This other person, the therapist, controls the situation to some extent: he indicates when the subject is to perform certain tasks and when the session is over. He understands the behavioral norms, the reinforcement contingencies, and the technical components of the environment, and he may provide instructions to the subject if the rules of behavior appear to be violated. Obviously, one great difference is that in psychoanalysis these factors are ancillary tools to ease the substantive work of the therapist; in REST, the technique is the central aspect of treatment. Another difference is that the standard psychoanalytic treatment does not involve severe stimulus reduction. It lasts for less than an hour, and even during this time the environment is more stimulating than that of a REST chamber. However, some workers have reported that profound sensory restriction can be helpful in analytic therapy. It would be interesting if such an environment were tried more widely by practicing psychoanalysts.

While the reduced-stimulation aspects of the psychoanalytic setting are easy to see, it has also been suggested that some of the therapeutic effects of the two approaches may overlap. For example, Kelman (1975), in a stimulating paper, argues that altered states of consciousness can occur during psychoanalysis. Such experiences occur as a result of increasingly free association and more openness and attentiveness to new experiences. The reports of his patients, and his interpretation of "avoidance of struggling, hanging on and letting go, or struggling against struggling . . . and finally containing struggling toward its solution on the way to more moments of communing" (p. 194) sound almost exactly like some of the reports of individuals undergoing water-immersion (Lilly, 1977; L. Perry, personal communication, August 1, 1978). The frequency of such experiences has not been ascertained, either among psychoanalytic patients or among people undergoing REST. We also do not know how much of a contribution such occurrences make to the total therapeutic process, although both Lilly and Kelman see this role as an important one.

HYPNOTHERAPY

Hypnotherapy is a form of treatment historically related to psychoanalysis, and it is a common experience for people using REST as a clinical technique to be asked whether it is in fact a form of hypnotic suggestion. This question is difficult to answer definitively. My own opinion is that the differences between the two approaches are much more significant than their similarities, but that the latter are by no means negligible.

The points of similarity lie in the history, effects, and uses of the two techniques. For example, the following passages, while written about hypnotherapy, are to a great extent applicable to REST:

[Hypnosis] is characterized by an increased ability to produce desirable changes in habit patterns, motivations, self-image, and life-style. Alterations may be produced in physiological functions, such as pain, that are usually inaccessible to psychological influence.

We do not know the earliest origin of hypnosis. It is perhaps as old as the ancient rites of healing known as 'temple sleep,' which may have utilized many principles of influence that underlie the modern practice of hypnotherapy. . . .

The suggested use of therapeutic hypnosis with certain problems was often met with severe rejections and hostility. . . . Doctrinaire rejection was all too often typical of the thinking of those days.

A conspicuous characteristic of research in the area of hypnotism is its relative isolation from empirical and theoretical work in other areas of psychology. . . . Until quite recently, research in hypnotism has been dominated by the notion of a special state that gives rise to extraordinary experiences and behaviors. (Barber, Spanos, and Chaves, 1974, pp. 140–141.)

The least known use of hypnosis is as a research tool, as a method for the experimental investigation of content areas other than hypnosis itself. (Levitt and Chapman, 1972, p. 85.)

Every writer on the subject agrees that hypnosis is a way of increasing suggestibility. It also intensifies the relationship between the therapist and the patient, induces alert relaxation, makes long-lost memories available again, has been characterized as "regression in the service of the ego" (Gill and Brenman, 1961), and may be to some as yet undefined extent affected by a variety of confounding factors such as expectancy (Rosenhan, 1967). The view that traditional hypnosis leads to a state of relaxation and peacefulness, along with the ability to focus one's attention, is defended by Edmonston (1977). He contrasts this phenomenon with alert trance, and argues that traditional ("neutral") hypnosis induces a state of consciousness which, while certainly a form of trance, is very closely akin to relaxation. All of these aspects are vividly reminiscent of the situation with regard to REST as a therapeutic and experimental procedure. Similarly, the wide variety of theories advanced to explain the effects of hypnosis, and the lack of closure on judging the relative superiority or areas of appropriateness of these theories, is reminiscent of the situation in the restricted stimulation literature (see e.g., Fromm and Shor, 1972).

In application, we find more parallels. It has been said that hypnosis itself is not a therapy, but merely prepares the way for more effective therapeutic interventions (e.g., Lee, 1970). And in fact, hypnosis is frequently used by therapists as part of a multicomponent approach. Some of the applications are very similar to those that have been tested under REST conditions: hypnotherapy has been used with psychotic and neurotic patients, as well as in the treatment of such behavioral problems as smoking and overeating (see Cheek and LeCron, 1968; Gordon, 1967, among others). The wide range of applications, and such features as the reduction of extranous stimulation, the induction of a state of relaxation, and the client's interpretation of the event as something unusual, again place hypnotherapy in close conjunction not only to REST but to other techniques discussed in this chapter, such as the therapeutic use of meditation (see also Wickramasekera, 1978).

Incidentally, hypnosis—like "sensory deprivation"—has also been implicated as a tool in interrogation and coercive indoctrination (Bowart, 1978; Gibson, 1977). But here, too, the actual data do not seem to support the claim (e.g., Orne, 1961).

But there are also important differences in the areas of application of the two techniques. Hypnosis has been widely used in dealing with physical illnesses, including allergies (e.g., Barber, 1978). Perhaps its most prominent medical use has been in the area of analgesia (Chaves and Barber, 1976). These do not seem to be appropriate problems to approach with the use of REST, particularly since pain sensitivity increases as a function of stimulus reduction. There are different methodological problems, such as the fact that a significant proportion of the population is either completely or to a great extent unhypnotizable, whereas with appropriate orientation the vast majority of volunteers can tolerate REST reasonably well. Incidentally, the reader is reminded that REST appears to have a facilitative effect on susceptibility to hypnotic induction (Gill and Brenman, 1959; Wickramasekera, 1977c), so that at least with patients who are hard to hypnotize a combination of the two techniques might prove useful.

One interesting question is the degree of similarity between REST and hypnosis from a theoretical standpoint. Traditionally, most writers have agreed that there is some special state of consciousness that mediates the dramatic effects of hypnosis. Of course, it has also been suggested that the consequences of REST are based upon an altered state of consciousness; but the evidence for this has been sparse (see Chapter 6).

On the other hand, some theories of hypnosis have also emphasized cognitive factors. Among these are the argument that the hypnotic state is primarily characterized by the subject's willingness and ability to suspend his usual reality orientation in favor of a temporary involvement in imagination and fantasy suggested by an external source (Hilgard, 1970; Shor, 1970). Other theorists have agreed with this view but reject the traditional concept that the change in reality orientation occurs in some special trance condition (Spanos and Barber, 1974). Barber's own experience as a hypnotic subject confirms the importance of the subject's active cognitive and imaginative involvement, as well as his perception of the situation as being useful and valuable (Barber, 1975). Leaving aside the question of trance or altered states of consciousness, the parallels between the hypnotic state and REST are clear. But then, it would be difficult to think of any major form of psychotherapy in which it is not necessary for the patient to have a positive attitude and a willingness to become actively engaged in the therapeutic process.

The next point is that hypnotic effects are very closely bound to the suggestions emanating from the hypnotist, with the reactions of the subject being essentially limited to obeying or rejecting the suggestion, and perhaps to elaborating upon it or rationalizing the behaviors that follow from it. Even those authors who reject the idea of an altered state of consciousness tend to agree that responses are dominated by the influence of the therapist or experimenter (Barber, 1969; Barber et al., 1974;

Sarbin and Coe, 1972). In the case of REST, it is true that there have been some therapeutic situations where such suggestion was important (see Chapters 8 and 10). However, the impact of suggestions from the experimenter has not been thoroughly established, and clearly is not comparable to the dominance of a hypnotist (see Suedfeld, 1969c). In the REST treatment of maladaptive lifestyles, the point is precisely that the patient uses the period of stimulus restriction to think about, evaluate, attempt to solve, and generally work through the problems involved in his behavior patterns, at most using some of the information provided by the therapist as an aid in this process. In the less strictly clinical applications of REST this point is even more clear-cut.

SLEEP THERAPY

Sleep-producing medication has been known and used from the very beginning of medical treatment of the mentally ill (Shaffer and Lazarus, 1952). Among the most frequently used modern techniques for inducing long-duration sleep have been electric current, sodium amytal, and sodium pentothal. In lower dosages, the same pharmaceutical agents have been used to produce borderline states between sleep and wakefulness, in which patients are more open to the discussion of sensitive issues with the therapist and in which negative affects are less disturbing. Long periods of sleep—usually at least 2 or 3 days—are used as disruptors of ongoing "programs" (in the sense of Miller, Galanter, and Pribram, 1960, or Tomkins, 1962).

Physiological danger is involved, with some probability of respiratory and cardiovascular problems occurring during sleep and convulsions upon withdrawal of the drug (Shaffer and Lazarus, 1952). Racamier, Carretier, and Sens (1959) also found negative psychological aftereffects in some cases, the crisis occurring between 1 and 3 days after sleep therapy. The symptoms included overwhelming anxiety and anguish, confused thought, depression, and psychomotor disturbances. Apparently, intensive psychotherapy and the use of drugs have been needed to enable patients to overcome this problem. Here, however, the argument is that this crisis is part of the therapeutic process (a suggestion that REST workers have not yet thought of).

The treatment has been judged useful with affective disturbances, schizophrenia, autism and catatonia, and with obsessive-compulsive syndromes. According to Pekarek and Svestkova (1967), sleep therapy combined with chemotherapy of various sorts has been shown to be of potential use in the treatment of psychoses, including schizophrenia.

However, the authors acknowledge that there has been insufficient research, and not even enough clinical experience, for definite conclusions to be drawn. Vidal and Vidal (1969) found that repeated sleep therapy during a 2-year session obtained at least some improvement in 36 of 48 patients. However, there was no control group, so that we do not know how much spontaneous recovery there might have been anyway. At any rate, they point out some of the pragmatic benefits of sleep therapy: it is easy and safe for preventing suicide and for associated chemotherapy, and apparently also facilitates the patient's openness to psychotherapeutic approaches.

A recent review (Loo, Sauvage, and Saba, 1971) discusses the best applications of the technique. Aside from its original use in manic-depressive psychosis, which the reviewers feel is now better treated chemically, it has been utilized in a range of neurotic disorders. The most positive results have been found for reactive depression and for neuroses involving somatic conversion such as physical pain or breathing problems. The argument is that its major use is as an introductory step, from which one goes on to psychotherapeutic procedures. Loo et al. also illustrate the environmental similarities with REST, sleep therapy taking place in isolated and soundproof rooms.

Apparently because of ideological factors and good empirical results, sleep therapy became a highly preferred technique in the Soviet Union (Andreev, 1952). Soviet workers have even applied sleep therapy with neurotics and what they call "borderline cases of neuro-psychological diseases" (Chumakova and Kirillova, 1967) in an outpatient clinic. After 10 years, they report good results with neurotics and with some organically ill individuals. The latter include patients suffering from head injuries, early cerebral arterial sclerosis, and some forms of rheumatic encephalitis. Neurotic children seem particularly responsive to sleep therapy. In the outpatient situation, the duration of sleep is only approximately 2 hours for adults and 1 hour for children. Twenty-five to 50 sessions are administered. The authors mentioned that sleep induced by drugs may have damaging side-effects; similarly, electrosleep may result in various neurological problems.

Murray (1965) concluded that sleep therapy seems to be effective for the treatment of affective disturbance, but (like REST) not for obsessions. Generally, the effects seem to be no more impressive than those found with psychotherapy. A third to a half of the patients improve significantly. Improvement is greater among individuals whose original complaints were less severe (the opposite of the findings of Adams using REST). The most prominent finding seems to be a decrease in tension and anxiety, and in their physiological consequences. Reduction of tension may result from protective inhibition, from the making up of sleep lost due to anxiety, from the regressive aspects of long sleep, and perhaps from increased opportunities for dreaming.

One theoretical argument (Banay, 1952) proposes that electrosleep removes the intensity of psychotic symptoms, so that they are replaced by merely neurotic forms of pathology, which can then in turn be treated by psychotherapy. In a way, electrosleep was based on a theory similar to that of Wolpe. It was posited that sleep and inhibition, which are identical processes, protect the individual from further pathological cerebral functioning, rest the cells of the brain, and help to destroy pathological connections and to replace them by normal ones (Lafitte, 1952).

Sleep therapy is in some ways similar to REST. There is the use of a nonstimulating environment, the relative quiescence of the patient, and the fairly long duration of the session. However, there are gross dissimilarities as well. Perhaps the most salient one is that REST is a relatively natural situation, whereas prolonged sleep is induced through the use of drugs or electrical current. One cannot but help wonder what the side- and aftereffects of the sleep-producing techniques may be above and beyond that of the therapy itself. Also, sleep therapies use repeated sessions, sometimes many of them over a long period of time, which REST therapists and researchers have not done. But the major difference, it seems to me, is in the immediate effects. The client in the reduced stimulation environment relaxes. But he also concentrates, remains relatively alert, and generates or learns ways of coping with his problem. All of these characteristics are directly contradictory to the unaware, inactive state of the sleeper. Thus, in spite of the surface parallels, I would not consider sleep therapy to be in any important way analogous to REST.

RELAXATION AND REFOCUSING THERAPIES

The next section deals with a family of techniques that have much in common with each other and with REST. In fact, it could reasonably be argued that REST actually belongs to the family. These methods induce a state of relaxation as a central aspect of therapy. Some of them claim to go beyond that, as in the altered states of consciousness reached in meditation; others combine the relaxation component with other features, as in the use of relaxation and systematic desensitization. However, as the reader will see, the similarities are great and obvious, and can be found in theoretical explanations, treatment procedures, problems attacked, and kinds of results.

Meditation

Many people, when they first encounter the literature concerning positive effects of REST, draw parallels between this technique and various currently popular forms of meditation (see Chapter 6). In fact, the two approaches do appear to have much in common. For example, the same kinds of biobehavioral disruptions have been successfully treated by both. Transcendental Meditation has been reported to be effective in the elimination of addictive behaviors, including cigarette smoking, the use of nonprescription drugs and hallucinogens, and heavy alcohol intake (Benson and Wallace, 1971; Shafii, Lavely, and Jaffe, 1974, 1975; Schuster, 1975–76). Patients in psychiatric hospitals who were taught to meditate showed decreases in the need for medication, improvements on a number of MMPI scales, better rapport with the therapist, increased ability to relax, more self-acceptance, and openness to new experiences and other people (Carrington, 1978). Practiced meditators adapt more effectively to stressful situations, as measured by subjective anxiety ratings and physiological responses (Goleman and Schwartz, 1976). Various forms of meditation have been used to treat generalized anxiety (Shapiro, 1976), phobias (Boudreau, 1972), and insomnia (Nicassio and Bootzin, 1974). A Zen meditation workshop has been shown to have positive effects on a range of self-report measures, including feelings of creativity, self-control, and anxiety; positive and negative self-statements; friendliness; and calmness. Hypnotic susceptibility also increased (Shapiro, undated). Not all of these measures showed significantly more improvement in the Zen group than in an untreated control group. However, strangely enough, Zen was also associated with a decrease in the self-reported appreciation of nature.

There are many other common features in the clinical literatures dealing with the two procedures. Meditation may be a good addition to multimodal treatment packages. In a recent book on the use of meditation as a therapeutic technique, several contributors emphasized the advisability of combining it with other procedures (Smith, 1977; Kristeller, 1977; Nuernberger, 1977; Ballentine, 1977). Unexpected beneficial side effects have been noted (Thorpe, 1977).

The therapeutic usefulness of meditation has been questioned, criticized, and rejected (e.g., J.C. Smith, 1975). Some of the reasons for this negative evaluation are similar to those found in the literature concerning REST. For example, there is a variety of techniques, all of which are labeled "meditation" and which do not necessarily resemble each other very closely—at least at first glance. The effects of such techniques should not be, but often have been, compared without appropriate attention to the methodological differences. (For readers who are interested in the various forms of meditation, and the meaning of the differences among them, the discussion by Carrington, 1978, is highly recommended.) Second, the literature abounds in studies that do not use appropriate control groups, that are extremely selective as to the subject populations included, and that fail to perform long-range followup data collection. As a result, workers in the field still are not sure about the optimal parameters, the actual effects, or the therapeutic permanence of the changes induced.

It has been argued that the more elaborate forms of meditation are really equivalent to deep relaxation or resting states (Michaels, Huber and McCann, 1976). Herbert Benson, one of the researchers who first established the reality of physiological changes accompanying Transcendental Meditation (Wallace and Benson, 1972), later came to believe that deep relaxation can have equivalent effects (Benson, 1975; see also Morse, Martin, Furst, and Dubin, 1977). This literature is parallel to the "stimulus reduction is nothing but . . ." arguments of the 1960s. In my opinion, there is another commonality that underlies some of the explicit criticisms. Both REST and meditation are perceived by many people as being so offbeat, weird, and out of the scientific mainstream as to be conceptually foreign; some of the reasons for the rejection are in fact attempts to rationalize this feeling.

Another shared problem is the tendency to assume that the effects of the experience are uniform from one person to another. This is a misleading assumption at best (see e.g., Pagano, Rose, Stivers, and Warrenburg, 1976). There have been reports of negative reactions, including serious thought disorder (French, Schmid, and Ingalls, 1975; Krishna, 1975; Lazarus, in press). Some people come to use meditation as a refuge and a focus for their entire life, without any decrease of stress or maladjustment (Carrrington, 1978; Cauthen and Prymak, 1977). At the other extreme, meditation can lead to an excessive lack of structure, depriving people of defenses upon which they used to depend (Carrington, 1978).

Meditation and environmental restriction have been explicitly compared. In her discussion of the relationships between REST and meditation, Carrington (1978) said: "Meditation might even be described in part as a form of self-imposed 'sensory deprivation,' as if, every time we meditated, we entered an 'isolation chamber' of our own making" (p. 228). As she points out, meditation reduces stimulation to a subnormal level, but certainly does not eliminate it—just as is the case with REST. The use of the mantra, staring at a particular object, gestures, concentration on breathing, and so on, create a monotonous stimulus environment, similar to that of some REST techniques. The effects, too, are in some ways similar. Meditators, like REST subjects, report vivid dream-like imagery. Carrington points out that these rarely are true hallucinations, apparently unaware of the fact that the same is true in "sensory deprivation." Other reports include distortion of the body image, disorganized thinking, and the like. It also appears that some personality traits are relevant to the response to both situations. Among these are field dependence and sensation-seeking.

There is a deeper level of meditation, called *samadhi*, which is a withdrawn state much more similar to severe stimulus reduction than is either the standard REST laboratory or the more common levels of meditation. It is said that in this condition, the unusual emotional, cognitive and physical symptoms reported by meditators disappear. This disappearance may parallel the fact that such symptoms are much more frequent in monotonous stimulation than in severely reduced stimulation experiments (see Schultz, 1965). Some of the subjective effects reported during *samadhi* are also present during profound stimulus reduction. These include perceptual clarity, increases in energy, and a changed perspective on life—all results that have been reported by REST subjects and patients. (One of the best-established firms manufacturing and marketing water-immersion tanks for private use is called the Samadhi Tank Co.) It has been argued (Myers, 1976) that both techniques increase the individual's access to primary process material. They facilitate the emergence of repressed emotions and open the individual to the possibility of new patterns of thought, attitude, emotion, and behavior.

Some of the conceptual analyses are also quite similar. One of the rationales for REST therapy with certain kinds of patients has been that it enables the individual to focus on specific important information, rather than being distracted by the normal bombardment of stimuli. This is exactly like the effect of meditation, attending to a specified target while ignoring everything else (Goleman, 1976). Meditation has been proposed as a way to achieve adaptive regression in the service of the ego (Shafii, 1973). Liberation from existing patterns and openness to new ones has been described as the end product of the meditation state (Suzuki, Fromm, and DeMartino, 1960), as well as of REST.

Another intriguing hypothesis has been advanced for the therapeutic usefulness of meditation (Benson, Greenwood, and Klemchuk, 1976). According to this view, there are situations in which people are constantly forced to attend to and react to stimuli. In other words, continuous behavioral adjustment is needed. This demand on the individual activates a series of psychophysiological reactions that increase arousal, and leads to the development of stress diseases such as addictive behaviors and hypertension. Benson and his coworkers propose that one way to reduce the problems arising from such environmental pressure is to inculcate what they call the relaxation response as an incompatible counterpart of the emergency reaction. Methods of doing so include the various forms of meditation that have been devised in many eras and many cultures.

Four major elements of the elicitation of the relaxation response are noted. A particular stimulus word or phrase is repeated covertly and continuously; the focus of attention is redirected to the technique, and away from distracting thoughts and emotions; the person is made physically comfortable; and a quiet, minimally stimulating environment is provided. The interesting aspect of this from our point of view is the overlap between the circumstances of the relaxation response and what happens in REST. The last two items, physical comfort and stimulus reduction, are integral parts of the REST procedure. The first—if not a mantra, at least some kind of monotonous, repetitive stimulus—has been externally provided in some REST studies. The second, teaching the participant to disregard distracting environmental or internal stimulation, has not been considered by REST researchers.

The usefulness of the relaxation response in therapy is cited by Benson and his co-authors in the areas of addictive behavior, hypertension, and headache, although only in the first case was there any controlled collection of objective data. The similarity between the two techniques is again implied by the fact that two of the three areas of application overlap, although there have not been controlled systematic investigations in each problem area in REST either. The implication, and some preliminary evidence, of usefulness in more severe psychiatric illnesses is also similar.

Benson's emphasis, of course, is on the relaxation aspect of meditation. This certainly is one component of many techniques, and is likely to be a useful one in dealing with a number of biobehavioral and biomedical problems (see also Parker, Gilbert, and Thoreson, 1978). Benson (1975) has proposed a physiological explanation for these relaxation effects based on Hess' (1957) "trophotropic response," the decrease of sympathetic nervous system activity to protect the organism against excessive stress and overreaction. Logically enough, other techniques such as autogenic training, relaxation suggested under hypnotic trance, and progressive relaxation, are listed as close analogues. By this time, it is perhaps superfluous to note that REST is not so identified.

However, this is only part of the story. We do not know whether relaxation is the crucial component of meditation in the context of behavioral medicine; and we do know that there are meditational techniques that lack the quietness and comfortable passivity that characterize the relaxation response. These include Sufi dancing, loud drumming and chanting, and even physical deprivation and pain. Trance states based on excessive stimulation are widely used in religious ritual (see Chapter 6), and have also been found in healing procedures (Akstein, 1977; Jilek, 1978).

Carrington points out that what these techniques, and those that do involve physical relaxation, have in common is also what they have in common with REST: "All these techniques close out the distractions of the outer world in much the same way as an 'isolation chamber' " (1978, p. 5). This is a negative way of putting the proposition that the common element is the refocusing of attention. In the normal environment, there are so many things claiming our interest and requiring a response that it is difficult if not impossible to hold one's thought concentrated on one's own condition, or on even a life-threatening problem. Meditation and related methods—such as contemplation and prayer, self-hypnosis, autogenic training, free association, progressive relaxation, and biofeedback—remedy the situation by training the individual to ward off the bombardment of external stimuli. What REST accomplishes is to interrupt this bombardment simply by removing the individual to a still and undemanding environment. From this point of view, the shared effect is a cognitive one, the increased ability to process only that information with which the individual wants to concern himself at the time.

Obviously, this is not an either-or proposition, nor is it an all-inclusive definition of the effects. Cognitive refocusing and relaxation can go on simultaneously, and both meditation and REST have a wide range of effects besides facilitating concentration. But this is an important aspect of all of these approaches, and one that logically appears to be implicated in many of their beneficial powers.

We can look at REST as an environmental inducer of some effects very similar to those generated internally by experienced meditators. One important difference, of course, is that many of the meditative exercises are not pragmatically feasible with certain clients—for example, those in states of profound psychosis (see e.g., Rosa, 1973)—whereas REST is not only possible but has been shown to be useful in such situations. The REST experience is much more concentrated and does not require long periods of training. Furthermore, it can produce therapeutic effects with a single session, rather than only after long and continuous practice. Thus, it appears to be a more practical approach from the point of view of wide applicability and lower effort.

On the other hand, meditation has some advantages as well. To begin with, individuals who are stressed by reduced stimulation (e.g., claustrophobics) may be able to benefit from meditation. Second, meditation and relaxation do not require specific facilities, at least not once the response has been thoroughly learned. Last and related to the previous point, the response, once learned, is immediately available as a stress reducer in a broader range of contexts and situations than is REST. One appropriate tactic, in my opinion, would be to combine these two methodologies. This might not only increase the ease and efficiency with which people learn the relaxation or meditation exercise, but would combine the benefits to be gained from both a concentrated and a more diffuse but more easily available technique.

Relaxation

Quite aside from meditation, it is well known that relaxation per se has beneficial effects in many cases. This is the argument pursued for several centuries by psychiatrists dealing with "maniacal" patients, which was generalized to a fairly wide range of mental problems by the early part of this century (e.g., Dercum, 1917). Jacobson (1934, 1938) developed the systematic approach to progressive relaxation, whose goal was to make the individual more aware of his own bodily processes and states. This technique was a prolonged and demanding one; Wolpe's (1958) modification led to much wider use and formed the basis of one of the major types of behavior modification. Wolpe not only developed a method for relaxation that was much briefer and more efficient than the original, he also shifted the emphasis of the training. Whereas Jacobson had originally viewed the learning of muscle relaxation as a specific conditioning technique against anxiety, the "systematic desensitization" method developed by Wolpe used relaxation as a conditioned response to what had previously been anxiety-arousing stimuli.

In recent years, this technique (sometimes in combination with others, such as biofeedback—see, e.g., Tarler-Benlolo, 1978) has been applied not only to classical problems of neurosis but also to the increasingly prevalent and serious symptoms of the stress diseases. Of course, the best-known use of relaxation in recent years has been as a component of behavior modification, preeminently with phobic patients. In the minds of many therapists, relaxation training followed by systematic desensitization procedures has become the treatment of choice for such problems. Although the data are somewhat mixed, there is good reason to think that this combined treatment is a very effective one, and further that its theoretical foundation is reasonably firm (see e.g., Lomont and Edwards, 1967; Beiman, Graham, and Ciminero, 1978a). Progressive relaxation, like meditation and REST, has a stress-reducing effect that goes beyond the immediate session (Goleman and Schwartz, 1976); this factor may lead to a useful role in the treatment of health-dysfunctional behaviors that are initiated by the experience of anxiety or tension (e.g., Parker, Gilbert, and Thoreson, 1978). A recent study showed that while relaxation alone lowered blood pressure in the natural environment and in a psychology clinic, it failed to do so in a medical setting. Pressure reduction in the latter environment occurred only after systematic desensitization (Beiman et al., 1978b).

A widely used book, with a record of instructions enclosed (Bernstein and Borkovec, 1973), summarizes some of the useful application of progressive relaxation. Some major categories are "tension-caused illnesses" (which I have been calling stress diseases), phobias, and chronic insomnia. The last of these is a problem for which REST would seem to be a natural treatment; as of this writing, no one has tried it. In addition, relaxation training has been reported to improve recall, particularly among highly anxious individuals and for difficult materials, and some evidence was cited about its usefulness with autistic and hyperactive children. Also interesting was a brief passage in which the authors discuss the positive effects of relaxation on the ability of clients to engage in therapeutic discussion of emotionally charged issues. The commonality between the relaxation and the REST approaches is obvious.

In the section on meditation, I have already discussed the point that both meditational and stimulus reduction techniques may owe some of their beneficial effects to the ability of the participant to relax. I am not going to repeat that discussion here. What I would like to point out is the use of REST-like conditions in progressive relaxation training. In their very widely-used manual, Bernstein and Borkovec (1973) made the following suggestions as to the appropriate physical setting. The ideal training environment is a sound-proof room, but if this is not available, the therapist should try to eliminate all visual and auditory stimuli from the outside. Windows, doors, drapes, and the like should be closed. Incidentally, the authors indicate that a steady hum, as from an air conditioner, is not a problem as long as it is not too loud; in the same way, both maximal achievable silence and a low but steady white noise have been used in REST conditions. As to visual input, Bernstein and Borkovec feel that complete darkness would be ideal, but that it is impractical because it may make the client anxious and also because the therapist needs to watch whether the client is relaxing properly. Instead, the light should be dimmed and the necessity for this should be explained to the client. The chair should be well-padded, and should enable the client to recline; at any rate, the crucial characteristic is that it be comfortable. The individual should remain relatively still, but should be encouraged to move slightly if there are problems with circulation as a result of immobility. Last, the client should be instructed to wear comfortable, loose clothing. Glasses, watches, and shoes are removed.

This list sounds like an almost exact duplication of the environmental prescription for a REST study or session. One interesting point is Bernstein and Borkovec's fear that clients who are already anxious might become more so at being placed in a completely dark room with a comparative stranger (the therapist). I wonder whether this is an exaggerated fear, or whether being put into a dark room by oneself is less stressful than being with a stranger. In either case, depending on whether visual observation is really crucial (or whether it could be replaced by, for example, infra-red closed circuit TV), the REST chamber appears to be an ideal situation for progressive relaxation training. In fact, the introduction to the manual's section on the physical setting is just about a perfect definition of the goals of REST: "Eliminate all sources of extraneous stimulation" (p. 17).

Even some of the problems are the same. Clients may experience strange feelings during relaxation. These include changes in body image and spatial orientation, fears of losing control of one's emotions, and signs of internal arousal. Intrusive, sometimes anxiety-producing thoughts also occur. Failure to follow instructions may include unnecessary movement, laughing, and talking.

Conceptually, too, the techniques are linked. Both appear to improve focused attention, although in relaxation training this tends to be more specifically restricted to the ongoing procedures than is the case in REST. The two overlap in the problems to which they may be applicable, as well as in their results. One obvious step is to conduct relaxation training under conditions of profound REST (see Chapter 8); another interesting procedure would be to evaluate the responses of people who have gone through relaxation training to the REST situation.

Edmund Jacobson, the originator of progressive relaxation, has recently (1970) argued that the combination of suggestion and relaxation in therapy tends to be counterproductive, since suggestion weakens the ability to relax. In REST work, "relaxation" is not used in the technical sense as Jacobson defines it. We do not know whether, in this situation, there is a counteraction between the two components. There may be in some cases, which might explain the lack of additive effects in the smoking plus message treatment combination. On the other hand, as the work on weight reduction shows, this is not a universal phenomenon. It may be that the relaxed state, as loosely defined and as encountered among REST participants, is not seriously diminished by message presentation. The other possibility is that REST itself prevents the antagonistic action of suggestion on relaxation. This hypothesis needs to be tested by the use of progressive relaxation training and exercises, and of therapeutic suggestion while the subject is in the REST chamber. There is at least the possibility that a powerful combination of suggestive therapy and relaxation would emerge under REST conditions (see Chapter 8).

Autogenic Therapy

This technique, developed by Schultz and Luthe (1969), emphasizes the gaining of control over one's own bodily and behavioral processes. It teaches "passive concentration" by the use of exercises and verbal formulae. After a while, with continuous practice, there is a shift to a spectator-like attitude, which the authors call "passive acceptance." During the early stages of training, the client gains control over heart rate and such feelings as heaviness of the limbs and temperature changes in the extremities, the abdomen, and the head. The changes, like those found with progressive relaxation, are the opposite of the physiological concomitants of stress, so that the technique should be useful for the prevention and treatment of tension-related illnesses.

The exercises are of two major types, physical and verbal. Physiological sensations go along with verbal formulae, which are called "standard exercises" or "orientations." The fundamental "peace" formula is "I am at peace" (Rosa, 1973). This is the general motto of the entire autogenic training process, and is practiced for a long time with the individual in a state of physical relaxation and rest. Eventually, two standard exercises are used to induce feelings of heaviness and warmth in the limbs (one at a time), and then generalizing these to the trunk. The third formula is for a calm and strong pulse; the fourth, for a peaceful and regular breath (although it is claimed that this is not really a breathing exercise); the fifth is for warmth in the solar plexus, generalized to the abdomen; and the sixth and last is coolness of the forehead, by contrast facilitating the feeling of warmth in the feet and accomplishing relaxed "deconcentration."

Autogenic training is a direct derivative of hypnosis and self-hypnosis. As Rosa (1973) says: "The goal of an AT session is a hypnotic state of light trance" (p. 4). The subject is aware of his senses, but does not engage in reflection and problem-solving. The entire effort (which ideally is really effortless) is to reach and then maintain a pleasant, relaxed state.

Clinically, autogenic training has been successfully used in the treatment of migraine headaches (Fahrion, 1978; Sargent, Green, and Walters, 1973) and some components of hypertension (Lantzsch and Drunkenmölle, 1975). Reductions in neuroticism and anxiety accompanied the diminution of dyslexic symptoms when standard functional and ortho-graphic training were supplemented by autogenic exercises (Frey, 1978). In a study using 152 participants in 6-week autogenic training courses, improvements were found on a large number of self-rated psychosomatic symptoms such as dryness of the mouth, "falling asleep" of the limbs, and disturbances of sleep or appetite. Statistically significant changes were found in 20 of the 103 items; 12 of these were in the direction of improvement (Susen, 1978).

In comparison with other techniques, autogenic training effectively re-duced anxiety scores on a mood adjective checklist in a study using psychiatric inpatients (Jessup and Neufeld, 1977). However, in the same study it had no effect on tension levels measured by frontalis muscle tension, heart rate, skin resistance, and hand and forehead temperature, nor on other aspects of mood and personality measured by the checklist. Four other relaxation procedures also failed to obtain significant changes. In contrast, a noncontingent tone control condition was associated with both heart rate and checklist alterations. Actually, this was not an appro-priate test of autogenic training, since only a brief introduction and prac-tice of the six standard autogenic phrases were used. In another compari-son study, Nicassio and Bootzin (1974) reported that autogenic training was as effective as progressive relaxation in treating insomnia, although the relaxation subjects improved more rapidly. Six months later, one component of the dependent variable still showed improvement: subjects were taking less time to fall asleep. However, other changes (including self-reports of improvement) had regressed to baseline.

The similarity between autogenic training and other relaxation (and some meditation) techniques is obvious. Carrington (1978) includes auto-genic training in her review of such methods and describes several in-stances in which it was used outside the clinical or experimental situation just as other relaxation procedures have been used. A writer who has had extensive practice with autogenic training, progressive relaxation, and various forms of meditation (Grim, 1975) found that the total relaxation experience, approximated but not quite reached through autogenic meth-ods, led toward the states described as the goal of meditation. The de-scription of the technique (Schultz and Luthe, 1969) certainly illustrates parallels between it and other exercises in this category, the emphasis being on relaxation and concentration, two major components of medita-tion noted previously.

Of course, these are also two of the major aspects of REST. The physical settings have identical goals. The very first page of the first volume in which autogenic training was described in English says: "The shift to the autogenic state is facilitated by conditions involving a signifi-

cant reduction of afferent and efferent impulses . . ." In the most direct
comparison (Wuermle, undated), changes in states of consciousness during autogenic training were compared with those during "sensory deprivation." These changes were measured by scales that included questions
about reported visual and auditory sensations, changes in thought and
concentration, feelings of euphoria, unreality and depersonalization, etc.
The data indicated very similar results for the two methods, and the
author concludes: "According to these results autogenic training can be
understood as a technique of self-induced sensory deprivation."

Biofeedback

It is not my intention to review here the literature on the therapeutic uses
of biofeedback. This technique, or rather set of techniques, is concerned
with enabling patients to monitor and modify physiological functions such
as blood circulation, heart rate, blood pressure, and muscle tension. This
is typically done through the use of electronic equipment, although the
absence of such apparatus does not exclude a particular method from this
category. For the interested reader, the annual series entitled *Biofeedback
and Self-Control*, published by Aldine, gives a thorough and current view
of progress.

In general, the biofeedback approach has been applied to many of the
same problems as the relaxation therapies; and like these, biofeedback
training usually occurs in an environment of moderately reduced stimulation. A generally unsuccessful attempt at alpha enhancement training
(Plotkin, 1978) led to the conclusion that "unusual experiences" were
largely due to stimulus reduction and suggestion. Subjects who underwent the biofeedback sessions in a condition of relatively profound REST
were more positive about the training than a partial-REST group.

In the treatment of stress diseases, various meditation and relaxation
procedures are sometimes combined with biofeedback. The two types of
training should complement each other and lead to more effective reduction of stress symptoms. There is evidence that electromyographic feedback from the frontalis muscle, in conjunction with meditation, can produce substantial decreases in muscle tension. Interestingly, biofeedback
training and practice are also associated with increases in internal locus of
control, obviously a relevant personality variable (Zaichkowsky and Kamen, 1978). This self-focusing effect, in which the individual responds to
biofeedback training with greater attributions to the self as a causal factor
in various events and experiences, has also been found with heartbeat
biofeedback (Fenigstein and Carver, 1978). Although the equivalent re-

search has not been carried out with REST subjects, introspective reports certainly support the view that such a shift occurs in the reduced stimulation environment as well.

Lloyd (1977) has recently presented an argument comparing the effects of REST with those of biofeedback. He suggests that a major source of stress problems is the difficulty of processing interoceptive cues (signal) against a constant background of environmental stimulation (noise). In therapy, REST reduces the amount of noise whereas biofeedback amplifies the signals. In both cases, the goal is to make the relevant signals easier to perceive and respond to. Lloyd goes on to advocate what he calls the "reduced sensory/perceptual environment (RSPE)" as a clinical tool for teaching people to modify their autonomic nervous system activity. The combination of procedures—reducing noise while strengthening the signal—may be doubly effective. This is why, as I have indicated, stimulus reduction is logically a contribution to the usefulness of many of the self-regulation therapies that have been applied in the treatment of stress diseases during the past 10 years. An explicit recognition of this factor, and systematic planning for environmental restriction in this context, would greatly reduce the apparent variability and confusion in methodological approaches to health psychology.

REST as a Refocusing Therapy

Julian Huxley, in commenting on criticisms of evolutionary theory as dehumanizing, rejected what he called "nothing butism." That is, the statement that human beings are animals does not imply that they are nothing but animals. In the same way, the fact that relaxation and meditation procedures overlap greatly with REST in technique, conceptual foundations, and results, does not mean that the two categories are redundant. The wide individual variations on all three of these dimensions within each category would negate any such conclusion. At the same time, however, the similarities are too close, too pervasive, and too important to be ignored. It would seem that we have reached the stage where the isolation of REST research and therapy from the progress being made in its more popular counterparts is a serious drawback.

The development of the refocusing approach may resolve one problem that has plagued REST advocates: no one knows where the technique fits into conceptual or taxonomic systems of therapeutic methods. Although REST can play a role in a wide variety of treatments, from the psychodynamic to the behavioral, it seems basically to fit into the group of self-management techniques generally described as attentional refocusing and relaxation. As the brief review above has pointed out, the specific procedures in the classification vary among themselves in many ways, and REST varies from the others; but the underlying relationship is there.

One major difference between REST and all of the other procedures is that it is much more stimulus-bound. The others in the category rely on the client's learning and applying certain principles to his own thoughts and actions, whereas in REST the initiation of change is brought about by the altered environment. This is an advantage in some ways, since it eliminates the need for lengthy, difficult, and sometimes unsuccessful training. REST does not depend on continued practice and application of the methods after the treatment is officially completed, and it can be used with individuals who for some reason cannot learn or who eventually stop practicing (the latter group posing a major problem for most techniques). On the other hand, it requires at least some special facilities and its use is precluded with another potential group of patients, those for whom the stimulus-reducing environment is so unpleasant as to be intolerable. Its advantages make it a valuable tool. Because it does not in itself require the exclusive concentration of the individual on any specific exercise, it is perhaps more flexible in possible combinations with other methods than is the norm.

The similarities have, of course, been recognized by users of the various techniques. The characterization of REST as an approach to biofeedback (Lloyd, 1977) has already been mentioned. In addition, Wickramasekera (1977a) has argued that the self-management relaxation techniques discussed in this section, and REST, can be combined to produce a learned reduction of arousal. In turn, low arousal conditions and REST potentiate cognitive control over the individual's physiological functioning, thus leading to the therapeutic changes that have been noted in the literature. In common with other theorists, he hypothesizes that this effect may be based on the inhibition of left-hemisphere dominance. Positive expectancy and openness to suggestion are also considered to be contributory factors to the effect. Clearly, this analysis seems compatible with the data, and incorporates the results of sensory reduction research and therapy into the general category of stress management.

Budzynski (1976) also cites low arousal as an effect common to these techniques, but emphasizes the role of such conditions ("twilight states of consciousness") in facilitating the assimilation of new material. Because of information processing changes, twilight state learning also leads to greater attitude change. This characterization of the effect is similar in some ways to the cognitive disorganization hypothesis advanced by Suedfeld (1972), although it relies much more heavily on the hypothesized induction of an altered state of consciousness. The evidence for such induction in standard REST situations is reviewed in Chapter 6; neither introspective reports nor objective data appear to support the view that drastic alterations in consciousness are commonly found during sensory reduction sessions.

One of the things that REST may accomplish is to bring home to the participant the close connections between his behavior and its outcomes. As Schwartz (in preparation) points out, many people in today's society have come to assume that their unhealthy styles of life will have no ill effects on them because of the great accomplishments of medicine. The fact that technology actually has succeeded in relieving us of many of the natural consequences of our behavior (for example by making available drugs that relieve pain or even discomfort) has made it easy for people to generalize this principle, which Schwartz calls "disregulation." It may be that REST, which focuses the individual's attention more directly upon his own experiences, fosters a realization of natural regulatory principles. Another analogy is that REST acts as an interruptor of ongoing maladaptive programs, as a reset button that clears the board for new and more beneficial approaches to life. There is a conceptual parallel with such drastic techniques as electroconvulsive therapy, but REST is painless, nontraumatic, and —most important—serves not *only* as a disruptor but also as an environment in which the desired patterns can be considered, evaluated, and selected.

Going through REST may be re-regulatory; this is not necessarily therapeutic in itself, and certainly is not necessarily pleasant. The individual may discover things he would prefer not to know about himself, may be distressed by the realization of how adverse the natural effects of his approach to life may be, and it is at least theoretically possible that he may become terribly discouraged. However, one would expect that in most cases the realization, which is both cognitive and affective, would lead to the consideration and adoption of more healthy habits. In my own studies, there is no evidence of despair about the possibilities of improvement. While many subjects reported that they had faced for the first time the fact that their smoking or overeating was damaging and even dangerous, very few felt that the situation was hopeless.

OTHER THERAPEUTIC APPROACHES

It is difficult, of course, to identify all of the therapeutic schools in which diminution of input plays a part. One of the problems is that such schools are proliferating so rapidly as to make it almost impossible to keep track of them all. For the most part, the techniques deriving from Gestalt approaches tend to maintain levels of stimulation at about normal, or to increase them greatly. For example, most of the recently popular intense group therapy marathons enforce constant social interaction, require the monitoring of a great deal of cognitively and affectively relevant information, and induce intense emotions. There are some uses of REST-type environments. For example, primal therapy (Janov, 1970) begins with 24 hours of isolation in a hotel room, during which no diversions are permitted and in fact even sleep may be prohibited. The point "is to deprive the patient of all his usual outlets for tension, while sleeplessness tends to weaken his remaining defenses: he has fewer resources to fight off his feelings. The aim is not to allow the patient to become distracted from himself" (p. 80). Janov's goal of concentrating the person's attention upon himself and his problems is similar to one of the outcomes of reduced stimulation therapy; but the atmosphere of increasing tension and discomfort is just the opposite of that used in REST work.

Theta rebirthing (Orr and Ray, 1977), another recent development, includes a retroactive attempt to eliminate birth trauma for those people who did not have the benefits of Leboyer birth methods (see Chapter 9). Patients go through "rebirthing", which involves complete submersion in water (breathing through a snorkel) and reliving some part of prenatal existence and the process of being born. The theory is that because the experience of birth is so traumatic, its sequelae linger on, flooding the unconscious mind with negative expectations and emotions. When the adult client goes back to that situation, it becomes more understandable and tolerable and the adverse effects are ameliorated. The parallels between this technique and water-immersion REST are obvious, but they may be superficial. However, just how rebirthing fits into the general class of procedures that we have been discussing is difficult to tell because, like most components of the "human potential" movement, it is very light on coherent theory, and even more so on objective and systematic evaluation.

It should be noted that Erika Fromm (cited in Kracke, 1967) had characterized the REST situation as being as close as one can get to the intrauterine environment in an experimental setting. According to many theorists, this should make it a totally pleasant and quiescent state. As we know, REST has both of these qualities for some subjects, either one for others, and neither for still others. One explanation for negative reactions is that intrauterine-like conditions are also associated with the traumatic sensation of the original birth experience. Or it may be that the evocation of primary process material, and perhaps the dependency and related aspects of fetal and early life, are overwhelmingly threatening for some subjects. This explanation, of course, ties in with data previously cited that REST is maximally pleasant for individuals who can adjust comfortably to regression in the service of the ego. The other way to adapt is to control the primary process. In two studies (Wright and Abbey, 1965; Wright and Zubek, 1969), Rorschach measures of such control were positively correlated with tolerance for a one week-long monotonous stimulation condition.

REST IN JAPANESE PSYCHOTHERAPY

Much of Japanese psychiatry is the adaptation or even direct adoption of Western techniques. These include the use of seclusion rooms in mental institutions (Jacobson and Berenberg, 1952); but, unlike most Western psychotherapists, the Japanese have used REST as a part of systematic treatment approaches. It may be that the tradition of meditation, so long a feature of Japanese thought and practice, makes the idea of stimulus reduction as a therapeutic situation more natural and palatable for the Japanese.

Aside from indigenous folk medicine, two modern Japanese innovations in psychotherapy have included REST as a major component. The first, most widely used, and best known of these is Morita therapy, begun in 1917 as a treatment for a type of neurosis called *shinkeishitsu.* Morita acknowledged that some of his ideas were based on Mitchell's (1877/1905) Rest Cure.

Morita Therapy. *Shinkeishitsu,* which has been translated as neurasthenia (Reynolds, 1976), shows itself in interpersonal problems such as inferiority feelings, shyness, introversion, hypochondria, and excessive sensitivity in social situations. Morita interpreted this syndrome as reflecting an excessive focusing upon inadequacies as opposed to the world in which the self must function and in which its problems must be solved. To reduce the symptoms, the therapist tries to lead the patient to see himself as similar to other people, and, in fact, as potentially superior because his desire to overcome his limitations is so much stronger (as demonstrated by the fact that it has led him to develop the neurotic symptoms).

Inpatient care is divided into three phases, the first of which is closest to REST. This is the phase of absolute bed rest, which typically lasts for approximately one week. The patient is placed alone in a comfortable but relatively bare room, with facilities for sanitation but not for recreation. The therapist comes in once or twice a day to see how the patient is progressing. Aside from this, there is no contact with other people.

Some present-day Morita therapists have shortened and deemphasized the bed rest period, varied the number and duration of visits from the therapist, introduced the use of Western psychotherapeutic techniques (e.g., the elicitation of transference) during those visits, and so on. One purpose of the bed rest period is for the subject to be open to his own thoughts and feelings without censorship or diversion, a rationale that is quite similar to some of those advanced for the use of more profound but shorter REST in Western studies. The patient is encouraged to think about his symptoms and problems, and to stay on the bed and continue the process even if he feels bored and has an urge to terminate the treatment.

The phase of bed rest also serves the purposes of improved diagnosis. If a patient cannot accept the restrictions, or does not get increasingly bored, he is diagnosed as suffering from something besides *shinkeishitsu* and subsequent treatment is modified accordingly. Also, the patient learns that even extreme feelings diminish over time, so that he becomes more open to change. His perfectionist criticisms of his own thoughts and feelings are reduced through the instructions and through the experience of suspending censorship. There is a parallel between bed rest and the relaxation response. Feelings of anxiety and other tension-arousing feelings are incompatible with lying down and relaxing, and may thus be weakened by reciprocal inhibition (Reynolds, 1976). Stimulus hunger also plays a role. Because the social contact between the therapist and the patient becomes so pleasurable for the latter, the bed rest phase provides the foundation for a good relationship between the two; and, because inactivity and lack of stimulation go on for so long, patients become more positive toward life (Iwai, Homma, Amamoto, and Asakura, 1978). This "desire for life" shapes their attitude toward the work therapy that characterizes the remainder of the treatment. Reports of pleasure about going to work after bed rest support this hypothesis.

The next phase of the treatment consists of light work and enjoyment of nature around the institution, coupled with keeping a diary and attending lectures and meetings. Heavy labor follows, usually manual work related to the maintenance of the institution, together with intense group interaction with other working patients. Finally, the patient is prepared for release. He is encouraged to reassume responsibility for his daily life and to reestablish contact with the environment outside the institution. There are ex-patient groups and magazines, and many of the former patients attend meetings after they terminate the treatment itself. These are the central techniques of intervention, although outpatient, group, and mail therapy based on Morita's principles have also been used.

It is difficult to evaluate the effectiveness of any one component of this multidimensional approach. Reynolds (1976) says that there have been some cases of suicide during the bed rest phase. Of course, one cannot tell whether this is in any way a causal relationship, since it is at this phase that patients tend to be most disturbed by their condition (after all, they have just taken the drastic step of entering an institution). While there are no controlled scientific studies of outcome for the total treatment, those followups that are reported by Morita therapists (and the reports of former patients) suggest relatively high improvement rates, in the neighborhood of 60% to 70%. Changes on personality tests have also been found in pre- to post-therapy comparisons.

Chang (1965) proposed that the function of bed rest is to enable (or perhaps force) the individual to stop avoiding himself and to face his own anxieties, depressions, and other problems. Ruminating about logical solutions to those problems eventually indicates that such solutions are not adequate, which leads to an insight about the relativity of logic and of one's own point of view. This explanation goes somewhat beyond that of Reynolds, and is more philosophical. In Chang's interpretation, the goal of therapy is for the patient to reach a state of enlightenment.

The inconsistency about the therapeutic goal is interesting, and one is tempted to speculate about the cultural differences between the two authors. What makes it even more intriguing is that Reynolds, who describes Morita as a philosophy of life that emphasizes the acceptance of oneself without trying to please everyone, also compares the technique to "lying-down Zen" (1976, p. 48). In that meditative technique, the monk goes through isolation, REST, and periodic interactions with the master—just the same procedures as are used in Morita therapy. Reynolds clearly perceives the similarity between the methods as well as their identical pragmatic aspects. For example, in both cases the isolated individual makes minimal demands on institutional resources and in fact is responsible for progressing toward the goal largely on his own. There are even some theoretical parallels. These include deemphasis of self-consciousness, focusing of attention, and encouragement of the natural flow of thought; understanding beyond intellectualization; daily practice of the principles and activities learned; the sharing of manual labor; redirecting the individual toward goals that he was not fully aware of in the beginning; and the need to extinguish the euphoria that follows the reaching of an insight. In spite of these recognized parallels, Reynolds does not interpret the goal of Morita therapy as equivalent to the Zen goal of enlightenment.

There is also a hint that Reynolds, at least, recognizes stimulus overload as an aspect of *shinkeishitsu*. In his chapter on Japanese national character, he argues that dependency, social sensitivity, and image projections are primary ways in which the self is defined by the Japanese.

Extreme levels of these traits produce a person who is excessively sensitive both to signals from others and to the signals that he himself is emitting. He is therefore so inundated with information to be processed, much of which is actually unimportant or irrelevant, that he loses track of central issues in social interaction. When he is dealing with many people simultaneously, the overload paralyzes his information-processing capabilities to the point of panic. This is one aspect of *shinkeishitsu*, anthropophobia, frequently treated in Morita therapy.

Reynolds discusses the alteration of subjective reality when a major change in orientation becomes necessary, a situation that one may presume characterizes individuals who need any form of therapy. As Reynolds indicates, there are two major ways of doing this. One is to change objective reality, and the other is to change the way in which one interprets that reality and responds to it internally. The former has been standard in the West; and, at least until the recent historical past, the latter has been more characteristic of the East. Although Reynolds does not point this out, one might argue that REST changes both of these aspects quite drastically. Thus, it may be one technique on which Eastern and Western psychotherapeutic approaches can converge. In fact, it could be tried quite explicitly as an integrative technique (Schuster, 1977).

Reynolds goes to some trouble to differentiate the bed rest period of Morita therapy from experimental REST. While reduction of sensory and social stimuli occurs in Morita treatment, it is not nearly as severe in nature as the reductions imposed in "sensory deprivation" laboratories. When Reynolds himself went through the Morita technique, he reported that it was quite pleasant. Of course, so do many subjects and patients going through more profound REST. But, as we know, stimulus reduction is always a matter of degree. It appears that a week of almost total isolation in one room would provide a fair degree of diminution, particularly for people who normally live in a highly technological and extremely crowded environment. It is interesting that some of the discussion of the bed rest period at least approaches recognizing its nature as an unfreezer, although a gentle one used with people who have already self-selected themselves as wanting to change. In that, the parallel with the uses of REST described in this book is obvious. Incidentally, just as in REST studies, there have been cases of individuals whose Morita cure was brought about by the bed rest period alone. One of these is Tomonori Suzuki, who went on to become a famous Morita therapist himself.

Chang (1974) reports that patients at first find bed rest to be a period of freedom from their normal obligations and responsibilities, just as Western patients react to REST, but the focusing on problems and their solutions develops and strengthens with time in the situation. These thoughts are pursued to their ultimate conclusion—unlike in the normal stimulus environment, where interruptions are so frequent and unavoidable. The patient then feels that he has attained an important insight, and typically experiences a period of tranquility. This happens again and again, as new problems and new insights are dealt with. However, about half-way through the week, the cycle begins to disappear. Apparently, stimulus-hunger takes over, and the patient is increasingly oriented towards entering the outside world. The second stage, which Reynolds characterizes as light work, is called the semi-bed-rest period by Chang, again an interesting difference in emphasis. Several hours per day are still spent in the bed rest situation, but the rest of the time the patient is permitted to wander around the grounds and observe nature. Light work, the keeping of a diary, and reading the classics are also permitted.

Another description of Morita therapy (Suzuki and Yamaguchi, 1974) also differs slightly from some of the others. For example, the bed rest period (*gajoku*) is described as being a period of lack of communication: while the therapist comes to visit the patient once a day, he does not converse with him at all! According to Suzuki and Yamaguchi, this is not enough to produce therapeutic change in a short time although according to Reynolds, Suzuki himself was cured in this way. Since "short time" is not defined, and Reynolds does not tell us whether the duration of bed rest in Suzuki's case was prolonged, the source of the inconsistency is uncertain.

Doi (1962) confirms that the therapist in classical Morita therapy does not speak to the patient during the bed rest phase. He, like Suzuki and Reynolds, points out the closeness of Morita therapy to Zen. Doi, a psychoanalyst, has tried to apply analytic treatment to patients coming to him with *shinkeishitsu* symptoms. He interprets the development of the neurosis as the consequence of a severe frustration of the wish to be loved. In this interpretation, the isolation of the patients and the conditions during work therapy fail to address or satisfy this need. But Doi thinks it possible that somehow the treatment enables the patient to transcend his dependence on the love of others, thus eliminating his symptoms. Some of the similarities between Freudian and Morita therapy are discussed by Reynolds and Yamamoto (1972). An obvious one is the important role of a respected and expert therapist, and another (not noted in the paper) is the use of stimulus reduction for at least some portion of the therapeutic procedure.

Naikan Therapy.   Another native school of therapy developed in Japan is *Naikan,* which literally means "looking inside" (Reynolds, 1976; 1978). Here, the subject is given a short lecture after having been oriented to

Naikan therapy by books, lectures, and so on. He then sits in a comfortable position in a small room or chamber, facing the wall, for approximately 20 hours. During this time, he is instructed to think about his relationship with other people, particularly his mother, sequentially exploring his own attitudes and interactions with such people during his past life. The therapist comes in approximately every hour for a few minutes, discusses the patient's insights, gives advice, or suggests a new topic for thought. This goes on, with breaks for eating, sleeping, and sanitation, every day for 6 to 10 days. After that time, the patient is encouraged to practice the technique in his normal life daily for an hour or so. As in Morita therapy, recent developments in the technique have made it less severe (e.g., at its inception, food and sleep deprivation were also imposed).

This procedure is apparently often employed in correctional institutions, particularly those dealing with young offenders. In the initial orientation, and again at the end of the intensive treatment, important people in the institution (the director, warden) demonstrate their support and approval. The therapists can be paraprofessionals, the major requirement being that they have themselves gone through the procedure.

The technique apparently has two major results. One is that the patient stops ruminating about disappointments and grievances for which his family, particularly his parents, had been responsible. Through repeated discussions with the therapist, who encourages a more empathic point of view, the patient eventually comes to a realization that his parents and others have loved and helped him, that he is therefore in debt to them, and that he should devote himself to repaying that debt through love and service to others. At the same time, he develops a close and grateful relationship with the therapist, who (unlike in Zen and Morita therapy) is a wise and gentle advisor rather than an authority figure.

Here, the goal of therapy is seen as the emergence of a central self which is moral and basically good. The therapy, just as in the Morita procedure, is characterized as an essentially educational process. Individuals who are ignorant of the appropriateness of being grateful, accepting one's obligations in society, and shouldering one's responsibilities, are brought to realize that the lack of such correct behavior causes problems and feelings of shame for other people. Their own moral self awakens and feels guilt (Reynolds, 1978), and the result is a pro-social change in attitude and behavior. The three major topics of thought during therapy, focusing in turn upon different people and different periods of life, are:

1. What the patient has received from others.
2. What he has done for those others in return.
3. Problems that he has caused for those others (Murase, 1972).

In *Naikan,* the major purpose of reduced environmental stimulation appears to be to focus the individual's ability to concentrate. This, of course, is one of its uses in Morita therapy, as well as in Western approaches of which it is a component. Other therapeutic aspects, such as relaxation, openness to therapeutic suggestion, increasing desire to interact with the real world, and so on, do not seem to be utilized.

Naikan, which is relatively recent in origin, has been used in mental hospitals and schools. However, its main use is in the rehabilitation of juvenile and adult criminals. Its effectiveness seems to be high, with recidivism rates of clients being significantly less than those of other prisoners. The difference ranges from approximately 33% to approximately 75% (Takeda, 1971). It is claimed that even habitual criminals, gangsters, and psychopaths can benefit from the procedure. As a rehabilitative application of REST, *Naikan* is not unique (see Chapter 3); but its systematic use and widespread acceptance are very unusual.

In a forthcoming book, Reynolds (in preparation) discusses several other Japanese techniques based on REST. These include *seiza* ("quiet sitting") and *shadan* (isolation therapy). In the former, patients are taught to sit and breathe "properly," and perform the exercise two or three times a day for half an hour at a time. The purpose is to use the healing forces within the body itself, and it is claimed that the technique has positive effects on a variety of physical, biobehavioral, and psychological problems. A state of calm alertness is supposedly one of the effects. *Shadan* therapy, using only bed rest as the procedure, is based on the same theoretical grounds. According to Reynolds, the fundamental processes used were first described in writings that are approximately 1000 years old.

The connection between this category of therapeutic approaches and Zen has been pointed out by almost all writers in the field. There are the shared goals of restoring equilibrium, of recognizing and eliminating causes of unnecessary needs and frustrations. Participants reduce their physical activity to a minimum while maintaining an alert state. To this end, a comfortable, quiet, adequately lit room is used. The light, and the principle that the eyes should remain open, prevents the meditator from falling asleep (Akishige, 1976). Zen meditators underestimate elapsed time (Chihara, 1976), improve their ability to concentrate without being distracted (Taniguchi, 1976), and transfer the control of some autonomic activity from lower to higher centers of the brain (Akishige, 1976). All of these can be aspects of psychotherapy (Hirai, 1975), and all of them have been at least theoretically implicated as possible consequences of REST. Zen meditators also tend to concentrate on a perceptual response, and a

Western study (Maupin, 1965) has shown that individuals who are relatively open to imagery and fantasizing respond more quickly to the meditation exercises. These, too, are parallels between the two procedures.

CONCLUSION

It should be clear that reduced stimulation has a long history in psychotherapeutic practice in the formal European tradition, as well as in other cultures. Furthermore, this aspect of treatment was recognized as important even in the very early days of treatment for behavioral disorders. Thus, the systematic use of REST is based on a long, consistent, and well-established history.

Current therapeutic procedures continue to incorporate features of environmental restriction. Present-day practitioners may not be as fully aware of this as were their predecessors, but even when the inclusion of this kind of manipulation is done without deliberate design, it is easily identifiable. Unfortunately, only rarely is there an attempt made to control the stimulus-reducing features of the therapeutic environment in any systematic manner, or to assess its contribution to the effectiveness of the therapy. One side-effect of this oversight is the further separation of REST research and application from mainstream clinical investigations, as exemplified by the frequent omission of relevant studies from otherwise thorough literature reviews. As I have indicated in Chapter 1, this tendency has had adverse effects on both lines of development. Workers using REST become discouraged, and the optimal features and applications of the procedure remain insufficiently clarified. At the same time, clinicians working toward the solution of various problems fail to modify or expand their procedures by using a technique that might significantly increase the beneficial impact of their treatments. Another group that sustains serious loss because of this situation, and whose loss in fact may be the most serious, is that of the clients whose potential gain from the better understanding and wider application of REST procedures is thwarted. In my opinion, given the striking universality of reduced stimulation as featured in many therapeutic traditions, and its theoretical and practical similarities to so many currently popular modes of treatment, the urgency of a movement toward integration is clear.

CHAPTER 8

REST with Noninstitutionalized Adults

This chapter addresses itself to the systematic use of stimulus reduction with clients who have problems that do not require institutionalization but that result in sufficient discomfort and distress (and sometimes physical danger) to warrant intervention. Applications in this group have included the use of REST to facilitate smoking cessation and weight reduction, with pilot studies in various other areas.

The treatment of noninstitutionalized individuals potentially involves many more patients, therapists, and behavioral problems than does work with the hospitalized mentally ill. In spite of this there has until recently been relatively little research on the use of REST in the outpatient situation. The clinical psychologists using stimulus reduction have tended to be staff members of hospitals, and have had easy access to institutionalized people and to convenient facilities. Because hospitals provide constant availability of patients with dramatic symptoms, greater environmental control, good financial and material support systems, and methodological efficiency, they have been a convenient site for clinical REST projects.

However, the use of REST with noninstitutionalized individuals has its own advantages. To begin with, volunteer clients tend to be highly motivated. They are dependable and cooperative in providing information, including follow-up data. Compared to psychotic inpatients, they can articulately discuss their problems, uncertainties, reactions to the treatment, and progress with the researcher/therapist. Last, because the dysfunctions being treated are relatively specific and limited, evaluation of the results can be based on objective evidence. This is more difficult to achieve in the therapy of hospitalized psychiatric patients, who tend to suffer from global or profound disturbances.

REST IN SMOKING CESSATION

The area of smoking was the first in which REST was systematically applied to the modification of health-dysfunctional habit patterns. The earliest such attempt of my own research team grew out of dissatisfaction with some of the aspects that the literature on persuasibility and restricted stimulation shared with the rest of the experimental attitude change literature (Suedfeld, Landon, Pargament, and Epstein, 1972). These problematic features include excessive reliance on rating scales and compliance with experimental instructions rather than using nonlaboratory behavior as the dependent variable; a concentration on peripheral attitudes, which have little if any relevance to the subject's daily life, or even on topics on which his original attitudes are neutral or nonexistent; and an ignoring of the need for followup data collection at fairly long durations after the experimental treatment.

There are many reasons for these shortcomings. To begin with, experimental investigations in social psychology, as in other areas, require relatively objective and quantifiable measures. Attitude scales and compliant behavior seem to provide this kind of datum. Furthermore, such measures are quite compatible with those used in other areas of psychological research. The use of unimportant topics has three obvious bases. One of these is an ethical problem, concerning the experimenter's right to change attitudes that are central in the subject's belief system, such as political or religious loyalties. Second, the data are much clearer if all subjects start out from approximately the same attitudinal position. This is most easily accomplished when one starts from a zero or neutral point. Third, and seldom explicitly admitted, was (and is) the doubt that most experimental social psychologists harbor concerning the efficacy of their techniques.

The fragility and nonreplicability of phenomena observed in social psychological laboratories is proverbial among investigators. Almost any review, in any subarea, will indicate that consistent effects are very rare indeed. This problem has, in the past decade, exploded in what has by now too often been called the malaise of social psychology. Discouragement has reached the point where some theorists have questioned whether social psychology can even theoretically aspire to be a science (Gergen, 1973). Even moderate critics have agreed that the power of social psychological manipulation in the laboratory is at best greatly limited. Obviously, if one wants to avoid "negative" results (i.e., those that fail to confirm the hypothesis at a statistically significant level), one must deal with phenomena as malleable as one can find. It is equally obvious that neutral or weakly held attitudes are easier to change than those to which the subject has a serious commitment.

The problem of followup is to a great extent a pragmatic difficulty. The investigator would like to finish the study as soon as possible, would like to avoid the erosion of the subject group, and may be worried about the possible effects of repeated testing. Secondarily, he again may have the fear that data collected any appreciable time after the experiment would demonstrate the impermanence of the changes that he managed to elicit originally.

It was not with any great faith in the potency of restricted stimulation as a technique for obtaining attitude change that I decided to abandon the traditional approach. Rather, I felt that my research group had exploited the neutral and peripheral attitude topic with which we had been working (the opinions of American university students about Turkey) as far as we wanted to, and was ready to test the boundary conditions for the restricted stimulation-persuasibility phenomenon (see Suedfeld, 1969b).

We then looked for an attitude topic that would meet these criteria: 1. Objective measures of change should be feasible. 2. Change should be possible without ethical qualms. 3. Followup data collection should be practical without having the subjects report back to the laboratory. We soon decided that research with a clinical focus would be the most appropriate. The modification of an unhealthy habit would fit the criteria mentioned above. Smoking seemed to be a convenient topic with which to start. With change in the number of cigarettes smoked as the major dependent variable, the first and the third criteria would be fulfilled. There was considerable evidence to show that smoking less—or not at all—would be beneficial for our subjects. Furthermore, such a change would not affect any basic ideological position. The second requirement, that of ethical acceptability, was thus met. Each subject could be used as his or her own control, with changes in smoking rate being measured from the pre-experimental baseline. Since the measure was a behavioral rather than a verbal one, the problem of initial equivalence across subjects became less crucial even though it was not completely solved.

My own conviction was that our experimental technique would not be powerful enough to produce any substantial change in smoking behavior. The literature on smoking cessation was not encouraging then (nor is it now—see Hunt and Bespalec, 1974; Hunt and Matarazzo, 1973). Standard psychotherapy, behavior modification, and re-focusing and relaxation techniques all seem to be of very limited effectiveness. For example, while some writers advocate hypnotherapy for smokers (e.g., Nuland and Field, 1970; Watkins, 1976; West, 1977), a review of 30 years of this treatment concluded that "most authors claim success but their procedures cannot be reproduced" (Johnston and Donoghue, 1971, p. 271). Research with meditation and relaxation techniques has generated some positive results, but there has not been enough of it for a reliable assessment. On the other hand, REST and the other relaxation and re-focusing procedures are conceptually relevant. Smoking seems to increase arousal and at the same time induce a feeling of relaxation (Frankenhaeuser, Myrsten, Post, and Johansson, 1971; Nesbitt, 1973—but cf. Shiffman and Jarvik, 1978—Schubert, 1965). Similar effects may be produced by restricted stimulation, which may thus serve as a temporary substitute. Since many smokers use cigarettes as a way of coping with tension, while others progress to the point where smoking becomes automatic for them, both relaxation and attentional refocusing should be appropriate modes of inducing change.

The only early attempt to use REST in this context had been unsuccessful. In that study (Patrick, 1965), the showing of an antismoking film was preceded by an hour of reduced stimulation. During a 3-hour social isolation period after the viewing of the film, the experimental subjects smoked less than did a group that had not seen the movie; however, there was no difference between their rate and that of another group of subjects who had seen the film without previous environmental restriction. It is difficult to ascribe this negative result to any particular factor. Patrick's subjects were psychiatric patients, the period of REST was very brief, the change in environment (being taken out of the REST condition to see the film) plus the film itself may have been stimulating enough to overcome whatever stimulus restriction effects had emerged, and a strong need for cigarettes may have arisen if the subjects found the post-presentation period of solitude punitive or anxiety-arousing.

We were not sure whether a representative sample of smokers would volunteer for a prolonged period in restricted stimulation. An additional difficulty was that because of environmental and safety considerations the subjects could not have cigarettes available in the chamber. Previous investigators had reported that there were smokers among their volunteers, and that such subjects did not seem to terminate the experiment prematurely because of the lack of cigarettes (Vernon, 1963; J. P. Zubek, personal communication, 1970). To check these informal accounts, a large class in introductory psychology was given a questionnaire which, among other things, measured the attitudes and the behaviors of the students in regard to cigarettes. These data were compared with some that had been collected from subjects in a previous REST experiment, unrelated to smoking, that had been run in our laboratory. We were pleased to find that the proportion of smokers was approximately 50% in each of the two groups. Furthermore, the Horn-Waingrow scale of smoking (1966) showed that the different types of smokers (habitual, positive affect, negative affect, and addicted) appeared in the same proportions in our two samples. Thus, since the REST subjects and the general student group showed essentially equivalent attitudes and behaviors related to smoking, we were reasonably confident that a fairly good sample of smokers could be obtained for our research.

Early Studies

The design of our first experiment consisted of the factorial variation of 24 hours of reduced stimulation and a 3-minute taped message which concentrated upon the adverse health effects of smoking. REST, here as in all of our subsequent work on smoking and obesity, meant lying on a bed in a dark, sound-reducing chamber. Water and liquid diet food were sipped ad lib through plastic tubes pinned near the subject's pillow. Getting up was permitted only when the subject had to use the chemical toilet placed near the bed. The contents of the message were based upon the then recently published Report of the Surgeon General of the United States. The content, style, and tone of the message were all factual and unemotional.

The tape was played approximately half an hour before the end of the REST session for the combined-treatment group. The message-only group heard it after reporting and being oriented to the laboratory. The REST-only group went for 24 hours without any input from the experimenters, while the control group received neither REST nor the message presentation. All of the subjects were given a measure of belief stability (see Koslin, Pargament, and Suedfeld, 1971), a scale of attitudes about smoking, and a question as to the extent to which they had missed smoking while participating in the experiment.

The attitude results were complex and somewhat unexpected. REST subjects showed less belief stability than did the nonconfined groups. This finding supported our hypothesis that REST is a general cognitive, and therefore belief, unfreezer (see Lewin, 1958; Suedfeld, 1972). However, there was also an interaction effect. As predicted, the message produced lower stability in the nonconfined condition; but it led to higher stability in the confined group. Subjects undergoing the combined treatment agreed with fewer items on the smoking scale, regardless of whether these items were favorable or unfavorable to smoking, than any of the other three groups. There were no differences between the confined and nonconfined groups on how much they had missed cigarettes during the previous 24 hours, in spite of the fact that the former had been completely deprived of cigarettes while the latter had not. On a 1–7 scale, none of the four groups had a mean score higher than the midpoint (4).

These data were interpreted as generally supporting the prediction that REST would impair the complex cognitive performance involved in maintaining belief stability in the face of a persuasive presentation. However, while the treatment induced uncertainty about the topic, it also provided information that reduced the general uncertainty and information need generated by stimulus reduction (Jones, 1969). The resulting approach-avoidance reaction may have led to reactance and a generally negative reaction to all of the attitude items regardless of their direction. Such an interpretation is compatible with findings that subjects with above-average intelligence (presumably including many of our college students) sometimes exhibit a boomerang effect in response to persuasive messages during sensory restriction (e.g., Myers et al., 1966). The prediction of a positive linear relationship between belief instability and agreement with anti-smoking statements was not completely confirmed although such a relationship did obtain both within the nonconfinement and the REST treatment.

Thus, stimulus reduction had greater effects on stability and opinion change than did the presentation of a persuasive message under normal conditions. This may have been a function of the generally disorganizing effect of the environment, of changes in arousal level, or of some other REST-specific factor. The finding that 24 hours without a cigarette did not lead to any discomfort among our confined subjects substantiated previous anecdotal reports. It also represents an interesting and as yet unexplained datum that deserves further investigation.

Even more interesting was the behavioral followup, which occurred 3 months after the experiment. The four groups had smoked approximately the same amount before the experiment. When they were telephoned 3 months later, ostensibly as part of a survey on the smoking behavior of college students, the two REST groups reported smoking 38% less than at baseline. In contrast, there was a 23% reduction in the message-only group, and essentially no change in the control group (omitting one subject who for some reason had increased his smoking rate by about 300%).

This was the real surprise. With a minimal persuasive intervention—a very short and undramatic message— and 3 months after the session, the REST subjects were still maintaining a significantly reduced consumption of cigarettes. We were also intrigued to see that there was no difference between those REST subjects who had heard the message and those who had not. This finding could be explained on the basis that the message was neither novel nor instructive, and that the measures administered immediately after the session may have concentrated the attention of all of the subjects on their smoking behavior. Explanations based on set, desire to please the experimenter, and other such artifacts appeared to be ruled out. These participants had initially volunteered in response to a general call for experimental subjects rather than because they wanted to stop smoking, and the followup was not identified with the initial experiment.

Although the results were promising, I was not yet convinced that the technique was a clinically useful one. One major problem constantly found in the smoking cessation literature is that almost any treatment can reduce smoking rate for a while, but almost none has resulted in significant reductions over a long period (see e.g., Greenwald, 1973; Levenberg and Wagner, 1976). As one reviewer said, "Even high immediate success rates generally fall off sharply over time" (Keutzer, Lichtenstein, and

Mees, 1968, p. 529); or, to borrow a highly similar concept, "It is, in reality, very easy to kill a dragon, but it is impossible to keep him dead" (Bramah, 1922/1972, p. 48).

The next step (Suedfeld and Ikard, 1973) was to improve the effectiveness of the messages, and to try the treatment out on a sample that was motivated to succeed but posed a real problem for smoking cessation intervention. Accordingly, more messages were written, of which eventually 18 were included in a study. Nine of them dealt with the health hazards caused by cigarettes, two with motivational factors in smoking cessation, and seven with how to solve problems that might arise from the decision to quit smoking. After each message, a brief comprehension test was administered to help focus the subject's attention on the presentation. We also included periodic reinforcements, of the form "Congratulations. You have now gone X hours without a cigarette. You are doing very well."

Subjects for a pilot study were recruited by means of an advertisement in a community newspaper. The five individuals selected to participate were early respondents to the advertisement, all of whom had smoked at least 30 cigarettes per day for a prolonged period of time, scored as psychologically addicted to smoking on the Tomkins-Ikard Smoking Scale (Ikard and Tomkins, 1973), and reported that they had previously attempted to quit smoking but were unable to do so on their own. All five underwent the combination of 24 hours of REST and interspersed messages presented over the intercom.

The results were mixed. All of the participants stopped smoking for a while, but two went back up to baseline levels within 2 months. These two had volunteered for the treatment in the first place for reasons other than wanting to quit smoking: one because he was interested in what the environment would be like, and the other to placate her teenage son, who kept "hassling" her to stop smoking. These two subjects also had slightly higher baseline smoking rates than did the other three. Of the other three subjects, one stayed abstinent from cigarettes during the 3-month followup period, although he smoked a few cigars; the other two maintained rates substantially below baseline up to 2 months, when they each had a brief "booster shot" consisting of 12 hours of reduced stimulation with a repetition of some of the earlier messages. During the 1-month followup after this experience, both of them remained completely abstinent. The three successful subjects reported that their craving for cigarettes had disappeared during the REST session and had not returned. The two who went back to smoking did so for other reasons, primarily as an aid in managing negative emotions.

Clearly, the treatment was partially successful. Given the nature of this particular sample, the findings were encouraging enough to justify continuing this line of research.

A Major Demonstration

The next experiment (Suedfeld and Ikard, 1974) combined features of the first two. From the first, we took the 2 × 2 design independently varying 24 hours of reduced stimulation and the presentation of messages; from the second, the recruitment of volunteers from the general community and the expanded message format. Several hundred people responded to newspaper and radio invitations to test a new, experimental method for smoking cessation. Each of these was sent an autobiographical data sheet, a questionnaire concerning smoking habits, and the Tomkins-Ikard Smoking Scale.

The sample selected contained approximately equal numbers of men and women, an age range of 25 to 55, and a wide variety of occupations, socioeconomic and educational levels, and home communities. All of the smokers were smoking at least 20 cigarettes per day (with a mean of 32), and had been doing so for at least 3 years (mean = 15). All of them scored as psychologically addicted or pre-addicted on the smoking scale. Except for keeping the sex distribution relatively equal, subjects were assigned randomly to each of the four treatment groups.

Ten messages were presented at approximately 1½ hour intervals. Seven of these were taken from Suedfeld and Ikard (1973). The other three represented a form of covert rehearsal and desensitization. The subject was asked to recall in detail the last emotional situation in which he or she had craved a cigarette. This time, a brief relaxation exercise was to be substituted at the point where the cigarette had been lit originally. One message did this for an experience of anger, one for anxiety, and one for joy. In addition to the ten substantive messages, there were five reinforcers of the type mentioned in the previous discussion. These were presented after 6, 10, 15, 20, and 23 hours of REST. Nonconfined subjects in the message presentation group were asked to stay at home, close to a telephone. The messages were played to them over the phone at the same intervals as they were played into the REST chamber. The nontreated control group was referred to other therapeutic facilities, including the American Health Foundation, which was one of the sponsors of this study.

Figure 8-1 shows smoking rates through a 2-year followup. There was no contact with the subjects between the end of the first and the end of

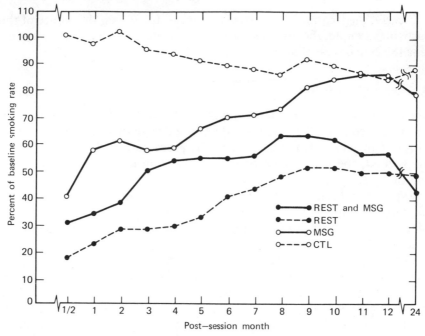

Figure 8.1.   Effects of REST and messages on cigarette smoking: Mean reduction from pre-treatment baseline. From P. Suedfeld in R. B. Stuart (Ed.), *Behavioral self-management: Strategies, techniques and outcomes*, New York: Brunner/Mazel, 1977.

the second years. Several of them moved during that period and were unreachable. Therefore, the 2-year data are based on about half of the original group. The immediate impact of all treatments was considerable, but—as usual—it did not remain stable for very long. All three curves began to creep upward, a trend that apparently reached asymptote before the end of the second year. At the end of one year, the two nonconfined groups had decreased their smoking by approximately 16%, compared to almost 50% for the two REST groups; a year after that, the two nonconfined groups were smoking an average of 18% under baseline compared to 55% for the two REST groups. In both cases, subjects who had heard the messages were smoking somewhat, but not significantly, less than their no-message counterparts. At the end of the first year of followup, the proportion of totally abstinent subjects was 27% among REST and 11% among nonconfined participants. At the end of the second year (based on a reduced sample), the equivalent figures were 39% and 16%. The main effect for REST remained highly significant throughout the entire followup period.

This study provided a major demonstration of the effectiveness of REST as a treatment for smoking. Some of its other findings were also of interest. One was the replication of the minimal effects of messages added to environmental restriction, even when these messages were more elaborate and intuitively appeared more helpful than the one presented in Suedfeld et al. (1972). This was the case in spite of having several subjects report, both in this study and in Suedfeld and Ikard (1973), that specific messages had been useful to them in maintaining their reduced smoking rate. One possible reason is that, on the whole, smoking cessation or reduction is not a technically difficult problem to solve and that these particular clients were already highly motivated to quit. Therefore, the messages served neither an instructional nor a motivational role of any significance.

Another interesting datum was that this treatment, unlike many others, does not seem to work on an all-or-none basis. While almost every subject is completely abstinent for at least the first week after REST, this rate decreases as it does in all smoking cessation techniques. However, reduced stimulation is peculiar in that people who have undergone it as part of a smoking cessation program frequently report long-term maintenance of smoking rates significantly below their baseline, even though they are not able to remain completely abstinent from cigarettes. This is in contrast to the experience of many smoking clinics, which find that baseline levels are rapidly re-attained if a client begins smoking again after the treatment is over.

Another interesting point is the low drop-out rate. Of the original group of 40, three REST subjects quit shortly after the beginning of the session. None of the REST subjects defaulted on the followup data collection up to a year. Two of the nonconfined subjects did fail to respond to the followup questionnaires. Thus, 72 of the original 77 participants went through whatever treatment they were assigned, and continued to respond to followups for one year.

It should also be noted that, unlike the projects typically reported in the literature, ours concentrated on psychologically addicted and pre-addicted smokers. Eisinger (1972) has confirmed that psychologically addicted smokers—who use cigarettes to enhance positive and reduce negative affect and for whom not to be smoking is itself a source of negative affect—are the least likely to quit smoking. The fact that we obtained both low attrition rates and high success rates with this extremely difficult sample is particularly striking.

A Treatment Package Including REST

The most recent study performed at my laboratory (Suedfeld and Best, 1977; Best and Suedfeld, in preparation) used a multimodal approach to the modification of smoking behavior. It included a combination of two behavioral methods, previously used by Allan Best: detailed monitoring of smoking, so that the client would become aware of the emotional and environmental contingencies that initiated the behavior in each specific instance, followed by one day of satiation smoking in which the participants were requested to smoke three times their normal rate. This has the effect of increasing the aversive consequences of smoking, such as nausea, headaches, and sore throat, even if the target rate is not reached (as it frequently was not by our subjects). Another component was 24 hours of REST, during which the messages used in Suedfeld and Ikard (1974) were presented. Since we were interested in comparing the relative and combined efficacy of the techniques, all of which had previously been established as useful, no untreated control group was included. The design included one group that participated in self-monitoring and satiation smoking, one group undergoing REST with messages, and one group that experienced the combination of all of these techniques.

Cigarette consumption went up in the early part of the followup period, but one year later the smoking rate of the combined treatment group was 50% of baseline. Both other groups reported actual increases. Figure 8-2 shows abstinence rates during one year. With either component by itself the proportion of subjects who remained totally abstinent drops to approximately a quarter, not significantly different from those found in the

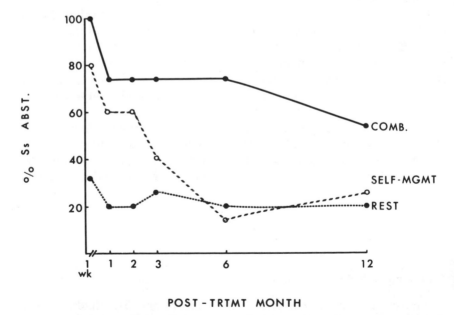

Figure 8.2.   Effects of REST and a behavioral self-management package on cigarette smoking: Percentage of subjects remaining abstinent. Data from Best & Suedfeld, in preparation.

general literature (Hunt and Matarazzo, 1973) and in previous studies using these specific techniques (Best and Steffy, 1975; Suedfeld and Ikard, 1974). The combined treatment, however, showed much better maintenance of the quit rate, remaining at 73% after six months and then dropping to 53% by the end of the year. In Fig. 8–2 (unlike in 8–1), higher percentages mean greater treatment success.

Unfortunately, it is very difficult to compare these findings with those of other workers, since the vast majority of the studies in the literature do not continue followup for as long as 12 months. However, the implication is of a level of success considerably above the average of other approaches. One of the few comparable findings was recently reported by Lando (1977), whose broad-spectrum technique called for six sessions over a 1-week period, followed by seven maintenance sessions during the next 2 months. The treatment consisted of indoctrination concerning the possibility of unlearning the smoking habit, satiation smoking for a week, rapid smoking for 25 minutes during each of the six treatment sessions, contractual management involving a money penalty for smoking, self-reward and self-punishment depending on whether the individual remained abstinent, booster treatment with rapid smoking upon relapse, group sessions in which problems were discussed and solutions offered, and general indications of group support and cohesiveness to help members maintain abstinence. With this elaborate multimodal technique, 76% of the clients—about the same as with our brief satiation/REST treatment—were still abstinent at the 6 month followup. No data have been reported for a longer interval.

In view of the many parallels between REST and systematic relaxation (see Chapter 7), we may consider a study whose design was very similar to that of Best and Suedfeld but used progressive relaxation rather than REST (Sutherland, Amit, Golden, and Rosenberger, 1975). Three groups of smokers were used, one each receiving progressive relaxation training and satiation smoking, and one group receiving both treatments. The combined relaxation and satiation condition demonstrated the most dramatic reduction of smoking rate at the end of the 6 weeks of active treatment, and was the only group that maintained a significant reduction in smoking rate during the 3-month followup. The final rate at the end of 3 months was over half of baseline.

It should be noted that the satiation smoking technique is not the same as "rapid smoking," in which the client has to inhale every 6 seconds for as long as he can (usually about 5 minutes) repeatedly during each treatment session (Schmahl, Lichtenstein, and Harris, 1972). This latter technique, which appears to be quite a successful one, has also aroused controversy as a possible health hazard (Hauser, 1974; Horan, Linberg, and Hackett, 1977).

Summary

Let us summarize these findings. Briefly, we established that 24 hours of REST could be instrumental in enabling even addicted smokers to terminate or at least reduce their use of cigarettes. The technique appeared to work without differential effects as a function of sex, age, socioeconomic background, educational level, baseline smoking rate (within the relatively narrow range represented by our participants), suggestibility as measured by Spiegel's eye-roll technique (1970), or intelligence. Reduced smoking seemed to be a feasible alternative for those who did not quit (see Frederiksen, Peterson, and Murphy, 1976). Most subjects lost their craving for cigarettes completely, even during long followup periods. Booster sessions including REST seemed to be useful, although the data on this point are indicative rather than definitive (cf. Relinger, Bornstein, Bugge, Carmody, and Zohn, 1977).

Evaluation of the Results

Smoking cessation is not a field for blind optimism. Many reviews and research papers have concluded that intervention has only marginal success, with abstinence rates at followups 6 months to a year later hovering between 20% and 30% (e.g. Hunt and Matarazzo, 1973). Although I do not think that the spreading of gloom is a very useful enterprise, particularly in a field where gloom is already pervasive, it might be appropriate to quote from recent publications testing various smoking cessation procedures. For the sake of brevity, all of the quotes are from titles or abstracts:

"No treatment combination led to reductions in smoking beyond controls for nonspecific factors, nor were reductions maintained over followup times" (Conway, 1977, p. 348).

"Smoking cessation: Long term irrelevance of mode of treatment" (Levenberg and Wagner, 1976).

"It was concluded that an immediate punishment technique was not effective and that 5, 7, or 9 days of therapy were not of sufficient duration for a high rate of success to be attained" (Nelson, 1977, p. 191).

"Although both experimental groups significantly relapsed between posttreatment and the 3-month follow-up, control subjects did not" (Relinger, Bornstein, Bugge, Carmody and Zohn, 1977, p. 245).

This is not a random sample, of course, and there are reports that justify somewhat more optimism. But the reason I quote them is to indicate that, even now, investigators are meeting failure after failure in attempts to enable people to stop smoking. In spite of this, and in spite of the fact that REST as a treatment for smoking has been shown to be reliably effective as well as economical, many practitioners, researchers, and reviewers continue to ignore the data.

How do the REST findings compare with others in the literature? This question might be answered in two ways: by looking at absolute success rates or by attempting to derive some kind of efficiency measure. The REST treatment used by Suedfeld and Ikard (1974) was certainly among the most powerful techniques reported in the literature; the more elaborate combined approach of Best and Suedfeld (in preparation) has had even better results. In comparison, Hunt and Bespalec (1974) indicated that the typical abstinence rate 6 months after treatment termination is about 20 to 30%. This is the case regardless of whether we are dealing with smokers, heroin addicts, or alcoholics. Rapid smoking, described as yielding "results far superior to previously reported methods" (Relinger et al., 1977, p. 245), yielded abstinence rates of approximately 60 to 64% in the first few studies, although this dropped off to essentially no effect by the end of the year in some later reports (e.g., Lando, 1975). REST has not yet been incorporated in any of the recently popular multimodal approaches. But even these have not been superior to the stimulus restriction technique: their 6-month abstention rates hover around 50 to 60%, and range up to about 75% in some rare cases (Lando, 1977; Tongas, 1977).

In terms of cost-effectiveness, REST is even more outstanding. Comparisons are difficult here because there are such extreme differences between techniques. The overwhelming majority require the client to be physically present at the clinic or laboratory a number of times, to devote considerable time and effort, and to invest a fair amount of money. In many programs therapist time is also used quite lavishly. In contrast, the REST procedure takes one day, and does not require major effort. One does not need to reveal one's emotions in a group setting, suffer from aversive stimuli, or the like. Most of our subjects have felt that the cessation of other activities for 24 hours is considerably less disruptive than repeated sessions, each for a smaller number of hours, on a larger number of days. This was explained partly on the basis of having to come for treatment only once, and partly on the basis that it is more convenient to clear one full day, perhaps on a weekend, than to give up portions of several.

The REST method also requires relatively little time and involvement from a fully qualified therapist, beyond perhaps the initial screening and orientation. The session can be monitored by a technician or paraprofessional staff member, and one such monitor can supervise many individual treatment rooms. Thus, a high level of efficiency can be obtained, logically resulting in reduced costs for the patient. The usefulness of techniques employing inexperienced, or even not fully qualified, personnel obviously has to be established (Levenberg and Wagner, 1976). In the case of REST, the major time investment can be done by technicians monitoring the chamber. Most other procedures, including those that can be combined with REST, use people of at least graduate student level.

The major investment, aside from the breaking of the psychological barrier that seems to prevent so many clinicians from considering REST as part of their repertoire, is the acquisition of the physical facility and equipment. This can be done very expensively, if one buys a chamber from any of several commercial manufacturers. However, such an elaborate set-up is probably unnecessary for clinical purposes. If one can find some rooms in a quiet location (in the inner core of a building or in a basement would be best from the point of view of sound reduction), the remaining steps are relatively easy and cheap. All needs are met by the total covering up of any windows (of course, in a location such as those suggested above, this may not be a problem), the installation of fiber board or other sound-absorbing material on the walls, floor, and ceiling, and the purchase of the necessary equipment (intercom and tape recorder, bed and bedding, and a chemical toilet, plus some furniture for the control room). In Chapter 11, R.A. Borrie gives more details of procedures and costs.

Obviously, I feel that the use of REST under such circumstances is very practical. Cost-effectiveness studies are rare in the literature. Unfortunately, the only one that has evaluated REST did so in a fallacious way. This was the report by Barnes (1976), who compared the effectiveness and expense of a REST treatment based on Suedfeld and Ikard (1974) with the Five-Day Plan popularized by the Seventh Day Adventists (see McFarland and Folkenberg, 1964). While the effectiveness of the two methods was comparable, the Five-Day Plan was judged to be the more economical ($8.06 per client completing the program vs. $33.25 for REST).

There are several problems with the computation on which this conclusion was based. It did not take into account the amount of time that clients have to divert from other activities in order to participate. More importantly, however, the figures were biased in two ways, both tending to the same result. First, the researcher received material and personnel at no charge from active Five-Day Plan clinics. The amount that would have had to be paid to obtain these necessary components commercially or in the normal run of a clinic was not included in the cost estimates. In fact, with the omission of permanent equipment and staff personnel costs, the cost per client completing the treatment would have been reduced to $6.50 for the REST group, lower than the per-unit cost of the Five-Day Plan.

Second, the total cost of setting up the REST facility and buying equipment and supplies was prorated over the relatively small number of subjects used in the study, thus greatly confusing the issue. In an ongoing clinic, the great majority of these expenses are incurred only at the onset; once the equipment has been purchased, future costs are minimal regardless of the number of clients treated. Therefore, to divide this expense by a small number of clients inflates the apparent cost substantially. A more valid calculation of the actual investment is presented in Chapter 11.

Younggren and Parker (1977) have reported on what they considered to be a very promising smoking clinic, lasting 4 weeks and using educational seminars and individualized aversion sessions (rapid smoking). Five Army Medical Corps men were used as the primary therapists, but their work was supplemented by medical and psychological lectures and also by the presentation of educational films. In spite of this prolonged and multidimensional approach, fewer than 40% of the patients who completed the program were still abstinent 6 months after it was over.

This is not an unusual finding; the only reason why I am citing it at such length is because it is one of the few studies in which some attempt to estimate cost per client was made. Unfortunately, that attempt reveals an inadequacy similar to that of Barnes (1976). The cost cited is approximately $1.20 per patient "short of the expense of the four personnel operating the program" (pp. 86–87). Aside from the confusion as to whether four or five therapists were actually involved, ignoring personnel costs is obviously a major accounting flaw. Furthermore, it is at least likely that other costs were also excluded. The clinic was held on an army base, so that overhead may not have been added to the cost; and the cost of guest lecturers, film rentals, and equipment purchase may or may not have been included. Since 31 individuals completed treatment, the estimate given in the paper came out to a total of approximately $37 for the entire program, not a very credible figure if all expenses were actually counted.

Evaluation of the Procedures

It has justly been stated that the literature on smoking cessation suffers from a great number of methodological flaws. Let us look at one analysis of the situation and see how the series of four REST studies measures up to the suggested criteria. The list of desirable attributes is taken from an influential review by Bernstein (1969; see also Bernstein and McAllister, 1976).

Control Treatment.   1. A "contact control" group, whose members are acceptable for inclusion in the study but are told that for some innocuous reason they cannot be treated. The untreated control group in Suedfeld and Ikard (1974) fits this criterion, as its members were told (truthfully) that we did not have the chamber facilities to include them.

2. An "effort control" group, whose members are asked to quit smoking on their own while they wait for the treatment. Not included in the studies.

3. An "expectation control" condition, where the subjects are asked to try to quit by themselves, but no future treatment is promised. No such group was included in any of the studies. The suggestion given to the untreated control group in Suedfeld and Ikard (1974) that they seek out other forms of assistance, and providing information as to where such assistance was available, is as close as we have come.

4. An "attention placebo" condition, in which the same degree of therapist involvement with the client is provided, but without active treatment. Again, no such treatment was specifically included in any of our studies. However, the comparison of the efficacy of various active treatments (Suedfeld and Best, 1977; Best and Suedfeld, in preparation) seems to fulfill at least some of the same functions.

Data Collection.   Bernstein indicates the importance of accurate information concerning the smoking behavior of the subjects before, during (not an issue in the REST conditions), and after treatment. This criterion was reasonably well met in Suedfeld and Ikard (1974), and even more so in the self-monitoring groups of Best and Suedfeld (in preparation). It has been suggested that self-monitoring may be reactive, and thus may affect the behavior itself. But this has not been empirically established, while the reliability of the technique has (e.g., Frederiksen, Epstein, and Kosevsky, 1975).

Another issue, not emphasized by Bernstein, is the length of followup. Three to 6 months seems to be the typical period in most published studies, with a much smaller number going on to 1 year and extremely few continuing beyond that. In view of the well-known rapid erosion of results over time, particularly after the first few months (Bernstein, 1969; Hunt and Matarazzo, 1973), such early termination casts doubt upon the usefulness of scientific inferences drawn from the data. Our own followup in one of the major studies went on for 2 years, showing essentially no change between the end of the first and the second. Accordingly, in the most recent study (Suedfeld and Best, 1978; Best and Suedfeld, in preparation) data collection was terminated at the end of the first year.

Orientation. Bernstein argues that instructions given to participants should be carefully designed to minimize falsification of self-report data that might arise out of a desire on the subject's part to please the experimenter, or for some similar reason. On the whole, I feel fairly safe in concluding that our data were not seriously affected by distorted self-reports. The suggestion made by Bernstein to use nonreactive measures of actual smoking behavior is of course a good one, but difficult to achieve without intruding upon the privacy of the subject. In our work, several procedures were used to attain honest reporting. In the first study (Suedfeld et al., 1972), the subjects did not know that a followup data collection would be made. When it did occur, it was not identified as being related to the original experiment. In Suedfeld and Ikard (1973), there was such close and personal contact between the five subjects and the experimental staff that falsification would almost certainly have been detected.

In Suedfeld and Ikard (1974), the instructions given to the volunteers were carefully designed around this crucial issue. Subjects were repeatedly informed that the treatment was an experimental one and that false reporting in either direction would be harmful. In one case it would lead to the continued expenditure of time, money, effort, and hope on a technique that was not effective, while in the other it would result in the abandonment of a useful treatment. The subjects were clearly told that the research staff had no particular stake in the outcome beyond wanting to know the actual effects of the procedure. This was repeated in each followup contact with the subjects. We have no way to ascertain that accuracy was in fact maintained, but there are some indirect indicators. One is that many subjects reported their smoking rates in very specific terms (e.g., 33 cigarettes per day rather than 30 or 35, as would be more likely if they were estimating, and as had been more common in the telephone survey used in Suedfeld et al., 1972). In many instances, they wrote detailed analyses and explanations of the effects that they had experienced and how this had changed or not changed their smoking behavior. Several subjects were personally known either to someone connected with the research staff or to other subjects, who verified the reports made by the participant.

Data Analysis. Another shortcoming noted in previous research is the failure to mention and include attrition rates in the data analysis. We did not find attrition to be a significant problem. In the first study, everyone whom we managed to reach by telephone responded to the question, and there is no reason to think that the remainder of the group were somehow unrepresentative. In the second study, all five of the subjects remained with us until the end of our data collection. In the third experiment, there was very little attrition during the first year and presumably nonselective attrition from then to the end of the second. Attrition was, however, a problem in the most recent research (Best and Suedfeld, in preparation), particularly in regard to subjects terminating the REST experience before the scheduled time. This appeared to be due to two factors. Many of the participants had volunteered for the smoking clinic without realizing that reduced stimulation, or in fact 24 hours spent away from home at one stretch, was to be a possible part of the program. Second, the orientation to REST, which was originally provided by individuals who worked in the clinic rather than in the reduced stimulation laboratory, in some cases did not allay the fears and anxieties of the subjects. Given the high rate of successful completion in the study immediately before this one (Suedfeld and Ikard, 1974), we feel that steps can be taken to avoid this problem.

The next question relates to the appropriate measure of results. We have followed the suggestion made by Bernstein, that success rates be based upon the number of subjects completing treatment, but that information with respect to excluded subjects be provided. We have also reported both the smoking rates (cigarettes per day) and the proportion of subjects remaining abstinent as dependent measures, and in one study have supplemented these with verbal measures of attitudes.

Replications.   Another issue, of course, is whether the technique can be used by other workers, and whether the same results can be obtained in other establishments. The evaluation of replicability depends to a great extent on the willingness of clinical practitioners to follow the identical procedure carefully, since experimental replications are relatively rare (partly because of the high premium that journals place on originality). Because of the reluctance of clinicians to use REST, to which I have repeatedly referred, and because of the relative recency of the use of this technique in behavioral medicine, replications have been unfortunately scarce. Most of the evidence for the efficacy of the technique in the realm of smoking cessation comes from my own research program. In addition, there have been two clinical facilities using this technique; however, neither has yet reported results on the basis of systematically collected data.

In the one reported replication of our research, Barnes (1976) used the design and the messages originated in Suedfeld and Ikard (1974). The REST chamber was somewhat different from ours, and white noise was used. Other major features were equivalent. The subjects were not selected to be addictive or negative affect smokers. Followup continued for only 6 months, at which time 58% of the subjects were completely abstinent. This was a considerably better finding than the equivalent data (35%) for the addicted smokers of Suedfeld and Ikard (1975), and bore out the effectiveness of the REST-message combination treatment.

The paper by Barnes is actually the only controlled replication of the study; however, Hennessy (1975) investigated the possibility that the same results could be obtained by the use of visual deprivation rather than global REST. All of the subjects spent 24 hours in a windowless, comfortably equipped room among whose furnishings there was a radio that they could play at will. Two groups wore an opaque black mask over the face to prevent visual perception. Half of the light-deprived subjects, and half of the confined but nondeprived control subjects, were permitted to smoke while in the chamber. As it turned out, there was an initial difference in smoking rates, with the two groups that were permitted to smoke reporting less cigarette usage during a pre-treatment monitoring phase. Although this difference was handled statistically by the use of analysis of covariance, it may have reflected some difference in the proportions of different types of smokers included in each group that would not have been eliminated by the statistical technique. Only a 1-month followup was performed. There was a significant reduction in post-treatment smoking rates, but the reduction did not differ as a function of treatment. Qualitative reports indicated that most subjects reported a lessened desire to smoke during the session and predicted that the experience would have a favorable effect on their ability to reduce smoking. These reports were not differentially distributed across treatment conditions. Among the various changes in mood and cognitive processes mentioned by the subjects, the group that was confined under conditions of normal visual input and availability of cigarettes reported a high level of negative affect.

It is difficult to specify the implications of this study for the therapeutic effectiveness of REST. The design eliminated the confounding of stimulus restriction and the absence of cigarettes, which could have been a substantive contribution to the literature. However, there are three major problems that detract from the value of the study. One is that the visually deprived subjects were in fact exposed to much more environmental stimulation than those in the studies of my own research group. To the extent that the elimination of such stimuli increases the power of the technique, we would have to say that Hennessy's treatment was a much weaker version of ours. It is true that on some dependent variables the effects of visual deprivation have been quite similar to those of global REST; but there is no reason to think that a highly resistant behavior such as smoking would be such a variable. Second, on the other side of the same coin, is the fact that the so-called control groups in Hennessy's study were actually confined groups. As a result, the difference in stimulus restriction was very much a matter of degree, and probably not of very striking degree. These two factors together help to explain the relative lack of effect: the "experimental" group was given a weak version of REST, while the "control" groups were given an only slightly weaker version. It is no wonder that there were no significant intergroup differences. The third problem, of course, is the short followup, which made it impossible to evaluate whether the changes would be differentially resistant to erosion over time.

A few years ago, a clinic in Vancouver, B.C. used the combination treatment (self-monitoring, satiation smoking, REST, and messages) plus individual counseling. This clinic, which offered the service to the community at large, developed a hierarchy of treatment intensities. They ranged from a standardized set of taped messages that the client was given to take home and present to himself in a stimulus-reduced room, to individualized messages, generated specifically on the basis of the client's specific smoking behaviors and problems, that were presented during a 24-hour REST session in a specially adapted room of the clinic. Unlike most clinical intervention programs, this one maintained data collection during a prolonged followup period, so that an objective evaluation of the effectiveness of the treatment will be possible.

A clinic in Ecuador, which is called *Bienestar* ("well-being"), combined REST, acupressure, messages, satiation smoking, and a low carbohydrate diet. Other techniques are added from time to time. As of the middle of 1978, 33 of their clients had been put into REST. Some problems were encountered at first, until the clinic staff realized that because of the altitude, the ventilation equipment had to be improved. Since then, there have been few problems with REST tolerance. This became particularly dramatic when a blanket, formed of alternate layers of organic and inorganic material and left in the sunshine for a while, was swathed around the ventilator. When such blankets are used, the clients report a much more pleasant experience. Whether this is a function of changes in ionization, smells from the blanket being blown into the room by the ventilating equipment, or some as yet unthought-of mediating variable, is not known. Of 13 smokers, only one is back to his baseline rate of cigarette consumption, and he has requested to go through the treatment again. Three others were smoking approximately five cigarettes per day, down from 40 or more. The nine others are apparently completely abstinent.

Some cultural aspects are interesting. To begin with, many of the clients want to go through the experience at the same time as a friend, and this is accomplished by the use of two chambers simultaneously. Also, there is some problem with followups, since the participants prefer not to hurt the therapist's feelings by giving her bad news. Apparently, this tendency was overcome only by hard work on the part of the staff. Last, the letter from the organizer of the clinic in which these details were communicated also pointed out "another interesting thing—everyone has shown up and only two people have been slightly late. . . . " This is a very unusual phenomenon in view of the time norms of Latin American countries (Ann Corcoran, personal communication, June 5, 1978).

Clearly, there has not been sufficient testing of this technique in laboratories and clinics other than our own. The apprehension that, as with so many other therapeutic innovations, the effect may be to some extent specific to our own group has not been allayed, although the findings of Barnes (1976) and of Cooper et al. (1977) are encouraging. So are the informal reports of the clinics using REST for the treatment of smokers. However, I would still place high priority on obtaining independent verification of the results.

DYSFUNCTIONS OF EATING BEHAVIOR

REST has been used with two behavioral problems connected with eating: anorexia nervosa and obesity. So far, not many studies have been done explicitly employing REST in these situations. However, the preliminary evidence has been positive.

Anorexia Nervosa

Anorexia nervosa, a pathological self-starvation based on an aversion to food or to weight gain, has been estimated to afflict between .24 and 1.6 per 100,000 population annually. Most of the patients are adolescents or young adult women. Death rates have been estimated at between 3 and 25% of the patients, a discrepancy partially explainable by different lengths of followup (Bemis, 1978). Its high incidence and life-threatening nature make it a serious problem.

There is a theory that anorexia nervosa is caused by disorders in the relationship between the child and the mother, specifically maternal deprivation which makes for a need to regress and be dependent in a warm relationship with some other person. However, the individual rejects this regression, along with the food that symbolizes the mother's nurturance. Given the possibility that reduced stimulation may induce regression and make it more acceptable (see Azima, Vispo, and Azima,

1961), one might argue from this psychoanalytic viewpoint that REST might be a useful technique in dealing with the problem.

In a recent review, Bemis (1978) evaluated a number of therapeutic approaches. Psychodynamic treatments seem to be of relatively low utility. Family therapy, which attempts to reorganize the family's interaction toward a more favorable pattern, has been tested only a few times but appears to be promising. Somatic remedies have included hormonal treatment, electroconvulsive shock, psychosurgery, and a variety of psychopharmacological agents. Some of these appear to be useful in remedying the abnormal physiological functioning that accompanies the behavioral problems; but they tend to leave other aspects of the syndrome, and the presumed precipitating causes, untouched. Furthermore, there has been little evidence for the superiority of any particular physiological theory or treatment. This vagueness casts doubt upon the ability of such approaches to identify the basic problem.

Behavioral interventions have included operant reinforcement, withdrawal of social reinforcement for not eating, and systematic desensitization. The results have been mixed and, as with so many other habit interruption techniques, there is a high rate of relapse during followup. The usual problems of small sample size, short followup, complicated treatment techniques that make it impossible to identify the effects of any particular component, and vague standards for selecting patients into programs characterize the literature.

Several studies have used some version of REST. Bachrach, Erwin, and Mohr (1965) isolated a patient in a bare room, without visitors or recreational facilities. An experimenter, who was present during all meals, rewarded the patient for eating, first verbally and then by extending privileges such as the possibility of watching television. In another study (Leitenberg, Agras, and Thomson, 1968), a similar technique was used with two patients. A baseline was established for each before the treatment started. After the baseline period, the staff was instructed to ignore anything the patient said about eating or physical problems. This procedure reduced food-related remarks but did not produce weight increase. The next phase was characterized by monitoring, with the patient counting each mouthful of food and being verbally rewarded for eating, and with desired activities made available as reinforcements for gaining weight. Then an extinction phase was instituted, in which no reinforcements were given. Both patients continued to eat at the same level as during the reinforcement period. All three of the patients in these two studies were discharged from the hospital after substantial weight gain. Weight gain was still maintained at the 4 and 9 month followups of the Leitenberg et al. (1968) project.

In another study, sensorially depriving a patient after each meal appeared to reduce the tension associated with eating. Food intake and body weight increased substantially (Lobb and Schaefer, 1971). The patient not only maintained normal weight for 4 months after the termination of the treatment, but her fear of becoming obese had completely disappeared, and she apparently abandoned a habit of excessive drinking. Unfortunately, as with a variety of other techniques, the gains appeared to be only temporary (L.G. Lobb, personal communication, 1973).

REST in the Treatment of Obesity

The usefulness of REST in the treatment of obesity was implied in a *New Yorker* article some years ago (Trillin, 1971): "Specialists can always make fat people thin through a variety of hospital treatments—treatments that a layman would probably summarize as solitary confinement—but once released the fat people almost invariably become fat again" (p. 58). Here is another area in which successful treatments are fairly rare (leaving aside surgical interventions, which have many undesirable characteristics). As with smoking, initial improvement is relatively easy to accomplish, but relapse is the rule rather than the exception (Kingsley and Wilson, 1977). Among the techniques tried and found wanting (see e.g. Leon, 1976) are group therapy including insight, emotional support, task orientation, and social pressure; individual psychodynamic therapy; hypnotherapy; a great variety of diets and periodic fasts; and behavioral methods including positive and aversive reinforcers of various types, contingency contracting, covert sensitization, and coverant control. Most of the reports leave a lot to be desired in term of appropriate controls, clear manipulations, and systematic long-term followups. Leon's (1976) review concludes that behavioral management and environmental control procedures are somewhat more effective than traditional therapies, but that the evidence is not clear.

While somewhat more optimistic about the effects of behavioral modification techniques, particularly in multi-component programs, Bellack (1977) criticizes the research aspects of the literature. There are problems with picking an appropriate dependent measure, and researchers handle treatment dropouts inconsistently in the data analysis and reporting. The majority of studies have been done on young, educated, and only slightly overweight individuals who are probably the easiest to treat successfully. It seems to be generally agreed that traditional psychotherapies have been ineffective, and one outstanding researcher has recently concluded: "Behavioral therapies have been no more effective than traditional ones in this regard" (Stunkard, 1977, p. 349).

There has been one study using stimulus reduction as a systematic treatment for overweight indivuals (Borrie, 1977; Borrie and Suedfeld, in press). Basing his design on the factorial study of REST and messages in smoking therapy (Suedfeld and Ikard, 1974) Borrie adapted the technique for weight reduction. In addition, he incorporated Schachter's idea (1971; Schachter and Rodin, 1974) that obese individuals tend to eat in response to external environmental cues rather than to interoceptive hunger signals. This external orientation leads to obesity because of the excess of food cues in the normal environment. Although considerable evidence has been generated to support this point of view, it has not yet been established as valid for all, or even most, obese individuals (Milich, 1975; Mahoney, 1975). However, the elimination of environmental eating cues is analogous to the elimination of smoking cues. Thus, whether or not Schachter's hypothesis is correct, REST can be expected to reduce the craving for food just as it does the craving for cigarettes. The importance of this effect obviously increases if Schachter is right.

In Borrie's study, members of the community were invited by radio and newspaper descriptions to participate "in an experimental weight loss program." The invitation was for women between the ages of 20 and 55 who were at least 25% over the optimal weight for their age and build. This information, as well as marital status and medical condition, was verified in a telephone interview. The actual percentages of overweight were between 25 and 130%. Subjects who were diabetic or hypoglycemic, or who did not meet the stated criteria, were excluded. Of those remaining, volunteers were matched for age, marital status, and percentage over desirable weight, and then assigned to the four treatment groups.

After considerable pretesting, and contact with the volunteer's physician and—where appropriate—spouse or living partner, each subject received a booklet for self-monitoring her eating for one week. The subject came to the laboratory. Biographical and demographic information was collected and weight and skinfold measures were taken. Then the subject received one of the following treatments:

1. 24 hours of REST, with sets of messages presented 3 hours and 20 hours after the beginning (see page 256 for details of the REST procedure).

2. 24 hours of REST, without messages but with instructions to concentrate on the problem of losing weight.

3. Presentation of the first set of messages, reporting back to the laboratory the following day to hear the second set.

4. No confinement and no messages.

There were two sets of messages. One, lasting an hour, discussed the problems of controlling urges and taking care of one's body. The presentation was followed by three exercises: a relaxation procedure, practice in raising awareness of the body, and rehearsal in dealing with emotional situations without eating. The second set, which lasted 45 minutes, contained information about nutrition, dieting, environmental control of eating behavior, and physical exercise. Before going home from the laboratory, all subjects received personal instruction in a diet and exercise program and were given a diet manual. The three treated groups also had the weight and skinfold measurements repeated.

No preexisting differences among the treatment groups reached acceptable level of statistical significance. The variables measured included age, height, weight, number of years overweight, two skinfold measures, number of children, years of education, various measures of field dependence and locus of control, suggestibility, self-monitored eating, self-reported amounts of drinking and smoking, and motives for and the perceived difficulty of losing weight.

Post-treatment weight loss is shown in Figure 8-3. The absolute weight loss was not great; however, it was significantly more for the group receiving the combination of REST and messages than in the other three conditions. This difference was still increasing at the end of the 6-month followup, with the combined treatment group continuing to lose weight at

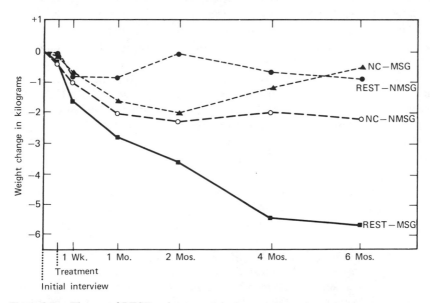

Figure 8.3. The use of REST and messages in the treatment of obesity. Data from Borrie & Suedfeld, in press.

that time. Unfortunately, because of the practical aspects of writing a dissertation, no longer-range followup was conducted.

Among the secondary measures, the predictor variables based on field orientation and locus of control failed to show a significant relationship with weight loss. This finding does not support Schachter's externality hypothesis. Demographic variables also seemed to be irrelevant. In fact, the only powerful predictors of eventual weight loss were the anticipated difficulty of losing weight (the more difficulty was anticipated, the more weight was lost) and a motivational factor (the less the motive for reducing was to please one's spouse, the more weight was lost). The last relevant factor, eating slowly after the treatment, was positively related to weight reduction.

Although the measures of externality failed to predict success, the two useful predictors were interesting. As with smoking (Suedfeld and Ikard, 1973), individuals whose primary motivation was to please someone else tended to fail. However, the finding that success was positively related to perceiving the attempt as difficult was somewhat unexpected. In a previous report (Eisinger, 1972), the ability to stop smoking was positively related to thinking that to do so would be easy. One difference between the two studies was that Eisinger's data were derived from individuals who quit by themselves, rather than participating in a controlled experimental or clinical study. We do not know whether the same relations would hold if the components (intervention versus self-management, and smoking versus obesity) were combined in different patterns.

Besides demonstrating that REST could be useful in a weight management program, this study also showed that messages presented during REST are not necessarily ineffective. In contrast to the smoking studies, Borrie's research showed a significant interaction between REST and the messages, rather than a REST main effect. Whether this was due to differences in subject population, to better messages, or to the fact that people trying to lose weight need more technical help in how to do so than people who want to quit smoking (not an unlikely hypothesis, since dieters still have to eat), remains to be established. The absolute level of loss was not dramatically high, although it was not much different from those reported with other techniques. Unlike in most studies, the rate of loss remained consistent and showed no reversal even at the end of 6 months.

It is highly probable that the results could be improved with the use of a multimodal approach that would combine the data collection followups with further counseling, behavioral and group techniques, and possibly brief booster periods in REST. Borrie has used the first two of these methods with seven overweight clients in a clinic program. Of these, three have provided followup data for at least 7 months, with net weight losses of 11.6, 16.7 and 5.5 kg. Another had lost 28.2 kg at the end of a 6-month followup. Followups available for the other 3 are at 3, 2, and 1 months after the session, with losses of 20.8, 7.9 and 2.8 kg respectively. Mean weight reduction for all clients was an impressive 0.62 kg (1.37 lbs) per week.

Although no controlled replications have yet been published, the Bien-estar Clinic (see pp. 272 to 273) has treated some overweight clients (Ann Corcoran, personal communication, June 5, 1978). Subjects undergoing 12 hours of REST as part of a treatment for obesity have averaged a 1.6 kg weight loss while in the chamber. They were given only weak lemon tea with artificial sweetener while they were there. Most of these individuals lost another 1.8 to 2.3 kg in the week after they came out. This report is encouraging, but not very meaningful without longer followup data.

PHOBIAS

Three studies used moderate periods of REST in an attempt to reduce a common type of fear, that of snakes. The rationale was that self-chosen exposure to pictures of snakes would be increased during REST and that the fear response would be inhibited by a positive reaction deriving from the reduction of stimulus hunger. This effect should transfer to the fear of snakes in general. The dependent measures in all of the experiments consisted of self-ratings and approach to a live boa constrictor, to which the third study added physiological recordings of electrodermal response and heart rate.

The first experiment (Suedfeld and Smith, 1973) used female college students who had reported a high level of fear of snakes. Setting the pattern for future studies, the procedure consisted of 5 hours of REST. After this time, there were nine 5-minute periods, 20 minutes apart, dur-ing which the subjects could push a button in order to see slides depicting snakes of various degrees of realism. Each slide was exposed for two seconds; there was no set interstimulus interval. In this particular study, the same slide was shown whenever the button was pressed within any particular 5-minute period. However, there was variation across periods. In one condition, the slides increased in realism (hierarchical order); in the other, they varied randomly (random order). The number and order of slides shown to each nonconfined control subject were yoked to one REST subject. Random presentation resulted in approximately 2½ times as many requests to see the slides, and a significantly closer approach to the live snake after the experiment. There was a significant positive correlation between the number of slides seen and increased approach to the snake.

In the second study (Suedfeld and Buchanan, 1974) another nonconfined condition was added, with slides presented on request to control for self-paced exposure to the slides. The hierarchical and random stimulus presentations were used again. As measured by approach to the snake and self-reported responsiveness on a fear survey, REST was significantly more effective in reducing fear than the other two treatments. The Subjective Stress Scale (Berkun, Bialek, Kern, and Yagi, 1962), which is a measure of general unpleasant affect, showed no change. An interaction effect was significant. In REST, random order of realism reduced fear more than did hierarchical order, with the opposite effect among nonconfined subjects. The latter datum, of course, is in line with the assumptions on which systematic desensitization procedures are normally based.

Both of these studies used student subjects who were fearful, but not necessarily phobic. Such analogue research has been criticized as not being generalizable to actual clinical situations (Cooper, Furst, and Bridger, 1969; see also Bates, 1970; Levis, 1970). Wherever the merits of that argument lie, we avoided the problem in the third experiment of the series (Suedfeld and Hare, 1977). Here, the participants were volunteers from the community who were actually snake phobic. This diagnosis was based on a combination of written and physiological measures. To be accepted, subjects had to score either 6 or 7 on the fear of snakes item of the Geer Fear Survey (Geer, 1965) as in the earlier experiments. But they also had to show a combination of mean heart rate acceleration of at least 5 beats per minute in response to 10 snake slides, with heart rate acceleration of no more than 1 beat per minute in response to 10 neutral slides. This measure was taken during a pre-experimental session (see Hare, 1973; Prigatano and Johnson, 1974). For comparison purposes, we included one group of subjects that met the self-report but not the physiological criterion. There were two REST groups, undergoing the procedure described above with a random order of presentation. The physiologically nonqualified subjects constituted one of these groups (REST$_2$). There were also two control groups. One received slide presentations yoked to subjects in the physiologically phobic REST category, but with the door open and the room dimly lit (sc); the other was untreated, with no slides (c).

The dependent measures included approach to the live snake, self-reports of fear, and measures of GSR and heart rate in response to slides, half of which depicted snakes and the other half neutral stimuli. The approach and self-report measures were administered before and at the end of the treatment for each group. The physiological measures were administered on the day before and the day after the experiment. The physiologically nonphobic group was exempted from the last measurement.

Figure 8-4 shows the results. On all indices, REST led to greater fear reduction than the other two conditions. This difference was significant on all measures for the phobic group, but not for the group that had reported high fear without demonstrating the psychophysiological signs of phobia. However, even among the latter subjects, the majority of measures showed significant changes. The differences between the physiologically phobic and nonphobic REST groups were so small as to lend support to the idea that, at least in the case of phobias, the analogue approach can be justified.

The psychophysiological changes were interesting. There was a positive and significant correlation between fear reduction as measured by approach and by GSR, and a similar relationship between self-report measures and heart rate. The correlations across these cells were not significant, even though the two psychophysiological measures were significantly correlated with each other and the approach measure was significantly correlated with each of the verbal tests. This is quite a complex outcome, with an intriguing specificity of relationship between certain

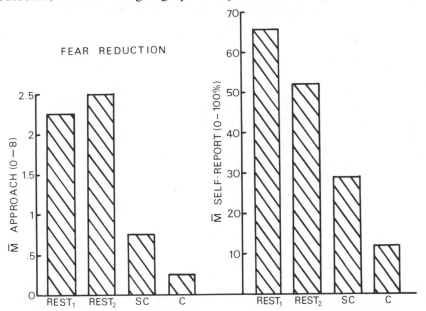

Figure 8.4. The effects of REST and slide exposure on fear of snakes. Data from Suedfeld & Hare, 1977.

kinds of psychophysiological and certain kinds of behavioral measures of fear reduction.

The results are also relevant to the perennial question of just how severe stimulus restriction has to be in order to achieve a therapeutic effect. The slide control subjects saw the same slides as the REST group, in the same order, in a dimly lit, quiet room. Nevertheless, they did not show as much change as the subjects undergoing complete darkness and the other aspects of experimental REST.

Since systematic followups were not conducted in any of these studies, the actual therapeutic effectiveness of the procedure remains unknown. Spontaneous reports from some participants in the last study indicated that at least three had maintained their gains, to the extent of significant changes in daily life (e.g., being able to go gardening, hiking, and walking in the park, which had been impossible before). In at least one other case, the improvement was not maintained.

Unfortunately, while some discussions have focused on the possibility of performing similar research with other phobias, no serious attempt has yet been made in this regard. The reader is warned that the one such publication in print at the moment—on REST as a treatment for claustrophobia—is a hoax (Suedfeld, 1976). Incidentally, would anyone be surprised that REST studies are omitted from reviews of the treatment of phobias (e.g., Mathews, 1978)?

OTHER THERAPEUTIC APPLICATIONS

Aside from these relatively systematic attempts to use REST in the therapy of noninstitutionalized adults, there have been a number of other studies reporting such interventions. For the most part, these represent a single foray into an area, which for some reason was not followed up by further research. However, the results were positive enough in almost every case that further investigation seems warranted.

Alcohol and Drug Abuse

The work on REST and smoking has implications for the treatment of alcoholism and drug abuse. There are mixed data as to the effects of social stimulation versus isolation on alcohol intake. Sensorially isolated rats show a reversal of the usual preference and choose to drink alcohol solution rather than pure water (Cole and Goldstein, 1971). However, isolated human subjects have demonstrated a suppression of alcohol use (Griffiths, Bigelow, and Liebson, 1973; Lobb and Schaefer, 1971) while both social and environmental stimulation have been shown to increase human alcohol consumption (Bigelow, Cohen, Liebson and Faillace, 1972; Cohen, Liebson and Faillace, 1972; Griffiths, Bigelow and Liebson, 1973; Keehn, 1970 but cf. Foy and Simon, 1978).

Alcohol Abuse. As with cigarette smoking, the first problem is to establish whether heavy drinkers and drug users would be willing to undergo periods of REST. Jacobson (1971) had shown that alcoholics could tolerate an hour of monotonous isolation. However, given our preference for longer durations, this was not sufficient evidence.

In a pilot study (Rank and Suedfeld, 1978), men who had admitted being alcoholic but who were at that time abstinent from liquor for between 2 and 10 weeks were recruited to participate in a 24-hour restricted stimulation study. The reason for selecting alcoholics in remission, in spite of the obvious questions about generalizability to active users, was to try to avoid some of the procedural, medical, and ethical problems that might otherwise be raised. At any rate, we found not only that the subjects completed the REST session without any trouble, but that their feelings about the experience were significantly more positive than ratings of their normal life environments. Aside from evidence for the acceptability of REST treatment with alcoholics, this finding may also throw some light on etiological factors. For at least some alcoholics (as opposed to nonalcoholic college students—see, e.g., Schwarz, Burkhart, and Green, 1978), excessive drinking may be a way to reduce stimulus overload in the ordinary milieu. REST, like other relaxation and refocusing therapies (Parker et al., 1978), may serve the same need sufficiently for self-directed change to become possible.

Recently, Cooper, McGraw, Pasternak, Paznak, and Adams (1977) directed their efforts to reducing alcohol intake in individuals who rated themselves as moderate to heavy social drinkers. Individuals who had experienced the symptoms of alcoholism were specifically excluded from this study. A six-group design was used. Two groups each received a brief message slightly over half-way through a $2^1/_2$ hour REST session. One of these messages was supportive, emphasizing the individual's ability to lead his life without depending on liquor; the other was a confrontation in which the negative aspects and effects of excessive drinking were discussed. A third group received REST without a message. The three nonconfinement conditions included one group hearing each of the two messages and one that merely filled out the scale of alcohol use twice. The dependent measure in all cases was the change in self-reported drinking from 1 week prior to the experience to 1 week after it.

The group receiving the confrontation message under restricted stimulation conditions reported a 30% reduction in alcohol intake on the retest. A 20% decrease occurred with the supportive message in REST. Changes in the groups that did not have either message-REST combination ranged from no reduction at all to a maximum of 7%. One other finding should encourage practitioners to try the method: after the session, REST subjects rated the therapist as being closer to their own ideal self (G.D. Cooper, personal communication, November 28, 1978).

Unfortunately, the summarized report is not entirely clear. For example, it appears that the interaction with therapists, consisting of pre- and post-sesssion interviews, played a role in the outcome. It is difficult to tell exactly what this role was, although from the brief description it sounds considerably more elaborate than the mere REST orientation and debriefing that were used in our own studies. The same group of researchers is now reported to be pursuing a study with actual alcoholics, which of course would be the real test of the applicability of the technique with this problem. As of the time of this writing, details and data are not yet available.

Other Drugs.   Work on drug abuse is even less advanced. There has been evidence, both from animal and human research, that REST conditions reduce or even eliminate the effects of various psychoactive drugs (see Chapter 10). This would appear to make REST (perhaps coupled with medical treatment) a suitable emergency intervention in cases of overdose and "bad trips." This possibility has been explored at an initial level with users of phencyclidine (PCP), a drug which in excessive dosages can cause uncontrollable anxiety, excitability, violence and symptoms of paranoia. Isolation and minimal stimulation from the environment are generally recommended to counteract the severity of this phase (Luisada and Brown, 1976; Petersen and Stillman, 1978).

A second possible application of REST is to ease the period of withdrawal from an addictive drug. The extrapolation is from the finding that addicted cigarette smokers do not suffer when tobacco is withheld from them during a REST experience of 24 hours or longer. It would seem reasonable to hypothesize that a similar low-stress reaction may be found with individuals addicted to other drugs, although there is no direct evidence bearing on this issue.

The last, and most intriguing suggestion, is that REST could be used in conjunction with other techniques for the treatment of drug abuse as it has been for the treatment of addictive smoking and other behavioral problems. A pilot study with three imprisoned drug addicts was initiated some years ago in conjunction with my own program. Because of administrative problems, the experiment was stopped before any conclusive results were obtained. At the present time, there seems to be no active research going on in this area.

Stuttering

In an exploratory study, Svab, Gross, and Langova (1972) demonstrated that social isolation in a small chamber led to improvement in the speech fluency of adult stutterers, both when reading aloud and during extemporaneous speech. When external monitoring of the subject's speech was reestablished in the normal environment, the improvement was maintained. Thus, the experience could be used as a therapeutic technique rather than merely to provide immediate relief from the stress of stuttering. However, the findings were not conclusive because of a lack of control over order effects. This problem was cleared up in a later study (Langova and Svab, 1973) which eliminated the possibility that either practice or adaptation was the cause of the improvement. The original results were replicated. In spite of these promising data, no further work seems to have been built upon the approach. As so frequently happens with studies using REST or one of its variants, these articles are not cited in reviews of behavioral methods for treating stutterers.

Hypertension

Hypertension, like obesity and smoking, is a widespread problem in Western society. In the United States, 15% to 30% of the population suffers from high blood pressure, which is associated with death and illness involving the cardiovascular system. At least 90% of all cases of hypertension are classified as "essential"; that is, there is no identifiable physiological cause. The suspicion is that the etiology is based primarily on environmental factors, and it seems appropriate that biobehavioral interventions be considered part of the treatment. It has been suggested that a multimodal behavioral treatment battery be developed (Schwartz and Shapiro, 1973). Some of the components used in previous work are treatments closely related to, and actually involving a degree of, REST. Autogenic training, biofeedback, meditation, hypnosis, and relaxation training have all been applied. The results have been promising, but mixed. Much of the literature suffers from inadequate controls or follow-ups (see Frankel, Patel, Horwitz, Friedewald, and Gaarder, 1978; Jacob, Kraemer, and Agras, 1977). It appears intuitively reasonable that arousal-modifying techniques might be useful for treating high blood pressure

(Steptoe, 1978). The person-environment interaction, which seems to be a factor in the onset of the condition (Shapiro, 1978), should be investigated as a possible factor in its cure (Lazarus, 1978). Both theoretically and on the basis of pilot data, it would seem reasonable for REST to be part of such clinical research programs.

In our laboratory, 3 pilot subjects have participated in a treatment combination including relaxation training and REST as a technique for reducing blood pressure. They had been referred to us by a psychiatrist specializing in biofeedback, to whom in turn they had been sent by their general practitioners. The patients were on heavy doses of medication. In spite of this, and in the absence of identifiable physiological causes, their blood pressure remained excessively high. Their condition had not changed markedly as a function of medical or psychiatric treatment. They agreed to participate in what was described as a preliminary test of a treatment that had been useful with other problems such as smoking, but had not been tested with regard to blood pressure.

Prior to entering the chamber, each subject had baseline measures taken on blood pressure and other physiological indices, was oriented to the REST environment, and was shown the biofeedback apparatus that was to be used in training during the session. The subject was told that, at a specified time during the session, he was to try to lower his own blood pressure and that if he was successful he would be informed by the sounding of a tone. Deep-muscle relaxation training was given, but no changes in blood pressure were found.

Reduced stimulation consisted of 24 hours of lying on a bed in a completely dark and sound-reduced chamber. Prior to the session, subjects were given brief relaxation training, and during the 24 hours in the chamber were repeatedly instructed to practice the relaxation technique. During the session, water and liquid diet food were available ad lib at the bedside, and a chemical toilet was located in the chamber. The stimulus reduction environment was only minimally disrupted for either feeding or use of the toilet. A technician in the next room constantly monitored the patient over the intercom in order to ensure that no problems arose. A physician was on call in case of medical complications. All three of the patients in this pilot study completed the REST session without any trouble or major signs of discomfort, anxiety, or other aversive reactions.

Immediately after entering the chamber, the subjects again received the deep-muscle relaxation instructions. They were encouraged to practice the exercise at will while in REST. Approximately 19 hours after entering a room, the biofeedback period began. Because of equipment malfunction, no actual biofeedback training occurred. The procedure remained as a placebo. Immediately afterward, a tape was played, concerning the reinterpretation and reduction of such negative emotions as anxiety and anger through techniques based on Rational-Emotive Therapy. At the end of 24 hours, the subjects were released and debriefed. Each was given a set of the relaxation training tapes to take home.

The first patient had a 30-year history of periodic attacks of dizzy spells and other symptoms possibly indicating cardiovascular problems. By 1975, he had suffered two moderate strokes and was receiving total disability payments. When first seen by our medical collaborator, he had been suffering from severe dizziness and tachycardia, had a blood pressure of 160/110, and was taking a variety of medications. One month after the REST treatment, he was taken off medication by his physician and was maintaining a blood pressure of 140/80. This improvement was eroded when his wife was killed in an automobile accident about 6 months later, and was further reversed by the court case arising from that accident. At the latest followup, about 1½ years after the REST session, he was taking very light doses of medication and had a blood pressure of 150/90. His physician felt that without the REST intervention the tragic death of the patient's wife would quite probably have led to a fatal stroke.

The second patient had been placed on anti-hypertensive medication approximately 4 years before her contact with our research facility. Her blood pressure at that time was 140/95, and she had been undergoing treatment for several years both for high blood pressure and for general stress responses arising from her troubled home life. Since psychotherapy was not helping, and the drugs were not succeeding in reducing her blood pressure, she was put into the REST program. After this session she was taken off medication except for an anti-depressant that she took before going to sleep. Her blood pressure went down to 110/70. She also solved most of the personal problems that had been bothering her, and showed general improvements in adjustment. These included a cessation of demanding and intrusive behavior toward her physician.

The third patient had a history of anxiety and depression. Within the past 10 years he had been treated for shortness of breath and increasing obesity as well as for hypertension. With considerable doses of medication, his blood pressure had been reduced from 150/100 to 140/90 prior to the REST treatment. Following REST, his blood pressure decreased. His medication was reduced by half. He also became dramatically more assertive and self-confident and began to solve some of the personal and family problems that had contributed to his unfavorable health situation. Approximately 1½ years after REST, he was still taking a half dosage of medication and was maintaining his blood pressure at 138/88. His personal life was apparently much better than it had been. At the present time, 2 years after the session, medication has been completely terminated.

Obviously, more research needs to be done on the use of REST with hypertensive patients, and such a project is being planned. However, the data collected so far seem to indicate that reduced stimulation is a useful technique not only in maintaining a lowered level of blood pressure even when medication is reduced or completely stopped, but also in the wider area of increased ability to cope with stress. This is a side-effect that we have found in our previous research with smokers, and may be one of the strengths of the technique. Many subjects report that the session enables them to think more clearly and deeply about their problems than they are normally able to do. They find it possible to generate, consider, and choose solutions that they had not thought of previously (see Suedfeld and Best, 1977).

General Psychotherapy

Lasaga (1975) has used brief periods of reduced stimulation in his office practice. The patient spends 2 to 5 minutes at the beginning of each therapy session in a REST condition, during which time he thinks about specific topics suggested by the therapist. Visual images and associated thoughts are then discussed. In 7 of the 10 patients with whom the technique was tested, the procedure elicited richer dynamic material than is usually obtained under the normal office conditions. In 3 of these cases Lasaga reports "a meaningful emotional abreaction" during the session. A similar use in group therapy settings is also described, but it is not clear whether it has actually been tried. However, Welter (1975) has reported that blindfolding the participants in a group discussion led to more anxiety at first but less at the conclusion, more willingness to take risks, and a higher degree of dealing with the "here and now." He concluded that visual deprivation might be a useful adjunct to psychotherapy. Lazarus (1968) has suggested that REST could be useful in the treatment of depression, making the patient more susceptible to therapeutic and other residual stimuli. This recommendation appears to be untested so far.

Suraci (1974), who served as his own REST subject, reported an interesting phenomenon. Previously repressed memories were suddenly brought into awareness in a manner so vivid that at times he mistook them for hallucinations. He rated the result of reliving these experiences as being comparable to those achieved in psychoanalysis. Changes occurred in his self-perception, motivation, and behavior.

As Chapter 7 pointed out, many standard therapeutic procedures are routinely performed in REST-like environments. In addition, some workers have noted the potential benefits of stimulus reduction for particular kinds of patients. For example, Horowitz (1976) suggests that such reduction should be a part of the treatment of people who are suffering the aftermath of a traumatic experience such as major surgery, divorce, or the death of a parent. Periodic exposure to profound REST could be one aspect of such treatments, as well as of other office procedures in psychotherapy.

Pseudo-REST via Hypnosis.   An interesting technique for obtaining reduced stimulation in the absence of special facilities was reported by Lazarus in 1963. This is to induce a hypnotic trance and to suggest to the subject that he or she feels no sensations, that the limbs are anesthetized, and so on. The last modality to be "switched off" would be audition, eliminating all sounds other than the voice of the therapist. During 5 to 15 sessions with each patient, Lazarus reported treatment success in 3 out of 4 cases of free-floating anxiety. All of these individuals had undergone previous treatment, including electroconvulsive therapy, chemotherapy, and various psychotherapeutic approaches, with little if any improvement. Followup periods varying from 2 weeks to 4 months indicated an elimination of the anxiety and some improvement in other symptoms. In one of these cases, ordinary hypnotic relaxation and sleep suggestion were first used for 5 sessions, with very slight improvement. Complete elimination of anxiety occurred after the administration of hypnotically-induced sensory deprivation. Incidentally, I have been told of one successful case of smoking cessation treatment using the same substitute for actual environmental reduction (I. Freilich, personal communication, June 1977).

There are problems with the induction of sensory reduction by means of hypnosis. These are essentially identical to those characterizing hypnotherapy in general. One difficulty is that it is not useful with all subjects. For example, Lazarus (1963) found that for the technique to work patients had to be highly amenable to hypnotic suggestion. Several of his anxious clients did not meet the criterion and could not be treated by this method. The fourth subject to undergo the treatment, although she was hypnotizable, experienced great anxiety when tactile sensations were hypnotically eliminated. This reaction was countered by the immediate reestablishment of tactile and kinesthetic awareness, and considerable reassurance during a period of emotional upset that followed. However, no permanent ill effect seems to have resulted.

The technique seems promising, particularly in view of the fact that other therapies had failed to help Lazarus's patients. His findings suggest two courses of research. One is to use hypnotically-induced "REST" in a wider variety of problem areas, and the other is to use real (i.e., environmentally induced) REST as a treatment for pervasive anxiety. Neither of these applications has been tried as yet.

Hypnosis in itself has similarities to REST, even when it is not used to duplicate the REST experience (see Chapter 7). Attention to distracting stimuli is minimized. Contact with the external world is maintained only through the therapist, just as it is in the isolation chamber. As a consequence, the subject's ability to concentrate on the therapeutic input is magnified (Kubie and Margolin, 1944; Reyher, 1964). It is probably not accidental that sensory deprivation appears to increase hypnotizability (Pena, 1963; Sanders and Reyher, 1969; Wickramasekera, 1969, 1970), although the data are not completely unequivocal (Levitt, Brady, Ottinger, and Hinesley, 1962).

A Neurological Problem: Esophoria

One research team (Martin, Roulsh, and Nicholson, 1967) used REST as a treatment for a medical rather than a behavioral or biobehavioral problem. The condition treated was esophoria, a tendency of the eyes to deviate inward, which is caused by a neurological imbalance. This defect is fairly common among college students, so that sufficient subjects could be found to participate. The usual treatment is a neuromuscular visual training procedure. The design of this study included (a) such training administered either after REST or after a period of patterned stimulation, (b) a pseudo-training procedure similar to the above but without one of the essential elements, again after either REST or stimulation, and (c) REST or stimulation without any subsequent training procedures. The most striking result was an interaction effect, showing that the visual training procedure administered after the 35-minute REST session was significantly superior to other treatment combinations in the correction of esophoria. This finding was interpreted in terms of the increase in attention and learning ability previously found with sensory restriction. Again, the study should be replicated and extended to other medical problems in which the learning of specific exercises can be an important curative approach.

CONCLUSION

REST has been used in the treatment of a variety of behavioral problems presented by noninstitutionalized clients. Of these, perhaps the most systematic program of research has been related to smoking cessation. The results have been reliable and positive. There have been high success rates, relatively few treatment dropouts, and favorable cost-effectiveness levels. Most of this literature stems from clinical research, but a few facilities have had success in offering this kind of service for a fee to the general public. Similarly, positive results have been found in studies on weight loss and the reduction of snake phobia. A series of single demonstration projects have indicated the usefulness of the technique with other problems, including anorexia nervosa, alcohol and other drug abuse, stuttering, esophoria, and symptoms found in general psychotherapeutic office practice. Clearly, additional research needs to be done before the utility of REST is firmly established in some of these areas. In the case of smoking, some of the guidelines are beginning to emerge. For example, the combination of REST with more traditional techniques appears to be fruitful. But many important procedural details remain to be established. Among the most urgent needs are the testing of various durations of REST, the nature and timing of therapeutic messages, and treatment combinations.

A large number of theoretical explanations have been offered, including formulations based on neuropsychological, cognitive, affective/motivational, and environmental variables. These are by no means mutually exclusive, nor has the literature reached a stage where hypotheses derived from different theories could be empirically tested against each other (see Chapter 12). From the point of view of clinical practice, this of course is a relatively abstract question. However, a multimodal behavioral engineering approach could define the range of theoretical formulations that would be useful as sources of ideas for the design of procedures directed toward specific problems (see Varela, 1971).

The continued call for more research is by now a cliché in psychology —almost every journal article uses it as a convenient final statement. But there is little doubt in my mind that such an exhortation, extending to clinical applications as well as to research, is particularly urgent in the case of REST. Stress diseases and behavioral problems present some of the most serious health problems in Western society, and it is clear that the reduced stimulation technique is a promising tool in dealing with them. Thus, it should be considered a potential treatment modality in a wide range of the problems with which health psychology and behavioral medicine have been concerned. Yet, for a variety of reasons that have been discussed in this book, very little of the necessary work has been done and even that by a relatively small group of people. A more receptive and open-minded attitude on the part of investigators, reviewers, practitioners, and opinion leaders in relevant fields might establish whether the conclusions advocated in this chapter are in fact correct, and thus lead either to the objectively justifiable abandonment of a dead end or—as I think likely—to a considerable improvement in the efficiency and power of the techniques available for treating many debilitating and even life-threatening conditions. According to the Director of the National Heart, Lung, and Blood Institute, some 164,000 lives have been prolonged by changes in behavioral patterns among the American population between 1968 and 1976 (". . . and NHLBI Director," 1978); with the kind of improvement in techniques to which I have referred, this effect could be even greater in the future.

CHAPTER 9

REST with Children

This chapter reviews the evidence that stimulus-restricted environments can have beneficial effects on children. One aspect of this issue is the provision for periods of solitude and input reduction in the everyday life of the normal child. For example, Larson (1978; Larson and Csikszentmihalyi, 1978) obtained about 5000 self-reports from 75 high school students. His respondents were alone during 26% of the sampled periods. During this time they felt relaxed, reflective, and less self-conscious. Their concentration was also better than when they were in company. Furthermore, adolescents who spent a moderate proportion (about 50%) of their waking time alone were better adjusted in terms of mood and self-image than those who were alone either more or less of the time. Historically, most texts on child-rearing and pedagogy have tended to ignore the need for, and the benefits of, reduced stimulation. Only recently has there been some growth in the explicit recognition that such conditions can be desirable. Children and adolescents need time to themselves, just as do adults, although how much of it they need varies from individual to individual and from situation to situation. Chapters 2 and 6 discuss the role of reduced stimulation as a facilitator of thought, creativity, and serenity in settings that are not specifically therapeutic. These points are equally applicable to young people. In contrast, this chapter addresses itself to more systematic and controlled uses of REST in early life.

A recent letter published in the American Psychological Association *Monitor* proposed "that the small child may need more quiet, unstimulated time alone than is suspected" (Rubin-Rabson, 1976, p. 44). This author, in discussing the merits of day-care centers, then went on to argue that some centers may not permit this kind of stimulus reduction and may press the child into premature socialization and learning experiences. Similar comments could be made about a wide variety of commonly encountered behavior settings for children.

STIMULUS REDUCTION IN INFANCY

The beneficial uses of reduced stimulation with infants have not been thoroughly explored. One clear possibility of such an application is implied by the concept of birth trauma: if the transition from the intrauterine to the external environment is in fact traumatic because of the sudden and drastic increase in sensory bombardment that it involves, one might reasonably hypothesize that an amelioration of this change may have benign effects. The psychoanalytic implications of "birth trauma" may not be necessary. There is evidence that high levels of perinatal stimulation are deleterious even in some infrahuman species (Newton, Foshee, and Newton, 1966; Newton, Peeler, and Newton, 1968).

Thus, there are both theoretical and empirical bases for the argument advanced by Leboyer (1974), which favors a delivery room procedure characterized by as gentle a transition from the intrauterine environment as is possible. The room is dimly lit and silent. People move slowly and gently, and the child is massaged slowly. Soon after emerging, the infant is put into a bath with water at body temperature, from which he is taken out to be wrapped in cloth. Many aspects of this procedure are reminiscent of experimental REST approaches, as well as of some cultures in which labor occurs in a dark "birthing hut" with a minimum of attendants. The technique was developed after Leboyer had spent some time in various Indian ashrams, where he learned reduced stimulation methods that were adaptable to obstetrical procedures in accordance with his belief in the adverse aftereffects of birth trauma. In the American edition of his book, Leboyer says, "What makes being born so frightful is the intensity, the boundless scope and variety of the experience, its suffocating richness" (1976, p. 15). This richness consists of overwhelming changes in stimulation—vision, audition, touch, temperature, and kinesthesia—added to the dramatic change from the liquid intrauterine to the atmospheric external environment. Leboyer's description of the delivery room "without violence" is, "Near-darkness . . . silence . . . darkness and quiet; what more is needed? Patience. Or more accurately, the learning of an extreme slowness that comes slowly to immobility" (p. 41).

It has been reported that infants born in this kind of environment have a mortality rate of 12% as opposed to the French national average of 20% (Guichard, 1976). A relatively large-scale study (Rapoport, 1976) used 120 "Leboyer" babies who were between 1 and 3 years old at the time. They had developed at a normal rate; furthermore, only four of them were reported to have posed any major problems for their parents, a very low figure indeed. Sleeping and feeding problems were relatively rare, and relationships between the infants and the parents seemed to be extraordinarily good.

Wilcox (1957; personal communication, February 5, 1974) has argued in favor of restricted stimulation for babies suffering from colic. This technique consists of minimal stimulation in the visual, auditory, and tactile modalities, tight pressure of the body except for the chest, and confinement in a posture with the head forward, knees up, and back bent. Without using sedative medication or manipulating feeding techniques, formulae, and so on, Wilcox has reported a cure rate of approximately 80%.

It is obvious that in this area, as in so many others related to the field of reduced stimulation, the empirical evidence upon which sensible decisions could be based has not yet been collected. In fact, even clinical observation and intelligent speculation are relatively scarce. It would seem clear that levels of stimulation below the adult norm may be beneficial for newborn infants; and, given the propensity of many older children to seek solitude and sensory reduction from time to time, there may be a more general benefit to be gained from deliberately arranging for, or at least not interfering with, such experiences.

REST IN THE TREATMENT OF PSYCHIATRIC ILLNESS IN CHILDREN

In view of the possibility that prolonged sensory restriction in infancy and childhood may have deleterious effects (Chapter 4) , the argument that REST may be beneficial for children with certain kinds of emotional problems seems at first glance paradoxical. However, one must remember the distinctions between the kinds of deprivation discussed in Chapter 4 and the relatively brief, carefully monitored periods of restriction used in therapy. The appropriate analogy perhaps is the chronic ingestion of some chemical throughout a number of years, which may lead to a poisoning of the system, as compared to the taking of controlled dosages of the same chemical during some circumscribed period as a remedy for illness or deficiency. Incidentally, this analogy once again illustrates the logical error committed by those who equate sensory restriction of the first sort with that advocated in this volume.

Autism

Given the favorable reaction of adult schizophrenics to reduced stimulation, perhaps the most obvious application of REST with children is in cases of infantile autism or childhood schizophrenia. We shall concentrate on autism, the focus of extensive theorizing, research, and clinical application. Kanner (1943, 1949) formulated the original description of the autistic syndrome and identified two crucial diagnostic signs: extreme detachment from other people and a strong negative reaction toward change and novelty in the environment. Most writers have accepted these two criteria, although it is clear that other symptoms are frequently found. Among these are unawareness of personal identity, preoccupation with particular objects, distortions of perception, motility, and speech, and developmental anomalies (see e.g. Ornitz and Ritvo, 1976).

One problematic point should be emphasized. This is the difficulty and uncertainty of diagnosis, which has plagued research on autism almost from the beginning. In many instances, the diagnostic category is used as a convenient label for a wide variety of symptoms. Thus, many institutions and many studies supposedly concerned with autistic children in fact deal with a wide range of problems including mental retardation, hyperactivity, and various psychotic syndromes.

The origin of the autistic syndrome has not been identified. The classical explanation (Kanner, 1949) is that the autistic child is cursed with parents who are cold and unemotional. But it would be equally feasible to hypothesize that the behavior of the autistic child extinguishes the demonstration of warmth on the part of the parents. Besides, there is no evidence that all—or even most—autistic children have parents of this sort (Margolies, 1977). Other theories have used the existence of an approach-avoidance conflict focused on the parents and various aspects of reinforcement history to explain the development of the syndrome. Some authors believe that autism is probably present at birth (Ornitz and Ritvo, 1976). Such theories usually connect the condition with neurophysiological malfunctions related to errors of modulation in the processes intervening between sensory inputs and perceptual-motor responses (Ornitz, 1974).

Schopler (1965) argues that autism is a cognitive disorder that involves a failure of the child to make the transition from near to distant receptor inputs (i.e., to vision and audition) as primary cues for behavior. This failure is accompanied by an inability to use auditory and visual stimuli as memory cues in the recognition and anticipation of subsequent events. As a result, fixation occurs at a level where repetitive proximate (touch, taste, and pain) stimulation remains the primary source of input. In Schopler's view, autism can result when this reduced sensitivity to distance reception, and consequent inadequate cortical arousal, are combined with a maternal environment that is also low in stimulation ("a 'cold, intellectual' mother who is not prone to initiate cuddling and handling especially with an unresponsive infant," p. 333). The sum effect of these factors is a state of chronic stimulus deprivation.

Somewhat related is the theory proposed by Rimland (1964) that autism results from a disturbance of the nervous system. The anomaly is centered on the reticular formation, and prevents the child from developing normal cognitive and conceptual linkages among the stimuli present in the environment at any particular time as well as between material learned in the past and novel events in the present (Schopler, 1965). If REST also affects reticular system functioning, there may be some connection between the original dysfunction and the temporary disruption due to environmental manipulation. Rimland (1964) specifically cites distorted perception of environmental stimuli, and compares autism with early sensory restriction.

Williams and Harper (1973) also identify stimulus deprivation as a causal factor. However, their hypothesized physiological component is somewhat less complex, consisting of visual or hearing loss. A disturbance of the parent-child interaction due to separation, depression on the part of the parent or the child, or similar instances of withdrawal, especially when combined with sensory deficits, may reduce the child's level of input below that necessary for proper development at given periods. According to these authors, deprivation of this sort at any particular stage of development makes the child more vulnerable to later stress. Besides, a period of isolation and withdrawal makes it more likely that the child will respond in the same way to stress on a subsequent occasion. The autistic syndrome is the end product of repeated occurrences of this sort, with abnormal behavior and perceptual defects becoming more marked the longer the condition is allowed to continue.

Moore and Shiek (1971) have proposed that autistic children have a subnormal ability to receive external stimuli, so that they suffer from sensory deprivation which in turn explains their inability to respond affectionately to other people, their repetitious and self-injurious behavior, and so on. It may also be that the problem involves reduced sensitivity and/or adaptation to environmental change. Baum (1978) reported that autistic children displayed particularly abnormal responses to changes in ambient light; their behavior in darkness was very much like their behavior under illumination. This is in contrast to the drastic changes observed in normal children.

As usual, environmental stimulation has been more directly implicated by some theorists. It has been hypothesized that the normal environment is excessively stimulating for autistic children, just as it is for schizophrenics. Their pathological behavior is a way of withdrawing from a level of input that they are unable to handle (Bettelheim, 1967; DesLauriers and Carlson, 1969). Actually, this interpretation is quite compatible with two of the major theoretical formulations in the area.

Lovaas's (e.g., 1977) concept of stimulus overselectivity is one of these. It posits that autistic children attend and respond to only one, arbitrarily selected, feature of a stimulus array. Under high input conditions, this one feature is probabilistically likely to be irrelevant to adaptive problem-solving. An information processing explanation (Hermelin and Wing, 1976) emphasizes the inability of the autistic child to encode and decode information appropriately and to generate or perceive structure, pattern and meaningfulness.

Both of these problems are characteristic of information processing breakdowns in situations of stimulus overload. Thus, if autism involves a dysfunction of the gating mechanism that normally protects the individual from excessive stimulus bombardment, the expected consequences would include overselectivity and information processing deficits. In either case, a reduction in the level of environmental input should compensate for the inability of the individual to screen out stimuli, and should therefore eliminate or alleviate the problem, at least temporarily. It would make sense that prolonged periods of REST would be both pleasant and beneficial for such patients. At this point, there is no basis for accepting any particular formulation as identifying either necessary or sufficient conditions in the actual development of the syndrome (Bosch, 1970).

There seems to be general agreement that environmental restriction per se is not a crucial etiological factor in autism (Bagshaw, Schwartzkroin, and Burk, 1974; William and Harper, 1974), nor in mental retardation, which frequently accompanies diagnoses of autism (Gunther, 1972). However, it may, if it occurs during some critical period, increase the vulnerability of children to these and other psychological malfunctions. An interesting idea, deserving of further research, is that impoverished dreaming and nocturnal imagery may be related to childhood psychosis (Gold and Robertson, 1975). The degree to which reduced stimulation results in changes in dreaming and waking imagery needs to be explored to see whether there is any relationship that could be either utilized or modified.

The evidence for these, as well as for other explanations of the nature of autism, is mixed. The psychodynamic thesis (King, 1975) that autism is the result of inadequate mother-child interactions early in life is contradicted by the differences between behavior shown by maternally deprived children and those diagnosed as autistic. The data have not always supported the hypothesized distortion of receptor dominance hierarchy (Goldfarb, 1964). A theory that some fetuses imprint on the intrauterine environment (Moore and Shiek, 1971) has been criticized on both theoretical and empirical grounds (Webb, 1972). One recent hypothesis that is being supported by the evidence is that autism and other severe psychopathological symptoms in childhood are related to high levels of prenatal stress and anxiety of the mother and discord in the family (Stott and Latchford, 1976; Ward, 1976, 1977). Physical illness—e.g., rubella—early in life, and sometimes undiagnosed, may also be involved. While there is little agreement about the etiology of the syndrome, and while a recent review concluded that "no etiologically based rational treatment is available that alters the course of the disease" (Ornitz and Ritvo, 1976, p. 618), the unusual orientation of these children to external stimulation (see also Litrownik, McInnis, Watzel-Pritchard, and Filipelli, 1978; Lovaas and Newsom, 1976) is worthy of a closer look.

If some abnormal reaction to environmental inputs is really involved in the development of this syndrome, one might expect that an alteration of the sensory environment would affect the behavior of autistic children and that an appropriate manipulation of input levels may prove therapeutic. One intuitively obvious intervention would be to try to compensate for hypothetical stimulus reduction by enriching the sensory world of the child. Some therapists have already adopted this approach. For example, in some case studies high levels of tactile stimulation have been administered with beneficial effects (Waal, 1955; Schopler, 1962). In an experimental study, Metz (1972) showed that autistic children preferred higher intensities of auditory stimulation than did either schizophrenic or normal subjects, a finding compatible with the hypothesis that autism involves a chronically low arousal level which the child may attempt to bring up toward optimal by seeking out stimulation or producing it himself (e.g., Rimland, 1964). Hung (1978) even used contingent self-stimulation as a reinforcer in successfully eliciting appropriate spontaneous speech. However, it should also be remembered that autistic children frequently ignore external stimuli and that self-stimulation may be a technique for blocking out environmental inputs (Stone, 1964).

One intriguing finding is the usefulness of structural therapy with autistic children (Ward, 1970, 1978). Structural therapy involves high levels of physical and verbal stimulation applied in a game-playing atmosphere, a great deal of novelty, and increased visits by parents. This treatment is based on the theory (as we have noted, not strongly supported by data) that autism has its roots in a lack of new and varied stimulation, just as is the case with symptoms arising in connection with rubella, blindness, and deafness. Ward (1978) reports that after 3 years of treatment, 12 of his 21 inpatient cases could be discharged from the structural therapy unit of the institution. They went to either normal or special schools or workshops, their development having progressed to the point where—although they were not up to age norms for cognitive and affective processes—more standard educational and therapeutic techniques were appropriate. The results were notably better than those for two units using standard psychodynamic therapy and play therapy in treating similar, although perhaps less disturbed, children.

If one accepts an optimal level of stimulation approach to the therapy of autistic patients, it would seem clear that one might expect either a positive or a negative orientation toward additional stimuli depending upon the environmental baseline level. At any rate, there appears to be a reasonable possibility that the usual levels of stimulation found in the environment tend to be too high rather than too low for the autistic child, and that REST may be employed beneficially with such patients. Recent discussions of the problem, emphasizing the unpleasantness of change and unpredictability for autistic individuals, certainly imply that this is feasible (see Kaufman, 1976; Ornitz and Ritvo, 1976). Although little systematic research has yet been undertaken, there is some supportive evidence.

To begin with, brief periods of immobilization have been used to decrease disruptive behavior and self-stimulation on the part of autistic children. Immobilization has usually been employed in conjunction with other behavior modification techniques such as verbal cues and physical punishment; however, a recent study (Bitgood, Crowe, Peters, and Suarez, 1976) used immobilization only. The patients were children categorized as "retarded/autistic." Immobilization occurred for 15 seconds each time the child attempted to leave his seat during treatment sessions focusing on a variety of instructional tasks. In three separate studies, the investigators found a significant decrease in attempts to leave the chair, the suppression of a variety of previously chronic self-stimulatory stereotyped behaviors, and a reduction of tantrum behavior. Only one child failed to show the effects. For three children, cessation of the immobilization procedure showed a recovery of the undesirable behavior to levels significantly lower than the original baseline, although three others recovered to the original level. When immobilization was then reintroduced, all children showed rapid decrease in the target behavior. It should also be noted as an important factor that "the emotional responding frequently cited as a negative side effect of punishment was observed in only one of the seven reported cases." Thus, it does not appear that immobilization was perceived as particularly aversive, and the authors did not note any negative side effect of the treatment. Rincover (1978) similarly reduced self-stimulation by preventing its normal sensory consequences through removal or masking (e.g., carpeting a surface to avoid auditory feedback, blindfolding the child to avoid visual feedback). This technique, which he calls "sensory extinction," implies that specific kinds, not only general levels, of stimulation are important.

In another relevant study (reported in Hutt, Hutt, Lee, and Ounsted, 1964), stereotyped behavior was found to increase as the complexity of the environment increased. Six autistic children, aged between 3 and 6 years, were observed, the primary focus of the investigation being on EEG patterns. The authors also noted that the behavior of the children was least "psychotic" while they were sitting in an unfurnished waiting room. It was concluded that stereotyped behavior "would be least likely when there was relative sensory deprivation" (p. 909). In contrast, brief social isolation unaccompanied by specific instructions was found to be unsuccessful in reducing the hyperactive behavior of an autistic child (Risley, 1968).

The apparent contradictions may reflect too gross a sampling procedure. Frankel, Freeman, Ritvo, and Pardo (1978) have reported that intelligence is a moderating variable in this context. High levels of stimulation increased stereotyped behavior among low-IQ autistic children while decreasing it among a higher IQ group. The implication is that this type of behavior may serve to reduce environmental complexity for the former, and increase it—providing a pleasant diversion—for the latter. Given similar interactions between IQ and stimulus variables in the experimental REST literature (see Chapt. 2), this finding may be a lead to more effective therapeutic manipulations of environmental input in the treatment of autism.

Margolies (1977) recently reviewed the usefulness of behavioral treatments of autism. Dismissing traditional forms of psychotherapy as unsuccessful, Margolies examined the behavioral interventions that have been attempted with the various components of autistic behavior. These treatments range from the first demonstrations that autistic children do in fact respond to reinforcement (the problem is the discovery of appropriate reinforcers) through the extinction of maladaptive behaviors and to the learning of more desirable ones. Several studies have used mild forms of REST in order to minimize distraction while the therapeutic process was going on (Hewett, 1965; Jellis, 1972), and even more employed periods of timeout that served both as reduced stimulation and as components in the reinforcement contingency program (Husted, Hall, and Agin, 1971; Jensen and Womack, 1967; Schell and Adams, 1968; Tramontana and Stimbert, 1970; Wetzel, Baker, Roney, and Martin, 1966; Wolf, Risley, Johnston, Harris, and Allen, 1967; Wolf, Risley, and Mees, 1964).

Margolies admits that not all of the interventions were successful, that some behavioral gains disappeared when the treatment program came to an end, and that very few of the studies incorporated any kind of control subjects or treatments. But he does conclude that approaches based on behavior modification have at least some utility. Interestingly, and perhaps not surprisingly given the general isolation of the REST literature from other relevant bodies of work, this otherwise thorough review does not mention the work of Schechter and his colleagues, which is described below.

Drawing on the work of Cohen (1963) and Charny (1963)—see pages

312 to 313—Schechter and his associates (Maier, 1970; Schechter, Shurley, Toussieng, and Maier, 1969, 1970; Schechter, Shurley, Sexauer, and Toussieng, 1969) used isolation and monotonous stimulation to treat three autistic boys. The idea was that in this situation the patients could relax their defenses, originally adopted to ward off "overwhelming" stimuli, and allow themselves to seek out and accept human contact. The isolation area was the size of a normal room. It contained only a mattress, a toilet, and a sink. Sound and light from the outside were muffled by heavy drapes. The windows were covered by insulation and fiberglass board. The room was dimly lit, and there was a constant hum from an electric fan. The temperature was controlled. The children were fed from a tray taken into the room by a staff member. This plus a 10 to 15 minute visit from the therapist twice a day was the only personal contact between the child and the staff.

The boys were left in the room for 40, 68, and 74 days. All were reported to have become more alert and much less defensive. All became closely involved with their therapist. Eventually, as time and isolation went on, and as the children began to manifest a desire for social interaction, verbal and tactile stimulation and signs of affection were provided. Interest in social contact and involvement grew and was extended to other staff members, and eventually to visitors including the children's parents. After release, the children were followed up for 12 to 24 months. All three constantly increased their social contacts and became functioning members of the family. They were attending nursery school and were enjoying and benefiting from their attendance. Thus, the technique was successful in reaching its stated goals.

One of the published papers (Maier, 1970) provided an extensive case study of one of these three boys. Maier wrote that the reduced stimulus environment had relieved the child "of the burden of trying to deal with what seemed to be overwhelming stimulation. He was surprisingly content in the room and was able to drop many of the defenses that separated him from other people. He did make significant progress toward developing more satisfactory object relationships and better social and intellectual skills."

One of the things that should be noted, particularly by those who have reservations about the ethical aspects of the treatment, is the change in the attitudes of staff members as the therapy progressed. Apparently, the nurses and other staff were quite dubious about isolating the children, and were anxious about how the boys would react. However, these concerns diminished as time went on and the patients showed no discomfort or side effects. In fact, they gave every evidence of liking the environment. It appeared that the children were comfortable and happy in the isolation room, for the most part not even trying to leave when the door was left open. They also remained physically healthy, ate well, and maintained their normal body weight. Furthermore, they demonstrated resistance to respiratory and other infections that struck the community. Besides, the therapeutic benefits of the treatment became constantly more salient. The growing dedication and enthusiasm of the therapist and the nursing staff, and the involvement of family members, were seen as being important aspects of the eventual success of the therapy. Initial hesitancy and anxiety are frequently found among staff members when REST procedures are first introduced; but in most cases of which I am aware the lack of negative consequences and the demonstrated benefits usually extinguish these adverse expectations fairly rapidly.

Obviously, more systematic research is needed on this particular application of REST. The work must be replicated with a larger number of patients, and with longer and more systematic followups. Also, the usefulness of the treatment should be compared with that of other approaches, and REST should be evaluated as a factor in therapeutic programs combining a number of techniques. Nevertheless, the theoretical and experimental bases for applying reduced stimulation to autistic children as a therapeutic method appear to be sound, and the preliminary data now available seem promising. It is to be hoped that a more extensive testing of the efficacy of this approach will not be long delayed, particularly in view of the fact that even now the prognosis for autistic children tends to be relatively poor.

What are we to make of the findings? The success of Schechter's treatment makes sense if one explains it from the theoretical viewpoint that autism involves the inability to cope with levels of stimulation as high as those normally found in the environment. Whatever the causes of such inability may be, its consequences are obviously remediable by lowering the stimulus load. But it is somewhat difficult to reconcile this with the positive findings reported for Ward's structural therapy. The progress of these children does not seem to have been as marked as those reported by Schechter et al. (1969); on the other hand, more patients were involved for a longer period of time. Let us take both sets of results as indicating a true change. What this might mean, it seems to me, is that techniques successfully focusing the attention of the autistic child on environmental factors are therapeutically effective. In the case of structural therapy, this is done by increasing the intensity of input, and thus the impact of the environment; incidentally, an analogous phenomenon may underlie the success of behavioral therapies based on strong aversive reinforcers (e.g., Lovaas, Schaeffer, and Simmons, 1965). REST, on the other hand, achieves the goal by reducing the level of stimulation to the point that the child's stimulus-hunger is aroused, and he seeks out and attends to those inputs that are made available. In view of the report that this is not an unpleasant situation for the children, there may be a philosophical basis for preferring it to intensive stimulation. REST motivates the patient himself to alter his behavior, rather than merely evoking a reaction to the stimulation that is forced upon him. The crucial need appears to be the performance of systematic and well-designed comparison studies, and possibly of treatment combinations.

Richer and Nicoll (1971), apparently unaware of the work done by Schechter and the other investigators mentioned above, developed a similar approach. Arguing that autistic children are more easily over-aroused than normals, and that their symptoms reflect escape or avoidance behavior, these writers set up an environment that would reduce the intrusiveness of stimulation and permit withdrawal. The room was divided into a number of connected parts in which a child could get away from others. A dark "retreat box" was included, but was rarely used. Ten institutionalized children, of whom 8 were autistic, spent most of their time in this unit, with a significant reduction in stereotyped behavior and increased social interaction. General improvements were found in other behaviors, such as playing together. Aside from demonstrating the usefulness of lowered stimulation in the treatment of disturbed children, this study also exemplified the value of an appropriate interdisciplinary approach: Richer is a psychologist and Nicoll an interior designer.

Aside from the use of REST as a global therapeutic agent, one might also consider it as a technique for achieving more limited goals. For example, we know that in the absence of distracting environmental stimulation, subjects become more able to learn and remember simple materials and even to identify simply concepts. This set of data could be the basis for investigations on whether reduced stimulation would be helpful in teaching autistic children specific stimulus-response connections, or particular ways of behaving in the presence of relevant cues. As one example, it appears that some of the abnormal behavior of these children may be a function of their responding to only a subset of the information available, and that under some circumstances they can be taught to respond to multiple rather than to unitary cues (Koegel and Schreibman, in press). Whether this learning could take place more efficiently in the REST environment is a question worth investigating.

Intellectual Dysfunctions

Some of the uses of REST with retarded children are described in the section on timeout procedures. However, we should also consider the possibility that reduced stimulation in contexts other than timeout may be useful. There is certainly anecdotal evidence to indicate that this might be the case. For example, the John F. Kennedy School for Mentally Retarded Children in Quebec has a room, situated away from noisy areas of the school and painted in monochromatic shades, in which 3 to 5 brain-damaged or autistic children are taught. The teacher has found that more stimulating environments, such as a normal classroom, distract these children, and that the reduction of visual and particularly of auditory input enables them to benefit more from instruction (Geraldine Schwartz, personal communication, June 30, 1973).

Several writers have advocated stimulus reduction to eliminate hyperactivity, lack of attention, and self-stimulation (e.g., Bower and Mercer, 1975; Glennon and Nason, 1974; Sachs, 1973; Strauss and Lehtinen, 1947). Some versions are more sophisticated than a mere global reduction of input. Strauss and Kephart (1955), for example, proposed a complete educational package, including changes not only in the environment but in the behavior of the teacher and in the type of material presented.

Apparently, schools in some jurisdictions routinely isolate children. Whether this is done to help them learn, or as a disciplinary measure, or both, differs from case to case. Recently, it was reported that over a period of several weeks a 13-year old Ontario pupil had spent 3 to 4 hours at a time in a booth constructed of cardboard. The booth contained a desk and a chair. The stated purpose was to help the boy concentrate, and according to the principal, his schoolwork did improve as a result ("Cardboard 'cell' boy," 1978). School authorities also stated that the booth, similar to study carrels in libraries, was like those used commonly in Ontario schools to help children concentrate. However, because of the mother's objection, the pupil was transferred to another class.

The issue of distractibility has attracted considerable attention among people working with the intellectually dysfunctional. Strauss and Lehtinen (1947), followed by Cruickshank, Bentzen, Ratzeburg, and Tannhauser (1961), advanced the view that children who are brain-injured and hyperactive have difficulty in concentrating attention on relevant stimuli. They recommended the use of individual cubicles, with a minimum of non-task oriented stimulation available, as a preferable learning environment for such children. Subsequent research has generated mixed data. The reduced stimulation cubicle may improve attention to the task (Shores and Haubrich, 1969), but it only sometimes improves performance (Cruikshank, Junkala, and Paul, 1967; Rost and Charles, 1967; Shores and Haubrich, 1969; Somerville, Jacobsen, Warnberg, and Young, 1974; see also Douglas, 1973). In fact, peripheral stimulation has also been reported to result in improvement (e.g., Browning, 1967; Carter and Diaz, 1971).

There have been many reports of unusually high distractibility among retardates and among hyperkinetic children, but some reviewers (Crosby, 1972; Rosenthal and Allen, 1978) found no such general factor. In Crosby's opinion, previous research suffered from a failure to distinguish between the effects of retardation and those of institutionalization, from the use of inappropriate distractor stimuli, and from the selection of tasks that require only periodic rather than continuous attention. In Crosby's study, a continuous vigilance and monitoring task was presented, with meaningfully related but task-irrelevant distractors. Institutionalized retarded subjects with brain damage showed the highest number of attention lapses, with their non-brain-damaged counterparts next. However, the retarded subjects did not show more responsiveness to the distractor stimuli than did normals. Crosby concludes that while some retarded people are highly distractible, others may be even less than normally so. The performance of the latter group, composed of individuals with chronically low arousal levels, could be improved by making the environment more stimulating. For distractible patients, with chronically high arousal, this may be counterproductive. We might add that for the latter group reduced stimulation may serve a beneficial function.

In one attempt to investigate the relevant personality variable, Somerville, Warnberg, and Bost (1973) identified 24 normal first grade school children who were rated by their teachers as distractible on a variety of dimensions and 24 who were rated as nondistractible. The experimental conditions included reduced stimulation (isolation in a small quiet room), increased stimulation (group testing with loud and diverse tapes playing and a variety of visual stimuli being shown), and normal stimulation (the children being tested in a room provided by the school without any modification of the environment). With these children, the stimulus environment did not significantly affect the rapidity of task performance. Quality of performance was unfortunately not scored, or at least not reported. However, the authors do note that distractible white students showed slow performance under high-stimulation conditions, while the same environment led to rapid performance for distractible black and nondistractible white pupils.

These data are difficult to interpret. It appears to be counterintuitive that some distractible students perform more rapidly under distracting conditions. We do not know whether this finding is replicable. The results might be altered if tasks differing in complexity were included, if the environmental manipulations were modified, or if the labeling and selection of the subject groups were done differently. At any rate, one can hardly disagree with the authors' conclusion that "the general acceptance of techniques involving stimulus reduction is unfounded or, at best, premature" (p. 184). At this stage, so is the general rejection of such techniques. This study was perhaps not modal in making the argument in favor of reduced stimulation intuitively appealing; but it certainly was in testing that argument inadequately.

A relevant formulation was proposed by Gordon and Haywood (1969), who differentiated between retardates suffering from physiological damage and those whose problem was ascribed to family or other social variables. Although these investigators did not manipulate environmental conditions, they manipulated the task (WISC and WAIS Similarities subtests) by administering an "enriched" version of the test to some subjects. Enrichment consisted of adding three stimulus words: that is, asking the subject to identify the concept common to five words as opposed to the usual two words. Gordon and Haywood reported that while stimulus enrichment did not affect the performance of normal nor of brain-damaged retarded subjects, it had a positive effect on the scores of children whose retardation was not due to organic causes. Their argument is that these children suffer from stimulus deprivation or "input deficit," leading to a reduced capacity of the information processing channels. This effect can be overcome by increasing the impact of the informational stimuli. However, a reanalysis of the Gordon and Haywood data, followed by further research (Friedrich, Libkuman, and Thomas, 1973), yielded different results. The two types of retarded subjects did not in fact differ in task performance on Similarities, as the input deficit hypothesis would require. Instead, enrichment was actually beneficial for both groups. Friedrich et al. maintain that the original reports were partly based on a failure to control for order effects in the presentation of the enriched and the standard versions of the test.

Jenkins, Gorrafa, and Griffiths (1972) pointed out that some of the criticisms of the reduced stimulation approach to teaching retarded children were based on a questionable assumption. This was that general achievement, as measured by standardized tests, was in fact the appropriate dependent variable. It has been found that scores on such tests are relatively insensitive to educational and environmental factors. Therefore, Jenkins et al. used a more appropriate measure, a direct performance index (the amount of work accomplished in a given period). On this criterion, children's performance in an environment of social isolation and reduced stimulation was in fact superior to work in a normal classroom. Not only was the difference statistically significant, but the direction was as predicted in 15 of the 16 individual comparisons.

Scott (1970) reported an interesting paradox: individual cubicles, cubicles with background music playing, and a normal classroom with background music playing all led to better performance on arithmetic problems than the standard classroom environment. The paradox was that stimulation in the three experimental conditions differed from the control situation in opposite directions. One might hypothesize that a reversed form of the curvilinear function between performance and arousal was operating, with the normal classroom as a nonoptimal level from which deviation in either direction was beneficial. Conversely, one may argue that there was a novelty or a Hawthorne effect. This could be tested by maintaining the subject in the unusual environments long enough for the novelty to wear off.

There are interesting data, supporting the view that a curvilinear function is involved, on increases in stereotyped behaviors (e.g., rocking). Retardates have been shown to increase these behaviors after high external stimulation such as noise and social interaction, as well as after high internal stimulation such as hunger. Immobilization and sensory reduction can have the same effect (Forehand and Baumeister, 1970; Guess, 1966; Tizard, 1968; Warren and Burns, 1970). Higenbottam and Chow (1975) performed an experiment in which immobilization, darkness, and noise were varied factorially. The effects of these three variables summated, although the moderate immobilization used did not have an effect by itself. This makes sense if one considers stimulus reduction as an arousal-increasing manipulation, although once again the question of environmental novelty as opposed to the specific nature of the environment is raised. This is particularly relevant because of the finding that rocking rate decreased after the first 5 minutes regardless of the environmental condition.

Relevant to the treatment of retarded children from a therapeutic or educational viewpoint are some studies that look at "social drive." Aside from the question of whether retardation can be attributed to social and/or stimulus deprivation in infancy (cf., Rosenheim and Ables, 1974), it does appear that retarded children are highly responsive to supportive social reinforcements (e.g., Mosley, 1971). Zigler and Williams (1963) found that among children whose retardation was not due to organic causes, those with the highest social motivation showed the greatest decrease in IQ during institutionalization. This datum was interpreted as implying that the IQ decrease was related to an abnormally high desire for social reinforcement among these children. It appeared that this kind of motivation is more marked among children whose experiences prior to institutionalization were relatively normal, but this finding was contradicted in a more recent study (Zigler, Balla, and Butterfield, 1968). In the latter report, institutionalized subjects showed an IQ increase rather than a decrease, and children with more favorable backgrounds showed less need for social reinforcement than did those from poor backgrounds. The authors used these differences to emphasize the importance of considering specific institutional variables.

Hyperactivity and Conduct Dysfunctions

Zentall (1975) has suggested that hyperactivity in children occurs as a homeostatic mechanism to increase stimulation when the environment is not providing a sufficiently high level. This is an alternative to the traditional view that the syndrome arises from brain damage that impairs the ability to screen out irrelevant stimuli and the ability to organize relevant stimuli meaningfully (e.g., Strauss and Lehtinen, 1947; Strauss and Kephart, 1955).

Zentall's optimal stimulation theory is based on the more general concepts proposed by motivation theorists in REST and other areas: particular levels of stimulation are optimal for particular individuals, who are motivated to restore these levels whenever the range of actual input becomes markedly discrepant from them. He goes on to postulate that children become overreactive in order to raise excessively low stimulation levels. This explanation is supported by evidence that the greatest amount of hyperactive behavior is found under such conditions as waiting for something to happen, having to perform highly structured but difficult tasks, being in environments that are low in novelty, and in general experiencing situations that can be described as relatively monotonous. The logical conclusion is that the syndrome should be treated not by environmental restriction, as the Strauss theory would imply, but rather by relatively high levels of environmental input. This theory also explains why it is that stimulating drugs "paradoxically" seem to reduce hyperactive behavior. There is nothing paradoxical about that result, since the medication raises stimulation level internally. Zentall also draws parallels between the behavior of hyperactive children and that of REST subjects. Both groups find difficulties with visual-motor tasks and motor coordination, and as time goes on in a particular task environment, both exhibit increased activity, difficulty in concentrating on a task, and so on.

Zentall and Zentall (1976) recommend that hyperactive children be placed in particularly stimulating environments. Their study, using 16 such children between the ages of 7 and 11, indicated that a relatively stimulating room did in fact lead to better performance on a cognitive-motor task (locating and circling particular letters of the alphabet in a large array). The children were also more successful in inhibiting locomotor activity when requested to sit still. The difference between the two rooms was somewhat confounded, unfortunately. From the description, the low-stimulation room appears to be considerably less pleasant than the one characterized by high stimulation (bare white walls and gray floors versus pictures, posters, signs, live mice in a cage, a three-dimensional scene, colored Christmas lights, and so on). This difference may or may not be relevant to the outcome of the study; but at the very least, it would seem appropriate that when the effects of low versus high stimulus level are compared, other characteristics should be equated as far as possible (cf. Russell and Mehrabian, 1975).

In one very interesting study (Kinnealey, 1973), 20 severely retarded hyperactive children were selected, 10 of whom had demonstrated an aversion to external stimuli while the other 10 had not. The first group avoided or escaped from stimulation, moving quickly and alertly, and demonstrating delicately modulated hand movements. The second was low in reactivity, exhibited rough hand movements, and enjoyed although they did not seek social contact. Rating the children's reactions to a variety of stimuli in different modalities, a number of raters reliably found differences in the direction supporting the original criterion on which the investigator had differentiated the two groups. These differences occurred in each of the modalities tested. Kinnealey uses her data to recommend different kinds of chemotherapeutic intervention, without reference to environmental alterations that might be helpful.

It is interesting that vestibular stimulation (the child being spun on a desk chair or rolled around on a large ball) elicited fewer aversive reactions from both of Kinnealey's groups than did input in other modalities, while auditory stimulation was particularly aversive, especially for the hyperreactive subjects (see also the comment from the John F. Kennedy School cited above). This study did not include nonretarded comparison subjects, but it has been shown that retarded children—unlike normals—show a preference for vibratory as opposed to visual stimulation (Ohwaki, Brahlek, and Stayton, 1973; Halliday and Evans, 1974). Further investigations of modality preferences and aversions might provide some useful clues as to the appropriate design of learning and living environments for hyperactive individuals.

As in timeout, possible use of brief periods of isolation to strengthen the social motivation of the subjects might be beneficial in improving learning and therapeutic interactions. Simpson and Nelson (1972) used cubicle isolation in conjunction with attention training and feedback about breathing rate. The three hyperactive children who participated in the study showed increased regularity in breathing, improvements on task performance, and greater ability to maintain concentration. Although these changes did not persist outside the cubicle, the results are promising enough to warrant a trial of a more elaborate REST-biofeedback-specific training package similar to that being prepared for hypertensive adults (see Chapter 8).

Von Hilsheimer has advocated relaxation training, sleep therapy, and arousal-reducing medication, among other techniques, in successfully working with adolescents suffering from learning disabilities and social maladjustment (Von Hilsheimer, 1971; Von Hilsheimer, Klotz, and Philpott, 1971). The use of methods so closely related to REST (see Chapter 7) raises the question of why there has been no attempt to include systematic stimulus reduction as one of the treatments. A partial answer may be provided by the fact that reviews of the literature on the behavioral treatment of retarded, hyperkinetic, learning disabled, and other maladjusted children tend to ignore or deemphasize studies in which environmental restriction is identified as a central manipulation, although they do deal with techniques such as relaxation and biofeedback, where restriction is imposed as part of another procedure (e.g., Hobbs and Lahey, 1977; Prout, 1977). For example, "functional relaxation training" in solitude and quiet has reduced restlessness and increased self-insight in mildly hyperactive children, leading to better school performance (Janz, 1978).

With conduct disorders, REST has most frequently been used in small doses under the rubric of timeout (see below). However, there have been some studies in which longer durations were utilized. Glynn (1957) reported on the use of solitude in a psychiatric inpatient unit for adolescent girls, with the rationale that this treatment protected the patients against overstimulation.

Glynn and his staff discovered that seclusion, often regarded only as a practical management device for minimizing the impact of impulsive, uncontrolled behavior, could be recognized and accepted as a valuable treatment technique once its therapeutic functions were clearly understood by staff and patients. Staff members learned that solitude could facilitate the processes of personality reorganization and the internalization of new ego controls. To accomplish these positive results, girls placed in seclusion received added staff attention, extra psychotherapy sessions, and more intensive intervention, interspersed with periods of aloneness.

Glynn found that when seclusion was viewed as a positive, therapeutic experience and not as a form of punishment, it was voluntarily requested by many girls on the unit (see also the section on prisons in Chapter 3). This occurred most often when girls reached some critical point in therapy and sensed that their own internal controls were inadequate. It was at these crucial junctures that the protective, less stimulating environment of the seclusion room served to provide a relief from unmanageable tensions and from the possibility of impulsive acting out and loss of control.

Glynn's paper contains generalized observations but no detailed data. He makes it clear that he conceives of seclusion as providing a reduced stimulus environment, a unique form of treatment that was particularly effective at critical points in therapy. His suggestions for using seclusion combined with intensified therapy and staff intervention have parallels in the procedures adopted by the Azima group (see Chapter 10), who gave their adult psychiatric patients a systematic combination of reduced stimulation and psychotherapeutic treatment.

A more recent use of reduced stimulation and isolation has been with children exhibiting severe character disorders. These patients, living in a residential treatment unit for seriously disturbed children, developed a subculture in which resistance to treatment became the norm. A program had to be devised to deal with the extreme acting-out behaviors that ensued (Cohen, 1963; Charny, 1963).

Cohen (1963) originally did not emphasize the sensory reduction aspect of this treatment. Rather, the goal was to remove the child from undesirable peer influences, to prove to the child that he was not omnipotent, to force an increase in anxiety and introspection and thereby facilitate psychotherapy, and to ensure the physical safety of both the child and the group. The technique was used in crisis situations where extreme acting out was occurring. The isolation room was lit only dimly, and was also sound-deadened. There was nothing in it except a mattress and sheets. One to 3 hours of staff contact were provided per day. Eventually, the procedural emphasis shifted to the control of the sensory environment, with a view toward minimizing external anchors. For example, routines were deliberately varied to remove time cues. Six children went through the procedure, which lasted as little as 2 months and as much as about 6, with a 3-month average.

Cohen reports that the children go through a definite pattern, starting with panic and anxiety over lack of access to manipulable adults, then going on to the rebuilding of defenses and the expression of anger. The next phase is a "loosening of personality organization," demonstrating the child's major problems with his self-image and with his relationship to his parents. Intense resistance to therapy and change follows before a final reorganization and the abandonment of defenses, ending in resocialization. The author notes that after the experience the children exhibited heightened interest in school work, social interaction, and recreational activities, presumably as a result of the stimulus hunger that was built up during the isolation period.

The outcome seems excellent: "In all instances, the children who were involved in this treatment procedure, after the relatively brief period of resocialization following isolation were sufficiently improved to be discharged either to their homes or to social agency type residences. . . . Follow-up information now extending over 2¹/₂ years indicates that all of them are still in the community" (p. 186). None of the subjects required rehospitalization during the 2¹/₂ year followup. In view of the fact that these children had very poor prognoses and backgrounds, this is quite impressive. Furthermore, the effects on the other family members also appeared to be good. One remark from a child who had been through the procedure is enlightening: "I was born in that room" (p. 185).

Working in the same institution, Charny (1963) reported in more detail on five of the cases, including children diagnosed as manifesting personality disorders, aggressiveness, and childhood schizophrenia. In all five cases, positive results were noted. Further, while all of the children at one point or another expressed negative reactions to being isolated, these reactions were not extreme nor permanent. The explanations offered for the results were essentially psychodynamic, citing regression in the service of the ego just as did the writings of the Azima group working with adult patients.

Morse and Wineman (1957) reported on the therapeutic use of social isolation in a summer camp for ego-disturbed boys. While their paper does not provide detailed research data, Morse and Wineman discussed practical applications of social isolation procedures and described the personality traits typical of boys who were most likely to benefit from such methods. They noted that some children in their camp were refractory to many traditional counseling and therapeutic techniques because of their aggressive, uncontrolled, antisocial conduct and the "alibi skills" that they used to avoid self-understanding and the acceptance of personal responsibility for their own actions.

According to these authors, about 5% of the boys in the camp seemed to be incorrigible behavior problems. Many institutions use some form of separation, isolation, or seclusion with such hard-core cases; these procedures are viewed as necessary but not therapeutic, and are seldom discussed publicly.

Morse and Wineman dissent from these views in their detailed report on the use of social isolation procedures. The procedures were employed with campers whose socially disruptive behavior required their removal from the group. During a pre-isolation interview, a senior therapist reviewed each boy's previous history of destructive behavior with him, and gave him a choice of either leaving the camp or going to live in an isolation cabin with a counselor. Almost all of the boys chose the isolation cabin.

In the cabin the child was removed from contact with other campers, but was intensively counseled by an adult. After 2 or 3 days of isolation and intensive counseling he could be returned to the group. Morse and Wineman found that "we can cut through the alibi network much faster and get down to issues" with these procedures. Therapeutic relationships with the counselor developed much more rapidly in the isolation cabin. The children became less suspicious, more open, and more likely to develop rapport with the staff.

Another relatively positive concept of solitude was employed in the treatment of aggressive and negativistic children by Wahler and Fox (1978). Four such boys between the ages of 5 and 8 underwent a treatment designed to increase the duration of solitary play with toys. Such play, scheduled during times of the day when the child usually exhibited problem behaviors, involved continuing attention to the toys even in the presence of other family members and avoiding communication with the latter. Social and nonsocial reinforcers were made contingent upon successfully completing such sessions. The children's behavior as rated by observers and by the parents, and the attitudes of the parents toward the child, improved. No such improvement was found when a similar contract was applied to cooperative social play sessions or television watching sessions. The beneficial change was temporary, but was reinstated when a timeout contingency was added to the solitary play contract. The use of the contract to teach acceptable and enjoyable solitary activity even in the presence of others is truly a step toward what Wahler (1978) has called "productive solitude." It is a pity that solitary play in children, like solitary creative activity in adults, has been denigrated for so long by Western society. Perhaps the balance is beginning to be restored. As Wahler and Fox assert, " 'Aloneness' need not therefore connote maladjustment. In fact, we think that a good case could be made to consider high rates of social interaction as questionable in value to the developing child'' (1978, p. 28).

"TIMEOUT": THE USES OF BRIEF REST

As early as 1957, reports were appearing concerning the systematic use of isolation rooms as areas for brief timeout, and even for somewhat longer periods of solitude used with disturbed children (Glynn, 1957; Morse and Wineman, 1957; Robinson, 1957). The so-called timeout procedure was originated on the basis that the removal of an individual from positive reinforcement, contingent upon some undesired behavior, would serve to extinguish that behavior. On a more cognitive level, one might interpret this as an information-processing task, in which the patient learns that the change in environment is a cue indicating that the therapist disapproves of a particular response. At any rate, the actual methodology frequently involves taking the individual from the environment in which his behavior has been observed to a special location, which is normally characterized by isolation and sometimes by reduced stimulation as well. The duration of timeout—that is, of being confined in the special environment—may last from a few minutes to several days, depending on the type of patient and the institution. As a rule, however, it is a matter of minutes or a few hours. The technique was transferred from original investigations with infrahuman species, where timeout was from reinforcement by food, to human experimental subjects and eventually to patients, timeout here usually being from some interesting and liked activity or from social interaction.

Whether timeout is really different from aversive reinforcement (i.e., whether it is in fact a form of punishment) is a controversial theoretical issue (see, e.g., Kaufman and Baron, 1968; Leitenberg, 1965). Interestingly, while the experience appears to meet the definitions of an aversive event with infrahuman animals, and while some writers seem uncritically to transfer this evaluation to human subjects, once again there is evidence that at least some patients react to it with positive affect. Unfortunately, even practitioners who use timeout sometimes assume that it is aversive. Worse yet, they frequently fail to evaluate its specific effects when it is used as a component in a multimodal treatment program (e.g., Drash, 1976). Thus, the systematic research as to how it can best be structured and used still needs to be done.

The most frequent therapeutic use of timeout procedures has been in the treatment of children, particularly to suppress hyperactivity, self-injury, tantrums, sterotyped movements, and antisocial behavior (e.g., Duker, 1975; Doleys, Wells, Hobbs, Roberts, and Cartelli, 1976; Reichle, Brubakken, and Tretreault, 1976; Sachs, 1973; Spitalnik and Drabman, 1976; Tyler and Brown, 1967). Studies with adults have shown effective reduction of delusional and hallucinatory speech (Davis, Wallace, Liberman, and Finch, 1976), have established fluent speech with stutterers (Costello, 1975), and have significantly reduced the variety of symptoms exhibited by psychiatric inpatients (Finch, Wallace, and Davis, 1976). Timeout can also have positive side-effects, with undesirable behaviors other than the target activity being reduced and desirable behavior emerging (Firestone, 1976).

There have been voices criticizing the procedure as being relatively ineffective, sometimes because timeout is actually positively reinforcing and may thus increase rather than decrease the occurrence of the undesired behavior (Martin, 1975; Steeves, Martin, and Pear, 1970). Some instances of ineffectiveness may be due to various environmental or treatment parameters that have not been pretested. It appears that there are unsuspected complexities in the use of the treatment (see Benoit and Mayer, undated; Burchard and Barrera, 1972; MacDonough and Forehand, 1973; Solnick, Rincover, and Peterson, 1977). Duration can also be a relevant factor (e.g., Hobbs, Forehand, and Murray, 1978).

One of the important aspects of timeout is that it may not be necessary for there to be an obvious situation of ongoing positive reinforcement which is interrupted by the imposition of timeout when inappropriate behaviors are emitted. For example, Pendergrass (1972) has described a study in which two retarded children were subjected to timeout if they engaged in undesired behaviors in their classroom. When the behavior occurred, the experimenter gave a verbal prohibition and then put the child into an isolation booth for 2 minutes. Misbehavior was significantly suppressed, even though the responses could easily have been emitted even in the isolation situation. The author interprets the results as indicating that being in a group setting was positively reinforcing for these children, even though they joined minimally in class activities, and that isolation was timeout from this source of pleasure. An alternative explanation is that the isolation situation helped to relieve some condition (e.g., a nonoptimal arousal level) that had been built up in the classroom and had led to the emission of the undesirable behavior, and that with repeated experience, the child learned to cope with those pressures in other ways.

A number of similar findings have been published with children whose behavior was difficult to control (e.g., Burchard and Barrera, 1972; Sachs, 1973; White, Nielsen, and Johnson, 1972). Murray (1976) has even described a timeout technique to be used by parents when children throw tantrums in public. The child's head and shoulders are covered with a coat or small blanket. He is isolated in a corner, a public restroom, or the family car. No data are provided to evaluate the effectiveness of any of these suggested procedures. However, they seem reasonable when one recalls the success of reduced stimulation in other settings and especially in view of the fact that tantrum behavior in small children is so commonly triggered by excessively high stimulation and arousal levels. Among other uses of timeout have been in the control of noncompliance at home, lack of attention and erroneous responses in classroom, and inappropriate behavior at meals (see Gast and Nelson, 1977; Hobbs and Goswick, 1977).

It should be emphasized that timeout does not necessarily involve either complete social isolation or stimulus reduction. For that matter, even removal to a completely different location is not necessary. Foxx and Shapiro (1978) and Barsness, Thompson, and Warrington (1977), among others, have used timeout procedures which were relatively nonintrusive and which involved no major change in the environment. The results appeared to be good; unfortunately, there has not been sufficient research to estimate the degree to which the nature and extent of environmental modification influenced the usefulness of the timeout experience.

Naturally, the use of timeout procedures has become quite controversial, and in the United States the courts have sometimes stepped in. Mostly, their involvement has been in the areas of professional supervision, duration of isolation, and conditions of the isolation environment. In their analysis of the problems involved, Gast and Nelson (1977) distinguished among three forms of timeout. The least disruptive is "contingent observation," where the individual is instructed to move away from the activity and observe the rest of the group. In another form of this procedure, the child is not removed but his ineligibility for reinforcement is signaled by the presence or absence of a colored ribbon or other marker. This technique was reported to be successful with severely retarded children (Foxx and Shapiro, 1978). Somewhat more drastic is "exclusion timeout," in which the individual is removed to another part of the room and may not be able to observe the group. "Seclusion timeout," in which the person is removed from the group area and isolated, is the most intensive form. Gast and Nelson claim that this version is the most commonly used, "potentially the most aversive," and possibly the most effective of the three.

Accordingly, it should be used only when the other techniques have failed to suppress disruptive behavior. The conditions under which it is applied (duration, environmental characteristics, supervision) should be closely controlled. The authors argue that before any timeout procedure is employed, consideration should be given to the desirability of warning the individual and of providing explanations as to why timeout is being used and how it may be terminated. The therapist or teacher should specify the behavioral contingencies for release from timeout. These recommendations are very similar to those proposed for the use of solitary confinement in correctional institutions (see Chapter 3), and may in fact increase the efficacy of the procedure as well as solving possible ethical problems (see e.g., Bernhardt, Fredericks, and Forbach, 1978).

To answer another criticism, that timeout is time wasted from the point of view of learning or therapy (Burchard and Barrera, 1972), Linkenhoker (1974) has proposed that patients undergoing timeout be asked to spend the time thinking about and verbally describing the nature of the problem that led them to this situation, how they feel about it, and what behaviors could have kept them from being put into timeout. This explanation, recorded on tape, would be reviewed by a group consisting of staff members and possibly peers. The perceptions of staff and the patient as to the circumstances surrounding the timeout period would be compared, and the feelings of the people involved thoroughly explored. In token economies, the patient could even be given some limited number of token reinforcers if his proposed solutions are appropriate and his observations show insight. This is an interesting suggestion, which would make the timeout procedure somewhat similar to those used in some REST studies, in Morita therapy, and in the program at the Walla Walla State Penitentiary, discussed elsewhere in this book. As yet, no systematic test of its efficacy has been made.

Rather than looking at timeout merely as a punitive experience, we might consider that the normal classroom or group environment is aversive for some of the individuals involved. Disruptive behavior may be a cue that their tolerance limit is being reached or exceeded, and removal from the situation is thus a way of enabling them to restore their balance. This is, of course, a more cognitive explanation than one based purely on reinforcement variables.

Another point to note is the possibility that social isolation, aside from suppressing undesired behaviors, may foster desired ones. Bernhardt, Fredericks, and Forbach (1978) found that when information was given as to the specific behavior being rewarded, timeout and praise were both effective in facilitating the learning of a discrimination task by preschool children. However, unlike Wahler (1969) and the researchers using REST with adult subjects, Bernhardt et al. did not find any additional increment in efficacy when the two techniques were combined. This may be a function of the age of the children, or of the fact that they were normal subjects learning an experimental task rather than patients learning new behavior patterns relevant to their problems.

The study by Bernhardt et al. is one of the few tests of combinatorial treatments of which timeout is one component. Parsons and Davey (1978) have shown that modeling was more effectively learned through a combination of social reinforcement and timeout than with reinforcement only. This is logical, given the well-established increase in the efficacy of social reinforcement following isolation (e.g., Endo, 1968; Eisenberger, 1970). The combined procedure may lead to increased social responsivity among children first subjected to timeout, just as it seems to do in the long-term isolation condition reported with autistic children. As a matter of fact, Altman (1971) has suggested brief isolation as a way to elevate depressed activity and particularly depressed social participation of the target individuals. The suggestion remains untaken by any researcher at the moment. Obviously, more work is necessary to establish the most effective uses of the method.

Controlled comparisons among various specific procedures are clearly necessary. Similar comparisons between timeout and other techniques such as aversive stimulation and overcorrection also need to be performed, so that the optimal techniques and combinations of techniques may be identified. For example, Sachs (1973) found that extinguishing undesired behaviors by ignoring them was more effective than isolation with the retarded child on whom the techniques were tested. In addition, ignoring misbehavior did not produce temper tantrums (isolation did).

CONCLUSION

Once again, it should be noted that the assumed aversiveness of REST, timeout and isolation procedures is mostly a matter of generalization from other situations, intuition, and claims in the course of litigation. In contrast to these sources of dubious information, the data show that brain damaged and autistic children, once they have had experience in the isolation setting, will repeatedly seek it out deliberately, particularly when they feel agitated or hyperactive (Murray, 1975). Pupils in schools that have instituted isolation rooms to provide timeout as a form of discipline find the environment both effective in helping them to catch up with their work and to stay out of trouble, and desirable to the point where they have been reported to seek isolation deliberately (Norman, 1977). One staff member in an institution for the mentally retarded, referring to the two seclusion rooms under heavy use at that center, says, "solitude is the best reinforcer we've got" (Catherine T. Dineen, personal communication, October 25, 1976).

From reviews of the literature on the treatment of retarded, hyperactive, autistic, and otherwise disturbed children (see e.g., Brundage-Aguar, Forehand, and Ciminero, 1977; Hobbs and Lahey, 1977), it is clear that none of the many medical, psychopharmacological, and behavioral techniques has been found to be a panacea. Most studies in this area use very few subjects, limited followups, and a lack of adequate controls and comparison groups; but there is no doubt that a period of isolation has been beneficial in many instances. The parameters, other environmental changes, and treatment combinations that would increase this efficacy need to be explored.

CHAPTER 10

Effects of Reduced Stimulation on Institutionalized Adult Patients

HENRY B. ADAMS
Area C Community Mental Health Center, Washington, D.C.

Let me begin on a personal note. In reviewing the literature for this chapter, I was struck by the discrepancy between the actual research findings, which were generally positive, and the widespread negative beliefs about "sensory deprivation" research which are more fully discussed in other chapters. These negative beliefs originated with the sensationalized and confusing early reports which erroneously linked "sensory deprivation" or restricted environmental stimulation with dissimilar psychological phenomena such as "brainwashing," coercive persuasion, mind control, torture, and the like. These erroneous beliefs were subsequently perpetuated by psychology textbooks, despite the fact that there was never any empirical evidence to support them.

In view of the prevalence of negative beliefs about "sensory deprivation" research, many readers may be skeptical of the predominantly positive findings presented in this chapter. These positive findings may seem to be at variance with what many well-informed readers have come to accept. It is reasonable to expect that searching questions will be raised about the statements and conclusions I have offered.

In an effort to anticipate these questions, I have provided much more detailed information in this review about research procedures and their rationale than is customary in surveys of the literature. I also made a special point of including the ideas of the original investigators by extensive paraphrasing and direct quotations. Many of their ideas are still quite novel and unfamiliar to most of the scientific community and the popular media. I believe that these ideas have much validity and that they deserve a fair hearing today, particularly since they failed to gain much acceptance when they first appeared many years ago.

GENERAL STATEMENTS

This chapter surveys research on the effects of REST on institutionalized adults, most of whom were hospitalized psychiatric patients. In a few of the studies reviewed here other kinds of subjects (noninstitutionalized or nonpsychiatric patients, or "normals") were used for baseline or control groups. However, publications involving only "normal" and/or noninstitutionalized subjects (which actually includes almost all the research literature on "sensory deprivation") were not included in this survey.

This chapter excludes studies of adults in correctional institutions, which are discussed in Chapter 3. It also omits the extensive literature on Japanese institutions that utilize what Reynolds (1976; in press) has termed "the quiet therapies": that is, techniques such as Morita psychotherapy, Zen meditation therapy, and so on, which systematically incorporate the use of reduced environmental stimulation (isolation, bed rest) as an integral part of their therapeutic procedures. This area is covered in Chapter 7. Research on reduced stimulation in the treatment of behavior disorders in institutionalized children and adolescents is reviewed in Chapter 9.

Each section of this chapter reviews a different topical area. The next section surveys research on the effects of REST on institutionalized adult patients. "REST" is a generic label which includes two distinctly different types of special stimulus environments that characteristically produce different psychological effects. Explicit distinctions are made between special environments generating (1) reduced stimulation and (2) monotonous stimulation.

In reduced stimulation environments, absolute levels of intensities of sensory stimulation are greatly reduced, usually by darkness, silence, isolated quiet rooms, and so on. In monotonous stimulation environments there is no reduction in absolute levels of sensory stimulation, but there is a reduction in the amount of stimulus patterning and/or variability. One example of monotonous stimulation is the use of translucent goggles in a brightly lit room, which eliminate meaningfully patterned visual stimulation while admitting diffuse, homogeneous bright light. The difference between these two conditions may be illustrated by the contrast between a silent, soundproof room, which provides greatly reduced levels of auditory stimulation, and relatively loud white noise, producing homogeneous, unvarying, monotonous auditory stimulation with no reduction in the absolute volume of sound.

The distinction between reduced stimulation and monotonous stimulation is important, since the psychological effects of these contrasting stimulus environments are quite different. I could find no reports of significant improvement in institutionalized adults exposed to conditions of monotonous stimulation, but there are many published reports of improvement after reduced environmental stimulation.

There follows a survey of the effects of reduced stimulation on chemically induced "psychoses" or psychotic-like reactions produced by phencyclidine (PCP) and LSD. No publications investigating the effects of monotonous stimulation on these chemically induced psychotic-like states have appeared thus far. That section includes an early group of research papers from controlled scientific settings and a later group of more impressionistic clinically-oriented papers from treatment settings, which appeared after a recent upsurge in the use of illicit PCP and LSD caused a rapid increase in the incidence of drug-induced psychotic reactions. The more recent clinical papers consistently recommended the use of reduced environmental stimulation as the treatment of choice for these dangerous psychotic states.

The following section reviews papers on differential effects of special stimulus environments. This section deals with differences among individuals and contrasts between groups in reactions to special stimulus environments, including not only reduced and monotonous stimulation—as defined above—but also the effects of varying noise levels in an ordinary mental hospital ward.

The last section, Conclusions, briefly summarizes major findings and considers some of their implications.

EFFECTS OF REST ON ADULT PSYCHIATRIC INPATIENTS

The first modern studies utilizing reduced environmental stimulation with hospitalized psychiatric patients were published by Azima and his associates (Azima and Cramer-Azima, 1956a, b; 1957; Azima, Vispo, and Azima, 1961). This group of investigators had been personally familiar with the pioneering McGill studies conducted by Bexton, Heron, and Scott (1954) under the direction of Hebb (1955, 1961).

Early Studies

Whereas the subjects in the work of Bexton et al. were male college students, the Azima group used as subjects hospitalized psychiatric patients of both sexes. Azima et al. reduced levels of visual stimulation by placing their subjects in a darkened, isolated hospital room, and reduced auditory stimulation by the use of heavy curtains in the room and by plugging the subjects' ears with cotton. Under these conditions absolute levels of visual and auditory stimuli were greatly reduced, a procedural modification whose significance was apparently not recognized at the time.

Recognizing that the needs and expectations of hospitalized inpatients anticipating some form of treatment differed from those of presumably "normal" college students, Azima et al. stated (1956a, p. 60) that their techniques differed in two major aspects from those used by Bexton et al. The first difference was "that of motivation, psychological attitude, and the nature of the subject-observer relationship, and the second, relative decrease of verbal communication." Before being exposed to reduced environmental stimulation, patients were told that these procedures were a means of investigation and treatment aimed at cutting down on the level of external stimulation, and that they could terminate the procedures at any time. The patients accepted the procedures as a method of recovery from their psychological handicaps.

The decrease in verbal communication was accomplished by cutting down on verbal interaction. Patients were checked every hour, but they were interviewed only once or twice a day, for 20 to 30 minutes each time. "This interview was conducted in a psychotherapeutic fashion. During the hourly checking time conversation was neither initiated nor encouraged, and if the patient began to talk he received no answer" (1956a, p. 61).

The first two published reports by Azima and Cramer-Azima (1956a, b) seem to be describing the same subjects, who received from 2 to 6 days of reduced stimulation. There were five depressives, in whom a "beneficial therapeutic effect was observed; in two this effect was permanent." Two obsessional neurotics manifested acute psychotic episodes that were treated with electric shock, "which resulted in improvement in both paranoid and obsessional features." The other eight cases "showed a moderate increase in motivation, socialization, and self-assertiveness."

The authors observed that two sets of changes occurred as a result of reduced stimulation (1956a, p. 122). The first was a "disorganization of psychic structure." The second was a process of reorganization, which "consisted of a marked change in mood in the depressed cases" and in most other cases involved "constructive aggression . . . with an increasing tendency to socialization and relationship-undertaking." They also found that "psychological tests showed up significant impairment in concentration and efficiency," in contrast to the impaired functioning on psychological tests reported by Bexton et al. in subjects exposed to monotonous stimulation.

A 1957 study by Azima and Cramer-Azima reported on results with four obsessional neurotics treated with the same procedures as in the two 1956 papers. Of the four subjects, one had a brief psychotic episode which subsided after electric shock treatment. The other three patients showed no changes in symptomatology, but they did show "an increase in their communicativeness and their desire to socialize."

A later paper by Azima, Vispo, and Azima (1961) described a modification of their earlier procedures. Using the same small quiet room and the same conditions of reduced stimulation, they fostered a more intense therapist-patient relationship which they called "anaclitic isolation." Before being placed in anaclitic isolation each patient selected was seen "for one or two weeks prior to isolation in one or more daily interviews to establish a positive transference relationship." Patients were told that this was a form of treatment where they could "rest from any external stresses, and where they have nothing to do but indulge in this rest and relaxation," which they could terminate at any time. Whereas patients in previous studies were seen only once or twice daily for interviews of 15 to 30 minutes, each patient in anaclitic isolation was seen three times a day in interviews lasting from 1 to $1^{1}/_{2}$ hours, during which the therapist fed the patient and took him to the bathroom, "encouraging a relationship of total dependency." During the therapist's absence, each patient was observed frequently by a nurse, who did not communicate verbally with the patient.

Azima et al. reported on 4 patients treated in anaclitic isolation, which aimed at systematically fostering dependency needs so as to provide deep regression and disorganization. Regression occurred in 3 patients, but a fourth went into a manic state and had to leave the situation. Azima et al. explained that their rationale in inducing regression was to induce a process of "uncovering" and "working through." This process of regression or disorganization was then followed by a process of progression and constructive personality reorganization in directions fostered by the therapist.

The four published reports by this group showed that the desired results were obtained consistently in a majority of the patients treated. There were wide individual differences, with a few patients showing substantial changes in "improved" directions. There were also failures, in which patients showed more severe symptomatology during or after the procedures. The investigators suggested many questions for future research, but there were no subsequent publications by this group.

Harris (1959) exposed a group of 12 hospitalized schizophrenics to conditions of reduced stimulation, during which they lay on a couch in a soundproofed cubicle, wearing opaque goggles and gloves fitted with cardboard cuffs. They were left alone in the cubicle for two periods, 30 minutes on the first day and about 2 hours on a subsequent day. These brief periods of exposure to reduced stimulation contrast with the procedures used by the Azima group, in which subjects had several days of exposure.

Harris observed that although previous publications had indicated that most normal subjects found exposure to reduced environmental stimulation unpleasant, his schizophrenic subjects "were more tolerant than normal subjects of these conditions, which tended to reduce the intensity of hallucinations" (p. 237). Harris noted substantial individual differences in the reactions of these schizophrenics. Several reported that their persistent hallucinatory symptoms diminished or disappeared while they were in the cubicle. On the other hand, two others reported feelings of distress while in the same cubicle.

Harris offered the suggestion that "some of the phenomena of schizophrenia have been explained on the grounds of an inability to deal with the inflowing stream of sensations and percepts and to extract meaning from them." He hypothesized that reduced environmental stimulation or "sensory deprivation" would not aggravate the schizophrenic's inability to cope with this stream of inflowing sensory stimulation, and that "it might even produce improvement by reducing the strain and bringing temporary relief to the mechanisms involved" (p. 235). Harris's positive results with this group of patients suggest that the reduction of environmental stimulation served to relieve them of pressures related to their inability to cope successfully with a normal stimulus environment.

A team of investigators at the Lafayette Clinic in Detroit reported results substantially similar to those obtained by Harris with schizophrenic patients. Two publications by this group (Cohen, Rosenbaum, Dobie and Gottlieb, 1959; Luby, Gottlieb, Cohen, Rosenbaum, and Domino, 1962) described an experiment involving four normal, one neurotic, two sociopathic, and three schizophrenic subjects. They were exposed to 1 hour of reduced stimulation, seated in a comfortable armchair located in a quiet, isolated (but not soundproofed) room, with ear plugs and padded ear phones to minimize auditory input. Tactual stimulation was reduced by bandages on the fingers and elbow-length mittens. Visual stimuli were minimized for some subjects by opaque blackened-out goggles, while others wore frosted goggles which permitted diffuse, unpatterned light perception.

At the beginning of the hour each subject was given the suggestion that unusual perceptions were appropriate in this situation. Subjects were observed continuously and their movements and verbalizations recorded. All were interviewed immediately after the end of the session.

The visual experiences described by the subjects were less vivid, less elaborate, and more commonplace than those reported in the McGill experiments of Bexton et al. (1954). Comparison of the effects of frosted translucent goggles with black goggles showed that visual sensory reactions occurred in 5 of the 6 subjects wearing frosted goggles, but in only 1 of the 4 subjects wearing black goggles. Neither condition generated true visual hallucinations, but the greater frequency of visual sensory reactions was viewed as consistent with other studies reporting more "abnormal visual phenomena . . . under conditions of diffuse stimulation (e.g., the McGill conditions) as contrasted with conditions of total visual blackout" (Cohen et al., 1959, p. 490). This may be viewed as one more instance of the difference in effects of reduced visual stimulation (black goggles), as compared with monotonous, unpatterned, homogeneous visual stimulation (frosted goggles).

However, the greatest differences were found in comparisons of the emotional responses of the subjects. Normal and neurotic subjects were generally more anxious and restless during restricted stimulation than the schizophrenics and sociopaths. "The most distinctive finding was that the psychotic subjects in poor reality contact showed the least discomfort and the most affectively sensitive reactions to the procedure. They regarded the experience as pleasant and comfortable, and retained calm composure throughout the hour. This was in marked contrast to the reactions of the nonpsychotic subjects as described above. While the schizophrenic subjects did report some hallucinatory perceptions, these were not different from their usual behavior outside the reduced stimulus environment. Reduction of sensory input did not exacerbate schizophrenic pathology, and in some cases it had an ameliorating effect" (Luby et al., 1962, p. 64). This paper added that "the inference can be drawn that the cognitive organization of schizophrenic subjects is characteristically 'geared down' so that they experience difficulty in the central accommodation of normal sensory inflow." Reduced stimulation may provide for the schizophrenic "a more balanced relation between input load and reception interpretation capacity. Schizophrenic withdrawal may represent an attempt by the patient to reduce input overload, resulting in a form of learned self-imposed sensory isolation."

Two related papers (Smith and Lewty, 1959; Smith, Thakurdas, and Lawes, 1961) contrasted responses to "sensory deprivation" in a group of normal subjects of both sexes with a group of chronic schizophrenics. The 1959 paper described reactions of 10 normal volunteers to experimental conditions which were a mixture of both reduced and monotonous stimulation. Subjects were placed in a soundproof room which minimized auditory input, and their hands and arms were covered with comfortable fur gauntlets and cotton gloves which reduced tactile stimulation. However, the room was lighted and subjects wore translucent goggles which eliminated patterned visual stimuli.

All subjects were visited four times daily for brief questioning, at which time the goggles, gauntlets, and gloves were removed and a meal set before them, which they ate in isolation after the interview. They remained in the soundproof room "as long as they could stand it; all knew that they could terminate the experiment at any time." They remained for periods from 4 to 92 hours, with an average of 29 hours for men and 49 hours for women.

The 1961 paper by Smith et al. reported the responses of 6 chronic schizophrenics exposed to the same set of conditions. The schizophrenics voluntarily remained much longer than any of the normal subjects, for periods ranging from 430 to 486 hours.

Both groups of subjects were rated on twelve items of mentation. The normals showed greatest disturbance on items indicating disordered thinking, agitation and restlessness leading to panic in some cases, body image disturbances, progressive loss of appetite, and dreams having nightmare quality. Ratings of schizophrenics on the same mentation items showed no evidence of disturbance or change on any item. Smith et al. observed that "all patients gave the impression of accepting these lengthy periods of isolation without any difficulties or upset."

In explaining these differences, Smith et al. suggested (1961, p. 843) that "normal subjects find great difficulty in adapting to or tolerating the stress of sensory isolation but schizophrenics find no difficulty. It appears to be their normal habitat. Normal subjects find increasing need for and attempt to obtain extrinsic physical and social stimuli. Schizophrenics have no such need and make no effort to obtain such stimuli."

The Richmond VA Hospital Program

Five large-scale investigations with hospitalized male psychiatric patients extending over a period of several years were conducted by a team of investigators in the Richmond, Virginia, Veterans Administration hospital. There were also informal exploratory studies in which normal subjects, including staff members, employees, and students, participated in the same procedures and were evaluated on the same measures of change as the psychiatric patients. The normals consistently showed little or no change following reduced stimulation, while substantial changes were found in patients exposed to the same conditions and evaluated by the same measures. Furthermore, positive changes were greatest among those patients who initially displayed the most severe symptomatology.

The first large-scale investigation was a pilot study in which 30 patients were exposed to a maximum of 6 hours of reduced environmental stimulation. They lay on a bed in a quiet, comfortable, air-conditioned hospital room with their eyes covered, ears plugged with cotton, and head wrapped in gauze, minimizing levels of visual and auditory stimuli. There was no interference with tactual or kinesthetic stimuli, since cuffs, gloves, and other restraints were not used. There was no social interaction with the experimenter during the period of reduced stimulation, and subjects were not fed during that period. They were free to leave at any time, but those who had not voluntarily terminated earlier were removed at the end of 6 hours. Of the 30 subjects, 12 remained for the full 6-hour period.

The results of the pilot study were published in three separate reports. The first (Gibby, Adams, and Carrera, 1960) reported changes in psychiatric symptomatology based on interview data, as rated on a 20-item symptom rating scale (Jenkins, Stauffacher, and Hester, 1959). Although there were changes in the directions of both reduced and increased symptomatology, changes in the "positive" direction (reduced symptomatology) were significantly greater than those in the opposite direction. "Positive" changes 1 day after reduced stimulation tended to persist 1 week later, while "negative" changes (increased symptomatology) tended to disappear during the same 1-week period. The positive changes reflected persisting internal modifications of a beneficial nature, while the negative changes appeared to be manifestations of a temporary upsurge of anxiety and emotional disturbance which later subsided.

In addition, there were a number of generalized qualitative changes in the behavior of these psychiatric patients outside the three interviews scheduled before and after reduced stimulation. They demonstrated an increased desire for social contacts and therapeutic relationships with the staff. They verbalized increased awareness of internal conflicts, new insights into personal difficulties, and recognition of their own role in the maladaptive behavior patterns that led to their hospitalization. After a period of reduced stimulation there was a less rigid utilization of repressive and inhibitory defenses. It appeared that the reduction of external stimulation "may have facilitated the reassessment of older maladaptive patterns, along with a reduction of previously well-established repressive and inhibitory defenses" (Gibby et al., 1960, p. 30).

The second pilot study paper (Cooper, Adams, and Gibby, 1962) reported on Rorschach changes in the same patients. Four measures of ego strength, based on Cartwright's (1958) modification of Klopfer's Rorschach Prognostic Rating Scale, were used in the data analysis. On all four measures the average patient changed in the direction of increased ego strength after reduced stimulation. Positive changes on three measures were statistically significant. Those whose initial scores indicated least ego strength tended to show the greatest increases afterward.

The third pilot study paper (Adams, Cooper, and Carrera, 1972) reported changes on the Wechsler Adult Intelligence Scale. The mean IQ score for patients in the study increased from 97 to 104 after reduced stimulation, which was highly significant statistically. Changes in IQ scores showed wide individual differences, and there were several significant correlations with other behavioral measures, which are summarized more fully in the section on differential effects.

The pilot study was open to the criticism that there was no control group, and that the changes observed might have been due to factors other than reduced stimulation. A second large-scale study was then initiated, which substantially replicated the pilot study but with the introduction of a matched control group and some additional personality measures (Cooper, Adams, and Cohen, 1965). There were 40 subjects, half in the experimental group and half in the control group. Their ages, educational levels, and psychiatric diagnoses were similar to the pilot study group. All 40 subjects were administered the Rorschach, MMPI, Interpersonal Check List (Leary, 1956, 1957), and Rotter Form Board (Rotter, 1942), and their interview behavior was rated on the same 20-item symptom rating scale used in the pilot study. Subjects in the experimental group were pretested and interviewed the first day, exposed to not more than 3 hours of reduced stimulation on the second day, and post-tested and interviewed again on the third day. Control subjects followed the same schedule except that they were not exposed to reduced stimulation. The interviewer did not know which subjects were assigned to the two groups, since the assignment to groups and the placement of subjects in the reduced stimulus environment was done by a second staff member in order to minimize possible interviewer bias.

Overt symptomatology was reduced in both groups, but the reduction in symptomatology was significantly greater in the experimental group. On the four psychological tests the control group showed no significant improvement, while the experimental group showed enhanced ego functioning, greater self-acceptance, and more effective utilization of defense mechanisms. Again there were substantial individual differences, with evidence that subjects showing greatest improvement were those least amenable to orthodox verbal psychotherapy. A special analysis of these individual differences was conducted, the results of which appear on pages 349–353. This study replicated the results of the initial pilot study, while use of a matched control group indicated that the observed changes resulted from reduced stimulation and not from extraneous artifacts.

A third study (Gibby and Adams, 1961) was based on the observation by many investigators that reduced environmental stimulation seems to induce a state of "stimulus hunger," in which receptiveness to new stimuli is greatly enhanced. It was suggested that if messages of a therapeutic nature were presented under conditions of reduced stimulation, increased stimulus hunger would render the patient more open and receptive to suggestion.

A total of 42 subjects with characteristics similar to those in the two preceding studies were randomly assigned to four groups. All subjects were administered a self-concept inventory (Brownfain, 1952) on Day 1 and Day 3. On Day 2 subjects in the experimental group were exposed to 4 hours of reduced stimulation under the same conditions as in the other two studies. During the session a standardized prerecorded message was presented, phrased in broad, general language aimed at improving the patient's conscious self-concept. Subjects in the three control groups received various combinations of these conditions. One control group heard the same standardized tape message while sitting alone in an office, the second received reduced stimulation without the message, while a third (test-retest) group received neither reduced stimulation nor a message.

The experimental group changed in positive directions on all four sets of self-concept ratings. On each set these changes were significantly greater than in any of the three control groups. The prerecorded message had far greater impact on subjects whose receptiveness had been increased by reduced environmental stimulation.

The fourth study (Hogan, 1963) was based on the rationale and procedures of the third. In place of the self-concept measures, Hogan employed two measures of decision-making ability. The standardized message prepared for two groups of subjects was both instructional and emotionally supportive, suggesting specific ways for subjects to improve their decision-making ability.

In most other respects the fourth study closely resembled the third. Characteristics of the 60 patients used as subjects were similar to the other three studies. Fifteen subjects were assigned to each of the four groups. On Day 1 all subjects were administered the two tests of decision-making ability (Hogan, 1963). On the morning of Day 2 subjects in the experimental group received 3 hours of reduced stimulation, during which the prerecorded instructional message was presented. The other three (control) groups had the same combination of conditions as in the third study, and were administered the two decision-making tests on the same schedule as the experimental group. On the afternoon of Day 2 the two tests of decision-making ability were repeated for all four groups.

Subjects in the two groups hearing the message showed significantly improved decision-making scores on post-testing. However, subjects in the experimental group, who heard the message under conditions of reduced stimulation, showed significantly higher scores on post-testing than subjects in the control group, who heard the same message in a normal stimulus environment. The improvement in scores on both measures of decision-making ability was significantly greater in the experimental group than in all three of the control groups.

A fifth study in this series (Adams, Robertson, and Cooper, 1966) investigated changes induced by individually prepared messages presented while subjects were in a reduced stimulus environment. Since the two preceding studies had shown that presentation of a standardized taped message during reduced stimulation produced significant changes in desired directions, it was thought that individual messages prepared specifically for each subject might be used to facilitate the processes of psychotherapy, overcoming resistances, enhancing insightful self-awareness, and fostering new interpersonal attitudes.

Subjects were 43 psychiatric inpatients, with essentially the same characteristics as in the four previous studies. All subjects were administered two personality measures, the MMPI and the Leary (1956, 1957) Interpersonal Check List (ICL). They were then assigned to one of three groups.

For every subject assigned to Group I, a separate individual message was prepared and recorded on tape. The content of each message was based on the subject's responses on the MMPI and ICL, scored and interpreted according to the Multilevel System of Interpersonal Diagnosis (Leary, 1956). Each message described (1) the subject's typical overt interpersonal behavior, (2) his conscious self-description, (3) his covert, preconscious attitudes, (4) his conception of the ideal person, and (5) the psychological significance of discrepancies among these four aspects of personality. There was also an explanation of the goals and purposes of the psychotherapy that was to be initiated immediately after the reduced stimulation and post-testing procedures were completed.

Each subject in Group I was exposed to 3 hours of the same conditions of reduced stimulation as in the four previous studies. After 2 hours the individually prepared taped message, which ran for about 15 minutes, was presented. The subject was then allowed 45 minutes to assimilate the contents of the message before being removed from the room. On the following day the ICL and MMPI were administered a second time to evaluate personality changes. Each subject in Group I then began individual psychotherapy with the same therapist whose voice he had heard on the taped message.

Subjects in Group II were administered the same two personality measures 2 days apart. On the intervening day they were exposed to 3 hours of reduced stimulation without the messages. Subjects in Group III served as a test-retest control group. They were given the ICL and MMPI twice, two days apart. During the intervening time they had the same routine ward activities as subjects in the other two groups.

Statistical analysis of changes from pretesting to post-testing showed that the number of significant differences among the three groups was several times greater than chance expectancy. After exposure to the combination of reduced stimulation and individual messages, subjects in Group I showed more realistic ideals, improved internal controls, diminished overall symptomatology, and a reduction of defensiveness and repression.

Subjects in Group II also showed improvement, but the pattern of changes was significantly different from Group I. They showed greater dominance, enhanced ego strength, less depression, greater conscious self-acceptance, and an outward display of increased personal adequacy. However, there was less of an increase on measures reflecting conscious insight and self-awareness than in Group I, while tendencies to deny personal shortcomings were greater.

Comparisons of Group III with the other two groups indicated that the significant changes in Groups I and II resulted from the message and/or conditions of reduced stimulation rather than from testing and retesting alone.

A later followup of one patient in Group I was published as an individual case study (Adams, 1965). This case study demonstrated that the combination of reduced stimulation and the individually prepared message rendered the patient willing to accept intensive outpatient psychotherapy for the first time. During the previous 10 years the patient had been hospitalized 6 times, but he had consistently rejected offers of intensive psychotherapy. After being presented during reduced stimulation with a message recommending psychotherapy, he remained in psychotherapy for the next 16 months. His need for hospitalization was reduced, since he had three admissions as an inpatient during the 13 months prior to the experience of reduced stimulation, but only one admission during the 30 months afterward.

A second individual case study (Adams, 1979) reports on a paranoid schizophrenic who made a full recovery from psychosis after being exposed to reduced stimulation 4 times during a 9-day period. Each exposure was relatively brief, ranging from 50 to 90 minutes, and each was voluntarily terminated by the patient. Except for the fact that this patient had repeated exposures to reduced stimulation and heard no messages, the conditions were the same as in the preceding studies.

Prior to the first experience the patient had shown the typical clinical symptoms of a full-blown paranoid schizophrenic psychosis. His MMPI profile and his interview behavior as rated on the 20-item symptom rating scale also indicated an acute psychotic break. During the 9 days when he was repeatedly exposed to a reduced stimulus environment, his interview behavior was rerated after each exposure. The MMPI was also administered several times. Both measures indicated a rapid drop in the severity of his psychiatric symptoms. At the end of this period, his symptoms had disappeared, he had gained insightful understanding of himself, and he requested individual psychotherapy for the first time. He was seen for 7 therapy sessions during the next 4 weeks, at which time he was discharged from the inpatient service, having maintained his recovery. He did not continue psychotherapy after his discharge, but returned to the outpatient service every 6 months for psychiatric medication. During the following 5 years he had no recurrence of the psychotic symptoms for which he had initially been hospitalized.

Robertson (1964, 1965) attempted to facilitate therapeutic changes in hospitalized psychiatric patients by the repeated use of several individually prepared tape messages, which were presented when the patients were exposed to reduced stimulation. His study was an extension of the same approaches and general rationale as in the study by Adams, Robertson, and Cooper (1966) described above. Subjects were 51 psychiatric patients at a state mental hospital in Michigan.

In Robertson's study the hospitalized psychiatric patients assigned to his Group I (reduced stimulation plus message) were interviewed and their behavior rated on the same 20-item symptom rating scale (Jenkins, et al., 1959) which was used in the studies by Gibby et al. (1960), Cleveland et al. (1963), and Cooper et al. (1965). They were given the MMPI and ICL and then told that they would be seen again a week later. Using data from the interview, the two personality tests, and the case history, a set of three individually prepared 20-minute messages was written and taped. On the Monday, Wednesday, and Friday of the week after the first interview, each subject received 3-hour sessions of reduced stimulation. The three pre-recorded messages were presented on those three days, one individual message during each session. One week after hearing the third message, each subject in Group I was interviewed a second time and rated again on the 20-item symptom rating scale, after which the MMPI and ICL were repeated. A period of almost 3 weeks elapsed between the initial interview and pretesting and the second interview and post-testing.

There were three other groups, on whom the same interview and test measures were obtained, with the same long time interval elapsing between the first and second sets of measures. Patients in Group II heard three individually-prepared messages without reduced stimulation. Group

III had reduced stimulation only, without any messages, while Group IV was a test-retest control group.

On the 20-item symptom rating scale all three of the treated groups showed significantly more improvement than the untreated control group, but the three treated groups did not differ significantly from one another. On the MMPI and ICL, subjects receiving reduced stimulation alone showed significantly greater increases on a measure of self-acceptance than the untreated controls, a result which replicated the findings of the 1966 study by Adams et al. There were no other significant results.

In evaluating Robertson's findings, it is important to note that he did not follow the same procedures in analyzing the MMPI and ICL data that were employed in the study by Adams et al., and consequently it is hard to make meaningful comparisons. A more serious difficulty is the fact that the time interval between the two measures of change (almost 3 weeks) was much greater than in any of the other studies reviewed in this section. The possibility of confounding extraneous variables is therefore greatly increased. Any questions which arise in evaluating Robertson's results could probably be resolved by a replication of his study, but with much shorter time intervals between measures of change and more measures of change immediately after each significant experimental treatment.

Monotonous Stimulation

With minor exceptions, the studies reviewed above involved a reduction in absolute levels of visual and auditory stimuli. By contrast, a study with patients in the Houston VA Hospital by Cleveland, Reitman, and Bentinck (1963) utilized conditions of monotonous stimulation. Subjects were placed in an isolated hospital room and fitted with translucent eye goggles, after which two overhead lights and a white noise generator were turned on. Under those conditions "there was no reduction in the absolute level of stimuli intensity. Instead, subjects were exposed to an unvarying, repetitive stimulus environment in which meaningful patterned cues had been minimized" (p. 456).

Cleveland et al. assigned 60 psychiatric inpatients to three groups of 20 each. A group of schizophrenics and a group of nonpsychotic patients were exposed to a maximum of 4 hours of the experimental condition of monotonous stimulation. A control group of schizophrenics did not receive monotonous stimulation.

All subjects were placed on a 3-day schedule. On Day 1 they were interviewed and their interview behavior rated on the same 20-item symptom rating scale (Jenkins et al., 1959) used by Gibby et al. (1960) in the Richmond VA studies. They were also given the Holtzman Inkblot Technique (Holtzman, Thorpe, Swartz, and Herron, 1961), the Draw-A-Person test, and the Bender Gestalt. On the morning of Day 2 a group of schizophrenics and a group of nonpsychotic patients were exposed to not more than 4 hours of monotonous stimulation. The subjects were free to leave early if they so desired, and of the 40 subjects in these two groups, 27 voluntarily terminated before the end of the 4-hour period. Immediately after the monotonous stimulation experience the psychological tests were repeated for the two experimental groups and a nonconfined control group of schizophrenics. On Day 3 the subjects were interviewed a second time and their behavior rated once again on the 20-item symptom rating scale.

Cleveland et al. found no significant changes on the symptom rating scale or on any of the three psychological tests in the two groups of subjects exposed to monotonous stimulation. They pointedly commented that their results had failed to replicate those reported in the pilot study conducted in the Richmond VA Hospital (Gibby et al., 1960; Cooper et al., 1962), which had obtained significant reductions on symptomatology on the same symptom rating scale and significant improvement in ego strength as shown by the Rorschach.

Schultz (1965, p. 117) contrasted these studies in his book and cited other research which demonstrated that behavioral impairments are usually more severe under monotonous stimulation ("perceptual deprivation") than reduced stimulation ("sensory deprivation"). He concluded that "the way is clear for a well-controlled study comparing the relative therapeutic values" of these two stimulus conditions.

Cooper et al. (1965), who used the same symptom rating scale as Cleveland et al., and who also had a matched control group of hospitalized VA psychiatric patients, did essentially replicate the findings of the Richmond pilot study. Cooper et al. found a number of significant positive changes in their experimental group after reduced stimulation, while Cleveland et al. found no significant changes after monotonous stimulation on the symptom rating scale or any of three psychological tests. Although the measures used were not identical, the 1965 Cooper et al. study and the 1963 Cleveland et al. study were similar in terms of the patients used, the VA hospital setting, the same 20-item symptom rating scale, and several other procedural details. The most important difference seems to be that one study used reduced stimulation while the other used monotonous stimulation. So far as the writer can determine, all the studies which reported improved functioning in psychiatric patients employed the former condition, and no papers have appeared reporting significant improvement in psychiatric patients after monotonous stimulation. Reviews of the literature by Schultz (1965), Brownfield (1965), and Zubek (1973) agree that monotonous conditions are more likely to impair functioning than a reduction in absolute levels of stimulation, and that improved functioning has been reported in many studies utilizing reduced stimulation but not in those which employed high levels of unvarying monotonous stimulation.

This differentiation is a fundamental issue to consider in evaluating the results obtained by Moran (1969), who set out to investigate the effects of "sensory deprivation" but actually investigated the effects of monotonous stimulation. Nevertheless, his study was in most respects carefully designed and well-controlled. In reviewing the literature, Moran included a section which made explicit distinctions between reduced patterning of sensory input (monotonous stimulation) and reduction in absolute levels of sensory input (reduced stimulation). He cited studies showing "significantly greater impairment on both intellectual and perceptual tests" under the former than under the latter conditions.

Although Moran seems to have been well aware of these differences, his study of the effects of "sensory deprivation" on learning in schizophrenics used monotonous stimulation exclusively. There were five matched groups of subjects, each consisting of 16 white male schizophrenics in a state mental hospital. Two groups of subjects received 1 hour and 3 hours respectively of "sensory deprivation,"—that is, monotonous stimulation. This condition was "essentially the same as that used at McGill, i.e., reduced patterning of sensory input" (p. 43). Subjects in these two groups lay on a bed in a lighted room, wearing translucent goggles which "admitted diffuse light but prevented patterned vision," and were exposed to constant auditory stimulation in the form of the "monotonous noise of an electric air conditioner placed on the floor below and behind the head of the subject." Two other groups had 1 and 3 hours respectively of social isolation without monotonous stimulation, while a fifth served as a test-retest control group. All subjects were given a battery of tests including (1) the Associate Learning subtests from the Wechsler Memory Scales I and II, (2) the Digit Symbol subtests from the Wechsler Adult Intelligence Scale and the Wechsler-Bellevue Form II, (3) the Benton Visual Retention Test (Benton, 1955), (4) a Logical Memory Test, (5) the Shipley Scale (Shipley, 1940), and (6) the Sensation-Seeking Scale (Zuckerman, Kolin, Price, and Zoob, 1964). The same tests were administered twice to all subjects in all groups, with 5 hours intervening between pretesting and post-testing.

Moran found no improvement on any measure, and concluded that the results "failed to support the hypothesis that sensory deprivation would improve" learning in schizophrenics.

It is unfortunate that Moran's experimental design failed to include a systematic comparison of the differing effects of reduced and monotonous stimulation. He had explicitly taken note of differences between the two conditions in reviewing the earlier research literature, but did not provide for investigation of these differences in designing his own study. However, his results are consistent with other research which found no significant improvement in psychiatric patients after exposure to monotonous stimulation.

A Treatment Combination

The importance of interpersonal influences in conjunction with reduced stimulation was emphasized in a study by Cooper, Adams, Dickinson, and York (1975). They felt that interpersonal experimenter influences might be maximized as a consequence of the increased receptivity of subjects following exposure to reduced stimulation. Cooper et al. conducted a clinical demonstration to show how changes in the interpersonal roles of experimenters, together with reduced stimulation, could induce lasting changes in the interpersonal behavior of patients. The study demonstrated two changes: (1) shifts in the interpersonal behavior of subjects after a combination of interviewer role-playing and reduced stimulation, and (2) a subsequent long-lasting reduction in the frequency of visits to a medical clinic for hypochondriacal complaints of a nonmedical nature.

Subjects were 20 male VA domiciliary patients who were selected on the basis of three criteria: (1) passive, antagonistic behavior, (2) frequent inappropriate medical clinic visits for largely hypochondriacal complaints, and (3) patients regarded themselves as more disabled than warranted by their physical condition. Selections were made jointly by a physician and a nurse. Ten subjects were assigned randomly to the demonstration group and 10 to an untreated baseline control group.

Subjects in the demonstration group were not told in advance of the planned procedures, which were short and simple. Each subject was interviewed in a psychologist's office and the interview recorded on tape for later analysis. Immediately after the interview each subject spent 2 hours lying on a comfortable bed in a quiet, darkened, air-conditioned room with eyes and ears covered. He was then removed by the same interviewer, who took him immediately to an office for a second tape-recorded interview.

In the two interviews each subject was free to discuss any topic he wished. However, the interpersonal role played by the interviewer was carefully prestructured according to the explicit criteria of the Interpersonal System (Adams, 1964; Carson, 1969; Foa, 1961; Leary, 1956, 1957). It was expected that this prestructuring of the interviewer's role would induce reciprocal shifts in the interpersonal role of the subject, according to the rationale of the Interpersonal System. Specifically, it was predicted that each subject's behavior during the second interview would show more dominance and affiliation. Edited samples from the taped interviews were analyzed and rated independently by two judges. The analysis showed statistically significant shifts in expected directions in the demonstration group but none in the untreated baseline group.

A later followup showed that 6 months after reduced stimulation the frequency of medical clinic visits had fallen 80% from the original level for the demonstration group. According to a physician's ratings, the relatively few visits by these subjects now represented appropriate medical complaints rather than hypochondriacal maneuvers. For the untreated baseline group the frequency of visits continued virtually unchanged during the same 6 month period. In addition, 11 sets of ratings on 7 behavioral variables were made by physicians and other staff members, none of whom knew which subject was assigned to which group. Ratings obtained before, 1 week after, and 6 months after reduced stimulation showed many statistically significant changes in "improved" directions, which persisted after 6 months in the demonstration group. There were no significant changes in the baseline group during the same period.

These changes are all the more impressive if one remembers that subjects in the demonstration group had only 2 hours of reduced stimulation, with short prestructured interviews immediately before and immediately afterward. There was no further treatment of a psychological nature (counseling, interviewing, therapy, etc.) at any time after the second interview.

REST IN THE TREATMENT OF PHENCYCLIDINE (PCP) PSYCHOSIS AND LSD PSYCHOSIS

This section deals mainly with the effects of reduced environmental stimulation on individuals who have taken the psychotomimetic drug phencyclidine. Many publications of the 1950s and 1960s used the manufacturer's trade name "Sernyl" to refer to phencyclidine, while papers published in recent years often refer to this drug as PCP. In the 1970s the illicit use of phencyclidine became widespread within the American drug culture. The label most often used in the drug culture to refer to phencyclidine is "angel dust," but Lerner and Burns (1978, p. 74) recently provided a list of other popular names. Most of the papers deal with psychological effects of reduced stimulation on individuals who have taken phencyclidine, but there is one case study of LSD psychosis, in which reduced stimulation reduced the severity of the patient's psychotic symptoms.

PCP Psychosis

Domino (1978) has given a historical account, beginning with the first work done with phencyclidine in the 1950s and continuing through the next two decades, during which illicit PCP usage became widespread. By 1978, according to Domino, PCP had become "the number one drug of abuse in the United States." Research on phencyclidine initially began with efforts to develop a better anesthetic. Domino wrote that in early work with monkeys the drug appeared to be "the best anesthetic agent I had ever seen," that it appeared very safe when compared with other anesthetics, and that "it caused serenity," which led the manufacturer to give the new drug the trade name of "Sernyl." It was tested as a general anesthetic and initially found effective for that purpose. Unfortunately, the drug also produced undesirable side effects, the most serious being that it induced psychotic-like symptoms in humans.

One early paper declared that "phencyclidine produced sensory deprivation" (Meyer, Griefenstein, and DeVault, 1959; Domino, 1978, p. 18). This formulation, based on early initial observations of human subjects, was not substantiated by later research, but some important relationships were consistently observed in research studies and clinical reports on the effects of reduced stimulation or "sensory deprivation" on human subjects who had taken phencyclidine. It was observed that (1) taking PCP (by ingestion, smoking, or "snorting") produced psychotic-like symptoms, (2) that the severity of these symptoms could be diminished by placing the individual in some kind of reduced stimulation environment with minimal social interaction, and (3) that these psychotic-like symptoms reappeared whenever the individual was returned to a normal sensory environment and normal social interaction after having been in a reduced stimulus environment.

Publications on phencyclidine and reduced stimulation fall into two groups. The first is a group of research studies carried out in controlled research settings, all published in the 1960s. The second is a group of case studies and clinically-oriented papers published in the 1970s, after the use of PCP had become commonplace in the illicit drug culture and PCP psychosis was being encountered with increasing frequency. These publications deal with the use of reduced stimulation in the management of psychotic reactions (at times quite severe and dangerous) in individuals hospitalized after taking large and/or unknown amounts of PCP. The more recent clinically oriented publications stress two points: (1) the hazards of PCP psychosis (paranoia, violence, loss of control, homicidal behavior, etc.), and (2) recommendations that reduced stimulation be employed as the treatment of choice for PCP psychosis.

The Earlier Research Studies. Two research papers by Cohen, Luby, Rosenbaum, and Gottlieb (1960) and Luby, Gottlieb, Cohen, Rosenbaum, and Domino (1962) reported that normal subjects who were given phencyclidine ("Sernyl") and then placed in a reduced stimulation environment responded to reduced stimulation "in the manner previously described as characteristic of schizophrenic subjects" by Harris (1959) and Cohen et al. (1959). When the drug was administered to normal subjects it produced "a predictable series of changes mimicking the primary symptoms of schizophrenia," resulting in schizophrenic-like deficits in primary attention and cognition.

Cohen et al. and Luby et al. reported that when normal subjects exposed to a normal sensory environment were given phencyclidine, they developed symptoms such as body image distortions, feelings of unreality and depersonalization, inability to maintain directed thinking, hypnagogic phenomena, catatonic-like posturing, and verbal descriptions of feeling "crazy" and "out of control." When phencyclidine was administered to schizophrenics, the drug caused a severe exacerbation of their psychotic symptomatology.

When normal subjects who had taken phencyclidine were exposed to reduced stimulation, the psychotic-like symptoms and other psychopathological effects resulting from the drug were greatly diminished. Subjects exposed to reduced stimulation stated that they felt calmer, experienced minimal anxiety, and regarded their experiences as pleasant. Symptoms such as nausea and catatonic posturing did not appear under conditions of reduced stimulation, but returned in several cases when subjects were removed from the reduced stimulus environment.

It was suggested that the state induced by phencyclidine resembled schizophrenia to the extent that normal subjects who took the drug tolerated reduced stimulation environments "in a manner similar to that reported . . . as characteristic of schizophrenic subjects" by earlier investigators who found that schizophrenics responded to reduced stimulation with less anxiety and more positive affect than normal subjects.

These observations may signify that the clinical psychosis of schizophrenia, like the model psychosis produced by Sernyl, engenders indiscriminate aversion to environmental sensory stimulation. Perhaps schizophrenic withdrawal is based upon the need to reduce or regulate normal levels of sensory influx which are too intense, too distorted, and hence too terrifying for the patient to tolerate. (Cohen et al., 1960, p. 348.)

Similar findings were reported by Lawes (1963), who administered phencyclidine ("Sernyl") to a group of 8 normal male volunteers from a mental hospital staff, explaining in advance that the drug might cause them to experience a mild schizophrenic-like psychosis. His subjects were exposed to three conditions: (1) normal environment (an interview room) and normal social interaction (conversation and untimed psychological tests); (2) reduced stimulation (soundproof room, dim lights and goggles, subjects lying on a mattress) and minimal social interaction; and (3) normal environmental stimulation (bright lights, open doors, subjects sitting up in chairs with reading and writing materials available) but minimal social interaction. Subjects were rated on the same 12 items of mentation used in the 1961 study by Smith et al., and on a specially constructed rating scale of 26 symptoms reported "to be prominent in early schizophrenia."

In terms of the 12 items of mentation, Lawes found (p. 245) that under condition (1) the ingestion of phencyclidine was followed by "considerable disturbances of behavior and a psychological process suggestive perhaps of a mild or early psychotic state." Under condition (2) (reduced stimulation and minimal social interaction), "phencyclidine led to little disturbance of behavior or of psychological process. It seemed rather to be associated with a readiness to tolerate, or even find pleasure, in the experimental conditions." Under condition (3) (normal environmental stimulation but minimal social interaction) "there was a degree of severity of disturbance intermediate between conditions [1] and [2] above, but clinically closer to [1]."

On the 26-item symptom rating scale Lawes found an average of 21 symptoms per subject under condition (1) but only 4 symptoms per subject under condition (2). Under condition (3) there was an average of 18 symptoms per subject.

To account for these results, Lawes suggested (p. 249) that in both schizophrenics and normal subjects given phencyclidine there is a "failure of the mechanism for exercising control of afferent flow and, in particular, failure to be able to inhibit or select it." This failure "would, under ordinary conditions, show as a difficulty in adaptation to and assimilation of the environment; a corollary is that this difficulty" could be diminished by reduced environmental stimulation and minimal social interaction. "Schizophrenics—and subjects to whom a schizophrenomimetic drug has been administered—can be envisaged as obtaining, in a similar way, under these conditions a very welcome 'holiday' from the impossible demands of normal life." Lawes added that controlled conditions of reduced environmental and social stimulation may have therapeutic value and that schizophrenics may react to these conditions as "personally satisfying and perhaps even . . . beneficial."

Later Clinically-Oriented Publication. The papers reviewed in this portion of the chapter are clinically oriented, reflecting the greatly increased incidence of PCP psychosis experienced in the 1970s. The first of these publications was an individual case study by Stein (1973), which stressed the need to minimize sensory influx in cases of phencyclidine psychosis. He reported the case of a young man hospitalized in a severely psychotic state following the ingestion of large amounts of illicitly-obtained PCP. The quantity ingested was far greater than that administered in any of the research studies reviewed above.

Stein noted that after the patient emerged from a comatose state induced by the drug, he showed disorientation, inappropriate affect, and regressive, schizophrenic-like behavior. Although he remained quiet, staring blankly so long as he was left to himself, the patient became agitated and excited when approached by family or staff members, becoming verbally and physically aggressive to the point where he had to be physically restrained.

After 8 days of hospitalization he was transferred to the psychiatric ward and isolated in a single room where verbal and physical contact were kept to the lowest feasible levels. This procedure was intended to avoid "the exacerbation of clinical symptoms when the patient was even minimally stimulated either verbally or physically." Reduced stimulation was clinically effective, for "within 36 hours the patient had reconstituted" (p. 590) and his psychotic symptoms had disappeared. He then revealed a history of extensive drug abuse, and later entered into daily group therapy sessions and occupational therapy. He subsequently remained free of any evidence of psychosis and was discharged after a short stay in the psychiatric ward.

Stein emphasized the need to minimize sensory stimulation, since the clinical symptoms in this case were aggravated by sensory influx. He added that treatment procedures for PCP psychosis should attempt to reduce stimulation to very low levels, while maintaining appropriate medical and psychiatric care.

Stein's clinical observations are consistent with previous research investigations in which small amounts of phencyclidine were administered to normal volunteers. However, the symptoms of psychosis described in Stein's case study were much more severe, perhaps reflecting greater amounts of the drug ingested by the patient.

In 1975 Luisada and Reddick presented a report to the American Psychiatric Association entitled "An Epidemic of Drug-Induced 'Schizophrenia.' " They described a sudden upsurge in hospital admissions "for what appeared to be unusually long, severe, and treatment-resistant . . . schizophrenic psychoses. . . . Violently aggressive behavior was characteristic of the onset, and the presenting picture was at first indistinguishable from a florid schizophrenic episode."

It was subsequently learned that these psychotic episodes appeared in individuals who had previously taken PCP. Luisada and Reddick reported that this initial "epidemic" lasted about a year, ending temporarily after a local clandestine drug laboratory was closed by a police raid. The authors reviewed the records of patients hospitalized during the "epidemic." From a larger number of individual case histories they selected 11 patients who had taken PCP but no other psychoactive drug, since they wished to evaluate the effects of PCP alone.

Among these 11 patients the classical symptoms of schizophrenia were present on admission. Agitation, fearfulness, hyperactivity, paranoia, confusion, and disorientation had been the most common symptoms, and many patients had been violent and extremely dangerous. During the first phase of their hospitalization "they were violently psychotic and required immediate isolation." Social isolation and reduced environmental stimulation had a calming effect and alleviated symptoms of acute panic, although there was no substantial overall improvement for several more days. During this initial phase they reacted strongly to ordinary social stimulation, such as being fed. During the second phase their behavior was more controlled but still unpredictable. In the third and final phase there was "rapid personality reintegration," during which symptoms of psychosis abated and most patients "achieved premorbid levels of functioning."

Luisada and Reddick stressed the need to minimize environmental stimulation and social interaction, particularly during the dangerous first phase of PCP psychosis. They recommended that "the patient should be isolated with minimal intrusion by ward staff. . . . The drug induces perceptual errors which result in the misinterpretation of innocuous stimuli as threatening, leading to extreme unpredictability."

In a 1976 publication Luisada and Brown described in detail the clinical case management procedures which they had found most effective with PCP psychosis. Their clinical observations were conducted on the same hospital unit as the 1975 Luisada and Reddick paper. However, the problems which developed due to increased supplies of illicit PCP in the local area had persisted, and "as a result, phencyclidine psychosis is presently the leading cause of inpatient psychiatric admissions in our catchment area" (p. 539). Luisada and Brown's 1976 paper was "based upon experience gained from treating in excess of 100 phencyclidine psychoses on an inpatient psychiatric ward over the past two years.'' This paper described in more detail the same three phases of recovery from PCP psychosis as Luisada and Reddick's 1975 report.

During the first phase patients are "dangerous, ambivalent, unpredictable, psychotic, and agitated.'' The immediate goals of treatment during this phase are (1) prevention of injury to the patient or others, (2) assurance of continuing treatment, (3) reduction of stimuli, (4) amelioration of the psychosis, and (5) reduction of agitation. To meet these goals Luisada and Brown recommended a controlled hospital inpatient environment, "preferably on an involuntary basis. Isolation in a locked bare seclusion room with frequent but unobtrusive observation is the treatment of choice. Seclusion not only safeguards other patients and staff, but also calms the patient through the reduction of stimuli which he can misperceive as threatening, particularly the sight of other people" (p. 542).

In the 1970s the use of phencyclidine within the drug culture rapidly increased, becoming overnight a major new social problem. Many authorities were alarmed by this development, since the available evidence suggested that PCP had become the leading drug of abuse in the United States.

Evidence of increasing PCP usage is provided by current data from the statistical reporting system known as the Drug Abuse Warning Network (DAWN), operated by the U.S. Drug Enforcement Agency. Nationwide statistics gathered from 900 hospital emergency rooms and other facilities indicate that PCP reactions were reported almost 10 times more frequently in 1978 than in 1973. Comparable figures on marijuana show a steady increase during the same period, but not nearly so great as those for PCP. In 1979 PCP usage was reported to DAWN more frequently than marijuana. DAWN's figures on heroin show a peak in 1975 and a 50% drop by early 1978, while data on PCP showed a steady rapid increase. These statistics, whatever their limitations, clearly show that PCP abuse (and consequently, the incidence of PCP-induced psychoses) has assumed the proportions of a major nationwide epidemic. Inevitably, there are far-reaching social consequences in such a development, and the long-term effects may be felt for many years in the future.

In response to this development, the National Institute of Drug Abuse published a volume in 1978 entitled *Phencyclidine (PCP) Abuse: An Appraisal*, containing 17 papers by many leading authorities on various aspects of this problem (Petersen and Stillman, 1978). The editors of this volume stated in a foreword that PCP abuse was expanding rapidly, and that there is good reason to believe that the standardized indicators of the extent of PCP use and of its adverse consequences represent serious underestimates of the seriousness of the problem. Clinical reports have also indicated that phencyclidine use can precipitate violent acting out and seriously self-destructive behavior as well as psychotic thinking and behavior. (Petersen and Stillman, 1978, p. v.)

Every contributor in the 1978 volume who discussed the clinical management of psychotic reactions due to PCP agreed on the need for reduced environmental stimulation in the early stages of PCP psychosis. Petersen and Stillman noted (p. 12) that

most clinicians advocate placing the patient in an isolated environment during this period, reducing sensory stimulation as much as possible in order to minimize the phase of excitability, irritability, anxiety, paranoia, and violence which often follows the obtunded or comatose phase. Needless to say, such isolation of the patient (in quiet rooms, etc.) cannot be at the expense of . . . monitoring . . . vital signs and . . . response to emergency life support management. Patients are often so unmanageable that restraints are necessary, and the help of four or five (not one) burly aides will often be needed to prevent injury to staff and patients.

Describing the treatment of youthful PCP users, Lerner and Burns (1978, p. 70) wrote that

under conditions of sensory isolation or reduced visual, auditory, and tactual stimulation, less disturbances of behavior and psychological processes were evident. Subjects experienced only minimal body image changes and felt more in control and less anxious. They were less productive verbally and appeared quieter and calmer. They reported experiencing 'nothingness' and 'emptiness.' When the sensory isolation was stopped, subjects were immediately aware of the perceptual distortions and became more disturbed. Some subjects then experienced nausea or exhibited catatonia.

Elsewhere in the same paper, Lerner and Burns advised (p. 111) that

the acutely confused patient is best managed by sensory isolation with observation at a distance. Minimizing verbal and tactile stimulation does not preclude the monitoring of vital signs . . . Ideally, the patient would be placed on a cushioned floor in a 'quiet room' with a monitor present.

A chapter by Luisada (1978) reiterated the need for reduced stimulation in the treatment of PCP psychosis, stressing the same points as the 1975 report by Luisada and Reddick and the 1976 paper by Luisada and Brown.

The publications in this section dealing with treatment and management of PCP psychosis, which appeared very recently when PCP abuse was rapidly increasing, were based on direct first-hand clinical observations of patients in treatment settings. None were planned or set up as controlled research projects. It is all the more impressive to find such unanimity of opinion that reduced stimulation procedures constitute the treatment of choice during the earlier and more dangerous phases of PCP psychosis. Many of these clinical publications also considered other treatments, such as halperidol, chlorpromazine, and other drugs, but they repeatedly recommended reduced stimulation as the single most effective treatment modality.

In one respect these clinical reports contrast with the earlier research reports, in which normal volunteers were given small amounts of phencyclidine in controlled settings. The earlier research workers did note the presence of psychotic-like symptoms, but in no cases did they describe the intense, violent, dangerous symptoms which are repeatedly mentioned in the clinical papers. This may reflect the ingestion of very large amounts of illicit PCP by those patients hospitalized for PCP psychosis, who were described in the clinical reports.

Nevertheless, the two sets of papers agreed that symptoms of psychosis resulting from PCP (regardless of amount) were substantially diminished whenever the total amount of social and environmental stimulation was significantly reduced. They also agreed that persons under the influence of this drug showed great increases in symptoms of mental disturbance if they were removed from a reduced stimulus environment and exposed to commonplace normal stimulation. The capacity to cope with normal environmental stimulation was always diminished following the administration of phencyclidine, but the degree of psychological disturbance resulting from this diminished coping capacity was much less if the total amount of sensory stimulation impinging upon the individual was reduced.

LSD Psychosis

A number of papers on the use of reduced stimulation in the treatment of PCP psychosis have appeared, but only one on its use in LSD psychosis. Metzner (1969) published a case study in which reduced stimulation was utilized in conjunction with daily counseling during one phase of the patient's hospitalization.

The patient, a young college-educated male, was admitted to a state mental hospital "in an acute psychotic episode induced or triggered by LSD." Shortly after his admission the therapist asked him "if he wanted to try sensory deprivation and he agreed." During the next 2 weeks the patient voluntarily participated in four sessions of "sensory deprivation," lying on a mattress in a quiet, lightproof room. Each session lasted about 2 hours, during which he was continuously monitored through an intercom. The room was unlocked and the sessions could be terminated by the patient, which he never did. "In fact, he asked several times for more sessions. Staff reports of this time indicate that he was generally quiet and cooperative."

Metzner wrote (p. 202),

It was my impression that the dark (and more or less silent) room enabled him to control somewhat the overwhelming flood of information-stimulation that was pouring in. . . . By eliminating external input, the task of sorting was made easier. He was definitely calmer and almost "in touch" when he emerged from the room.

Metzner added that "the calm induced by the sessions in the dark room usually did not survive the return to the ward, where the stimulation caused by interaction with the other patients and staff would send the patient back on his 'trip,' " that is, cause his psychotic symptoms to reappear.

As an explanation for the patient's improvement Metzner suggested (p. 205) that exposure to a reduced stimulus environment "reduces stimulus flooding and provides opportunity for more adequate coding and sorting of information by the overloaded circuits." He reasoned that the reduction in the total amount of sensory stimulation impinging upon the patient should facilitate a process of constructive personality reorganization, "enabling the person to piece together the fragmented elements of his universe." He thought that this process of reorganization should "be more permanent and psychologically satisfying to the patient."

Unfortunately, Metzner was unable to follow through on these ideas, since his patient was transferred to another unit where the reduced stimulation procedures could not be continued. However, it is noteworthy that in this one case of LSD-induced psychosis, the patient's response to reduced stimulation was much like the typical pattern reported in cases of PCP psychosis. In both disorders, symptoms of drug-induced psychosis were alleviated when patients were placed in reduced stimulus environments, and the psychotic symptoms reappeared as soon as these patients were returned to normal stimulus environments.

DIFFERENTIAL EFFECTS OF SPECIAL STIMULUS ENVIRONMENTS

Many papers reviewed in this chapter suggested that the effects of both reduced and monotonous stimulation varied substantially, and that the beneficial, therapeutic effects of reduced stimulation were substantially greater for some types of individuals than others. These suggestions were offered in an impressionistic fashion, with little systematic supporting data. The papers reviewed in this section deal with these varying effects more systematically, presenting data collected specifically for the purpose of determining differential effects of special stimulus environments.

Stimulus Reduction

Two early studies with normal subjects should be mentioned. In the first, Grunebaum, Freedman, and Greenblatt (1960) exposed a group of college students to 8 hours of reduced stimulation. They were interviewed before and after this experience, and their interviews were recorded and rated for purposes of statistical analysis. A wide range of individual differences was found. Grunebaum et al. concluded (p. 880) that the reduced stimulation environment "is an ambiguous situation which the subject structures according to his own personality and handles with his habitual adaptive and defensive resources."

The second early study of individual differences was conducted by Goldberger (1961), who commented that the psychological effects of reduced and monotonous stimulation had been investigated mainly within a neuropsychological framework, and individual differences and their personality correlates were generally neglected. Goldberger analyzed individual personality differences in relation to varying reactions to monotonous stimulation. He exposed 14 male college students to 8 hours of monotonous stimulation (white noise, translucent eye coverings, gloves and cuffs over hands and forearms). They were given the Rorschach before this experience and interviewed and asked to complete a questionnaire afterward. The Rorschach data showed many significant correlations with reactions to monotonous stimulation, reflecting individual differences in personality. Goldberger concluded that individuals differ significantly in their ability to handle "primary process" thinking, since measures of this ability were significantly related to each individual's pattern of responses to a monotonous stimulation environment. In selecting his subjects, Goldberger screened out all those showing evidence of "too-precarious adjustment." Although he found a substantial range of individual differences among normal subjects, he obtained no data on individuals with significant psychopathology, since his screening procedures deliberately eliminated all such subjects.

The two studies cited above included no institutionalized subjects, in contrast with those reviewed below. Some statements in those studies regarding the importance of individual differences seem applicable to institutionalized patients. However, studies of institutionalized patients also provide important new information, particularly the fact that the beneficial, therapeutic effects of special stimulus environments seem to be much greater among institutionalized patients than among "normals." The findings on individual differences point up the need for individualized assessment and treatment in future clinical applications.

The first published study which systematically analyzed differential effects of reduced stimulation on institutionalized psychiatric patients was a paper by Cooper et al. (1962). This publication was one of three reports on hospitalized male psychiatric patients in the Richmond, Virginia, VA Hospital, whose subjects and procedures are more fully described on pages 327–334. All subjects were administered the Rorschach one day before and one day after exposure to not more than 6 hours of reduced stimulation. The Rorschach protocols were scored and analyzed using Cartwright's modification of Klopfer's Rorschach Prognostic Rating Scale (Cartwright, 1958). After reduced stimulation the subjects as a group showed significant increases on the Rorschach measures, which were interpreted by Cooper et al. (p. 216) as reflecting increased "concern with real human relations, the ability to empathize with others, well-controlled emotional responsiveness, and adequate reality contact."

Analysis of individual differences found highly significant inverse correlations between initial Rorschach scores and changes after reduced stimulation. Subjects with lowest initial scores, which indicated least adequate functioning, tended to show the most improvement on the same Rorschach scores afterward. Cooper et al. concluded that "subjects who initially functioned least adequately were those who derive the most benefit" from exposure to reduced stimulation. The authors added that the Rorschach measures they used "have been employed with great success in predicting the degree of improvement resulting from conventional verbal types of psychotherapy . . . Higher scores on these Rorschach measures indicate a greater degree of improvement following conventional verbal psychotherapy." They reasoned that if exposure to reduced stimulation had produced the same psychological changes as orthodox verbal psychotherapy, there would have been significant positive relationships between initial scores on the Rorschach measures and subsequent changes on the same measures. "But exactly the opposite relationship was found. This suggests that subjects who have relatively low scores on the Rorschach measures of ego strength, which means that they would be relatively poor candidates for traditional verbal psychotherapy," were the ones who derived the greatest benefit from reduced sensory stimulation. Cooper et al. added that techniques involving reduced stimulation may be "therapeutically most useful in patients for whom orthodox techniques of verbal psychotherapy are relatively unfruitful."

The second part of the paper by Cooper et al. (1965), the first part of which was reviewed earlier, included an analysis of individual differences in hospitalized psychiatric patients. These authors found that an experimental group of patients exposed to reduced stimulation subsequently showed improved overall functioning and increased receptiveness for conventional psychotherapy, whereas a matched control group showed no comparable changes. When comparisons were made between individuals who showed the greatest improvement—as measured by Klopfer's Rorschach Prognostic Rating Scale—and those showing least improvement, significant personality differences were found. Those showing most improvement after reduced stimulation had

(1) poorly integrated and relatively unsuccessful defense mechanisms, (2) low verbal productivity and limited ability to relate verbally to others or deal symbolically with problems, (3) reliance on primary repression as a defense and tendencies to act out behaviorally when repression fails, (4) a tendency to regard themselves as helpless and dependent, and (5) intrapunitive ways of handling hostility. These traits are not typical of patients with the best prognosis for traditional verbal psychotherapy (p. 116).

By contrast, individuals showing least improvement were characterized by

(1) moderately well-integrated and effective defense systems, (2) comparatively adept social skills and the ability to relate comfortably on a verbal level, (3) reliance on complex and elaborate defense systems utilizing isolation, intellectualization, reaction-formation, and projection, and (4) a tendency to attribute to others the responsibility for their own difficulties.

Cooper et al. observed (p. 117) that the patients who showed least improvement after reduced stimulation "resembled patients usually selected for traditional verbal psychotherapy far more than" those showing the most improvement.

They also urged that future investigations of the effects of reduced stimulation consider each individual's

characteristic defenses to a far greater extent than has been done. The generally positive effects observed here seem largely a function of the personality characteristics of the psychiatric inpatients used. A group of college students or well-integrated outpatients might have shown very different results.

The authors suggested (p. 116) that reduced stimulation as a therapeutic technique "may have properties quite different from orthodox verbal psychotherapies," and recommended use of the Rorschach and other personality measures to select patients who might derive the most benefit.

Adams et al. (1972) conducted an elaborate statistical analysis of individual differences in behavioral reactions of 30 psychiatric inpatients, each of whom received not more than 6 hours of REST. They were administered the MMPI and the Wechsler Adult Intelligence Scale (WAIS), and their interview behavior was rated on a 20-item symptom rating scale. While in the reduced stimulation environment they were rated on a Behavioral Anxiety index. Following exposure to reduced stimulation the WAIS was administered a second time, and the interviews and symptom ratings were repeated. The MMPI was not given a second time.

With the use of these measures, several indices of change and of behavioral reactions before, during, and after reduced stimulation were developed. These indices were correlated with MMPI and WAIS scores, and many significant relationships were found. The full report of this investigation is long and detailed, and it offers many possible interpretations for interrelationships which emerged from analysis of the data. Only the most important findings are summarized below.

In this study the average patient presented substantial psychiatric symptomatology before being exposed to reduced stimulation, but experienced only moderate anxiety while in the reduced stimulation environment. There were changes in the directions of both diminished and increased symptomatology following REST, although diminished symptoms were much more frequent than increases. After reduced stimulation the average WAIS IQ score increased about 7 points; again there were wide individual differences. There were four different behavioral measures; each one showed a distinctive pattern of correlations with scales of the MMPI.

In discussing their findings Adams et al. (1972) placed greatest emphasis on their Symptom Reduction Index, which they viewed as a global indicator of improvement. This index showed highly significant positive correlations with an index of gross symptomatology, indicating that patients displaying the most symptom reduction after REST initially had the most severe symptoms. The authors reported significant correlations with MMPI scales, which they interpreted as evidence that patients having the greatest symptom reduction "tended to be (1) more impulsive and open to new experiences, (2) more spontaneous and less inhibited in their interpersonal relationships, (3) emotionally less rigid and repressed, and (4) had more severe symptoms to begin with" (p. 210). Those showing least symptom reduction "were seen as (1) relatively impervious to new experiences and novel environmental influences, (2) guarded, rigid, and overcontrolled in their personal relationships, (3) emotionally defensive, repressed, and inhibited'' (p. 211), and (4) initially displayed relatively little overt psychiatric symptomatology.

Adams et al. (1972) observed that data obtained from the MMPI and Symptom Reduction Index were generally consistent with Rorschach results reported in two previous papers by Cooper et al. (1962, 1965). These three studies essentially agreed that individuals with more severe initial symptoms, more openness to new environmental influences, and stronger tendencies toward impulsive acting out were most likely to show symptomatic improvement after reduced stimulation. They also provided evidence that the characteristics of patients who improve the most after REST differ from those typical of patients usually considered most suitable for verbal psychotherapy.

Adams et al. found no significant relationships between their Symptom Reduction and Symptom Increase indices. They observed that reductions in psychiatric symptomatology after reduced stimulation tended to persist over extended periods of time, whereas increases in symptomatology after exposure to reduced stimulation were temporary in nature and tended to disappear relatively quickly. They concluded that transient increases in symptomatology after REST should not be regarded as contraindications to the use of this technique. Their MMPI data suggested that these short-lived increases in symptoms of mental disorder following exposure to reduced stimulation were most pronounced in poorly integrated, resentful, hypersensitive individuals with a precarious, marginal adjustment, who could be precipitated into transitory personality disturbances by relatively mild environmental stresses.

The Behavioral Anxiety index, developed as a measure of average anxiety levels during exposure to reduced stimulation, showed several unexpected relationships with other measures. Subjects with more education manifested significantly greater anxiety while in the REST environment, and the strength of this relationship was further increased when the effects of differences in IQ were partialed out. Subjects who experienced greatest anxiety during exposure to reduced stimulation had the greatest increases in IQ scores afterward, suggesting that anxiety during the experience had a facilitating effect on intellectual functioning. Subjects showing greater anxiety had lower scores on the Barron Ego-Strength scale, which is widely used as a measure of prognosis for psychotherapy. This relationship was interpreted as indicating that the subjects rendered most anxious by exposure to REST were those who would be expected to have the poorest prognosis for conventional verbal therapy. Yet, those were the same subjects whose IQ scores (and intellectual functioning) improved the most after reduced stimulation. This finding was viewed as another indication that REST procedures may be most effective for persons who are considered unsuitable for conventional verbal types of psychotherapy.

Adams et al. (1972) suggested that these new procedures might ultimately render possible significant therapeutic benefits among formerly unreachable segments of the population, who might have been written off previously as unpromising candidates for older conventional procedures. This would be particularly true for those whose lack of verbal fluency, social naiveté, impulsive acting out, and severe overt symptomatology render them relatively poor prospects for the verbal (and often rather intellectualized) types of psychotherapy now in widest use.

Brownfield's 1966 study related individual differences in reactions to reduced stimulation among normal subjects and hospitalized psychiatric patients to the general concept of optimal stimulation levels. His data suggest that every individual has a characteristic optimal stimulation requirement, that there is a wide range of individual differences in these requirements, and that individual reactions to REST are a function of these characteristic requirements for sensory stimulation.

Citing previous research, Brownfield observed that many normal subjects exposed to a reduced stimulation experience discomfort, anxiety, and occasional impairment of mental functioning, while in contrast.

mental patients seem frequently to experience reduction or elimination of already active delusions and hallucinations, subsequent development of more adequate and "normal" secondary processes and, where depression is clearly identifiable, reduction of anxiety with reported feelings of discomfort. Within groups of both normal and disturbed Ss, individual differences are also noted; all Ss show varying degrees of tolerance for anxiety, discomfort, and tedium. Thus there seems to be some general factor operating in both groups which characterizes one more than the other and which accounts for the observed differences within and between the two; it is hypothesized that this factor is the "optimal stimulation requirement" (p. 28).

As a measure of this factor Brownfield used the Sensation-Seeking Scale (SSS) developed by Zuckerman, Kolin, Price, and Zoob (1964) to quantify the construct of optimal stimulation level. The SSS was devised as a measure of differential needs for stimulation. Scores on the SSS reflect generalized stimulus-seeking tendencies rather than specific behavioral traits. Brownfield set out to determine differential effects of REST among normal subjects and hospitalized psychiatric patients in terms of stimulus requirements. The SSS was used to identify high, middle, and low sensation (stimulation) seekers.

This study had two phases. In the first phase the SSS was administered to 70 randomly selected patients in a state mental hospital and 70 normals.

Subjects with high scores on the SSS were classified as Sensation-Seeking and those with low scores as Sensation-Avoiding. The SSS data showed that Sensation-Seeking was more characteristic of normals, while Sensation-Avoiding typified mental patients as a group; females were less Sensation-Seeking than males; with increasing age all subjects tended to become more Sensation-Avoiding. There was a wide range of individual differences within each category.

In the second phase of the study Brownfield selected two small groups of subjects who had extremely high (Sensation-Seeking) and extremely low (Sensation-Avoiding) scores on the SSS. Each group included both normals and psychiatric patients. In the second phase all subjects in the two extreme groups were exposed to reduced stimulation in a quiet, dark, comfortably ventilated room for periods of 6 to 24 hours.

While in this room, all the "Sensation-Seekers" reported more discomfort, anxiety, and boredom than the "Sensation-Avoiders." The latter group "tolerated the experimental conditions quite well, subsequently reporting that they felt better, i.e., more comfortable, relaxed, calmer, less anxious, etc." (p. 33). In subsequent followup interviews, high scorers on the SSS said they would not wish to undergo the same procedure again, whereas low scorers "seemed eager to re-volunteer" and repeat the experience.

Reports of unusual mental phenomena during exposure to reduced stimulation were related to differences between Sensation-Seeking and Sensation-Avoiding tendencies. Sensation-Seekers "frequently experienced reduced visual, auditory, and kinesthetic sensations, though there was nothing like the vivid, well-organized hallucinations earlier investigators have sometimes reported" (p. 33). By contrast, none of the Sensation-Avoiding subjects "described any strange or unusual experiences of any sort approaching those reported by the Sensation-Seeking Ss. Fantasies and delusional ideas were very common among the high scorers" but not among the low scorers. "The Sensation-Avoiding Ss reported only comfortable and relaxed feelings, slept soundly, and said they could think out their problems better in isolation without distraction from the environment."

Brownfield said

the fact that some Ss were disturbed mental patients and others were normals had relatively little bearing on individual response differences; the relevant variable appeared to be Sensation-Seeking or Sensation-Avoiding as determined by scores on the SSS, which in turn seems to reflect differential optimal stimulation requirements.

He suggested that

distui bed individuals, as well as the aging, are or become preoccupied with reducing stimulation and tension to an optimal level, while among normal individuals
and younger persons, increasing stimulation to higher levels is characteristic,

and that optimal stimulation levels seem to decrease in mental disturbance. He added that

if allowed to withdraw from 'normal' environmental interactions on both the
sensory and perceptual planes, the Sensation-Avoiding person seems to regain,
perhaps from relief from sensory overstimulation, the ability to re-engage normally with the environment, as evidenced by reported improvement

during and after exposure to a reduced stimulation environment.
   Brownfield hypothesized that

mental patients, among whom more Sensation-Avoiding Ss were found, are more
receptive and responsive to environmental stimulation than are normals, and that
a broadening of receptivity to a wider range of stimuli from the environment
results in 'overloading' and produces consequent maladaptive behavior and cognitive disorganization (p. 35).

He suggested that a reduced stimulation environment

besides possibly enhancing suggested therapeutic effects, may provide patients
with reduction of a kind of sensory overload in which the normal environment
imposes too high a level of stimulation for Sensation-Avoiding Ss to be able to
function as if they were normal and adaptive (i.e., Sensation-Seeking).

When exposed to reduced stimulation, mental patients "show signs of an
adaptive homeostatic process and appear to approach more normal
modes of functioning" (p. 36). He concluded that "the clinical treatment
of mentally disturbed individuals, including milieu therapy, ought to be
predicated on a recognition of individual optimal stimulation requirements, and procedures should be adjusted to insure that those requirements can be met" (p. 37).

Other Procedures

The last two studies to be reviewed here are not fully comparable with
those discussed above, since they did not utilize the same conditions of
reduced sensory stimulation in quiet, dark environments. But they did
demonstrate clearly the differential effects of special stimulus environments.
   The first of these two studies, conducted by Reitman and Cleveland
(1964), involved the use of monotonous stimulation rather than reduced
stimulation, with the same experimental conditions as in the 1963 study

by Cleveland et al. described earlier. As previously noted, empirical research evidence indicates that monotonous stimulation often produces disruptive effects on organized mental functioning and seems to have little or beneficial effect on psychiatric patients, in contrast to reduced stimulation. However, Reitman and Cleveland did find significant differential effects among psychiatric patients resulting from monotonous stimulation. In their published report, these authors referred to their condition as "sensory deprivation," making no distinction between the conditions of monotonous stimulation they used and the conditions of reduced stimulation employed by other investigators. Later writers have made this distinction explicit.

Reitman and Cleveland reported changes in measures of body image after exposure to monotonous stimulation in schizophrenics and nonpsychotic mental patients. In their study 20 schizophrenics and 20 nonpsychotic patients in a VA psychiatric hospital received not more than 4 hours of monotonous stimulation, while a control group of 20 hospitalized schizophrenics was administered the same measures of body image but not exposed to monotonous stimulation.

Subjects receiving monotonous stimulation lay on a bed in an isolated hospital room. They were fitted with translucent eye goggles. Two overhead lights and a white noise generator created an unvarying, homogeneous stimulus environment which minimized meaningfully patterned cues without reducing absolute levels of light and sound. Measures of body image were obtained one day before and immediately after monotonous stimulation. The same measures were obtained on the control group following the same 2-day schedule.

Reitman and Cleveland's schizophrenic control group showed no significant changes on any measures, while the other two groups showed many significant changes. The changes were generally in opposite directions, indicating differential effects. After monotonous stimulation (1) schizophrenics showed increased somesthetic sensitivity, while the nonpsychotic subjects showed decreased sensitivity; (2) estimates of their own height were significantly greater after monotonous stimulation in nonpsychotic subjects than in the schizophrenics; (3) estimates of three body dimensions increased in the nonpsychotic subjects, but decreased in the schizophrenics; (4) judgments of the size of body parts increased in nonpsychotics but diminished in the schizophrenics; and (5) on the Holtzman inkblot test schizophrenics showed increased barrier and decreased penetration scores, while the nonpsychotic subjects changed in the opposite directions on the Holtzman test.

Reitman and Cleveland interpreted these divergences as evidence that their experimental stimulus conditions led to a reintegration or "firming up" of the body image among schizophrenics, while causing a disintegration or breakdown of the body image of the nonpsychotic subjects. These conditions appeared to the authors as "a disorganizing experience for nonpsychotic subjects, in which normal incoming stimuli useful in orienting and determining one's body boundaries are diminished. In consequence, perceived body boundaries are rendered vague and limitless," whereas for schizophrenics the same stimulus conditions were regarded by those authors as "an experience providing the schizophrenic patient with a uniform, nonthreatening pattern of stimuli which, so to speak, offers him a chance to pull himself together" (p. 175). Their rationale for the positive changes in schizophrenics is not inconsistent with other research, in which reduced stimulation was employed, but it is possible that the disorganization in their nonpsychotic subjects resulted from the fact that Reitman and Cleveland used experimental conditions of monotonous rather than reduced stimulation. A replication comparing these two experimental stimulus conditions could determine whether the differences between the schizophrenic and nonpsychotic subjects were due to the differing stimulus environments.

Ozerengin and Cowen (1974) demonstrated the differential effects of noise levels on two groups of hospitalized schizophrenics. Their study was limited to the effects of varying noise levels only, and no sensory modalities other than audition were involved. They began with the observation that noise has unpleasant, stressful properties as well as stimulating properties which may be beneficial for certain individuals, depending "not only on the quality and volume of the sound but also on the receptivity of the listener as a function of his emotional state and social conditions" (p. 241). They cited research showing that schizophrenics have lower noise tolerance than normals and that schizophrenics constitute a homogeneous population in this respect. They advised that "it is often advantageous to divide schizophrenic subjects into two groups: (a) withdrawn and (b) active, when establishing a therapeutic regime," and hypothesized that "a noisy, more stimulating environment might be beneficial to the withdrawn patient while a quieter environment might help the active ones."

Two groups of physically healthy schizophrenic mental hospital patients were selected, composed of 15 withdrawn and 15 active subjects per group, with comparable sex and age distributions. Both groups were placed in a large, quiet hospital room, in which the noise level was kept in the range of 40 to 60 db for 3 hours each morning for a period of 6 weeks. Their behavior was evaluated using three measures: (1) a psychological test, the Detroit Test of Learning Aptitude, which was individually administered to every subject: (2) a 10-item scale for rating each patient's motor activity and verbal productivity; and (3) a daily clinical evaluation of each patient, including requirements for psychiatric medication.

At the end of 6 weeks all subjects in both groups continued going to the same hospital room daily, but the noise level in the room was increased to an average range of 80 to 90 decibels. This was accomplished by maintaining the radio, TV set, and record player at full volume. (Sound levels were monitored with a sound meter at 15-minute intervals throughout all phases of the study.) The same three measures were utilized in the noisy phase of the study.

Ozerengin and Cowen found sharply contrasting effects of varied noise levels on the two groups of schizophrenics. For the withdrawn group (who showed autism, withdrawal, disorganization, and low verbal productivity), the noisy environment led to increased motor and verbal performance, improved perceptual organization, improved sleep patterns, and diminished hallucinations. As a consequence of their clinical improvement in the noisy environment, the withdrawn subjects required less psychiatric medication. But when the active schizophrenics (who displayed restlessness, anxiety, and disorganization) were exposed to the noisy environment, their motor and verbal performance decreased while their conceptual disorganization, anxiety, and restlessness were heightened, resulting in an increase of 40% in their medication requirements.

The quiet environment also produced contrasting effects on the two groups. The withdrawn group showed

considerable regression with heightened autism, seclusiveness, more conceptual disorganization, and disturbed sleep patterns with increased hallucinations. The active group in the quiet environment showed improved performance, decreased anxiety, more conceptual organization, less hallucinations, better sleep patterns; motor and verbal productivity increased.

The authors commented (p. 243) that

the stimulant effects of noise should be distinguished from its stress attributes and. . . that the overall effect depends markedly upon the emotional and psychological status of the listener. A quiet environment appears to produce some improvement both clinically and psychologically in active schizophrenics . . . but is deleterious to the withdrawn patients. Conversely, a noisy environment appears to be therapeutic in most respects measured for withdrawn patients, but is antitherapeutic for the active subjects in that they require more medication in this noisy environment.

They concluded that their findings were of

direct clinical interest in optimizing the treatment and maintenance of mentally ill patients. The common practice of sending irritable and disturbed patients to a 'disturbed ward' with its attendant noise and activity, would appear to be deleterious to this group of patients, resulting in increased medication requirements and/or a slower recovery. It is suggested that such hyperactive patients be placed in a calm and quiet environment instead of a 'disturbed ward'. . . . Conversely, the withdrawn patient might improve more rapidly in a more stimulating . . . setting.

Implications of the Findings

Some general comments are in order regarding the broader significance of research on differential effects. Many investigators who conducted research on the effects of special stimulus environments have observed wide differences between individuals and/or groups in reactions to these environments. Yet there are few studies in which data on differential effects were sytematically collected, analyzed, and correlated with other relevant variables. It is impressive that every systematic study of differential effects reviewed here has reported clear-cut statistically significant results even though a variety of measures were used and many different attributes of individuals and groups were examined.

Unfortunately the neglect of these differential effects remains one of the most serious deficiencies in this area of research. In a 1966 paper, Adams, Robertson, and Cooper commented on the fact that many investigators in the field of "sensory deprivation" had made some mention of individual differences, while few had systematically followed up on these leads. Adams et al. expressed the opinion (p. 264) that

the many contradictory, inconsistent research findings reported in the literature might be a consequence of the wide range of individual differences in the ways subjects are affected by exposure to the same objective experimental conditions of reduced sensory input.

They suggested that the most fruitful research strategy "would involve questions of greater specificity, e.g., how, under what conditions, and for what types of individuals may these procedures be most effectively applied?" These authors called for

careful, systematic investigation of promising variables, specifying the objective stimulus conditions, characteristics of individual subjects, techniques used, and the nature of changes observed in personality, mental functioning, and overt behavior for different types of individuals. No one study can reasonably be expected to provide a definitive answer to all these questions. However, the steady accumulation and pooling of results from many independent investigations could in time lead to the development of an extensive body of systematic knowledge and a repertoire of techniques for the effective utilization of what now appears to be a promising new therapeutic approach.

CONCLUSIONS

In summing up, let us consider the papers surveyed in this review separately by sections, since each section focussed on a different topical area.

One section dealt with effects of special restricted stimulus environments on institutionalized adults, mostly psychiatric patients, although a few studies also included some noninstitutionalized and/or normal subjects as controls. Distinctions were drawn between REST environments involving reduced stimulation (reduction in absolute levels of sensory stimulation, such as darkness, silence, etc.) and those involving monotonous stimulation (continuous, unvarying stimulation of a homogeneous nature, e.g., white noise, diffuse unpatterned light, etc.). A few investigators used experimental stimulus conditions combining both reduced and monotonous stimulation, and judgments had to be made as to whether the stimulus conditions described by these investigators consisted primarily of reduced or monotonous stimulation.

Using these criteria, 20 of the 22 papers reviewed were categorized as having employed largely or exclusively conditions of reduced sensory stimulation. The other two involved conditions of monotonous stimulation.

Of the 20 studies using reduced stimulation, 18 reported some kind of positive change (improved mental functioning, reduced psychiatric symptomatology, etc.) in institutionalized adults. Thirteen of these reports also noted that negative changes (increased symptomatology or impaired mental functioning) did occur in a minority of subjects, but all 13 observed that changes of a positive nature were more frequent and more salient than those in the opposite direction. In other words, exposure to reduced stimulation led to improvement for a majority of the institutionalized adult subjects, but a minority failed to improve and some got worse.

One study noted that psychiatric patients showed indications of improvement in a reduced stimulus environment, whereas normals showed impaired functioning and emotional disturbance when exposed to the same environment. In two related studies, one involving schizophrenics and the other involving a group of normals, exposure to REST produced disturbances of mentation in normals but no significant disturbances or impairment in the schizophrenics; furthermore, the schizophrenics voluntarily remained in the restricted stimulus environment for very long periods, while the normals quit much sooner. These studies pointed up the differential effects of special stimulus environments on psychiatric patients as contrasted with normals.

Many investigations reviewed did not include control groups or statistical tests of significance in their procedures. Only 6 papers employed both control groups and tests of significance. All 6 reported that subjects exposed to reduced stimulation (sometimes in conjunction with prerecorded taped messages) subsequently showed significantly more changes in desired positive directions than controls.

Two studies involved the use of monotonous rather than reduced stimulation. Both were well-designed and included control groups and statistical tests of significance. In both studies there were no significant changes on any measures in psychiatric patients following exposure to monotonous stimulation. These results are consistent with earlier research findings (Brownfield, 1965; Schultz, 1965; Zubek, 1973) which suggested that monotonous stimulation ("perceptual deprivation") is far more likely to produce impaired mental functioning and less likely to lead to improvement in psychiatric patients and other kinds of subjects than reduced stimulation ("sensory deprivation").

None of the papers reported improvement in every single subject after reduced stimulation. They consistently described a general pattern in which the majority showed improvement (which was very great in a few cases), while a minority showed no improvement, and a few subjects got worse after the experience. Comparable findings have also been reported in studies with children and adolescents institutionalized for behavior disorders. These are reviewed in Chapter 9.

The publications reviewed in the next section dealt with effects of reduced environmental stimulation on chemically-induced psychotic-like states caused by the drugs PCP and LSD. All reported that the severity of these drug-induced "psychotic" reactions diminished whenever the affected individuals were placed in a reduced stimulus environment. Some also noted that these psychotic-like symptoms, which diminished under reduced environmental stimulation, reappeared when the affected individuals were returned to a normal, ordinary environment.

These observations held up consistently despite the fact that the studies showed considerable diversity in terms of the settings in which they were conducted and the aims of their authors. When the drugs PCP and LSD first appeared, they were used by a number of responsible scientific investigators to study drug-induced model psychotic states. Three papers reviewed here were formal research investigations in which normal subjects were administered relatively small amounts of PCP, closely watched at all times, and exposed to reduced stimulation. All the subjects showed psychotic-like symptoms after taking PCP, and in every case the severity of these symptoms was diminished under conditions of reduced stimulation.

Both PCP and LSD were subsequently withdrawn from legal use with human subjects, but both continued to be illegally produced and sold within the illicit drug culture. Obviously, the makers and sellers of illegally manufactured PCP are not deterred by ethical concerns. Immense profits can be made by selling illegal PCP on the street and in the drug culture, overriding any ethical or moral qualms. Even the heavy criminal penalties for trafficking in PCP have not been very effective deterrents. The incidence of PCP psychosis in the United States has increased sharply in recent years, and in some areas it has become the leading cause of admission to mental hospitals. As a result, psychotic reactions induced by these drugs have been encountered with increasing frequency in clinical treatment settings, where they must often be dealt with as high-risk emergencies.

The most recent group of publications consisted of case reports and generalized observations and comments based on first-hand clinical experience in treating cases of PCP psychosis in hospital settings, often under emergency conditions. Many of these papers offered relatively little systematic statistical data, but there were many accounts drawn from clinical experience which stressed the dangers, the severity, and the unpredictability of PCP psychosis. It should be emphasized that these clinical reports were describing drug-induced psychotic reactions in which the drug had been obtained illegally.

Because of the circumstances in which PCP is distributed and consumed in illicit settings, the papers dealing with clinical treatment of PCP psychosis could not be conducted in the manner of the traditional psychological experiment. The orderly, systematic administration of large dosages of PCP to subjects was an ethical impossibility, and consequently methodological niceties such as control groups, statistical tests, systematic data collection, control of intervening variables, and so on, were out of the question. The authors of the clinical papers on PCP psychosis were forced by events of follow less systematic data-collection procedures than are customary in most other good scientific research. Nevertheless, considering the dangerous nature of these drug-induced psychotic reactions, the requirements for quick emergency responses, and the ethical issues connected with hazardous drugs such as PCP, these clinical studies with all their methodological limitations may be the best that are realistically possible, given the circumstances.

The one case study of LSD psychosis reviewed in the section reported that the symptoms of LSD psychosis, like those of PCP psychosis, were alleviated under conditions of reduced stimulation, but that they reappeared when the patient was returned to the stimulus environment of a normal hospital ward.

The literature on reduced stimulation in the treatment of PCP and LSD psychosis reflects the difficulties due to real external circumstances. In contrast to the studies reviewed in the earlier section, none of the case reports or clinical studies involved the use of control groups or statistical tests of significance.

From the standpoint of research methodology and procedures, the papers reviewed in the subsequent section on differential effects contrast with these clinical publications. All of these were conducted in research-oriented settings, in which extensive measurements of personality, behavior, and other variables were obtained and the resulting data subjected to statistical analysis. A wide variety of measures was used in these studies but despite this diversity every paper surveyed reported statistically significant differential effects. The results indicate that special stimulus environments, including both reduced and monotonous stimulation, as well as variations in noise levels alone, produce widely varying effects on different individuals and groups of subjects. Any ultimate applications of special stimulus environments for treatment purposes must take into account the wide range of effects which these stimulus environments can produce in different subjects.

Research papers on the use of REST with psychiatric patients reported that patients presenting more severe symptomatology showed significantly greater improvement after exposure to reduced stimulation, as reflected in a variety of different measures. Some data suggested that reduced stimulation environments may produce greatest therapeutic effects in psychiatric patients who are relatively unpromising candidates for other forms of therapy.

An important personality dimension considered by one study was that of sensation-seeking versus sensation-avoiding. Exposure to reduced stimulation produced anxiety, boredom, discomfort, and strange sensations in "sensation-seekers," while "sensation avoiders" found the same environment comfortable, pleasant, and relaxing, providing a place where they could think out their problems without distraction.

Two other studies illustrated the differential effects of special environments which did not involve substantially reduced levels of sensory stimulation. One study showed that the effects of monotonous stimulation on schizophrenics, as reflected in measures of body image, differed significantly from the effects on nonpsychotic subjects. A second study found that differing noise levels (with no other sensory modalities being involved) produced significantly different effects on two contrasting groups of hospitalized schizophrenics. Increased noise levels produced improvement in withdrawn schizophrenics, whereas restless, agitated schizophrenics got worse in a noisy environment but showed significant improvement when placed in a quiet environment.

The authors of several papers reviewed in the section urged far more systematic investigation of the differential effects of special environments, observing that relatively little research has been conducted on differential effects. Much of the apparent confusion, inconsistency, and contradiction in the research literature may be due to a failure to consider the importance of these effects. The lack of systematic attention to the differential effects of REST and other special stimulus environments is indeed one of the most serious omissions in this area of research.

CHAPTER 11

A Practical Guide to Clinical REST[1]

RODERICK A. BORRIE
Vancouver, B.C.

In the course of developing any new technique for application in a therapeutic setting there is invariably an assortment of problems and pitfalls that plague the practitioner at every step. In this respect REST is no different from other new methods, although some of the specific problems associated with REST are unique. While we do not claim to have solved or even identified all of the possible difficulties, we have been able to deal successfully with the problematic situations that have arisen over the past few years. It is the purpose of this chapter to provide the interested reader with specific information pertaining to the establishment of a REST facility and with our suggestions regarding the handling of potential REST clients.

It is our hope that by reading this chapter as a type of professional's manual, the interested therapist will be able to apply these techniques with as few hindrances as possible. By disseminating this technology that we have found to be so effective we hope to encourage practitioners to use REST in their practice and to add further refinements and new applications. With the sharing of elaborations and improvements of the technique, the state of the science will progress at a much more rapid pace.

The organization of this chapter will follow a logical progression from acquiring and setting up the necessary equipment to the evaluation of the efficiency of REST. Naturally the problems did not arise in the neat order in which they are presented, nor are they likely to occur for you in the same sequence. After discussing the actual establishment of a REST facility we shall consider the planning of the individual client's session and how to prepare the client for the experience. The next area is the

---

[1]This chapter is based primarily on procedures used in the REST laboratory at The University of British Columbia. The chapter incorporates some portions of an unpublished paper prepared by P. Bruce Landon.

session itself and methods of directing the client's experience. Finally, we shall take up the question of followup and evaluation of the efficacy of REST.

SETTING UP A REST FACILITY

There are several different types of REST facilities available today. The environment we have used and found most convenient is the sound-proofed, darkened chamber. The client lies on a comfortable bed in the completely lightless, soundless room. The room is self-sufficient in that the client has immediate access to a toilet, food, and water. Our chamber has an intercom system to the outside, speakers connected to one tape recorder, and a microphone connected to another. We have also added at various times other equipment such as projectors, light displays, and different controls for the client.

The Treatment Room

There are several alternative methods of creating REST facilities. Perhaps the easiest is the lightproof, soundproof chamber which is the one that we have used. Although we are less familiar with the problems associated with other techniques, it is quite possible that one of these methods may better meet the specific needs of a particular client or therapist. One of these alternatives is the tank isolation technique devised by J.C. Lilly (1956, 1977). In the most recent version of this device the individual floats in a high-density solution contained in a covered tank approximately the size of a bed. The tank is light- and sound-proof and does not use any communication equipment to the outside. The uses of this method have primarily been of an introspective and meditative nature rather than a therapy directed by a practitioner. The tanks are commercially available from Leela Designs, the Samadhi Tank Company, and other commercial firms. The most complete source of information on the use and manufacture of isolation tanks is Lilly's book *The Deep Self* (1977); the newsletter *Float* has also published relevant information.

Stimulus Reduction Chambers.   The chambers we use are commercially available from the Industrial Acoustics Corporation. The sound isolation rooms marketed by this and other companies vary considerably in size, weight, standard features, and optional equipment. Industrial Acoustics will also build chambers to the buyer's specifications.

An alternative to the commercial REST chamber is the creation of an appropriate setting within an existing facility. Adequate suites can be found in most psychiatric, hospital, and correctional institutions. For use in noninstitutionalized applications, it is possible to modify a suite in a medical office building, a hotel, or even one's own house. An excellent degree of light removal and a fair degree of sound reduction can be achieved by fitting windows and doors with leaded vinyl curtains. These are readily available from most acoustic supply companies and are quite portable. The important aspect of the installation is to achieve complete seals around sources of outside light. Sound cannot be completely removed, but distracting building or traffic noise can be masked somewhat by the use of low levels of white noise. Alternatively, sessions can be scheduled for low-noise periods such as weekends.

The technique of using hotel suites which also contain a room for the monitor has been explored by Dr. P.B. Landon, who claims that it is nearly as effective as the more total reduction of stimuli in the commercially available REST chambers. Portable intercom and tape recorder systems are easily installed between the rooms. Dr. Landon has also tried to set up this situation in the client's own bedroom, but has found that clients generally tend to be more distractible in their own homes.

A third alternative is one that can be used in almost any setting and may be quite effective for short periods. This involves using light-eliminating goggles and headphones with low levels of white noise. Therapeutic communications can easily be presented by means of the headphones. After long periods, the goggles and headphones would probably become uncomfortable. They also restrict movement to some extent. We are not aware of this technique having been used in a therapeutic setting.

The type of facilities used will depend on a number of different variables. Deciding whether to buy, build, or rent depends partially upon one's needs and resources. Aside from financial considerations there are the questions of the client's and monitor's comfort and safety, the desirability and preferred types of communication, the degree of freedom from interruptions, the prevention of distractions, the length of sessions desired, and the basic objectives of the therapy.

Furnishings. The chamber itself should be furnished at least with a bed, a portable toilet, thermos bottles for food and water, a light, a speaker or speakers, and an intercom to the monitor's room. It is vital to have a comfortable bed. We have found that a firm mattress with a board under it receives the fewest complaints. However, it seems impossible to avoid some complaints. Lying on even the most comfortable bed for 24 hours is bound to produce some discomfort. Incidentally, fitted bottom sheets are essential for such a long stay in bed. Arrangements can probably be made with a local laundry to pick up and deliver your linen on a regular schedule. An extra pillow and an extra blanket should be provided in addition to the standard bedding.

A portable chemical toilet, toilet paper, and some sort of damp towel for washing the hands should be located very close to the bed. We put ours at the foot of the bed so the client can feel his way there along the bed and never have to walk far in the darkness. Male clients should be warned to sit on the toilet when urinating. Most of these toilets are odorless if used properly and kept clean, and most importantly are completely silent. A minor but unpleasant problem is the task of cleaning them out. We have solved this by requesting at the orientation to the REST session that the client be responsible for emptying the toilet at the completion of the session. Careful supervision of the clients' dismantling of these toilets can avoid unhappy accidents. A further solution to this unpleasantness is to simply request that the client defecate before beginning the REST session.

Our manner of handling the client's nutritional needs without adding undesired stimulation is to provide liquid food and water in thermos bottles. This procedure avoids the auditory, tactile, and kinesthetic input from unwrapping, handling, and chewing the food. To reduce gustatory and olfactory stimuli, we use a fairly bland yet nutritionally balanced liquid food. Our current choice is vanilla Metrecal, a liquid diet drink which comes in convenient six-ounce cans. We place the thermos bottles in a cooler near the head of the bed to prevent their being overturned. Free access to the food and water is available through plastic tube "straws" that run from each thermos and are attached with large pins to the bottom sheet near the pillow. The "straws" are available as long rolls of half inch, sterile plastic tubing that can be cut to the desired length. In this way the client need only turn his head to one side to drink. We usually put two cans of cool Metrecal in one thermos and leave two unopened cans in the cooler with an opener in case the client wishes more. Two cans usually suffice, although we had one hungry client who consumed 10 cans in 24 hours. The other thermos is filled with drinking water. If the client needs more food or water, the monitor enters the chamber without turning on the light and deposits the additional supply in the thermos.

The speakers are connected to a tape recorder located in the monitor's room. The intercom is used for communication with the monitor and for the monitor's auditory surveillance of the client. If it is desirable to tape record all of the client's responses, a microphone connected to a second tape recorder can be attached to the wall above the head of the bed. Both tape recorders are located and controlled in the monitor's room. Some other furnishings are not absolutely necessary but can be useful or soothing for the client. A chair and small table can be used by the client to fill out forms while becoming acclimated to the room before the session. A rug between the toilet and the bed makes getting up to use the toilet a bit more comfortable. We have also found that both internal and external decoration can ease some of the client's apprehension of the impending unusual experience. Posters and wall hangings, even though they cannot be seen once the REST session begins, add a homey, more comfortable feeling to the room when it is first entered. We have even wallpapered the outside of our chambers to prevent them from looking quite so much like walk-in freezers. This is all designed to give the client as positive a set as possible, since worry and apprehension about the experience can interfere with the purpose of the session.

Cost. The major cost concern is obviously the chamber itself. Elaborate commercial versions can cost up to $6000, or even more for double-walled models. It is much cheaper to sound- and light-proof a regular room. The cost of such a conversion is difficult to estimate, since it depends on location, traffic flow, thickness of existing walls, and so on. However, in reasonably appropriate circumstances it can probably be done for less than $1000.

Necessary equipment can be purchased for under $500 per chamber (see Table 11–1). The control room costs about the same to equip, except that data-recording devices, timers, scales, etc. may need to be added. Extra furniture—desks, chairs, coat-racks, filing cabinets—are also necessary. The estimates do not include recording tapes and expendable supplies and services such as food, laundering, plastic tubing, toilet paper, etc. These cost less than $5 per 24-hour session, to which the pay of the monitor should be added.

Table 11.1. Chamber Equipment

Item	Cost
Bed	$150
Chemical toilet	50
Intercom	50
Tape recorder	150
Food and water containers	10
Bedding	50
Total	$460

Location

It is important in the placement of REST chambers to try to use an already quiet location in the building. While the lightproofing of the chamber is absolute, the soundproofing still lets in a very low level of ambient noise from the surrounding building. For instance we discovered that some clients could determine when it was morning from the increase in noise due to the renewal of activity throughout the building. While the noise is very slight, it is certainly detectable when one has been in complete quiet for a number of hours.

Another consideration in installing REST facilities is the location of quarters for the monitor on duty and the availability of a lavatory. Since a monitor is on duty while the client is undergoing REST it is important to provide a control room for the chamber or chambers (one control room will serve for several REST chambers) that is also self-sufficient. In other words, a bed, desk, chairs, books, refrigerator (with food and beverages), telephone, and perhaps a radio should all be right in the control room. A lavatory should be close by so that the monitor will only have to leave the control room briefly if at all. This is important because it is unnerving for the client in need of something to call for the monitor and receive no reply. Further discussion of this follows under "Preparing the client." A convenient lavatory is handy for the client's use prior to and following the REST session.

The Control Room

The monitor's room should also contain controls for each chamber and all the equipment that is connected to the chambers. The most basic controls are the light switches and the intercom system. We have found it useful to use rheostatic switches that make the change in and out of complete darkness more gradual. Avoiding a sudden change is most important at the termination of the session when the client is extremely relaxed, dark adapted, and light sensitive. The intercom is simple and quite inexpensive. It is also possible to have one installed by Industrial Acoustics as an optional extra. The system should be at least two-way, with the line from the REST chamber to the monitor's room being continuously open. This eliminates the need for the client to fumble around for a button to press when wishing to communicate and also provides the monitor with an ongoing sound check on the client. Any excess movement or verbalization can be monitored in this way, and if necessary the monitor can then check with the client for possible problems. One instance where this was consequential was when one of our clients had purposely neglected to disclose her fear of darkness. After a brief period in REST she began to cry continuously but had no intention of terminating early. With some persuasion she agreed that it would be best for her if she ended the session. The intercom line from the monitor to the client is kept closed except when the communication button is pushed. A possibility that we have considered but not yet used is to have a third intercom line between two REST chambers so that two clients undergoing REST simultaneously could communicate when they wished. This might be valuable in such areas as marriage counseling.

Other essential equipment includes tape recorders, probably two or more depending on the number of chambers being attended. One tape recorder should be for playing of recorded materials into the chamber, while the other is for recording the subject's responses. The machine for playing tapes should have an additional speaker with separate volume control in the monitor's room so that the running of the tape can be followed without being too intrusive to the monitor's activities. Further equipment depends on the nature of the treatment planned for the individual client. It may include event counters, motion detectors, slide or movie projectors, and various physiological measurement devices, just to name a few of the possibilities.

PLANNING THE SESSION

Once the REST facility is set up, there are many preliminary and planning tasks that must be taken care of before any client actually goes through a REST session. The actual recruitment and selection of noninstitutionalized clients who would benefit from REST can be problematic and certainly has some problems that must be managed—such as the initial contact and first interview. Scheduling each client's session and working out an individual program also requires careful forethought. Preparing the client himself for the session includes orienting him to the facility, building up his confidence, alleviating fears and misgivings, and giving him instructions in how to involve himself in the experience in the most constructive way. Each of these problems is discussed in more detail below.

Recruitment and Selection

If a therapist has advertised or gained a reputation that he is using REST for the treatment of particular problems, his first contact with the patient is likely to be on the telephone. It is important to describe the technique carefully and positively as it is the client's first impression of REST. After ascertaining that REST might be useful in solving the client's problem, it would be wiser to concentrate on allaying the client's fears and doubts and encouraging him to come in for an interview rather than describing the details of the REST program.

Once a client comes in for an interview, the major tasks are to assess the client's situation, to judge the suitability of REST for his problem, and to present a very clear description of the entire treatment program. The last should include the specifics of the REST session and a mention of previous results and expected benefits. In this it is good to be very specific. Otherwise, clients may expect the technique to be a sort of "magical cure" because it is so novel and unusual. One problem is that clients may not keep their first interview appointment. REST is such an unknown quality that some clients may have considerable trepidation regarding the experience. Such individuals may back out at the last minute. In these cases it is best to call them back and give more reassurance.

In the screening of subjects for REST we cannot be sure who would and who would not benefit from the experience. Individual differences in the response to REST make it very difficult to predict reactions. Research on personality traits related to such reactions is incomplete. The even more complex task of predicting who will benefit therapeutically is still unanswered. Actually, this is one area in which we hope other users of REST will add to the body of knowledge about the technique.

However, we do know a few of the types of clients who will probably not enjoy or benefit from the REST session maximally, at least not without special handling prior to the session. The first type includes those who are looking for a magical or instant cure and see REST as just such a cure. While it is true that REST can be very effective, it seems to be so mainly with people who are motivated to help themselves. Those who wish to place responsibility for their problem totally on someone or something else will often be disappointed by the results. These clients should be helped to develop a more realistic attitude before going into REST. Another related problem is the client who, although he has made a commitment to use REST with you, is unable to defend his decision to others at home because of poor self-esteem. This client may devalue his own REST experience in order to support the opinion of those other people. The third type of subject who should not use REST includes those with certain phobias, claustrophobia being the obvious one. Such fears will make for a terrifying rather than a relaxing and comfortable experience. A less obvious problem is that of the extremely dependent person who fears to be separated for any length of time from family or important others. After several hours of REST, one such woman began to be concerned with how her family was getting on without her. This concern became exaggerated to the point that she was hearing the voices of her children calling her. She left in an agitated state. Based on the work of other researchers, we would also discourage the use of REST with obsessive-compulsive clients. Several reports of severe disturbance with such cases have been published. One other point is that some clinicians have found REST to be particularly effective with patients who were relatively less educated, intelligent, and verbal than the people who usually benefit the most from psychotherapy. These data were collected with a VA hospitalized group, but they may be kept in mind when assessing the suitability of a client who on the basis of standard criteria does not seem to be a good candidate. In screening clients, specific questions and perhaps tests should be directed to these issues as well as to possible medical problems that might exclude them from REST (e.g., a need for frequent medication). In questionable cases, a medical clearance can be required.

Scheduling the Session and Preparing the Client

There are a number of basic considerations in coordinating the necessary resources for a successful session. First, it is good to keep a 24-hour log for each REST facility to ascertain the availability of each chamber. It is probably best to leave at least an hour between scheduled sessions because of the time required for debriefing the last client and getting the chamber ready for the next.

The availability of monitors is another essential concern. It is possible to use monitors on a continuous basis (i.e., one for the entire 24 hour period) or on a shift basis. On a continuous basis it is difficult for the monitor to work two or more sessions in a row; so, in either case, a pool of available monitors is necessary. Monitors do not have to be therapists themselves, but they should be carefully instructed in running the equipment, dealing with the client, and handling any problems that might occur (see the section on "Running the session").

The availability of the client's time is also a prime concern. The client should not only leave the 24 hours open for the REST session itself, but he should also have some period afterward in which there will be no pressing demands made upon him. He should make arrangements with his family to take care of any tasks or demands that could become worrisome during REST. Some clients have difficulty removing themselves from the worries of everyday tasks and they need extra assurance that everything will run smoothly in their brief absence.

One final consideration in the scheduling of the REST session is to maintain an element of flexibility regarding the day the client is scheduled. Other important events in the client's life should be carefully considered. While some of these can be anticipated in advance and taken into consideration in planning, others cannot be predicted. For example, family problems can arise that put the client into a mental state that would affect the whole REST session and perhaps even make it countertherapeutic. On such occasions the client should be gently excused and rescheduled for a later date when the current crises should have subsided enough to be of less central concern.

Actually preparing the client with the proper mental set for the REST session is a crucial factor. One reason is that the client is about to do something he has never attempted before, and is likely to be very concerned with "getting ready" and "doing it right." Another reason is that the attitudes, concerns, mood, and expectations that the client has upon entering REST will have a profound and pervasive influence on his reactions. One researcher has described the setting as a "walk-in inkblot": each participant creates his own individual experience within the unstructured environment.

Transportation arrangements should be made in advance. Since REST may leave the client feeling somewhat disoriented, it is preferable to use some transportation other than driving his own car. The best alternative is to have a family member or good friend drive the client home, since crowds of strangers on public transport can be bothersome for someone in a sensitized or contemplative state. Plans might also be made to spend a period of time immediately following REST in some enjoyable, quiet sensory experience such as walking through a park or garden.

Clients should bring comfortable bed clothes and personal toiletries for freshening up after the session. They are not allowed to take into the chamber any personal items that may be distracting, such as watches, purses, bags, and excess jewelry. They should be instructed to leave such items at home if it would be worrisome not to have them in the chamber. One of our clients spent much of her REST time worrying about a purse that she had had to leave in the control room. It may be desirable to use individual lockers or containers when dealing with more than one client at a time.

The client may suffer from anxiety, confusion, and embarrassment regarding the impending REST session. Anxiety and confusion can be alleviated by giving a full explanation of what will happen, in the actual sequence. The probable range of feelings and thoughts that the client may have during the session, and the experiences that previous clients have had, should be discussed. Embarrassment can arise from the feeling that other people, particularly the client's friends, may view going into REST as an extreme or weird technique. Some clients are so worried about this reaction that they keep their decision to go through REST a secret from others around them. Information about the many subjects who have gone through this treatment can counteract this feeling. The client should be encouraged to tell others about what he is going to do. This serves several purposes. It eases the client's worry about the upcoming session, it increases the client's commitment to the program, and it strengthens the client's belief that he will benefit from the experience. It also confronts and reduces the client's embarrassment.

Preparing Appropriate Communications

Tailoring a client's session to his needs requires careful analysis of his present problems and an ordering of priorities for dealing with those problems. It is possible for the message to actually hinder the client's progress if it is poorly targeted. We have found that the most effective method of message preparation is to work closely with the client, getting him to do much of the planning for himself. Standardized messages can be used, but should be screened prior to use. Sometimes when a client can focus on one objectionable point within the message, his critical reaction will reduce the impact of otherwise acceptable material.

The purpose of messages in REST is to help instill and strengthen desired or newly acquired attitudes regarding the problem behavior and the actions to be taken by the client to solve the problem. Therefore the selection of material is crucial. It must be able to fit within the client's existing system of values and beliefs in order to be completely and enthusiastically accepted. For instance, with one client anti-smoking messages may center around the desire to completely control one's own life and not be controlled by an unthinking habit; for another client the same program may be oriented toward good health and the need to be responsible for one's own body; still another client may be more motivated by the removal of a dirty habit and the anticipation of improved senses of taste and smell. The goal is the same in all three cases, but the messages used for one client would not be as effective for the others. For this reason it is a good idea to obtain some measure of the client's values and beliefs (e.g., the Rokeach Values Scale). Another technique, of course, is the use of a standard, multi-approach set of messages. This does, however, run the risk of having a personally objectionable piece of information negate the acceptable information by association.

With guidance, the client may generate messages directed toward his own therapeutic goals. The actual writing of the messages may be a therapeutic experience in itself. In order to assist the client in making up the messages, it is helpful to have a catalogue of prepared messages that can be used as examples or can be edited to suit the client. Such a catalogue should include as many approaches to the problem as possible, to help the client identify the approaches that would be most relevant for him. By editing, any undesirable portions of the prepared messages can be removed or adjusted to make the material more acceptable. In some cases it is desirable to have the client himself, or a close friend or relative, make the actual recordings. The client's preference is important in this matter.

While there is little formal research evidence regarding the best sequencing, content, and structure of therapeutic messages in REST, it is possible to take advantage of the existing literature in the technology of attitude change in general. A number of good reviews are available (e.g., McGuire, 1969; Zimbardo, Ebbesen, and Maslach, 1977), summarizing some of the research findings on what sort of persuasion works with whom. Varela (1971) has put together some persuasion techniques that combine the findings from several areas of attitude research. The suggestions from the attitude change literature are many and can be confusing to one not familiar with the area. If there is a single rule of thumb to follow, it is to keep the message simple, logically sound, and within the client's point of view.

In the REST situation, simply structured messages—that is, those with fewer points or points of view—may be more effective than complex messages. To take advantage of the client's focused attention in REST, it is a good idea to limit the number of message topics to between 5 and 9. This avoids confusion and forgetting of the material. It is better to repeat a few messages at different times rather than to continue giving new information and thereby provide more material than can be processed at one time. If in preparing the client's program it is found that the amount of material the client wishes to cover in a single session may be overwhelming, it is quite feasible to plan for further REST sessions. If multiple sessions are decided upon for this reason, it is important to separate the material into logically relevant groupings, and to separate the sessions with a reasonable amount of time. Actually, it is a good idea to set up behavioral improvement goals for the first session that must be achieved before proceeding with the second session.

There are reasons other than having a large amount of material to cover for having more than one REST session. With a long-term behavioral problem—such as weight loss—which requires continued motivation and effort, it may be helpful to use additional REST sessions as boosters to the original. In these cases, the original message material that the client felt had been most beneficial would be emphasized in the booster session. It is not necessary to plan booster sessions at the outset of the client's program. The option should be left open and the decision left to the client. It should be remembered that the actual impact of booster sessions has not been empirically established.

RUNNING THE REST SESSION

The client's first visit to the REST facility should not be on the day of the actual session. It should take place at some earlier interview session. The client should be taken on an informal tour of the establishment, and have the procedure and anticipated experiences described by the therapist. The purpose of this session is mostly to reduce the client's fears of the chamber and to answer any questions the client may have. The monitor's room should be included on this tour.

On the day of the actual REST session the client should be given a more detailed orientation. Detailed explanations, demonstrations, and practice should deal with exactly how to use the toilet, how to get food and water, and how to communicate over the intercom. The client should be shown where the microphone and the speakers are located, and the location and function of any other equipment being used. If there is equipment present that is not being used with this client, its function or nonfunction should also be explained. The client should also be taught how to exit from the chamber if he should wish to terminate the session. The major goal of this orientation procedure is to make the client feel at ease in the situation. Therefore, the person in charge of the orientation should use a relaxed, yet professional and assured, style of presentation. It may be desirable for portions of the process to be memorized from a brief script.

If possible, the client should have a chance to meet the monitor or monitors who will be on duty during the session. Personal acquaintance, possibly on a first name basis, makes the experience more comfortable. Using first names is particularly helpful when the monitor addresses the client during the session. The job of the monitor should be thoroughly explained, and the client should be assured about the continuous presence of the monitor. Mention should be made of the fact that the monitor may not respond immediately to a call from the client because of being at the toilet or having to get up if the call happens to be at night. In this case the client should merely wait for a short while and try again. The client should be also reassured about the security of personal effects and valuables that must be left in the control room.

It is important to be accepting of the client's nervousness and concern. These reactions are perfectly normal. The usual range of experiences and feeling in REST should be summarized for the client again. He should be warned that at different times he may feel relaxed, anxious, bored, or quite comfortable, and may at times engage in problem solving, reminiscing, fantasizing, daydreaming, or wondering about the purpose of the REST session. The possibility of becoming uncomfortable with the situation and deciding to leave should be mentioned as an infrequent but quite natural occurrence, and it should be added that in such an instance one should feel free to leave the chamber, emphasizing that there is no stigma involved. The ease of exit should be demonstrated and the fact that the doors cannot be locked should be mentioned. It should be pointed out that the desire to leave is frequently only temporary. Therefore, the client should wait and be really sure of his desire to terminate the session before doing so.

In the chamber the client is instructed to lie quietly on the bed for the whole session. But comfort is more important than lack of motion, so he should feel free to move around on the bed to some extent if it makes him more comfortable. The client is told that the monitor has been instructed to keep communications to the essentials. For example, a monitor is not allowed to tell the client the time. Unless he is in need of something (e.g., more liquid food or water), or feeling ill, the client is asked not to communicate with the monitor. In some cases it is desirable to arrange for the presentation or repetition of messages on the client's request, and this may be another possible communication, although it would be better done by pushing a button or switch. If the client feels upset with the situation, he may call the monitor, ask to have the light turned on, or leave immediately.

Sometimes the client will ask the monitor a question mainly to hear another voice. The monitor should respond in a warm, friendly manner, but be brief and remind the client of the need to remain still and quiet. Too cursory or formal handling of the client in this situation can be misinterpreted and lead to the client becoming hostile toward the staff, a feeling that may counteract the therapeutic effect of the session. A number of other possible thoughts can become exaggerated preoccupations and distract the client from the major purpose of the REST session. These can include troublesome aspects of the session, concerns about upcoming events, worrying about business and family activities during the 24-hour period, or ruminating about side issues like how to get home or whether the keys have been locked in the car. These concerns can become a major annoyance that can contribute to general discomfort with the situation. Physical aches and pains may also lead to an early termination of the sessions. For this reason it is important to query the client about current worries, even trifling ones, and give advice about what he should do if he starts focusing continually on a disturbing issue. By trying to accept the concern, rather than denying it, and going over it from several vantage points, one can usually move on to more important matters fairly rapidly.

When everything is ready for the beginning of the REST session, the client should be allowed to use the outside toilet facilities. He should be then given a period alone in the chamber in which to change into bed-clothes and get settled on the bed. When he is ready, any last questions should be answered. The client is then left alone in the chamber, the door is closed, and the lights are turned out. Once REST has begun, it is good to focus the client's attention on his treatment. We have found it useful to begin the session with a progressive relaxation exercise with instructions for dealing with any anxieties that may occur during or after the session. Since even trivial aspects of instructions or recordings can become exaggerated in REST, it is necessary to be warm and supportive in all communications.

Message presentations can be set at specific intervals, or be given at the request of the client. It is a good idea to wait a few hours before the initial presentation, to allow REST conditions to raise stimulus need and increase the client's ability to concentrate on the message. An exception can be made for the relaxation exercise, which is chiefly to put the client at ease in the novel situation. Another consideration here is to avoid having the presentations too close to each other in time, since frequent interruptions will tend to reduce the effect produced by the REST conditions. The sequencing of messages should follow an order that will be logical to the client and which suits the practitioner's own insights about the client's program.

A small but consistent percentage of clients (approximately 5% in a 24-hour exposure) will request early termination of the REST session. Monitors should be thoroughly instructed in the handling of such cases. Many of these people will be anxious and upset, not only over whatever it was about REST that disturbed them but also about not having completed the session. The monitor should be soothing, comforting, and reassuring about the normality of such reactions. The monitor should also have available the phone numbers of the therapist in case the client wishes to talk directly with him. The client should be kept occupied with the therapist or monitor for at least 45 to 90 minutes before releasing him into the hustle and bustle of the outside world. If termination occurs at night, the client may choose to go back to bed in the REST chamber with the door open until morning. It is also possible that after a brief respite from REST or even just a period with the lights on the client may wish to continue the REST session. This should be permitted only when the therapist is assured that the client is calm and may benefit from such a continuation. In any case it is important to arrange an early followup appointment for these clients to discuss their experience and their feelings about it. It may be helpful for the client to practice deep breathing relaxation exercises either at the REST facility or upon arriving home.

It is generally useful to provide the client with a capsule summary of his program shortly before the normal completion of his REST session. This presentation can incorporate a discussion of how elements of the REST experience can be transferred to the world outside. Such useful factors include the messages, the relaxation exercise, and any insights the client may have gained. The client should be congratulated on his accomplishment and reminded of the ritual significance of the event as a starting point of a new set of habits. The lights should be slowly returned to normal or slightly below normal illumination level and a period of time allowed for the client to become more alert, to get up, and to dress. The client can be told to come out whenever he feels ready. Usually the first thing he wants to do is freshen up in the bathroom. Once the client is feeling more alert, he and the therapist can discuss the feelings, thoughts, fantasies and dreams that the client has experienced during REST. The therapist should make note of the client's reactions to specific message material: which items were most memorable, most interesting, most influential, and so on. It is a good idea to record as much of the client's post-session reaction as possible since it is useful information that may be forgotten at a later date. This can include emotions, thoughts, feelings, dreams, and insights. It is interesting to compare these first reactions with later remembered reactions to the experience, and the material can also be used to identify problems and construct future messages.

It is a good idea for the client to have prepared some quiet, restful, nondemanding activity for the period immediately following REST. This is important since the client is likely to be feeling somewhat disoriented. The client should be told that it is common for sensations to seem more intense, more vivid, more engrossing, and possibly more emotion-arousing. The client may not wish to be in the company of others for a while. Therefore it may be good to plan to ease gradually back into social situations. Another reason for the planning of the post-REST period is that it can be structured to allow the client to reflect calmly on the recent events and their significance in his life. Finally, before releasing the client to go home, arrangements should be made for followup checks either in person or over the phone.

EVALUATING REST EFFECTS

Gains from REST are potentially very far-reaching, in that the client may benefit in areas other than that targeted by his program. For this reason, thorough documentation of the client's pre-REST condition as well as of progress following REST is advisable. The gains from REST may also involve a "sleeper effect." The full benefit may not be noticed until some time well after the session itself. Therefore it is wise to collect followup material for long periods after the session. Good long-range data also provide a confirmation of the long-term effects of REST. Such information can be useful in explaining the benefits of REST to prospective clients.

In documenting the outcome of REST, it is important to include material that is amenable to statistical analysis. Even though that may not be an initial concern of the therapist, it could be extremely useful at some future date. For example, outside funding for research is difficult to receive without such data. Without the accurate analysis that inferential statistics provide, it is possible to overlook the discovery of some important interaction such as between a type of message and a particular personality trait. Also, accurate documentation with statistical analysis is the best answer to any professional or public concern that may surround a new and unfamiliar technique such as REST. Finally, thorough data collection and analysis provides an effective mode to share the discoveries that a therapist may want to communicate to interested colleagues.

In conclusion, we would like to add some final words of advice to potential users of the REST technique. First, since it is a relatively new method in therapy, one should be open to its novel uses. These include its application to new problems and its incorporation in multimodal procedures with different therapeutic methods. One must also keep an open mind about the REST procedure, in full or in part, as the data accumulate. Service may need to be delivered to an expanding volume of client requests, and with regard to an increasing diversity of problems. Finally, it is highly advisable to establish and maintain liaisons with other professionals using REST in related areas of service in order to share ideas and data, and to further develop the efficiency of the service being provided.

CHAPTER 12

Some Final Considerations

This last chapter considers once again what we know about restricted stimulation as an experimental and clinical technique. Relevant theories are explored in some detail. One other concern is why the public, both lay and professional, has been so resistant to the idea that environmental restriction should be explored and used in clinical settings. In examining this issue, I shall look at some of the related literature and at the evidence concerning the actual stressfulness of REST.

REST: MANY FACTS, MANY THEORIES

I have pointed out several times in earlier chapters the ties between REST research and theoretical systems related to psychopathology and behavioral dysfunction. While the conceptual bases of REST as a therapeutic technique can be quite elaborate, there are two major gaps. One of these is that it has been very difficult indeed to generate strong hypotheses in which the superiority of one theoretical formulation over another can be clearly demonstrated. The other is that psychology and its cognate disciplines have many conceptual frameworks that may be relevant to the understanding and proper utilization of REST, but that have not been explored in this regard. Consequently, the experiments and the applications that would be deduced from these theories have not been performed.

The first of these problems is not solvable at the present time. One reason for this is that we do not know enough about REST itself, nor about its neurophysiological and other effects, to be able to make very specific predictions as to behavioral outcomes. Another and more fundamental reason is that it is quite possible to visualize a situation in which theoretical explanations at various levels (neurological, cognitive, environmental) all are valid and efficient in explaining some portion of REST effects. If this is the case, then the whole idea of testing theories against each other becomes meaningless and self-defeating. At this stage I would prefer to leave the attempts to explain what happens in REST complex, multilevel, and flexible, even though this state of affairs may distress those colleagues for whom a clear-cut theoretical structure is a psychological necessity.

I would like, however, to consider the second issue. One aspect of this is the difficulty of categorizing sensory deprivation research in any particular subarea of experimental psychology, and similarly of assigning restricted stimulation therapy to any of the standard treatment classifications. As I mentioned in Chapter 7, REST certainly has much in common with relaxation and refocusing therapies such as those involving meditation, relaxation training, and biofeedback. Theoretical propositions related to these should therefore also hold implications for the use and understanding of REST. Some of these are pretty straightforward; others are more complicated and related to issues which have not been adequately considered in the therapeutic literature. The history of research on stimulus restriction has consistently demonstrated the interplay between data collection and theory-building. The original impetus for the development of the technique was basically theoretical, stemming from the desire to modify then-dominant concepts of perception, motivation, and learning. Once the field became popular, investigators proceeded from their own diverse theoretical starting points. But the accumulation of data soon outstripped the attempts at explanation. By 1963, a major contributor could refer to the field as "facts without a theory" (Vernon, 1963). In the definitive book edited by Zubek, there were two chapters dealing with theoretical formulations; but the author of one of them still felt that "facts have increased geometrically while theories have remained static" (Zuckerman, 1969c, p. 407).

In the 25 years that have elapsed since the first publications, some of the "facts" have turned out to be misunderstandings, artifacts, or nonreplicable findings. Others have become firmly established, and sometimes better understood. As a result of these developments, some theoretical statements have been disconfirmed while others still remain consistent with empirical knowledge. But it is certainly true that no overarching conceptual system of how stimulus reduction affects the organism has been developed. Rather, bits and pieces of various more general theoretical constructs have been usefully applied to the literature. There have also been a few such constructs developed specifically to deal with stimulus restriction effects and phenomena. Most of these need to be tested considerably more than they have been before their validity and their place in the analysis of the data can be established.

What is true of the experimental literature is equally true of the clinical work reviewed in this book. As we have seen, REST is a condition that characterizes or accompanies many therapeutic and quasi-therapeutic situations. For the most part, practitioners belonging to particular schools of thought tend to assimilate the stimulus characteristics of their procedures into the basic theory of human behavior and psychotherapy that underlies their approach. Many other workers have proceeded from an essentially atheoretical point of view. They are pragmatists, and for them the beneficial effects of REST are sufficient to justify its use. No ties with theoretical postulates are necessary. The first part of this statement seems persuasive from the point of view of a helping profession: if the procedure works, it is justified (note that "works" covers not only efficacy but also related issues such as ethically acceptable procedures and an absence of dangerous side-effects). At the same time, however, a better understanding of where these effects fit into a more general analysis of behavior and behavioral dysfunction would not only make the data more valuable to psychology as a science, but could lead to improvements in their application to the problems faced by the clinician. Thus, a good theory could indeed be practical as well as enlightening.

It is clear that no universally acceptable theoretical position has yet been proposed. In my opinion, it is unlikely that one ever will be. In fact, given that health-related behavior is complex, multiply determined, and many-dimensional, no such all-inclusive theory can reasonably be expected. Rather, I think that what we need is a multilevel theoretical approach that looks at influences and contributions of factors ranging from the neurophysiological to the social.

In much of the book so far, I have emphasized cognitive and affective models. But to arrive at an adequate theoretical explanation of the findings, we must abandon the idea of using only one level of abstraction whether this one level be based on cognition, emotion, regression, changes in the brain, or any other intervening factor. Instead we need to view the organism as a complex, multimodal biobehavioral system interacting with the REST environment. This does not, of course, preclude concentrating on one or another variable at a given time; but it mandates that the theorist bear in mind the totality of the organism with which he is dealing. An explanation at any level must be at least compatible with explanations at other levels.

The workers cited in this book have explanations based on an incredible diversity of points of view: behavioral, cognitive, psychoanalytic, "humanistic," transcendental. In fact, it is difficult to think of a theory that someone has not attempted to fit to REST data (or vice versa). In this section, I shall look at some of the postulates that appear to be the most relevant to the findings on the clinical uses of stimulus reduction. However, I shall concentrate on those theories that are relatively specific in addressing themselves to the effect of sensory reduction, and particularly those that have inspired recent work in the field. This approach precludes attention to some of the theories considered in detail in the theoretical chapters of Zubek's book (Suedfeld, 1969c; Zuckerman, 1969c), such as the use of psychoanalytic and ego-psychological concepts by clinical investigators—for example, those working at Allan Memorial Hospital (Azima, Lemieux, and Cramer-Azima, 1962) and New York University (Goldberger and Holt, 1958). Further, the reader may note that in discussing theoretical explanations I have focused on their relevance to REST with noninstitutionalized adult patients. This area appears to me representative of clinical applications in general. Because of its relative abundance of objective data, it is also the most useful domain in which theories can be evaluated.

Neuropsychological Hypotheses

An early analysis (Lindsley, 1961) argued that the neurophysiological locus of sensory deprivation effects was in the brainstem, particularly in the reticular formation. This system, and specifically its activating component, is relevant to the attentional shifts and changes in arousal of more central areas and to the monitoring and processing of sensory inputs. It is thus likely to play a role in some of the effects of REST. For example, "with the exceptional conditions of sensory deprivation, literally a void would be created with vigorous striving for necessary stimulation to keep the ARAS [ascending reticular activating system] and, in turn, the cortex, going on an activated basis so that one's past or present may be reviewed" (p. 176). Here is a neuropsychological explanation for stimulus hunger, as well as for the vivid memories, explorations of the self, and other phenomena reported by REST subjects. The formulation is also centrally relevant to theories that relate REST effects to changes in the general arousal or activation of the organism (see Suedfeld, 1969c; Zuckerman, 1969c).

Another suggestion on the neurophysiological level is related to Lindsley's hypothesis that stimulus reduction affects the brainstem in a massive way. As behaviors are first learned and then become overlearned and essentially automatic, the originally important factor of cortical control over movements becomes less crucial. Examples would be the gradual change as an adolescent male first begins to shave his facial hair, exercising great care and attending completely to the activity, and eventually progressing to the point where he can perform the same chore without paying much attention and almost without looking; an individual repeatedly driving his car over a particular route, until at last he can arrive at his destination with no memory of the actual drive (unless some unusual event or emergency situation occurs, in which case attention is suddenly refocused); or, more pertinent to our interests, the learning of such behaviors as smoking. Habitual smokers, those who frequently light up without even thinking about it, are common. Many of our own subjects reported that it was not unusual for them to find themselves with a cigarette in their mouth without any memory of taking it out of the pack, lighting it, and starting to smoke.

If stimulus restriction in fact disrupts the accustomed functioning of the brainstem, it may be that control over at least some of these behaviors is once again redirected back to the cortex. This would serve to reduce the automatic quality of the act, requiring the individual to focus his attention on it and enabling him to extinguish it if he so desires.

There is at present no hard evidence confirming the theory on a neurophysiological level. This would be difficult to do with current techniques. On a behavioral level, however, one relevant test would be to see whether similar changes occur in the case of other habitual behaviors. We do know from other reports and from our own observation that such activities as driving are to some extent disrupted after the subject comes out of REST. In fact, we ask our participants not to drive a car for at least a few hours after the end of the session. Unfortunately, we have not in the past attempted to collect data on whether changes analogous to those with smoking have occurred in other areas.

In an extremely interesting chapter, Budzynski (1976) has subsumed REST effects under the phenomena of what he calls twilight states of consciousness. These states are referred to by sleep researchers as hypnagogic or hypnopompic, and we have already seen that some of the reported perceptual experiences in REST may be in fact twilight state experiences. Budzynski argues that this condition, which has also been referred to as reverie, the preconscious, and transliminal experience, can serve to increase creativity, make dreams more vivid, call back long-lost memories and lead to relaxation and the ability to concentrate. Increased learning ability and suggestibility are also cited, and in one paper the possibility of using this situation as an aid to smoking and weight-loss therapy has been suggested (Barber, 1957). Wickramasekera (1977c) has indicated that this factor is common to sensory restriction, autogenic training, progressive relaxation, symbolic systematic desensitization, biofeedback, and hypnotherapy.

Perhaps the most intriguing aspect of this argument is a theoretical one. Budzynski proposes that twilight states are essentially those in which arousal is relatively low, with high production of EEG waves in the theta range. Subjects can be taught to produce theta rhythms through biofeedback, and the state can also be produced by autogenic exercises and monotonous stimulation (Bertini, Lewis, and Witkin, 1969). He then proposes that twilight learning takes place in the nondominant hemisphere. The descriptions of memory and images, the inability of subjects to verbalize that which they have learned—even though test performance shows that they have actually learned this material—and the high level of nonverbal performance support this interpretation. Supposedly, what happens in the low-arousal condition is that the critical, analytic, logical functions are diminished, pointing to a reduced role of the dominant hemisphere. This happens much more slowly with the holistic activities of the minor hemisphere. It would certainly be fascinating if one could test this hypothesis more directly; but even without that, some explicit attempt to test it in the REST environment would be an important step towards explaining the neurophysiological substrates of the "sensory deprivation" effect. Theoretically, as arousal decreases, there is a difference in the thresholds at which the activity of the two hemispheres is diminished, this threshold occurring at an earlier point with the dominant hemisphere. It is in the interval between the stage at which the dominant hemisphere is affected and the point at which the minor hemisphere is affected that the type of functioning to which Budzynski refers becomes prominent. Wickramasekera (1977a) similarly proposes that the critical, analytic functioning of the dominant hemisphere is temporarily inhibited by the low-arousal techniques (including REST), giving greater scope to holistic information processing and a fresh and different definition of various events or stressful stimuli. It is this redefinition that leads to the potential for therapeutic change.

This point of view ties in nicely with that advanced by Watzlawick (1978), which is that therapists have to learn to communicate in right-hemisphere terms, while blocking off left-hemisphere information processing (of course, this may be reversed for individuals with left side—right hemisphere—dominance). Once again, if this hypothesis is valid, REST may fulfill the function of potentiating right-hemisphere communication. This may explain the experience of imagery and primary process on the one hand, and the fuller communication with the therapist following REST on the other.

There is, of course, considerable doubt as to the appropriateness of ascribing such clear-cut differences to hemispheric functioning. But whether the neuropsychological constructs are correct or not, we can at least say that REST sometimes seems to act as the functional equivalent of the hypothetical shift in the activity of the brain.

Luria's (1973) neuropsychological theorizing also has implications for the understanding of REST phenomena. It appears that all three of the functional units to which he refers (those governing activation, information processing, and regulatory activity) are affected by stimulus reduction. The unit for regulating activation, alertness, or the orienting reflex is involved because it is clear that states of arousal change under REST conditions and that investigative activity, which Luria considers to be an outgrowth of the orienting reflex, increases as a function of stimulus hunger. Structurally, the units involved are the reticular formation and limbic system, the nonspecific nuclei of the thalamus, the caudate nucleus, and the hippocampus. Because the close link between the orienting reflex and memory is ascribed to this area of the brain stem, and because the changes in activation are closely tied in with such memory phenomena as unusually vivid redintegration of past experiences, it seems likely that there is some involvement here when the individual is in a restricted environment.

The functional unit that deals with the reception, analysis and storage of information, located in the posterior part of the cerebral cortex, is also involved. This is particularly true in relation to the role of these areas for synthesizing stimuli into percepts; that is, the tertiary zones of this system. This process not only changes sequentially received stimuli into a simultaneously processed pattern, it is also involved in the transformation of such patterns to symbolic processing. This region is crucial in moving from concrete perception to abstract thought, a transition that is also likely to be affected by REST.

The general regulatory control exercised by the tertiary portions of the frontal lobes, however, is probably the most relevant to our concerns. For one thing, it has been shown that lesions of the frontal lobes can prevent organisms from inhibiting responses to irrelevant stimuli. To the extent that such an ability interferes with various human processes, including for example therapeutic interactions, one would expect that REST (in which irrelevant stimuli are minimized) would be beneficial for individuals with this problem. At a wider level, the frontal cortex is involved in the control of activation, which in turn is connected with all forms of conscious behavior.

It is clear, of course, that all complex behaviors are based on the integrative working of all of the three systems. But the connection between REST and behavior appears to be more obviously related to some functions than to others. For example, the automatization of motor behavior appears to be closely linked to the motor structures of the anterior parts of the brain and the lateral zones of the frontal cortex. To the extent that REST disorganizes these preprogrammed sequences of activity (see, for example, the section on smoking behavior) it may be that the neuropsychological level of explanation should focus on these areas. Disturbances characterized by loss of motivation for complex thinking have been connected with disturbances of the lateral zones of the frontal cortex; affective outbursts and disinhibition with the orbital cortex; and disturbances of the interaction between the cortex and the reticular formation with the medial zones of the frontal lobes.

Once again, the argument must remain on a hypothetical basis. Neuropsychological studies of the effects of environmental restriction have been quite crude. Primarily, they have consisted of taking EEG measurements before, during, and/or after a session of REST. There have been no systematic attempts to look at the localization of changes in brain functioning, much less at the relationship between such localization and changes in psychological and behavioral functions. Clearly, these are necessary steps in the explication of environmental effects at this particular level of theory; clearly also, given the wide individual differences in response to REST, some attempt should be made to investigate whether in different individuals given neural processes have varying thresholds of responsivity or liability to change as the environment is manipulated.

Cognitive Explanations

Robertson (1961, 1962) has proposed an explanation based on the idea that the reduction of external stimulation leads to increased focusing of attention on internal material, including memories, awareness of problems, and ways of solving those problems (see also Schultz, 1965). This material is normally kept from consciousness by the availability, urgency, and impact of environmental inputs. As the individual becomes more and more preoccupied with his own consciousness, the thoughts, emotions, and residual stimuli become increasingly separated from context and other structural anchors. As a result, the subject becomes less critical of any remaining input. If this input consists of persuasive messages, being less critical means being more suggestible. A cognitive analysis has frequently been considered in the use of sensory restriction with relatively severe psychotic patients. In particular, it explains why schizophrenic adults and autistic children appear to benefit from REST (see Chapters 9 and 10). It has been widely speculated that both of these conditions involve the malfunctioning of some kind of gating mechanism that allows the normal individual to screen out a large proportion of incoming stimuli as being irrelevant to ongoing problem-solving and adaptation processes, and therefore not calling for a response. The inability of schizophrenic and autistic patients to perform this selection and screening process effectively leads to the maladaptive patterns that characterize these conditions (e.g., Buss and Lang, 1965; Hermelin and Wing, 1976; Lovaas, 1977). Obviously, stimulus reduction helps to solve this problem at least temporarily by eliminating the bombardment of irrelevant stimuli, thus making relevant ones (such as therapeutic communications) more salient and more likely to be processed. In addition, such an environment should also be relatively pleasant for these individuals, since the stimulus overload that characterizes their experiences in "normal" conditions is alleviated.

The next explanation is derived from the known effects of reduced stimulation on cognitive performance. As noted in Chapter 2, reviews and experiments have established that REST has a reliable disruptive effect on complex thinking. Taking this finding one step further, Suedfeld (1972) has argued that the attempt to maintain one's pattern of attitudes and beliefs in the face of a powerful persuasive presentation—that is, one that is factual, seems legitimate, and is presented in a convincing way—is a complex cognitive task. It calls for processing and evaluating the components of the message, comparing each one with the counterpart in one's own pre-existing set of beliefs and opinions, and marshaling counterarguments, qualifications, and other techniques for resisting change. There is direct evidence (Suedfeld, Tetlock, and Borrie, in preparation) that in at least some cases stimulus reduction significantly impairs the generation of counterarguments. Evaluating one's own beliefs, deriving the implications of each one for appropriate emotional reactions to a particular topic, and then ordering all of the known facts, arguments and preferences in the development of some final set of attitudes is also a complex task. To the extent that these processes are impaired, the belief structure becomes unstable (see Koslin et al., 1971), and the stage of attitude change that Lewin called "unfreezing" occurs. By this process, the probability of change in the system is raised.

If REST is a general disruptor of complex cognitive functioning, one may extrapolate that under appropriate conditions it would have destabilizing effects on resistance to persuasion. We thus hypothesize that REST can bring about the "unfreezing" stage of the attitude change process. This proposition was supported most directly by a study in which 24 hours of darkness and silence, even without the presentation of any attitude-related messages, caused significant decreases in belief stability on both a central and a peripheral attitude (Tetlock and Suedfeld, 1976). An attitude structure, once unfrozen to some extent, is then more susceptible to being changed. This is one explanation of the generally reliable finding that stimulus restriction increases persuasibility (Suedfeld, 1969b).

The next step in this extrapolation is that health-related attitudes, and the behavior patterns based on them, follow the same pattern as the attitudes investigated under purely experimental conditions. According to cognitive disorganization theory and its derivatives, we would therefore expect that clients would be more likely to change or abandon attitudes that have supported their unhealthy activities, and consequently to abandon the activities themselves, when appropriate messages are presented in a REST situation.

Once again, the data are mixed. To begin with, the evidence that belief instability occurs is not as clear-cut in health-related persuasions using REST as in straight experimental studies. Suedfeld et al. (1972) found the lowest levels of instability among confined no-message subjects, moderate levels among confined and nonconfined subjects who heard the anti-smoking message, and the highest levels among nonconfined message subjects. On the other hand, Silverstein and Suedfeld (1976) did find higher instability among REST subjects hearing anti-smoking messages. Attitude scores are similarly confusing, with the study by Suedfeld et al. (1972) failing to support the hypothesis and that by Silverstein and Suedfeld (1976) providing partial confirmation. As to the relationship between attitude change and behavior change, messages made no difference in the effectiveness of the treatment for smoking (Suedfeld et al., 1972; Suedfeld and Ikard, 1974) but did have a significant positive effect in the case of weight reduction (Borrie, 1978).

Presumably, the importance of this factor would depend on how novel and convincing the arguments are. Perhaps even more important is the degree to which the messages contain concrete and effective behavioral guidelines and tactics that the subject can use after leaving the clinic or laboratory. This is particularly true when the habit being attacked requires systematic tactics for extinction, as in the case of inappropriate dietary and exercise patterns.

Even if unfreezing and changing have occurred, the crux of the matter is still refreezing, or the establishment of a stable attitudinal and behavioral system in the new pattern. As the relapse rates indicate, this is the crucial problem with all clinical interventions in health habits. Because of our relatively high level of success, it appears that the REST treatment is more effective than most in this regard. However, there is obviously room for improvement. It has been suggested, and future research may test, that keeping clients in the laboratory for some time (perhaps a day) after release from REST would be useful. This period would be devoted to reinforcing the changes obtained during the reduced stimulation session, providing support and further information as needed. Followups that provide therapy, not merely further data, might also be useful and have been adopted to some extent in clinical work. Another possibility is the use of booster sessions in REST. These have helped some subjects and have been requested by many others (Suedfeld and Ikard, 1973, 1974) even though the efficacy of boosters in conjunction with other techniques is under criticism (Relinger et al., 1977).

The concept that stimulus reduction is a general unfreezer, which is supported by the findings of Tetlock and Suedfeld (1976), would explain the "nonspecific" effect that has appeared to perturb some reviewers (e.g., Bernstein and McAlister, 1976). I think that what the treatment does is to make the individual more open to the possibility of change. The kind of change, if any, that ensues is a function of the context (e.g., the client knows that he is participating in a smoking cessation clinic), the specific materials presented (messages, attitude measures, behavioral self-report forms that concern smoking), and his own personal motives (the fact that he cannot quit smoking has been bothering him, so he spends time in the chamber working on that problem). This explains the generalizability of the technique, both in experimental and clinical settings.

In a way, this hypothesis is related to Bem's early ideas about attitudes (e.g., 1965). The decreased stability of the attitude/belief system that occurs as a consequence of REST, and subsequent attitude change, probably are not made manifest to the subject, have no effects, and may disappear soon after the treatment. To prevent such relapse, the therapist should make a specific attempt to measure the change, make the client aware of it, reinforce it, and base behavioral changes on it.

One of the possible reasons for the effectiveness of restricted environmental stimulation therapy may have been implied in the recent report by Cooper, McGraw, Pasternak, Pasnak, and Adams (1977). This paper dealt with the use of brief stimulus restriction and messages on the alcohol intake of moderate to heavy social drinkers. Some of these subjects had an actual drinking problem. The more effective of the two messages was a confrontation indicating that a heavy drinker is already in trouble, even if he is not actually an alcoholic. In a brief description of this study ("Sensory deprivation experiments with problem drinkers," 1977), the senior author was quoted as saying: "That message . . . tends to be an absolute bomb-out if you give it to people outside of the procedure— everybody says that couldn't possibly apply to me. [Within the procedure] it was the most effective message—really bypassing some preliminary stages of therapy and getting into a kind of confrontation very early on, which, of course, is one of the valuable things" (page 7).

In terms of Fishbein's (1976, 1977) levels of belief analysis, what this implies is that Levels 1 and 2 (awareness and general acceptance) are bypassed and Level 3 (personalized acceptance) is reached immediately. According to the model, a person may be aware of a particular argument (e.g., he may know that according to some authority excessive drinking is harmful), and may even accept the argument in general (he may believe that excessive drinking is in fact harmful), but may not necessarily accept it in a personalized way (that is, he may nevertheless believe that his own excessive drinking will not harm him). Judging by Cooper's remarks, it may be that the confrontation message is rejected and disbelieved on the personalized level by control subjects, but that the use of REST enables it to make the kind of impact that results in a determination to change. Whether a similar process is involved in the smoking and other REST-message treatments remains to be investigated.

It has also been suggested (Tomkins, 1968) that, at least for addicted smokers, the analogy of a programmed sequence is appropriate. The sequence, which has been overlearned through a great number of repetitions, may include some environmental stimulus that focuses the individual on his craving for a cigarette, which in turn engages a series of behaviors connected with smoking. When a cigarette is not available toward the end of this process, the sequence recycles with ever-increasing degrees of stress and anxiety. If the first step is eliminated from the repertoire, the rest of the sequence may also be deleted. REST provides a unique combination of cigarette deprivation and relaxation. Afterwards, a post-session return to stressful situations, cues related to cigarettes, and so on will not be enough to reconstitute the programmed sequence. This approach would explain why even those subjects who go back to smoking cigarettes report that the craving seems to have been extinguished.

Affective-Motivational Explanations

I must admit to a bias in favor of cognitive levels of analysis (the reader may already have noticed this). Aspects of information processing, however, interact with changes at the affective level. If, as has been hypothesized so frequently, REST is a situation in which secondary process loses its predominance in the adult, a flooding of the affective channels may result. In a therapeutic situation, emotions about the problem, its origins, impact, possible solutions, and possible perpetuation, may fill the mind of the subject. We do not yet know what the effects of stimulus restriction on imagery really are, although there is some hope that investigations using modern techniques in imagery research will shortly be undertaken. But if the anecdotal evidence concerning the vividness and impact of such experiences is at all accurate, it is quite possible that the effects of REST on beneficial changes in behavior are related to the emotion-laden remembering and imagining centered around the undesirable habit.

For some patients, this can be extremely unpleasant. In fact, it may explain the adverse reactions of obsessive-compulsive patients who, faced with this flooding and bereft of their usual defenses, can be psychologically overwhelmed. At the moment, there are no data to cite on this issue; but there may well be some kind of curvilinear function between the degree of negative affect aroused in the chamber and the usefulness of the experience in behavioral change. If the subject does not suffer some anxiety, remember some pain, imagine some frustration or even serious illness, the motivational level (unless it is extremely high to begin with) may not be sufficient to propel a change. On the other hand, too great a flood of unpleasant emotion may cause the individual to leave the environment or at least to switch his train of thought onto other tracks. Somewhere between these extremes, there may be a level where fantasizing and emotive recall can play a role in supporting the patient's determination to get rid of his habit.

Along with this, positive emotions can be aroused in connection with the projected improvement in behavior patterns. In our smoking studies, some messages were based on Spiegel's (1970) exhortation to protect one's own body from being poisoned and on various other health-related concepts. Some people responded with euphoria about the physical, psychological, social, and financial benefits to be gained from quitting. Several subjects remembered (again with great positive affect) how physically fit they had been in the past, how they were able to engage in sports and other activities that had become difficult for them. Others imagined the pleased reaction of their family and friends after their success, or contemplated what they could do with the money they would save by no longer buying cigarettes. Similar positive reactions were found among individuals suffering from obesity, hypertension, and phobias.

We have not done very much to strengthen the role of emotions in the therapeutic use of REST. In fact, we have not even investigated this variable, beyond recording spontaneous remarks made by subjects. But as the profession becomes increasingly aware of the importance of affect and of imagery, and their relevance to therapy (e.g., Ahsen, 1977; Singer, 1974), the exploration of this issue has gained in priority.

One interesting point is that according to Tomkins's (1968) analysis there is a positive correlation between the amount of suffering undergone in connection with giving up smoking and the likelihood that abstention will be permanent. Tomkins further points out the tremendous craving for a cigarette that addicted smokers feel whenever they are deprived, and the intensification of this craving when cigarettes are seen, smelled, or mentioned (as in the messages presented during REST) One might predict that our subjects, for whom giving up the habit by means of REST did not seem to be at all stressful, should be quite likely to relapse. Yet we have found that this is not the case.

Apparently, the major counterforce to the craving for a cigarette (and perhaps for similar feelings related to other substances) is the experience of strong positive affect. It has been suggested that any situation evoking such feelings—a vacation, for example—may be put to therapeutic use in reducing the craving. However, there is no evidence of permanent change as a result, as there is with REST.

Another peculiarity of the REST treatment is that many people keep smoking at very low rates after the experience. This is contrary to Tomkins's (1968) hypothesis that one cigarette will re-addict formerly addicted smokers who have quit. Tomkins argues that for addicted smokers the awareness that they are not smoking, or that they are planning to quit, leads to negative affect, which is reduced by smoking. In order for smoking cessation to occur successfully, one must modify this link. In our work, this seems to be accomplished. The unavailability of cigarettes in the REST chamber does not arouse unpleasant feelings, and quitting or cutting down becomes feasible. What seems to happen is that for many subjects the tie between the awareness of nonsmoking and the negative emotions usually connected with that awareness is broken. One does not have to worry about breaking the sequence in which anxiety and tension due to not having a cigarette lead the individual to go out and get one if the lack of cigarettes ceases to arouse anxiety and tension.

Another factor contributing to therapeutic effectiveness may be the arousal of stimulus hunger as a result of reduced environmental stimulation (Jones, 1969). Attitude change researchers generally assume that people are motivated to maintain their existing attitudes unchanged. After a period of REST, novel information opposing the subject's beliefs would be listened to carefully for the first time, would take on positive incentive and reward value because it reduces the state of stimulus hunger, and therefore might become acceptable. Change in the target attitude might follow. The evidence regarding this hypothesis in experimental tests has been negative so far. In those studies that measured recall and evaluation of the messages, there was no indication that stimulus-deprived individuals either remembered the content better or rated it more favorably than did control subjects (e.g., Silverstein and Suedfeld, 1976; Suedfeld and Borrie, 1978a). This may, however, have been a function of inadequate measures of memory and evaluation.

In contrast, Landon (personal communication, July 24, 1978) noted that instructions as to how to behave in the chamber were remembered at 90% efficiency by clinic clients who heard them presented over the earphones after the experiment had begun, as opposed to only 50% by clients who received the instructions in a group setting prior to entering the experimental room.

The finding that informational/persuasive messages increased the effect of REST with obese patients but not with smokers may also be related to stimulus hunger. The messages concerning dieting and exercising were probably more novel for the listeners than were those dealing with the adverse health effects of cigarettes. This is a post hoc analysis, since we do not as yet have adequate systematic ratings of how novel or informative the subjects perceived the messages to be.

The differences in message impact may have been related to specific content. Giving up smoking is an easy task compared to losing weight. For one thing, it is possible never to smoke again; it is not possible never to eat again. Thus, it may be that the technical information contained in the weight-loss messages was useful in solving the cognitive/behavioral problem of weight reduction. By comparison, the smoking messages were simple. Their only technical content was the brief relaxation exercise. We would expect that more elaborate relaxation training, or any other pragmatically useful and informative material, would have an added effect beyond that provided by REST itself.

It is perhaps most likely that stimulus hunger played a critical role in the studies dealing with snake fear. The rationale of this work drew directly on the hypothesis that stimulus hunger would lead the subjects to expose themselves voluntarily to normally aversive stimuli, which would be less (or not at all) aversive under these conditions. An added refinement of the stimulus hunger explanation is related to the order of slide presentation. Jones (1969) has argued that stimulus hunger is primarily a need for information, and that the most positive sets of inputs are those that are highest in information value and lowest in predictability. The validity of this hypothesis in the snake phobia research is supported by the finding that a random order of realism in the presentation of the snake slides was more effective in reducing post-confinement fear than was a hierarchical order, although the latter was more effective with unconfined phobic subjects (Suedfeld and Buchanan, 1974).

It is also possible that the REST session may have changed the criteria by which subjects evaluated fear, rather than the fear response itself. That is, internal reactions may be interpreted differently after the treatment, and thus lead to different behaviors, just as in one study formerly painful stimuli were reinterpreted as not being painful after acupuncture (Clark and Yang, 1974). This hypothesis, however, is contradicted by the finding that in our work physiological changes were significantly correlated with the behavioral ones (Suedfeld and Hare, 1977). It appears that REST brought about a change in the actual internal experience, not only in the cognitive/affective judgments about the experience. Cognitive dissonance may have been another factor. The subject's knowledge that he had deliberately decided to see a normally aversive slide could have aroused dissonance. This state could then have been reduced by a cognitive reorganization to the effect that the stimulus was not really very unpleasant after all.

Another motivational aspect of REST is that the client increasingly produces his own stimuli in order to maintain an appropriate level of overall stimulation. Since he enters the situation with the intention of modifying his maladaptive behavior patterns, one likely way of spending the time is to engage in thought, imagination, and planning related to the central problem. This kind of cognitive/affective rehearsal may be a factor in the cessation or modification of the habit pattern, another possibility that has not been empirically explored.

Arousal and Environmental Factors

In the REST chamber there are no recurrent, schedule-controlled behavior patterns. This fact is relevant because the activity levels of both human and infrahuman subjects have been found to increase during the intervals between schedule-controlled responses (Wallace and Singer, 1976a). When habitual smokers are engaging in schedule-controlled behaviors, and cigarettes are present, the rate of smoking between the required responses increases, presumably as one specific outlet of the general increase in excitability that leads to higher levels of movement in general (Wallace and Singer, 1976b). A similar mechanism may operate in eating patterns.

An environmental factor that probably helps to reduce the stress of not smoking and unexciting food is the removal of cues that normally initiate consummatory behavior (Epstein and Collins, 1977). External evokers of either positive or negative affect are minimized, and conditioned stimuli (e.g., a cup of coffee, the table set for a meal) are absent. Even the most naturally related stimuli, the sight and smell of cigarettes and of food, are removed. But there is a problem with this explanation, as there is with the argument that smoking serves the function of reducing involvement with the external situation (Clark, 1977). If this were true, it would explain why REST serves as an acceptable substitute, so that cigarettes are not craved during the session. However, neither of these theories accounts for the long-range effects of the treatment.

Another explanation is related to the neuropsychological concepts mentioned earlier. Basically, it is the cognitive counterpart of returning behavioral control from the brainstem to the cortex—that is, from habitual and almost automatic patterns to voluntary actions. In this view, REST functions as a rapid deconditioning procedure which puts the client back to where he was when he first started smoking or overeating. He then has the choice whether he wants to re-initiate the pattern. Actually, the neurophysiological part of this explanation is not a crucial component. "De-automatization," the process of refocusing attention on routine behaviors and thoughts, is a valid concept regardless of the specific brain functions that underlie it (see p. 386; Gill and Brenman, 1961; Hartmann, 1939/1958). This kind of change has been cited in some explanations of altered states of consciousness (Deikman, 1966) and of the effects of REST (Taylor, 1973).

While there are no direct data bearing on this theory as it relates to our work, it is compatible with some of the anecdotal reports of our subjects. Many of them—in fact, most—reported that the great craving for a cigarette when none was available had disappeared in and after REST, and did not come back. The driven quality of their smoking had disappeared. Even those who later went back to smoking in order to manage anxiety or some other negative affect usually reported that they must now think and deliberately proceed to light a cigarette. They do not crave the smoke, nor do they find themselves holding a cigarette in their hand without having been aware of taking it out as had been the case prior to their REST experience.

Another part of the treatment that is likely to be significant is the enforced abstinence from cigarettes (and from favored foods) during the REST session. Most of our subjects, particularly those who are addicted smokers, find even a short period without smoking to be extremely unpleasant; yet they are able to tolerate 24 hours of such deprivation while in the chamber, and apparently experience little if any suffering. Why this happens, and why the low level of distress persists after the session, we do not know.

Regardless of the explanation, the phenomenon should not be ignored. If withdrawal symptoms are a major cause of relapse (Shiffman and Jarvik, 1978), the fact that they are inhibited by REST may be an important therapeutic factor. One way to test how important it is might be to let the subjects smoke in the stimulus-restricted environment. However, this is neither practical nor safe, since smoking would provide stimulation that would interfere with REST and pose a ventilation and fire hazard as well. Conversely, nonconfined subjects could be kept in an environment where cigarettes are not available. Since many of our participants had previously gone for a day or more without cigarettes in their normal circumstances, without feeling either a reduction in stress or achieving a subsequent change of their smoking patterns, it is not likely that this would have an effect equivalent to the one found among restricted subjects. We do have some analogous data. Preliminary findings in two projects indicate that favored foods become less liked after having served as part of the subject's diet during a 24-hour REST session. The change persists for at least several weeks afterward.

It has also been proposed that high levels of arousal may contribute to the efficacy of therapy. Among the procedures that lead to such levels are sensory overload, sleep deprivation, the administration of appropriate drugs, and perhaps REST. Excessive stimulation is a salient component of many currently popular group methods, although it is not always clearly conceptualized as such by the practitioners involved. So far, no systematic attempt has been made to assess its importance in the total procedure and outcome.

There is some information about the effect of sleeplessness, which has also been incorporated in some marathon techniques. Svendsen (1976) used one night of sleep deprivation, either on one or on several occasions, with 77 manic-depressive psychotics. Participants included both out-patients and institutionalized patients. Lasting improvements were re-ported in 29% of the cases, and temporary improvements in 38%. The major effect seemed to be the reduction of suicidal impulses, depressed moods, sleeping difficulties, and motor inhibition. Treatments given twice a week for a maximum of six sessions were the most effective. There was no difference in improvement as a function of previous and concurrent chemotherapy, previous episodes of depression, or uni- versus bipolarity of the symptoms. No side effects, EEG changes, or symptom substitu-tions were found. Vogel, Thompson, Thurmond and Rivers (1973) de-prived their patients only of REM sleep. Again, positive results were reported.

Aside from some of the almost mystical treatment that REM sleep has received, much of which is unsupported by reliable evidence, sleep and REM sleep deprivation may be viewed as forms of stimulus overload and excessive arousal. Experimental sleep deprivation has been found to be unpleasant and stressful, leading to deteriorated task performance on a variety of measures even when the subject spends the entire sleepless period in bedrest. Partial sleep deprivation, where the subject is permitted to get only a portion of the sleep he needs or where the schedule of sleeping is disrupted, also leads to cognitive deterioration and to de-creases in reported well-being, as well as to irritability and regression. Prevention of REM sleep is less generally disruptive, either on task per-formance or on subjective emotional state (for a review, see Naitoh, in press). Deprivation and interruption of sleep have also been widely used as torture techniques to break down the resistance of prisoners.

One can see why arousal-increasing treatments could be beneficial for patients who chronically suffer from insufficient arousal levels. Conversely, individuals whose problem is based on chronically high arousal would probably be further damaged by environmentally-dictated increments. One intriguing paradox is that there seems to be no agreement on whether schizophrenia is associated with excessively low levels of input and activation (Brawley and Pos, 1967) or with excessively high levels (Mednick, 1958). The evidence seems to indicate that there is in fact no one answer to this question. While information processing characteristics of schizophrenic patients are certainly different from those of the normal population, the direction of the deviation is not consistent among people exhibiting the symptoms of schizophrenia (see Chapman and Chapman, 1973).

It is also possible to manipulate arousal more directly, by administering chemical substances that activate or deactivate the biological system. As in the case of environmental modifications, the therapist does not necessarily recognize that the effect of the drug is mediated by changes in arousal level. However, there has been one very interesting series of studies where this point has been explicitly emphasized. Hoehn-Saric and his co-workers (Hoehn-Saric, Frank, and Gurland, 1968; Hoehn-Saric, Liberman, Imber, Stone, Frank, and Ribich, 1974; Hoehn-Saric, Liberman, Imber, Stone, Pande, and Frank, 1972) have argued that psychotherapy is a process of persuasion, and that increases in arousal make the recipient more susceptible to persuasive attempts. Accordingly, they produced higher arousal in neurotic patients by using drugs, and—as they had expected—found an increase in the acceptance of persuasive therapeutic communications related to the patients' adjustment problems.

Whether or not REST can be called an arousal-increasing manipulation is a controversial issue (for example, cf. Zuckerman, 1969c and Suedfeld, 1969c), but there is no doubt that it shares at least some effects with such treatments. If one takes this point of view, one should consider arousal induction, possibly by REST (a demonstratedly effective facilitator of attitude change), as a potential component of persuasive psychotherapy. Thus, it could be combined with group methods (see Beutler, Jobe, and Elkins, 1974; Rotter, 1968; Samler, 1969). One might reasonably argue that effects similar to those brought about in the Hoehn-Saric studies can be among those induced by REST.

Buchsbaum (1976), basing his work on the theory of sensory augmentation and reduction (Petrie, 1979), has spoken of a "sensoristat" that controls the degree to which the brain acts either to enhance or to diminish the intensity of incoming stimulation. In clinical application, he has shown that manic-depressive cycles are related to augmentation, as the individual in the manic phase seeks out and generates high levels of stimulation. The argument is that the sensoristat is working incorrectly, so that it continues to augment inputs even when there is an excessively high level. Appropriate treatment would seem to be a reduction of the augmentation response, as by drugs; an alternative would be to reduce the actual external level of stimuli, as by REST. Some schizophrenics are also augmenters, and one may hypothesize that their case is analogous to the manic-depressives mentioned above, except that they do not even need to increase the environmental load since they are already taking it in at a level far above that of the average individual. This may explain why REST seems to be pleasant and beneficial for schizophrenic patients. One interesting sidelight is that Buchsbaum identifies these individuals as the least likely to recover quickly, while other schizophrenics who are reducers have a better prognosis. One advantage of this approach is that it spans the psychological and neurological levels: augmentation and reduction can be measured by evoked potentials, and its basis may lie in the biochemical environment of the brain (particularly the level of endorphins).

Wickram (1970) has argued that the usefulness of sensory restriction in therapy lies in its ability to arouse anxiety. According to him, the most effective contributor to the success of any psychotherapeutic technique is increased persuasibility, and this in turn is a function of some level of anxiety. This hypothesis is quite compatible with others that relate motivational arousal and persuasibility to therapeutic success. What makes it really interesting is the demonstration of learning on the part of the author. In this early paper, he emphasized the anxiety-inducing nature of REST; after reading the literature that appeared during the next several years, he modified his position, ascribing the usefulness of REST to its relaxation-like effects (Wickramasekera, 1977a). I can only express my regret that other writers on this topic were not as diligent in keeping up with the literature, nor as open-minded in incorporating new findings into their theoretical proposition.

Other Explanations

It is possible that REST reduces or eliminates some of the adverse physiological effects of cigarette deprivation, or conversely, compensates for the desired effects of cigarettes, so that deprivation is less unpleasant than is usually the case. We know, for example, that smoking increases arousal as measured by a variety of psychophysiological indices (Knott and Venables, 1977; Myrsten, Elgerot, and Edgren, 1977). The first of these papers hypothesizes that smokers become dependent on cigarettes because their baseline arousal level is too low, and smoking helps to raise it (see also Schubert, 1965). If REST either serves the same function, or somehow makes low cortical arousal less aversive, the absence of stress among even addicted smokers in REST becomes understandable. It has also been proposed that smoking reduces distraction by stimuli that are extraneous to problems and activities at hand (Friedman, Horvath, and Meares, 1974), another problem that would not arise during REST, thus presumably reducing the need for cigarettes. But there is still the mystery of why the effects persist after the end of the session.

Another argument is that REST provides a placebo, in that participants feel that they have gone through an elaborate and demanding procedure, believe in its efficacy for that reason, and change their behavior accordingly. One aspect of this change would be the reduction of cognitive dissonance that might result from having participated and failed to change. There are several problems with this explanation which lead me to discount it. To begin with, many of the subjects who stopped smoking or reduced their rates substantially after REST had previously participated, without success, in one or more smoking cessation programs. Most of these were at least as demanding as ours in time, effort, and money. Second, the description of the REST treatment to our participants has always emphasized that the technique is experimental, and that we do not know whether or not it will work. It is difficult to reconcile this with the so-called placebo effect. Third, in one study (Suedfeld et al., 1972), the subjects did not even know that the experiment was concerned with smoking until the end of their REST session, and had not originally volunteered in order to quit smoking. Last, it appears that a message-only group (Suedfeld and Ikard, 1974) felt that they had actually undergone treatment. At least, they did not afterward seek other forms of help to any greater extent than the confined subjects. In spite of this, their rate of change was significantly lower than those of REST participants. Incidentally, those members of the untreated control group in the same study who took our advice to try other forms of clinical intervention reported a mean smoking rate reduction of 14.1% after such assistance. This change was not significantly different from the average for all nonconfined subjects. Of course, it may still be argued the REST is a particularly dramatic treatment. So far, no appropriate dramatic controls have been used to test the importance of this feature.

Sarbin and his co-workers (Sarbin and Adler, 1970; Sarbin and Nucci, 1973) suggested a treatment for smoking (which would presumably be relevant to other problems as well) based on role theory. In this proposal, the central argument is that the individual must go through a ritual process in which his old self as a smoker is replaced by a new self in which smoking has no place. Thus, rather than being a cured smoker or temporarily arrested smoker, the patient becomes a nonsmoker. Among other procedures, this transformation would include a group of comrades spending 2 weeks together undergoing various rituals. The isolation of the group from the outside world is tangentially related to our concerns. More relevant is the fact that REST serves as some sort of rite of passage, less dramatic, prolonged, and ritualistic than that proposed, but nevertheless with some shared features. Among these is the feeling of a strange and difficult situation successfully surmounted and the providing of an experience that can serve as the point of clear demarcation between the previous and the new selves. A very interesting discussion of this approach to psychotherapy and to other types of personality change is presented by Boyanowsky (1977; see also Chapter 6).

Last, we may consider the general implications of "refocusing" as a consequence of REST. Do people find a new ability to determine and control their own behaviors? Introspective reports have frequently indicated that they do, but there is no easy way to test the hypothesis objectively. The finding that REST led to increases in field independence among alcoholics (Jacobson, 1971) is consonant, though. It would be interesting to see whether changes occur on related personality measures such as tests of internal-external locus of control and origin-pawn self-perceptions (deCharms, 1968). It may be that we have a procedure that increases self-efficacy (Bandura, 1977). REST may enable the participant to attain a more positive attitude toward his ability to initiate successful coping behavior, an expectation that may well be the precursor of actual success (see, e.g., Corn, 1978).

Needed: Some Theoretical Integrations

To tie some of these levels of explanation together, we may hypothesize that the effect of REST on the brainstem changes the relationship between stimuli and responses so that the individual now more closely monitors his behavior, thus increasing his volitional control over it. At a cognitive level, the recognition that the automatic and driven quality of the behavior has diminished is related to more complex decision–making about the initiation of renewed habits, and to a greater awareness and consideration of the information and techniques making it possible not to return to the previous habit pattern. At the affective level, this realization is connected with an increased feeling of mastery and competence and a diminution of the feelings of helpless craving. Such effects as stimulus hunger and undisturbed concentration, and a number of environmental aspects of REST, may also contribute in varying degrees. The particular role of each of these factors varies with the personality of the client, the nature of the problem being addressed, and the details of the treatment procedure.

It is sad that the decline in the volume of REST research generally coincided with the development of theoretical and methodological innovations that could be very important to the area. Among these are recent work on imagery, both in basic research and in therapy, emphasizing the importance of the stream of affect and cognition; the much more detailed understanding of the brain that came about with single-neuron recording, evoked potentials, and increasingly accurate localization of functions; findings concerning perceived control versus helplessness as factors in adjusting to the environment; attribution theory and its explanations of how individuals present and explain to themselves the situation in which they are and the behavior in which they engage; better theoretical explications of various levels of memory, attention, and information processing; and a host of techniques and ideas related to behavioral and cognitive change. All of these came too late to be incorporated into the better understanding and wider utilization of the effects of REST. It is to be hoped that these words are too final and too pessimistic. New researchers may take advantage of these theories and techniques to improve the work on REST, while conversely they or others may increasingly use REST to explore interesting variables related to the substantive questions raised above.

THE DEMONOLOGY OF REST

This appears to be the ideal place to look at some of the criticisms of REST, both in experimental research and in clinical application. Many of these criticisms are in fact based on a lack of attention to any of the data published after the first few years of sensory deprivation research, and in some cases on a willful ignoring of such data. Unfortunately, these distortions have seriously affected the popular view of sensory restriction and have hampered the progress of research and application in this area.

Stimulus Reduction in Fiction

Solitude and restricted stimulation have played important parts in many fictional works. With a few exceptions like *Robinson Crusoe*, such novels and stories have focused on prisoners in solitary confinement (e.g., *The Count of Monte Cristo, A Tale of Two Cities*, "The Pit and the Pendulum"). Until the past few years, most authors emphasized the suffering of the victim. But the reactions that they described were essentially the same as one would expect in any stressful situation. The specific nature of the environmental restriction seemed to produce no idiosyncratic symptoms.

In more modern fictional treatments of stimulus reduction we find several distinct lines of thought. The earliest, and even now by far the most frequent, has been dominant in books of adventure and mystery: stimulus reduction as torture and brainwashing (e.g., Deighton, 1962; Duncan, 1975; Hayes, 1973; Keating, 1966; Kennaway, 1963; West, 1974; see Smith, 1975). Some science fiction writers have fallen into the same mode (e.g., Anderson, 1977). The sources of this approach are easy to identify. They lie in the widely disseminated semi-popular writings of the 1950s. For the most part, novelists and scriptwriters have completely distorted the effects of "sensory deprivation." It is not at all unusual for fictional secret agents who are supposedly seasoned, trained, and highly competent to go completely berserk, become disoriented, and give up all resistance after even a few hours of REST. Anyone familiar with the actual research literature might suggest to these authors that their espionage agencies would do better hiring randomly selected college sophomores, who have shown much greater ability to tolerate stimulus reduction.

Only a few novelists have treated stimulus reduction and confinement in a less alarmist fashion. A treatment by William Golding (1959) is excellent in communicating the detailed and prolonged reverie and vivid recall reported by some individuals who have undergone prolonged isolation and sensory restriction. His fictional prisoner, waiting in a dark isolation cell and fearing torture, relives his life in great detail and achieves deep insights. In a recent book (Langton, 1978), darkness, restricted movement, and social isolation do not seem to faze the victim at all. He is much more worried by, and takes realistic steps to counter, a lack of food and water and the threat that his enemy might come to finish him off. In view of the fact that he is in this environment for something over 6 weeks, such an omission of psychological effects seems to be on the sanguine side. A better approach was taken in *Risk,* a novel by the outstanding mystery writer Dick Francis (1977). The hero of this book undergoes several periods of isolation and greatly reduced stimulation. His reactions reflect fear and stress, and competence in coping with both. He engages in physical and mental exercises, not unlike those actually reported both by long-term solitary prisoners and by a few experimental subjects; and in the final analysis, his behavior is effective.

A recent novel by Chayefsky (1978) is the first in which a REST researcher is actually the hero. For him, experiments with water immersion constitute the first step in deep studies of altered states of consciousness. Eventually, after he has experienced various shamanistic procedures, he comes to combine the tank with a mysterious and mystical drug. The results are quite dramatic. He regresses, not only psychologically but also physically, to become a member of the species from which humanity had originally descended. At the last, he appears as pure energy. Fortunately, his wife loves him and—redeemed by the love of a good woman—he leaves us in the end with a mixed but generally optimistic prognosis.

More relevant although less dramatic is the presentation by Chaim Potok (1969). One of Potok's heroes is a clinical psychologist who, faced with the deteriorating state of a schizophrenic adolescent, uses profound REST over a long period to achieve contact with the patient. Potok even cites some of the relevant literature, and obviously understands its implications. At one point, a character says: "a state of deprivation not only brings on regressive disorganization but also promotes a constructive reorganization of deeper resources within a person. . . . The regression it induces is utilized by the person in the service of ego development" (p. 285). The treatment is effective, and the patient begins to communicate with those around him. The rationale is not unrelated to those of real researchers using REST in such situations. The long period of reduced stimulation and human contact increases stimulus hunger and social hunger to the point where the boy drops some of his well-learned defenses and becomes amenable to more standard forms of psychotherapy. The pain and anguish of the boy's relatives, the uncertainty and involvement of the therapist, are all well portrayed. Unfortunately, the reactions of the patient are presented only at second hand. Given what we know of the actual behavior of autistic children under REST conditions (Schechter et al., 1969), his actual suffering as inferable by the reader is probably exaggerated.

One last comment has to be made about the contributions of fiction to the REST literature. One book stands alone in providing a way of coping with the environment that, while I am sure it is not too uncommon among subjects, has never been systematically explored. Pent up in solitary confinement by an implacable enemy, the picaresque Harry Flashman (Fraser, 1975) thinks of how other people have dealt with such situations: singing, reciting poetry, or working out mathematical formulae. Being neither artistically nor intellectually inclined, he does not consider these to be very useful. "So instead I compiled a mental list of all the women I'd had in my life . . . and to my astonishment there were four hundred and seventy-eight of them, which seemed rather a lot, especially since I wasn't counting return engagements. It's astonishing, really, when you think how much time it must have taken up" (p. 298). Flashman is, of course, a coward, a cheat, and an unrepentant sexist; but he does manage to fill in the empty time of solitary confinement.

Distortions of REST in the Professional Literature

In the professional literature, criticisms of "sensory deprivation" procedures are frequently related to attacks on the use of solitary confinement. These discussions, which tend to be very fervent, are usually based on political and/or humanitarian grounds. To support their points of view, the critics are usually not content with putting the argument in terms of its real basis. Rather, they attempt to convince the public that segregation of prisoners can be empirically demonstrated to be cruel (that is, to have dramatic negative effects on all or most individuals). Many of these attacks carry a tone of fervent morality, frequently ignoring arguments on the other side (Lucas, 1976) or broadly condemning as torture any procedure that involves isolation (e.g., Komitee gegen Folter, 1974). In the absence of evidence as to the general effects of solitary confinement these authors equate it with REST, which is at most only tangentially relevant. Citations of the REST literature in this context tend to be very selective, with major emphasis on the early findings of stress and anxiety responses. Little or no attention is paid to more recent work, using improved procedures, which demonstrates some of the beneficial effects of stimulus reduction.

In view of the gross differences between prison units and experimental or clinical REST situations, it is really futile to guess about the extent to which data from one are generalizable to the other. The therapeutic benefits of REST have been obtained in motivated and cooperative volunteers by professionals who are perceived as trying to help, and who use conditions of brief but drastic sensory reduction. This situation can obviously not be used to predict the reactions of convicts who are placed by people whom they perceive as antagonists, and against their own will, into an environment that is strikingly more varied and stimulating than that of the REST chamber, even if it is less so than the normal world. The cognitive, perceptual, affective, and other phenomena obtained under conditions of experimental stimulus reduction likewise cannot be assumed to occur in the average segregation unit. A more detailed discussion of these points is presented in Chapter 3.

Some Misleading Arguments. The use of solitude as a component in techniques of indoctrination and interrogation has given rise to much criticism. This is partly due to wide publicity given to the alleged use of stimulus reduction in situations of intensive interrogation and indoctrination, and partly to the historical fact that one of the main concerns of the first sensory deprivation research group at McGill University was "dismay at the kind of 'confessions' being produced at the Russian Communist trials" (Hebb, 1961, p. 6).

Some critics carry the attack to a logical absurdity. From the unproven assumption that solitary confinement is generally harmful, they conclude that REST should not be used in research or therapy. After discussing the treatment of suspected terrorists in Northern Ireland, Shallice (1972a) claims that sensory deprivation may be "an Orwellian use of psychology" and that the continued publication of REST research is dangerous. Another author buttressed her attack on REST research with the statement "that much of the vast and rapidly increasing literature on sensory deprivation experiments emanate [sic] from studies done in the U.S. and funded by military contracts" (Fields, 1976b, p. 54). This remark contrasts amusingly with her condemnation of guilt by association on the first page of the same paper. Even less logical is the argument that REST should not be used in a therapeutic setting because it can also be abused as a torture (Fields, 1976c).

Some segments of the popular press have also taken up the cry. One author writing in a Canadian magazine (Swan, 1974) was apparently determined to find her country guilty of being involved in torture, even though it did not appear on the Amnesty International list of such nations. To accomplish this, she mentioned John Zubek's research, mostly concerned with the perceptual effects of REST, as though it were somehow relevant. This article, like the propaganda barrage issued in Germany against the use of solitary confinement with the Baader-Meinhof gang, was seized upon by ideologues and led to threats, harassment, and personal derogation of the researchers.

Even aside from misconceptions and sometimes seemingly deliberate distortions, such writings reveal an elitist and antiscientific philosophy. This point of view is summed up in the argument that because knowledge that is useful may also be misused, it should be suppressed or withheld. We are then to accept that there is some particularly wise individual (i.e., the person advancing the argument) who is capable of balancing the possible benefits against the possible drawbacks and making an appropriate decision for the general good.

Politics and Polemics. It should also be noted that the critics seriously distort the sensory deprivation literature itself. McGuffin (1974) criticizes "sensory deprivation torture"—and includes under that label some 20 techniques that obviously involve stimulus overload or general disorientation as well as 2 that reduce stimulation level. McGuffin is not a behavioral scientists, and may perhaps be excused. But Shallice is not only a professional psychologist; he has evidently read the research, and there-

fore can hardly claim ignorance. Yet, he equates reported visual sensations with hallucinations (1972a, p. 294). He ignores the fact that the
sources he cites make the distinction very clear indeed, and have shown
that RVSs during restricted stimulation do not have the pathological implications of the term "hallucination." Charitably, we may call this a
difference in interpretation. But there is also gross distortion. In discussing the work of the Azima group (p. 396), Shallice mentions only the
psychotic episodes suffered by some neurotic patients undergoing
"perceptual deprivation" in a therapeutic program. Inexplicably and
inexcusably for a scientific reviewer, he never alludes to the majority of
subjects, who benefited from the REST treatment.

Shallice, Fields, McGuffin, and others appear to think that any research
conducted in the Western world, particularly if it is funded by Western
military agencies, is suspect. McGuffin expresses suspicions regarding
any research program that studies sensory deprivation "at various col-
leges, institutes and universities [funded] by large corporations, 'chari-
table societies' and 'private benefactors' etc. all part of a sinister and at
times as in the case of Vietnam, genocidal, military-industrial complex"
(p. 39). One wonders what source of research funds McGuffin would find
acceptable. The political basis of some criticisms is also revealed in the
closing passages of the article by Shallice, where he says: "The objective
long-term interests of the scientific community are in the rationally
planned, socially conscious application of science, not the way it is used
by capitalism" (1972a, p. 402).

It must be pointed out, on the other hand, that there are more balanced
views of the relationship between REST and solitary confinement. These
have frequently been expressed by individuals and groups closely connected with the fight against torture. Two Chilean refugees, psychologists
who have examined political prisoners in that country, presented a very
moving paper on torture at the 1976 International Congress of Psychology
(Vasquez and Resczczynsky, 1976). But when asked about REST, they
specifically denied any desire to interfere with scientific research in the
field (personal communication, July 22, 1976). A similar attitude was expressed by the International Secretariat of Amnesty International (Mar-
guerite Garling, personal communication, May 21, 1974).

The Case of Ulster.   That internees in Northern Ireland were deliberately
mistreated cannot be disputed. Nor can the fact that some of them suffered serious adverse consequences as a result, although the frequency
and the extent of disability have not been established. However, as Chapter 3 indicates, the evidence clearly shows that excessive rather than
inadequate stimulation was the method primarily used to "soften up" the

suspects. Although the difference between sensory reduction and sensory flooding seems to have escaped Shallice, other analysts of the same situation have pointed out the error (e.g., Boyanowsky, 1977).

Two interesting items serve to highlight the inappropriateness of indicting REST research. Both of these are drawn from a book by Rona M. Fields (1976a). In one passage, Fields claims that 60% of the former internees whom she tested evidenced some brain damage. But, in spite of her previous accusations about "sensory deprivation" being a crucial factor, she says: "This would also, of course, be as much a direct product of beatings on and around the head as it could be a product of the sensory deprivation and hooding treatments. There is absolutely no way to differentiate" (p. 84). Most people, unlike Fields, can differentiate pretty well between a period of darkness and silence and the experience of being beaten on the head. Furthermore, most objective evaluators would probably feel that "beatings on and around the head" are much more likely to produce brain damage than is sensory deprivation (even had sensory deprivation been used with these prisoners). According to Fields, the beatings were coupled with hooding which supposedly decreased the supply of oxygen to the brain and the CNS, a second plausible explanation of brain damage that does not involve the effects of sensory reduction. A footnote on the same page of Fields's book admits: "After I had conducted interviews with and tests on six of these cases, several important facts emerged. Strictly speaking, these were not sensory-deprivation cases, since they were continually subjected to noise treatment. . . . The treatment included sounds of screaming, which were variously interpreted by the subjects as their friends' distress, and which intensified their own anxieties and forebodings."

One might expect that, in view of these passages in her own book, Fields would be careful to use the term "sensory deprivation" only where it is truly appropriate, and even more to make the distinction between techniques such as hooding and the experimental or therapeutic REST procedure. If one did expect that, one would be disappointed.

Incidentally, since hooding is probably the only component of the Ulster technique that could even remotely be connected with sensory deprivation, it should be noted that Fields mentions only 14 prisoners who in fact went through this experience. This represents less than 10% of the number of detainees whom Fields has studied through psychological tests and clinical interviews, and well under 1% of the total number of internees in Northern Ireland. Given Fields's finding that a majority of her sample was suffering from long-term physical and/or psychological damage, one might again wonder about the justification for the claim that "sensory deprivation torture" was a significant factor in the results.

Those readers who are still worried may be somewhat reassured by the fact that the most recent, knowledgeable, and comprehensive book on behavior control (London, 1977) does not even bother to list "sensory deprivation" (or any variant of that term) in its index, which otherwise covers the widely used techniques in this area from drugs and electricity on the one hand to hypnosis, propaganda, and conditioning on the other.

Ironically, there has also been another interpretation of the Ulster techniques (Watson, 1977). The author of this analysis, while giving the usual nod in the direction of sensory deprivation experiments and Western investigations into techniques of Communist brainwashing, goes on to argue that the British "hybrid" procedure was more efficient than either of those. Part of this superiority was the outcome of using methods described in the well-known Stanford prison "simulation" (Haney, Banks, and Zimbardo, 1973). A reading of the literature that describes the Ulster and the Stanford procedures certainly supports the argument that there are great similarities between them, much greater than those between the Ulster conditions and experimental REST procedures. The irony is that the principal investigator in the Stanford work is a dedicated advocate of prison reform, who has used his simulation as the basis for numerous instances of intervention on behalf of prisoners (see Zimbardo, 1975).

What should the critics do now? Should they attack the Stanford demonstration because it is so similar to actual torture and may in fact have served as a model? Or should they focus instead on the beneficial effects that may result from the social advocacy that it has also supported? Of course, this dilemma is very similar to that related to the attacks on REST: that is, should benefits be suppressed because of possible, or even actual, abuses? The reasonable solution, recognizing that the technique itself is neutral and that one can defend its positive contributions while opposing its debasement for evil purposes, so far seems to be beyond the scope of some social scientists.

A Methodological Note.   One issue of which too little has been made in the past is the difference between reduced and monotonous stimulation. The data are fairly clear that stimulus reduction (e.g., darkness and silence) is less stressful, less disruptive, and therapeutically more effective than is monotonous stimulation (e.g., constant diffuse light and white noise). This difference is more striking in studies with human subjects than with infrahuman animals (compare Chapters 2 and 10 with Chapter 5). In the present context, the former is obviously the more important.

One issue is whether in fact monotonous stimulation is a condition that should be categorized with stimulus reduction. That it has been so categorized is in some sense a historical accident: since the original McGill research employed homogeneous light and noise, and since that particular program became the forerunner of "sensory deprivation," the identity was assumed as axiomatic by most people. In some ways, the two are certainly similar. Many of the features are common in that the subject is alone, confined to a bed in a small room, with the stimulus load controlled as the main independent variable, and so on. Furthermore, and significantly from the point of view of motivational theories, the information load in both cases is greatly reduced.

On the other hand, the difference in sensory input level may be a crucial issue. It is difficult to ascertain whether monotonous stimulation experiments reduce, leave unchanged, or actually increase the auditory input, since under normal conditions people are usually not exposed to constant noise for long periods of time. Visual input may be reduced if the illumination level in the room is normal and is diminished by the goggles; on the other hand, if the goggles merely eliminate patterned vision without decreasing illumination level, or if the ambient lighting is brighter than usual, the net intensity may be at least as high as or even higher than normal.

Conceiving of at least a substantial portion of monotonous stimulation experiments as being studies of overload rather than underload helps to explain some of the differences in the data. We know from the few systematic studies on excessive stimulation that it has more adverse effects on cognitive and other functions than traditional stimulus reduction manipulations; that subjects rate it as more unpleasant and are more eager to terminate it; and that it is distracting and has the effect of impairing introspection and processes of decision-making. The first two of these comparisons result in conclusions identical to those obtained from comparing sensory reduction and sensory monotony and the third would explain why the latter condition fails to have therapeutic utility. As a last point, such a reclassification would also make more sense when one turns to the literature on intensive indoctrination and interrogation. It is quite clear that the vast majority of such procedures involves intense stimulation rather than abnormally low stimulation, reductions being mostly useful to magnify "emergence trauma" (see Chapter 4) when the prisoner is removed and suddenly immersed in stimulus bombardment. In fact, some of the components of monotonous experimental environments are replicated, as in the white noise that characterized some of the Ulster procedures.

The classification of the monotonous stimulus condition as a sensory overload rather than a sensory reduction method is tentative, and its validity must be tested with actual measurements of stimulus load in the various situations. This is particularly true in that the change would mean a major break with tradition in this research area, seeing that the very first techniques used with human subjects in fact used monotony. It also would identify a major difference between the human and infrahuman research findings, a point that may not be too unpalatable in view of the copious evidence that cognitive mediation is very important in the human response to environmental manipulation. However, if data justify this reclassification, the conceptual and empirical confusion that now exists in some areas would be reduced, and the inappropriate analogies that some people have drawn between REST and the mistreatment of prisoners might be even more clearly invalidated.

SOME ANSWERS TO THE CRITICS

As we have seen previously, REST has been used by only a relatively small proportion of behavioral scientists and mental health practitioners. For the researcher or therapist who wants to start working with REST, it is well to be prepared for negative attitudes. Some of the reasons for this lack of popularity are mentioned in Chapter 1. However, two of the major sources of criticism are worth dealing with in some detail. Both have been widely discussed and have at least some face validity.

The first criticism is that REST is aversive, stressful, and perhaps even dangerous to the participant. This argument is usually based on some acquaintance with the highly publicized early results of negative affects and bizarre reactions. If the charge were true, one would obviously want to ensure that the possible benefits of any particular application of REST would outweigh its dangers. The crucial problem here, of course, is to establish just how realistic these fears are. The second source of criticism is a more clearly ethical one, and stems primarily from the fact that solitary confinement and other stimulus-reducing procedures have been cited as parts of torture techniques in various countries. These reports have led some critics to equate REST research and even therapy with torture, a position that can be countered on both empirical and logical grounds.

How Stressful is REST?

The answer to this question has important implications for such research issues as the role of personality differences in response to restricted stimulation, the motivational consequences of the treatment, and so on. Even more important, the likelihood that REST will be adopted for widespread therapeutic use, and the likelihood that such adoptions will be approved by professional bodies and accepted by the public depend to a significant extent on how it will be answered. The widely disseminated and wholly fallacious idea that restricted stimulation is extremely stressful for all participants has greatly aided the efforts of those propagandists who have argued against the use of the technique. It is time for a more objective look at the evidence.

Some Research Problems.   There can of course be no doubt that restricted stimulation is unpleasant for some people, nor that for a variety of cultural reasons even the thought of a prolonged period in this kind of environment may seem quite threatening. The early sensory deprivation researchers tended to emphasize the degree to which their subjects showed symptoms of stress on such indicators as early voluntary termination, rating scales, and verbal statements. The major difficulty in interpreting these reports is that many of them naively disregarded one or more crucial issues. Among these neglected variables are the effects of experimental procedures other than stimulus reduction itself, subject expectancy, and appropriate baseline or control data with which the consequences of REST could be compared (see Chapter 2 for a detailed discussion of these issues).

It was once standard practice for sensory deprivation researchers to require subjects to sign a legal form promising not to hold the institution responsible for physical or mental damage suffered during the course of the experiment. Subjects were prevented from familiarizing themselves with the experimental environment and apparatus under relatively normal conditions before the beginning of the actual experimental session. Laboratories prominently featured a "panic button"—so identified—for the subject's use if he desired to terminate the session. It is quite certain that such procedures significantly raised the subject's feeling of disorientation, strangeness, and threat—and thus his level of stress and anxiety—even before REST began. The logical outcome was an unmeasured but possibly dramatic increase in the occurrence of negative reactions (cf. Orne and Scheibe, 1964; Suedfeld, 1975).

To illustrate the issue of inadequate comparison data, we may cite a report by Smith and Lewty (1959). This paper was published during the earliest stage of REST research. The authors noted that subjects experienced anxiety and "panic" attacks, depression, tension, agitation, and nightmares. Some of these were experienced by all or most subjects, others primarily by those who quit the session relatively early, and still others by only a few subjects. This sounds fairly formidable. However, there was no attempt to establish whether under experimental conditions these phenomena were experienced by a higher proportion of individuals, were more intense, and/or were found more frequently, than they are in the normal environment. In this regard, it should be noted that for a considerable proportion of the history of sensory restriction research, many experimenters failed to include adequate control or baseline comparisons. Although it is true that the problem of identifying baselines is sometimes a difficult one (see Rossi, 1969), it is impossible to evaluate the actual meaning of the findings in the absence of such baselines. This is especially important in view of several later findings that phenomena once considered to be specifically related to restricted environments are actually quite frequently found under normal circumstances.

The role of expectancy in the response to REST is a controversial topic. Some authors feel that expectancy effects are not particularly important (e.g., Zuckerman, 1969a, b), while others argue that they are very important indeed (e.g., Jackson and Pollard, 1962). It is quite likely that the actual impact of different expectations is a function of the dependent variable being considered. It may be, for example, that relatively discrete and objectively measurable processes, such as perceptual and cognitive performance, are relatively stable regardless of set. More general and subjective aspects of the response may be comparatively vulnerable. Reports of anxiety and of unpleasant symptoms would be classified among the latter phenomena, and a number of authors have reported that deliberately induced set does affect reports of this sort (reviewed in Suedfeld, 1969c). In one study (Suedfeld, Landon, Epstein and Pargament, 1971), subjective stress ratings significantly reflected either high- or low-stress expectations inculcated as part of the procedure, but set did not affect performance on a learning task.

Findings Concerning Stress. Keeping in mind these shortcomings in much of the literature, let us look at the findings. Endurance time, one of the most frequently used measures of stressfulness, is—as one might expect—multiply determined, and therefore may not be an adequate index. But the argument that tolerance of confinement is to some extent a measure of stress certainly seems intuitively reasonable. It is also supported at least indirectly by studies showing that duration is significantly associated with such measures as restlessness, stimulation seeking, subjective stress ratings, and negative responses on a variety of paper-and-pencil scales (Myers, 1969).

Some interesting generalities have been found. For example, approximately one-third of the subjects fail to complete the prescribed period in studies between 2 and 14 days in duration. With some exceptions, this figure does not change much as a function of the actual scheduled duration nor of environmental manipulations (see Zubek, 1973; Zuckerman,

1964). The proportion of successful completers in shorter studies has varied widely, as a function of both of the influences mentioned above. Obviously, some of the experiments that last only a few minutes have 100% successful completion rates. But for studies in the 24 to 48 hour range, procedural aspects appear to become very salient. A full orientation to the chamber, coupled with detailed and reassuring instructions, both administered by calm and supportive personnel, seem to have significant impact. In my own laboratory, which emphasizes these details, 90% or more of the subjects usually complete the entire chamber session (Suedfeld, 1975).

A number of studies (see Myers, 1969) have addressed themselves to the more refined measurement of stress in restricted stimulation environments. As a general rule, scales of symptomatology, subjective stress, anxiety, and somatic complaints show a higher incidence of negative feelings on the part of REST than of control subjects. However, it should be pointed out that while these differences may be significant, they are relative. In the vast majority of studies, the experimental subjects do not actually indicate very high levels of stress, anxiety, etc. Responses rarely if ever approach the extreme anchor point of the measures. Most of the time, they tend to be in the range between neutral and slightly anxious or symptomatic. This crucial fact has unfortunately been obscured by the tendency of investigators to report only mean differences (or at best mean scale scores) and levels of statistical significance.

In addition, there have been a large number of studies in which no increase in negative symptoms was found as a function of REST, in which the results were mixed (see e.g., Myers et al., 1966), or in which no difference was seen between experimental and control groups (e.g., Suedfeld, in press). Even the water immersion procedure, originally reputed to be the most stressful of all, can be quite innocuous and even enjoyable given the right ancillary conditions (Hoffman, 1976; Kammerman, 1977b). There can be no question that some subjects react adversely, and even very adversely, to the situation; there are equally well-established data that some find it extremely enjoyable and seek it out repeatedly. As far as the general subject population is concerned, it is now very clear that REST is neither universally nor extremely stressful.

Perhaps an even more frightening possibility, that REST may damage the mental health of subjects, was raised by the once frequent use of terms such as "sensory deprivation psychosis," and was also implied by the legal release forms used by early researchers. This is obviously a crucial point. If the technique is in fact dangerous to a significant proportion of participants, one would find it difficult to justify using it unless the subject himself stood to benefit so much as to outweigh the peril. Because of the widespread fears in this respect, I recently undertook a literature review and a survey to assess the actual findings in regard to serious adverse outcomes (Suedfeld, 1977a).

Published reports had mentioned several instances in which psychiatric patients who underwent REST took a turn for the worse. Most of these individuals were obsessive-compulsive neurotics undergoing anaclitic therapy at Allan Memorial Hospital in Montreal, in the program directed by the late Hassan Azima. There was only a single case of a subject, not previously under psychiatric care, who needed treatment within a short period after completing a REST session (Curtis and Zuckerman, 1968). This man's test scores before the experiment had shown "poor adjustment, hostility, defensiveness, lack of insight, and insecurity in personal relationships" (p. 256); his childhood had been marked by serious physical and verbal hostility within the family, and the use of isolation and confinement as punishments. His current life was characterized by solitude and lack of involvement with other people. Although he did not quit the REST experiment early, he was stressed by the fact that the procedure included being strapped down in a form-fitting cocoon which prevented bodily movement. He developed delusions which lasted for several days, and states of anxiety and depression which lasted for several weeks. All of these symptoms were relieved after treatment. The personality characteristics of this young man were strikingly similar to those of a subject in another experiment, involving confinement in a respirator (Mendelson, Kubzansky, Leiderman, Wexler and Solomon, 1961), who also developed delusions. Among the symptoms common to both men was the conviction that they were being drugged by the researchers. The subject described by Mendelson et al., however, did not need formal therapy to get over his reaction. Besides the parallels in personality, another point may be significant: both of these cases occurred in studies using extreme physical immobilization. No equivalent phenomena have been reported under the more standard REST conditions that characterize the vast majority of studies.

In the survey, which incorporated responses from 19 of the major laboratories active between 1958 and 1974, there were reports of a few subjects who in the opinion of the experimenter required reassurance and support. However, no case of anyone needing clinical intervention was cited by the respondents (see Table 12-1). Thus, there has been only one instance where a subject not already under treatment needed professional help after a REST session. This occurrence was unique among well over 3000 subjects who had participated in the work of the laboratories surveyed. This gives us a rate of less than 3/100ths of 1% for severe psychological aftereffects with normal subjects (Suedfeld, 1977). Clearly, the

Table 12.1. Reports on Adverse Effects of Experimental REST: Survey Results

Laboratory	Years Active	Techniques Used	Duration of Session	Approx. No. of Subjects	Major Subject Population	Serious Adverse Effects	Other Relevant Observations
1	1958–70	Darkness, silence.	Up to 2 wks.	100	Eye operation patients	0	Some instances of "acting out"; exhibitionism, masturbation.
2	1963–74	Darkness, silence.	8–72 hrs.	400	Volunteers	0	Early termination rate 5–10%.
3	1965–69	Darkness, silence.	4 hrs.	150	College students	0	Early termination rate 10%.
4	1956–72	Darkness, silence.	12–48 hrs.	370	Servicemen	0	Some subjects observed overnight after release: no problems.
5	1972–74	Darkness, silence.	6 hrs.	20	Psychiatric patients	0	1 subject required 1/2 hr interview after session.
6	1971–74	Darkness, diffuse noise.	5 hrs.	40	Volunteers	0	
7	1958–69	Darkness, silence.	Up to 2 wks.	500	College students	1	1 other subject required "reassurance."
8	1964–67	Diffuse light, silence.	24–48 hrs.	36	Volunteers	0	
9	1963–70	Darkness, silence; water immersion; diffuse light and noise.	Up to 2 days	75	College students	0	3–4 immersed subjects required conversation, shower, and meal to regain poise.
10	1961–72	Diffuse light and noise.	3–48 hrs.	100	College students	0	Early termination rate 3%.

11	1951–58, 1969–73	Diffuse light and noise.	Up to 1 wk.	45	College students	0	
12	1955–74	Water immersion.	Up to 8 hrs.	300	Volunteers	0	
13	1969–73	Darkness, silence.	Up to 6 hrs.	155	Psychiatric patients	0	Some subjects showed increased symptoms; most decreased.
14	1959–74	Darkness, silence; diffuse light and noise; variations.	Up to 3 wks.	614	College students	0	
15	1963–67	Darkness, silence.	Up to 1 day	75	Volunteers	0	
16	1961–65	Diffuse light and noise.	Up to 2 days	55	College students	0	
17	1958–62	Darkness, silence.	Up to 3 days	55	College students	0	
18	1955–66	Water immersion; diffuse light and noise.	Up to 8 hrs.	100	College students, patients, actors, etc.	1	Severely obsessive-compulsive subject developed paranoid symptoms.
19	1958–63	Diffuse light and noise.	Up to 8 hrs.	162	College students	0	1 subject reported emotional problems a year after participating; no connection with experiment was established.

[1]From P. Suedfeld, Using environmental restriction to initiate long-term behavior change in R. B. Stuart (Ed.), *Behavioral self-management: Strategies, techniques and outcomes.* New York: Brunner/Mazel, 1977. Pp. 230–257.

fear that REST poses an appreciable danger to the mental health of subjects or clients is not supported by the evidence.

The Ethics of REST Research

Let us now turn from the empirical questions to the moral ones. Fields (1976a, page 57) says that the ethics of scientists should be examined from three basic perspectives: the value of the research, which according to her is "often answered by the nature and source of its funding"; whether the research procedure is ethical in terms of such things as the willing participation of the subjects and informed consent; and the dissemination of the information, that is, "Who will use it and for what purpose?" Of these, the first criterion is so nebulous as to be useless, the second is relevant and specific, and the third distorts the nature of scientific communication.

It is proverbially difficult to judge the value of a piece or program of research, with the exception of a relatively few dramatic contributions that transform a science. In fact, even these sometimes are not judged at their true worth at the time that they are first published, Mendel's work on genetics being one famous example. Scientists have found peer judgment to be a useful approximation for evaluative purposes. By this criterion, REST research has clearly been felt to have contributed something worthwhile to psychology and to related fields.

To judge research by the source of its funds is not only to impute guilt by association, but also represents a deliberate ignoring of relevant facts. The norm in recent American science has been for basic researchers to submit proposals to granting agencies, so that in the first instance the program is specifically based on the scientist's own interest. Granting agencies, in turn, have had such a wide variety of concerns as to make the classification of any experiment as virtuous or wicked on the basis of its sponsor fairly ridiculous. As one example, the Stanford prison demonstration (Zimbardo, 1975) was financed by a grant from the Office of Naval Research, an arm of the American military system. That project has generated information and publicity leading to some amelioration of prison conditions and has been followed by further work sponsored by the United States government, conferences financed by the Navy, and so on. One would presume that those who are in favor of making incarceration less rigorous would approve highly of this project, in spite of its "tainted" money. The Office of Naval Research, of course, has also sponsored work on conflict resolution, on the maximization of efficient decision-making under stressful conditions, and on the improvement of work environments, among a whole host of other projects performed during the past several decades. One wonders if either Fields or her allies would really argue that the Zimbardo study and the hundreds of other investigations are to be denigrated on this basis.

The second criterion is an appropriate one, and one that REST research fully meets. There is some evidence (Marks, 1978) that D. Ewen Cameron, in an early attempt to produce personality change in psychiatric patients, used stimulus reduction as well as LSD, electro-convulsive shock, sleep therapy, and a variety of psychoactive drugs. This massive combined procedure (which he called "psychic driving") was apparently quite stressful and of dubious therapeutic effectiveness. Cameron's procedures would certainly not meet today's ethical standards for therapy or research and were questionable even then, some 25 years ago. It is also possible that military and intelligence agencies in various countries (including the CIA, which funded some of Cameron's work) may have financed or conducted other research in which restricted stimulation was used in an unethical fashion. If so, such experiments have not been published and their existence is a matter of speculation.

At any rate, there is nothing about REST that makes it more susceptible to being abused than any other experimental or therapeutic technique. There are few if any ethical problems in the hundreds of articles and books that form the scientific literature in this area. There is not one published experiment using stimulus restriction with human subjects where the individuals were not volunteers, and where they did not have the right to terminate the REST session and leave the room or tank whenever they wanted to. Further, there is not a single example of deception in the sense that the subjects were misled as to what the nature of the experimental environment was going to be. It is therefore difficult to see how REST research can be faulted on that ground.

As to the third criterion, it is the tradition in Western science (aside from projects in which national security is involved) to publish one's findings fully with the expectation that they will then be available to anyone who cares to read the literature. It may be true that some kinds of research knowledge are put to uses of which the original researcher might disapprove, but the knowledge is supposed to belong to the storehouse of human information, not to some preferred person or subgroup. By the same token, of course, uses of which some researchers might approve would be disliked by other scientists. There is no justification for assuming that researchers are uniquely qualified to dictate or control the possible uses of knowledge that they produce. Scientific expertise does not ensure civic virtue, morality, or wisdom.

Speaking of REST specifically, there seems to be no direct evidence that the information generated from this research tradition has in fact changed the techniques used by the police and other authorities of which Fields disapproves. She infers that such applications were made from the fact that solitary confinement and environmental monotony have sometimes been combined with much more elaborate, traumatic, harmful, and inhumane methods in the treatment of prisoners. Extrapolating from this fact to the accusations that she has made is, of course, to confuse association with causation. This elementary fallacy apparently does not bother Fields and her fellow critics. At the same time, they manage to ignore the well-established fact that REST research has also been read by designers, architects, and organizational psychologists, with subsequent improvement of environmental conditions in work places, hospitals, institutions for children, housing developments, and prisons. Psychotherapists have read the literature and designed powerful clinical techniques that have used REST to help many people even to the point of saving their lives (as in the case of smokers at great risk from lung cancer and obese individuals whose weight is a serious strain on the cardiovascular system).

Thus, the criteria proposed by Fields are by no means adequate for judging scientific research. However, even if one were to accept these standards, the acceptability of REST work seems to be firmly established. The use of stimulus restriction and isolation as adjuncts to torture by some governments does not in any way reflect upon either the ethicality or the efficacy of these techniques in experimental and therapeutic settings. It is ludicrous to argue that a procedure which has been sometimes abused or misused should therefore not be used beneficially.

It is difficult to understand why stimulus reduction is picked out for such illogical attacks. For example, the Ulster reports on which the polemics of Shallice and his colleagues are based document, very clearly and explicitly, the routine use of sleep deprivation in the mistreatment of detainees. Lack of sleep has also been implicated in many other situations where prisoners have been abused and where no claim has been made that stimulus reduction was involved. Yet, no one has so far published an article recommending that the world rise up in righteous wrath and abolish research on the effects of sleep deprivation; nor do I know of any accusations that by implication equate sleep deprivation researchers with extermination camp personnel at Auschwitz, as was done for REST researchers in an unpublished letter to the editor of *Psychology Today* (Fields, 1976c).

This appears to be a peculiar lack of logic on the part of some social scientists. Fields (1976c) strongly implies that REST researchers are guilty of torture, and Laub (1974) quotes a German sociologist who argues that such techniques as urinalysis and infrared photography are imperialistic because they were used by the United States military in Vietnam.

Not all disciplines are prone to this kind of confusion. For example, there have been reliable reports that the drilling of healthy teeth has been used as a torture technique. In spite of this, the dentistry journals have published no exhortations to the effect that the use of drills in dental therapy, or research on improved drilling equipment, is evil and should be given up. As Laub points out, people who do research on poisons are not the same as poisoners, nor is their research equivalent to murder. This is a lesson in logic that some of the more impassioned critics of REST and social isolation research might do well to study, with an extension. Here, the appropriate analogy is research on drugs—including medicinal ones; not merely poisons. The critics, and the reader, might be reminded of Freud's comment on the possible abuses of psychotherapeutic procedures: "No medical remedy is proof against misuse: if a knife will not cut, neither will it serve a surgeon" (Freud, 1920/1943, p. 403).

CONCLUSION

Gaines and Vetter (1968), in a summary of the therapeutic REST literature up to that time, noted the overwhelmingly positive reports with a wide variety of patients and diagnostic categories. More recent reviews have found very similar patterns. A tally of the clinical studies reported in this book indicates almost universal positive effects, in spite of the extremely wide range of problems and types of patients involved. It therefore seems logical to argue that REST is now more than a merely experimental procedure in the therapeutic context. The subsequent ignoring of these findings by the great majority of clinical researchers and practitioners remains inexplicable.

In a way, early findings in the "sensory deprivation" literature foreshadowed the rich applied potential. Changes in cognitive processes, in imagery, in motivation, in the ongoing flow of thought and emotion, can all be turned to beneficial use. Depending on the problem being faced, it is appropriate to consider carefully the creative use of stimulus restriction, building therapeutic progress on the foundation of its ability to modify more basic functions. In some cases, it may serve well as the only therapeutic method used; however, my guess is that its most appropriate and most common application will be as one component of multimodal treatment. In this role, we know that REST has the ability to increase the power of more traditional approaches, including behavioral as well as verbal therapies, to facilitate the client's consideration of and involvement with new ways of thinking, feeling, and acting. It can also improve interaction with the therapist and enhance the learning of new and adaptive techniques for solving problems.

Several methodological aspects of optimal utilization still have to be worked out. For example, we have not established the best period of stimulus restriction. This is an important practical point, since the procedure may be made more generally acceptable and more economical if it were found that the same effects could be obtained with a shorter duration. And, of course, a period either longer or shorter than those now used might increase the success rate.

Another aspect of many of the REST approaches that needs further research is the type of message presented. As we have seen, messages do not always have a measurable effect. One obvious point is that their impact and usefulness should be increased by careful design and repeated testing. But there are other issues as well. For example, are individually designed messages superior to standard ones? As described in Chapter 10, both have been used but there have been no broad-range direct comparisons. We are also not sure about the most effective rule for timing the presentations. Should they be massed shortly after the beginning of the session, so that subjects have the remainder of the confinement to think about them? Would it be better to present them toward the end of the session, when REST effects may be at their highest, thus leading to maximum impact for the messages? Or perhaps they should be phased throughout the entire session? Might "demand feeding" be even better, ensuring that presentations occur when the client wants them?

Another set of questions concerns problems for which REST treatment has not been tried, but might be relevant. For example, there is the possibility that it could counteract or prevent memory losses following electroconvulsive therapy. It might increase the efficiency and applicability of such procedures as hypnotherapy, relaxation training, and biofeedback. It should obviously be tested with a variety of maladaptive behaviors that are related to problems which have already been shown to be responsive to REST: addictive behaviors other than smoking and overeating, phobias other than fear of snakes, and so on. At the same time, an attempt should be made to evaluate the cost-effectiveness of the treatment, preferably in a way that is sophisticated enough to give us reliable figures for REST carried out in various settings (psychiatric hospitals, community mental health centers, private offices, schools, correctional institutions).

The bases of the effectiveness of the treatment also need considerable research. I have repeatedly indicated the complexity of the theoretical approaches to REST effects and the lack of any resolution as to the testability, validity, or fruitfulness of the various systems.

One related point that should be investigated and explained is the apparent nonspecificity of some of the effects. It appears that many of the relaxation techniques, including REST, have a wide range of effects on behavior, cognition, and affect, rather than being restricted to the specific focal issue. This has been shown in the experimental REST literature by Tetlock and Suedfeld (1976), in a study where belief destabilization ("unfreezing") was found even without any attitudinal message. In the clinical context, this kind of general imapct has been criticized as indicating that the techniques rely on a placebo effect. For example, Jessup (1978) has charged that autogenic feedback for migraine is essentially a placebo treatment.

The degree to which nonspecificity should be characterized as placebo is open to debate, as is the whole idea of placebos in psychotherapy (Kirsch, 1978; O'Leary and Borkovec, 1978). For example, one might argue that the techniques are general in their impact because they work on a general mediating variable such as arousal; one would not call an arousal-modifying behavioral treatment a placebo any more than one would characterize an arousal-modifying pharmacological agent that way (see Wickramasekera, 1977b). It may also be that methods applied with the intention of altering a focal behavior can be generalized by the patient to other behaviors. In this case, the label of positive transfer, generalization, or (in a more medical sense) side effects might be more appropriate. In any case, there is evidence that the effectiveness of the treatment is not dependent upon expectancy or set, although these may be factors in its total impact. The term placebo therefore seems unjustified. There is another labeling problem here. "Placebo" has a derogatory connotation, and "nonspecificity" should be clearly distinguished from it. After all, if medicine ever did discover the universal panacea, its effects would by definition be nonspecific; but it would hardly be classifiable as a placebo.

Obviously, there are many promising beginnings in this field, but very few have been followed far enough to be evaluated definitively. Much research remains to be done. Replications have to be performed, combinations of REST with a variety of other treatments should be tested, the list of problems with which the technique has been tried must be expanded, and parametric work must be performed to ascertain such important facts as optimal confinement durations, types and degrees of sensory reduction, background and personality factors that may be predictors of success or failure, and the like. What the field needs is a great deal of the kind of systematic investigation that Gary E. Schwartz and I have termed "creatious": that is, "creative and cautious." Creativity is needed to get rid of old misconceptions and self-set limits; caution, to avoid the excessive optimism that has so frequently made both professionals and the public think that the journey has been accomplished when in actuality only the first step has been taken.

References

Adams, H. B. "Mental illness" or interpersonal behavior? *American Psychologist*, 1964, *19*, 191–197.

Adams, H. B. A case utilizing sensory deprivation. In L. P. Ullmann and L. Krasner (Eds.), *Case studies in behavior modification*. New York: Holt, Rinehart and Winston, 1965.

Adams, H. B. Recovery from psychosis following reduced environmental stimulation. Unpublished manuscript, 1979.

Adams, H. B., Cooper, G. D., and Carrera, R. N. Individual differences in behavioral reactions of psychiatric patients to brief partial sensory deprivation. *Perceptual and Motor Skills*, 1972, *34*, 199–217.

Adams, H. B., Robertson, M. H., and Cooper, G. D. Sensory deprivation and personality change. *Journal of Nervous and Mental Disease*, 1966, *143*, 256–265.

Adelson, E., and Fraiberg, S. Gross motor development in infants blind from birth. *Child Development*, 1974, *45*, 114–126.

Ader, R. Effects of early experience and differential housing on behavior and susceptibility to gastric erosions in the rat. *Journal of Comparative and Physiological Psychology*, 1965, *60*, 233–238.

Adler, M. [Cognitive changes during the course of a four-week social isolation experiment.] *Zeitschrift für experimentelle und angewandte Psychologie*, 1973, *20*, 521–528.

Ahsen, A. *Psycheye: Self-analytic consciousness. A basic introduction to the natural self-analytic images of consciousness, eidetics*. New York: Brandon House, 1977.

Akishige, Y. The principles of psychology of Zen. In Y. Akishige (Ed.), *Psychological studies on Zen* (Vol. 2). Tokyo: The Zen Institute of Komazawa University, 1977.

Akstein, D. Socio-cultural basis of terpsichoretrancetherapy. *American Journal of Clinical Hypnosis*, 1977, *19*, 221–225.

Al-Issa, I. Social and cultural aspects of hallucinations. *Psychological Bulletin*, 1977, *84*, HCF9s70–583.

Allekian, C. I. Intrusions of territory and personal space: An anxiety-inducing factor for hospitalized persons—An exploratory study. *Nursing Research*, 1973, *22*, 236–241.

Altman, I. *The environment and social behavior*. Monterey, California: Brooks/Cole, 1975.

Altman, I., and Haythorn, W. W. The ecology of isolated groups. *Behavioral Science,* 1967, *12,* 169–182.

Altman, R. The influence of brief social deprivation on the activity of mentally retarded children. *Training School Bulletin,* 1971, *68,* 165–169.

Altshuler, K. Z. Studies of the deaf: Relevance to psychiatric theory. *American Journal of Psychiatry,* 1971, *127,* 97–102.

Amnesty International *Report.* London: Amnesty International Publications, 1977.

". . . And NHLBI Director estimates 164,000 lives prolonged by habit shifts." *Behavior Today,* December 25, 1978, *9* (50), p. 5.

Anderson, P. *Agent of the Terran Empire.* London: Coronet, 1977.

Andreev, A. L. [Reorganization of the curative activity of the Kashchenko Hospital in the light of I. P. Pavlov's theory.] *Zhurnal Neuropatologii i Psikhiatrii,* 1952, *52,* 52–56.

Angermeier, W. F., Phelps, J. B., and Reynolds, H. A. The effect of differential early rearing upon discrimination learning in monkeys. *Psychonomic Science,* 1967, *8,* 378–379.

Anson, P. F. *The call of the desert.* London: SPCK, 1964.

Antista, B., and Jones, A. Some beneficial consequences of brief sensory deprivation. Paper read at the meeting of the Western Psychological Association, Sacramento, Calif., 1975.

Arberry, A. J. *Sufism: An account of the mystics of Islam.* Winchester, Mass.: Allen and Unwin, 1950.

Ardrey, R. *The territorial imperative.* New York: Atheneum, 1966.

Arlow, J. Unconscious fantasy and disturbances of conscious experience. *Psychoanalytic Quarterly,* 1969, *38,* 1–27.

Armen, J.-C. *Gazelle-boy.* London: Bodley Head, 1974.

Ashton, R. Infant state and stimulation. *Developmental Psychology,* 1976, *12,* 569–570.

Association for Legal Justice *Newsletter.* Belfast, Northern Ireland, 1972–1974.

Axelrod, S. Effects of early blindness: Performance of blind and sighted children on tactile and auditory tasks. *American Foundation for the Blind Research Series,* 1959, *9* (Whole No. 7).

Azima, H., and Cramer-Azima, F. J. Effects of the decrease in sensory variability on body scheme. *Canadian Psychiatric Association Journal,* 1956, *1,* 59–72. (a)

Azima, H., and Cramer-Azima, F. J. Effects of partial isolation in mentally disturbed individuals. *Diseases of the Nervous System,* 1956, *17,* 117–122. (b)

Azima, H., and Cramer-Azima, F. J. Studies on perceptual isolation. *Diseases of the Nervous System* (Monograph Supplement), 1957, *18,* 80–85.

Azima, H., Lemieux, M., and Cramer-Azima, F. J. [Sensory isolation: Psychopathological and psychoanalytic study of regression and body schema.] *L'Évolution Psychiatrique*, 1962, *2*, 259–282.

Azima, H., Vispo, R., and Azima, F. J. Observations on anaclitic therapy during sensory deprivation. In P. Solomon et al. (Eds.), *Sensory deprivation*. Cambridge: Harvard University Press, 1961.

Bachrach, A. J., Erwin, W. J., and Mohr, J. P. The control of eating behavior in an anorexic by operant conditioning techniques. In L. P. Ullmann and L. Krasner (Eds.), *Case studies in behavior modification*. New York: Holt, Rinehart and Winston, 1965.

Badger, R. *Teaching guide: Infant learning program and teaching guide: Toddler learning program*. Paoli, Pennsylvania: Instructo, 1971.

Baekeland, F. Laboratory studies of effects of presleep events on sleep and dreams. *International Psychiatry Clinics*, 1970, *7*, 49–58.

Bagshaw, M. H., Schwartzkroin, P., and Burk, E. D. Dissociation of motor and cardiac orienting reactions in autistic children. *Psychophysiology*, 1974, *11*, 220–221.

Ballentine, R. M., Jr. Holistic therapy. In Swami Ajaya (Ed.), *Meditational therapy*. Glenview, Illinois: Himalayan International Institute, 1977.

Banay, R. S. Electrically induced sleep therapy. *Confinia Neurologica*, 1952, *12*, 356–360.

Bandura, A. Self-efficacy: Toward a unifying theory of behavioral change. *Psychological Review*, 1977, *84*, 191–215.

Banks, R. K., and Cappon, D. Developmental deprivation and mental illness: "A study of 20 questions." *Child Development*, 1963, *34*, 709–718.

Barash, D. P. Human ethology: Personal space reiterated. *Environment and Behavior*, 1973, *5*, 667–672.

Barber, T. X. Experiments in hypnosis. *Scientific American*, 1957, *196*, 54–61.

Barber, T. X. *Hypnosis: A scientific approach*. New York: Van Nostrand Reinhold, 1969.

Barber, T. X. Responding to "hypnotic" suggestions: An introspective report. *American Journal of Clinical Hypnosis*, 1975, *18*, 6–22.

Barber, T. X. Hypnosis, suggestions, and psychosomatic phenomena: A new look from the standpoint of recent experimental studies. *American Journal of Clinical Hypnosis*, 1978, *21*, 13–27.

Barber, T. X., Spanos, N. P., and Chaves, J. F. *Hypnosis, imagination, and human potentialities*. New York: Pergamon, 1974.

Barner, P., Fink, G., Naske, R., and Stacher, G. [Influence of autogenic relaxation on the motility of the oesophagus.] *Zeitschrift für Psychosomatische Medizin und Psychoanalyse*, 1974, *20*, 384–390.

Barnes, L. J. *Comparative effectiveness of a Five-Day Plan and a sensory deprivation program on reduction and abstinence from cigarette smoking*. Unpublished master's thesis, Dalhousie University, 1976.

Barnes, T. C. Isolation stress in rats and mice as a neuropharmacological test. *Federation Proceedings,* 1959, *18,* 365.

Baron, A., DeWaard, R. J., and Lipson, J. Increased reinforcement when timeout from avoidance includes access to a safe place. *Journal of Experimental Analysis of Behavior,* 1977, *27,* 479–494.

Barron, F. An ego-strength scale which predicts response to psychotherapy. In G. S. Welsh and W. G. Dahlstrom (Eds.), *Basic readings on the MMPI in psychology and medicine.* Minneapolis: University of Minnesota Press, 1956.

Barsness, L., Thomson, A., and Warrington, M. *Eliminating disruptive behavior through timeout stimulus control in autistic children.* Mimeographed manuscript, H. C. Anderson School, Minneapolis, 1977.

Bates, H. D. Relevance of animal-avoidance analogue studies to the treatment of clinical phobias: A rejoinder to Cooper, Furst, and Bridger. *Journal of Abnormal Psychology,* 1970, *75,* 12–14.

Batini, C., Palestini, M., Rossi, G. F. and Zanchetti, A. EEG activation patterns in the midpontine pretrigeminal cat following sensory deafferentation. *Archives of Italian Biology,* 1959, *97,* 26–32.

Baum, J. [The behavior of autistic children in darkness.] *Bibliotheca Psychiatrica,* (Basel), 1978, *157,* 66–74.

Baxter, J. C. Interpersonal spacing in natural settings. *Sociometry,* 1970, *33,* 444–456.

Beach, F. A., and Jaynes, J. Effects of early experience upon the behavior of animals. *Psychological Bulletin,* 1954, *51,* 239–263.

Bearwald, R. R. *The effects of stimulus complexity and perceptual deprivation or stimulus overload on attention to visual stimuli.* Unpublished Ed. D. dissertation, Indiana University, 1976.

Behar, L., and Stephens, D. Wilderness camping: An evaluation of a residential treatment program for emotionally disturbed children. *American Journal of Orthopsychiatry,* 1978, *48,* 644–653.

Behar, M. P., and Zucker, D. R. Sensory awareness exercises for the visually handicapped. *New Outlook for the Blind,* 1976, *70,* 146–148.

Beigel, H. C. The influence of body position on mental processes. *Journal of Clinical Psychology,* 1952, *8,* 193–199.

Beiman, I., Graham, L. E., and Ciminero, A. R. Self-control progressive relaxation training as an alternative nonpharmacological treatment for essential hypertension: Therapeutic effects in the natural environment. *Behaviour Research and Therapy,* 1978, *16,* 371–375. (a)

Beiman, I., Graham, L. E., and Ciminero, A. R. Setting generality of blood pressure reductions and the psychological treatment of reactive hypertension. *Journal of Behavioral Medicine,* 1978, *1,* 445–453. (b)

Bellack, A. S. Behavioral treatment for obesity: Appraisal and recommendations. *Progress in Behavior Modification,* 1977, *4,* 1–38.

Bem, D. J. An experimental analysis of self-persuasion. *Journal of Experimental Social Psychology*, 1965, *1*, 199–218.

Bemis, K. M. Current approaches to the etiology and treatment of anorexia nervosa. *Psychological Bulletin*, 1978, *85*, 593–617.

Bendheim, S. Freud wouldn't recognize today's analyst's office. New York *Times*, 2 September 1979, Section 8, pages 1–2.

Benoit, R. B., and Mayer, G. R. *Timeout: Guidelines for its selection and use.* Mimeographed paper, Department of Guidance and Pupil Personnel Services, California State University at Los Angeles, undated.

Benson, H. (with M. Z. Klipper). *The relaxation response.* New York: Avon, 1975.

Benson, H., Greenwood, M. M., and Klemchuk, H. The relaxation response: Psychophysiologic aspects and clinical applications. *International Journal of Psychiatry in Medicine*, 1975, *6*, 87–98.

Benson, H., and Wallace, R. K. Decreased drug abuse with transcendental meditation: A study of 1862 subjects. In *Congressional Record*, 1971, Series. No. 92–1.

Benton, A. L. *The revised visual retention test: Manual.* Iowa City: State University of Iowa, 1955.

Bentz, J. E. Short-term sensory reduction used as a therapeutic aid in enhancement of self-concept. *Psychological Reports*, 1978, *42*, 1299–1304.

Berdyaev, N. *Solitude and society.* London: Centenary Press, 1938.

Berg, S. W., and Richlin, M. Injuries and illnesses of Vietnam War POWs. IV: Comparison of captivity effects in North and South Vietnam. *Military Medicine*, 1977, *141*, 757–761.

Berkson, G. Animal studies of treatment of impaired young by parents and the social group. Paper read at a Conference on the Blind Child in Social Interaction: Developing Relationships with Peers and Adults. New York City, 1973.

Berkun, M. M., Bialek, H. M., Kern, R. P., and Yagi, K. Experimental studies of psychological stress in man. *Psychological Monographs*, 1962, *76*(15, Whole No. 534).

Berlyne, D. E. *Conflict, arousal and curiosity.* New York: McGraw-Hill, 1960.

Berlyne, D. E. Curiosity and exploration. *Science*, 1966, *153*, 25–33.

Bernhardt, A. J., Fredericks, S., and Forbach, G. B. Comparison of effects of labeled and unlabeled praise and time-out upon children's discrimination learning. *Psychological Reports*, 1978, *42*, 771–776.

Bernicot, L. *The voyage of Anahita—Single-handed round the world.* London: Hart-Davis, 1953.

Bernstein, D. A. Modification of smoking behavior: An evaluative review. *Psychological Bulletin*, 1969, *71*, 418–440.

Bernstein, D. A., and Borkovec, T. D. *Progressive relaxation training: A manual for the helping professions.* Champaign, Illinois: Research Press, 1973.

Bernstein, D. A., and McAlister, A. The modification of smoking behavior: Progress and problems. *Addictive Behaviors,* 1976, *1,* 89–102.

Bernstein, L. The reversibility of learning deficits in early environmentally restricted rats as a function of amount of experience in later life. *Journal of Psychosomatic Research,* 1972, *16,* 71–73.

Bernstein, P. I want to be alone. *Penthouse,* 1976, *8*(1), 45.

Bertini, M., Lewis, H. B., and Witkin, H. A. Some preliminary observations with an experimental procedure for the study of hypnagogic and related phenomena. In C. T. Tart (Ed.), *Altered states of consciousness.* New York: Wiley, 1969.

Best, B., and Roberts, G. Early cognitive development in hearing impaired children. *American Annals of the Deaf,* 1976, *121,* 562–564.

Best, J. A., and Steffy, R. A. Smoking modification procedures for internal and external locus of control clients. *Canadian Journal of Behavioural Science,* 1975, *7,* 155–165.

Best, J. A. and Suedfeld, P. Restricted environmental stimulation therapy and self-management in smoking cessation. In preparation.

Bettelheim, B. Feral children and autistic children. *American Journal of Sociology,* 1959, *64,* 455–467.

Bettelheim, B. *The empty fortress: Infantile autism and birth of self.* New York: Free Press, 1967.

Beutler, L. E., Jobe, A. M., and Elkins, D. Outcomes in group psychotherapy: Using persuasion theory to increase treatment efficiency. *Journal of Consulting and Clinical Psychology,* 1974, *42,* 547–553.

Bexton, W. H., Heron, W., and Scott, T. H. Effects of decreased variation in the sensory environment. *Canadian Journal of Psychology,* 1954, *8,* 70–76.

Biase, D. V., and Zuckerman, M. Sex differences in stress responses to total and partial sensory deprivation. *Psychosomatic Medicine,* 1967, *29,* 380–390.

Biderman, A. D. *March to calumny: The story of American POWs in the Korean War.* New York: Macmillan, 1963.

Bigelow, G. E., Cohen, M., Liebson, I., and Faillace, L. A. Abstinence or moderation? Choice by alcoholics. *Behaviour Research and Therapy,* 1972, *10,* 209–214.

Bigelow, G. E., Liebson, I., and Griffiths, R. R. Alcoholic drinking: Suppression by a brief time-out procedure. *Behaviour Research and Therapy,* 1974, *12,* 107–115.

Bishop, M. *Saint Francis of Assisi.* Boston: Little, Brown, 1974.

Bitgood, S. C., Crowe, M. J., Peters, R. D., and Suarez, Y. Brief immobilization: Decreasing disruptive and self-stimulatory behaviors. Paper read at the meeting of the American Psychological Association, Washington, D.C., 1976.

Blakemore, C., and Cooper, G. F. Development of the brain depends on the visual environment. *Nature* (London), 1970, *5,* 477–478.

Blanck, G. Psychoanalytic technique. In B. B. Wolman (Ed.), *The therapist's handbook.* New York: Van Nostrand Reinhold, 1976.

Blank, H. R. Reflections on the special senses in relation to the development of affect with special emphasis on blindness. *Journal of the American Psychoanalytic Association,* 1975, *23,* 32–50.

Blazer, J. A. An experimental evaluation of "transcendence of environment." *Journal of Humanistic Psychology,* 1962, *3,* 49–53.

Bolin, R. H. *An investigation of sensory deprivation in immobilized orthopedic patients.* Unpublished master's thesis, University of Iowa, 1972.

Bombard, A. *The voyage of the Heretique.* New York: Simon and Schuster, 1953.

Bondy, S. C., and Morelos, B. S. Stimulus deprivation and cerebral blood flow. *Experimental Neurology,* 1971, *31,* 200–206.

Bone, E. *Seven years' solitary.* New York: Harcourt, Brace, 1957.

Bornstein, M. Analysis of a congenitally blind musician. *Psychoanalytic Quarterly,* 1977, *46,* 23–37.

Borrie, R. A. *The use of sensory deprivation in a programme of weight control.* Unpublished Ph.D. dissertation, University of British Columbia, 1977.

Borrie, R. A. Sensory deprivation used as part of a weight loss program. Paper read at the meeting of the Western Psychological Association, San Francisco, California, 1978.

Borrie, R. A. and Suedfeld, P. Restricted environmental stimulation therapy in a weight reduction program. *Journal of Behavioral Medicine,* in press.

Bosch, G. [*Infantile autism: A clinical and phenomenological-anthropological investigation taking language as the guide.*] Heidelberg: Springer Verlag, 1970 (cited in Margolies, 1977).

Bossley, M. I. Privacy and crowding: A multidisciplinary analysis. *Man-Environment Systems,* 1976, *6,* 8–19.

Boudreau, L. Transcendental meditation and yoga as reciprocal inhibitors. *Journal of Behavior Therapy and Experimental Psychiatry,* 1972, *3,* 97–98.

Bourne, L. E., Jr., and Dominowski, R. L. Thinking. *Annual Review of Psychology,* 1972, *23,* 105–130.

Bowart, W. *Operation mind control.* New York: Dell, 1978.

Bowden, D. M., and McKinney, W. T. Behavioral effects of peer separation, isolation and reunion on adolescent male rhesus monkeys. *Developmental Psychobiology,* 1972, *5,* 353–362.

Bower, K. B., and Mercer, C. D. Hyperactivity: Etiology and intervention techniques. *Journal of School Health,* 1975, *45,* 195–212.

Bowlby, J. *Attachment and loss. Vol. 2: Separation.* New York: Basic Books, 1973.

Boyanowsky, E. O. The psychology of identity change: A theoretical framework for review and analysis of the self-role transformation process. *Canadian Psychological Review*, 1977, *18*, 115–127.

Brackbill, Y. Continuous stimulation and arousal level in infancy: Effects of stimulus intensity and stress. *Child Development*, 1975, *46*, 364–369.

Brackbill, Y., and Douthitt, T. C. The development of response to continuous auditory stimulation in rats treated neonatally with 6-Hydroxydopamine. *Developmental Psychobiology*, 1976, *9*, 5–15.

Brady, J. Comment in *Report of the National Commission for the Protection of Human Subjects of Biomedical and Behavioral Research*. Washington, D.C., 1976.

Bramah, E. The dragon of Chang Tao. In L. Carter (Ed.), *Discoveries in fantasy*. New York: Ballantine, 1972 (original publication 1922).

Brand, I. *The "separate" or "model prison," Port Arthur*. West Moonah, Australia: Jason, 1975.

Brawley, P. and Pos, R. The information underload (sensory deprivation) model in contemporary psychiatry. *Canadian Psychiatric Association Journal*, 1967, *12*, 105–124.

Breger, L. Comments on "Building social behavior in autistic children by use of electric shock." *Journal of Experimental Research in Personality*, 1965, *1*, 110–113.

Bromberg, W. *From shaman to psychotherapist: A history of the treatment of mental illness*. Chicago: Regnery, 1975.

Bromwich, R. M. Stimulation in the first year of life? A perspective on infant development. *Young Children*, 1977, *32*, 71–82.

Brossard, M., and Decarie, T. G. The effects of three kinds of perceptual-social stimulation on the development of institutionalized infants: Preliminary report of a longitudinal study. *Early Child Development and Care*, 1971, *1*, 211–230.

Brown, J., and Hepler, R. Stimulation—A corollary to physical care. *American Journal of Nursing*, 1976, *76*, 578–581.

Brownfain, J. J. Stability of the self-concept as a dimension of personality. *Journal of Abnormal and Social Psychology*, 1952, *47*, 597–606.

Brownfield, C. A. *Isolation: Clinical and experimental approaches*. New York: Random House, 1965.

Brownfield, C. A. Optimal stimulation levels of normal and disturbed subjects in sensory deprivation. *Psychologia*, 1966, *9*, 27–38.

Browning, R. M. Effect of irrelevant peripheral visual stimuli on discrimination learning in minimally brain-damaged children. *Journal of Consulting and Clinical Psychology*, 1967, *31*, 371–376.

Bruinsma, Y., and Tees, R. C. The effect of bias-rearing on transfer after form discrimination training in the rat. *Bulletin of the Psychonomic Society*, 1977, *10*, 433–435.

Brundage-Aguar, D., Forehand, R., and Ciminero, A. R. A review of treatment approaches for hyperactive behavior. *Journal of Clinical Child Psychology*, 1977, *6*, 3–10.

Bruner, A. The Penetang experiment. *Weekend Magazine*, March 26, 1977. Pp. 9–12.

Buchsbaum, M. Self-regulation of stimulus intensity: Augmenting/reducing and the average evoked response. In G. E. Schwartz and D. Shapiro (Eds.), *Consciousness and self-regulation: Advances in research* (Vol. I). New York: Plenum, 1976.

Buchwald, J. S., and Brown, K. A. The role of acoustic inflow in the development of adaptive behavior. *Annals of the New York Academy of Sciences*, 1977, *290*, 270–284.

Budzynski, T. H. Biofeedback and the twilight states of consciousness. In G. E. Schwartz and D. Shapiro (Eds.), *Consciousness and self-regulation: Advances in research* (Vol. I). New York: Plenum, 1976.

Burchard, J. D., and Barrera, F. An analysis of timeout and response cost in a programmed environment. *Journal of Applied Behavior Analysis*, 1972, *5*, 271–282.

Burney, C. *Solitary confinement* (2nd ed.). London: Colin MacMillan, 1961.

Busch, F. *Problem-solving deterioration as a function of creativity, structure, and sex, in a situation of low-level, unpatterned stimulation (sensory deprivation).* Unpublished Ph.D. dissertation, University of Massachusetts, 1966.

Buss, A. H., and Lang, P.J. Psychological deficit in schizophrenia: I) Affect, reinforcement, and concept attainment. *Journal of Abnormal Psychology*, 1965, *70*, 2–24.

Busse, T. V., Ree, M., Gutride, M., Alexander, T., and Powell, L. S. Environmentally enriched classrooms and the cognitive and perceptual development of Negro preschool children. *Journal of Educational Psychology*, 1972, *63*, 15–21.

Butler, R. A. The effect of deprivation of visual incentives on visual exploration motivation in monkeys. *Journal of Comparative and Physiological Psychology*, 1957, *50*, 177–180.

Butler, R. A. The differential effect of visual and auditory incentives on the performance of monkeys. *American Journal of Psychology*, 1958, *71*, 591–593.

Byrd, R. E. *Alone.* New York: Putnam, 1938.

Cahn, C. H. Seclusion and restraint of the mentally ill. *Douglas*, 1975, *10*(1), 3–5.

Calhoun, K. S., Prewett, M. J., Peters, R. D., and Adams, H. E. Factors in the modification by isolation of electroconvulsive shock-produced retrograde amnesia in the rat. *Journal of Comparative and Physiological Psychology*, 1975, *88*, 373–377.

Campbell, B. A., and Coulter, X. The ontogenesis of learning and memory. In M. Rosenzweig and E. Bennet (Eds.). *Neural mechanisms of learning and memory.* Cambridge: MIT Press, 1976.

Caplan, R. D., Cobb, S., French, J. R. P., Jr., Van Harrison, R., and Pinneau, S. R., Jr. *Job demands and worker health: Main effects and occupational differences.* Washington, D.C., Department of Health, Education and Welfare (NIOSH) Publication # 75-160, 1975.

"Cardboard cell boy moved." Vancouver *Sun,* May 8, 1978, p. A-9.

Carlson, N. A. Statement before the House Committee on the Judiciary, Subcommittee on the Courts, Civil Liberties and the Administration of Justice, 1974.

Carolan, R. H. Sensory stimulation and the blind infant. *New Outlook for the Blind,* 1973, *67,* 119–126. (a)

Carolan, R. H. Sensory stimulation in the nursing home. *New Outlook for the Blind,* 1973, *67,* 126–130. (b)

Carpenter, P. B. The effects of sensory deprivation on behavior in the white rat. *Dissertation Abstracts,* 1960, *20,* 3396.

Carrington, P. *Freedom in meditation.* Garden City, New York: Anchor, 1978.

Carson, R. C. *Interaction concepts of personality.* Chicago: Aldine, 1969.

Carter, J. L., and Diaz, A. Effects of visual and auditory background on reading test performance. *Exceptional Children,* 1971, *38,* 43–50.

Cartwright, R. D. Predicting response to client-centered therapy with the Rorschach Prognostic Rating Scale. *Journal of Counseling Psychology,* 1958, *5,* 11–15.

Casler, L. The effects of extra tactile stimulation on a group of institutionalized infants. *Genetic Psychology Monographs,* 1965, *71,* 135–175. (a)

Casler, L. The effects of supplementary verbal stimulation on a group of institutionalized infants. *Journal of Child Psychology and Psychiatry,* 1965, *6,* 19–27. (b)

Casler, L. Perceptual deprivation in institutional settings. In G. Newton and S. Levine (Eds.), *Early experience and behavior.* Springfield, Ill.: Thomas, 1968.

Cauthen, N. R., and Prymak, C. A. Meditation versus relaxation: An examination of the physiological effects of relaxation training and of different levels of experience with transcendental meditation. *Journal of Consulting and Clinical Psychology,* 1977, *45,* 496–497.

Cattell, R. B. *A new morality from science: Beyondism.* New York: Pergamon, 1972.

Cegalis, J. A., Leen, D., and Solomon, E. J. Attention in schizophrenia: An analysis of selectivity in the functional visual field. *Journal of Abnormal Psychology,* 1977, *86,* 470–481.

Chang, S. C. The cultural context of Japanese psychiatry and psychotherapy. *American Journal of Psychotherapy,* 1965, *19,* 593–606.

Chang, S. C. Morita therapy. *American Journal of Psychotherapy,* 1974, *28,* 208–221.

Chapman, L. J. and Chapman, J. P. *Disordered thought in schizophrenia.* Englewood Cliffs, New Jersey: Prentice Hall, 1973.

Charny, I. W. Regression and reorganization in the "isolation treatment" of children: A clinical contribution to sensory deprivation research. *Journal of Child Psychology and Psychiatry*, 1963, *4*, 47–60.

Chase, J. B. *Retrolental fibroplasia & autistic symptomatology*. New York: American Foundation for the Blind Research Report No. 24, 1972.

Chaves, J. F., and Barber, T. X. Hypnotic procedures and surgery: A critical analysis with applications to "acupuncture analgesia." *American Journal of Clinical Hypnosis*, 1976, *18*, 217–236.

Chayefsky, P. *Altered states*. New York: Harper and Row, 1978.

Cheek, D. B., and LeCron, L. M. *Clinical hypnotherapy*. New York: Grune and Stratton, 1968.

Chichester, F. *Gypsy Moth circles the world*. London: Hodder and Stoughton, 1967.

Chihara, T. Psychological studies on Zen meditation and time-experience. In Y. Akishige (Ed.), *Psychological studies on Zen* (Volume 2). Tokyo: The Zen Institute of Komazawa University, 1977.

Chow, K. L., Riesen, A. H., and Newell, F. W. Degeneration of retinal ganglion cells in infant chimpanzees reared in darkness. *Journal of Comparative Neurology*, 1957, *107*, 27–42.

Chow, K. L., and Stewart, D. L. Reversal of structural and functional effects of long-term visual deprivation in cats. *Experimental Neurology*, 1972, *34*, 409–433.

Chumakova, L. T., and Kirillova, Z. A. Electrosleep as an effective outpatient treatment on nervous and psychological disorders. *Excerpta Medica: Proceedings of the 1st International Symposium on Electrotherapeutic Sleep*, 1967, 205–209.

Church, G., and Carnes, C. D. *The pit: A group encounter defiled*. New York: Pocket Books, 1973.

Clancy, H., and McBride, G. The isolation syndrome in childhood. *Developmental Medicine and Child Neurology*, 1975, *17*, 198–219.

Clark, B., and Graybiel, A. The break-off phenomenon. *Journal of Aviation Medicine*, 1957, *28*, 121–126.

Clark, R. R. *A social interaction theory of cigarette smoking and quitting*. Oceanside, New York: Dabor, 1977.

Clark, W. C., and Yang, J. C. Acupunctural analgesia? Evaluation by signal detection theory. *Science*, 1974, *184*, 1096–1098.

Cleveland, S. E., Reitman, E. E., and Bentinck, C. Therapeutic effectiveness of sensory deprivation. *Archives of General Psychiatry*, 1963, *8*, 455–460.

Clifford, W. The "separate system" revisited. *Australian and New Zealand Journal of Criminology*, 1978, *11*, 179–181.

Cohen, B. D., Rosenbaum, G., Dobie, S. I., and Gottlieb, J. S. Sensory isolation: hallucinogenic effects of a brief procedure. *Journal of Nervous and Mental Disease*, 1959, *129*, 486–491.

Cohen, M., Liebson, I. A., and Faillace, L. A. A technique for establishing controlled drinking in chronic alcoholics. *Diseases of the Nervous System,* 1972, *33,* 46–49.

Cohen, R. L. Developments in the isolation therapy of behavior disorders of children. In J. H. Masserman (Ed.), *Current psychiatric therapies* (Vol. 3). New York: Grune and Stratton, 1963.

Cohen, S. I., Silverman, A. J., Bressler, B., and Shmavonian, B. Problems in isolation studies. In P. Solomon et al. (Eds.), *Sensory deprivation.* Cambridge: Harvard University Press, 1961.

Cole, C. W., and Goldstein, G. S. Consumption of ethanol as a function of sensory isolation. *Learning and Motivation,* 1971, *2,* 363–370.

Colorado Outward Bound School. Information pamphlet. Denver, Colorado, 1977.

Compton Committee. *Report of the Enquiry into Allegations Against the Security Forces of Physical Brutality in Northern Ireland Arising out of Events on 9th August, 1971.* London: Her Majesty's Stationery Office, 1971.

Comptroller General of the United States. *Behavior modification programs: The Bureau of Prisons' alternative to long term segregation.* Washington, D.C., 1975.

Conquest, R. *The great terror: Stalin's purge of the Thirties.* London: Macmillan, 1968.

Conway, J. B. Behavioral self-control of smoking through aversive conditioning and self-management. *Journal of Consulting and Clinical Psychology,* 1977, *45,* 348–357.

Cooke, K. *What cares the sea.* New York: McGraw-Hill, 1960.

Coon, D. L. Effects of informational and evaluative sets on reported visual sensations in a sensory deprivation environment. Paper presented at the meeting of the Rocky Mountain Psychological Association, Las Vegas, Nevada, 1973.

Cooper, A., Furst, J. B., and Bridger, W. H. A brief commentary on the usefulness of studying fears of snakes. *Journal of Abnormal Psychology,* 1969, *74,* 413–414.

Cooper, G. D., Adams, H. B., and Cohen, L. D. Personality changes after sensory deprivation. *Journal of Nervous and Mental Disease,* 1965, *140,* 103–118.

Cooper, G. D., Adams, H. B., Dickinson, J. R., and York, M. W. Interviewer's role-playing and responses to sensory deprivation: A clinical demonstration. *Perceptual and Motor Skills,* 1975, *40,* 291–303.

Cooper, G. D., Adams, H. B., and Gibby, R. G. Ego strength changes following perceptual deprivation. *Archives of General Psychiatry,* 1962, *7,* 213–217.

Cooper, G. D., McGraw, J., Pasternak, R., Pasnak, R., and Adams, H. B. A new treatment for alcohol abuse: Preliminary report. Unpublished manuscript, George Mason University, 1977; summarized in *Alcoholism and Alcohol Education,* July 27, 1977, pp. 7–8.

Cooper, J. The Gros Ventre of Montana. In V. Flannery (Ed.), *Religion and ritual.* Washington, D.C.: Catholic University, 1956.

Cooper, R. M., and Zubek, J. P. Effects of enriched and restricted environments on the learning ability of bright and dull rats. *Canadian Journal of Psychology*, 1958, *12*, 159–164.

Cormier, B. M., and Williams, P. J. Excessive deprivation of liberty as a form of punishment. Paper presented at the meeting of the Canadian Psychiatric Association, Edmonton, Alberta, 1966.

Corn, R. Self-efficacy: Cognitive mediator of smoking cessation. Paper read at the meeting of the American Psychological Association, Toronto, 1978.

Costello, J. The establishment of fluency with time-out procedures: Three case studies. *Journal of Speech and Hearing Disorders*, 1975, *40*, 216–231.

Cox, D. N. *Psychophysiological correlates of sensation seeking and socialization during reduced stimulation.* Unpublished Ph.D. dissertation, The University of British Columbia, 1977.

Coyle, I. R., and Singer, G. The interaction of post-weaning housing conditions and prenatal drug effects on behaviour. *Psychopharmacologia (Berlin)*, 1975, *41*, 237–244.

Crasilneck, H. B., and Hall, J. A. *Clinical hypnosis: Principles and applications.* New York: Grune and Stratton, 1975.

Creighton, T. *Complexity preferences and preference shifts in rats as a function of early visual experience.* Unpublished master's thesis, University of British Columbia, 1969.

Creighton, T., and Tees, R. C. The effects of early visual deprivation on selective attention in the rat. *Bulletin of the Psychonomic Society*, 1975, *5*, 504–506.

Creutzfeldt, O. D., and Aeggeland, P. Neural plasticity in visual cortex of adult cats after exposure to visual patterns. *Science*, 1975, *188*, 1025–1027.

Crosby, K. G. Attention and distractibility in mentally retarded and intellectually average children. *American Journal of Mental Deficiency*, 1972, *77*, 46–53.

Cruikshank, W. M., Bentzen, F. A., Ratzeburg, F. H., and Tannhauser, M. T. *A teaching method for brain-injured and hyperactive children.* Syracuse, New York: Syracuse University Press, 1961.

Cruikshank, W. M., Junkala, J., and Paul, J. The preparation of teachers of the brain-injured and hyperactive children. Unpublished manuscript, Syracuse University, 1967 (cited in Zentall, 1975).

Culver, C. M., Cohen, S. I., Silverman, A. S. and Shmavonian, B. M. Cognitive structuring, field dependence-independence, and the psychophysiological response to perceptual isolation. In J. Wortis (Ed.), *Recent advances in biological psychiatry.* New York: Plenum, 1964.

Cummins, R. A., Livesey, P. J., Evans, J. G. M., and Walsh, R. N. A developmental theory of environmental enrichment. *Science*, 1977, *197*, 692–694.

Cummins, R. A., Walsh, R. N., Budtz-Olsen, O. F., Konstantinos, T., and Horsfall, C. R. Environmentally induced changes in the brains of elderly rats. *Nature*, 1973, *243*, 516–518.

Curtis, G. C., and Zuckerman, M. A psychopathological reaction precipitated by sensory deprivation. *American Journal of Psychiatry*, 1968, *125*, 255–260.

Curtiss, S. *Genie: A psycholinguistic study of a modern-day "wild child."* New York: Academic Press, 1977.

Dallett, J. O. *The effects of sensory and social variables on the recalled dream: Complementality, continuity, and compensation.* Unpublished Ph.D. dissertation, University of California, Los Angeles, 1973.

Dahl, H. Observations on a natural experiment: Helen Keller. *Journal of the American Psychoanalytic Association,* 1965, *13,* 533–550.

D'Atri, D. A. Psychophysiological responses to crowding. *Environment and Behavior,* 1975, *7,* 237–252.

Dauterman, W. L., Shapiro, B., and Suinn, R. M. Performance tests of intelligence for the blind reviewed. *International Journal for the Education of the Blind,* 1967, *17,* 8–16.

Davenport, J. W., Gonzalez, L. M., Carey, J. C., Bishop, S. B., and Hagquist, W. W. Environmental stimulation reduces learning deficits in experimental cretinism. *Science,* 1976, *191,* 578–579.

Davis, K. Extreme social isolation of a child. *American Journal of Sociology,* 1940, *45,* 554–565.

Davis, K. Final note on a case of extreme isolation. *American Journal of Sociology,* 1947, *52,* 432–437.

Davis, J. R., Wallace, C. J., Liberman, R. P., and Finch, B. E. The use of brief isolation to suppress delusional and hallucinatory speech. *Journal of Behavior Therapy and Experimental Psychiatry,* 1976, *7,* 269–275.

Davis, S. F., Beighley, B. G., Libretto, J. S., Mollenhour, M. N. and Prytula, R. E. Contrafreeloading as a function of early environmental rearing conditions. *Bulletin of the Psychonomic Society,* 1975, *6,* 595–597.

David-Neel, A. *Magic and mystery in Tibet.* New Hyde Park, New York: University Books, 1965.

Daw, N. W., and Wyatt, H. J. Raising rabbits in a moving visual environment: An attempt to modify directional sensitivity in the retina. *Journal of Physiology* (London), 1974, *240,* 309–330.

Day, C. *This simian world.* New York: Knopf, 1920.

Deaton, J. E., Berg, S. W., Richlin, M., and Litrownik, A. J. Coping activities in solitary confinement of U.S. Navy POWs in Vietnam. *Journal of Applied Social Psychology,* 1977, *7,* 239–257.

deBeaumont, G., and deTocqueville, A. *On the penitentiary system in the United States and its application in France.* Carbondale, Illinois: Southern Illinois University, 1964. (Originally published 1833.)

deCharms, R. *Personal causation: The internal affective determinants of behavior.* New York: Academic Press, 1968.

Deighton, L. *The Ipcress file.* London: Hodder and Stoughton, 1962.

Deikman, A. J. Deautomatization and the mystic experience. *Psychiatry,* 1966, *29,* 324–338.

Dennis, W. The significance of feral man. *American Journal of Psychology*, 1941, *54*, 425–432. (a)

Dennis, W. Review of A. Gesell's *Wolf-child and human-child. Psychological Bulletin*, 1941, *38*, 889–893. (b)

Dennis, W. Causes of retardation among institutional children: Iran. *Journal of Genetic Psychology*, 1960, *96*, 47–59.

Dennis, W. *Children of the crèche.* New York: Appleton-Century-Crofts, 1973.

Dennis, W., and Dennis, S. G. Development under controlled environmental conditions. In W. Dennis (Ed.), *Readings in child psychology.* New York: Prentice-Hall, 1951.

Dercum, F. X. *Rest, suggestion and other therapeutic measures in nervous and mental diseases* (2nd ed.). Philadelphia: Blakiston, 1917.

DeRopp, R. S. *The master game.* New York: Dell, 1968.

Descartes, R. *Discourse on method.* In *R. Descartes' Philosophy and theology.* London: Dent, 1912. (Originally published 1637.)

DesLauriers, A. M., and Carlson, C. F. *Your child is asleep: Early infantile autism: etiology, treatment, parental influences.* Homewood, Illinois: Dorsey, 1969.

Devereaux, G. *Reality and a dream: Psychotherapy of a Plains Indian.* New York: International Universities Press, 1951.

Dickens, C. *American notes.* In A. Land (Ed.), *The works of Charles Dickens* (Vol. 28). New York: Scribner's, 1907. (Originally published 1843.)

Dicks, H. V., Williams, A. H., Storr, C. A., and Wall, P. D. Comments submitted to Lord Parker's Committee on Interrogation Procedures, 1972.

Dittrich, A. [Comparison of altered states of consciousness induced by short-duration sensory deprivation and $(-)-\Delta$ [9]-trans-tetrahydrocannabinol.] *Zeitschrift für experimentelle und angewandte Psychologie*, 1975, *22*, 547–560.

Dodwell, P. C., Timney, B. N. and Emerson, U. F. Development of stimulus-seeking in dark-reared kittens. *Nature*, 1976, *260*, 277–280.

Doty, B. H. The effect of cage environment upon avoidance responding of aged rats. *Journal of Gerontology*, 1972, *72*, 358–360.

Dohrenwend, B. S., and Dohrenwend, B. P. Stress situations, birth order, and psychological symptoms. *Journal of Abnormal and Social Psychology*, 1966, *71*, 215–223.

Dohrenwend, B. S., Feldstein, S., Plosky, J., and Schmeidler, G. R. Factors interacting with birth order in self-selection among volunteer subjects. *Journal of Social Psychology*, 1967, *72*, 125–128.

Doi, L. T. Morita therapy and psychoanalysis. *Psychologia*, 1962, *5*, 117–123.

Doleys, D. M., Wells, K. C., Hobbs, S. A., Roberts, M. W., and Cartelli, L. M. The effects of social punishment on noncompliance: A comparison with time-out and positive practice. *Journal of Applied Behavior Analysis*, 1976, *9*, 471–482.

Dolliver, R. H. Concerning the potential parallels between psychotherapy and brainwashing. *Psychotherapy: Theory, Research and Practice,* 1971, *8,* 170–174.

Domino, E. F. Neurobiology of phencyclidine—an update. In R. C. Petersen and R. C. Stillman (Eds.), *Phencyclidine (PCP) abuse: An appraisal.* Washington, D.C.: U.S. Government Printing Office, 1978.

Douglas, V. I. Sustained attention and impulse control: Implications for the handicapped child. In J. A. Swets and L. L. Elliott (Eds.), *Psychology and the handicapped child.* Washington, D.C.: HEW Office of Education, 1973.

Downs, F. S. Bedrest and sensory disturbances. *American Journal of Nursing,* 1974, *74,* 434–438.

Doyle, L. J. (Transl.) *St. Benedict's rule for monasteries.* Collegeville, Minnesota: Liturgical Press, 1948.

Drake, G. L. and Herzog, T. R. Free-looking time for randomly generated polygons with experimenter present: Effects of content and duration of foreperiod. *Perceptual and Motor Skills,* 1974, *39,* 403–406.

Draper, W. A. and Bernstein, I. S. Note on the behavior of rhesus monkeys after release from a total body cast. *Perceptual and Motor Skills,* 1963, *17,* 368.

Drash, P. W. Treatment of hyperactive two-year-old children. Paper presented at the meeting of the American Psychiatric Association, Miami Beach, 1976.

Drever, J. Early learning and the perception of space. *American Journal of Psychology,* 1955, *68,* 605–614.

Duffy, E. The psychological significance of the concept of "arousal" or "activation." *Psychological Review,* 1957, *64,* 265–275.

Duker, P. Intra-subject controlled time-out (social isolation) in the modification of self-injurious behaviour. *Journal of Mental Deficiency Research,* 1975, *19,* 107–112.

Duncan, R. L. *Dragons at the gate.* New York: William Morrow, 1975.

Ecclestone, C., Gendreau, P., and Knox, C. Solitary confinement of prisoners: An assessment of its effects on inmates' personal constructs and adrenocortical activity. *Canadian Journal of Behavioural Science,* 1974, *6,* 178–191.

Edmonston, W. E., Jr. Neutral hypnosis as relaxation. *American Journal of Clinical Hypnosis,* 1977, *20,* 69–74.

Egerton, W., and Kay, J. H. Psychological disturbances associated with open heart surgery. *British Journal of Psychiatry,* 1964, *110,* 433–439.

Ehlers, W., Knebusch, R. E., Revenstorff, D., and Brengelmann, J. C. [Suggestibility as a therapeutic factor in various forms of smoking therapy.] *Archiv für Psychologie,* 1975, *127,* 210–219.

Eisen, N. H. Some effects of early sensory deprivation on later behavior: The quondam hard-of-hearing child. *Journal of Abnormal and Social Psychology,* 1962, *65,* 338–342.

Eisenberg, L., and Kanner, L. Early infantile autism, 1943–1955. *American Journal of Orthopsychiatry,* 1956, *26,* 556–566.

Eisenberger, R. Is there a deprivation-satiation function for social approval? *Psychological Bulletin*, 1970, *74*, 255–275.

Eisinger, R. A. Psychosocial predictors of smoking behavior change. *Social Sciences and Medicine*, 1972, *6*, 137–144.

Elkin, A. P. *The Australian aborigines* (4th ed.). Sydney: Angus and Robinson, 1964.

Ellan, P. and Mudi, C. *Sopranino*. New York: Norton, 1953.

Ellenberger, H. F. Behavior under involuntary confinement. In A. H. Esser (Ed.), *Behavior and environment: The use of space by animals and men*. New York: Plenum, 1971.

Ellis, A. *Reason and emotion in psychotherapy*. New York: Lyle Stuart, 1962.

Ellis, M. J. *Why people play*. Englewood Cliffs, New Jersey: Prentice-Hall, 1973.

Ellis, R. Unusual sensory and thought disturbances after cardiac surgery. *American Journal of Nursing*, 1972, *72*, 2021–2025.

Ellis, R., Jackson, C. W., Jr., Rich, R., Hughey, G.-A., and Schlotfeldt, R. M. Suggestions for the care of eye surgery patients who experience reduced sensory input. Paper read at the American Nurses' Association Regional Conferences, Philadelphia and Kansas City, 1968.

Elonen, A. S., and Cain, A. C. Diagnostic evaluation and treatment of deviant blind children. *American Journal of Orthopsychiatry*, 1964, *34*, 625–633.

Emmons, T. D., and Webb, W. W. Subjective correlates of emotional responsivity and stimulation seeking in psychopaths, normals, and acting-out neurotics. *Journal of Consulting and Clinical Psychology*, 1974, *42*, 620.

Endo, G. T. Social drive or arousal: A test of two theories of social isolation. *Journal of Experimental Child Psychology*, 1968, *6*, 61–74.

English, D. Anthony home: "I'm as sick as a dog." Adelaide *Advertiser*, October 22, 1977, p. 1.

Enzensberger, H. M., and Michel, K. M. (Eds.) [*Torture in the Federal Republic of Germany: On the situation of political prisoners.*] Kursbuch 32. Berlin: Kursbuch/Rotbuch Verlag, 1973.

Epstein, L. H., and Collins, F. L., Jr. The measurement of situational influences of smoking. *Addictive Behaviors*, 1977, *2*, 47–53.

Erdelyi, M. H. A new look at the New Look: Perceptual defense and vigilance. *Psychological Review*, 1974, *81*, 1–25.

Ernst, P. A., Beran, B., Safford, F., and Kleinhauz, M. Isolation and the symptoms of chronic brain syndrome. *The Gerontologist*, 1978, *18*, 468–474.

Ernst, P. A., and Badash, D. Psychiatric problems of the aged: A new approach more useful for both patient and doctor. *Israel Annals of Psychiatry and Related Disciplines*, 1977, *15*, 12–15.

Ewbank, R. The behavior of animals in restraint. In M. W. Fox (Ed.), *Abnormal behavior in animals*. Philadelphia: Saunders, 1968.

"Ex-Viet POW keeps vow." New Haven *Register*, May 26, 1978.

Eysenck, H. J. (Ed.). *The measurement of personality*, Baltimore, Maryland: University Park Press, 1976.

Eysenck, S. B. G., and Eysenck, H. J. *Manual for the Eysenck Personality Inventory*. San Diego, California: Educational and Industrial Testing Service, 1963.

Fahrion, S. L. Autogenic biofeedback treatment for migraine. *Research and Clinical Studies in Headache*, 1978, *5*, 1–11.

Fantz, R. L. Ontogeny of perception. In A. M. Schrier, H. F. Harlow, and F. Stolinitz (Eds.), *Behavior of non-human primates: Modern research trends* (Vol. 2). New York: Academic Press, 1965.

Farber, I. E., Harlow, H. F., and West, L. J. Brainwashing, conditioning, and DDD (debility, dependency and dread). *Sociometry*, 1957, *20*, 271–285.

Farley, F. H., and Sewell, T. Test of an arousal theory of delinquency. *Criminal Justice and Behavior*, 1976, *3*, 315–320.

Favazza, A. R. Feral and isolated children. In S. Sanker (Ed.), *Mental health and children* (Vol. 1). New York: PJD Publications, 1975.

Favazza, A. R. Feral and isolated children. *British Journal of Medical Psychology*, 1977, *50*, 105–111.

Federal Prisoners' Coalition. Brainwashing U.S. prisoners. A letter to United Nations Economic and Social Council, 1972. Reprinted in *Rough Times*, 1973, *3*(4), 6–7.

Fenigstein, A., and Carver, C. S. Self-focusing effects of heartbeat feedback. *Journal of Personality and Social Psychology*, 1978, *36*, 1241–1250.

Ferster, C. B. Positive reinforcement and behavioral deficits of young children. *Child Development*, 1961, *32*, 437–456.

Fickess, F. L. *Effects of a program of sensory stimulation upon patient recovery and welfare*. Unpublished doctoral dissertation, Catholic University, 1975.

Fields, R. M. *Society under siege: A psychology of Northern Ireland*. Philadelphia: Temple University Press, 1976. (a)

Fields, R. M. Torture and institutional coercion: Northern Ireland—A case study. Paper prepared for presentation at the meeting of the American Sociological Association, New York, 1976. (b)

Fields, R. M. Letter to the editors, *Psychology Today*, June 2, 1976. (Unpublished) (c)

Finch, B. E., Wallace, C. J., and Davis, J. R. Behavioral observations before, during, and after brief isolation (time-out). *Journal of Nervous and Mental Disease*, 1976, *163*, 408–413.

Fineman, J. A. B., Kuniholm, P., and Sheridan, S. Spasmus nutans: A syndrome of auto-arousal. *Journal of the American Academy of Child Psychiatry*, 1971, *10*, 136–155.

Firestone, P. The effects and side effects of timeout on an aggressive nursery school child, *Journal of Behavior Therapy and Experimental Psychiatry*, 1976, *7*, 79–81.

Fishbein, M. *Consumer beliefs and behavior with respect to cigarette smoking: A critical analysis of the public literature.* A report prepared for the staff of the Federal Trade Commission, Washington, D.C., 1977.

Fishbein, M. Persuasive communication: A social psychological perspective on factors influencing communication effectiveness. In A. E. Bennett (Ed.) *Communications between doctors and patients.* London: Oxford University Press, 1976.

Fiske, D. W., and Maddi, S. R. (Eds.) *Functions of varied experience.* Homewood, Illinois: Dorsey, 1961.

Fisman, M. The brain stem in psychosis. *British Journal of Psychiatry,* 1975, *126,* 414–422.

Fitzgerald, R. G. Visual phenomenology in recently blind adults. *American Journal of Psychiatry,* 1971, *127,* 109–115.

Fitzgerald, R. G., and Long, I. Seclusion in the treatment and management of severely disturbed manic and depressed patients. *Perspectives in Psychiatric Care,* 1973, *11,* 59–64.

Flaherty, B. E. (Ed.) *Psychophysiological aspects of space flight.* New York: Columbia University Press, 1961.

Foa, U. G. Convergences in the analysis of the structure of interpersonal behavior. *Psychological Review,* 1961, *68,* 341–353.

Forehand, R., and Baumeister, A. Body rocking and activity level as a function of prior movement restraint. *American Journal of Mental Deficiency,* 1970, *74,* 608–610.

Forgays, D. G., and McClure, G. N. A direct comparison of the effects of the quiet room and water immersion isolation techniques. *Psychophysiology,* 1974, *11,* 346–349.

Forgus, R. H. Early visual and motor experience as determiners of complex maze-learning ability under rich and reduced stimulation. *Journal of Comparative and Physiological Psychology,* 1955, *48,* 215–220.

Forgus, R. H. Advantage of early over later perceptual experience in improving form discrimination. *Canadian Journal of Psychology,* 1956, *10,* 147–155.

Fortune, R. *Omaha secret societies.* New York: Columbia University Press, 1932.

Fox, M. W. The effects of short term social and sensory isolation upon behavior, EEG and averaged evoked potentials in puppies. *Physiology and Behavior,* 1967, *2,* 145–151.

Fox, M. W. Socialization, environmental factors and abnormal behavioral development in animals. In M. W. Fox (Ed.), *Abnormal behavior in animals.* Philadelphia: Saunders, 1968.

Fox, M. W., Inman, O., and Glisson, S. Age differences in central nervous effects of visual deprivation in the dog. *Developmental Psychobiology,* 1968, *1,* 48–54.

Fox, S. S. Self-maintained sensory input and sensory deprivation in monkeys: A behavioral and neuropharmacological study. *Journal of Comparative and Physiological Psychology,* 1962, *55,* 438–444.

Foxx, J. R. Witchcraft and clanship in Cochiti therapy. In A. Kiev (Ed.), *Magic, faith, and healing.* New York: Free Press, 1964.

Foxx, R. M., and Shapiro, S. T. The timeout ribbon: A non-exclusionary timeout procedure. *Journal of Applied Behavior Analysis,* 1978, *11,* 125–136.

Foy, D. W., and Simon, S. J. Alcoholic drinking topography as a function of solitary versus social context. *Addictive Behaviors,* 1978, *3,* 39–41.

Fozard, J. L., and Popkin, S. J. Optimizing adult development: Ends and means of an applied psychology of aging. *American Psychologist,* 1978, *33,* 975–989.

Fraiberg, S. Parallel and divergent patterns in blind and sighted infants. *Psychoanalytic Study of the Child,* 1968, *23,* 264–300.

Fraiberg, S. Separation crisis in two blind children. *Psychoanalytic Study of the Child,* 1972, *26,* 355–371.

Fraiberg, S., and Freedman, D. A. Studies in the ego development of the congenitally blind child. *Psychoanalytic Study of the Child,* 1964, *19,* 113–169.

Fraisse, P. Temporal isolation, activity rhythms, and time estimation. In J. Rasmussen (Ed.), *Man in isolation and confinement.* Chicago: Aldine, 1973.

Francis, D. *Risk.* London: Michael Joseph, 1977.

Francis, R. D. The effect of prior instructions and time knowledge on the toleration of sensory isolation. *Journal of Nervous and Mental Disease,* 1964, *139,* 182–185.

Francis, R. D., and Diespecker, D. D. Extraversion and volunteering for sensory isolation. *Perceptual and Motor Skills,* 1973, *36,* 244–246.

Frankel, F., Freeman, B. J., Ritvo, E., and Pardo, R. The effect of environmental stimulation upon the stereotyped behavior of autistic children. *Journal of Autism and Childhood Schizophrenia,* 1978, *8,* 389–394.

Frankel, B. L., Patel, D. J., Horowitz, D., Friedewald, W. T., and Gaarder, K. R. Treatment of hypertension with biofeedback and relaxation techniques. *Psychosomatic Medicine,* 1978, *40,* 276–293.

Frankenhaeuser, M., and Gardell, B. Underload and overload in working life: A multidisciplinary approach. Unpublished paper, University of Stockholm, 1973.

Frankenhaeuser, M., and Johansson, G. On the psychophysiological consequences of understimulation and overstimulation. *Reports* from the Psychological Laboratories, University of Stockholm, Supplement No. 25, August 1974.

Frankenhaeuser, M., Myrsten, A.-L., Post, B. and Johansson, G. Behavioural and physiological effects of cigarette smoking in a monotonous situation. *Psychopharmacologia,* 1971, *22,* 1–7.

Fraser, G. M. *Flashman in the great game.* London: Barrie and Jenkins, 1975.

Fraser, T. M. *The effects of confinement as a factor in manned space flight.* Washington, D.C.: NASA Technical Report No. 511, 1966.

Frederiksen, L. W., Epstein, L. H., and Kosevsky, B. P. Reliability and controlling effects of three procedures for self-monitoring. *Psychological Records,* 1975, *25,* 255–264.

Frederiksen, L. W., Peterson, G. L., and Murphy, W. D. Controlled smoking: Development and maintenance. *Addictive Behaviors,* 1976, *1,* 193–196.

Freedman, D. A. The influence of congenital and perinatal sensory deprivations on later development. *Psychosomatics, 1968, 9,* 272–277.

Freedman, D. A. Congenital and perinatal sensory deprivation: Some studies in early development. *American Journal of Psychiatry,* 1971, *127,* 1539–1545.

Freedman, D. A. On the limits of the effectiveness of psychoanalysis: Early ego and somatic disturbances. *International Journal of Psychoanalysis,* 1972, *53,* 363–370.

Freedman, D. A. Congenital and perinatal sensory deprivation: Their effect on the capacity to experience affect. *Psychoanalytic Quarterly,* 1975, *44,* 62–80.

Freedman, D. A., and Brown, S. L. On the role of coenesthetic stimulation in the development of psychic structure. *Psychoanalytic Quarterly,* 1968, *37,* 418–438.

Freedman, D. A. and Cannady, C. Delayed emergence of prone locomotion. *Journal of Nervous and Mental Disease,* 1971, *153,* 108–117.

Freedman, D. A., Cannady, C., and Robinson, J. S. Speech and psychic structure: A reconsideration of their relation. *Journal of the American Psychoanalytic Association,* 1971, *19,* 765–779.

Freedman, D. A., Montgomery, J. R., Wilson, R., Bealmear, P. M., and Salve, M. A. Further observations on the effect of reverse isolation from birth on cognitive and affective development. *Journal of the American Academy of Child Psychiatry,* 1976, 15, 593–603.

Freedman, J. L. *Crowding and behavior.* San Francisco: Freeman, 1975.

Freeman, R. D. Psychiatric aspects of sensory disorders and intervention. In P. Graham (Ed.), *Epidemiological approaches in child psychiatry.* London: Academic Press, 1977.

Freireich, E. J., Bodey, G. P., Rodriguez, V., Gehan, E. A., Smith, T., Hester, J. P., and McCredie, K. B. A controlled clinical trial to evaluate a protected environment and prophylactic antibiotic program in the treatment of adult acute leukemia. *Transactions of the Association of American Physicians,* 1975, *88,* 109–119.

French, A. P., Schmid, A. C., and Ingalls, E. Transcendental meditation, altered reality testing, and behavioral change: A case report. *Journal of Nervous and Mental Disease,* 1975, *161,* 55–58.

Freud, A., and Burlingham, D. *Infants without families.* New York: International Universities Press, 1944.

Freud, S. Further recommendations in the technique of psycho-analysis. In *Collected papers* (Vol. 2). London: Hogarth, 1924. (Original publication 1913.)

Freud, S. *A general introduction to psychoanalysis.* Garden City: New York, Garden City Publishing Company, 1943. (Original English publication, 1920.)

Frey, H. [Improving the spelling performance of dyslexics through autogenic training.] *Zeitschrift für Entwicklungspsychologie und Pädagogische Psychologie,* 1978, *10,* 258–264.

"Friar Jim reborn in solitary confinement." Vancouver *Province*, August 9, 1975.

Friedman, C. J., Handford, A. H., and Settlage, C. Child psychological development: The adverse effects of physical restraint. Paper read at a meeting of the American Psychiatric Association, Philadelphia, 1964.

Friedman, C. J., Sibinga, M. S., Steisel, I. M., and Sinnamon, H. M. Sensory restriction and isolation experiences in children with phenylketonuria. *Journal of Abnormal Psychology*, 1968, *73*, 294–303.

Friedman, J., Horvath, T., and Meares, R. Tobacco smoking and the stimulus barrier. *Nature*, 1974, *248*, 455–456.

Friedrich, D., Libkuman, T., and Thomas, A. Input deficit and stimulus enrichment: A replication-with-extension. *American Journal of Mental Deficiency*, 1973, *77*, 687–693.

Fromm, A. and Shor, R. E. (Eds.) *Hypnosis: Research developments and perspectives*. Chicago: Aldine–Atherton, 1972.

Fuller, J. L. Effects of experiential deprivation upon behavior in animals. *Transactions of the Third World Congress of Psychiatry*. Toronto: University of Toronto Press, 1964.

Fuller, J. L. Experiential deprivation and later behavior. *Science*, 1967, *158*, 1645–1652.

Furth, H. G. *Thinking without language*. New York: Free Press, 1966.

Gaddis, T. E. *Birdman of Alcatraz*. London: Gollancz, 1957.

Gaines, L. S., and Vetter, H. J. Sensory deprivation and psychotherapy. *Psychotherapy: Theory, Research and Practice*, 1968, *5*, 7–12.

Gaines, R. Experiencing the perceptually-deprived child. *Journal of Learning Disabilities*, 1969, *11*, 9–15.

Gale, A. "Stimulus hunger": Individual differences in operant strategy in a button-pressing task. *Behaviour Research and Therapy*, 1969, *7*, 265–274.

Ganz, L. Orientation in visual space by neonates and its modification by visual deprivation. In A. H. Riesen (Ed.), *The developmental neuropsychology of sensory deprivation*. New York: Academic Press, 1975.

Ganz, L., and Riesen, A. H. Stimulus generalization to hue in dark-reared macaque. *Journal of Comparative and Physiological Psychology*, 1962, *55*, 92–99.

Garrison, F. H. *An introduction to the history of medicine* (3rd ed.). Philadelphia: Saunders, 1921.

Gast, D. L., and Nelson, C. M. Legal and ethical considerations for the use of time-out in special education settings. *Journal of Special Education*, 1977, *11*, 457–467.

Geer, J. H. The development of a scale to measure fear. *Behaviour Research and Therapy*, 1965, *3*, 45–53.

Gendreau, P., and Carlson, F. Response bias factors and the sensoristatic model of sensory restriction. *Canadian Journal of Psychology*, 1974, *28*, 32–36.

Gendreau, P., Ecclestone, J., and Knox, C. Solitary confinement of prisoners: An assessment of its effects on the personal constructs and stress level of inmates. Unpublished manuscript, Trent University, 1972.

Gerdes, L. The confused or delirious patient. *American Journal of Nursing,* 1968, *68,* 1228–1233.

Gergen, K. J. Social psychology as history. *Journal of Personality and Social Psychology,* 1973, *26,* 309–320.

Gerlach, K. A. Environmental design to counter occupational boredom. *Journal of Architectural Research,* 1974, *3,* 15–19.

Gesell, A. *Wolf-child and human-child.* New York: Harper and Brothers, 1941.

Gibby, R. G., and Adams, H. B. Receptiveness of psychiatric patients to verbal communication: An increase following partial sensory and social isolation. *Archives of General Psychiatry,* 1961, *5,* 366–370.

Gibby, R. G., Adams, H. B., and Carrera, R. N. Therapeutic changes in psychiatric patients following partial sensory deprivation. *Archives of General Psychiatry,* 1960, *3,* 33–42.

Gibson, E. J. *Principles of perceptual learning and development.* New York: Appleton-Century-Crofts, 1969.

Gibson, H. B. *Hypnosis: Its nature and therapeutic uses.* London: Peter Owen, 1977.

Gill, M. M., and Brenman, M. *Hypnosis and related states.* New York: International Universities Press, 1959, 1961.

Gillman, A. E. Handicap and cognition: Visual deprivation and the rate of motor development in infants. *New Outlook for the Blind,* 1973, *67,* 309–314.

Girodo, M. Yoga meditation and flooding in the treatment of anxiety neurosis. In G. R. Patterson, I. M. Marks, J. D. Matarazzo, R. A. Myers, G. E. Schwartz, and H. H. Strupp (Eds.), *Behavior change.* Chicago: Aldine, 1975.

Glass, D. C., and Singer, J. E. *Urban stress.* New York: Academic Press, 1972.

Glass, J. D. Alpha blocking: Absence in visuo-behavioral deprivation. *Science,* 1977, *198,* 58–60.

Glennon, C. A., and Nason, D. E. Managing the behavior of the hyperkinetic child: What research says. *Reading Teacher,* 1974, *27,* 815–824.

Globus, A. Brain morphology as a function of presynaptic morphology and activity. In A. H. Riesen (Ed.), *The developmental neuropsychology of sensory deprivation.* New York: Academic Press, 1975.

Glynn, E. The therapeutic use of seclusion in an adolescent pavilion. *Journal of the Hillside Hospital,* 1957, *6,* 156–159.

Godfrey, A. B. Sensory-motor stimulation for slow-to-develop children: A specialized program for public health nurses. *American Journal of Nursing,* 1975, *75,* 56–59.

Goebel, P. [The significance of the lack of the visual information system for the development of blind infants.] *Praxis der Kinderpsychologie und Kinderpsychiatrie,* 1975, *24,* 218–221.

Goffman, E. *The presentation of self in everyday life.* New York: Anchor, 1959.

Gold, M. S., and Robertson, M. F. The night/day imagery paradox of selected psychotic children. *Journal of the American Academy of Child Psychiatry,* 1975, *14,* 132–141.

Goldberg, B., Lobb, H., and Kroll, H. Psychiatric problems of the deaf child. *Canadian Psychiatric Association Journal,* 1975, *20,* 75–83.

Goldberger, L. Reactions to perceptual isolation and Rorschach manifestations of the primary process. *Journal of Projective Techniques,* 1961, *25,* 287–302.

Goldberger, L., and Holt, R. R. Experimental interference with reality contact (perceptual isolation): Method and group results. *Journal of Nervous and Mental Disease,* 1958, *127,* 99–112.

Goldberger, L., and Holt, R. R. *A comparison of isolation effects and their personality correlates in two divergent samples.* WADC Tech. Report 61–417, Contract AF33 (616)-6103. Wright-Patterson AFB, Ohio, 1961. (a)

Goldberger, L., and Holt, R. R. Experimental interference with reality contact: Individual differences. In P. Solomon et al. (Eds.), *Sensory deprivation.* Cambridge: Harvard University Press, 1961. (b)

Goldfarb, W. Effects of psychological deprivation in infancy and subsequent stimulation. *American Journal of Psychiatry,* 1945, *102,* 18–33.

Goldfarb, W. Emotional and intellectual consequences of psychologic deprivation in infancy: A revaluation. In P. H. Hoch and J. Zubin (Eds.), *Psychopathology of childhood.* New York: Grune and Stratton, 1955.

Goldfarb, W. *Childhood schizophrenia.* Cambridge, Mass.: Harvard University Press, 1961.

Golding, W. *Free fall.* New York: Harcourt Brace and World, 1959.

Goldman, R. Rest: Its use and abuse in the aged. *Journal of the American Geriatrics Society,* 1977, *25,* 433–438.

Goldstein, A. G. Hallucinatory experience: A personal account. *Journal of Abnormal Psychology,* 1976, *85,* 423–429.

Goldstein, K. M. Stimulus reinforcement during sensory deprivation. *Perceptual and Motor Skills,* 1965, *20,* 757–762.

Goldstein, K. M., and Blackman, S. *Cognitive style: Five approaches and relevant research.* New York: Wiley, 1978.

Goleman, D. *The varieties of the meditative experience.* New York: Irvington, 1977.

Goleman, D. J. Meditation and consciousness: An Asian approach to mental health. *American Journal of Psychotherapy,* 1976, *30,* 41–54.

Goleman, D. J., and Schwartz, G. E. Meditation as an intervention in stress reactivity. *Journal of Consulting and Clinical Psychology,* 1976, *44,* 456–466.

Goodacre, N. W. *Experiment in retreats.* London: Mowbray, 1970.

Gordon, A. M. Psychological aspects of isolator therapy in acute leukaemia. *British Journal of Psychiatry,* 1975, *127,* 588–590. (a)

Gordon, A. M. Psychological adaptation to isolator therapy in acute leukaemia. *Psychotherapy and Psychosomatics,* 1975, *26,* 132–139. (b)

Gordon, A. M. The effect of treatment environments. *Journal of Psychosomatic Research,* 1976, *20,* 363–366.

Gordon, C., and Gaitz, C. N. Leisure and lives: Personal expressivity across the life span. In R. H. Binstock and E. Shanas (Eds.), *Handbook of aging and the social sciences.* New York: Van Nostrand Reinhold, 1977.

Gordon, J. E. and Haywood, H. C. Input deficit in cultural-familial retardates: Effect of stimulus enrichment. *American Journal of Mental Deficiency,* 1969, *73,* 604–610.

Gorry, T., Chibucos, T., and Bell, R. Visual and tactual variation seeking in the rat: Intermodal effects of early rearing. *Developmental Psychobiology,* 1971, *4,* 123–132.

Gottlieb, G. Ontogenesis of sensory function in birds and mammals. In E. Tobach, L. R. Aronson, and E. Shaw (Eds.), *The biopsychology of development.* New York: Academic Press, 1971.

Gottlieb, G. The roles of experience in the development of behavior and the nervous system. In G. Gottlieb (Ed.), *Studies on the development of behavior and the nervous system* (Vol. 3). New York: Academic Press, 1976.

Graham, R. L. *Dove.* London: Sphere, 1974.

Greenough, W. T., Fass, B., and DeVoogd, J. J. The influence of experience on recovery following brain damage in rodents: Hypothesis based on developmental research. In R. N. Walsh and W. T. Greenough (Eds.), *Environments as therapy for brain dysfunction.* New York: Plenum, 1975.

Greenwald, A. G. Consequences of prejudice against the null hypothesis. *Psychological Bulletin,* 1975, *82,* 1–20.

Grey, A. *Hostage in Peking.* London: Michael Joseph, 1970.

Griffiths, R. R., Bigelow, G. E., and Liebson, I. Alcohol self-administration and social interaction in alcoholics. Paper read at the meeting of the American Psychological Association, Montreal, August 1973.

Grim, P. F. Relaxation, meditation, and insight. *Psychologia—An International Journal of Psychology in the Orient,* 1975, *18,* 125–133.

Grissom, R. J. Facilitation of memory by experiential restriction after learning. *American Journal of Psychology,* 1966, *79,* 613–617.

Gross, J., Kempe, P., and Reimer, C. C. [Insanity as a result of sensory deprivation and isolation.] In W. Schulte and R. Tolle (Eds.), *Wahn.* Stuttgart: G. Thieme, 1972.

Gross, J., and Svab, L. Social isolation and sensory deprivation and their judicial psychological aspects. Unpublished manuscript, Psychiatric Research Institute, Prague, 1967.

Grunebaum, H. U., Freedman, S. J., and Greenblatt, M. Sensory deprivation and personality. *American Journal of Psychiatry,* 1960, *116,* 878–882.

Gruneberg, N. H. Origins of head-rolling (spasmus nutans) during early infancy:

Clinical observations and theoretical implications. *Psychosomatic Medicine,* 1964, *26,* 162–171.

Guess, D. The influence of visual and ambulation restrictions on stereotyped behavior. *American Journal of Mental Deficiency,* 1966, *70,* 542–547.

Guichard, M.-T. [The Leboyer babies.] *Psychologie,* 1976 (No. 8), 33–38.

Gunther, W. [Recent insights into the causes of mental impairment.] *Praxis der Kinderpsychologie und Kinderpsychiatrie,* 1972, *21,* 41–48.

Gunzburg, A. L. The physical environment of the mentally handicapped. *British Journal of Mental Subnormality,* 1977, *22,* 1–6.

Guthrie, E. R. *The psychology of human conflict.* New York: Harper and Brothers, 1938.

Haenel, T., and Nagel, G. A. [The psychology of tumor patients with agranulocytosis under treatment in an isolated-bed system.] *Schweizerische Medizinische Wochenschrift,* 1975, *105,* 839–843.

Haggard, E. A. Some effects of geographic and social isolation in natural settings. In J. E. Rasmussen (Ed.), *Man in isolation and confinement.* Chicago: Aldine, 1973.

Haggard, E. A., Ås, A., and Borgen, C.-M. Social isolates and urbanites in perceptual isolation. *Journal of Abnormal Psychology,* 1970, *76,* 1–9.

Hall, E. T. *The hidden dimension.* Garden City, New York: Doubleday, 1966.

Hall, E. T. Environmental communication. In A. H. Esser (Ed.), *Behavior and the environment: The use of space by animals and men.* New York: Plenum, 1971.

Halliday, G. W., and Evans, J. H. Somatosensory enrichment of a deaf, blind, retarded adolescent through vibration. *Perceptual and Motor Skills,* 1974, *38,* 880.

Halpin, Glennelle, Halpin, Gerard, and Torrance, E. P. Effects of blindness on creative thinking abilities of children. *Developmental Psychology,* 1973, *9,* 268–274.

Haney, C., Banks, W. C., and Zimbardo, P. G. A study of prisoners and guards in a simulated prison. *Naval Research Reviews,* September 1973, 1–17.

Hare, R. D. Orienting and defensive responses to visual stimuli. *Psychophysiology,* 1973, *10,* 453–464.

Harlow, H. F., and Harlow, M. K. The effect of rearing conditions on behavior. *Bulletin of the Menninger Clinic,* 1962, *26,* 213–224.

Harlow, H. F., and Suomi, S. J. Social recovery by isolation reared monkeys. *Proceedings of the National Academy of Sciences,* 1971, *68,* 1534–1538.

Harlow, H. F., and Suomi, S. J. Induced depression in monkeys. *Behavioral Biology,* 1974, *12,* 273–296.

Harper, D. W., and Bross, M. The effect of unimodal sensory deprivation on sensory processes: A decade of research from the University of Manitoba. *Canadian Psychological Review,* 1978, *19,* 128–144.

Harrell, L. E., and Balagura, S. The effect of dark and light on the functional recovery following lateral hypothalamic lesions. *Life Sciences,* 1974, *15,* 2079 –2087.

Harrington, G. M., and Kohler, G. R. Sensory deprivation and sensory reinforcement with shock. *Psychological Reports,* 1966, *18,* 803–808.

Harris, A. Sensory deprivation and schizophrenia. *Journal of Mental Science,* 1959, *105,* 235–237.

Harris, J. W. Sensory isolation and aversive self-stimulation with light, sound and shock. *Dissertation Abstracts,* 1969, *30,* 2440.

Hartmann, H. *Ego psychology and the problem of adaptation.* New York: International Universities Press, 1958. (Original publication, 1939.)

Harvey, O. J., Hunt, D. E., and Schroder, H. M. *Conceptual systems and personality organization.* New York: Wiley, 1961.

Hatwell, Y. [*Sensory deprivation and intelligence.*] Paris: Presses Universitaires de France, 1966.

Hauser, R. Rapid smoking as a technique of behavior modification: Caution in selection of subjects. *Journal of Consulting and Clinical Psychology,* 1974, *42,* 625.

Havens, J. Psychology and religious retreats. *Pastoral Psychology,* 1969, *20,* 45–52.

Hayes, R. *The Hungarian game.* New York: Avon, 1973.

Heaton, P. *The singlehanders.* New York: Hastings House, 1976.

Hebb, D. O. *The organization of behavior.* New York: Wiley, 1949.

Hebb, D. O. Drives and the C.N.S. (conceptual nervous system). *Psychological Review,* 1955, *62,* 243–254.

Hebb, D. O. Introduction to W. Heron, "Cognitive and physiological effects of perceptual isolation." In P. Solomon, et al. (Eds.), *Sensory deprivation.* Cambridge, Mass.: Harvard University Press, 1961.

Heck, S. T. Workshops in the wilderness facilitating existential solitude. Paper read at the meeting of the Western Psychological Association, 1976; published by the Institute for the Study of Aloneness. Tempe, Arizona. (a)

Heck, S. T. *An investigation of the effects of therapeutically induced isolation on aloneness.* Unpublished doctoral dissertation, Arizona State University, 1976. (b)

Hein, A., Gower, E., and Diamond, R. M. Exposure requirements for developing the triggered component of the visual-placing response. *Journal of Comparative and Physiological Psychology,* 1970, *73,* 188–192.

Heinemann, L. G. Visual phenomena in long sensory deprivation. *Perceptual and Motor Skills,* 1970, *30,* 563–570.

Held, R., and Bossom, J. Neonatal deprivation and adult rearrangement: Complementary techniques for analyzing plastic sensory-motor coordinations. *Journal of Comparative and Physiological Psychology,* 1961, *54,* 33–37.

Held, R., and Hein, A. Movement-produced stimulation in the development of visually guided behavior. *Journal of Comparative and Physiological Psychology*, 1963, *56*, 872–876.

Henderson, N. D. Short exposures to enriched environments can increase genetic variability of behavior in mice. *Developmental Psychobiology*, 1976, *9*, 549–553.

Henderson, R. *Single-handed sailing: The experiences and techniques of the lone voyagers*. Camden, Maine: International Marine Publishing Co., 1976.

Hennessy, T. D. *Visual deprivation as a therapeutic tool in the treatment of smoking behavior*. Unpublished master's thesis, University of Manitoba, 1975.

Henrichs, T. The effects of brief sensory reduction on objective test scores. *Journal of Clinical Psychology*, 1963, *19*, 172–176.

Hermelin, B. and Wing, L. Coding and the sense modalities. In L. Wing (Ed.), *Early childhood autism* (2nd ed.). Elmsford, N.Y.: Pergamon, 1976.

Heron, W. Cognitive and physiological effects of perceptual isolation. In P. Solomon et al. (Eds.), *Sensory deprivation*. Cambridge: Harvard University Press, 1961.

Heron, W., Tait, G., and Smith, G. K. Effects of prolonged perceptual isolation on the human electroencephalogram. *Brain Research*, 1972, *43*, 280–284.

Hess, W. R. *The functional organization of the diencephalon*. New York: Grune and Stratton, 1957.

Hewett, F. M. Teaching speech to autistic children through operant conditioning. *American Journal of Orthopsychiatry*, 1965, *35*, 927–936.

Hewitt, D., and Rule, B. G. Conceptual structure and deprivation effects on self concept change. *Sociometry*, 1968, *31*, 386–394.

Hewitt, F. D., and Hill, W. F. The effects of sensory and activity deprivation on choice of an incentive. *Psychonomic Science*, 1967, *7*, 195–196.

Higenbottam, J. A., and Chow, B. Sound-induced drive, prior motion restraint, and reduced sensory stimulation effects on rocking behavior in retarded persons. *American Journal of Mental Deficiency*, 1975, *80*, 231–233.

Hilgard, J. R. *Personality and hypnosis*. Chicago: University of Chicago Press, 1970.

Hill, E. *The great Australian loneliness*. Melbourne: Robertson and Mullens, 1940.

Hill, W. F. Effects of activity deprivation on choice of activity incentive. *Journal of Comparative and Physiological Psychology*, 1961, *54*, 78–82.

Hilliard, S. *Man in Eastern religion*. London: Epworth, 1946.

Hinde, R. A., and Spencer-Booth, Y. Effects of brief separation from mothers on rhesus monkeys. *Science*, 1971, *173*, 111–118.

Hinderliter, C. F., Smith, S. L., and Misanin, J. R. A reduction of ECS-produced amnesia through post-ECS sensory isolation. *Bulletin of the Psychonomic Society*, 7, 542–544.

Hinkle, L. E., and Wolff, H. G. Communist interrogation and indoctrination of "enemies of the state." *Archives of Neurology and Psychiatry,* 1956, *76,* 115–174.

Hinton, W. *Hundred day war: The cultural revolution at Tsinghua University.* New York: Monthly Review Press, 1972.

Hirai, T. *Zen meditation therapy.* Tokyo: Japan Publications, 1975.

Hirsch, H. V. B. Visual perception in cats after environmental surgery. *Experimental Brain Research,* 1972, *15,* 405–423.

Hirsch, H. V. B., and Spinelli, D. N. Modification of the distribution of receptive field orientation in cats by selective visual exposure during development. *Experimental Brain Research,* 1971, *12,* 509–527.

Hirt, M. We must all fight medical crimes. Vancouver *Sun,* June 18, 1973, p. 6.

Hobbs, S. A., Forehand, R., and Murray, R. G. Effects of various durations of timeout on the noncompliant behavior of children. *Behavior Therapy,* 1978, *9,* 652–656.

Hobbs, S. A., and Goswick, R. A. Behavioral treatment of self-stimulation: An examination of alternatives to physical punishment. *Journal of Clinical Child Psychology,* 1977, *6,* 20–23.

Hobbs, S. A., and Lahey, B. B. The behavioral approach to "learning disabled" children. *Journal of Clinical Child Psychology,* 1977, *6,* 10–14.

Hoehn-Saric, R., Frank, J. D., and Gurland, B. J. Focused attitude change in neurotic patients. *Journal of Nervous and Mental Disease,* 1968, *147,* 124–133.

Hoehn-Saric, R., Liberman, B., Imber, S. D., Stone, A. R., Pande, S. K., and Frank, J. D. Arousal and attitude change in neurotic patients. *Archives of General Psychiatry,* 1972, *26,* 51–56.

Hoehn-Saric, R., Liberman, B., Imber, S. D., Stone, A. R., Frank, J. D., and Ribich, F. D. Attitude change and attribution of arousal in psychotherapy. *Journal of Nervous and Mental Disease,* 1974, *159,* 234–243.

Hoffman, P. *Sensory reduction: A senior project report.* Unpublished manuscript, Friends World College, 1976.

Hogan, T. P. *The effects of brief partial sensory deprivation and verbal communication on decision-making ability.* Unpublished Ph.D. dissertation, Catholic University of America, 1963.

Holland, J. Acute leukemia: Psychological aspects of treatment. In F. Elkerbout, T. Thomas, and A. Zwaveling (Eds.), *Cancer chemotherapy.* Leyden: Leyden University Press, 1971.

Holt, R. R., and Goldberger, L. Assessment of individual resistance to sensory alteration. In B. E. Flaherty (Ed.), *Psychophysiological aspects of space flight.* New York: Columbia University Press, 1961.

Holtzman, W. H., Thorpe, J. S., Swartz, J. D., and Herron, B. W. *Inkblot perception and personality.* Austin: University of Texas Press, 1961.

Honigmann, J. *Culture and ethos of Kasha society.* New Haven, Connecticut: Yale University Press, 1949.

Hood, R. W., Jr. Eliciting mystical states of consciousness with semistructured nature experiences. *Journal for the Scientific Study of Religion*, 1977, *16*, 155–163.

Hoover, E. L. Far out: Confronting the panic and promise of total isolation. In J. C. Lilly, *The Deep Self*. New York: Simon and Schuster, 1977.

Horan, J. J., Linberg, S. E., and Hackett, G. Nicotine poisoning and rapid smoking. *Journal of Consulting and Clinical Psychology*, 1977, *45*, 344–347.

Horn, D., and Waingrow, S. The Horn-Waingrow scale. In *Behavior and attitudes*. U.S. Public Health Service Questionnaire, 1966.

Horowitz, M. J. *Stress response syndromes*. New York: Aronson, 1976.

Hrdlicka, A. *Children who run on all fours*. New York: McGraw Hill, 1931.

Hummel, C. F. Solitude-in-wilderness: A poignant quiet, a sublime identity? Paper read at the meeting of the American Psychological Association, San Francisco, 1977.

Hung, D. W. Using self-stimulation as reinforcement for autistic children. *Journal of Autism and Childhood Schizophrenia*, 1978, *8*, 355–366.

Hunt, H. T. *A phenomenological and an experimental approach to altered states of consciousness: The effects of suggestion, isolation, and visual contemplation.* Unpublished doctoral dissertation. Brandeis University, 1971.

Hunt, H. T., and Chefurka, C. M. A test of the psychedelic model of altered states of consciousness: The role of introspective sensitization in eliciting unusual subjective reports. *Archives of General Psychiatry*, 1976, *33*, 867–876.

Hunt, J. McV. *Intelligence and experience*. New York: Ronald, 1961.

Hunt, J. McV. Motivation inherent in information processing and action. In O. J. Harvey (Ed.), *Motivation and social interaction: Cognitive determinants.* New York: Ronald, 1963.

Hunt, J. McV. Environmental programming to foster competence and prevent mental retardation in infancy. In R. N. Walsh and W. T. Greenough (Eds.), *Environments as therapy for brain dysfunction*. New York: Plenum, 1976.

Hunt, J. McV., Mohandessi, K., Ghodssi, M., and Akiyama, M. The psychological development of orphanage-reared infants: Interventions with outcomes (Tehran). *Genetic Psychology Monographs*, 1976, *94*, 177–226.

Hunt, W. A., and Bespalec, D. A. An evaluation of current methods of modifyng smoking behavior. *Journal of Clinical Psychology*, 1974, *30*, 431–438.

Hunt, W. A., and Matarazzo, J. D. Three years later: Recent developments in the experimental modification of smoking behavior. *Journal of Abnormal Psychology*, 1973, *81*, 107–114.

Husted, J. R., Hall, P., and Agin, B. The effectiveness of time-out in reducing maladaptive behavior of autistic and retarded children. *Journal of Psychology*, 1971, *79*, 189–196.

Hutt, C., Hutt, S. J., Lee, D., and Ounsted, C. Arousal and childhood autism. *Nature*, 1964, *204*, 908–909.

Hymovitch, B. The effects of experimental variations on problem solving in the rat. *Journal of Comparative and Physiological Psychology*, 1952, *45*, 313–321.

Ignatieff, M. *A just measure of pain: Penitentiaries in the Industrial Revolution in England, 1759–1810.* Unpublished doctoral dissertation, Harvard University, 1976.

Ikard, F. F., and Tomkins, S. S. The experience of affect as a determinant of smoking behavior: A series of validity studies. *Journal of Abnormal Psychology,* 1973, *81,* 172–181.

Inhelder, B. *The diagnosis of reasoning in the mentally retarded* (2nd ed.). New York: John Day, 1968.

Insel, P. M., and Lindgren, H. C. *Too close for comfort: The psychology of crowding.* Englewood Cliffs, New Jersey: Prentice-Hall, 1978.

"Into the tank." *Newsweek,* March 13, 1978, p. 98.

Irwin, O. C. Infant speech: Effect of systematic reading of stories. *Journal of Speech and Hearing Research,* 1960, *3,* 187–190.

Isaac, W. Evidence for a sensory drive in monkeys. *Psychological Reports,* 1962, *11,* 175–181.

Itard, J.-M.-G. [*Reports and memoirs of the savage of Aveyron.*] Paris, 1894. (Reprinted edition, originally published partly in 1801 and partly in 1806.) Translated and published as *The wild boy of Aveyron.* New York: Appleton-Century-Crofts, 1962.

Iwai, H., Homma, A., Amamoto, H., and Asakura, M. Morita psychotherapeutic process. *Psychotherapy and Psychosomatics,* 1978, *29,* 330–332.

Jackson, C. W., Jr. Clinical sensory deprivation: A review of hospitalized eye-surgery patients. In J. P. Zubek (Ed.), *Sensory deprivation: Fifteen years of research.* New York: Appleton-Century-Crofts, 1969.

Jackson, C. W., Jr., and Ellis, R. Sensory deprivation as a field of study. *Nursing Research,* 1971, *20,* 46–54.

Jackson, C. W., Jr., Ellis, R., Hughey, G. A., and Schlotfeldt, R. M. Auditory deprivation: Stapedectomy patients who reported social change due to hearing impairment versus those who did not. Paper presented at the meeting of the American Psychological Association, Washington, D.C., 1971.

Jackson, C. W., Jr., and Pollard, J. C. Sensory deprivation and suggestion: A theoretical approach. *Behavioral Science,* 1962, *7,* 332–342.

Jackson, C. W., Jr., and Pollard, J. C. Some nondeprivation variables which influence the "effects" of experimental sensory deprivation. *Journal of Abnormal Psychology,* 1966, *71,* 383–388.

Jacob, R. G., Kraemer, H. C., and Agras, W. S. Relaxation therapy in the treatment of hypertension. *Archives of General Psychiatry,* 1977, *34,* 1417–1427.

Jacobson, A., and Berenberg, A. N. Japanese psychiatry and psychotherapy. *American Journal of Psychiatry,* 1952, *109,* 321–329.

Jacobson, E. *You must relax.* New York: McGraw, 1934.

Jacobson, E. *Progressive relaxation.* Chicago: University of Chicago Press, 1938.

Jacobson, E. *Modern treatment of tense patients.* Springfield, Illinois: Thomas, 1970.

Jacobson, G. R. Effect of brief sensory deprivation on field dependence. *Journal of Abnormal Psychology*, 1966, *71*, 115–118.

Jacobson, G. R. *Sensory deprivation and field dependence in alcoholics.* Unpublished doctoral dissertation, Illinois Institute of Technology, 1971.

Jacobson, J., Fasman, J., and DiMascio, A. Deprivation in the childhood of depressed women. *Journal of Nervous and Mental Disease*, 1975, *160*, 5–14.

"Jailed Cubans tell of 3 years silence." Vancouver *Sun*, 1978.

Janet, P. [*Psychological medicine.*] Paris: Alcan, 1919.

Janov, A. *The primal scream. Primal therapy: The cure for neurosis.* New York: Dell, 1970.

Janz, G. [Functional relaxation therapy applied to children suffering from disturbances of concentration.] *Praxis der Kinderpsychologie und Kinderpsychiatrie*, 1978, *27*, 201–205.

Jellis, T. The back projection of kaleidoscopic patterns as a technique for eliciting verbalizations in an autistic child: A preliminary note. *British Journal of Disorders of Communication*, 1972, *7*, 157–162.

Jenkins, J. R., Gorrafa, S., and Griffiths, S. Another look at isolation effects. *American Journal of Mental Deficiency*, 1972, *76*, 591–593.

Jenkins, R. F., Stauffacher, J., and Hester, R. A symptom rating scale for use with psychotic patients. *Archives of General Psychiatry*, 1959, *1*, 197–204.

Jenkins, R. F., Stauffacher, J., Hester, R. A., Cohen, B. D., Luby, E. D., Rosenbaum, G., and Gottlieb, J. S. Combined sernyl and sensory deprivation. *Comprehensive Psychiatry*, 1960, *1*, 245–248.

Jenkins, S., and Norman, E. *Filial deprivation and foster care.* New York: Columbia University Press, 1972.

Jensen, G. D., and Womack, M. G. Operant conditioning techniques applied in the treatment of an autistic child. *American Journal of Orthopsychiatry*, 1967, *37*, 30–34.

Jessup, B. A. Autogenic feedback for migraine: Predominance and characteristics of placebo improvers. Paper read at the meeting of the American Psychological Association, Toronto, August 1978.

Jessup, B. A., and Neufeld, R. W. J. Effects of biofeedback and "autogenic relaxation" techniques on physiological and subjective responses in psychiatric patients: A preliminary analysis. *Behavior Therapy*, 1977, *8*, 160–167.

Jilek, W. G. *Salish Indian mental health and culture change: Psychohygienic and therapeutic aspects of the guardian spirit ceremonial.* Toronto: Holt, Rinehart and Winston, 1974.

Jilek, W. G. A quest for identity: Therapeutic aspects of the Salish Indian guardian spirit ceremonial. *Journal of Operational Psychiatry*, 1977, *8*, 46–51.

Jilek, W. G. Native renaissance: The survival and revival of indigenous therapeutic ceremonials among North American Indians. *Transcultural Psychiatric Research Review*, 1978, *15*, 117–147.

Joffe, J. M., Rawson, R. A., and Mulick, J. A. Control of their environment reduces emotionality in rats. *Science,* 1973, *180,* 1383–1384.

John Howard Society of Ontario. Brief: Use of Dissociation in Federal Penitentiaries, November 1975.

Johnson, D. L. *Sensory deprivation phenomena in patients with cervical spinal cord injuries.* Unpublished Ph.D. dissertation, University of Oregon, 1976.

Johnston, E., and Donoghue, J. R. Hypnosis and smoking: A review of the literature. *American Journal of Clinical Hypnosis,* 1971, *13,* 265–272.

Jones, A. Stimulus-seeking behavior. In J. P. Zubek (Ed.), *Sensory deprivation: Fifteen years of research.* New York: Appleton-Century-Crofts, 1969.

Jones, G., and Pasnak, R. Light deprivation and visual-cliff performance in the adult cat. *Psychonomic Science,* 1970, *21,* 278–279.

Jones, R. O. Delirium as a basic clinical problem. *Drug Therapy,* 1974, *4,* 38–41.

Kagan, J. Emergent themes in human development. *American Scientist,* 1976, *64,* 186–196.

Kagan, J., and Klein, R. E. Cross-cultural perspectives on early development. *American Psychologist,* 1973, *28,* 947–961.

Kahoe, R. D. (Ed.) Wilderness therapy: A special issue of *Wilderness Psychology Newsletter,* 1979 (February).

Kallman, W. M., and Isaac, W. Altering arousal in humans by varying ambient sensory conditions. *Perceptual and Motor Skills,* 1977, *44,* 19–22.

Kammerman, M. (Ed.) *Sensory isolation and personality change.* Springfield, Illinois: Charles C Thomas, 1977. (a)

Kammerman, M. Personality changes resulting from water suspension sensory isolation. In M. Kammerman (Ed.), *Sensory isolation and personality change.* Springfield, Illinois: Thomas, 1977. (b)

Kandel, E. J., Myers, T. I. and Murphy, D. B. Influence of prior verbalization and instructions on visual sensations reported under conditions of reduced sensory input. Paper presented at the annual meeting of the American Psychological Association, Washington, D.C., 1958.

Kanner, L. Autistic disturbances of affective contact. *Nervous Child,* 1943, *2,* 217–250.

Kanner, L. Problems of nosology and psychodynamics of early infantile autism. *American Journal of Orthopsychiatry,* 1949, *19,* 416–426.

Katz, R. A solo survival experience. Excerpt from R. Katz, *Preludes to growth: An experiential approach.* New York: Macmillan, 1973.

Katz, V. Relationship between auditory stimulation and the developmental behavior of the premature infant. *Nursing Research Conference,* 1971, *7,* 103–107.

Kaufman, A., and Baron, A. Suppression of behavior by timeout punishment when suppression results in loss of positive reinforcement. *Journal of the Experimental Analysis of Behavior,* 1968, *11,* 595–607.

Kaufman, B. N. *Son-rise.* New York: Warner, 1976.

Keating, H. R. F. *The dog it was that died.* Harmondsworth, England: Penguin, 1966.

Keehn, J. D. Reinforcement of alcoholism: Schedule control of solitary drinking. *Quarterly Journal of Studies in Alcohol,* 1970, *31,* 28–39.

Kellerman, J., Rigler, D., and Siegel, S. E. The psychological effects of isolation in protected environments. *American Journal of Psychiatry,* 1977, *134,* 563–565.

Kelly, G. A. *The psychology of personal constructs* (2 vols.). New York: Norton, 1955.

Kelman, H. Altered states of consciousness in therapy. *Journal of the American Academy of Psychoanalysis,* 1975, *3,* 187–204.

Kelvin, P. A social-psychological examination of privacy. *British Journal of Social and Clinical Psychology,* 1973, *12,* 48–61.

Kemp, B. J. Reaction time of young and elderly subjects in relation to perceptual deprivation and signal-on versus signal-off conditions. *Developmental Psychology,* 1973, *8,* 268–272.

Kennaway, J. *The mind benders.* London: Pan, 1963.

Kennedy, A. E. C. The effects of deafness on personality: A discussion based on the theoretical model of Erik Erikson's eight ages of man. *Journal of Rehabilitation of the Deaf,* 1973, *6,* 22–33.

Keutzer, C. S., Lichtenstein, E., and Mees, H. L. Modification of smoking behavior: A review. *Psychological Bulletin,* 1968, *70,* 520–533.

King, P. D. Early infantile autism: Relation to schizophrenia. *Journal of Child Psychiatry,* 1975, *14,* 666–682.

Kingsley, R. G., and Wilson, G. T. Behavior therapy for obesity: A comparative investigation of long-term efficacy. *Journal of Consulting and Clinical Psychology,* 1977, *45,* 288–298.

Kingsley, S. *The hermits.* New York: McClellan and Co., undated.

Kinnealey, M. Aversive and nonaversive responses to sensory stimulation in mentally retarded children. *American Journal of Occupational Therapy.* 1973, *27,* 464–471.

Kirsch, I. The placebo effect and the cognitive behavioral revolution. *Cognitive Therapy and Research,* 1978, *2,* 255–264.

Kitamura, S. Studies on sensory deprivation, IV, Part 8. General discussions and concluding remarks. *Tohoku Psychologica Folia,* 1965, *24,* 35–37.

Klaus, M. H., and Kennell, J. H. Mothers separated from their new born infants. *Pediatric Clinics of North America,* 1970, *17,* 1015–1037.

Klein, H., and Moses, R. Psychological reaction to sensory deprivation in patients with ablatio retinae. *Psychotherapy and Psychosomatics,* 1974, *24,* 41–52.

Klein, J. *Susto:* The anthropological study of diseases of adaptation. *Social Science and Medicine,* 1978, *12,* 23–28.

Klein, M., and Stern, L. Low birth weight and the battered child syndrome. *American Journal of Diseases of Children,* 1971, *122,* 15–18.

Knott, V. J., and Venables, P. H. EEG alpha correlates of non-smokers, smokers, smoking, and smoking deprivation. *Psychophysiology,* 1977, *14,* 150–156.

Koegel, R. L., and Schreibman, L. Teaching autistic children to respond to simultaneous multiple cues. *Journal of Experimental Child Psychology,* 1977, *24,* 299–311.

Koestler, A. *Darkness at noon.* London: Cape, 1940.

Köhle, K., Simons, C., Dietrich, M., and Durner, A. Investigation of behavior of leukemia patients treated in germfree isolators. In J. B. Henneghan (Ed.), *Germfree Research.* New York: Academic Press, 1973.

Köhle, K., Simons, C., Weidlich, S., Dietrich, M., and Durner, A. Psychological aspects in the treatment of leukemia patients in the isolated-bed system "Life Island." *Psychotherapy and Psychosomatics,* 1971, *19,* 85–91.

Köhler, W. *The mentality of apes.* New York: Harcourt, Brace, 1927.

Kohut, H. The psychoanalytic treatment of narcissistic personality disorders. *Psychoanalytic Study of the Child,* 1968, *23,* 86–113.

Komitee gegen Folter. [Torture through sensory deprivation: Analysis and documents.] Hamburg, Federal Republic of Germany, 1974.

Konrad, K., and Melzack, R. Novelty-enhancement effects associated with early sensory-social isolation. In A. H. Riesen (Ed.), *The developmental neuropsychology of sensory deprivation.* New York: Academic Press, 1975.

Korner, A. F. Early stimulation and maternal care as related to infant capabilities and individual differences. *Early Child Development and Care,* 1973, *2,* 307–327.

Kornfeld, D. S. Psychiatric problems of an intensive care unit. In J. S. Todd (Ed.), *Symposium on intensive care units.* The Medical Clinics of North America. Philadelphia: Saunders, 1971.

Kornfeld, D. S., Zimberg, S., and Malm, J. R. Psychiatric complications of open-heart surgery. *New England Journal of Medicine,* 1965, *273,* 287–292.

Koslin, B. L., Pargament, R., and Suedfeld, P. An uncertainty model of opinion change. In P. Suedfeld (Ed.), *Attitude change: The competing views.* Chicago: Aldine–Atherton,1971.

Kouretas, D. The Oracle of Trophonius: A kind of shock treatment associated with sensory deprivation in ancient Greece. *British Journal of Psychiatry,* 1967, *113,* 1441–1446.

Kracke, W. H. The maintenance of the ego: Implications of sensory deprivation research for psychoanalytic ego psychology. *British Journal of Medical Psychology*, 1967, *40*, 17–27.

Kramer, J. A reporter in Europe. *New Yorker*, 1978, *54* (No. 5), 44–87.

Kramer, M., Chamorro, I., Green, D., and Knudtson, F. Extra tactile stimulation of the premature infant. *Nursing Research*, 1975, *24*, 324–334.

Krishna, G. Meditation: Is it always beneficial? Some positive and negative views. *Journal of Altered States of Consciousness*, 1975, *2*, 37–47.

Kristeller, J. L. Meditation and biofeedback in the regulation of internal states. In Swami Ajaya (Ed.), *Meditational therapy*. Glenview, Illinois: Himalayan International Institute, 1977.

Kristeller, J. L. Perceptual and regressive effects of LSD. Unpublished paper, Yale University, 1978.

Krivitsky, W. G. *In Stalin's secret service*. New York: Harper, 1939.

Krushinski, I. V. *Animal behavior*. New York: Consultant Bureau, 1962.

Kubie, L. S. *Practical and theoretical aspects of psychoanalysis*. New York: International Universities Press, 1950.

Kubie, L. S., and Margolin, S. The process of hypnotism and the nature of the hypnotic state. *American Journal of Psychiatry*, 1944, *100*, 611–622.

Kubzansky, E., and Leiderman, P. H. Sensory deprivation: An overview. In P. Solomon et al. (Eds.), *Sensory deprivation*. Cambridge, Mass.: Harvard University Press, 1961.

Kulig, J. W. Ontogeny of memory: Examination of a behavioral explanation. *Bulletin of the Psychonomic Society*, 1977, *9*, 278–282.

Kurie, G. D., and Mordkoff, A. M. Effects of brief sensory deprivation and somatic concentration on two measures of field dependence. *Perceptual and Motor Skills*, 1970, *31*, 683–687.

Lacey, J. I. Somatic response patterning and stress: Some revisions of activation theory. In M. H. Appley and R. Turnbull (Eds.), *Psychological stress*. New York: Appleton-Century-Crofts, 1967.

Lafitte, V. [Sleep therapy.] *Bulletin du Groupe d'Étude Psychologie de l'Université de Paris*, 1952, *4* (Sp. No.), 97–100. (*Psychological Abstracts*, 1953, *27*, Abstr. # 829.)

Lambert, W., and Levy, L. H. Sensation seeking and short-term sensory isolation. *Journal of Personality and Social Psychology*, 1972, *24*, 46–52.

Lando, H. A. A comparison of excessive and rapid smoking in the modification of chronic smoking behavior. *Journal of Consulting and Clinical Psychology*, 1975, *43*, 350–355.

Lando, H. A. Successful treatment of smokers with a broad-spectrum behavioral approach. *Journal of Consulting and Clinical Psychology*, 1977, *45*, 361–366.

Landon, P. B. The unimportance of experimenter bias in sensory deprivation research. *Perceptual and Motor Skills*, 1976, *42*, 619–624.

Landon, P. B., and Suedfeld, P. Information and meaningfulness needs in sensory deprivation. *Psychonomic Science*, 1969, *17*, 248.

Landon, P. B., and Suedfeld, P. Complex cognitive performance and sensory deprivation: Completing the U-curve. *Perceptual and Motor Skills,* 1972, *34,* 601–602.

Landon, P. B., and Suedfeld, P. Complexity as multidimensional perception: The effects of sensory deprivation on concept identification. *Bulletin of the Psychonomic Society,* 1977, *10,* 137–138.

Lane, H., and Pillard, R. *The wild boy of Burundi.* New York: Random House, 1978.

Langova, J., and Svab, L. Reduction of stuttering under experimental social isolation: The role of adaptation effect. *Folia Phoniatrica,* 1973, *25,* 17–22.

Langton, J. *The Memorial Hall murder.* New York: Harper, 1978.

Lantzsch, W., and Drunkenmölle, C. [Research analyzing the circulation of patients with essential hypertension between the first and second standard exercises of autogenic training.] *Psychiatria Clinica,* 1975, *8,* 223–228.

Larson, R. *The significance of solitude in adolescents' lives.* Unpublished Ph.D. dissertation, University of Chicago, 1978.

Larson, R., and Csikszentmihalyi, M. Experimental correlates of time alone in adolescence. *Journal of Personality,* 1978, *46,* 677–693.

Lasaga, J. I. The therapeutic use of sensory deprivation. Paper read at the meeting of the Southeastern Psychological Association, Atlanta, Georgia, 1975.

Latané, B., Nesbitt, P., Eckman, J., and Rodin, J. Long- and short-term social deprivation and sociability in rats. *Journal of Comparative and Physiological Psychology,* 1972, *81,* 69–75.

Laub, G. [Researchers are all criminals.] *DZ,* February 8, 1974, p. 23.

Lavie, P., and Webb, W. B. Time estimates in a long-term time-free environment. *American Journal of Psychology,* 1975, *88,* 177–186.

Lawes, T. G. G. Schizophrenia, "Sernyl", and sensory deprivation. *British Journal of Psychiatry,* 1963, *109,* 243–250.

Lawson, R. B., and Frey, W. F. Effects of short-term sensory isolation upon stereoscopic size and distance. *Perceptual and Motor Skills,* 1971, *32,* 571–577.

Lazarus, A. A. Sensory deprivation under hypnosis in the treatment of pervasive ("free-floating") anxiety: A preliminary impression. *South African Medical Journal,* 1963, *37,* 136–139.

Lazarus, A. A. Learning theory and the treatment of depression. *Behavioural Research and Therapy,* 1968, *6,* 83–89.

Lazarus, A. A. Psychiatric problems precipitated by transcendental meditation (TM). *Psychological Reports,* in press.

Lazarus, H. R., and Hagens, J. H. Prevention of psychosis following open-heart surgery. *American Journal of Psychiatry,* 1968, *124,* 1190–1195.

Lazarus, R. S. Strategy for research in hypertension. *Journal of Human Stress,* 1978, *4,* 35–40.

Leary, T. *Multilevel measurement of interpersonal behavior.* Berkeley: Psychological Consultation Service, 1956.

Leary, T. *Interpersonal diagnosis of personality.* New York: Ronald, 1957.

Lebedinsky, A. V., Levinsky, S. V., and Nefedov, Y. G. [General principles concerning the reaction of the organism to the complex environmental factors existing in spacecraft cabins.] Paper read at XVth International Aeronautics Congress, Warsaw, 1964. Translated from Russian by NASA, TTF-273. Cited in J. P. Zubek (Ed.), *Sensory deprivation: Fifteen years of research.* New York: Appleton-Century-Crofts, 1969.

Lebipp, E. E., Brady, J. P., Ottinger, D. R., and Hinesley, R. Effect of sensory restriction on hypnotizability. *Archives of General Psychiatry,* 1962, 7, 343–344.

Leboyer, F. [*For birth without violence.*] Paris: Le Seuil, 1974.

Leboyer, F. *Birth without violence.* New York: Knopf, 1976.

Lebron-Rodriguez, D. E., and Pasnak, R. Induction of intellectual gains in blind children. *Journal of Experimental Child Psychology,* 1977, 24, 505–515.

Leckart, B. T., Levine, J. R., Goscinski, C., and Brayman, W. Duration of attention: The perceptual deprivation effect. *Perception and Psychophysics,* 1970, 7, 163–164.

Leckart, B. T., Glanville, B., Hootstein, E., Keleman, K., and Yaremko, R. M. Looking time, stimulus complexity, and the perceptual deprivation effect. *Psychonomic Science,* 1972, 26, 107–108.

Lee, J. A. *Sectarian healers and hypnotherapy.* Toronto, Ontario: The Queen's Printer, 1970.

Lee, R. E., and Ball, P. A. Some thoughts on the psychology of the coronary care unit patient. *American Journal of Nursing,* 1975, 75, 1498–1501.

Leff, J. P., and Hirsch, S. R. The effects of sensory deprivation on verbal communication. *Journal of Psychiatric Research,* 1972, 9, 329–336.

Leiderman, H., Mendelson, J. H., Wexler, D., and Solomon, P. H. Sensory deprivation—Clinical aspects. *Archives of Internal Medicine,* 1958, 101, 389–396.

Leiderman, P. H., and Seashore, M. J. Mother-infant neonatal separation: Some delayed consequences. *Parent-Infant Interaction,* CIBA Foundation Symposium 33 (New Series). Amsterdam: ASP, 1975.

Leitenberg, H. Is time-out from positive reinforcement an aversive event? A review of the experimental evidence. *Psychological Bulletin,* 1965, 64, 418–421.

Leitenberg, H., Agras, W. S., and Thomson, L. E. A sequential analysis of the effect of selective positive reinforcement in modifying anorexia nervosa. *Behaviour Research and Therapy,* 1968, 6, 211–218.

Leites, N., and Bernaut, E. *Ritual of liquidation.* Glencoe, Illinois: Free Press, 1954.

Lenneberg, E. H. *Biological foundations of language.* New York: Wiley, 1967.

Leon, G. R. Current directions in the treatment of obesity. *Psychological Bulletin,* 1976, *83,* 557–578.

Lerner, S. E., and Burns, R. S. Phencyclidine use among youth: History, epidemiology, and acute and chronic intoxication. In R. C. Petersen and R. C. Stillman (Eds.), *Phencyclidine (PCP) abuse: An appraisal.* Washington: U.S. Government Printing Office, 1978.

Lessac, M. S. *The effects of early isolation and restriction on the later behavior of beagle puppies.* Unpublished doctoral dissertation, University of Pennsylvania, 1965.

Lesser, S. R. and Lesser, B. R. Personality differences in the perceptually handicapped. *Journal of the American Academy of Psychiatry,* 1972, *11,* 458–466.

Levenberg, S. B., and Wagner, M. K. Smoking cessation: Long-term irrelevance of mode of treatment. *Journal of Behavior Therapy and Experimental Psychiatry,* 1976, *7,* 93–95.

Levin, J. Arousal and hallucinatory activity under two isolation conditions. *Perceptual and Motor Skills,* 1974, *391,* 443–450.

Levin, J., and Brody, N. Information–deprivation and creativity. *Psychological Reports,* 1974, *35,* 231–237.

Levine, A. S., Siegel, S. E., Schreiber, A. D., Hauser, J., Preisler, H., Goldstein, I. M., Seidler, F., Simon, R., Perry, S., Bennett, J. E., and Henderson, E. S. Protected environments and prophylactic antibiotics: A prospective controlled study of their utility in the therapy of acute leukemia. *New England Journal of Medicine,* 1973, *288,* 477–483.

Levine, E. S., and Wagner, E. E. Personality patterns of deaf persons: An interpretation based on research with the Hand Test. *Perceptual and Motor Skills,* 1974, *39,* 1167–1236 (Monograph Supplement 4-V39).

Levine, J. R., Pettit, A., and Leckart, B. T. Listening time and the short-term perceptual deprivation effect. *Bulletin of the Psychonomic Society,* 1973, *1,* 11–12.

Levine, S. Stimulation in infancy. *Scientific American,* 1960, *202,* 80–86.

Levine, S., and King, D. L. The effect of auditory restriction during pregnancy on offspring survival. *Psychonomic Science,* 1965, *3,* 275–276.

Levine, S., and Wiener, S. G. Malnutrition and early environmental experience: Possible interactive effects on later behavior. In R. N. Walsh and W. T. Greenough (Eds.), *Environments as therapy for brain dysfunction.* New York: Plenum, 1976.

Levinson, R. B., Ingram, G. L. and Azcarate, E. "Aversive" group therapy: Sometimes good medicine tastes bad. *Crime and Delinquency,* 1968, *14,* 336–339.

Levis, D. J. The case for performing research on nonpatient populations with fears of small animals: A reply to Cooper, Furst, and Bridger. *Journal of Abnormal Psychology,* 1970, *76,* 36–38.

Levison, C. A., and Levison, P. K. Effects of early visual conditions on stimulation-seeking behavior in young rhesus monkeys. *Psychonomic Science,* 1971, *22,* 145–147.

Levison, C. A., Levison, P. K., and Norton, H. P. Effects of early visual conditions on stimulation-seeking behavior in infant monkeys. *Psychonomic Science,* 1968, *11,* 101–102.

Lévi-Strauss, C. *The elementary structures of kinship.* London: Eyre and Spottiswoode, 1968.

Levitt, E. E., and Chapman, R. H. Hypnosis as a research method. In E. Fromm and R. E. Shor (Eds.), *Hypnosis: Research developments and perspectives.* Chicago: Aldine–Atherton, 1972.

Levitt, E. E., Brady, J. P., Ottinger, D. R., and Hinesley, R. Effect of sensory restriction on hypnotizability. *Archives of General Psychiatry,* 1962, *7,* 343–344.

Lewin, K. Group decision and social change. In G. E. Swanson, T. M. Newcomb, and E. L. Hartley (Eds.), *Readings in social psychology,* revised edition. New York: Holt, 1952.

Lewis, B. J. Sensory deprivation in young children. *Child: Care, Health and Development,* 1978, *4,* 229–238.

Lewis, D. *Ice bird.* Glasgow: Fontana, 1975.

Lewis, L., and Coser, R. L. The hazards in hospitalization. *Hospital Administration,* 1960, *5,* 25–45.

Lichstein, L., and Sackett, G. P. Reactions of differentially raised rhesus monkeys to noxious stimulation. *Developmental Psychobiology,* 1971, *4,* 339–352.

Lifton, R. J. *Thought reform and the psychology of totalism.* New York: Norton, 1961.

Lilly, J. C. Mental effects of reduction of ordinary levels of physical stimuli on intact, healthy persons. *Psychiatric Research Reports, No. 5.* Washington, D.C.: American Psychiatric Association, 1956, 1–9.

Lilly, J. C. Discussion of paper by J. T. Shurley. Profound experimental sensory isolation. *American Journal of Psychiatry,* 1960, *117,* 544–545.

Lilly, J. C. *The center of the cyclone: An autobiography of inner space.* New York: Julian, 1972.

Lilly, J. C. *The deep self.* New York: Simon and Schuster, 1977.

Lindsley, D. B. Common factors in sensory deprivation, sensory distortion, and sensory overload. In P. Solomon et al. (Eds.), *Sensory deprivation.* Cambridge: Harvard University Press, 1961.

Linkenhoker, D. D. Increasing the effectiveness of time-out from reinforcement. *Psychotherapy: Theory, Research and Practice,* 1974, *11,* 326–328.

Lipowski, Z. J. The conflict of Buridan's ass or some dilemmas of affluence: The theory of attractive stimulus overload. *American Journal of Psychiatry,* 1970, *127,* 273–279.

Litrownik, A. J., McInnis, E. T., Wetzel-Pritchard, A. M., and Filipelli, D. L. Restricted stimulus control and inferred attentional deficits in autistic and retarded children. *Journal of Abnormal Psychology,* 1978, *87,* 554–562.

Lloyd, A. J. *RSPE isolation—another approach to biofeedback?* Unpublished manuscript, Letterman Army Institute of Research, 1977.

Lloyd, A. J., and Shurley, J. T. The effects of sensory perceptual isolation on single motor unit conditioning. *Psychophysiology,* 1976, *13,* 340–344.

Lobb, L. G., and Schaefer, H. H. Successful treatment of anorexia nervosa through isolation. *Psychological Reports,* 1971, *30,* 245–246.

Lockard, R. B. Self-regulated exposure to light by albino rats as a function of rearing luminance and test luminance. *Journal of Comparative and Physiological Psychology,* 1963, *56,* 558–564.

Lockard, R. B., and Haerer, H. Time course of change in light preference resulting from prolonged exposure to adapting stimuli. *Journal of Comparative and Physiological Psychology,* 1968, *65,* 529–531.

Lomont, J. F., and Edwards, J. E. The role of relaxation in systematic desensitization. *Behaviour Research and Therapy,* 1967, *5,* 11–25.

London, H., Schubert, D. S. P., and Washburn, D. Increase of autonomic arousal by boredom. *Journal of Abnormal Psychology,* 1972, *80,* 29–36.

London, P. *Behavior control* (Rev. ed.). New York: New American Library, 1977.

Loo, P., Sauvage, J., and Saba, S. [Sleep therapy.] *Annales Médico-Psychologiques,* 1971, *2,* 367–390.

Lopata, D. J., and Pasnak, R. Accelerated conservation acquisition and IQ gains by blind children. *Genetic Psychology Monographs,* 1976, *93,* 3–25.

Lore, R. K. The activity drive hypothesis: Effects of activity restriction. *Psychological Bulletin,* 1968, *70,* 566–574.

Lovaas, O. I. *The autistic child: Language development through behavior modification.* New York: Wiley, 1977.

Lovaas, O. I., and Newsom, C. D. Behavior modification with psychotic children. In H. Leitenberg (Ed.), *Handbook of behavior modification and behavior therapy.* Englewood Cliffs, N.J.: Prentice-Hall, 1976.

Lovaas, O. I., Schaeffer, B., and Simmons, J. Q. Building social behavior in autistic children by use of electric shock. *Journal of Experimental Research in Personality,* 1965, *1,* 99–109.

Lowenthal, M. F. Social isolation and mental illness in old age. *American Sociological Review,* 1964, *29,* 54–70.

Lowenthal, M. F., and Haven, C. Interaction and adaptation: Intimacy as a critical variable. *American Sociological Review,* 1968, *33,* 20–30.

Lowenthal, M. F., Thurner, M., and Chiriboga, D. *Four stages of life: A psychological study of men and women facing transitions.* San Francisco: Jossey-Bass, 1975.

Lowrey, L. G. Personality distortion and early institutional care. *American Journal of Orthopsychiatry*, 1940, *10*, 576–585.

Lubow, R. E., Rifkin, B., and Alek, M. The context effect: The relationship between stimulus pre-exposure and environmental pre-exposure determines subsequent learning. *Journal of Experimental Psychology: Animal Behavior Processes*, 1976, *2*, 38–47.

Luby, E. D., Gottlieb, J. S., Cohen, B. C., Rosenbaum, G., and Domino, E. F. Model psychoses and schizophrenia. *American Journal of Psychiatry*, 1962, *119*, 61–67.

Lucas, R. C. Wilderness policy and management problems: Possible applications of psychology. Paper read at the annual meeting of the American Psychological Association, Toronto, August, 1978.

Lucas, W. E. Solitary confinement: Isolation as coercion to conform. *Australian and New Zealand Journal of Criminology*, 1976, *9*, 153–167.

Luisada, P. V. The phencyclidine psychosis: Phenomenology and treatment. In R. C. Petersen and R. C. Stillman (Eds.). *Phencyclidine (PCP) abuse: An appraisal*. Washington: U.S. Government Printing Office, 1978.

Luisada, P. V., and Brown, B. I. Clinical management of the phencyclidine psychosis. *Clinical Toxicology*, 1976, *9*, 539–545.

Luisada, P. V., and Reddick, C. An epidemic of drug-induced "schizophrenia." Paper presented at annual meeting of the American Psychiatric Association, Anaheim, California, May, 1975.

Luria, A. R. *The working brain: An introduction to neuropsychology*. Harmondsworth: Penguin, 1973.

McAninch, W. S. Penal incarceration and cruel and unusual punishment. *South Carolina Law Review*, 1973, *25*, 579–603.

McCain, G., Cox, V. C., and Paulus, P. B. The relationship between illness complaints and degree of crowding in a prison environment. *Environment and Behavior*, 1976, *8*, 283–290.

McClannahan, L. E., and Risley, T. R. Design of living environments for nursing-home residents: Increasing participation in recreation activities. *Journal of Applied Behavior Analysis*, 1975, *8*, 261–268.

McClure, G., and Forgays, D. G. Human sex differences in extreme isolation. *Perceptual and Motor Skills*, 1975, *40*, 387–391.

MacDonough, T. S., and Forehand, R. Response-contingent time out: Important parameters in behavior modification with children. *Journal of Behavioral Therapy and Experimental Psychiatry*, 1973, *4*, 231–236.

MacDougall, J. C., and Rabinovitch, M.S. Early auditory deprivation and sensory compensation. *Developmental Psychology*, 1971, *5*, 368.

McFarland, J. W., and Folkenberg, E. J. *How to stop smoking in five days*. Englewood Cliffs, New Jersey: Prentice-Hall, 1964.

McGuffin, J. *The guineapigs*. Harmondsworth: Penguin, 1974.

McGuire, W. J. The nature of attitudes and attitude change. In G. Lindzey and E. Aronson (Eds.), *Handbook of social psychology* (Vol. 3). Reading, Mass.: Addison-Wesley, 1969.

McKenna, V. V. Effects of perceptual deprivation and variation on cognitive styles. Paper read at the meeting of the Eastern Psychological Association, New York City, 1971.

McKinney, W. T. Primate social isolation. *Archives of General Psychiatry,* 1974, *31,* 422–426.

MacNeil, L. W., and Rule, B. G. Effects of conceptual structure on information preference under sensory-deprivation conditions. *Journal of Personality and Social Psychology,* 1970, *16,* 530–535.

McPhee, J. *Coming into the country.* New York: Farrar, Straus and Giroux, 1976.

Mahoney, M. J. The obese eating style: Bites, beliefs, and behavior. *Addictive Behaviors,* 1975, *1,* 47–54.

Maier, W. J. Sensory deprivation of an autistic boy. *American Journal of Psychotherapy,* 1970, *25,* 228–245.

Mallenby, T. W. Direct measurement techniques with hard-of-hearing children. *Environment and Behavior,* 1974, *6,* 117–122.

Malson, L. *Wolf children.* New York: New Left Books, 1972.

Margetts, B. L. African ethnopsychiatry in the field. *Canadian Psychiatric Association Journal,* 1968, *13,* 521–538.

Margetts, B. L. Canada—Indian and Eskimo medicine; with notes on the early history of psychiatry among French and British colonists. In J. G. Howells (Ed.), *World history of psychiatry.* New York: Brunner/Mazel, 1975.

Margolies, P. J. Behavioral approaches to the treatment of early infantile autism: A review. *Psychological Bulletin,* 1977, *84,* 249–264.

Marjerrison, G., and Keogh, R. P. EEG changes during brief periods of perceptual deprivation. *Perceptual and Motor Skills,* 1967, *24,* 611–615.

Marks, J. *The search for the Manchurian candidate: The CIA and mind control.* New York: Times Books, 1978.

Marlatt, G. A., and Marques, J. K. Meditation, self-control and alcohol use. In R. B. Stuart (Ed.), *Behavioral self-management: Strategies, techniques and outcomes.* New York: Brunner/Mazel, 1977.

Martin, D. G., Roush, P., and Nicholson, J. The increased effect of a visual training procedure after sensory restriction. *Psychonomic Science,* 1967, *8,* 229–230.

Martin, G. Brief time-outs as consequences for errors during training periods with autistic and retarded children: A questionable procedure. *Psychological Record,* 1975, *25,* 71–89.

Marum, D. D. Reproduction and ratio-production of brief duration under conditions of sensory isolation. *American Journal of Psychology,* 1968, *81,* 21–26.

Mason, W. A. Early social deprivation in the nonhuman primates: Implications for human behavior. In D. Glass (Ed.), *Environmental influences*. New York: Rockefeller University Press, 1968.

Mathews, A. Fear reduction research and clinical phobias. *Psychological Bulletin*, 1978, *85*, 390–404.

Mathews, A. S., and Albino, R. C. The permanence of the temporary—An examination of the 90- and 180-day detention laws. *South African Law Journal*, 1966, *83*, 16–43.

Mattson, M. R., and Sacks, M. H. Seclusion: Uses and complications. *American Journal of Psychiatry*, 1978, *135*, 1210–1213.

Maupin, E. W. Individual differences in response to Zen meditation exercise. *Journal of Consulting Psychology*, 1965, *29*, 139–145.

Mayers, K. S., Robertson, R. T., Rubel, E. W., and Thompson, R. T. Development of poly-sensory responses in association cells of kittens. *Science*, 1971, *171*, 1037–1038.

Meadow, K. P. The development of deaf children. In E. M. Hetherington, J. W. Higgin, R. Kron, and A. H. Stein (Eds.) *Review of child development research*, Vol. 5. Chicago, Ill.: University of Chicago Press, 1975.

Medical Research Council Applied Psychology Research Unit, Cambridge University. Publications, 1970–1977.

Mednick, S. A. A learning theory approach to research in schizophrenia. *Psychological Bulletin*, 1958, *55*, 316–327.

Mehrabian, A. A questionnaire measure of individual differences in stimulus screening and associated differences in arousability. *Environmental Psychology and Nonverbal Behavior*, 1977, *1*, 89–103.

Meier, G. W., and McGee, R. K. A re-evaluation of the effect of early perceptual experience on discrimination performance during adulthood. *Journal of Comparative and Physiological Psychology*, 1959, *52*, 390–395.

Melzack, R. Effects of early perceptual restriction on simple visual discrimination. *Science*, 1962, *137*, 978–979.

Melzack, R., and Burns, S. K. Neurophysiological effects of early sensory restriction. *Experimental Neurology*, 1965, *13*, 163–175.

Melzack, R., and Scott, T. H. The effects of early experience on the response to pain. *Journal of Comparative and Physiological Psychology*, 1957, *50*, 155–161.

Mendelson, J. H. The effects of sensory deprivation on deaf subjects. *Naval Research Reviews*, 1964, *17*, 15–20.

Mendelson, J. H., Kubzansky, P. E., Leiderman, P. H., Wexler, D., and Solomon, P. Physiological and psychological aspects of sensory deprivation—A case analysis. In P. Solomon et al. (Eds.), *Sensory deprivation*. Cambridge, Mass.: Harvard University Press, 1961.

Merrien, J. *The lonely voyagers*. London: Putnam, 1954.

Merton, T. *The silent life*. New York: Farrar, Straus and Giroux, 1957.

Metz, J. R. Stimulation-level preferences of autistic children. *Journal of Abnormal Psychology*, 1967, *72*, 529–535.

Metzner, R. A note on the treatment of LSD psychosis: A case report. *Psychotherapy*, 1969, *6*, 201–205.

Meyer, J. S., Griefenstein, F., and Devault, M. A new drug causing symptoms of sensory deprivation. *Journal of Nervous and Mental Disease*, 1969, *129*, 54–61.

Meyer, M. E., and Collins, M. D. Light deprivation and sensory reinforced behavior in chicks. *Perceptual and Motor Skills*, 1971, *32*, 602.

Michaels, R. R., Huber, M. J., and McCann, D. S. Evaluation of transcendental meditation as a method of reducing stress. *Science*, 1976, *192*, 1242–1244.

Michal-Smith, H. Sensory deprivation: A new approach to emotional problems of the child with a hearing loss. *Journal of Speech and Hearing Disorders*, 1962, *27*, 290–294.

Milgram, S. The experience of living in cities. *Science*, 1970, *167*, 1461–1468.

Milich, R. S. A critical analysis of Schachter's externality theory of obesity. *Journal of Abnormal Psychology*, 1975, *84*, 586–588.

Miller, A. R., Stewart, R. A., and Kiker, V. The facilitative effects of shock and sensory deprivation on bar-pressing during extinction. *Psychonomic Science*, 1968, *10*, 113–114.

Miller, G. A., Galanter, E., and Pribram, K. H. *Plans and the structure of behavior.* New York: Holt, 1960.

Miller, M. Observation of initial visual experience in rats. *Journal of Psychology*, 1948, *26*, 223–228.

Mills, S. R. *PREP:A preparation programme designed to minimize distress of institutional relocation on the elderly.* Unpublished M.A. thesis, University of British Columbia, 1978.

Mineka, S., and Kihlstrom, J. F. Unpredictable and uncontrollable events: A new perspective on experimental neurosis. *Journal of Abnormal Psychology*, 1978, *87*, 256–271.

Mineka, S., and Suomi, S. J. Social separation in monkeys. *Psychological Bulletin*, 1978, *85*, 1376–1400.

Mitchell, S. W. *Fat and blood: An essay on the treatment of certain forms of neurasthenia and hysteria.* Philadelphia: Lippincott, 1877/1905.

Monod, T. [The life of Sidi Mohamed Ould Sidia with the ostriches for ten years, related by himself.] *Notes Africaines*, Dakar, 1945.

Moor, P. Telling you like it is. Paper presented at a meeting of the British Columbia Mental Retardation Institute, Vancouver, 1970.

Moore, D. F., and Shiek, D. A. Toward a theory of early infantile autism. *Psychological Review*, 1971, *78*, 451–456.

Moran, T. C. *The effects of brief sensory deprivation on the learning efficiency of chronic schizophrenic patients.* Unpublished Ph.D. dissertation, St. John's University, 1969.

Morris, R. H. A play environment for blind children: Design and evaluation. *The New Outlook for the Blind*, 1974, *68*, 408–414.

Morrison, H., and McKinney, W. T. Environments of dysfunction: The relevance of primate animal models. In R. N. Walsh and W. T. Greenough (Eds.), *Environments as therapy for brain dysfunction*. New York: Plenum, 1976.

Morse, D. R., Martin, J. S., Furst, K. L., and Dubin, L. L. A physiological and subjective evaluation of meditation, hypnosis and relaxation. *Psychosomatic Medicine*, 1977, *39*, 304–324.

Morse, W. C., and Wineman, D. The therapeutic use of social isolation in a camp for ego-disturbed boys. *Journal of Social Issues*, 1957, *13*, 32–39.

Mosley, J. L. Social deprivation and the performance of retarded and nonretarded subjects on the Rectilinear Dot Progression Task. *American Journal of Mental Deficiency*, 1971, *76*, 92–100.

Murase, T. Naikan therapy. Paper read at a conference on Culture and Mental Health in Asia and the Pacific, Honolulu, 1972.

Murie, J. Pawnee Indian society. *Anthropology Papers*. New York: American Museum of Natural History, 1914, *11*, 543–644.

Murphy, D. B., Hampton, G. L., and Myers, T. I. Time estimation error as a predictor of endurance in sustained sensory deprivation. Paper read at the meeting of the American Psychological Association, St. Louis, Missouri, 1962.

Murphy, J. M. Psychotherapeutic aspects of shamanism on St. Lawrence Island, Alaska. In A. Kiev (Ed.), *Magic, faith, and healing*. New York: Free Press, 1964.

Murray, E. J. *Sleep, dreams, and arousal.* New York: Appleton-Century-Crofts, 1965.

Murray, M. E. Secondary effects of isolation in brain-damaged and autistic children. *Behavior Therapy*, 1975, *6*, 711–712.

Murray, M. E. Modified time-out procedures for controlling tantrum behaviors in public places. *Behavior Therapy*, 1976, *7*, 412–413.

Myers, T. I. Tolerance for sensory and perceptual deprivation. In J. P. Zubek (Ed.), *Sensory deprivation: Fifteen years of research*. New York: Appleton-Century-Crofts, 1969.

Myers, T. I. Meditation as a therapeutic process. Unpublished paper. Behavior Research Institute, 1976.

Myers, T. I., and Kushner, E. N. Coping with primary process and tolerance for sensory deprivation. Unpublished manuscript, Naval Medical Research Institute, Bethesda, Maryland, 1970.

Myers, T. I., Murphy, D. B., Smith, S., and Goffard, S. J. *Experimental studies of sensory deprivation and social isolation*. HumRRO Technical Report 66-8. George Washington University, 1966.

Myklebust, H.R. *The psychology of deafness*. New York: Grune and Stratton, 1964.

Myrsten, A.-L., Elgerot, A., and Edgren, B. Effects of abstinence from tobacco smoking on physiological and psychological arousal levels in habitual smokers. *Psychosomatic Medicine*, 1977, *39*, 25–38.

Naitoh, P. *Sleep-loss in man*. Springfield, Illinois: Thomas, in press.

Naranjo, C., and Ornstein, R. E. *On the psychology of meditation*. New York: Viking, 1971.

National Aeronautics and Space Administration. Conference on Long-Duration Space Flight, Washington, D.C., 1964.

Nelson, S. K. Behavioral control of smoking with combined procedures. *Psychological Reports*, 1977, *40*, 191–196.

Nesbitt, P.D. Smoking, physiological arousal, and emotional response. *Journal of Personality and Social Psychology*, 1973, *25*, 137–144.

"News Roundup." *Behavior Today*, 1979, *10*(4), 7.

Newton, N., Foshee, D., and Newton, M. Experimental inhibition of labor through environmental disturbance. *Obstetrics and Gynecology*, 1966, *27*, 371–377.

Newton, N., Peeler, D., and Newton, M. Effect of disturbance on labor: An experiment using 100 mice with dated pregnancies. *American Journal of Obstetrics and Gynecology*, 1968, *101*, 1096–1102.

Nicassio, P., and Bootzin, R. A comparison of progressive relaxation and autogenic training as treatments for insomnia. *Journal of Abnormal Psychology*, 1974, *83*, 253–260.

Nissen, H. W., Chow, K. L., and Semmes, J. Effects of restricted opportunity for tactual, kinesthetic, and manipulative experience on the behavior of a chimpanzee. *American Journal of Psychology*, 1951, *64*, 485–507.

Norman, L. S. Pupils like discipline idea, too. *Prince Georges Journal*, 1977.

Norris, J. E. The inconsistent older adult: Another casualty of social isolation. Paper read at the annual meeting of the Canadian Psychological Association, Ottawa, June 1978.

Norris, M., Spaulding, P., and Brodie, F. *Blindness in children*. Chicago: University of Chicago Press, 1958.

Nuernberger, P. Yoga and biofeedback: A treatment program. In Swami Ajaya (Ed.), *Meditational therapy*. Glenview, Illinois: Himalayan International Institute, 1977.

Novak, M.A., and Harlow, H.F. Social recovery of monkeys isolated for the first year of life: 1. Rehabilitation and therapy. *Developmental Psychology*, 1975, *11*, 453–465.

Nuland, W., and Field, P. B. Smoking and hypnosis: A systematic clinical approach. *International Journal of Clinical and Experimental Hypnosis*, 1970, *18*, 290–306.

O'Conner, J. Solo. *Mountain Gazette*, June 1974 (No. 22), 16–17.

O'Connor, N. Children in restricted environments. In G. Newton and S. Levine (Eds.), *Early experience and behavior*. Springfield, Illinois: Thomas, 1968.

Ohwaki, S., Brahlek, J. A., and Stayton, S. E. Preference for vibratory and visual stimulation in mentally retarded children. *American Journal of Mental Deficiency*, 1973, *77*, 733–736.

O'Leary, K. D. and Borkovec, T. D. Conceptual, methodological, and ethical problems of placebo groups in psychotherapy research. *American Psychologist*, 1978, *33*, 821–830.

Oleson, D. S., and Zubek, J. P. The effect of one day of sensory deprivation on a battery of relatively unstructured cognitive tests. *Perceptual and Motor Skills*, 1970, *31*, 919–923.

Olsen, L. *Wilderness Psychology Newsletter* and personal communications, 1975–1979.

Olson, E. V. The hazards of immobility. *American Journal of Nursing*, 1967, *67*, 780–797.

O'Neil, P. M., and Calhoun, K. S. Sensory deficits and behavioral deterioration in senescence. *Journal of Abnormal Psychology*, 1975, *84*, 579–582.

Orne, M. T. The potential uses of hypnosis in interrogation. In A. D. Biderman and H. Zimmer (Eds.), *The manipulation of human behavior.* New York: Wiley, 1961.

Orne, M. T. On the social psychology of the psychological experiment with particular reference to demand characteristics and their implications. *American Psychologist*, 1962, *17*, 776–783.

Orne, M. T., and Scheibe, K. E. The contribution of non-deprivation factors in the production of sensory deprivation effects: The psychology of the panic button. *Journal of Abnormal and Social Psychology*, 1964, *68*, 3–12.

Ornitz, E. M. The modulation of sensory input and motor output in autistic children. *Journal of Autism and Childhood Schizophrenia*, 1974, *4*, 197–215.

Ornitz, E. M., and Ritvo, E. R. The syndrome of autism: A critical review. *American Journal of Psychiatry*, 1976, *133*, 609–618.

Ornstein, R. E. *On the experience of time.* Harmondsworth, England: Penguin, 1969.

Orr, L., and Ray, S. *Rebirthing in the new age.* Millbrae, California: Celestial Arts, 1977.

Osaka, R. (Ed.) *Environmental psychology research.* Nagoya University Research Institute of Environmental Medicine, 1976, *1*, unpaged.

Oster, C. Sensory deprivation in geriatric patients. *Journal of the American Geriatrics Society*, 1976, *24*, 461–464.

Oster, C. Signs of sensory deprivation versus cerebral injury in post-hip-fracture patients. *Journal of the American Geriatrics Society*, 1977, *25*, 368–370.

Ozerengin, M. F., and Cowan, M. A. Environmental noise level as a factor in the treatment of hospitalized schizophrenics. *Diseases of the Nervous System*, 1974, *35*, 241–243.

Pagano, R. R., Rosc, R. M., Stivers, R. M., and Warrenburg, S. Sleep during Transcendental Meditation. *Science*, 1976, *191*, 308–310.

Paivio, A. *Imagery and verbal processes.* New York: Holt, 1971.

Palmer, R.D. Visual acuity and stimulus-seeking behavior. *Psychosomatic Medicine,* 1970, *32,* 277–284.

Paloczi-Horvath, G. *The undefeated.* Boston: Atlantic-Little-Brown, 1959.

Paloutzian, R. F. and Ellison, C. W. Emotional, behavioral and physical correlates of loneliness. Paper read at the UCLA Research Conference on Loneliness, Los Angeles, California, May, 1979.

Pangborn, R. M. and Sharon, I. M. Visual deprivation and parotid response to cigarette smoking. *Physiology and Behavior,* 1971, *6,* 559–561.

Panton, Y., and Fischer, R. Hallucinogenic drug-induced behavior under sensory attenuation. *Archives of General Psychiatry,* 1973, *28,* 434–438.

Papageorgiou, M. G. Incubation as a form of psychotherapy in the care of patients in ancient and modern Greece. *Psychotherapy and Psychosomatics,* 1975, *26,* 35–38.

Parker Committee. *Report of the Committee of Privy Councillors Appointed to Consider Authorized Procedures for the Interrogation of Persons Suspected of Terrorism.* London: Her Majesty's Stationery Office, 1972.

Parker, J. C., Gilbert, G. S., and Thoreson, R. W. Anxiety management in alcoholics: A study of generalized effects of relaxation techniques. *Addictive Behaviors,* 1978, *3,* 123–127.

Parker, J.L. Introversion/extraversion and children's aversion to social isolation and corporal punishment: A note on failure to replicate Eysenck. *Australian Journal of Psychiatry,* 1972, *24,* 131–143.

Parmelee, P., and Werner, C., Lonely losers: Stereotypes of single dwellers. *Personality and Social Psychology Bulletin,* 1978, *4,* 292–295.

Parson, D. J., and Spears, N. E. Long-term retention of avoidance learning by immature and adult rats as a function of environmental enrichment. *Journal of Comparative and Physiological Psychology,* 1972, *80,* 297–303.

Parsons, H. McI. Work environments. In I. Altman and J. F. Wohlwill (Eds.), *Human behavior and environment: Advances in theory and research* (Vol. 1). New York: Plenum, 1976.

Parsons, J., and Davey, G. C. L. Imitation training with a 4-year-old retarded person. *Mental Retardation,* 1978, *16,* 241–244.

Pastalan, L. A. Statement to the U.S. Senate Special Committee on Architectural Barriers, 1971.

Pastalan, L. A., Mautz, R. K., and Merrill, J. The simulation of age related losses: A new approach to the study of environmental barriers. In W. P. E. Preiser (Ed.), *Proceedings of the Environmental Design Research Association* (Vol. I). Stroudsburg, Pennsylvania: Dowden, Hutchinson and Ross, 1973.

Patchett, R. F. Auditory pattern discrimination in albino rats as a function of auditory restriction at different ages. *Developmental Psychology,* 1977, *13,* 168–169.

Patrick, R. O. Partial sensory depatterning and propaganda assimilation. *Dissertation Abstracts*, 1965, *26*, 3488–3489.

Pekarek, L., and Svestokova, H. The treatment of psychoses by the combination of sleep therapy, ataractics and antidepressants. *International Journal of Neuropsychiatry*, 1967, *3*, 72–76.

Pell, E. (Ed.) *Maximum security: Letters from prison*. New York: Dutton, 1972.

Pelletier, K. R., and Garfield, C. *Consciousness East and West*. New York: Harper and Row, 1976.

Pena, F. *Perceptual isolation and hypnotic susceptibility*. Unpublished Ph.D. dissertation, Washington State University, 1963.

Pendergrass, V. E. Timeout from positive reinforcement following persistent, high-rate behavior in retardates. *Journal of Applied Behavior Analysis*, 1972, *5*, 85–91.

Peplau, L. A., and Perlman, D. (Chairmen) UCLA Research Conference on Loneliness. Los Angeles, California, May, 1979.

Peretti, P. O., Suss, L., and Aderman, M. Effect of sensory isolation upon intracranial self-stimulation by Sprague-Dawley rats. *Psychological Reports*, 1971, *28*, 863–868.

Peters, J., Benjamin, F. B., Helvey, W. M., and Albright, G. A. A study of sensory deprivation, pain, and personality relationships for space travel. *Aerospace Medicine*, 1963, *34*, 830–837.

Peters, R. D., Calhoun, K. S., and Adams, H. E. Modification by environmental conditions of retrograde amnesia produced by ECS. *Physiology and Behavior*, 1973, *11*, 889–892.

Petersen, R. C., and Stillman, R. C. (Eds.) *Phencyclidine (PCP) abuse: An appraisal*. Washington: U.S. Government Printing Office, 1978.

Petrie, A. *Individuality in pain and suffering* (2nd ed.). Chicago: University of Chicago Press, 1979.

Phillips, E. L. Contributions to a learning theory account of childhood autism. *Journal of Psychology*, 1957, *43*, 117–124.

Piaget, J. Need and significance of cross-cultural studies in genetic psychology. In B. Inhelder and H. H. Chipman (Eds.), *Piaget and his school: A reader in developmental psychology*. New York: Springer-Verlag, 1976.

Pillyard, A. *Spiritual exercises and their results*. London: Macmillan, 1927.

Pinneau, S. R. The infantile disorders of hospitalism and anaclitic depression. *Psychological Bulletin*, 1955, *52*, 429–452.

Pishkin, V., and Shurley, J. T. Sensory deprivation and operant conditioning in rats. *Psychonomic Science*, 1966, *5*, 283–284.

Plantade, A., and Girardin, P. [Infantile psychosis and deafness.] *Revue de Neuropsychiatrie Infantile*, 1976, *24*, 697–705.

Plotkin, W. B. Long-term eyes-closed alpha-enhancement training: Effects on alpha amplitudes and on experiential state. *Psychophysiology,* 1978, *15,* 40–52.

Plutchik, R., Karasu, T. B., Conte, H. R., Siegel, B., and Jerrett, I. Toward a rationale for the seclusion process. *Journal of Nervous and Mental Disease,* 1978, *166,* 571–579.

Potok, C. *The promise.* Greenwich, Connecticut: Fawcett, 1969.

Potter, C. F. *The great religious leaders.* New York: Simon and Schuster, 1958.

Powell, L. F. The effect of extra stimulation and maternal involvement on the development of low-birth-weight infants and on maternal behavior. *Child Development,* 1974, *45,* 106–113.

Prescott, J. W. Early somatosensory deprivation as an ontogenetic process in the abnormal development of the brain and behavior. In E. T. Goldsmith and J. Moor-Jankowski (Eds.), *Medical primatology.* Basel: Karger, 1971.

Prescott, J.W. Developmental neuropsychophysics. In J. W. Prescott, M. S. Read, and D. B. Coursin (Eds.), *Brain function and malnutrition: Neuropsychological methods of assessment.* New York: Wiley, 1975.

Prescott, J. W. Somato-sensory deprivation and its relationship to the blind. In Z. S. Jastrzembska (Ed.), *The effects of blindness and other impairments on early development.* New York: American Foundation for the Blind, 1976.

Pribram, K. H. *Languages of the brain.* Englewood Cliffs, New Jersey: Prentice-Hall, 1971.

Pribram, K. H. Operant behaviorism: Fad, fact-ory, and fantasy? In H. Wheeler (Ed.), *Beyond the punitive society.* San Francisco: Freeman, 1973.

Price, J. The oral personality in partial sensory deprivation, social isolation and confinement: Electrodermal activity and task performance measures. Unpublished manuscript, State University of New York at Buffalo, undated.

Prigatano, G. P., and Johnson, H. J. Autonomic nervous system changes associated with a spider phobic reaction. *Journal of Abnormal Psychology,* 1974, *83,* 169–177.

Prince, R. Indigenous Yoruba psychiatry. In A. Kiev (Ed.), *Magic, faith, and healing.* New York: Free Press, 1964.

Proshansky, H., Ittelson, W. H., and Rivlin, L. G. (Eds.) *Environmental psychology.* New York: Holt, Rinehart & Winston, 1970.

Prout, H. T. Behavioral intervention with hyperactive children: A review. *Journal of Learning Disabilities,* 1977, *10,* 20–25.

Putnam, N., and Yager, J. Traction intolerance syndrome: A psychiatric complication of femoral fractures. *International Journal of Psychiatry in Medicine,* 1978, *8,* 133–143.

Quackenbush, J. F. Letter in the *Wilderness Psychology Newsletter,* May 31, 1977.

Quay, H. C. Psychopathic personality as pathological stimulation-seeking. *American Journal of Psychiatry,* 1965, *122,* 180–183.

Racamier, P. C., Carretier, L., and Sens, C. [The aftermath of sleep therapy.] *L'Évolution Psychiatrique*, 1959, *2*, 305–330.

Raffetto, A. M. Experimenter effects on subjects' reported hallucinatory experiences under visual and auditory deprivation. Paper read at the meeting of the Midwestern Psychological Association, Chicago, Ill., 1968.

Rainer, J. D., and Altshuler, K. Z. (Eds.) *Psychiatry and the deaf.* Washington, D.C.: HEW, 1967.

Rainer, J. D., and Altshuler, K. Z. A psychiatric program for the deaf: Experiences and implications. *American Journal of Psychiatry*, 1971, *127*, 103–108.

Ramey, C. T., Starr, R. H., Pallas, J., Whitten, C. F., and Reed, V. Nutrition, response-contingent stimulation, and the maternal deprivation syndrome: Results of an early intervention program. *Merrill-Palmer Quarterly*, 1975, *21*, 45–53.

Rank, D., and Suedfeld, P. Positive reactions of alcoholic men to sensory deprivation. *International Journal of the Addictions*, 1978, *13*, 805–813.

Rapaport, D. The theory of ego-autonomy: A generalization. *Bulletin of the Menninger Clinic*, 1958, *22*, 13–35.

Rapoport, D. [For birth without violence: Results of a first study.] *Bulletin de Psychologie*, 1976, *29*, 552–560.

Rasmussen, J. E. (Ed.) *Man in isolation and confinement.* Chicago: Aldine, 1973.

Raviv, S., Sharan, S., and Strauss, S. Intellectual development of deaf children in different educational environments. *Journal of Communication Disorders*, 1973, *6*, 29–36.

Reed, G. F. Preparatory set as a factor in the production of sensory deprivation phenomena. *Proceedings of the Royal Society of Medicine*, 1962, *55*, 1010–1014.

Reed, G. F. Sensory deprivation. In G. Underwood and R. Stevens (Eds.), *Aspects of consciousness.* London: Academic Press, in press.

Reichle, J., Brubakken, D., and Tetreault, G. Eliminating perseverative speech by positive reinforcement and time-out in a psychotic child. *Journal of Behavior Therapy and Experimental Psychiatry*, 1976, *7*, 179–183.

Reidman, S. R., and Green, C. C. *Benjamin Rush: Physician, patriot, founding father.* London: Abelard-Schuman, 1964.

Reitman, F. B., and Cleveland, S. E. Changes in body image following sensory deprivation in schizophrenic and control groups. *Journal of Abnormal and Social Psychology*, 1964, *68*, 168–176.

Relinger, H., Bornstein, P. G., Bugge, I. D., Carmody, T. P., and Zohn, C. J. Utilization of adverse rapid smoking in groups: Efficacy of treatment and maintenance procedures. *Journal of Consulting and Clinical Psychology*, 1977, *45*, 245–249.

Reusch, J. *Psychiatric care.* New York: Grune and Stratton, 1964.

Reyher, J. Brain mechanisms, intrapsychic processes and behavior: A theory of hypnosis and psychopathology. *American Journal of Clinical Hypnosis,* 1964, *7,* 107–119.

Reynolds, D. K. *Morita psychotherapy.* Berkeley: University of California Press, 1976.

Reynolds, D. K. Naikan therapy—An experiential view. *Internal Journal of Social Psychiatry,* 1978, *23,* 1093/1–1093/6.

Reynolds, D. K. *The quiet therapies.* Honolulu: University of Hawaii Press, in press.

Reynolds, D., and Yamamoto, J. East meets West: Moritist and Freudian psychotherapies. In J. H. Masserman (Ed.), *Research and relevance (Science and psychoanalysis,* Vol. 21). New York: Grune and Stratton, 1972.

Richer, J. M. and Nicoll, S. The physical environment of the mentally handicapped: IV. A playroom for autistic children and its companion therapy project—a synthesis of ideas from ethology, psychology, nursing and design. *Journal of Mental Subnormality,* 1971, *17,* 132–143.

Richardson, J. T. E. Nonparametric indexes of sensitivity and response bias. *Psychological Bulletin,* 1972, *78,* 429–432.

Richardson, S. A. The influence of severe malnutrition in infancy on the intelligence of children at school age: An ecological perspective. In R. N. Walsh and W. T. Greenough (Eds.), *Environments as therapy for brain dysfunction.* New York: Plenum, 1976.

Riege, W. H. Environmental influences on brain and behavior of year-old rats. *Developmental Psychobiology,* 1971, *4,* 157–167.

Riesen, A. H. Excessive arousal effects of stimulation after early sensory deprivation. In P. Solomon, et al. (Eds.), *Sensory deprivation.* Cambridge: Harvard University Press, 1961.

Riesen, A. H. Effect of visual deprivation on perceptual function and neural substrate. In J. Ajuriaguerra (Ed.), *Désafférentation expérimentale et clinique.* Geneva: George, 1965.

Riesen, A. H. Neuropsychological consequences of altered sensory inputs. In K. H. Pribram and E. D. Broadbent (Eds.), *Biology of memory.* New York: Academic Press, 1971.

Riesen, A. H. (Ed.) *The developmental neuropsychology of sensory deprivation.* New York: Academic Press, 1975.

Riesen, A. H., and Aarons, L. Visual movement and intensity discrimination in cats after early deprivation of pattern vision. *Journal of Comparative and Physiological Psychology,* 1959, *52,* 142–149.

Riesen, A. H., Dickerson, G. P., and Struble, R. G. Somatosensory restriction and behavioral development in stumptail monkeys. *Annals of the New York Academy of Sciences,* 1977, *290,* 285–294.

Riesen, A. H., and Zilbert, D. E. Behavioral consequences of variations in early sensory environments. In A. H. Riesen (Ed.), *The developmental neuropsychology of sensory deprivation.* New York: Academic Press, 1975.

Rimland, B. *Infantile autism*. New York: Appleton-Century-Crofts, 1964.

Rincover, A. Sensory extinction: A procedure for eliminating self-stimulatory behavior in developmentally disabled children. *Journal of Abnormal Child Psychology*, 1978, *6*, 299–310.

Risley, T. R. The effects and side-effects of punishing the autistic behaviors of a deviant child. *Journal of Applied Behavior Analysis*, 1968, *1*, 21–34.

Ritchie, S. Van A. *Modification of hypnotic susceptibility through sensory deprivation and stress*. Unpublished Ph.D. dissertation, Brigham Young University, 1976.

Ritvo, E. R. (Ed.) *Autism: Diagnosis, current research, and management*. New York: Halsted Press, 1976.

Robertson, A. D., and Inglis, J. The effects of electroconvulsive therapy on human learning and memory. *Canadian Psychological Review*, 1977, *18*, 285–307.

Robertson, J. *Young children in hospital*. London: Tavistock, 1958.

Robertson, M. H. Theoretical implications of sensory deprivation. *Psychological Record*, 1961, *11*, 33–42.

Robertson, M. H. Sensory deprivation and some therapeutic considerations. *Psychological Record*, 1961, *11*, 343–347.

Robertson, M. H. Facilitating therapeutic changes in psychiatric patients by sensory deprivation methods. Final progress report to Research Foundation of the National Association for Mental Health, November 30, 1964.

Robertson, M. H. Therapeutic effectiveness of verbal communication under conditions of perceptual isolation. *APA Convention Proceedings*, 1965, 259–260.

Robinson, F. (Ed.) *Psychiatric inpatient treatment of children*. Washington, D. C.: American Psychiatric Association, 1957.

Rogers, D. L. *Information seeking behavior in the tactile modality*. Unpublished Ph.D. dissertation, Arizona State University, 1975.

Rogow, S. M. Speech development and the blind multi-impaired child. *Education of the Visually Handicapped*, 1973, *4*, 105–109.

Rogow, S. Retardation among blind children. In R. E. Mordy and J. G. Cull (Eds.), *Mental retardation and physical disability*. Springfield, Illinois: Thomas, 1974.

Rolston, H. III. Lake Solitude: The individual in wildness. *Main Currents*, March-April, 1975, *31*(4), 121–126.

Rosa, K. R. *You and AT* Autogenic Training—The revolutionary way to relaxation and inner peace*. New York: Saturday Review/Dutton, 1973.

Rosen, H., and DiGiacomo, J. N. The role of physical restraint in the treatment of psychiatric illness. *Journal of Clinical Psychiatry*, 1978, *39*, 228–232.

Rosen, R. D. *Psychobabble: Fast talk and quick cure in the era of feeling*. New York: Atheneum, 1977.

Rosenhan, D. On the social psychology of hypnosis research. In J. E. Gordon

(Ed.), *Handbook of clinical and experimental hypnosis.* New York: Macmillan, 1967.

Rosenheim, H. D., and Ables, B. S. Social deprivation and "mental retardation." *Child Psychiatry and Human Development,* 1974, *4,* 216–226.

Rosenthal, R. The effect of the experimenter on the results of psychological research. In B. Maher (Ed.), *Progress in experimental personality research* (Vol. 1). New York: Academic Press, 1964.

Rosenthal, R. *Experimenter effects in behavioral research.* New York: Appleton-Century-Crofts, 1966.

Rosenthal, R. H., and Allen, T. W. An examination of attention, arousal, and learning dysfunctions of hyperkinetic children. *Psychological Bulletin,* 1978, *85,* 689–715.

Rosenzweig, M. R. Environmental complexity, cerebral change, and behavior. *American Psychologist,* 1966, *21,* 321–332.

Rosenzweig, M. R. Effects of environment on development of brain and of behavior. In E. Tobach, L. R. Aronson, and E. Shaw (Eds.), *Biopsychology of development.* New York: Academic Press, 1971.

Rossi, A. M. General methodological considerations. In J. P. Zubek (Ed.), *Sensory deprivation: Fifteen years of research.* New York: Appleton-Century-Crofts, 1969.

Rossi, A. M. Note on GSRs as operants during sensory deprivation. *Perceptual and Motor Skills,* 1971, *33,* 722.

Rossi, A. M., Nathan, P. E., Harrison, R. H., and Solomon, P. Operant responding for visual stimuli during sensory deprivation: Effect of meaningfulness. *Journal of Abnormal Psychology,* 1969, *74,* 188–192.

Rost, K. J., and Charles, D. C. Academic achievement of brain injured and hyperactive children in isolation. *Exceptional Children,* 1967, *34,* 125–126.

Rothschild, B. F. Incubator isolation as a possible contributing factor to the high incidence of emotional disturbance among prematurely born persons. *Journal of Genetic Psychology,* 1967, *110,* 287–304.

Rotter, J. B. Level of aspiration as a method of studying personality. *Journal of Experimental Psychology,* 1942, *31,* 410–422.

Rotter, J. B. Beliefs, social attitudes, and behavior: A social learning analysis. In R. Jessor and S. Feshbach (Eds.), *Cognition, personality, and clinical psychology.* San Francisco: Jossey-Bass, 1968.

Rubens, R. L., and Lapidus, L. B. Schizophrenic patterns of arousal and stimulus barrier functioning. *Journal of Abnormal Psychology,* 1978, *87,* 199–211.

Rubenstein, C. M., and Shaver, P. A factor-analytic exploration of experience of adult loneliness. Paper read at the UCLA Research Conference on Loneliness, Los Angeles, California, 1979.

Rubin, M. Auditory deprivation in infants. *Journal of Communication Disorders,* 1972, *5,* 195–204.

Rubin-Rabson, G. Home v. daycare. *American Psychological Association Monitor*, 1976, 7 (September–October), 44.

Rush, B. *Essays: Literary, moral and philosophical* (2nd ed.). Philadelphia: Bradford, 1806.

Russell, J. A., and Mehrabian, A. Task, setting and personality variables affecting the desire to work. *Journal of Applied Psychology*, 1975, *60*, 518–520.

Rutter, M. *Maternal deprivation reassessed.* Harmondsworth, England: Penguin, 1972.

Ryugo, D. K., Ryugo, R., Globus, A., and Killackey, H. P. Increased spine density in auditory cortex following visual or somatic deafferentation. *Brain Research*, 1975, *90*, 143–146.

Sachs, D. A. The efficacy of time-out procedures in a variety of behavior problems. *Journal of Behavior Therapy and Experimental Psychiatry*, 1973, *4*, 237–242.

Sackett, G.P. Effects of sensory deprivation level, visual complexity, and age upon light contingent responses during rearing. *Animal Behavior*, 1965, *13*, 393–399.

Sackett, G. P. Monkeys reared in isolation with pictures as visual input: Evidence for an innate releasing mechanism. *Science*, 1966, *154*, 1470–1473.

Sackett, G. P. Response to stimulus novelty and complexity as a function of rats' early rearing experiences. *Journal of Comparative and Physiological Psychology*, 1967, *63*, 369–375.

Sackett, G. P. Abnormal behavior in laboratory reared rhesus monkeys. In M. W. Fox (Ed.), *Abnormal behavior in animals.* Philadelphia: Saunders, 1968.

Sackett, G. P., Keith-Lee, P., and Treat, R. Food versus perceptual complexity as rewards for rats previously subjected to sensory deprivation. *Science*, 1963, *141*, 518–520.

Sadat, A. *In search of identity.* New York: Harper and Row, 1978.

Salinger, W. L., Schwartz, M. A., and Wilkerson, P. R. Selective loss of lateral genicular cells in the adult cat after chronic monocular paralysis. *Brain Research*, 1977, *125*, 257–263.

Salzarulo, P. [Quantitative data on nighttime fast sleep in normal and experimental sensory deprivation.] *Boll. Soc. Ital. Biol. sper. [Bulletin of the Italian Society for Experimental Biology]*, 1971, *47*, 559–561.

Salzarulo, P. Afternoon sleep in sensory deprivation: An EEG and polygraphic investigation in man. *Physiology and Behavior*, 1972, *8*, 1135–1140.

Sameroff, A. J. Early influences on development: Fact or fancy? *Merrill-Palmer Quarterly*, 1975, *21*, 267–294.

Sameroff, A. J., and Chandler, M. J. Reproductive risk and the continuum of caretaking casualty. In F. D. Horowitz, M. Hetherington, S. Scarr-Salapatek, and G. Siegel (Eds.), *Review of child development research* (Vol. 4). Chicago: University of Chicago, 1975.

Samler, J. Change in values: A goal in counseling. *Journal of Counseling Psychology*, 1960, 7, 32–39.

Sanders, R. S., and Reyher, J. Sensory deprivation and the enhancement of hypnotic susceptibility. *Journal of Abnormal Psychology*, 1969, 74, 375–381.

Sapir, E., and Swadesh, M. *Native accounts of Nootka ethnography.* Bloomington, Indiana: Indiana University Research Center of Anthropology, Folklore and Linguistics, 1955.

Sarbin, T. R., and Adler, N. Self-reconstitution processes: A preliminary report. *Psychoanalytic Review*, 1970, 57, 599–616.

Sarbin, T. R. and Coe, W. C. *Hypnosis: A social psychological analysis of influence communication.* New York: Holt, Rinehart and Winston, 1972.

Sarbin, T. R., and Nucci, L. Self-reconstitution processes: A proposal for reorganizing the conduct of confirmed smokers. *Journal of Abnormal Psychology*, 1973, 81, 182–198.

Sargant, W. *Battle for the mind* (Rev. ed.). Baltimore: Penguin, 1961.

Sargant, W. *The unquiet mind.* London: Pan, 1971.

Sargent, J. D., Green, E. E., and Walters, E. D. Preliminary report on the use of autogenic feedback training in the treatment of migraine and tension headaches. *Psychosomatic Medicine*, 1973, 35, 129–135.

Sayegh, Y., and Dennis, W. The effect of supplementary experiences upon the behavioral development of infants in institutions. *Child Development*, 1965, 36, 81–90.

Scarr-Salapatek, S., and Williams, M. L. The effects of early stimulation on low birth-weight infants. *Child Development*, 1973, 44, 94–101.

Schachter, S. *Emotion, obesity and crime.* New York: Academic Press, 1971.

Schachter, S., and Rodin, J. *Obese humans and rats.* Potomac, Maryland: Erlbaum, 1974.

Schädelin, J. [Experiences with the isolation of leukemic patients.] *Schweizerische Medizinische Wochenschrift*, 1975, 105, 1792–1804.

Schaffer, H. R., and Emerson, P. E. The development of social attachments in infancy. *Monographs of the Society for Research in Child Development*, 1964, 29, (Whole No. 1).

Schapiro, H., Britt, L. G., Gross, C. W., and Gaines, K. J. Sensory deprivation on visceral activity: III. The effect of olfactory deprivation on canine gastric secretion. *Psychosomatic Medicine*, 1971, 33, 429–435.

Schapiro, H., Gross, C. W., Nakamura, T., Wruble, L. D., and Britt, L. G. Sensory deprivation on visceral activity: II. The effect of auditory and vestibular deprivation on canine gastric secretion. *Psychosomatic Medicine*, 1970, 32, 515–521.

Schapiro, H., Wruble, L. D., Britt, L. G., and Bell, T. A. Sensory deprivation on visceral activity: I. The effect of visual deprivation on canine gastric secretion. *Psychosomatic Medicine*, 1970, 32, 379–396.

Schechter, M. D., Shurley, J. T., Sexauer, J. D., and Toussieng, P. W. Perceptual isolation therapy: A new experimental approach in the treatment of children using infantile autistic defenses. A preliminary report. *Journal of Child Psychiatry*, 1969, *8*, 97–139.

Schechter, M. D., Shurley, J. T., and Toussieng, P. W. Autism revisited. *Journal of the Oklahoma State Medical Association*, 1970, *63*, 299–300.

Schechter, M. D., Shurley, J. T., Toussieng, P. W., and Maier, W.J. Sensory isolation therapy of autistic children: A preliminary report. *Journal of Pediatrics*, 1969, *74*, 564-569.

Scheckenbach, A. F. The START program. Paper presented at the meeting of the American Psychological Association, Washington, D.C., 1976.

Schein, E. H. *Coercive persuasion*. New York: Norton, 1961.

Schell, R. E., and Adams, W. P. Training parents of a young child with profound behavior deficits to be teacher-therapists. *Journal of Special Education*, 1968, *2*, 439–454.

Schimpff, S. C., Greene, W. H., Young, V. M., Fortner, C. L., Jepsen, L., Cusack, N., Block, J. B., and Wiernik, P. H. Infection prevention in acute nonlymphocytic leukemia: Laminar air flow room reverse isolation with oral, nonabsorbable antibiotic prophylaxis. *Annals of Internal Medicine*, 1975, *82*, 351–358.

Schmahl, D. P., Lichtenstein, E., and Harris, D. E. Successful treatment of habitual smokers with warm, smoky air and rapid smoking. *Journal of Consulting and Clinical Psychology*, 1972, *38*, 105–111.

Schmale, A. The sensory deprivations: An approach to the study of the induction of affects. *Journal of the American Psychoanalytic Association*, 1974, *22*, 626–642.

Schneirla, T. C. Aspects of stimulation and organization in approach withdrawal processes underlying vertical behavior development. In D. S. Lehrman, R. A. Hinde, and E. Shaw (Eds.), *Advances in the study of behavior* (Vol. 1). New York: Academic Press, 1965.

Schoen, K. F. A new prison in a system encouraging alternatives. Paper read at an international seminar on Long-term Imprisonment, Montreal, October 1977.

Schopler, E. The development of body image and symbol formation through bodily contact with an autistic child. *Journal of Child Psychology and Psychiatry*, 1962, *3*, 191–202.

Schopler, E. Early infantile autism and receptor processes. *Archives of General Psychiatry*, 1965, *13*, 327–335.

Schroder, H. M., and Suedfeld, P. (Eds.) *Personality theory and information processing*. New York: Ronald, 1971.

Schroder, H. M., Driver, M. J., and Streufert, S. *Human information processing*. New York: Holt, Rinehart and Winston, 1967.

Schubert, D. S. P. Arousal seeking as a central factor in tobacco smoking among college students. *International Journal of Psychiatry*, 1965, *11*, 221–225.

Schulman, C. A., Richlin, M., and Weinstein, S. Hallucinations and disturbances of affect, cognition, and physical state as a function of sensory deprivation. *Perceptual and Motor Skills,* 1967, *25,* 1001–1024.

Schultz, D. P. *Sensory restriction: Effects on behavior.* New York: Academic Press, 1965.

Schultz, J. H., and Luthe, W. Autogenic methods. In W. Luthe (Ed.), *Autogenic therapy* (Vol. 1). New York: Grune and Stratton, 1969.

Schulz, R. Effects of control and predictability on the physical and psychological well-being of the institutionalized aged. *Journal of Personality and Social Psychology,* 1976, *33,* 563–573.

Schulz, R., and Hanusa, B. H. Long-term effects of control and predictability-enhancing interventions: Findings and ethical issues. *Journal of Personality and Social Psychology.* 1978, *36,* 1194–1201.

Schuster, R. Meditation: Philosophy and practice in a drug rehabilitation setting. *Drug Forum,* 1975–76, *5,* 163–170.

Schuster, R. Towards a synthesis of Eastern psychology and Western psychotherapy. *Psychotherapy,* 1977, *14,* 3–13.

Schwartz, G.E. *The disregulated species.* New York: Summit, in preparation.

Schwartz, G. E., and Shapiro, D. Biofeedback and essential hypertension: Current findings and theoretical concerns. *Journal of Seminars in Psychiatry,* 1973, *5,* 493–503.

Schwartz, G. E., and Weiss, S. M. Editorial: What is behavioral medicine? *Psychosomatic Medicine,* 1977, *39,* 377–381.

Schwartz, G. E., and Weiss, S. M. (Eds.) *Proceedings of the Yale Conference on Behavioral Medicine.* Washington: U.S. Department of Health, Education and Welfare, Publication No. (NIH) 78-1424, 1978.

Schwarz, R. M., Burkhart, B. R., and Green, S. B. Turning on or turning off: Sensation seeking or tension reduction as motivational determinants of alcohol use. *Journal of Consulting and Clinical Psychology,* 1978, *46,* 1144–1145.

Schwitzgebel, R. A comparative study of Zulu and English reaction to sensory deprivation. *International Journal of Social Psychiatry,* 1962, *8,* 220–225.

Scott, T. J. The use of music to reduce hyperactivity in children. *American Journal of Orthopsychiatry,* 1970, *40,* 677–680.

Sedman, G. "Brain-washing" and "sensory deprivation" as factors in the production of psychiatric states. The relation between such states and schizophrenia. *Confinia Psychiatrica,* 1961, *4,* 28–44.

Seligman, M. E. P. *Helplessness: On depression, development, and death.* San Francisco: Freeman, 1975.

"Sensory deprivation experiments with problem drinkers getting quick results." *Alcoholism and Alcohol Education,* 1977, *6* (10), 7–8.

Serafetinides, E. A., Shurley, J. T., Brooks, R., and Gideon, W. P. Electrophysiological changes in humans during sensory isolation. *Aerospace Medicine,* 1971, *42,* 840–842.

Shaffer, G. W., and Lazarus, R. S. *Fundamental concepts in clinical psychology.* New York: McGraw–Hill, 1952.

Shafii, M. Adaptive and therapeutic aspects of meditation. *International Journal of Psychoanalytic Psychotherapy,* 1973, *2,* 364–382.

Shafii, M., Lavely, R., and Jaffe, R. Meditation and marijuana. *American Journal of Psychiatry,* 1974, *131,* 60–63.

Shafii, M., Lavely, R., and Jaffe, R. Meditation and the prevention of drug abuse. *American Journal of Psychiatry,* 1975, *132,* 942–945.

Shallice, T. The Ulster depth interrogation techniques and their relation to sensory deprivation research. *Cognition,* 1972, *1,* 385–405.(a)

Shallice, T. Dual functions of consciousness. *Psychological Review,* 1972, *79,* 383–393. (b)

Shapiro, A. P. Behavioral and environmental aspects of hypertension. *Journal of Human Stress,* 1978, *4,* 9–17.

Shapiro, D. H., Jr. Meditation and behavioral self-control strategies applied to a case of generalized anxiety. *Psychologia,* 1976, *19,* 134–138.

Shapiro, D. H., Jr. *Behavioral and attitudinal changes resulting from a "Zen experience" workshop and Zen meditation.* Mimeographed manuscript, Stanford University, undated.

Shapiro, D. L. *Structural aspects of visual imagery in altered states of consciousness: A study of regressive styles.* Unpublished doctoral dissertation, University of Michigan, 1972.

Sharma, A. Modern isolation research and the concept of *Pubbenivasanussatinana,* or retrocognition. *International Philosophical Quarterly,* 1978, *18,* 335–339.

Sheehan, S. Annals of crime: A prison and a prisoner. III. You wouldn't understand. *New Yorker,* 1977, *53* (No. 8), 123–202.

Shiffman, S. M., and Jarvik, M. E. Withdrawal symptoms: The first week is the hardest. Paper read at the meeting of the American Psychological Association, Toronto, 1978.

Shiffman, S. M., and Jarvik, M. E. Cigarette smoking, physiological arousal, and emotional response: Nesbitt's paradox reexamined. Paper read at the meeting of the American Psychological Association, Toronto, 1978.

Shipley, W. C. A self-administering scale for measuring intellectual impairment. *Journal of Psychology,* 1940, *9,* 371–377.

Shirley, M. M. A behavior syndrome characterizing prematurely born children. *Child Development,* 1939, *10,* 115–128.

Shor, R. E. The three factor theory of hypnosis as applied to the book reading fantasy and to the concept of suggestion. *International Journal of Clinical and Experimental Hypnosis,* 1970, *18,* 89–98.

Shore, E. Sensory deprivation, preconscious processes and scientific thinking. *American Journal of Orthopsychiatry,* 1971, *41,* 574–580.

Shore, E. Sensory deprivation, preconscious processes and scientific thinking. Unpublished manuscript, Albert Einstein Medical Center, Philadelphia, Pennsylvania, undated.

Shores, R. E., and Haubrich, P. A. Effect of cubicles in educating emotionally disturbed children. *Exceptional Children,* 1969, *36,* 21–24.

Shurley, J. T. Stress and adaptation as related to sensory/perceptual isolation research. *Military Medicine,* 1966, *131,* 254–258.

Shurley, J. T. The hydro-hypodynamic environment. *Proceedings of the Third World Congress of Psychiatry,* Vol. 3. Toronto: University of Toronto, 1963.

Siegel, R. K. Hallucinations. *Scientific American,* 1977, *237,* 132–140.

Silverstein, C., and Suedfeld, P. Complexity of the environment, the message, and the conceptual structure of the subject as factors in persuasibility: Attitude manipulation in restricted environments, IX. Unpublished manuscript, University of British Columbia, 1976.

Silvestri, D. (Letter) Wilderness therapy. *Wilderness Psychology Newsletter,* April 1978 (No. 4).

Simpson, D. D., and Nelson, A. E. Breathing control and attention training: A preliminary study of a psychophysiological approach to self-control of hyperactive behavior in children. Unpublished paper, Texas Christian University, 1972.

Singer, J. L. *Imagery and daydream methods in psychotherapy and behavior modification.* New York: Academic Press, 1974.

Singer, J. L., and Streiner, B. F. Imaginative content in the dreams and fantasy play of blind and sighted children. *Perceptual and Motor Skills,* 1966, *22,* 475–482.

Singer, R. G. Confining solitary confinement: Constitutional arguments for a "new penology." *Iowa Law Review,* 1971, *56,* 1251–1296.

Skeels, H. M. Adult status of children with contrasting early life experience. *Monographs of the Society for Research in Child Development,* 1966, *31,* 1–65.

Skeels, H. M., and Dye, H. B. A study of the effects of differential stimulation of mentally retarded children. *Proceedings of the American Association on Mental Deficiency,* 1939, *44,* 114–136.

Skinner, B.F. *Beyond freedom and dignity.* London: Jonathan Cape, 1972.

Slocum, J. *Sailing alone around the world.* New York: Century, 1900.

Slomin, V., and Pasnak, R. The effects of visual deprivation on the depth perception of adult and infant rats and adult squirrel monkeys *(Saimiri scurea). Vision Research,* 1972, *12,* 623–626.

Smith, A. *Powers of mind.* New York: Random House, 1975.

Smith, G. W. *A defence of a system of solitary confinement of prisoners adopted by the State of Pennsylvania.* Philadelphia: Philadelphia Society For Alleviating the Miseries of Public Prisons, 1833.

Smith, J. C. Meditation as psychotherapy: A review of the literature. *Psychological Bulletin*, 1975, *82*, 558–564.

Smith, J. C. Yoga and stress. In Swami Ajaya (Ed.), *Meditation therapy*. Glenview, Illinois: Himalayan International Institute, 1977.

Smith, M. Wild children and the principle of reinforcement. *Child Development*, 1954, *25*, 115–123.

Smith, S. Clinical aspects of perceptual isolation. *Proceedings of the Royal Society of Medicine*, 1962, *55*, 1003–1005.

Smith, S., and Lewty, W. Perceptual isolation using a silent room. *Lancet*, 1959, *2*, 342–345.

Smith, S., Thakurdas, H., and Lawes, T. G. G. Perceptual isolation and schizophrenia. *Journal of Mental Science*, 1961, *107*, 839–844.

Solkoff, N., and Matuszak, D. Tactile stimulation and behavioral development among low-birthweight infants. *Child Psychiatry and Human Development*, 1975, *6*, 33–37.

Solkoff, N., Yaffe, S., Weintraub, D. and Blase, B. Effects of handling on the subsequent development of premature infants. *Developmental Psychology*, 1969, *1*, 765–768.

Solnick, J. V., Rincover, A., and Peterson, C. R. Some determinants of the reinforcing and punishing effects of timeout. *Journal of Applied Behavior Analysis*, 1977, *10*, 415–424.

Solomon, E. G., and Bumpus, A. K. The running meditation response: An adjunct to psychotherapy. *American Journal of Psychotherapy*, 1978, *32*, 583–592.

Solomon, P., Kubzansky, P. E., Leiderman, P. H., Mendelson, J. and Wexler, D. (Eds.) *Sensory deprivation*. Cambridge, Mass.: Harvard University Press, 1961.

Solomon, R. L., and Lessac, M. S. A control group design for experimental studies of developmental processes. *Psychological Bulletin*, 1968, *70*, 145–150.

Somerville, J. W., Jacobsen, L., Warnberg, L., and Young, W. Varied environmental conditions and task performance by mentally retarded subjects perceived as distractable and nondistractable. *American Journal of Mental Deficiency*, 1974, *79*, 204–209.

Somerville, J. W., Warnberg, L. S., and Bost, D. E. Effects of cubicles versus increased stimulation on task performance by first-grade males perceived as distractable and nondistractable. *Journal of Special Education*, 1973, *7*, 169–185.

Sommer, R. *The end of imprisonment*. New York: Oxford University Press, 1976.

Spanos, N. P., and Barber, T. X. Toward a convergence in hypnosis research. *American Psychologist*, 1974, *29*, 500–511.

Sperber, M. A. Sensory deprivation in autoscopic illusion, and Joseph Conrad's "The secret sharer." *Psychoanalytic Quarterly*, 1969, *43*, 711–718.

Spiegel, H. A single-treatment method to stop smoking using ancillary self-hypnosis. *International Journal of Clinical and Experimental Hypnosis,* 1970, *18,* 235–250.

Spigelman, M. N. Effects of age at onset and length of blindness on auditory spatial learning in the rat. *Canadian Journal of Psychology,* 1969, *23,* 292–298.

Spigelman, M. N., and Bryden, M. P. Effects of early and late blindness on auditory spatial learning in the rat. *Neuropsychologia,* 1967, *5,* 267–274.

"Spiritual paths basis for matching up prison pen-pals." *Unitarian Universalist World,* September 15, 1978, p. 9.

Spitalnik, R. and Drabman, R. A classroom timeout procedure for retarded children. *Journal of Behavior Therapy and Experimental Psychiatry,* 1976, *7,* 17–21.

Spitz, R. A. Hospitalism: An inquiry into the genesis of psychiatric conditions in early childhood. *Psychoanalytic Study of the Child,* 1945, *1,* 53–74.

Spitz, R. A. Hospitalism: A follow-up report. *Psychoanalytic Study of the Child,* 1946, *2,* 113–117. (a).

Spitz, R. A. Anaclitic depression. *Psychoanalytic Study of the Child,* 1946, *2,* 313–342. (b)

Spitz, R. A. Anxiety in infancy: A study of its manifestations in the first year of life. *International Journal of Psychoanalysis,* 1950, *31,* 138–143.

Sprague, J. M., Chambers, W. W., and Stellar, E. Attentive, affective and adaptive behavior in the cat. *Science,* 1961, *133,* 165–173.

Starker, S. Fantasy in psychiatric patients: Exploring a myth. *Hospital and Community Psychiatry,* 1979, *30,* 25–30.

Steeves, J. M., Martin, G., and Pear, J. Self-imposed time–out by autistic children during an operant training program. *Behavior Therapy,* 1970, *1,* 371–381.

Stein, J. I. Phencyclidine induced psychosis. The need to avoid unnecessary sensory influx. *Military Medicine,* 1973, *138,* 590–591.

Stephens, J. *Society of the alone: Freedom, privacy, and utilitarianism as dominant norms in the SRO.* Mimeographed paper, Department of Anthropology and Sociology, University of Queensland, 1974.

Steptoe, A. New approaches to the management of essential hypertension with psychological techniques. *Journal of Psychosomatic Research,* 1978, *22,* 339–354.

Sterritt, G. M., Camp, B. W., and Lipman, B. S. Effects of early auditory deprivation upon auditory and visual information processing. *Perceptual and Motor Skills,* 1966, *23,* 123–130.

Stewart, N. J. *Psychological effects of immobilization and social isolation on hospitalized orthopedic patients.* Unpublished master's thesis, University of Saskatchewan, 1977.

Stokols, D. A social-psychological model of human crowding phenomena. *Journal of the American Institute of Planners,* 1972, *38,* 72–83.

Stolk, J. M., Conner, R. L., and Barchus, J. D. Social environment and brain biogenic amine metabolism in rats. *Journal of Comparative and Physiological Psychology,* 1974, *87,* 203–207.

Stone, A. A. Consciousness: Altered levels in blind retarded children. *Psychosomatic Medicine,* 1964, *26,* 14–19.

Stott, D. H., and Latchford, S. A. Prenatal antecedents of child health, development, and behavior. *Journal of the American Academy of Child Psychiatry,* 1976, *15,* 161–191.

Strauss, A. A., and Kephart, M. *Psychopathology and education of the brain-injured child* (Vol. 2). New York: Grune and Stratton, 1955.

Strauss, A. A., and Lehtinen, L. E. *Psychopathology and education of the brain-injured child* (Vol. 1). New York: Grune and Stratton, 1947.

Streufert, S., and Streufert, S. C. *Behavior in the complex environment.* Washington, D.C.: Winston/Wiley, 1978.

Stunkard, A. J. Behavioral treatment of obesity: Failure to maintain weight loss. In R. B. Stuart (Ed.), *Behavioral self-management: Strategies, techniques and outcomes.* New York: Brunner/Mazel, 1977.

Sturt, M. *The psychology of time.* London: Kegan Paul, 1925.

Suedfeld, P. Birth order of volunteers for sensory deprivation. *Journal of Abnormal and Social Psychology,* 1964, *68,* 195–196.

Suedfeld, P. Anticipated and experienced stress in sensory deprivation as a function of orientation and ordinal position. *Journal of Social Psychology,* 1968, *76,* 259–263.

Suedfeld, P. Introduction and historical background. In J. P. Zubek (Ed.), *Sensory deprivation: Fifteen years of research.* New York: Appleton-Century-Crofts, 1969. (a)

Suedfeld, P. Changes in intellectual performance and in susceptibility to influence. In J. P. Zubek (Ed.), *Sensory deprivation: Fifteen years of research.* New York: Appleton-Century-Crofts, 1969. (b)

Suedfeld, P. Theoretical formulations: II. In J. P. Zubek (Ed.), *Sensory deprivation: Fifteen years of research.* New York: Appleton-Century-Crofts, 1969. (c)

Suedfeld, P. Sensory deprivation stress: Birth order and instructional set as interacting variables. *Journal of Personality and Social Psychology,* 1969, *11,* 70–74. (d)

Suedfeld, P. Evanescence of sensory deprivation effects: A comment on Oleson and Zubek's 'Effect of one day of sensory deprivation. . . .' *Perceptual and Motor Skills,* 1971, *33,* 753–754.

Suedfeld, P. Attitude manipulation in restricted environments: V. Theory and research. Symposium paper read at the XXth International Congress of Psychology, Tokyo, 1972.

Suedfeld, P. Social isolation: A case for interdisciplinary research. *Canadian Psychologist,* 1974, *15,* 1–15. (a)

Suedfeld, P. Solitary confinement in the correctional setting: Goals, problems, and suggestions. *Corrective and Social Psychiatry,* 1974, *20,* 10–20. (b)

Suedfeld, P. The clinical relevance of reduced sensory stimulation. *Canadian Psychological Review,* 1975, *16,* 88–103.

Suedfeld, P. The use of sensory deprivation in the treatment of claustrophobia: Another study in the development of a panacea. *Worm Runner's Digest,* 1976, *18,* 93–95.

Suedfeld, P. Using environmental restriction to initiate long-term behavior change. In R. B. Stuart (Ed.), *Behavioral self-management: Strategies, techniques and outcomes.* New York: Brunner/Mazel, 1977. (a)

Suedfeld, P. Environmental effects on violent behaviour in total institutions. In E. Fattah (Ed.), *Violence in Canadian society.* Unpublished manuscript, 1977. (b)

Suedfeld, P. Solitary confinement as a rehabilitative technique: Reply to Lucas. *Australian and New Zealand Journal of Criminology,* 1978, *11,* 106–112.

Suedfeld, P. Stressful levels of environmental stimulation. In I. G. Sarason and C. Spielberger (Eds.), *Stress and Anxiety,* Vol. 6. New York: Wiley, 1979.

Suedfeld, P., and Best, J. A. Satiation and sensory deprivation combined in smoking therapy: Some case studies and unexpected side-effects. *International Journal of the Addictions,* 1977, *12,* 337–359.

Suedfeld, P., and Borrie, R. A. Sensory deprivation, attitude change, and defense against persuasion. *Canadian Journal of Behavioural Science,* 1978, *10,* 16–27. (a)

Suedfeld, P., and Borrie, R. A. Altering states of consciousness through sensory deprivation. In A. A. Sugerman and R. E. Tarter (Eds.), *Expanding dimensions of consciousness.* New York: Springer, 1978. (b)

Suedfeld, P., and Buchanan, E. Sensory deprivation and autocontrolled aversive stimulation in the reduction of snake avoidance. *Canadian Journal of Behavioural Science,* 1974, *6,* 105–111.

Suedfeld, P., Glucksberg, S., and Vernon, J. Sensory deprivation as a drive operation: Effects upon problem solving. *Journal of Experimental Psychology,* 1967, *75,* 166–169.

Suedfeld, P., Grissom, R., and Vernon, J. The effects of sensory deprivation and social isolation on the performance of an unstructured task. *American Journal of Psychology,* 1964, *77,* 111–115.

Suedfeld, P., and Hare, R. D. Sensory deprivation in the treatment of snake phobia: Behavioral, self-report, and physiological effects. *Behavior Therapy,* 1977, *8,* 240–250.

Suedfeld, P., and Ikard, F. F. Attitude manipulation in restricted environments: IV. Psychologically addicted smokers treated in sensory deprivation. *British Journal of Addiction,* 1973, *68,* 170–176.

Suedfeld, P. and Ikard, F. F. The use of sensory deprivation in facilitating the reduction of cigarette smoking. *Journal of Consulting and Clinical Psychology,* 1974, *42,* 888–895.

Suedfeld, P., Landon, P. B., Epstein, Y. M., and Pargament, R. The role of experimenter and subject expectations in sensory deprivation. *Representative Research in Social Psychology*, 1971, *2*, 21–27.

Suedfeld, P., Landon, P. B., Pargament, R., and Epstein, Y. M. An experimental attack on smoking: Attitude manipulation in restricted environments, III. *International Journal of the Addictions*, 1972, *7*, 721–733.

Suedfeld, P., Ramirez, C., Clyne, D., and Deaton, J. E. [The effects of involuntary social isolation on prisoners.] Paper read at the XVIth Interamerican Congress of Psychology, Miami Beach, Florida, 1976.

Suedfeld, P., and Roy, C. Using social isolation to change the behaviour of disruptive inmates. *International Journal of Offender Therapy and Comparative Criminology*, 1975, *19*, 90–99.

Suedfeld, P., and Russell, J. A. (Gen. Eds.), *The behavioral basis of design* (2 vols.). Stroudsburg, Pa.: Dowden, Hutchinson and Ross, Book 1, 1976, Book 2, 1977.

Suedfeld, P., and Smith, C. A. Positive incentive value of phobic stimuli after brief sensory deprivation: Preliminary report. *Perceptual and Motor Skills*, 1973, *36*, 320.

Suedfeld, P., and Vernon, J. A. Attitude manipulation in restricted environments: II. Conceptual structure and the internalization of propaganda received as a reward for compliance. *Journal of Personality and Social Psychology*, 1966, *3*, 586–589.

Suedfeld, P., Rank, D. S., and Rank, A. D. Hedonic value of visual stimuli after visual and sensory deprivation as a function of their information value and social content. Unpublished manuscript, The University of British Columbia, 1977.

Suedfeld, P., Tetlock, P. E., and Borrie, R. A. The effects of restricted stimulation and a distracting task on counterarguing and attitude change. In preparation.

Sugimoto, S. [The effect of prolonged lack of sensory stimulation upon human behaviour.] *Japanese Journal of Aerospace Medicine and Psychology*, 1967, *4*, 61–66.

Sugimoto, S. Some considerations on experimental research of sensory restriction. In R. Osaka (Ed.), *Environmental Psychology Research*. Nagoya University Research Institute of Environmental Medicine, 1976, *1*, unpaged. (a)

Sugimoto, S. Some considerations on experimental research of sensory restriction. *Annual Report of the Research Institute of Environmental Medicine*, Nagoya University, 1976. (b)

Sugimoto, S., and Kida, M. Changes in perceptual experiences during sensory deprivation. *Annual Report of the Research Institute of Environmental Medicine*, Nagoya University, 1968, *16*, 91–98.

Sugimoto, S., Kida, M., and Teranishi, T. Frequency changes of alpha brain waves during 3 days sensory deprivation. *Annual Report of the Research Institute of Environmental Medicine*, Nagoya University, 1969, *17*, 73–78.

Sugimoto, S., Kida, M., Teranishi, T. and Yamamoto, A. [Time estimation during prolonged sensory deprivation.] *Japanese Journal of Aerospace Medicine and Psychology,* 1968, *6,* 1–5.

Suomi, S. J. Surrogate rehabilitation of monkeys reared in total social isolation. *Journal of Child Psychology and Psychiatry,* 1973, *14,* 71–77.

Suomi, S. J. Social "deprivation" and "enrichment" in laboratory-reared rhesus monkeys. Paper read at the meeting of the American Psychological Association, Toronto, 1978.

Suomi, S. J., and Harlow, H. F. Depressive behavior in young monkeys subjected to vertical chamber confinement. *Journal of Comparative and Physiological Psychology,* 1972, *80,* 11–18.

Suppes, P. A survey of cognition in handicapped children. *Review of Educational Research,* 1974, *44,* 145–176.

Suraci, A. Environmental stimulus reduction as a technique to effect the reactivation of crucial repressed memories. *Journal of Nervous and Mental Disease,* 1964, *138,* 172–180.

Susen, G. R. [Experienced effectiveness of autogenic training.] *Zeitschrift für Psychosomatische Medizin und Psychoanalyse,* 1978, *24,* 379–383.

Sutherland, A., Amit, Z., Golden, M., and Roseberger, Z. Comparison of three behavioral techniques in the modification of smoking behavior. *Journal of Consulting and Clinical Psychology,* 1975, *43,* 443–447.

Suzuki, D. T. Zen in relation to Buddhism generally. In W. Barrett (Ed.), *Zen Buddhism: Selected writings of D. T. Suzuki.* Garden City, New York: Doubleday, 1956.

Suzuki, D. T., Fromm, E., and DeMartino, R. (Eds.). *Zen Buddhism and psychoanalysis.* New York: Grove, 1960.

Suzuki, T., and Yamaguchi, T. On Morita therapy. Paper read at the 1st International Symposium on Non-verbal Aspects and Techniques of Psychotherapy, Vancouver, Canada, 1974.

Svab, L., and Gross, J. The effect of being observed in experimental sensory deprivation: Expression of emotions in verbal content and in psychomotor behavior. In M. Moravek and J. Dvorak (Eds.), *Some problems of aviation and space medicine.* Prague: Universitas Carolina, 1967.

Svab, L., Gross, J., and Langova, J. Stuttering and social isolation: Effect of social isolation with different levels of monitoring on stuttering frequency (A pilot study). *Journal of Nervous and Mental Disease,* 1972, *155,* 1–5.

Svendsen, K. Sleep deprivation therapy in depression. *Acta Psychiatrica Scandinavica,* 1976, *54,* 184–192.

Swan, S. World torture, 1974. *The Canadian Magazine,* March 30, 1974.

Swets, J. A. The relative operating characteristic in psychology. *Science,* 1973, *182,* 990–1000.

Tabbel, J. *The compact history of the Indian wars.* New York: Tower, 1967.

Tait, G. A. *The effects of perceptual deprivation on the human EEG.* Unpublished doctoral dissertation, McMaster University, 1977.

Takeda, R. The participation of private citizens in crime prevention: The case of the Naikan-ho in Japan. Resource Material Series No.2, UNAFEI, November 1971, 145–150.

Taniguchi, Y. Psychological studies on concentration and no-contrivance. In Y. Akishige (Ed.), *Psychological studies on Zen* (Vol. 2). Tokyo: The Zen Institute of Komazawa University, 1977.

"Tanking it up—A new form of relaxation." *Washington Post,* December 3, 1978, p. G22.

Tarler-Benlolo, L. The role of relaxation in biofeedback training: A critical review of the literature. *Psychological Bulletin,* 1978, *85,* 727–755.

Tart, C. T. Introduction. In C. T. Tart (Ed.), *Altered states of consciousness.* New York: Wiley, 1969.

Taub, E. Movement in nonhuman primates deprived of somatosensory feedback. In J. F. Keogh (Ed.), *Exercise and Sports Science Reviews* (Vol. 4). Santa Barbara: Journal Publishing, 1977.

Taylor, A. Institutionalized infants' concept formation ability. *American Journal of Orthopsychiatry,* 1968, *38,* 110–115.

Taylor, E. I. *Psychological suspended animation.* Unpublished master's thesis, Southern Methodist University, 1973.

Taylor, E. I. Sensory deprivation and inner exploration: The transformation of a paradigm. Paper read at the annual meeting of the Southwestern Psychological Association, Fort Worth, Texas, April 1977.

Tees, R. C. Effects of early auditory restriction in the rat on adult pattern discrimination. *Journal of Comparative and Physiological Psychology,* 1967, *63,* 389–393.

Tees, R. C. Effect of early restriction on later form discrimination in the rat. *Canadian Journal of Psychology,* 1968, *22,* 296–301.

Tees, R. C. Effect of visual deprivation on development of depth perception in the rat. *Journal of Comparative and Physiological Psychology,* 1974, *86,* 300–308.

Tees, R. C. Mammalian perceptual development. In G. Gottlieb (Ed.), *Studies on the development of behavior and the nervous system* (Vol. 3). New York: Academic Press, 1976.

Tees, R. C., and Cartwright, J. Sensory preconditioning in rats following early visual deprivation. *Journal of Comparative and Physiological Psychology,* 1972, *81,* 12–20.

Tees, R. C., and Midgley, G. Recovery of function after early sensory deprivation in the rat. *Journal of Comparative and Physiological Psychology,* 1978, *92,* 768–777.

Teller, W. M. (Ed.) Rearing of non-identical twins with lymphopenic hypogammaglobulinaemia under gnotobiotic conditions. *Acta Paediatrica Scandinavica,* 1973, Supplement 240.

Tetlock, P. E., and Suedfeld, P. Inducing belief instability without a persuasive message: The roles of attitude centrality, individual cognitive differences, and sensory deprivation. *Canadian Journal of Behavioural Science,* 1976, *8,* 324–333.

Thackray, R. I., Bailey, J. P., and Touchstone, R. M. Physiological, subjective, and performance correlates of reported boredom and monotony while performing a simulated radar control task. In R. R. Mackie (Ed.), *Vigilance: Theory, operational performance and physiological correlates.* New York: Plenum, 1977.

Thoenig, R. H. Solitary confinement—punishment within the letter of the law, or psychological torture? *Wisconsin Law Review,* 1972, 223–237.

Thompson, W. R., and Grusec, J. E. Studies of early experience. In P. H. Mussen (Ed.), *Carmichael's manual of child psychology* (Vol. 1). New York: Wiley, 1970.

Thompson, W. R., and Heron, W. The effects of restricted early experience on the problem-solving capacity of dogs. *Canadian Journal of Psychology,* 1954, *8,* 17–24.

Thompson, W. R., and Melzack, R. Early environment. *Scientific American,* 1956, *194,* 38–42.

Thomson, L. R. Sensory deprivation: A personal experience. *American Journal of Nursing,* 1973, *73,* 266–268.

Thor, D. H. Total suppression of irritable aggression in rats by sensory deprivation. *Psychological Reports,* 1975, *37,* 432–434.

Thorpe, T. J. Effects of Hatha Yoga and meditation on anxiety and body image. In Swami Ajaya (Ed.), *Meditational therapy.* Glenview, Illinois: Himalayan International Institute, 1977.

Tittle, C. R. Prisons and rehabilitation: The inevitability of disfavor. *Social Problems,* 1974, *21,* 385–395.

Tizard, B. Observations of overactive imbecile children in controlled and uncontrolled environments: II. Experimental studies. *American Journal of Mental Deficiency,* 1968, *72,* 548–553.

Tizard, B., and Hodges, J. The effect of early institutional rearing on the development of eight year old children. *Journal of Child Psychology and Psychiatry,* 1978, *19,* 99–118.

Tobias, J. J. *Nineteenth-century crime: Prevention and punishment.* Newton Abbot (Great Britain): David and Charles, 1972.

Toffler, A. *Future shock.* New York: Random House, 1970.

Tomalin, N., and Hall, R. *The strange voyage of Donald Crowhurst.* London: Hodder and Stoughton, 1970.

Tomkins, S. S. *Affect imagery consciousness* (2 vols.). New York: Springer, 1962.

Tomkins, S. S. A modified model of smoking behavior. In E. F. Borgatta and R. R. Evans (Eds.), *Smoking, health, and behavior.* Chicago: Aldine, 1968.

Tomlinson-Keasey, C., and Kelly, R. R. The development of thought processes in deaf children. *American Annals of the Deaf,* 1974, *119,* 693–700.

Tongas, P. N. The long-term maintenance of nonsmoking behavior. In M. E.

Jarvik, J. W. Cullen, E. R. Gritz, T. N. Vogt and L. J. West (Eds.), *Research on smoking behavior.* Rockville, Md.: NIDA Research Monograph # 17, Dept. of Health, Education and Welfare, 1977.

Toynbee, A. Great expectations. In H. Wheeler (Ed.), *Beyond the punitive society.* San Francisco: Freeman, 1973.

Tramontana, J., and Stimbert, V. E. Some techniques of behavior modification with an autistic child. *Psychological Reports,* 1970, *27,* 498.

Treffert, D. A. Sane asylum: An alternative to the mental hospital. Paper presented at the meeting of the American Psychiatric Association, Miami Beach, 1976.

Trillin, C. The ordeal of Fats Goldberg. *The New Yorker,* July 3, 1971, 57–63.

Tuber, D. S., Hothersall, D., and Voith, V. L. Animal clinical psychology. *American Psychologist,* 1974, *29,* 762–766.

Turkewitz, G., Gilbert, M., and Birch, H. G. Early restriction of tactile stimulation and visual functioning in the kitten. *Developmental Psychobiology,* 1974, *7,* 243–248.

Turner, R. S. Laminar air flow: Its original surgical application and long-term results. *The Journal of Bone and Joint Surgery,* 1974, *56a,* 430–435.

Tyler, V. O., Jr., and Brown, G. D. The use of swift, brief isolation as a group control device for institutionalized delinquents. *Behaviour Research and Therapy,* 1967, *5,* 1–9.

Tyre, R. H. Teaching "The Lord of the Rings." *Media and Methods,* 1978, *15,* 18–20.

Underhill, E. *Mysticism.* New York: Dutton, 1961 (Original publication, 1911).

Valzelli, L. Drugs and aggressiveness. In S. Carattini and P. Shore (Eds.), *Advances in pharmacology* (Vol. 5). New York: Academic Press, 1967.

Valzelli, L., and Bernasconi, S. Differential activity of some psychotropic drugs as a function of emotional level in animals. *Psychopharmacologia* (Berlin), 1971, *20,* 91–96.

Van der Kolk, B., and Hartmann, E. Sensory deprivation and subsequent sleep. Paper read at the meeting of the Association for the Psychophysiological Study of Sleep, Denver, Colorado, 1968.

Van Hof-Van Duin, J. Development of visuomotor behavior in normal and dark-reared cats. *Brain Research,* 1976, *104,* 233–241.

Vantour Committee. Report of the Study Group on Dissociation. Ottawa: Ministry of the Solicitor General of Canada, 1975.

Varela, J. A. *Psychological solutions to social problems: An introduction to social technology.* New York: Academic Press, 1971.

Varela, J. A. Social technology. *American Psychologist,* 1977, *32,* 914–923.

Vasquez, M., and Resczczynsky, K. The psychology of torture: The Chilean case. Paper presented at the XXIst International Congress of Psychology, Paris, 1976.

Vaughan, C. S. The development and use of an operant technique to provide evidence for visual imagery in the rhesus monkey under sensory deprivation. *Dissertation Abstracts*, 1966, *21*, 61–91.

Venator, E. R. Effects of auditory input complexity on attention in the rat. Paper presented at the meeting of the Southeastern Psychological Association, Atlanta, Georgia, April, 1967.

Vernon, J. *Inside the black room*. New York: Potter, 1963.

Vernon, J., and McGill, T. E. Utilization of visual stimulation during sensory deprivation. *Perceptual and Motor Skills*, 1960, *11*, 214.

Vernon, M. Relationship of language to the thinking process. *Archives of General Psychiatry*, 1967, *16*, 325–333.

Vidal, G., and Vidal, B. [Treatment of depressive states through the sleep-amitrybtyline association cure.] *Annales Médico-Psychologiques*, 1969, *1*, 816–817.

Vitgood, S. C., Crowe, M. J., Peters, R. D. and Suarez, Y. Brief immobilization: Decreasing disruptive and self-stimulatory behaviors. Paper presented at the meeting of the American Psychological Association, Washington, D.C., 1976.

Vives R., J. and Reyes P., N. I. [Effects of tardy stimulation in children with early affective lack.] *Acta Psiquiátrica y Psicológica de América Latina*, 1978, *24*, 58–64.

Vogel, G. W., Thompson, F. C., Thurmond, A., and Rivers, B. The effect of REM deprivation on depression. *Psychosomatics*, 1973, *14*, 104–107.

Von Hilsheimer, G. Effectively engineering the learning disability classroom. Presentation to the Delaware Valley Association for Learning Disabilities, Philadelphia, 1971.

Von Hilsheimer, G., Klotz, S. D., and Philpott, W. D. *Doctor, teacher, parent, child: A balanced biological, existential, and nutritional approach to children who have trouble in school*. San Rafael, California: Academic Therapy Publications, 1971.

Vygotsky, L. *Thought and language*. Cambridge, Massachusetts: Massachusetts Institute of Technology, 1962.

Waal, N. A special technique of psychotherapy with an autistic child. In G. Caplan (Ed.), *Emotional problems of early childhood*. New York: Basic Books, 1955.

Wachs, T. D. The relationship of infants' physical environment to their Binet performance at $2^{1}/_{2}$ years. *International Journal of Behavioral Development*, 1978, *1*, 51–65.

Waddell, H. *The desert fathers*. New York: Sheed and Ward, 1942.

Wadeson, H., and Carpenter, W. T. Jr. Impact of the seclusion room experience. *Journal of Nervous and Mental Disease*, 1976, *163*, 318–328.

Wadeson, H., and Carpenter, W. T., Jr. Unpublished research, summarized in *Human Behavior*, 1977, *6*, 34–35.

Wahler, R. G. Setting generality: Some specific and general effects of child behavior therapy. *Journal of Applied Behavior Analysis*, 1969, *2*, 239–246.

Wahler, R. G. Productive solitude: Its generalization properties in the treatment of aggressive children. Paper presented at the annual meeting of the American Psychological Association, Toronto, 1978.

Wahler, R. G., and Fox, J. J., III. Solitary toy play: A desirable family treatment component for aggressive-oppositional children. Unpublished manuscript, University of Tennessee, 1978.

Walk, R. D. 'Visual' and 'visual motor' experience: A replication. *Journal of Comparative and Physiological Psychology*, 1958, *51*,785–787.

Walker, N. D. *Crime and punishment in Britain* (Rev. ed.). Edinburgh: T. and A. Constable, 1968.

Wallace, M., and Singer, G. Schedule induced behavior: A review of its generality, determinants and pharmacological data. *Pharmacology, Biochemistry and Behavior*, 1976, *5*, 483–490. (a)

Wallace, M., and Singer, G. Adjunctive behavior and smoking induced by a maze solving to schedule in humans. *Physiology and Behavior*, 1976, *17*, 849–852. (b)

Wallace, R. K., and Benson, H. The physiology of meditation. *Scientific American*, 1972, *226*, 84–90.

Walsh, R. N., and Cummins, R. A. Mechanism mediating the production of environmentally induced brain changes. *Psychological Bulletin*, 1975, *82*, 986–1000.

Walsh, R. N., and Cummins, R. A. Neural responses to therapeutic environments. In R. N. Walsh and W. T. Greenough (Eds.), *Environments as therapy for brain dysfunction*. New York: Plenum, 1976.

Walsh, R. N. and Greenough, W. T. (Eds.) *Environments as therapy for brain dysfunction*. New York: Plenum, 1976.

Walters, C., Shurley, J. T., and Parsons, O. A. Differences in male and female responses to underwater sensory deprivation: An exploratory study. *The Journal of Nervous and Mental Disease*, 1962, *135*, 302–310.

Walters, R. H., Callaghan, J. E., and Newman, A. F. Effects of solitary confinement on prisoners. *American Journal of Psychiatry*, 1963, *119*, 771–773.

Walton, D., and Latané, B. Visual versus physical social deprivation and affiliation in rats. *Psychonomic Science*, 1972, *26*, 4–6.

Ward, A. J. The application of structural therapy to the residential treatment of early infantile autism. *Schizophrenia*, 1970, *2*, 92–102.

Ward, A. J. *Childhood autism and structural therapy*. Chicago: Nelson-Hall, 1976.

Ward, A. J. Prenatal stress and childhood psychopathology. Paper read at the meeting of the American Orthopsychiatric Association, New York, 1977.

Ward, A. J. Early childhood autism and structural therapy: Outcome after 3 years. *Journal of Consulting and Clinical Psychology*, 1978, *46*, 586–587.

Warren, D. H. Blindness and early development: What is known and what needs to be studied. *New Outlook for the Blind*, January 1976, *70*, 5–16.

Warren, D. H. *Blindness and early childhood development.* New York: American Foundation for the Blind, 1977.

Warren, S. A. and Burns, N. R. Crib confinement as a factor in repetitive and stereotyped behavior in retardates. *Mental Retardation, 1970, 8,* 25–28.

Wathney, S. E. *Effects of sensory isolation on self-actualization.* Unpublished doctoral dissertation, California School of Professional Psychology, Fresno, 1978.

Watkins, H. H. Hypnosis and smoking: A five session approach. *International Journal of Clinical and Experimental Hypnosis, 1976, 24,* 381–390.

Watson, P. *War on the mind: The military uses and abuses of psychology.* New York: Basic Books, 1977.

Watts, A. W. *The way of Zen.* New York: Vintage, 1957.

Watzlawick, P. *The language of change: Elements of therapeutic communication.* New York: Basic Books, 1978.

Wax, T. M. Effect of age, strain, and illumination-intensity on activity and self-selection of light-dark schedules in mice. *Journal of Comparative and Physiological Psychology, 1977, 91,* 51–62.

Webb, R. A. A comment on Moore and Shiek's "Toward a theory of early infantile autism." *Psychological Review, 1972, 79,* 278–279.

Weinberg, M. M. *Effects of partial sensory deprivation on involuntary subjects.* Unpublished Ph.D. dissertation, Michigan State University, 1967.

Weinraub, M. and Lewis, M. The determinants of children's responses to separation. *Monographs of the Society for Research in Child Development, 1977, 42,* (4, Whole No. 172).

Weiss, R. J. (Ed.) *Loneliness: The experience of emotional and social isolation.* Cambridge, Mass.: MIT Press, 1973.

Weissberg, A. *The accused.* New York: Simon and Schuster, 1951.

Weitzenhoffer, A. M. Hypnotism and altered states of consciousness. In A. A. Sugerman and R. E. Tarter (Eds.), *Expanding dimensions of consciousness.* New York: Springer, 1978.

Wells, D. A. The use of seclusion on a university hospital psychiatric floor. *Archives of General Psychiatry, 1972, 26,* 410–414.

Welter, R. E. *An exploratory study of small leaderless groups where vision has been temporarily deprived.* Unpublished Ph.D. dissertation, California School of Professional Psychology, San Diego, 1975.

Wendt, R. H., Lindsley, D. F., Adey, W. R., and Fox, S. S. Self-maintained stimulation in monkeys after long-term visual deprivation. *Science, 1962, 139,* 336–338.

Wessman, A. E. and Gorman, B. S. The emergence of human awareness and concepts of time. In B. S. Gorman and A. E. Wessman (Eds.), *The personal experience of time.* New York: Plenum, 1977.

West, L. J. A general theory of hallucinations and dreams. In L. J. West (Ed.), *Hallucinations.* New York: Grune and Stratton, 1962.

West, L. J. Hypnosis in the treatment of the smoking habit. In M. E. Jarvik, J. W. Cullen, E. R. Gritz, T. M. Vogt, and L. J. West (Eds.), *Research on smoking behavior.* Rockville, Maryland, NIDA Research Monograph # 17, Department of Health, Education and Welfare, 1977.

West, M. *The salamander.* Richmond Hill, Ontario: Simon and Schuster, 1974.

Westin, A. *Privacy and freedom.* New York: Atheneum, 1970.

Wetzel, R. J., Baker, J., Roney, M., and Martin, M. Outpatient treatment of autistic behavior. *Behaviour Research and Therapy,* 1966, *4,* 169–177.

White, B. L., and Castle, P. W. Visual exploratory behavior following postnatal handling of human infants. *Perceptual and Motor Skills,* 1964, *18,* 497–502.

White, G. D., Nielsen, G., and Johnson, S. M. Timeout duration and the suppression of deviant behavior in children. *Journal of Applied Behavior Analysis,* 1972, *5,* 111–120.

White, R. Motivation reconsidered: The concept of competence. *Psychological Review,* 1959, *66,* 297–333.

Wickram, I. Goals and some methods in psychotherapy: Hypnosis and isolation. *American Journal of Clinical Hypnosis,* 1970, *13,* 95–100.

Wickramasekera, I. Effects of sensory restriction on susceptibility to hypnosis. *International Journal of Clinical and Experimental Hypnosis,* 1969, *17,* 217–224.

Wickramasekera, I. Effects of sensory restriction on susceptibility to hypnosis: A hypothesis and more preliminary data. *Journal of Abnormal Psychology,* 1970, *76,* 69–75.

Wickramasekera, I. Psychophysiological stress reduction procedures and a suggestion hypothesis: Sensory restriction and low arousal training. Paper read at the meeting of the American Association for the Advancement of Tension Control, 1977. (a)

Wickramasekera, I. The placebo effect and medical instruments in biofeedback. *Journal of Clinical Engineering,* 1977, *2,* 227–230. (b)

Wickramasekera, I. On attempts to modify hypnotic susceptibility: Some psychophysiological procedures and promising directions. *Annals of the New York Academy of Sciences,* 1977, *296,* 307–314. (c)

Wickramasekera, I. Psychophysiological stress reduction procedures and a suggestion hypothesis: Sensory restriction and low arousal training. Paper read at the meeting of the American Psychological Association, Toronto, 1978.

Wiesel, T. N., and Hubel, D. H. Comparison of the effects of unilateral and bilateral eye closure on cortical unit responses in kittens. *Journal of Neurophysiology,* 1965, *28,* 1029–1040.

Wilcox, J. W. A practical approach to treatment of colic. Paper read at the meeting of the Southwestern Pediatric Society, 1957.

Wilkins, W. Parameters of therapeutic imagery: Directions from case studies. *Psychotherapy: Theory, Research and Practice,* 1974, *11,* 163–171.

Wilkins, W. L. Prisoners of war and their adaptation during and following confinement. Paper presented at the annual meeting of the American Psychological Association, Montreal, Canada, 1973.

Williams, C. A functional analysis of stereotypy in the the rubella child—Introduction and background to the problem. Paper read at the Leonard Conference on Research into Visual Handicap. Cambridge University, January, 1972. London: The Southern Regional Association for the Blind *Conference Report* No. 62, 131–145.

Williams, S., and Harper, J. A study of aetiological factors at critical periods of development in autistic children. *Australian and New Zealand Journal of Psychiatry*, 1973, 7, 1–6.

Williams, S., and Harper, J. A study of etiological factors at critical periods of development in autistic children. *International Journal of Mental Health*, 1974, 3, 90–99.

Wilson, L. M. Intensive care delirium: The effect of outside deprivation in a windowless unit. *Archives of Internal Medicine*, 1971, 130, 225–226.

Wilson, M., Warren, J. M., and Abbott, L. Infantile stimulation, activity and learning by cats. *Child Development*, 1965, 36, 843–853.

Wilson, M., Wilson, W. A., and Sunenshine, H. Perception, learning and retention of visual stimuli by monkeys with inferotemporal lesions. *Journal of Comparative and Physiological Psychology*, 1968, 65, 404–412.

Wilson, T. Creating a diversified activity program in a small psychiatric institution for children. *Child Care Quarterly*, 1977, 6, 248–258.

Wohlwill, J. F. The virtues of a nonresponsive environment. Paper submitted for the programme of the Wilderness Conference, 1973.

Wohlwill, J. F. Human adaptation to levels of environmental stimulation. *Human Ecology*, 1974, 2, 127–147.

Wolf, M., Risley, T., Johnston, M., Harris, F., and Allen, E. Application of operant conditioning procedures to the behavior problems of an autistic child: A follow-up and extension. *Behaviour Research and Therapy*, 1967, 5, 103–112.

Wolf, M. M., Risley, T. R., and Mees, H. Application of operant conditioning procedures to the behavior problems of an autistic child. *Behaviour Research and Therapy*, 1964, 1, 305–312.

Wolfe, T. The me decade and the third great awakening. *New Times*, 1977, 1(1), 9–15 and 66–77.

Wolpe, J. *Psychotherapy by reciprocal inhibition.* Stanford, California: Stanford University Press, 1958.

"Woman fails in attempt to swim around Manhattan." New York *Times,* September 25, 1975, p. 1, 53.

Wood, P. B. *Dreaming and social isolation.* Unpublished doctoral dissertation, University of North Carolina, 1962.

Wood, W. E., and Greenough, W. T. Effects of grouping and crowding on learning in isolation reared adult rats. *Bulletin of the Psychonomic Society,* 1974, 3, 65–67.

Wright, D. *Deafness.* New York: Stein & Day, 1969.

Wright, N. A., and Abbey, D. S. Perceptual deprivation tolerance and adequacy of defenses. *Perceptual and Motor Skills,* 1965, *20*, 35–38.

Wright, N. A., and Zubek, J. P. Relationship between perceptual deprivation tolerance and adequacy of defenses as measured by the Rorschach. *Journal of Abnormal Psychology,* 1969, *74*, 615–617.

Wuermle, O. N. [An experimental comparison between the effects of autogenic training and sensory deprivation in the production of altered states of consciousness.] Unpublished paper, Department of Clinical Psychology, Psychological Institute, University of Zürich, undated.

Wurmbrand, R. *Sermons in solitary confinement.* London: Hodder and Stoughton, 1969.

Yaremko, R. M., Glanville, B., Rofer, C. P., and Leckart, B. T. Tactile stimulation and the short-term perceptual deprivation effect. *Psychonomic Science,* 1972, *26*, 89–90.

Yarmolenko, A. V. Characteristics and significance of touch for people who have lost their vision, hearing, and speech. *Soviet Psychology,* 1976, *15*, 3–58.

Yarrow, L. J. Maternal deprivation: Toward an empirical and conceptual reevaluation. *Psychological Bulletin,* 1961, *58*, 459–490.

Yarrow, L. J., Rubenstein, J. L., Pedersen, F. A., and Jankowski, J. J. Dimensions of early stimulation and their differential effects on infant development. *Merrill-Palmer Quarterly of Behavior and Development,* 1972, *18*, 205–218.

Yerkes, R. M., and Dodson, J. D. The relation of strength of stimulus to rapidity of habit-formation. *Journal of Comparative and Neurological Psychology,* 1908, *18*, 459–482.

Younggren, J. N. and Parker, R. A. The smoking control clinic: A behavioral approach to quitting smoking. *Professional Psychology,* 1977, *8*, 81–87.

Youngs, J. P., Jr. Experiential deprivation: A response. *American Annals of the Deaf,* 1975, *120*, 553–554.

Zaichkowsky, L. D., and Kamen, R. Biofeedback and meditation: Effects on muscle tension and locus of control. *Perceptual and Motor Skills,* 1978, *46*, 955–958.

Zajonc, R. B., and Morrissette, J. The role of uncertainty in cognitive change. *Journal of Abnormal and Social Psychology,* 1960, *61*, 168–175.

Zentall, S. Optimal stimulation as theoretical basis of hyperactivity. *American Journal of Orthopsychiatry,* 1975, *45*, 549–563.

Zentall, S. S., and Zentall, T. R. Activity and task performance of hyperactive children as a function of environmental stimulation. *Journal of Consulting and Clinical Psychology,* 1976, *44*, 693–697.

Zern, D. S. An interpretation of the effects of stimulation on development: Its role as a resolvable disequilibrator. *Genetic Psychology Monographs,* 1974, *90*, 325–347.

Zigler, E., Balla, D., and Butterfield, E. C. A longitudinal investigation of the relationship between preinstitutional social deprivation and social motivation in institutionalized retardates. *Journal of Personality and Social Psychology,* 1968, *10,* 437–445.

Zigler, E., and Butterfield, E. C. Motivational aspects of changes in I. Q. test performance of culturally deprived nursery school children. *Childhood Development,* 1968, *39,* 1–14.

Zigler, E., and Williams, J. Institutionalization and the effectiveness of social reinforcement: A three-year follow-up study. *Journal of Abnormal Social Psychology,* 1963, *66,* 197–205.

Zimbardo, P. G. The human choice: Individuation, reason, and order versus deindividuation, impulse and chaos. In W. J. Arnold and D. Levine (Eds.), *Nebraska Symposium on Motivation.* Lincoln: University of Nebraska Press, 1969.

Zimbardo, P. G. Statement in the case of Spain et al. versus Procunier et al., June, 13th, 1974.

Zimbardo, P. G. Transforming experimental research into advocacy for social change. In M. Deutsch and H. A. Hornstein (Eds.), *Applying social psychology: Implications for research, practice, and training.* New York: Wiley, 1975.

Zimbardo, P. G., Ebbesen, E. B., and Maslach, C. *Influencing attitudes and changing behavior.* Reading, Mass.: Addison-Wesley, 1977.

Ziskind, E. An explanation of mental symptoms found in acute sensory deprivation: Researches, 1958–1963. *American Journal of Psychiatry,* 1965, *121,* 939–946.

Ziskind, E., Jones, H., Filante, W., and Goldberg, J. Observations on mental symptoms in eye patched patients: Hypnagogic symptoms in sensory deprivation. *American Journal of Psychiatry,* 1960, *116,* 893–900.

Zubek, J. P. Counteracting effects of physical exercises performed during prolonged perceptual deprivation. *Science,* 1963, *142,* 504–506.

Zubek, J. P. (Ed.) *Sensory deprivation: Fifteen years of research.* New York: Appleton-Century-Crofts, 1969. (a)

Zubek, J. P. Sensory and perceptual-motor processes. In J. P. Zubek (Ed.), *Sensory deprivation: Fifteen years of research.* New York: Appleton-Century-Crofts, 1969. (b)

Zubek, J. P. Physiological and biochemical effects. In J. P. Zubek (Ed.) *Sensory deprivation: Fifteen years of research.* New York: Appleton-Century-Crofts, 1969 (c).

Zubek, J. P. [Behavioral and physiological effects of prolonged sensory and perceptual deprivation.] *Revista Interamericana de Psicología,* 1972, *6,* 151–200.

Zubek, J. P. Behavioral and physiological effects of prolonged sensory and perceptual deprivation: A review. In J. E. Rasmussen (Ed.), *Man in isolation and confinement.* Chicago: Aldine, 1973.

Zubek, J. P., Aftanas, M., Hasek, J., Sansom, W., Schludermann, E., Wilgosh, L., and Winocur, G. Intellectual and perceptual changes during prolonged perceptual deprivation: Low illumination and noise level. *Perceptual and Motor Skills*, 1962, *15*, 171–198.

Zubek, J. P., Aftanas, M., Kovach, K., Wilgosh, L., and Winocur, G. Effect of severe immobilization of the body on intellectual and perceptual processes. *Canadian Journal of Psychology*, 1963, *17*, 118–133.

Zubek, J. P., Bayer, L., Milstein, S., and Shephard, J. M. Behavioral and physiological changes during prolonged immobilization plus perceptual deprivation. *Journal of Abnormal Psychology*, 1969, *74*, 230–236.

Zubek, J. P. and Bross, M. Depression and later enhancement of the critical flicker frequency during prolonged monocular deprivation. *Science*, 1972, *176*, 1045–1047.

Zubek, J. P., Hughes, G. R., and Shephard, J. M. A comparison of the effects of prolonged sensory deprivation and perceptual deprivation. *Canadian Journal of Behavioural Science*, 1971, *3*, 282–290.

Zubek, J. P., and MacNeill, M. Effect of immobilization: Behavioral and EEG changes. *Canadian Journal of Psychology*, 1966, *20*, 316–336.

Zubek, J. P., and MacNeil, M. Perceptual deprivation phenomena: Role of the recumbent position. *Journal of Abnormal Psychology*, 1967, *72*, 147–150.

Zuckerman, M. Perceptual isolation as a stress situation. Paper read at the meeting of the Eastern Psychological Association, Philadelphia, Pennsylvania, 1964.

Zuckerman, M. Variables affecting deprivation results. In J. P. Zubek (Ed.), *Sensory deprivation: Fifteen years of research*. New York: Appleton-Century-Crofts, 1969 (a).

Zuckerman, M. Hallucinations, reported sensations, and images. In J. P. Zubek (Ed.), *Sensory deprivation: Fifteen years of research*. New York: Appleton-Century-Crofts, 1969. (b)

Zuckerman, M. Theoretical formulations: I. In J. P. Zubek (ed.), *Sensory deprivation: Fifteen years of research*. New York: Appleton-Century-Crofts, 1969. (c)

Zuckerman, M. The sensation seeking motive. In B. Maher (Ed.) *Progress in experimental personality research, Vol. 7*. New York: Academic Press, 1974.

Zuckerman, M., Kolin, E. A., Price, L., and Zoob, I. Development of a sensation-seeking scale. *Journal of Consulting Psychology*, 1964, *28*, 477–482.

Zuckerman, M., Persky, H., and Link, K. E. The influence of set and diurnal factors on autonomic responses to sensory deprivation. *Psychophysiology*, 1969, *5*, 612–624.

Index